Invenrelation

Shih Yu Chang

August 24, 2013

美商EHGBooks微出版公司
www.EHGBooks.com

EHG Books 公司出版

Amazon.com 總經銷

2013 年版權美國登記

未經授權不許翻印全文或部分

及翻譯為其他語言或文字

2013 年 EHGBooks 第一版

ISBN-13：978-1-62503-054-2

Contents

0.1 Preface 10

1 Why Adoption Mathematical Operations for Invention   14

2 Components for Things to be Invented   20

   2.1 Abstraction 20

     2.1.1 Measuring the Goodness of an Abstraction 22

     2.1.2 Abstraction Expansion 24

     2.1.3 Abstraction Generalization 26

   2.2 Elements 27

     2.2.1 Space and Time 28

     2.2.2 Substances 29

     2.2.3 Force and Energy 30

     2.2.4 Concepts and Knowledge 34

   2.3 Attributes 38

   2.4 Sets 40

     2.4.1 Sets and Their Components 40

     2.4.2 Subsets and Supersets 41

     2.4.3 Set Operations 41

     2.4.4 Product Sets 42

   2.5 Relations 43

   2.6 Algebraic Model for Invenrelation and Examples 45

   2.7 Information Collection 49

     2.7.1 Information Sending and Receiving 49

     2.7.2 Information Classification and Search 51

3 Invention Process by Basic Operations   **54**

  3.1 Four Elementary Arithmetics 54

     3.1.1 Addition and Substraction 54

     3.1.2 Multiplication and Division 59

  3.2 Product 66

  3.3 Quotient 72

  3.4 Varieties 78

     3.4.1 Lattices 78

     3.4.2 Groups 85

     3.4.3 Rings 88

     3.4.4 Fields 97

     3.4.5 Linear Algebras 101

  3.5 Quasivarieties 105

  3.6 Approximation 110

4 Relations and Actions   **118**

  4.1 Associations by Relations 119

     4.1.1 Composition of Associations 119

     4.1.2 Associations by Functions 120

     4.1.3 Association Examples 122

  4.2 Permutations by Actions 126

     4.2.1 Group Actions 127

     4.2.2 Permutation Representations of Groups 128

     4.2.3 Permutation Invention Examples 128

5 Plurioperad   **132**

  5.1 Motivations of Plurioperad 132

  5.2 Definition of Plurioperad 134

  5.3 Existence of Plurioperads 135

     5.3.1 Regular Algebraic Systems 135

     5.3.2 Free Plurioperads Construction 136

     5.3.3 The Existence Theorem of Plurioperads 136

     5.3.4 Differential Rules for Plurioperads 142

5.4   Invention Examples Rooted From Plurioperads 145

6   Analogy by Invengory   154

6.1   Analogy 154

6.2   A Mathematical Language for Analogy 155

     6.2.1   Invengory Definition 156

     6.2.2   Relations in an Invengory 159

     6.2.3   Objects Constructions 160

     6.2.4   Functors and Their Transformations 174

     6.2.5   Set-Valued Functor 179

     6.2.6   Universal Property 186

     6.2.7   Adjoints 187

6.3   Examples of Analogies 193

7   Multi-Analogy by Multi-Invengory   202

7.1   Multi-invengory 203

     7.1.1   Plain Invengory 205

     7.1.2   Structure Invengory 225

7.2 n-fold Invengory 235

7.3   Examples of Multiple Analogies 239

     7.3.1   Organization Design 239

     7.3.2   Puzzle Design 242

     7.3.3   Flow Chart Design 244

8   Evaluation Invenrelational Process Equationally   249

8.1   Motivation of Gluing Design for Invenrelational Process 249

8.2   Equations Definable Objects 251

     8.2.1   One-Sorted Representation of Many-Sorted Algebras 251

     8.2.2   Infinite Algebraic Systems 256

     8.2.3   Finite Algebraic Systems 263

8.3   Closed Construction for Oriented Complexes 272

     8.3.1   Construction Methods of Oriented Complexes 272

     8.3.2   Closed Construction Theorem 275

	8.3.3	Constructions from Group Actions	282
8.4		Evaluation Gluing Design Equationally	286
	8.4.1	Definition of Generalized ω-Invengories	286
	8.4.2	Gluing Design Evaluation Theorem	288
8.5		Example: Invenrelation Evolution Characterization	290
	8.5.1	Cobordism Model for Invenrelation Evolution Processes	290
	8.5.2	Vector Spaces Assignment	293

9 Derivability 296

9.1		Rules of Equational Deduction	296
	9.1.1	Many-Sorted Algebras and Terms	297
	9.1.2	Equations of MSA	300
	9.1.3	Rules of MSA Deduction	303
9.2		Derivability in One Invengory	303
9.3		Generalized Invenrelation Processes	305
9.4		n-Invengory Derivability	310
	9.4.1	Derivability : SISO Invenrelation Steps	311
	9.4.2	Derivability : MIMO Invenrelation Steps	324
9.5		Invenrelation Complexity	345

10 Unification of Perspectives 346

10.1		Perspectives	346
	10.1.1	A Model for Parameterized Algebraic Invenrelation Systems	347
	10.1.2	Conditions for Extension Theorem	348
10.2		Chain Rule of Isomorphism	352
	10.2.1	Isomorphisms between Labeled Sequences	352
10.3		Cancelation Rule	363
	10.3.1	Commutative Hexagon Lemma	364
	10.3.2	First Commutative Triangle Lemma	367
	10.3.3	Second Commutative Triangle Lemma	372
	10.3.4	Proof of Cancelation Rule and its Implications	380
10.4		Extension of Algebraic Invenrelation Systems through Perspectives	383
	10.4.1	Expression $\chi_{-,-}$, ρ_- and $\alpha_{\mathfrak{S}_{[k]}}$ by $\Upsilon_{-,-}$	383

10.4.2 Linearity of $\Upsilon_{-,-}$ 390

10.4.3 Extension Theorem of Algebraic Invenrelation Systems 394

10.5 Example 399

11 Invenrelation Networks   **404**

11.1 Coordinating Invenrelation Networks 405

    11.1.1 Advantages of Adopting CINs 405

11.2 Random Invengory 413

    11.2.1 Random Functions and Relations 413

    11.2.2 Random Invengory Definition 415

    11.2.3 Random Functor 416

11.3 Building Block: Tensor Product of Random Multi-invengories 417

11.4 Tensor Product of n-MIMO Random Invengories 423

    11.4.1 Monad Structure on MIMO Invengory 423

    11.4.2 Distributive Tensors 425

    11.4.3 Correspondence between Tensors and Plurioperads 432

    11.4.4 Induction to Higher Dimension 439

    11.4.5 n-MIMO Tensor Theorem 442

11.5 Example: A Network of Invenrelators with 2-MIMO Invengory 448

    11.5.1 Generators 450

    11.5.2 Naturality relations 452

    11.5.3 Functorial relations 454

    11.5.4 Identity relations 459

    11.5.5 Interchange relations 459

12 Final Remarks   **462**

12.1 Education 462

    12.1.1 Importance of Education 462

    12.1.2 Capabilities Required to Apply Invenrelation: Abstraction and Mathematics 463

12.2 Research 467

    12.2.1 Random 468

    12.2.2 Computer Implementation and Invenrelation Networks 471

    12.2.3 New Methods and Mathematical Representation 476

    12.2.4 New Knowledge Representation 478

12.3 Industry 478

    12.3.1 Intellectual Property 479

    12.3.2 Business 480

    12.3.3 Art 482

    12.3.4 Articles for Daily Use 483

12.4 Ethical Issues 485

List of Figures

1.1   Mathematical Operations for Invention Procedures 16

2.1   Abstracting out components 23

2.2   Elements → Attributes → Sets → Relations after abstraction 50

3.1   Increasing more axles (tires) to carry a heavier cargo. 58

3.2   Adjusting the distance between axles to carry a cargo with different shape (different center of mass). 58

3.3   Up subfigure: narrower baby door. Down subfigure: wider baby door. 60

3.4   The construction components. 63

3.5   A condo with 6 rooms. 65

3.6   Two family types. 66

3.7   A yoke with parallel structure. 71

3.8   A ball obtained by quotient operation. 73

3.9   A torus obtained by quotient operation. 74

3.10   L-shaped tile. 76

3.11   L-shaped tile decomposition of 15 squares 76

3.12   A hierarchical network with three levels (four Voronoi cells at the 0-th level). Nodes located within the dashed circle form a peer group. 79

3.13   A table for switch on-off relations. 82

3.14   Upper part: the original circuit. Lower part: the equivalent new circuit. 84

3.15   Timing diagram to transmit a packet successfully in IEEE 802.11. 91

3.16   Markov chain for backoff counter and contention window stage. 93

3.17   State diagram representation of the 802.11 MAC protocol. Transform variables X and Y are omitted for simplicity. 95

3.18 A reaction network example 104

3.19 (1) Two related entities, (2) An entity with an attribute, (3) A relationship with an attribute, (4) Primary key 109

3.20 Replacement = Subtraction + Addition 117

4.1 A relation decomposition example. 123

4.2 Permuation: Warrior or Coward 131

5.1 A plurioperad example. 137

5.2 Laugh and cry face made by plurioperads 148

5.3 Composition example of symmetric plurioperads. 149

5.4 Example for $((f_1, f_2), f_3, (f_4, f_5))$. 150

5.5 Fault tree modules. 151

5.6 Snowman from various snowballs 153

6.1 Product of Invengory. 162

6.2 Co-product of Invengory. 163

6.3 Multiple product diagram. 164

6.4 Pull back definition. 165

6.5 Pull back example 1. 166

6.6 Pull back example 2. 167

6.7 Push out definition. 167

6.8 Push out example. 168

6.9 The relations between the product $\prod_{v \in V} D_v$ and the product $\prod_{(v \to v') \in E} D_{v'}$. 171

6.10 Diagram of uniqueness. 172

6.11 Commutative diagram. 173

6.12 The diagram commutes in **D** with respect to all indices i, j and k. 178

6.13 Commutative diagram. 182

6.14 Commutative diagram. 184

6.15 Analog comparison between lamps and waterwheels for series connection. 196

6.16 Analogy 201

7.1 Different types of relations. 203

7.2 More complex input and output relation. 204

7.3   The example for map $(1, 2, 2, 3) \longrightarrow 1$. 207

7.4   MIMO invengoty example. 224

7.5   Organization design by decision tree. 241

7.6   A simple example about rectangular puzzle. 243

7.7   A flowchart for the registration procedure in an university. 246

7.8   The symbols $\circ_1$ and $\circ_0$ represent flowcharts attach along to a one dimensional
(arrow) object and a zero dimensional (dot) object, respectively. 247

7.9   Multi$-$Analogy 248

8.1   A two-folds evolution of invenrelation spaces composed by parts L, L' and M, M'. . 251

8.2   Examples of generalized ω-invengory: (a) $f \circ_0 g$, (b) $f \#_0 g \#_0 h$, (c) $(f \#_0 g) \circ_0 (f' \#_0 g')$ 288

8.3   Different views from different observation positions. 291

8.4   Pasting of cobordisms along boundaries. 294

8.5   Elementary 2 dimensional pieces 294

9.1   A semigroup example, automata. 302

9.2   Oriented complexes with neighbor dimension 1. 306

9.3   Oriented complex for an invenrelation procedure. 310

9.4   Meta-procedures. 310

9.5   Derivability of a SISO system. 317

9.6   Relation for one component. 321

9.7   Sequential and parallel relation chains. 321

9.8   Assemble relation chains. 322

9.9   General association identity. 324

9.10 Derivability of a MIMO system. 344

10.1 Invention Perspective Taking 403

11.1 Communication model. 411

11.2 Three components of CIN. 414

11.3 CIN 461

12.1 Three basic ingredients for invenrelation. 466

12.2 Possible future industries for brain-sports. 481

0.1 Preface

The **Dissertatio de arte combinatoria** is an early work authored by Gottfried Leibniz published in 1666 in Leipzig. It is an extended version of his doctoral dissertation, written before the author had seriously endeavored to study mathematics. The main spirit behind the book is that of an alphabet of human thought, which is attributed to Descartes. All concepts can be composed by a relatively small number of simple concepts, just as words are combinations of letters. All truths could be expressed as proper combinations of concepts, which can be decomposed into simple ideas, making the analysis much easier. So wonderful "invention technique" (the Art of invention) becomes possible: the concept that all possible ideas can be mechanically produced. Accordingly, we can not only explore the known, but the unknown can also be pursued further through more profound study. This beautiful dream had lived in Leibniz mind for the whole of his remainder life. The purpose of this book is try to realize this goal. Invenrelation indicates that the invention ideas can be composed by a serious of relations among thoughts mathematically.

We begin by explaining the motivations why we adopt mathematics to characterize invention procedures in Chapter I. In Chapter II, we begin by understanding the constitutive elements with their properties and relations for things to be invented (or problems to be solved) through abstraction method. Basically, the following four components for things to be invented could be abstracted: constitutive elements, attributes possessed by these constitutive elements, sets composed by some constitutive elements according to particular requirements of attributes and relations between these sets. In order to manipulate these abstracted components mathematically during an invention procedure, an algebraic model about these components is addressed. Since all components required for things to be invented require comprehensive information collection, we also discuss the meaning about information and its classification. We provide basic algebraic structures which help us to model invention process. Basically, algebraic structures could be classified by the following three kinds: arithmetic, varieties and quasivarieties. We will provide several invention examples by applying these basic algebraic structures.

Association method is a popular method that applies associative mental mechanism to generate creative ideas. The mental operation of association is try to make conceptual connections among different things; then creative ideas are excited by these connections. The physiological mechanism of association is a temporary connection among neuron models. The more knowledge and experiences one has, the more neuron models his/her brain saves. It becomes much easier to obtain useful ideas through association. The notion of relation originated from mathematics is suitable to provide a characterization for association since the concept of a relation adopted in mathematics is to figure out the relation (association) between two given sets. In order to comprehend more associative relations, the notion of relation is defined to provide more powerful association methods for creating new things. Permutation, which is an ordering of a certain number of elements of a given set, is an important relation among objects in a given set. These notions will be discussed in Chapter IV. From discussions in previous chapters, the input sets in the algebraic model of invenrelation form a finite sequence, i.e., a one dimensional array. In order to process more complicated invention procedure, we have to propose more delicate algebraic operations for inputs which form as some higher dimensional geometrical objects, e.g., grids, trees or pasting structures. Plurioperads are such kind of algebraic operations to be addressed in Chapter V.

Analogy has been claimed as the core for invention. The purpose of Chapter VI is to describe a mathematical language to describe an analogical invention procedure. Invengory theory, stemmed from category theory, provides us a language to describe analogical procedure of invention. Moreover, analogies can be extended to contain more than one analogical sources. The concept about multi-invengory theory will be introduced at Chapter VII. The main difference between multi-invengory theory and invengory theory is that the domain of a relation is not just a single object (invengory theory) but a finite sequence of objects (multi-invengory theory).

In order to evaluate invenrelational processes equationally, the main goal of Chapter VIII is to apply oriented complexes to characterize invenrelational processes. We begin by introducing the motivation behind modelling invenrelational processes through gluing cells formed by n-fold invengory. Then, we discuss the conditions required for objects in n-fold invengory to be defined equationally. Finally, the definition of oriented complexes and their construction rules are provided to prepare the main theorem in this chapter, which discusses the required conditions to evaluate invenrelational processes equationally. The main purpose of Chap. VIII is to provide conditions for evaluating invenrelational processes equationally. In order to solve invention problems through mathematical calculation systematically, it is more convenient to introduce variables to represent components of things to be invented first and one, then, can perform computation over these variables. The purpose of Chapter IX is to answer the basic question about derivability between terms related to variables. We will present the necessary conditions for derivability between algebraic invention terms in different invengory of algebraic invention systems. At the end, we discuss the problem about derivation complexity in such systems.

Perspective taking, as generated by prosocial motivation, encourages individuals to develop ideas that are useful as well as novel after adopting others perspectives. The main purpose of Chapter X is to provide a systematic way to enlarge ones perspectives domain and its associated algebraic invention systems (invenrelations). At the beginning of this chapter, we suggest that perspective can help individual to increase his/her creativity through perspective taking and propose a model for algebraic invenrelation systems parameterized by perspectives. Two important technical results required to show our extension theorem of parameterized algebraic invenrelation systems are discussed further. Finally, we show that one can expand ones perspectives domain and its associated algebraic invenrelation systems by keeping his/her model of algebraic invenrelation systems parameterized by perspectives (extension theorem of parameterized algebraic invenrelation systems).

With globalization, the economy, information and the people at different local area are getting closer than before. With this trend, a more radically superior mode of invenrelation than before is generated due to globalization. Such invenrelation mode is coordinating invenrelation networks (CIN). Thanks to the maturity of communication network technology, organizations at different local area are allowed to invent together. Coordinating invenrelation begins when organizations come together to invent common objects or solve common problems that are beyond the scope, scale or capabilities of individual organizations. Chapter XI is initiated by introducing three basic ingredients about coordinating invenrelation networks. Then concepts about random relations and random functors, which are used to model uncertain effect from information communication, are presented. Finally, the tensor product of many-sorted algebra (MSA) multi-invengories which plays as a building block for higher dimensional tensor product is introduced to describe the product of invention procedures (n-MIMO invengories).

Last Chapter (Chapter XII), we first mention the importance of education and two key capabilities, abstraction and mathematics, in applying invenrelation. Then, we propose several research topics about invenrelation. These topics can be classified into following categories: randomness of objects and relations in invenrelation systems, computer implementation issues, new invention methods and their relation with mathematics, and knowledge representation. Industrial Revolution was a period over the 18th and 19th centuries where changes in manufacturing, mining, agriculture, transportation, and technology had a deep effect on the social, economic and cultural conditions of the times. It began in the United Kingdom, then generally spread throughout Western Europe, North America, Asia, and eventually the rest of the world. At those times, inventions and scientific discoveries played an important role in modernization of the world, when an era of global industrial liberalization played a significant role in the scientific advancement of the world. It all began with the advancement of the liberal invention of humans after the Renaissance, which eventually led to the industrial revolution. We select following areas in industry to discuss possible future stories affected by invenrelation. They are intellectual property, business, art and articles for daily use. Invention or creation may be regarded as the most difficult (or advanced) function of our brains. If machines which apply invenrelation to invent or create new things are widely deployed in our world, we will suffer an Age of invention explosion. Finally, we will point out several ethical issues about such Age.

And finally, I would like to show my deep appreciation to my family members, especially, Mina, Andrew and Ray, during past years in preparing this book. Without their support and love, it is impossible for me to finish this book. They have always been there to encourage me when I needed them.

Chapter 1

Why Adoption Mathematical Operations for Invention

The first step of understanding any phenomena is to find out what objects are included in these phenomena, namely, to establish a taxonomy. For those various existing methods of *representation*, people have not accomplished such desired purpose. For different kinds of representations for problems, we only have rough and imperfect knowledge. In addition, we even know a little about the difference meaning between representation ways. We are particularly concerned about fields in knowledge representation and problems solving since there exists some significant insufficiencies in theory within these areas. The difference caused by representation has been recognized by people for a long time. For example, we understand clearly that it becomes easier to do arithmetic calculation by the Arabic number system instead of using Roman number system. However, we still do not know how to explain this mystical phenomenon theoretically. By reviewing the total kinds of mathematical conclusions, we observe that they are just rules or objects implied by premises. Therefore, all mathematical derivations could simply be considered as a procedure of transformations about representations. These transformations clarifies the true but originally blurry objects. This perspective could be adopted to the procedures of solving problems. Problems solving indicates that problems should be represented in proper ways which enable solutions clearly to be understood. If we can organize such similar processes to solve problems, representation will become the most important issue to deal with. Even such viewpoint maybe too exaggerative, however, issues about how to generate proper representations and how representations contribute to the process of problems solving will become necessary essences in future invention and design theory.

Many great scientists have contemplated the problem about mathematical representations from different perspectives. Since the time of the ancient Greeks, thought has been given to the exact nature of mathematical representations. What are their roles and status in reality? Most importantly, are they invented or discovered? Leopold Kronecker stood for the side of invention: "God created the natural numbers; all the rest is the work of Man." Charles Hermite, by contrast, stood for the side of discovery: "There exists, if I am not mistaken, an entire world, which is the totality of mathematical truths, to which we have access only with our mind, just as a world of physical reality exists, the one like the other independent of ourselves, both of divine creation." The German great physicist Heinrich Hertz further explained : "One cannot escape the feeling that these mathematical formulas have an independent existence and an intelligence of their own, that they are wiser that we are, wiser even than their discoverers, that we get more out of them than was originally put into them." G. H. Hardy concluded what many mathematicians today have a tendency to believe: " ... that mathematical reality lies outside us, that our function is to discover or observe it, and that the theorems which we prove, and which we describe grandiloquently as our creations, are simply the notes of our observations." Niels Bohr calls common language is not identical to our daily language which often makes ambiguity. For this reason, he refers to the special role played by mathematical representation in science. According to Bohr, we can use mathematics not as a "separate branch of knowledge," but rather as "a refinement of general language" in order "to represent relations for which ordinary verbal expression is imprecise or cumbersome". In particular, "just by avoiding the reference to the conscious subject which infiltrates daily language", the use of mathematical symbols secures the unambiguity of definition required for objective description [1]. Martin Gardner makes the claim that: "Mathematics is not only real, but it is the only reality. [The] ... entire universe is made of matter... And matter is made of particles... Now what are the particles made out of? They're not made out of anything. The only thing you can say about the reality of an electron is to cite its mathematical properties. So there's a sense in which matter has completely dissolved and what is left is just a mathematical structure." All these ideas are inspirational. Now, we wish to reveal our reasons to develop an invention theory based on mathematics.

The power about the function of mathematical expression is indicated by using a simple and univocal form to describe mathematical facts. Then, we can liberate mathematics away from words bondage. Otherwise, any widespread statements have become lots of cumbersom languages,

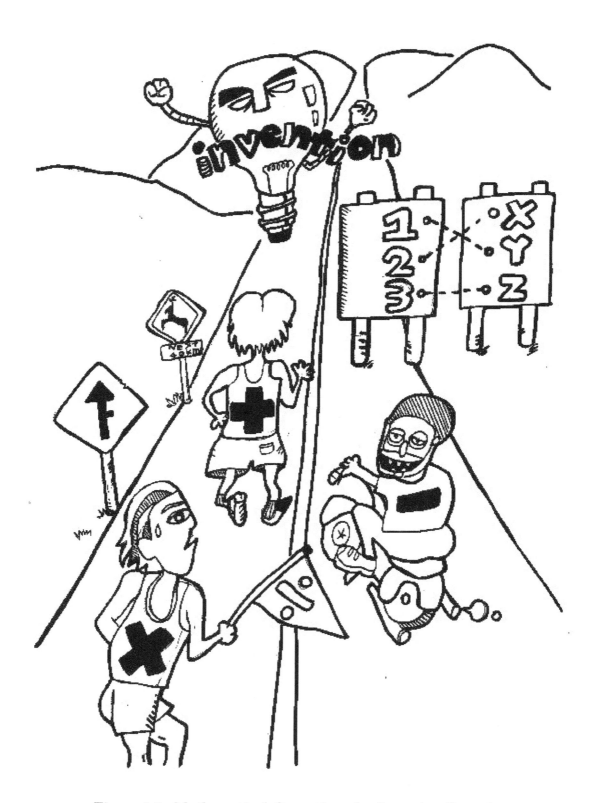

Figure 1.1: Mathematical Operations for Invention Procedures

which are easily affected by ambiguity and misunderstanding in language usage. Particular significance is that the meaning of symbols is man-made. It is not like that words inevitably involve traditional meaning. Words have kinds of inhibitions since they were used through the history. But symbols have not.

From cognitive perspective, the cognitive meaning of mathematical representation is that the structure of written symbols acting as visual elements directly involves cognitive processes and possesses irreplaceable functions. If we agree that the former thinking processes basically depend on the closed processes of permuting and combining the inner language and the imaginary formats, the import of mathematical representation makes the corresponding cognitive processes become open by incorporating consciousness and presentation elements simultaneously.

If we consider all information in our world as a database, we can reduce our internal memory structure significantly by associating everything in our world to a data structure. The external mathematical symbols not only provide a tool to help our memory, but also stimulate our human cognitive mechanism to explore knowledge. The most important thing is that mathematical representation can provide cognition a kind of new, indispensable and irreplaceable perspective factors in discovering new cognitive space.

General speaking, it is more easier to perform calculation than deductions. Everyone may have such experience: it is much simpler to solve complicated arithmetic problems by algebraic expressions. No wonder Gottfried Wilhelm Leibniz admitted that mathematical logics enabled two arguing philosophers stop debate and helped them to obtain correct answers peacefully through mathematical symbols. The essence of calculation is to perform deduction through manipulating meaningful symbols. Equivalently, calculation is a procedure of operational thinking for specific formats or operational thinking for symbols. However, the procedures of calculation shares the same structure with the corresponding deduction procedures. In fact, the process to confirm calculation rules is to verify the corresponding calculation satisfying the deduction argument. This explains why we adopt symbols and calculation rules (mathematics) to perform creation procedures since this will provide a new and easier way for invention.

An invention procedure about applying some mathematical concepts in creation is *Equivalent Transformation*, developed by Prof. Ichikawa in 1944. Equivalent Transformation is a method based on objective existing equivalences between things to implement technological creation by discarding the dross and selecting the essential parts. From Prof. Ichikawa's long-term observation and research, those equivalent factors and equivalent transformations exist in nature ubiquitously, e.g., a butterfly or a silkworm experiencing the process from a larva into a pupa, and a pupa into an imago.

Let A_0 be the existing objects, namely, the prototype of Equivalent Transformation; $c\varepsilon$ denotes the equivalent factors of composition, which ε is the equivalent factor and c is the constraint condition of ε; Σa denotes the conditions in A_0 to be removed; Σb denotes the required various special conditions to carry out new technological functions from A_0; B represents the constituent of equivalent transform, namely the created new object; v_i represents some technological requirements or targets, these terms can be used to represent Equivalent Transformation by the following formula:

$$\sum a$$
$$A_0 \uparrow \overset{c\varepsilon}{==} B$$
$$\uparrow$$
$$v_i \to \sum b$$

To apply Equivalent Transformation in technological innovation, one should based on the given technological requirements or targets v_i to transform A_0 to B by removing component Σa from A_0, adding Σb and keeping equivalent constituent elements $c\varepsilon$. For example, let us consider the design for a parking tower. According to Equivalent Transformation, the thinking process is provided as following:

First step is to define technological targets. According to technological requirements of designing a parking lot which occupies a small area with large capacity, we confirm that the technological goal is a tower structure. Second step is to define commonality elements (ε). We abstract the specific requirement of parking as storing items into a tower structure (ε). Third step is to define every prototype which includes ε functions, (A_0). We select "a watchtower" to represent an object with the tower structure (A_0). Fourth step is to decompose A_0 and find out the equivalent constraint conditions c of ε, namely, the elevating transfer mechanism through the center of a watchtower $(c\varepsilon)$. Fifth, we delete the inherent special conditions (Σa), such as transparent windows in a watchtower. Sixth, we import the needed special conditions (Σb) in the storage of cars, such as the multilevel structure. Finally, we would generate a complete design idea about a parking lot with the tower structure (B).

However, Equivalent Transformation only use mathematical concepts like addition, subtraction and equivalence. There are much more dedicated mathematical operations and concepts can be adopted in invention procedure, e.g., multiplication, quotient and relation. This observation motivates us to develop invenrelation theory.

Chapter 2

Components for Things to be Invented

In this chapter, we begin by recognizing the constitutive elements with their properties and relations for things to be invented (or problems to be solved) through abstraction method, the central topic in Sec. 2.1. Basically, the following four components for things to be invented could be abstracted: constitutive elements (Sec. 2.2), attributes possessed by these constitutive elements (Sec. 2.3), sets composed by some constitutive elements according to particular requirements of attributes (Sec. 2.4) and relations between these sets (Sec. 2.5). In order to manipulate these abstracted components mathematically during an invention procedure, an algebraic model about these components is discussed in Sec. 2.6. Since all components required for things to be invented require comprehensive information collection, we discuss the meaning about information and its classification in Sec 2.7. We begin by addressing to the concept of *abstraction*.

2.1 Abstraction

Abstraction is the process of recognizing essential parts and regulations of things based on human sense and perception and appearance of things. Abstraction is one of the fundamental ways that we deal with complexity. The purpose of abstraction enable us to develop concepts, classification ways and theorems (or principles) about our interesting things. The term of *abstract-* originated from Latin and the primary meanings for such term is separation, exclusion and extraction from things. For a short example, we may abstract a leather football to the idea of a ball retains only the information on general ball characteristics, eliminating the characteristics of that particular ball.

In the procedure of knowledge discovery, abstraction indicates the extraction out those basic and common properties from interesting things and the acquirement of concepts, classification ways and theorems (or principles) related to the interesting things after skipping out those non-essential components and connections inside interesting things. Since abstraction is a high level thought process by reflecting objective facts according to human sense and perception and appearance of things, such thought process is a jumping (or discontinuous) thought process from the perceptual recognition to the rational recognition. Recognizing things from appearances only can explain the association between outside behavior and phenomenons, one has to use abstraction method in order to procure new concepts, classification ways and theorems (or principles) related to the interesting things. Although the abstraction process has made human beings away from direct sensible things, it has upgraded our recognition for interesting things from the perceptual awareness to the rational comprehension. Hence, abstraction is able to reflect intrinsic characteristics for interesting things more deeply, correctly and completely.

There are two basic features of abstraction: objective concrete and subjective abstraction formulation. Abstraction is the unification of abstraction (subject) and concretion (object). Objective targets are represented by conceptual languages and formalized symbols through subjective abstraction. Therefore, the results of abstraction discover the essential components of objective targets and interrelations among essential components. The purpose of invenrelational abstraction is for invention computation which is different from metaphysical abstraction. Invenrelational abstraction procedure belongs to the range of dialectical thought methods because invenrelational abstraction not only extracts intrinsic elements and interrelationships from interesting things, but also develops concepts, classification ways and theorems (or principles) based on strict logical flow and mathematical derivation. Metaphysical abstraction is an isolated, fractional and detached (from objective targets) thought method, hence, some results obtained from metaphysical abstraction are void and rigid. If one adopts abstraction procedure improperly, one may make mistakes by treating subjective abstraction results as objective facts, misunderstanding superficial circumstances as essential principles or inferring the whole thing from partial (or even biased) evidence.

Invenrelational abstraction is executed by the following two phases. The first phase is to transform the perceptual information into abstraction thought. By means of collection and manipulation for the perceptual information which is generated from interesting things, one could formulate out new concepts and(or) principles. The second phase is to realize computational tasks involved in invention process by converting those concepts and principles obtained from the first phase into mathematical objects. The results received from such invenrelational abstraction could be utilized to the scientific explanation and prediction and these results have to be verified carefully through practice.

There are also several similar definitions about abstraction. We list some of them here for readers' kind references. Keene suggested that abstraction arises from a recognition of similarities between certain objects, situations, or processes in the real world, and the decision to concentrate upon these similarities and to ignore for the time being the differences [2]. Snyder defines an abstraction as a simplified description, or specification, of a system that emphasizes some of the system's details or properties while suppressing others [3]. An excellent abstraction is one that emphasizes the details that are significant to the inventors and suppresses details that are, at least for the moment, immaterial or diversionary. Hendler recommended the meaning of abstraction by "a concept qualifies as an abstraction only if it can be described, understood, and analysed independently of the mechanism that will eventually be used to implement it [4]." Booch defined an abstraction as follows: an abstraction denotes the essential characteristics of an object that distinguish it from all other kinds of objects and thus provide crisply defined conceptual boundaries, relative to the perspective of the viewer [5].

Some remarks have to be addressed here about abstraction. First, one has to collect the perceptual information as comprehensive as possible and tries to confirm the validity of such collected information. Second, essential elements and their interconnection have to be extracted from the collected perceptual information by removing fake or incomplete parts. Third, the lower level of abstraction must be derived from the higher level of abstraction. Otherwise, such abstraction could be invalid or unreasonable and one has to correct it.

2.1.1 Measuring the Goodness of an Abstraction

In general, a system should be built with a minimum set of unchangeable parts; those parts should be as general as possible; and all parts of the system should be associated within a framework. With computational development for invenrelation, these parts are the elements, attributes and sets that make up the key abstractions of the system (a thing to be invented), and the framework is provided by those relations among sets. We suggest the following four criterions in measuring the quality of an abstraction: sufficiency, completeness, primitiveness and compatibility.

Figure 2.1: Abstracting out components

For sufficiency, we mean that the abstraction captures enough characteristics of the things to permit meaningful and efficient interaction. Completeness indicates that the abstraction captures all of the meaningful characteristics of interesting things. Whereas sufficiency implies a minimal requirement for capturing characteristics of interesting things, a complete abstraction is one that covers all aspects of the interesting things. Completeness is a subjective matter, and it can be overdone. Providing all meaningful relations for a particular abstraction overwhelms the inventor and is generally unnecessary, since many high-level relations can be composed from low-level ones. For this reason, we also suggest that the abstraction to be primitive. Primitiveness means that the abstracted things are basic enough to be acted as generators for other related things. Compatibility is a notion borrowed from structured design. It measures the strength of association established by a connection from one abstraction of things to another.

2.1.2 Abstraction Expansion

In general, abstraction procedure will focus on some particular aspect of interesting things. If we extend the abstraction procedure from one aspect to other aspects and figure out their mutual relationships, such procedure is namely as *abstraction expansion*. This is a dialectical method by considering many aspects of interesting things theoretically. Abstraction expansion originated from German philosopher Hegel and his primary exposition is an extension procedure from thoughts (ideas) in minds to practical manners in external world. According to this train of thought, a philosophical system based on idealism is constructed by [6]. Marx reformed Hegel's primary thought from the perspective of materialism. Marx considered that practical manners or concrete things discussed in external world have still to be governed by abstraction thoughts in minds [7].

Abstraction expansion begins with the most simple or essential part of interesting things and expands toward more complicated or more concrete concepts through theoretical development until the whole aspects and their relationships of interesting things are reproduced in our minds. During the procedure of abstraction expansion, there are four basic portions involved in such procedure. They are *initial, intermediate, final* and *logical order*. Each portion of these four portions has its own properties to satisfy.

The initial portion of abstraction expansion is the beginning part for later theoretical formulation and derivation. The initial portion must satisfy one of the following characteristics: (1) the simplest part of interesting things; (2) the most general part of interesting things; (3) the constitutional part of interesting things and (4) the contradictory part which exists in the whole evolution of interesting things. In the book of *The Wealth of Nations*, which is considered as Adam Smith's magnum opus and the first modern work of economics, Smith treat *value* concept as the most basic and general part in deriving his whole theory, the kernel of Classical economics. After setting up this value concept as initial point, various economical concepts and their relationships could be mastered through value concept. We have to make sure that the initial portion of abstraction expansion is the ultimatum of the whole abstraction procedure, however, the depth of abstraction should be confined in a reasonable degree.

The intermediate portion of abstraction expansion is a serious of interconnection concepts or principles between the initial portion and the final portion. This portion has the following properties: (1) From the procedure of abstraction expansion, every part of the intermediate portion has relative abstraction property with respect to its preceding and succeeding parts. The preceding part has fewer aspects of interesting things to be abstracted compared to its succeeding part. On the other hand, the succeeding part has more aspects of interesting things to be abstracted. (2) The intermediate portion of abstraction expansion can connect the initial portion and the final portion through logical flow and make the all portions (initial, intermediate and final) into a thought system.

The final portion of abstraction expansion is the last step for the abstraction expansion procedure where the whole aspects and their relationships of interesting things are rebuilt in our minds.

During the entire procedure of abstraction expansion, logical order among concepts and principles has to be obeyed. Logical order has based on inner relationships among abstracted things, hence, our thoughts cannot jump wantonly in the procedure of abstraction expansion. Following rules may be helpful for us to unravel logical order among abstracted concepts and principles: (1) Various concepts and principles may be ordered by the understanding level for abstracted targets from the perspective of human knowledge history. (2) Association relationships among abstracted concepts and principles could also be adopted to arrange their logical order.

The complete procedure of abstraction expansion not only reflects the practical evolution procedure of objective things, but also possesses rigorous logical flow associated to each involved concepts and principles. The method of abstraction expansion could also be applied in constructing scientific systems theoretically.

2.1.3 Abstraction Generalization

From previous discussion, we understand that the abstraction procedure is to decompose the interesting things and examine their components carefully followed by removing secondary or non-intrinsic aspects and extracting essential attributes and their relationships. Thereafter, such thought procedure will empower us to develop concepts, classification ways and theorems (or principles) about our interesting things. Abstraction procedure is rooted from applying a serious of fundamental philosophical methods, e.g., analysis, synthesis, comparison and classification, to investigate characteristics and their relationships for the interesting things. Compared to perceptual recognition, the concepts obtained from abstraction is not vacuous, contrarily, more complete and insightful recognition for interesting things can be won. For example, natural numbers have been abstracted for two main purposes: counting, e.g., there are 6 apples on the table and ordering, e.g., this is the 3rd largest city in the world. This shows that the function of abstraction can disclose more essential parts of interesting things.

Abstraction generalization is to expand some particular intrinsic characteristics and principles obtained from abstraction procedure based on the original interesting things to all other things which share the same characteristics and principles of the original interesting things. Consequently, abstraction generalization may lead to new discoveries of scientific results since more widespread concepts about such characteristics and principles are obtained. Usually, scientific outcomes are commenced from experienced generalization followed by theoretical generalization.

At the stage of abstraction generalization based on experiences, one begins by observing each individuals thoroughly, then compares their identical (or similar) and different (or dissimilar) parts to get more generic recognition for these individuals. This procedure is an upgrade from recognizing of individuals characteristics to recognize attributes possessed by the kind which contains these interesting individuals. In the phase of experience-based abstraction generalization, generalization is executed by induction and the results obtained by suchlike experience-based generalization are experienced laws.

After the stage of experience-based abstraction generalization, one can include results obtained from experience-based abstraction generalization into the theoretical derivation and build a more comprehensive knowledge system by associating experienced-based generalization results with other related laws and (or) theories. Once the propositions about generalizations can be deduced from a theoretical system, such propositions will be provided with theoretical generalization properties and these may become theorems or laws after strict verifications. In summary, the whole procedure of abstraction generalization are composed by means of analysis, synthesis, comparison and classification.

Abstraction and generalization are mutual related with tight connection. Abstraction is the foundation of generalization and we cannot accomplish generalization without the materials obtained from the abstraction stage. On the other hand, generalization could be beneficial for scientific abstraction sometimes. This mutual dialectical relationship between abstraction and generalization keeps increasing broadness and profoundness of human knowledge.

2.2 Elements

To abstract the constitutive elements is the first step in forming mathematical objects in inven-relation theory. These constitutive elements could be treated as atoms for things to be invented. Atomism is a natural philosophy that developed in several ancient traditions. For examples, the Greek constitutive elements (*Earth, Water, Air, Fire, and Aether*) are proposed from pre-Socratic times and persisted throughout the Middle Ages and into the Renaissance, influencing European culture and thought deeply. The Greek five elements are sometimes associated with the five platonic solids. The Chinese had a somewhat different series of constitutive elements, namely *Fire, Earth, Water, Metal and Wood*, which were understood as different types of energy which interact destructively and constructively, rather than the Greek notion of different kinds of material.

In order to make the later theoretical formulation and derivation conveniently, we suggest the following guidances in abstracting constitutive elements:

- The simplest part of things to be invented.

- The most general part of things to be invented.

- The building blocks of things to be invented.

- The most basic part of things to be invented.

The following subsections are provided to readers about possible candidates of constitutive elements for things to be invented. The ways for elements abstraction listed below are not the only ways to extract elements for things to be invented. We can automatically adjust our range for elements abstraction in order to manipulate components for things to be invented easily. For example, the concept of filed in physics is expressed as a physical quantity associated to each point of space and time, which will be provided in detail in Sec. 2.2.1. Hence, a complete description of a field requires space, time and some values which characterize the strength of the interesting physical phenomenon (three basic elements: space, time and concept of number). A field can be classified as a scalar field, a vector field, or a tensor field, according to whether the value of the field at each point is a scalar, a vector, or tensor, respectively. For example, the electrical field is a vector field: specifying its value at a point in spacetime requires three numbers, the strength of electrical field in each direction at that point.

2.2.1   Space and Time

The concept of space is considered to be important in understanding of the physical universe although disagreement continues between philosophers over whether it is itself an entity, a relationship between entities, or part of a conceptual framework. For examples, classical physical space is the boundless, three-dimensional extent where things and events occur and have relative position and direction. In 1905, Albert Einstein published a paper on a special theory of relativity, in which he proposed that space and time be combined into a single construct known as spacetime. Hence, space discussed by modern physicists becomes four-dimensional. In mathematics, one may define a space with different dimensional mathematical objects and underlying mathematical structures associated to these objects. We abstract the meaning of space based on the aforementioned examples as: space was a collection of relations between things in which relations are given by their distance and direction from one another.

Geometry is the study of shapes and configurations. It attempts to understand and classify spaces in various mathematical contexts. For a space with lots of symmetries, the study will focuses on properties which are still invariant under the symmetrical operation of the space. Since space is endowed with relations which are provided by distance and direction among things in space, geometry, one major subject of mathematics, could be applied in solving the problems related to space.

Similar to space, time has been an another major subject of religion, philosophy, and science, but defining it in a proper manner which is applicable to all fields of study has consistently eluded the greatest scholars. Historically, there are two distinct sentiments on time from those prominent philosophers. One party treat time as part of the fundamental structure of the universe, a dimension in which events occur in a sequential order. Time travel, in this view, becomes a possibility as other "times" persist like frames of a film strip, spread out across the time axis. Sir Isaac Newton subscribed to this realist view, and hence it is sometimes referred to as Newtonian time [8]. The other viewpoint is that time does not relate to any kind of container that events or things "moving through", nor to any entity that "flows", but that it is instead part of a basic mental structure within which humans sequence and compare events or things. This second view, supported by Gottfried Leibniz and Immanuel Kant, states that time is neither an event nor a thing, and thus is not itself measurable nor can it be traveled.

From numerous definitions about time, I prefer to adopt the *"operational definition of time"*, in which we defines one standard unit time as a duration for completing a certain number of periodical events (such as the passage of a free-swinging pendulum). This definition is highly useful in the conduct of both advanced experiments and everyday affairs of life.

2.2.2 Substances

Many philosophies have used a set of archetypal classical elements to act as the simplest essential parts to constitute all substances. In chemistry, substances are divided into three categories: pure chemical elements, pure chemical compounds and mixtures of chemical elements or compounds.

An element is a chemical substance that is made up of a particular kind of atoms and hence cannot be separated further by a chemical reaction into a different element. However, it can be transformed into another element through a nuclear reaction. Hence, all of the atoms in a sample of an element have the same number of protons, though they may be different isotopes, with different number of neutrons. There are about 120 known elements, about 80 of which are stable existing in natural world.

A pure chemical compound is a chemical substance that is composed of a particular set of molecules or ions. A chemical compound is composed by at least two or more chemical elements through a chemical reaction. A chemical compound can be either atoms bonded together in molecules or crystals in which atoms, molecules or ions form a crystalline lattice. Compounds made up primarily on carbon and hydrogen atoms are called organic compounds, and all others are called inorganic compounds. Organic compounds play important roles in biochemistry and its applications.

Mixtures contain more than one chemical substance (chemical element or chemical compound), and they do not have a fixed composition. In principle, they can be separated into the component substances by purely physical processes. Butter, soil and wood are common examples of mixtures.

In modern physics, the subatomic particles become a new classes of elementary particles, which are particles with no substructure. Elementary subatomic particles are divided in three classes: quarks and leptons (particles of matter), and gauge bosons (force carriers, such as the photon).

2.2.3 Force and Energy

Force

From general experience, we recognize that the following fact: the motion of a body is a direct result of its interaction with the other bodies surround it. For instances, there is an interaction with the ball and bat controlled by a person when a person strikes a ball. The motion of an electron around a nucleus is provided by its electric interaction with the nucleus. The Moon moves around the Earth is the result of mutual gravitational interaction. Even in much smaller scale size, protons and neutrons are bound together tightly by their mutual strong interaction. Interactions are often represented quantitatively by an abstract concept-*force*. Three laws of motion were first formulated by great Sir Issac Newton at 17th century. We have to note that those laws formulated by Newton are only proper for motion speed much less than light speed. If the motion speed is closer to light speed, the theory of relativity proposed by Albert Einstein has to be adopted.

From Newton's second law of motion, the magnitude of force is equal to the changing rate of momentum. There are various kinds of force existing around us during our daily life. When we walk, our feet apply force on the ground. When we try to move bodies, our hands may push or pull bodies. We must apply force to tight up a rope when we try to bind something. Most transportation, e.g., boats, cars and airplanes, is powered by engine where gases are exploded to generate kinetic energy for transportation. Besides these, we can easily think of several other instances where forces are generated and applied. However, an important question is: where do these force come from?

From microscopic perspective, force is the result of statistical behaviors of atoms if we analyze the interaction between elementary particles. One of the important accomplishment of the last decades is to simplified all forces observed in nature into some fundamental interactions between the basic elements of matter. This indicates that forces are manifestations of the fundamental forces when a very large number of particles are considered. These basic forces are: gravitation, electromagnetic, strong interaction and weak interaction. From Newton's third law of action and reaction, any fundamental forces are associated with some particular matters since any matter that is the origin of a force is also the matter that can be acted upon by such a force. Different types of fundamental forces have different kinds of matters associated with them: *mass* is the matter of the gravitational force; *electrical charge* is the matter of the electric (or electromagnetic) force; the *color charge*, which is a property of quarks, is the matter of the strong force; and the weak interaction has its own matter named as *weak charge*. Since not all particles have these four matters involved and this is why particles are affected distinctly by these four fundamental interactions.

It is important to consider the action distance with respect to these four fundamental interactions. For example, strong forces do not generate measurable effects in ordinary experiments since the strong interactions happen within the range around 10^{-15} m. This explains the face that the strong force wad not discovered until the 1930s. Compared to strong forces, the gravitational and electric forces have been recognized for several hundred of years. Due to long range action of the gravitational and electric forces, many phenomena we observe in the world are the results of these two forces. We can state that very large structures in the universe are governed by gravitational force, e.g., solar system and galaxy. For very small structures in the universe, for examples, neutrons and protons, they are regulated by strong and weak interactions. For structures in the universe with size in between (atoms, molecules, liquids and solids), electric forces are responsible for most facts and chemical reactions found in the daily life. For instance, friction, viscosity and gas pressure are the result of electric actions between large numbers of atoms and molecules.

We summarize these four basic forces in the following table:

Forces	Relative Strength	Range	Matter
gravitation	1	∞	mass
electromagnetic	10^{36}	∞	electric charge
weak	10^{24}	10^{-18} m	weak charge
strong	10^{38}	10^{-15} m	color charge

Energy

Different from force, which may be easier to be recognized from ordinary life, the concept of energy has not been formulated clearly until 19th century. In physics, energy is a scalar physical quantity that quantifies the work that can be performed by a force. Different forms of energy exist in the following form, e.g., kinetic, potential, thermal, electromagnetic, gravitational, sound and elastic energy, and they are named by the related force. Another similar concept related to energy is power which denotes for the rate at which work is performed. Energy may not be created nor destroyed for any isolated system. This principle is called *the conservation law of energy*. According to energy conservation law, the total inflow of energy into an isolated system must equal to the total outflow of energy from the system, plus the change in the energy contained within the system. Any form of energy can be transformed into another form, for example, heat energy is transformed into mechanical energy in engine. However, the *law of conservation of energy* must be obeyed in process of energy transfer.

The notion of energy is widespread in all sciences. In biology, any living organism depends on an external source of energy to survive. For green plants, they perform oxygenic photosynthesis and anoxygenic photosynthesis to obtain energy from the Sun. For animals, they require an intake of food or nutrition to gain chemical energy and transform the original chemical energy into body heat and work made by animals. For meteorological phenomena like wind, hail, snow, rain, lightning, hurricanes and tornadoes, all of them are results of energy transformations brought about by solar energy on the atmosphere of the Earth. In geology, earthquakes, continental drift, mountain ranges and volcanoes, are phenomena that can be attributed to the internal energy of the Earth. In cosmology and astronomy, the phenomena of solar activity, stars, nova, supernova and quasars are energy transformations of matter in universe. Energy in such transformations is either from gravitational action of matter into various classes of astronomical objects (stars, black holes, etc.), or from nuclear fusion of lighter elements.

In the following, we will discuss different forms of energy. Mechanical energy may be the most famous form of energy since it can be easily sensed from our daily life. Basically, mechanical energy can be classified into potential energy and kinetic energy. The potential energy is a very general term, because it exists in all force fields, such as gravitation, electrostatic and magnetic fields. Potential energy is referred as the energy obtained by a body due to its position in a force field. The kinetic energy of an object is the extra energy which it possesses due to its mobility.

It is defined as the work needed to accelerate a body of a given mass from static condition to its current velocity.

Thermal energy of some matter is the energy associated with the microscopical random motion of particles constituting the matter. For example, in case of monoatomic gas it is just a kinetic energy of motion of atoms of gas as measured in the reference frame of the center of mass of gas. In case of many-atomic gas, the rotational and vibrational energy are involved. In the case of liquids and solids, the potential energy of interaction between atoms is engaged. Many processes involving exchanges of energy between a piece of mater and its environment can be analyzed without explicitly considering the atomic or molecular structure of matter. The study of such processes is the central topic of thermodynamics. Many macroscopic phenomena such as temperature, heat and pressure are related to molecular properties from theory of thermodynamics. Thermodynamics is very important for engineering development since heat engines are developed at about the same time due to the mature of thermodynamics theory. There are two main laws governing thermodynamics: the first law of thermodynamics, an expression of the principle of conservation of energy, states that energy can be transformed (changed from one form to another), but cannot be created or destroyed; the second law of thermodynamics is an expression of the universal principle of entropy, asserting that the entropy of an isolated system which is not in equilibrium will tend to increase over time and approach a maximum value at equilibrium.

Electrical related energy is composed by the following kinds: electrostatic energy, electricity energy and electromagnetic energy. The electrostatic energy of charges with a particular configuration is defined as the work which must be applied against the Coulomb force to rearrange charges from infinite separation to this configuration. If an electric current passes through a resistor, electricity energy is generated to increase the heat of the resistor. The amount of electricity energy due to an electric current can be expressed as

$$\text{electricity energy} = I^2 Rt, \tag{2.2.1}$$

where I is the current (in amperes), R is the resistance value (in Ohms) and t is the time for which the current flows (in seconds). Electromagnetic radiation is a phenomenon that takes the form of self-propagating waves in a vacuum or in matter. It consists of electric and magnetic field components which oscillate perpendicularly in phase to each other and perpendicular to the direction of radiation (energy) propagation. Electromagnetic radiation is classified into several types according to the wavelengh of its wave; these types include (by decreasing order of wave-length): radio waves, microwaves, terahertz radiation, infrared radiation, visible light, ultraviolet radiation, X-rays and gamma rays. Electromagnetic radiation carries energy and momentum to matter with which it interacts.

Chemical energy is the energy related to atoms in molecules and this is defined as a work done by electrical forces during re-arrangement of mutual positions of electrons and protons in the process of chemical reaction. If the chemical energy of a system decreases during a chemical reaction, the difference is transferred to the surroundings in form of heat or light. On the other hand, if the chemical reaction makes the difference of chemical energy of a system, then the difference is provided by the surroundings. For example, when two oxygen atoms react to form a dioxygen molecule, the chemical energy decreases by 498 KJ per mole.

Nuclear energy is obtained by splitting (fission) or merging together (fusion) of the nuclei of atom(s). Nuclear energy was first discovered by French physicist Henri Becquerel in 1896, when he observed that photographic plates stored in the dark near uranium were grown dark like X-ray plates. The energy from the Sun, also called solar energy, is an example of nuclear energy (fusion energy). In the Sun, the process of hydrogen fusion converts about 4 million metric tons of solar matter per second into light, which is radiated into space, but, during this process, the number of total protons and neutrons in the Sun does not change. In this system, each of the helium nuclei which are formed in the process is less massive than the four protons from they are formed, but there are no particles or atoms destroyed in the process of turning the nuclear potential energy into light.

2.2.4   Concepts and Knowledge

Concept is a knowledge unit for a group of interesting things through abstraction procedure by reflecting the common properties among these interesting things. Hence, concept is an abstract and universal thought with respect to interesting things. Concept is also the basic element of a proposition, as the word is the basic semantic element in a sentence. Concept is the carrier of meanings, not those who take the initiative of meanings. A single concept can be expressed in any number of languages; terminology is the representation of the concept which enables human beings to recognize the concept. In a sense, the language-independent property of passing concept among persons makes translation possible. In other words, various terminologies used by different languages have the same meaning for a concept, because they expressed the same concept.

From the historical development perspective, concepts are arisen from language usage. Such concepts are called vocabulary concepts since these concepts correspond lexical symbols in natural languages. For example, concepts for RED, SMILE, and LARGE, belong to vocabulary concepts. The main reason for the interest in vocabulary concepts is that it is common to think that words or phrases in natural languages inherit their meanings from he concepts they are used to express. Since more and more vocabulary concepts are proposed during the procedure of historical development, one may classify these vocabulary concepts based on some rules, relations, or similarities among these concepts. Hence, a structure is introduced due to classification for these vocabulary concepts. We say that primitive (or atomic) concepts are ones that are basic concepts without a specific structure. In contrast, concepts which are not primitive concepts are named as complex concepts. What exactly it means to describe that a concept has, or lacks, an associated structure is the main concern of the next paragraph.

Two main models for conceptual structure are presented here. The first is called as *Containment Model*. For this model, one concept is a structured complex of other concepts just in case it has other concepts as proper parts. For instance, a concept A might be composed of the concepts X, Y and Z, then an occurrence of A will also induce appearances of X, Y and Z since X, Y and Z are contained in A and A cannot happen without components X, Y and Z. For instance, the concept *drinking water* could not be emblemed without *drinking* or *water* being tokened. The word "water" is a structural element of the phrase "drinking water" in the sense that it is a proper part of the sentence. Consequently, one cannot convey a token of the phrase "drinking water" without thereby uttering a token of the word "water". The other model for conceptual structure is called *Inferential Model*. According to this perspective, one concept is a structured complex of other concepts just in case it stands in a special relation to other concepts, generally, by some types of inferential disposition. With this model, the concept A may still occur without the appearances of its partial concepts X, Y and Z. For example, the concept "GREEN" may have a structure to imply the concept of "color", but on the Inferential Model, one could deal with the concept GREEN without having to token the concept COLOR. For example, one may link GREEN with environmental protection and energy-saving concepts.

Basically, there are two perspective views about appearance of concept : concept as abstraction V.S. concept as mental representation. The best way to distinguish these two perspective views for concepts can be considered as the distinction between *sense* and *reference*, which is proposed by the nineteenth-century German philosopher Gottlob Frege. Such distinction between sense and reference is generally applied to expressions of every size and semantic class. For example, "silver"(sense) and "element with atomic number 47"(reference) may refer to the same thing, but under different perspective views for concepts description. Similarly, "Samuel Clemens"(sense) and "Mark Twain"(reference) indicate the same individual, but their ways to specifying a concept are dissimilar. Following three points are listed to characterize the difference between sense and reference [9].

- Senses are the mental contents of linguistic expressions. This point is associated to what has come to be known as *Frege's Puzzle*. Frege inquires how two equivalent statements, "the morning star is the morning star" and "the morning star is the evening star", could be different in mental content. Both are identical statements concerning referential terms indicating the planet Venus. The first statement is only a truism, however, the second statement is an important discovery from astronomical observation. Based on Frege's interpretation to this puzzle, literal expressions involved in these statements have senses and the dissimilarities in mental contents correspond to differences between the senses they express.

- Senses determine references. According to Frege's explanation, human linguistic and conceptual access to the world is interfered by the senses of the expressions in our language. A sense determines the reference of an expression through our comprehension of a sense. For example, "a white dog' refers to the object it dose because this expression has the sense it does.

- Senses are the indirect referents of expressions in deliberate contexts. Some linguistic context, e.g.,... feel that... (or other propositional attitude statements), have special properties since their meanings have to be associated with the original intention of presenters. Outside of these contexts, one can freely substitute referential terms without affecting the truth value of the sentence, e.g., the morning star is bright $\rightarrow$ the evening star is bright. Let us consider another situations where substitutions are not possible since the truth value may be changed after a substitution, e.g., "Tom feels that the morning star is bright." $\nrightarrow$ "Tom feels that the evening star is bright.". This situation suggests that expressions do not refer to their customary senses in such contexts, but rather to their customary senses. Since the expressions have different customary senses, they have different references in these contexts.

After clarifying the notions of concepts, the term *knowledge* can be illuminated by concepts.

The definition of knowledge is a matter of on-going debate among philosophers, social scientists and historians. Knowledge may be generated in the following situations: (1) the record for accumulated experiences, (2) the arranged facts with respect to some logical order, and (3) recognized behaviors or status. The classical definitions about knowledge were proposed since Greek times, for instances, by great philosophers Plato and Socrates. Plato believed that we learn in this life by recollecting knowledge originally acquired in a previous life, and that the soul already has all knowledge, and we learn by remembering what in fact the soul already knows. Plato suggested three analyses of knowledge, all of which he proposed were rejected by another great Greek philosopher Socrates. The first is that "knowledge is equivalent to perception." Socrates rejected this by saying that we can perceive without knowing and we can know without perceiving. For example, we can see and hear the usage of a foreign language by foreigners without knowing it. Since we can perceive without knowing, then knowledge cannot be identical to perception. Plato's second analysis is that true belief is knowledge. Socrates disproved this by describing that when a jury believes a defendant is guilty by just hearing the prosecuting attorney's rambling, rather than of any solid evidence, it cannot be said to know that the accused is guilty even if the accused has guilty. Hence, the jury's beliefs cannot be treated as knowledge. Plato's third analysis is that true belief accompanied by reasonable statements is knowledge, whereas true belief disassociated by a rational account is not recognized as knowledge. All interpretations of account are deemed inadequate. These analyses prove to be an excellent example of the attacking the inadequate theories of knowledge, but it does not prove an answer to what knowledge is.

The above classical definition about knowledge, described but not ultimately endorsed by Plato, specifies that a statement must meet three criteria in order to be considered knowledge: it must be justified, true, and believed. Until last century, various modern definitions about knowledge are proposed. In the end of 1940s, Wittgenstein clarified the difference between belief and knowledge hinted from Moore's paradox. For example, one can say "He believes it, but it isn't so", but not "He knows it, but it isn't so". Wittgenstein went on to argue that these did not correspond to distinct psychological states, but rather to distinct ways of talking about conviction. What is different here is not the psychological state of the speaker, but the circumstances in which they are engaged. For instance, on this account, to know that wood is burning is not to be in a particular state of mind, but to perform a particular action with the statement that wood is burning. Wittgenstein tried to skip the difficulty of definition by looking to the way "knowledge" is used in natural languages. He proposed the notion of *family resemblance* to describe the structure characteristics of various concepts among a knowledge field.

In 1990s, Purser and Pasmore defined knowledge as a collection of things which are used to make decisions, e.g., facts, models, schema, opinions and intuitions. Badaracco defined knowledge as all truths, principles, ideas and information obtained from human activities. Besides, Davenport defined knowledge as complexes with flow nature based on the characteristics of knowledge. It may include structured experience, values, processed information by vocabularies or figures, opinions from experts and frameworks provided to assess and integrate new experiences. More recently, Japanese scholar N. Ikujiro recognized knowledge as a pluralistic concept with multiple levels of significance. Knowledge involves belief, commitment and actions and it can be classified into the implicit and explicit knowledge.

By summarizing above numerous definitions of knowledge, knowledge is *a collection of organized concepts* and the size of such collection is determined by the number of concepts associated to the interesting knowledge. A concept map is a diagram help us to comprehend the relationships among concepts. Concept maps are graphical tools for organizing and representing knowledge. Concept maps, in general, are composed by boxes or circles and directed arrows among them. Concepts, usually expressed as boxes or circles, are connected with labelled arrows in a downward-branching hierarchical structure. The relationship between concepts can be associated by linking phrases such as "gives rise to", "is required by,", "results in" or "contributes to". If two associated concepts are related to quantity, mathematical relations, e.g., greater, smaller or equal, will be used to articulate these two concepts. An industry standard that implements formal rules for designing such diagrams is the Unified Modeling Language (UML) [10].

2.3   Attributes

In this section, we will begin to discuss the notion of attributes, or properties. Every element abstracted out for things to be invented has a number of properties since there is no formless element without useful properties for invention. In general, an attribute used to describe any elements is represented by several predicates.

Some attributes are inherent attributes of individuals, for example, radioactivity and comprehensibility. Such kinds of properties are called as intrinsic properties *intrinsic attributes*. On the other hand, some attributes are attributes related to various substantial individuals. For example, solubility is the attribute of a solid, liquid, or gaseous chemical substance called solute to dissolve in a liquid solvent to form a homogeneous solution. The solubility of a substance strongly depends on the used solvent as well as on temperature and pressure. The pressure also affects the solution whether it is gas or liquid, like temperature. So, in the definition of solubility we also need to specify the background pressure and temperature for solving procedure. The extent of the solubility of a substance in a given solvent is measured as the saturation concentration where adding more solute will not increase the concentration of the solution further. Therefore, there are four elements involved in attribute about solubility: solute, solvent, pressure and temperature. Such attributes are called *mutual attributes*.

A mutual attribute of an element may or may not depend causally on some other element involved. For example, velocity of a moving element is a mutual attribute because this attribute is related to both the moving element and the reference frame, nevertheless, the moving behavior is not introduced by the reference frame. Similar frame-depend mutual attributes appeared in science include distance, duration, gravity field strength and many other physical and chemical properties. Another category of mutual attributes, e.g., color and loudness perceptible by human beings, are special kind of mutual attributes since they depend not only on the background environment with respect to the target element but also on the subjectivity of observers. We name such kinds of attributes as *subjective attributes*.

If some attributes are related to quantity, structure, space, and variation of elements, four main subjects of mathematics, e.g., arithmetic, algebra, geometry, and analysis, can be adopted to describe these attributes formally and rigorously. In summary, we can classify all attributes into the following six categories:

- Non-mathematical Intrinsic Attribute

- Non-mathematical Mutual Attribute

- Non-mathematical Subjective Attribute

- Mathematical Intrinsic Attribute

- Mathematical Mutual Attribute

- Mathematical Subjective Attribute

2.4 Sets

2.4.1 Sets and Their Components

In our daily lives as well as in our inventional work, we often deal with elements involved and make statement such as, "The students in this class are sophomore and Electrical Engineering majors," "Chairs can be made from wood, stone or metal" and "Not all materials float on water". We would like to abstract some of basic concepts dealing with the many different elements and their attributes (or properties) and establish certain common terminology for dealing with them.

In the first statement, we are referring to students who possess the two attributes of being a Electrical Engineering major and of being a sophomore. This indicates the concept of *and* which is used to collect objects which have more then one attributes. In the second statement, the concept of *or* is adopted here to indicate that there are three possible materials used (simultaneously or non-simultaneously) to make chairs. In order to exclude some objects which have some specified attributes from the original collection of objects, the concept of *negation* is required as shown at the third sentence. Our examples illustrate the many situations on which we deal with several classes of objects and wish to refer to those objects that belong to some or all classes. The notion of *set* is then established to indicate a collection of elements with desired attributes and we can form a new set from the original sets by a serious of set operation related to the concept of *and, or* and *negation.*

Therefore, a set is a collection of objects based on some attributes. In general, we use the capital alphabets, e.g., A, B, C,...., to represent the name of a set and use the following notation to denote for a set, named as S:

$$S = \{s | s \text{ has certain attributes}\}, \tag{2.4.1}$$

where s is the component of the set S. If each component at a set has its own name, another way to express such set will by a list. For example, the set of vowels in English is

$$S = \{a, e, i, o, u\}. \tag{2.4.2}$$

In general, the components in a set are those elements suggested in Sec. 2.2.

Two sets A and B are equal, written $A = B$, if they consist of the same elements. It is equivalent to say that each component of A belongs to B and each component of B belongs to A. For example, the set $A = \{\text{real roots of } x^2 - 3x + 2 = 0\}$ and $B = \{1, 2\}$ are equal. If the number of components in a set is finite, such set is called a finite set; otherwise, a set is called an infinite set.

In any application of the sets, all sets under discussion are subsets of a fixed set. This particular set is called *universal set* and often denoted by symbol U. It is also suitable to define a set which contains nothing. This set is named as *empty or null set*, represented as $\emptyset$, is considered to be a finite set and a subset of every other set.

2.4.2 Subsets and Supersets

A set A is a subset of a set B (or, equally, B is a superset of A), expressed as $A \subset B$ or $B \subset A$, if each element in A also belongs to B; that is if $x \in A$ implies $x \in B$. For example, consider the sets $A = \{1, 3, 5, 7, \cdots\}$, $B = \{3, 6, 9, 12, \cdots\}$ and $C = \{$prime number greater than 2$\}$, Then $C \subset A$ since every prime number greater than 2 is odd. But set B not belongs to set A since the component $6 \in B$ but 6 not $\in A$. For any three sets A, B and C, we have the following three facts: (1) $A \subset A$, (2) if $A \subset B$ and $B \subset A$ then $A = B$, and (3) if $A \subset B$ and $B \subset C$ then $A \subset C$. These three facts can be verified easily from definitions.

2.4.3 Set Operations

From those statements examples provided in the beginning part of Sec. 2.4.1, we observe that there are three concepts involved in changing the components of the original sets, which are *and, or, negation*. Hence, there are also three operations about sets, namely *intersection, union, complement*, corresponding to the three concepts of *and, or, negation*.

The *intersection* of two sets A and B, denoted as $A \bigcap B$, is the set of components which belong both A and B. If $A \bigcap B = \emptyset$, then A and B are said to be *disjoint* sets. The *union* of two sets A and B, denoted by $A \bigcup B$, is the set of all elements which belong to A or B. The *complement* of a set A, denoted as A^c, is the set of components which do not belong to A. The *relative complement* of a set B with respect to A (or called the *difference* of A and B), denoted as $A \backslash B$, is the set of components which belong to A but which do not belong to B.

Sets under the above operations satisfy various laws or identities, for example, we have the following identity, namely *distributive law*, as $A \bigcap (B \bigcup C) = (A \bigcap B) \bigcup (A \bigcap B)$. The proof is given below as

$$A\bigcap(B\bigcup C) = \{x : x \in A \text{ and } x \in B\bigcup C\}$$
$$= \{x : x \in A \text{ and } \{x \in B \text{ or } x \in C\}\}$$
$$= \{x : \{x \in A \text{ and } x \in B\} \text{ or } \{x \in A \text{ and } x \in C\}\}$$
$$= (A\bigcap B)\bigcup(A\bigcap B). \tag{2.4.3}$$

In summary, we use the following table to represent those basic laws and identities satisfied by sets operations.

Laws	Union	Intersection
Idempotent	$A\bigcup A = A$	$A\bigcap A = A$
Associative	$(A\bigcup B)\bigcup C = A\bigcup(B\bigcup C)$	$(A\bigcap B)\bigcap C = A\bigcap(B\bigcap C)$
Commutative	$(A\bigcup B) = (B\bigcup A)$	$(A\bigcap B) = (B\bigcap A)$
Distributive	$A\bigcup(B\bigcap C) =$ $(A\bigcup B)\bigcap(A\bigcup C)$	$A\bigcap(B\bigcup C) =$ $(A\bigcap B)\bigcup(A\bigcap C)$
Identity	$A\bigcup\emptyset = A, A\bigcup U = U$	$A\bigcap\emptyset = \emptyset, A\bigcap U = A$
Complement	$A\bigcup A^c = U, (A^c)^c = A$	$A\bigcap A^c = \emptyset, U^c = \emptyset, \emptyset^c = U$
De Morgan	$(A\bigcup B)^c = A^c\bigcap B^c$	$(A\bigcap B)^c = A^c\bigcup B^c$

2.4.4   Product Sets

The product, also known as Cartesian product, of two sets A and B, denoted as $A \times B$, is the set of all ordered pairs of the form (a, b) where $a \in A$ and $b \in B$. For example, the product of the 13-component set of standard playing card ranks Ace, King, Queen, Jack, 10, 9, 8, 7, 6, 5, 4, 3, 2, and the four-component set of card suits $\{\spadesuit, \heartsuit, \diamondsuit, \clubsuit\}$, is the 52-element set of all possible playing cards (Ace, $\spadesuit$), (King, $\spadesuit$), ..., (2, $\spadesuit$), (Ace, $\heartsuit$), ..., (3, $\clubsuit$), (2, $\clubsuit$). The corresponding product set has $52 = 13 \times 4$ elements.

If the two original sets, say A and B, are not identical, the product set is not commutative because the ordered pairs (a, b) is not equal to (b, a), where $a \in A$ and $b \in B$. The product set is not associative since the triple ordered pairs $(a, (b, c))$ is not equal to $((a, b), c)$. Considering the product operation with intersection operation, we have $(A\bigcap B) \times (C\bigcap D) = (A \times C)\bigcap(B \times D)$. However, in general, we do not have $(A\bigcup B) \times (C\bigcup D) = (A \times C)\bigcup(B \times D)$.

42

The concept of product set can be extended to any finite number of sets. The product set of the sets $B_1, B_2, \cdots, B_n$, expressed as

$$B_1 \times B_2 \times \cdots \times B_n \qquad (2.4.4)$$

consists of all n ordered tuples $(b_1, b_2, \cdots, b_n)$ where $b_i \in B_i$ for each $1 \leq i \leq n$.

2.5 Relations

The concept of sets have been provided in Sec. 2.4. Since each set is formed by collecting elements with specific attributes, the concept of *relation* between particular sets is induced by exploring the interaction between components in these sets. There are numerous examples about relations existing in various areas of our life and science. In sociology, a social relation refers to an association between two, three or more individuals (e.g. a social group). This association may be based on love, regular business interactions, or some other types of social commitment. Social relationships take place in a great variety of contexts, such as family, friends, marriage, associates, work, clubs, neighborhoods, and churches. Social relations, obtained from individual agency, form the basis of the social structure. Therefore, social relations are always the basic objects to analysis by social scientists. In anthropology, kinship is a relationship generated by descent and marriage, while usage in biology includes descent and mating. Human kinship relations through marriage are commonly called "affinity" in contrast to "descent" (also called "consanguinity"). In civil countries, the doctrine of legitime plays a similar role, and makes the lineal descendants of the dead person forced heirs. Rules of kinship and descent also have crucial political aspects, especially under monarchies, where they determine the order of succession, the heir apparent and the heir presumptive. By considering components in sets as nations in our current world, international relations, which is a branch of political science, is to study foreign affairs and global issues among nations.

We considered the concept of an ordered pair of components in Sec. 2.4.4. A *binary relation* from the set A to set the B is defined as a subset of product set $A \times B$. A binary relation provides the intuitive notion that some of the components in A are related to some of components in B. If R denotes for the binary relation from A to B and the ordered pair (a, b), where $a \in A$ and $b \in B$, is in R, then we say that the component a is related to the component b. For example, let $A = \{a, b, c\}$ be a set of three students and let $B = \{MA_1, MA_2, MA_3, MA_4, MA_5, MA_6\}$ be set of six candidate courses. The cartesian product $A \times B$ provides all possible pairings of students and courses taken. The relation R_1, which is (a, MA_1), (a, MA_2), (b, MA_1), (b, MA_2), (b, MA_3), (c, MA_4), (c, MA_5) and (c, MA_6), describes the courses taken by all students. Another relation R_2, which is (a, MA_2), (a, MA_4), (b, MA_1), (b, MA_3), (c, MA_5) and (c, MA_6), states the courses that the students are interested in. Then the binary relation $R_1 \bigcap R_2$, which is (a, MA_2), (b, MA_1), (b, MA_3), (c, MA_5) and (c, MA_6), indicates the courses that the students are taking and also interested in. The binary relation $R_1 \bigcup R_2$, which is (a, MA_1), (a, MA_2), (a, MA_4), (b, MA_1), (b, MA_2), (b, MA_3), (c, MA_4), (c, MA_5) and (c, MA_6), demonstrates the courses that the students are either taking or interested in. Finally, the binary relation $R_1 \backslash R_2$, which is (a, MA_1), (b, MA_2) and (c, MA_4), represents the courses that the students are taking but not interested in.

A particular case of binary relation is formed by the subset of product set $A \times B$, where $A = B$. Such binary relation over a set A could also be named as *endorelation* over A. In the following, we introduce several important properties for binary relations over a set A.

1. *Reflexive*: $\forall a \in A$, the ordered pair (a, a) belongs to the relation,

2. *Symmetric*: For $a_1, a_2 \in A$, if the ordered pair (a_1, a_2) is in a relation, then (a_2, a_1) is also in this relation.

3. *Asymmetric*: For $a_1, a_2 \in A$, if the ordered pair (a_1, a_2) is in a relation, then (a_2, a_1) is NOT in this relation.

4. *Antisymmetric*: For $a_1, a_2 \in A$, if both the ordered pairs (a_1, a_2) and (a_2, a_1) are in a relation, then $a_1 = a_2$.

5. *Transitive*: For a_1, a_2 and $a_3 \in A$, if both the ordered pairs (a_1, a_2) and (a_2, a_3) are in a relation, then (a_1, a_3) is also in this relation.

6. *Total*: For $\forall a_1, a_2 \in A$, either (a_1, a_2) or (a_2, a_1) is in a relation.

A relation is called an *equivalent relation* if it is reflexive, symmetric and transitive. A relation which is reflexive, antisymmetric and transitive is called a *partial order*. A partial order relation with total property is called a *total order*, *linear order* or *a chain*. A total order relation in which every nonempty set has a least element is called a *well-order relation*.

As binary relations characterizes the relationship between pairs of components from two sets, we may extend ternary relations to describe the relationship among triples of components from three sets. A *ternary relation* among three sets A, B, and C, denoted as $A \times B \times C$, is a subset of product of three sets A, B, and C. For example, if $A = \{a, b\}$, $B = \{c, d\}$ and $C = \{1, 2\}$, we then have

$$A \times B \times C = \{(a, c, 1), (a, c, 2), (a, d, 1), (a, d, 2),$$
$$(b, c, 1), (b, c, 2), (b, d, 1), (b, d, 2)\}. \qquad (2.5.1)$$

In general, an *n-ary relation* among n sets $A_1, A_2, \cdots, A_n$ is defined as a subset of product set $A_1 \times A_2 \times \cdots \times A_n$. Equivently, an n-ary relation among sets $A_1, A_2, \cdots, A_n$ is a set of ordered n-tuples in which the first term in a component from the set A_1, the second term is a component from set A_2, and the n-th term is a component from set A_n. Without loss of generality, we may regulate the previous $n - 1$ sets as the input for an n-ary relation and the n-th set as the output for this n-ary relation. Such agreement will enable us easier to consider mathematical function concept as a special case of relation concept.

2.6 Algebraic Model for Invenrelation and Examples

From previous discussion, constitutive elements, attributes possessed by these constitutive elements, sets formed according to attributes of elements and relations among sets are abstracted out as components for things to be invented. In order to manipulate these components mathematically during an invention procedure, an algebraic model about these components is proposed in this section.

There are two family of sets in this algebraic model, denoted as $\mathbb{S}$ and $\mathbb{F}$. The family $\mathbb{S}$ is composed by sets S_i where i is the index for sets in $\mathbb{S}$. The index i belongs to the index set I (or called by proper names). The family $\mathbb{F}$ is made up by relations f_ω where ω is the index for different relation. The index ω belongs to the index set Ω (or called by appropriate names). For each ω, the relation f_ω is a $n(\omega) + 1$-ary relation where $n(\omega)$ is an positive integer depending on the index ω. Let $S_{i_{1,\omega}}, S_{i_{2,\omega}}, \cdots, S_{i_{n(\omega),\omega}}$ be those $n(\omega)$ sets at the input of the relation f_ω and the set $S_{i_{n(\omega)+1,\omega}}$ is the output of the relation f_ω, then f_ω can be expressed as

$$f_\omega : S_{i_{1,\omega}} \times S_{i_{2,\omega}} \times \cdots \times S_{i_{n(\omega),\omega}} \to S_{i_{n(\omega)+1,\omega}}, \qquad (2.6.1)$$

in which $i_{j,\omega}$ is the corresponding index with respect to the index set of $\mathbb{S}$ (I) for the j-th set associated with $n(\omega) + 1$-ary relation f_ω. The family $\mathbb{S}$ is produced by collecting constitutive elements followed by classifying them into different sets S_i based on their attributes. After figuring out relations among sets in $\mathbb{S}$, the family $\mathbb{F}$ can also be determined.

We will provide several examples to conclude key points of this section. The first example illustrates the abstraction results for basic components with respect to things to be invented. The second example provides an algebraic model shown by (8.2.1) to describe resultant force of a object acted by two or more forces. Actually, this algebraic model is a vector space and such concept is used extensively in mathematics and engineering applications. The third example is about applying the algebraic model for combination invention, one important method for creating new things. In example 2, we note that the abstraction procedure for elements or attributes may be omitted if we can clearly define our sets used in the algebraic model.

Example of Abstraction

Elements Abstraction: Individuals that represent constitutional entities of a problem domain or solution-domain. For a composer, notes with various kinds of time duration and staves are constitutional elements abstracted from music.

Attributes Abstraction: Abstract expressionism artists often extract out significant attributes from their interesting things, e.g., special forms, colors and lines of interesting things, and manipulate their masterpieces by exaggerating these abstracted attributes.

Sets Abstraction: In biology, a biological system (or Organ system) is a group of organs that work together to perform a certain kinds of tasks. Such biological system is formed by a *Set* of organs by abstracting those similar physiological attributes and functions shared by organs. Common biological systems, such as those presented in mammals and other animals, studied in human anatomy, are the circulatory system, the respiratory system, the nervous system, etc. The organ systems of the human body include the musculoskeletal system, cardiovascular system, digestive system, endocrine system, integumentary system, urinary system, lymphatic system, immune system, respiratory system, nervous system and reproductive system.

Relations Abstraction: Galileo Galilei, an great Italian scientist, who did many significant scientific contributions in fields of physics, mathematics and astronomy. In his study about the law of free falling bodies, he abstracted out two sets of variables in describing a falling body, the falling distance and the elapsed time. Moreover, he abstracted out the relationship between the falling distance and the elapsed time as : an initially-stationary object which is allowed to fall

46

freely under gravity drops a distance which is proportional to the square of the elapsed time.

Algebraic Model for Forces

An applied force has both direction and magnitude. In order to describe force by its applied direction and magnitude, the family $\mathbb{S}$ is composed by two kinds of sets V and F, where V is the set of vectors and F is the set of real numbers (scaler). In physics, the net force acted on an object by several forces can be expressed as the vector addition among these forces. For relation about the set V, we have

$$\overbrace{V \times V \times \cdots \times V}^{\text{the number of } V \text{ is the number of applied forces}} \to V, \qquad (2.6.2)$$

where the *vector addition* is the relation between the set of input forces and the set of resultant force. The magnitude of a force is described by a real number with a force unit, e.g., Newton. Since the basic arithmetic operations about real numbers are addition, subtraction, multiplication and division, the relations about the set F for basic arithmetic operation become

$$F + F \to F, \ F - F \to F, \ F \cdot F \to F, \text{ and } F \div F \to F. \qquad (2.6.3)$$

The Eq. (2.6.3) can be extended to consider more than two sets of F as the input of an arithmetic relation. It can be written as

$$\overbrace{F \times_1 F \times_2 \cdots \times_j F}^{\text{the number of set } F} \to F, \qquad (2.6.4)$$

where each $\times_k$ for $1 \leq k \leq j$ represents a basic arithmetic operation selected from addition, subtraction, multiplication and division. In addition, we need to have the following relation to describe the situation of adjusting the magnitude of a force without changing its direction. Such relations are $F \times F \times V \to V$ and $F \times V \times V \to V$ and we have to obey the following rules in these two relations. They are

$$(\lambda\mu)\vec{a} = \lambda(\mu\vec{a}),$$

$$(\lambda + \mu)\vec{a} = \lambda\vec{a} + \mu\vec{a},$$

$$\lambda(\vec{a} + \vec{b}) = \lambda\vec{a} + \lambda\vec{b}, \qquad (2.6.5)$$

where λ, μ are scalers in F and $\vec{a}, \vec{b}$ are vectors in V.

47

Algebraic Model for Combination Invention

Combination invention is a method to create new things through assembling components with different functions. Combination invention treats final products as combination of several components or modules with specific functions according to some rules. The following steps are involved in this procedure: the first step is to collect and classify all possible components for things to be invented, the second step is to combine these components with respect to some rules or principles. From Eq. (8.2.1) and the first step of combination invention, the sets of S_i are composed by all possible components for things to be invented, where the index i is used to distinguish different type of components for things to be invented. The relation f_ω is determined by principles or rules to combine sets of components $S_{i_{1,\omega}}, S_{i_{2,\omega}}, \cdots, S_{i_{n(\omega),\omega}}$ into final set of creation $S_{i_{n(\omega)+1,\omega}}$, where the index ω is used to represent different combination ways for components.

Suppose we are given a problem to create a new dinning tool which enable us easier to enjoy different kinds of foods, e.g., noodles, meat balls, steaks or soups, without switching between assorted dining tools. The constitutive elements for designing new tableware are those dining tools used or known by general audience, for example, dishes, sauce boats, glassware, and cutlerys (knives, forks, spoons, chopsticks and so on) used to set a table for eating a meal. If we wish to design a new dining tool with handle which makes us effortless to control such new dining tool, the set of components for new dinning tool is formed by eliminating those elements of tableware without handle. Here, we adopt the attribute of "handles" to screen out our sets for algebraic model as written by Eq. (8.2.1). Some possible components in such set are knives, forks, spoons and chopsticks. If we use S_{handle} to represent a set which consists of all tableware with handles and denote S_{new} as the set for created items through a combination method, we have the following algebraic model for combination invention by assemble two components from set S_{handle}. It is

$$f_{\text{handle}} : S_{\text{handle}} \times S_{\text{handle}} \to S_{\text{new}}, \qquad (2.6.6)$$

where f_{handle} is a relation which represents a way of combination by adhering two dinning tools from set S_{handle} together through their handle. Therefore, possible new dining tools in set S_{New} may be knife-chopstick, fork-chopstick, spoon-chopstick, knife-spoon, fork-spoon and knife-fork. Two patent applications in U.S.A (D384,249 and D386,050) about using combination invention for creating new dining tools have obtained their patent rights at 1997.

In summarize, we can use the Fig. 2.2 to illustrate the procedure to abstract a food chain from a grassland.

2.7 Information Collection

In order to survive, enjoy life and solve problems, we need various kinds of information. Therefore, we can understand the importance of information. Information is not only quite important to our mankind, but also is indispensable to all living beings in the world. Proper operations and balance of all systematic functions of living beings depends on adjusting their reactions based on surrounding environment information collected by several sense organs. Some information sensed by living beings are favorable, however, some collected information are unfavorable. Hence, proper adjustments are able to promote our living capability. For our human beings, we can go one step further by applying information to change the environment and our thoughts in order to create a more comfortable world to live within. At the initial step of invention, we also have to collect information about constitutive elements, attributes possessed by these constitutive elements, sets developed based on attributes of elements and relations among sets before forming algebraic models for invention. In conclusion, information collection is very important!

2.7.1 Information Sending and Receiving

In order to transmit and receive the information, we must have an intact and open communication system, i.e., we are capable to grasp information source, information, information conveyers, transmission channels, recipients and their perceptual ability. Blemish in such communication system is that there are many obstacles existing in this procedure of information transmission. The first obstacle is that experience and background of information conveyers and accepters will affect the transmitted information. Primitive information may be distorted and changed due to other reasons. The most common reasons to alter information during a communication procedure are listed as follows:

- Languages used by conveyer and accepter are different.

- Lack of understanding basic knowledge of information.

- The method used to retrieval information is not capable enough.

49

GRASSLAND   ELEMENT

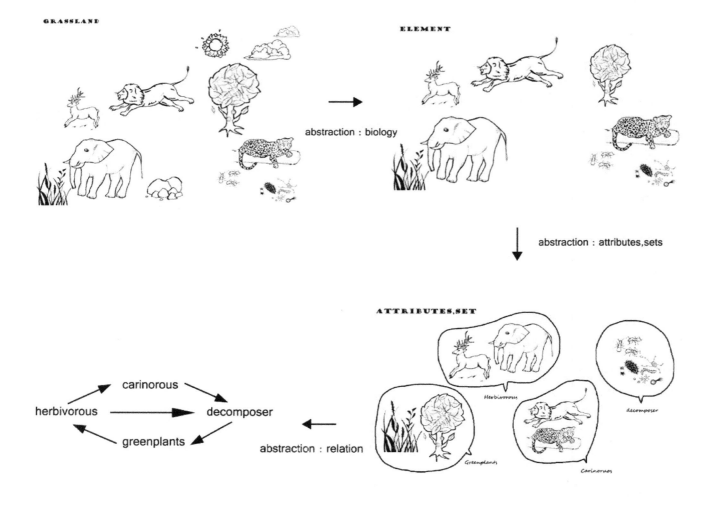

abstraction : biology

abstraction : attributes,sets

ATTRIBUTES,SET

carinorous

herbivorous   decomposer

greenplants

abstraction : relation

- Too much or too strong noises, interferences or mistakes are produced.

Open communicative channels make people apt to obtain information. Especially, it becomes more important when one wishes to make the best decision in a very short time. Excellent information communicative method can save a lot of time for us since we can adjust our reactions properly and promptly according to the acquired information.

2.7.2   Information Classification and Search

Due to the growth of information and the improvement of communication facilities, we are facing a global information overload. Our senses and brains have suffered unprecedented pressure and we may describe that we are in the era of information explosion.

The human brain is not unalterable since our intelligence can grow up gradually. However, we still have many time and mental limits when we deal with information from various areas. How could we avoid to be drowned in such information floods? Although nobody can master every thing, we have to learn how to discover and search useful information.

Actually, we would be more relax since there is much information in the world which is not direct related to our problem. Fundamentally, we must be able to organize, classify and investigate the things that we really need to understand. We should face "the information explosion" by extracting the key ideas through contracting, replacing, contacting or deleting those unnecessary parts from obtained information. The following suggestions are provided to screen out useful information:

- Evaluating what information you need and the processing methods, try to increase your own capacity for absorbing information.

- Selecting useful information by sorting obtained information with respect to its importance.

- Focus at interesting problems and try to avoid distractions and interferences from the background environment.

- Using any information sources efficiently to store and search information, e.g., computers, notebook, assistants or friends.

From the birthday of ones life, he/she begins to receive information consistently and form his/her own personal experience and background knowledge gradually every day. Most information may come from ones job and daily habit, such first-hand materials often become strong mental belief in personal consciousness and subconsciousness because we participate these activities over a long period of time. This information also includes various feelings acquired by sense organs. Besides, we also obtain a lot of second hand information through sharing knowledge, intelligence and experience with others. These kinds of information are often intellectual which are not information obtained from sense organs.

For convenient purposes, we may classify information roughly into the following six categories and we can clearly identify the category for our information in hand.

- Essential regulations, rules and knowledge among the universe.

- Evolution progress in history.

- Memory composed by personal firs-hand sensed materials.

- Information required and news happened in daily life .

- New products and discoveries in art, science and technology.

- Conjectures and unknowns claimed by people.

Among the above six kinds of information, the former two categories are stable and static and they are slowly accumulated by thousands of years. The following two types are about personal interests and mental development. Information collected by these two types will vary proportionally with respect to the personal growth and change. The last two kinds will be altered according to new developments in art, science and technology. In the past decade, the growth of information amount in the world is much more than the sum of information amount in the past few hundred years and it has been recorded in various forms, such as books, films, videos, audio tapes, microfiches or computer disks. Our future generations will have the opportunity to access these valuable information assets.

Different kinds of information are required to solve problems, change things, and engage in creation, we must be able to retrieve existing information. There are many basic research results about information retrieval have been finished in the past 50 years, and numerous information searching technologies are developed. This kind of ambition to seek information is very important. By utilizing known information prepared by great knowledge pioneers, we could enlarge our knowledge domain constantly. In this age, we have enjoyed the most convenient way to access these information achievements compared to any other age in the whole civil history.

An information retrieval process begins when a inventor enters a query into the data system. Queries are formal statements for required information, for example, key words strings in web search engines. In such information retrieval process, a query does not uniquely identify a single object in the data system. Most likely, several objects may match the query, perhaps with different degrees of relevancy. Most information retrieval systems compute a numeric score on how well each object in the database associated to the query, and rank the objects according to this score. Most popular performance measures are: *Precision*, which is the fraction of the documents retrieved that are relevant to the user's information need; *Recall*, that is the fraction of the documents that are relevant to the query that are successfully retrieved; and *Fall-Out*, which measures the proportion of non-relevant documents that are retrieved out of all non-relevant documents available. The top ranking objects are presented to the inventor. The process may then be iterated if the inventor wishes to refine the query.

An object is an entity that is represented by information in a data system. User queries are matched against the database information. Depending on the inventors requirements, the data objects may be, for instances, text documents, images, or videos. To save the space of an information retrieval system, the data objects themselves are not kept or stored directly in the information retrieval system, instead, are represented in the system by information surrogates or catalogues.

The most serious problem in information retrieval is to decide proper queries and select useful information from query results. It is easy to collect a whole heap of information, however, the real significant information for inventors are quite few in general. This issue needs inventors' experiences and wisdom to assess collected information through analyzing the relevance among collected information. The more important information inventors get, the higher opportunity for inventors to solve problems perfectly. Following suggestions are given to help inventors to process information for solving new problems.

- Establishing more efficient information retrieval systems and expanding more channels to access information.

- Organizing obtained information and figuring out its relation with the problems in mind.

- Selecting useful information to solve the problems or to create new things.

Chapter 3

Invention Process by Basic Operations

In this chapter, we provide basic algebraic structures which help us to model invention process. Basically, algebraic structures could be classified by the following three kinds: arithmetics, varieties and quasivarieties.

3.1 Four Elementary Arithmetics

Mathematically, there are four basic arithmetic operations for two sets of numbers. In Sec. 3.1.1, we study an invention procedure by using the concept of addition and substraction. Another invention way about applying the notion of multiplication and division is discussed in Sec. 3.1.2.

3.1.1 Addition and Substraction

Addition is a mathematical operation that represents combining collections of components from the same set together into a larger collection. It is expressed by the plus sign, $+$. For example, if we are given 3 apples from the set of apples and the other two apples from the same set of apples, there are $3 + 2 = 5$ apples. Besides counting of apples, addition can also represent combining other physical and abstract quantities from same set using different systems of objects: negative numbers, fractions, irrational numbers, vectors, geometrical objects and more. Hence, if we wish to create a new thing with components from the same set and the combination of components is under the same structure relation among components, the addition concept from mathematics may be utilized to create a new thing. The algebraic model for invention procedure which adopts addition operation can be expressed as

$$+ : S \times S \to S_{\text{new}}, \qquad (3.1.1)$$

where S denotes for the set of components used to create a new thing and S_{new} is the set of invented new things. We have to be careful in performing addition operation. In order to add components which can be described by some units system, they must first be expressed with common unit. For example, if a measure of 5 feet is extended by 3 inches, the sum is 63 inches, since 60 inches is equal to 5 feet. On the other hand, it is usually meaningless to add 3 meters and 5 square meters, since their units are incomparable,

Below, we discuss about properties of addition operation. We say that an addition operation is *commutative* if one can change the order for dealing with summands and the result will be the same after order exchange. Symbolically, if s_1 and s_2 are any two components of S, then

$$s_1 + s_2 = s_2 + s_1. \qquad (3.1.2)$$

The fact that addition is commutative is known as the "commutative law of addition".

The *associative* property is raised when one tries to define repeated addition. Should the expression $s_1 + s_2 + s_3$ be defined to mean $(s_1 + s_2) + s_3$ or $s_1 + (s_2 + s_3)$? That addition is associative tells us that the choice of definition is irrelevant. For any three components $s_1, s_2, s_3 \in S$, it is true that

$$(s_1 + s_2) + s_3 = s_1 + (s_2 + s_3). \qquad (3.1.3)$$

For example, $(2 + 1) + 3 = 3 + 3 = 6 = 2 + 4 = 2 + (1 + 3)$.

When adding zero (0) to any number, the quantity does not change; zero is the identity element for addition, also names as the *additive identity*. In symbols, for any $s \in S$, we have

$$s + 0 = 0 + s = s. \qquad (3.1.4)$$

Some addition operation may satisfy the above properties. For example, if we restrict components of set S as those familiar mathematical objects like real numbers, vectors, angle degrees and so on. However, some addition operation may not satisfy properties of commutativity and associativity, e.g., the chemical reactions. If we want to mix sulfuric acid (H_2SO_4) and water safely, we have to add sulfuric acid into water to avoid getting a serious acid burn since sulfuric acid reacts very vigorously with water. Given three chemical elements, C, O_2 and H_2, the chemical reaction results for the following two reaction procedure will be different:

$$(C + 2H_2) + 2O_2 \rightarrow CH_4 + 2O_2 \quad \rightarrow \quad CO_2 + 2H_2O,$$
$$C + (H_2 + \frac{1}{2}O_2) \rightarrow C + H_2O \quad \rightarrow \quad CO + H_2, \tag{3.1.5}$$

where those coefficients in front of each reactant represent ratio of moles required by each reactant.

Subtraction is another one of the four basic arithmetic operations. It is the inverse operation of addition indicates that if we start with any original component and add any component and then subtract the same component we added, we return to the original component we started with. Subtraction is denoted by a minus sign $(-)$ in general. The algebraic model for invention procedure which adopts substraction operation can be expressed as

$$- : S \times S \rightarrow S_{\text{new}}, \tag{3.1.6}$$

where S denotes for the set of components used to create a new thing and S_{new} is the set of obtained new things. Subtraction is not associative or commutative, thereafter, it is important to specify the order of components in substraction operations. Following examples, although they are simple, are provided to demonstrate an invention procedure applying addition and substraction.

Example 1 *A semi-trailer is a trailer without a front axle. It obtains its mobility by a road tractor through a detachable front axle assembly known as a dolly, or by the tail of another truck. A semi-trailer is normally equipped with landing gear (legs which can adjust their length) to support it when it is uncoupled. There are many types of semi-trailers in use designed to carry wide range of various products, e.g., refrigerator, reefer, tanker and cars hauler. There are some advantages to use semi-trailers for cargo transportation; 1. In the event of a breakdown, a tractor unit can be exchanged quickly and the load delivered to its destination without much delay. 2. The semi-trailers can be coupled and uncoupled quickly, allowing them to be shunted for loading and to be trunked between factories. 3. Because of the longer overall length of the cargo bed, a semi-trailer can haul longer objects, for example, pipes, tree trunks, beams, railway track, than an ordinary trailer.*

Most semi tractors have two or three axles having twin wheels on each side. If the cargo is not so heavy, the basic configuration has eight wheels (two axles). However, if the cargo is heavy, we have to add four more wheels (one axle) to support carried cargo. The algebraic model for configuration design of axles can be formulated as

$$S \pm S \to S_{spt}, \tag{3.1.7}$$

where S is the set of axles and S_{spt} represents the set of axles used to support cargo. Such binary operation becomes an addition operation if one want to increase the loading capability of a semi-trailer and substraction operation if one want to decrease the loading capability of a semi-trailer.

The cargo semi-trailer usually has two tandem axles at the rear. Many semi-trailers are equipped with movable tandems that can be set to adjust the weight on each axle through varying the mutual distance between two axles for load balance. The algebraic model for the position of an axle with respect to the end of a semi-trailer can be written as

$$S \pm S \to S_{td}, \tag{3.1.8}$$

where the first (left) S denotes for the original distance between the tandem axle to the end of a semi-trailer, the second (right) S indicates the distance shift of tandem and the set S_{td} represents the set of all possible distance between the movable tandem axle to the end of a semi-trailer. This binary operation becomes addition operation if we wish to increase the distance between the tandem axle and the end point of the semi-trailer when cargo is put at the middle part of the semi-trailer. On the other hand, if cargo is put near the end of the semi-trailer, we adopt substraction operation to decrease the distance between the tandem axle and the end point of the semi-trailer. In Fig. 3.1, we show that more axles (tires) required to carry a heavier cargo. We indicates how to adjust the distance between axles to carry cargos with different center of mass in Fig. 3.2.

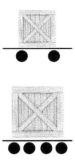

Figure 3.1: Increasing more axles (tires) to carry a heavier cargo.

Figure 3.2: Adjusting the distance between axles to carry a cargo with different shape (different center of mass).

Example 2 *For safety reason, families with babies often try to prepare* baby door gates *to confine babies in their room or keep them away from dangerous regions, e.g., kitchen or stairs. The gate height is approximately 78 centimeters and width of a baby door gate can be adjusted from 72 centimeters to 100 centimeters by adding or removing extension plates in order to fit variations width requirement determined from interior design. The algebraic model for proper design of a baby door gate can be expressed as*

$$S \pm S \to S_{gate}, \tag{3.1.9}$$

where S is the set of extension plates and S_{gate} represents the set of all possible arrangements of a baby door gate. Such binary operation becomes addition operation if one want to fit the baby door gate for a wider region by adding more extension plates and substraction operation if one want to fit the baby door gate for a narrower region by removing away more extension plates. In upper part at the Fig. 3.3, we show the baby door for the entrance door with narrower door width. We add plates for the baby door mounted at the entrance door with wider door width at the lower part at the Fig. 3.3.

3.1.2 Multiplication and Division

The concept of multiplication comes from repeated addition. For instance, we have

$$\overbrace{4+4+4+4+4}^{\text{5 times of number 4}} = 5 \cdot 4 = 20. \tag{3.1.10}$$

If we hope to create a new thing with components from the same set by repeating the combination of components under the same structure relation among components, the multiplication concept from mathematics is adopted to create a new thing. The algebraic model for invention procedure which adopts multiplication operation can be expressed as

$$\cdot : N \times S \to S_{\text{new}}, \tag{3.1.11}$$

where N is the set of numbers which represent the repeating times of the addition operation, S denotes for the set of components used to create a new thing and S_{new} is the set of invented new things. The multiplicative identity is 1; anything multiplied by one is itself.

For set N composed by integers, fractions, and real numbers, multiplication has certain properties. The order in which two components from N and S are multiplied has the same result. We have $n \cdot s = s \cdot n$, where $n \in N$ and $s \in S$. Since expressions solely involving

Figure 3.3: Up subfigure: narrower baby door. Down subfigure: wider baby door.

multiplication are invariant with respect to order of operations, i.e., $(n_1 \cdot n_2) \cdot s = n_1 \cdot (n_2 \cdot s)$ for $n_1, n_2 \in N$ and $s \in S$. By consider associative property jointly with the commutativity, we also have $(n_1 \cdot s) \cdot n_2 = n_1 \cdot (s \cdot n_2)$ and $(s \cdot n_1) \cdot n_2 = s \cdot (n_1 \cdot n_2)$. Given $s_1, s_2 \in S$ and $n \in N$, the multiplication operation expressed by Eq. (3.1.11) is *left-distributive* over $+$ since $n \cdot (s_1 + s_2) = (n \cdot s_1) + (n \cdot s_2)$. The multiplication operation expressed by Eq. (3.1.11) is also *right-distributive* over $+$ since $(n_1 + n_2) \cdot s = (n_1 \cdot s) + (n_2 \cdot s)$, where $n_1, n_2 \in N$ and $s \in S$. We have to note that the component $s \in S$ may not have its multiplicative inverse since it is not always proper to have an identity component in set S_{new}. However, if the set S is a special set, e.g., a set of real number except 0, we always have multiplicative inverse for any component in such set.

Division is another one of the four basic arithmetic operations. It is the inverse operation of multiplication which demonstrates the process or result of dividing an original thing into separate parts equally. Division is represented by a division sign ($\div$) in general. From Eq. (3.1.11), there are two interpretations to exhibit the inverse operation of multiplication. These two ways of division is classified by the kinds of divisors, numbers or components belonged to the subset of the original thing. The algebraic model for invention procedure which involves divisors as numbers can be expressed as

$$\div_{\text{nb}} : S \times N \to S_{\text{new}}, \tag{3.1.12}$$

where S denotes for the set of components of the original thing, N is the set of numbers and S_{new} is the set of new things which are identical between each other. However, the components in the set of S_{new} are parts in the set of S. The other algebraic model for invention procedure whose divisors are components belonged to the subset of the original thing can be expressed as

$$\div_{\text{sb}} : S \times S_{\text{sb}} \to N, \tag{3.1.13}$$

where S denotes for the set of components of the original thing, S_{sb} indicates the components belonged to the subset of the original thing and N is the set of numbers which represent the number of identical parts of the original thing.

Some attention has to be paid for the algebraic model for invention procedure which involves divisors as numbers. The results obtained by Eq. (3.1.12) may not be unique. For example, if we try to separate a regular convex polygon (a convex polygon has identical corner angles and identical edges) into two equally parts by a cut through the center of a regular polygon, there are infinite ways to separate a regular convex polygon with even number of edges into two identical parts. When divisors are numbers, this is an advantage for an invention procedure utilizing division to generate various kinds of new things due to non-uniqueness, however, we have to be careful in performing later computational invention procedure based on results obtained from Eq. (3.1.12) by specifying clearly what are divided results. Similar to properties of substraction, both division operations (for divisors as numbers or components belonged to the subset of the original thing) are not associative or commutative. Following examples are presented to illustrate invention procedures related to multiplication and division.

Example 3 *Packaging is the science, art and technology of enveloping or protecting products for distribution, storage, sale, and usage. The following reasons make packaging become more important in nowadays commercial world. 1. The products enclosed in the package could avoid disturbances from surrounding environment, e.g., vibration, temperature or humidity. 2. Some products without a fixed shape, like liquids, powders or seeds, require packing for shipping. 3. Words and figures can be printed on packages to carry information for users about usage, transportation, recycle, or dispose of products. Products related to public health, for instance, foods or drugs, are regulated by government to provide necessary information on their packages. 4. Packaging can reduce the security risks of shipment, for example, packages pilferage or malicious behaviors applied to packages.*

Some products made up by small items are typically grouped together in one package for reasons of efficient shipping and marketing, e.g., candies or animals fodder. However, it may not proper to open the whole package by only using a small portion of the whole product due to storage or protection issues of products. The concept of division operation could be applied to invent a new package with smaller size compared to the original product which, nevertheless, is suitable for usage at a time. From algebraic model for division procedure when divisors are numbers implied by Eq. (3.1.12), we can chose a suitable number from the set N to generate a new package with proper size. In this situation, the set of S_{new} is composed by packages with different sizes. The sale in separate (or individual) packing applies the aforementioned idea exactly.

Example 4 *In the fields of architecture and civil engineering, building is the act of constructing structures for some purposes, for instance, living, transportation or commerce. Generally, a building is composed by bases, roofs, pillars, beams, walls, doors and windows. In this example, four basic arithmetic operations are applied to design building structures.*

Suppose we are required to design a condo consisting multiple dwellings where each unit is individually owned. Five components, which are a base (B), a roof (R), a wall (W), a wall with entrance door (WD) and a wall with window (WW), are used for each unit as shown by Fig. 3.4. In order to describe the physical size and the placement for each component of a dwelling unit, a 7-tuple expression is used to characterize the physical size and the placement for each component. The first three elements of this 7-tuple expression represent the thickness, the length and the height of the construction object [1]. The fourth to sixth elements of this 7-tuple expression denote for the location coordinates for the center of a construction object. The last element of this 7-tuple expression is a unit vector used to represent the orientation of the construction object. For example, a wall with the thickness T, the length L and the height H placed at the position (x, y, z) is represented as $(T, L, H, x, y, z, \vec{n})$, where the unit vector $\vec{n}$ indicates the orientation of this wall.

Figure 3.4: The construction components.

A wall having windows or doors within it has to reserve spaces for windows or doors by hollowing some parts from the original wall. The subtraction operation can be adopted to form a new construction object representing a wall having windows or doors within it. We also assume that each window or door is a rectangular parallelepiped and can also be expressed as a 7-tuple expression. For instance, if we want to have a window with parameters $(T_W, L_W, H_W, x_W, y_W, z_W, \vec{n}_W)$

---

[1]We assume that each construction object is a rectangular parallelepiped. Of course, we may consider other shapes of construction objects by using their geometrical parameters in such object expression

on the wall with parameter $(T, L, H, x, y, z, \vec{n})$, the construction object for such wall with window, shown as WW, is expressed as $(T, L, H, x, y, z, \vec{n}) - (T_W, L_W, H_W, x_W, y_W, z_W, \vec{n}_W)$.

Based on above expression for construction objects, a dwelling unit for a condo assembled by base, roof, front wall with an entrance door, back wall, left wall with a window on it and right wall with another window on it can be obtained by addition and substraction operations expressed as following:

$$
\begin{aligned}
a\ dwelling\ unit \ =\ & Base + Roof + Wall + Wall\ with\ Door + \\
& Wall\ with\ Window,\ No.\ 1 + \\
& Wall\ with\ Window,\ No.\ 2 \\
=\ & (T_B, L_B, H_B, x_B, y_B, z_B, \vec{n}_B) + \\
& (T_R, L_R, H_R, x_R, y_R, z_R, \vec{n}_R) + \\
& (T_W, L_W, H_W, x_W, y_W, z_W, \vec{n}_W) + \\
& [(T_{WD}, L_{WD}, H_{WD}, x_{WD}, y_{WD}, z_{WD}, \vec{n}_{WD}) - \\
& (T_D, L_D, H_D, x_D, y_D, z_D, \vec{n}_D)] + \\
& [(T_{WW_1}, L_{WW_1}, H_{WW_1}, x_{WW_1}, y_{WW_1}, z_{WW_1}, \vec{n}_{WW_1}) - \\
& (T_{W_1}, L_{W_1}, H_{W_1}, x_{W_1}, y_{W_1}, z_{W_1}, \vec{n}_{W_1})] + \\
& [(T_{WW_2}, L_{WW_2}, H_{WW_2}, x_{WW_2}, y_{WW_2}, z_{WW_2}, \vec{n}_{WW_2}) - \\
& (T_{W_2}, L_{W_2}, H_{W_2}, x_{W_2}, y_{W_2}, z_{W_2}, \vec{n}_{W_2})].
\end{aligned} \tag{3.1.14}
$$

From a dwelling unit, we can apply multiplication operation to form a condo with multiple dwellings. A condo with 3 dwelling units at the direction along the wall with door, 2 dwelling units at the direction along the wall with window and 2 floors can be generated by multiplication operation as

$$
a\ condo = 3\ \cdot_{WD} 2\ \cdot_{FR}\ a\ dwelling\ unit, \tag{3.1.15}
$$

where $\cdot_{WD}$ and $\cdot_{FR}$ indicate the multiplication operations representing duplication of a dwelling unit along the direction of the wall with door 3 times, and the vertical direction of the dwelling twice, respectively. The result condo of Eq. (3.1.15) is depicted in Fig. 3.5.

If a dwelling space is not big enough for a family with larger members size, such family may require two dwelling units which are juxtaposed together in a condo. Given the number of such family, the division operation, as expressed by Eq. (3.1.13), could be applied to find out the proper

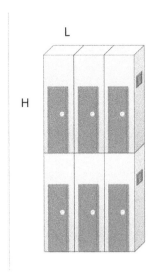

Figure 3.5: A condo with 6 rooms.

space constituted by two dwellings in the condo determined by Eq. (3.1.15). Since the divisor in Eq. (3.1.13) is composed by elements (subset) of the condo, there are two possible subsets of the condo that each subset has two dwelling units juxtaposed together. They are

$$family\ space_1 = 2 \cdot_{FR} (Base + Roof + Wall + Wall\ with\ Door$$
$$+\ Wall\ with\ Window,\ No.\ 1 + Wall\ with\ Window,\ No.\ 2), \tag{3.1.16}$$

or

$$family\ space_2 = 3 \cdot_{WD} (Base + Roof + Wall + Wall\ with\ Door$$
$$+\ Wall\ with\ Window,\ No.\ 1 + Wall\ with\ Window,\ No.\ 2). \tag{3.1.17}$$

The Eq. (3.1.16) indicates that the space for a larger family is composed by two dwellings arranged in two floors. The other case is for the three dwellings units arranged along the direction of the wall with door. Hence, we have

$$a\ condo \div_{sb} family\ space_1 = 3, \tag{3.1.18}$$

or

$$a\ condo \div_{sb} family\ space_2 = 2, \tag{3.1.19}$$

which means that there are 6 identical space composed by two dwelling units for a larger family. The results from Eqs. (3.1.18) and (3.1.19) are illustrated by Fig. 3.6.

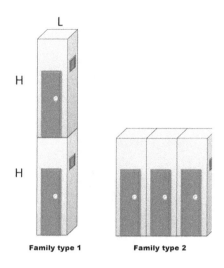

Figure 3.6: Two family types.

3.2 Product

The algebraic model for invention procedure which adopts multiplication operation is expressed by Eq. (3.1.11), the multiplier set in Eq. (3.1.11) is composed by numbers. Here, we attempt to enlarge the possible components of the multiplier set from numbers to other objects which will be adopted to invent new things. Such operation is named as a product operation. The algebraic model for product operation according to a combination method can be written as

$$\bullet\text{Combination Method} : S_1 \times S_2 \rightarrow S_{\text{new}}, \tag{3.2.1}$$

where $\bullet_{\text{Combination Method}}$ denotes for the product operation which organizes the components from two sets S_1 and S_2 in some particular combination method. The components in the set S_1 may or may not be equal to the components in the set S_2. Moreover, if we restrict the new thing S_{new} to the subset which is constructed by elements of the i-th set, the components from the i-th set will be obtained. This is called the projection property of the product operation. It can be written as

$$\pi_i : S_{\text{new}} \rightarrow S_i, \tag{3.2.2}$$

where π_i is the projection operation to components from the i-th set. Essentially, the product of a family of sets according to a specific combination method is to produce a new thing which possesses the same attributes to each of the given sets.

In the following, properties of product operation are explored. A product operation is *commutative* if one can change the order for dealing with multipliers and the result will be the same after order exchange. Symbolically, if s_1 and s_2 are any two components of S_1 and S_2 respectively, then

$$s_1 \bullet_{\text{Combination Method}} s_2 = s_2 \bullet_{\text{Combination Method}} s_1. \tag{3.2.3}$$

The commutativity of production operation, in general, holds if components in sets S_1 and S_2 are substances.

The *associative* property is raised when one tries to define repeated product operation. Given $s_1 \in S_1$, $s_2 \in S_2$ and $s_3 \in S_3$, respectively, the associativity of product operation, $\bullet_{\text{Combination Method}}$, requires that

$$(s_1 \bullet_{\text{Combination Method}} s_2) \bullet_{\text{Combination Method}} s_3 =$$
$$s_1 \bullet_{\text{Combination Method}} (s_2 \bullet_{\text{Combination Method}} s_3). \tag{3.2.4}$$

In general, the product operation $\bullet_{\text{Combination Method}}$ may be associative or not, which depends on properties of three sets S_1, S_2, S_3 and the combination method used to assemble these three sets.

Example 5 *If three sets S_1, S_2 and S_3 are identical sets composed by building blocks which can only be assembled with the orientation constraint, the order to assemble blocks s_1 and s_2 first or to assemble blocks s_2 and s_3 first makes no difference for the final result.*

However, let us consider another case where associativity dose not valid again. Given the component s_1 as Red color, the component s_2 as a wooden ball and the component s_3 as Black color, the product operation is to apply given color to cover the whole wooden ball, denoted as $\bullet_{color}$. Then we have

$$(s_1 \bullet_{color} s_2) \bullet_{color} s_3 = Black\ wooden\ ball, \tag{3.2.5}$$

and

$$s_1 \bullet_{color} (s_2 \bullet_{color} s_3) = Red\ wooden\ ball. \tag{3.2.6}$$

It is clear to see that the different order to perform production $(s_1 \bullet_{color} s_2)$ and $(s_2 \bullet_{color} s_3)$ introduces the different final result.

The combinatorial creation is a way to invent a new thing through assembling two or more than two items, or methods properly. Some inventors even admit that the only way to invent is to assemble known items or methods properly. Generally speaking, the items or methods used to assemble a new thing do not have any particular constraints, one can assemble any two or more than two items or methods willfully. For instance, one may assemble two items with different functions or objectives, two items with different structures, two items with different materials, two methods with different principles, two items with different status, two methods with different procedures, two different colors, two different shapes, two different sounds, two different tastes, etc. Not just only two items or methods, one may also assemble three or more items or methods jointly. Besides, there are various ways to assemble two things, such as association, amalgamation, union, coalition, compound or minglement, etc.

There are three characteristics for combinatorial creation:

(1) Divergent:

During the procedure of combinatorial creation, we cannot restrict our thoughts only at some particular things, on the contrary , we have to consider any possible candidate components used to assemble a new thing by divergent thinking. Divergent thinking is a thought method used to generate creative things by exploring items from various sorts. Many possible solutions could be figured out in a short amount of time when unexpected relations, originally, are drawn. Psychologists have observed that a person with high IQ alone does not guarantee his/her creativity. Instead, personal habit to think new solutions based on divergent thinking is more important.

(2) Selective:

During the process of combinatorial creation, it may not proper to assemble two things unchangeably without choosing their useful aspects. Inventors have to select only those useful parts from original things to assemble new thing creatively.

(3) Synthetical:

Given a group of original items, there are various ways to assemble these items into a new thing. Hence, one needs to compare those assemble methods and select one of them which satisfies mostly to our goals. Basically, there are three kinds of combinatorial creation: (a) Appendix to a main body: One adds an appendix according to the original main body to increase, perfect or supply functions of the original main body. (b) Assemble by same items: The new thing is created by assembling two or more identical things. (c) Assemble by different items: The new thing is created by assembling at least two different kinds of things.

During the procedure of combinatorial creation, we cannot restrict our thoughts only at some particular aspects of the original things or kinds of combinatorial components, instead, we have to consider more perspectives of the original things or species of combinatorial components and study their advantages and disadvantages. An excellent combinatorial creation is the result obtained by assemble items which can reserve the advantages and remove the disadvantages of the original items.

Example 6 *The desk lamp is used to help readers reading their documents brightly. Some persons may have the following problems during reading, like to fall sleep easily or be annoyed by insects. Traditionally, freshening agents and insect-resist agents are chemical agents adopted to energize human beings and prevent attacks from insects. Moreover, the effect to spread chemical substances would be more significant if the containers for freshening agents or insect-resist agents can be installed at an environment with higher temperature compared to room temperature.*

By applying product operation for set constituted by desk lamps and set composed by chemical agents through appending containers of agents to the bulb mounting seat (combination method), a new style of desk lamp is created which not only provides light for readers but assists readers to avoid falling sleep or be stung by insects during their study also. The container of chemical substances is appendixed to the bulb mounting seat in order to obtain an environment with higher temperature. The algebraic model for such product operation can be written as

$$S_{desk\ lamp} \bullet_{Container\ appendixed\ to\ bulb\ mouting\ seat}$$
$$S_{container\ with\ chemical\ substances} \to S_{new\ desk\ lamp}, \tag{3.2.7}$$

where $\bullet_{Container\ appendixed\ to\ bulb\ mouting\ seat}$ *denotes for the product operation which assembles the components from set* $S_{desk\ lamp}$ *(desk lamp) and* $S_{container\ with\ chemical\ substances}$ *(container with chemical substances, e.g., freshening agents or insect-resist agents), respectively.*

Example 7 *A yoke is a beam made by wood or steel which is used between a pair of animals, e.g., horses, oxen, donkeys, to allow them to pull a load or to plow fields together. There are several types, used in different cultures, and for different types of animals. There are three types* *of yoke. The first one is called as a bow yoke since it is a shaped wooden or steel crosspiece bound to the necks of a pair of animals. It is held on the animals' necks by an oxbow. The second one is named as a withers yoke. A withers yoke is a yoke that fits just in front of the withers of the animal. The yoke is held in position by straps, either alone or with a pair of wooden staves either side of the animals withers. A head yoke is the third kind of yoke which fits onto the head of the animal. It usually fits behind the horns, and has carved-out sections into which the horns fit; it may be realized by a single beam attached to both animals, or each animal may have a separate short beam.*

The invention of yoke is an example by applying product operation for two identical sets, which is composed of an equipment to control the movement of animals. In order to pull a load or to plow fields more powerfully, one have to think a good way to control a group (pair) of animals. By applying product operation for two animal control equipments through combining them parallelly or vertically with respect to the front side of the controller, a new equipment to control a group of animals (yoke) is formed. The algebraic model for such product operation can be expressed as

$$S_{single\ animal\ controller} \bullet_{parallel\ combination} S_{single\ animal\ controller}$$
$$\rightarrow S_{parallel\ yoke}, \qquad (3.2.8)$$

where two single animal controllers are combined in parallel direction. For case that two single animal controllers are combined in vertical direction, the corresponding algebraic model is formulated as

$$S_{single\ animal\ controller} \bullet_{vertical\ combination} S_{single\ animal\ controller}$$
$$\rightarrow S_{vertical\ yoke}. \qquad (3.2.9)$$

The Fig. 3.7 shows a parallel yoke.

Example 8 *Catalog method is a method that compulsorily links the two unrelated products or ideas (sets) together and then leads to a new product or idea through a creative product of these two sets. The method is similar with couple listing method. The method is very simple, we only need to open product samples or other printed matters, such as patent specifications or products catalogs, and select a statements, item or topic randomly; we use the identical method to select the second statement, item or topic randomly and associate both of them into an integrated object*

Figure 3.7: A yoke with parallel structure.

through an invented new relation among these two statements, items or topics. The algebraic model for such product operation can be expressed as

$$S_{\text{an item collected from one catalog (set)}} \bullet_{\text{new relation}}$$
$$S_{\text{an item collected from another catalog (set)}} \to S_{\text{new item}}, \qquad (3.2.10)$$

where $\bullet_{\text{new relation}}$ *determines what new item will be produced. In Chap. V later, we will give more detailed studies about relation.*

The feature of this invention method is that the new thought is generated between two unrelated things originally, hence, the variability becomes larger and it is able to enforce someone to exceed the limit of personal experiences, which makes one easier to enlighten personal inspiration and generate a new idea. One thing to be careful when someone performs such method to create a new thing. Since the associated objects are often lack of some inner or familiar relation, sometimes, the obtained new ideas are unreasonable or feasible deformities. One have to be careful in verifying and refining such new ideas through logical analysis and current knowledge or culture backgrounds. Catalog method can be applied in designing a new product, reforming an old product, new advertising contents, and conceiving an article, etc.

3.3   Quotient

In arithmetic, a quotient is the result of a division . For example, when dividing 9 by 3, the quotient is 3, while 9 is called the dividend, and 3 the divisor. For integers, the quotient indicates as the number of times the divisor divides into the dividend. The concept of quotient can be extended to deal with more abstract mathematical spaces, e.g., quotient sets, quotient spaces, or quotient algebraic structures whose elements are the equivalence classes of some equivalence relation on another set, space, or algebraic structure. Since the idea of quotient is helpful for constructing new sets out of the original set, we will illustrate notions about quotient from mathematical definitions and provide two examples to demonstrate how to apply quotient concept to invent new things.

Given a set S and an equivalence relation $\sim$ on S, the equivalence class of an element x in S is the subset of all elements in S which are equivalent to x:

$$[x] = \{s \in S | s \sim x\}. \tag{3.3.1}$$

The set of all equivalence classes in S given an equivalence relation $\sim$ is usually represented as $S/\sim$ and called the quotient set of S by $\sim$. This operation can be thought as the act of "dividing" the input set by the equivalence relation. One way in which the quotient set accords with division is that if S is finite and all equivalence classes have same size, then the cardinality of $S/\sim$ is the quotient of the cardinality of S by the cardinality of an equivalence class. The quotient set can be treated as the set S with all the equivalent points identified. From basic properties of an equivalence relation, any two equivalence classes are either equal or disjoint. It follows that the set of all equivalence classes of S forms a partition of S, i.e., every element of S belongs to one and only one equivalence class. Conversely, every partition of S also defines an equivalence relation over S. In other words, if $\sim$ is an equivalence relation on a set S and x and y are two elements, then the following three statements are equivalent: $x \sim y$, $[x] = [y]$ and $[x] \cap [y] \neq \emptyset$.

In the sequel, two examples about applying quotient idea are provided. The first is about applying quotient idea to construct new geometrical objects from the original geometrical object. The second example is to identify some portion of the original problem into a subproblem, therefore, the original problem can be dealt more efficient through hierarchical structure.

Example 9 *In topology and geometry of mathematics, a quotient space is the result of identifying or "pasting together" certain points of a given space. The points to be identified are specified* by an equivalence relation. This is a basic tool in order to construct new spaces from given ones. Quotient space can be described as following: Let X be a geometrical space and let X^* be a partition of X into disjoint subsets whose union is X. We also have a surjective map $q : X \to X^*$ [2] that sends each element of X to the element of X^* containing it. Under such map q, the space X^* is called Quotient space of X. Two examples below are provided to construct new space from the original space.

(1) Let X be the closed unit disk,

$$X = \{(x, y) | x^2 + y^2 \leq 1\}, \tag{3.3.2}$$

where (x, y) is the coordinate representation for a point in $\mathbb{R}^2$. And, let X^* be the partition of X into two parts: (a) $\{(x, y) | x^2 + y^2 < 1\}$ and (b) $\{(x, y) | x^2 + y^2 = 1\}$. The quotient of the two dimensional disk by gluing the boundary becomes a two dimensional sphere, shown by Fig. 3.8.

(2) Let X be the unit square,

$$X = \{(x, y) | (x, y) \in [0, 1] \times [0, 1]\}, \tag{3.3.3}$$

where (x, y) is the coordinate representation for a point in $\mathbb{R}^2$. And, let X^* be the partition of X into the following six parts: (a) $\{(x, y) | 0 < x < 1, 0 < y < 1\}$, (b) $\{(x, y) | 0 < x < 1, y = 0\}$, (c) $\{(x, y) | 0 < x < 1, y = 1\}$, (d) $\{(x, y) | x = 0, 0 < y < 1\}$, (e) $\{(x, y) | x = 1, 0 < y < 1\}$ and (f) Four points set: $\{(0, 0), (0, 1), (1, 0), (1, 1)\}$. It is easy to observe that the union of these sets becomes X. The torus can also be described as a quotient of the square under the identification $(x, y) \sim (x + 1, y) \sim (x, y + 1)$, shown by Fig. 3.9.

From these two expositions of quotient space, we can construct totally different geometrical space from the original space. $\square$

---

[2]Surjective map is a function map if its image is equal to its range (codomain).

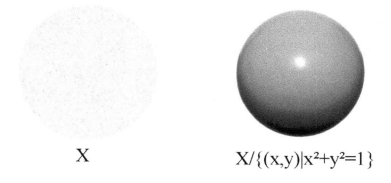

X   X/{(x,y)|x²+y²=1}

Figure 3.8: A ball obtained by quotient operation.

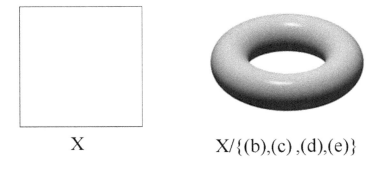

X   X/{(b),(c) ,(d),(e)}

Figure 3.9: A torus obtained by quotient operation.

Example 10 *We often get stuck when we face a difficult or big problem. One important problem solving technique is to break the original problem into simpler or smaller subproblems and we solve these subproblems first and organize the final results (solutions of the original problem) based on the solutions of these subproblems. In computer science, divide and conquer (D & C) is an important algorithm design paradigm inspired by such spirit. If the partitioned subproblem is still not easy to solve, one can recursively to partition the subproblem into smaller and easier subproblems. We can use tree structure to demonstrate the procedure of recursive partition of the original problem.*

(1) In this example, we wish to show any $2^n \times 2^n$ chessboard where n is any positive integer with one square removed can be tiled with L-shaped triominoes. First, we have to recognize that any 2×2 chessboard with one square removed can be tiled with an L-shaped triomino. Consider a $2^{k+1} \times 2^{k+1}$ chessboard with one removed square as shown by part (a) of Fig. 3.10. We identify each $2^k \times 2^k$ chessboard into a subproblem. Note that one of these 4 $2^k \times 2^k$ chessboards has a square removed. Moveover, we can think that the other three quadrants are also $2^k \times 2^k$ chessboards with one square removed if an L-shaped triomino is put at the center of the original $2^{k+1} \times 2^{k+1}$ chessboard, as plotted in part (b) at Fig. 3.10. Then, the answer to show that any $2^{k+1} \times 2^{k+1}$ chessboard with one removed square can be tiled is reduced to show the tiling problem for square with size $2^k \times 2^k$. By applying the arguments of mathematical induction where we assume that any $2^k \times 2^k$ chessboard with one square removed can be tiled, we can tile each any $2^{k+1} \times 2^{k+1}$ chessboard with one square removed by above explanations about partitioning the original chessboard into 4 smaller chessboards. We provided a 4×4 chessboard partition example in part (c) at Fig. 3.11.

$\square$

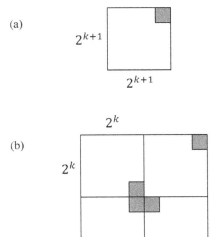

(a)

2^{k+1}

2^{k+1}

(b)

2^k

2^k

Figure 3.10: L-shaped tile.

(c)

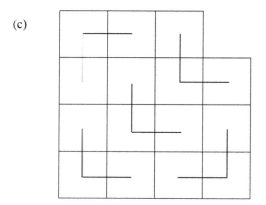

Figure 3.11: L-shaped tile decomposition of 15 squares

(2) The scalable ad hoc networks draw a lot of research interest nowadays [11]. A hierarchical routing algorithm was proposed to solve the problems induced by a lot of network nodes [12]. Usually, two main concerns incurred in a hierarchical network are the efficiency of the routing algorithm and the size of the required communication overhead (routing table size) [13, 14]. As the number of network nodes becomes very large, the algorithm complexity and the routing table size reduce significantly with the help of the hierarchical structure [15, 16]. The central idea of hierarchical network structures is to group (identify) a subset of the original set of nodes and organize these subsets properly.

In general, the hierarchical network with large number of nodes is modeled by using Poisson point process [17] in $\mathbb{R}^2$. All the nodes in the network are represented as points which are uniformly distributed in a finite region B (observed window). Let Φ_0 be a homogeneous Poisson process in $\mathbb{R}^2$ with intensity λ_0 which characterizes the population of the nodes in the region B. Without loss of generality, we may assume that the region B is a unit area. Hence, there are λ_0 nodes in the observed network in average. Let $\Phi_1, \Phi_2, \cdots, \Phi_{N-1}$ be $N-1$ two-dimensional independent Poisson processes with intensities, $\lambda_1, \lambda_2, \cdots, \lambda_{N-1}$, which are also independent of Φ_0. These $N-1$ processes correspond to the higher-level nodes in the hierarchical network, which allow us to define an N-level hierarchical network. Usually. there are a lot of subscribers in a network. Hence, we propose to use the point processes to model the population of the network nodes for each hierarchical level and study the network performance accordingly.

The point process Φ_i, for $1 \leq i \leq N-1$, represents the nodes at the i-th level in the hierarchy. In practical communication networks, the point process Φ_0 is used to model the network subscribers and the point process Φ_i is modeled as the network distributors at level i. According to the least-distance hierarchical principle [18], for $1 \leq i \leq N-1$, the relationship between the nodes in two adjacent levels is established by associating each point of Φ_{i-1} with the point of Φ_i which is the closest in physical distance. Thus, the nodes of Φ_i are called the cluster *nodes of Φ_{i-1} and the nodes of Φ_{i-1} are called their corresponding* subscribers. *Recall that a* Voronoi Cell *with respect to the point process Φ_i centered at x where x is a point in B, denoted as $V_x(\Phi_i)$, is the convex polygon defined as*

$$V_x(\Phi_i) = \{y \in \Phi_i | x \text{ is the closet point of } \Phi_i \text{ from } y\}. \tag{3.3.4}$$

Equivalently, each point of Φ_{i-1} located within $V_x(\Phi_i)$ has an arc connecting it to point x. We denote Peer Group *for level i, where $0 \leq i \leq N-1$ with respect to Voronoi Cell $V_x(\Phi_i)$, to* represent all nodes in the Voronoi Cell $V_x(\Phi_i)$. Let us consider a point $x_1 \in \Phi_1$ where the node x_1 corresponds to a level 1 node. The Peer Group (for level 0) that x_1 represents corresponds to the set of nodes at level 0 which lie in the Voronoi Cell $V_{x_1}(\Phi_0)$. The Peer Groups for level 0 are in turn partitioned according to each node form Φ_1 and represented by level 1 nodes. Let us further consider a point $x_2 \in \Phi_2$ where the node x_2 corresponds to a level 2 node. The Peer Group for level 1 that x_2 represents corresponds to the set of nodes at level 1 which lie in the Voronoi Cell $V_{x_2}(\Phi_1)$. Similarly, the Peer Groups for level 1 are also in turn partitioned according to each node form Φ_2 and represented by level 2 nodes. This procedure is repeated iteratively to build a hierarch network with N levels according to N point processes $\Phi_0, \Phi_1, \cdots, \Phi_{N-1}$. For example, the aforementioned network with three hierarchical levels is illustrated in Figure 3.12.

The number of total nodes is n at the first level and the number of nodes at the second level is $\frac{n}{10}$ if we partition the total number of nodes into 10 parts and the network is formed as a hierarchical network with two levels. Then the routing complexity using Dijkstra algorithm is Cn^2 where C is a constant if we do not apply hierarchical structure. However, the complexity to find out the shortest path between two given nodes will be $2C(\frac{n}{10})^2 + 10^2 C$ through hierarchical routing technique. We observe that the complexity reduces as only 3% of the non-hierarchical scheme if the number of nodes is large, say $n = 100$. $\square$

3.4 Varieties

In an invention procedure, we may need more complicated algebraic operations then aforementioned operations, e.g., arithmetic, product, quotient. For practical example, one will mix three or more (not just two) different chemical compounds to generate new compounds. Through collecting all identities required by an algebraic model for some invention procedures, *a variety of algebras* is formed by such set of identities. In this section, we will introduce several classes of algebraic structures and invention procedures associated to them.

3.4.1 Lattices

In order to model human reasoning mathematically, George Boole proposed an important class of algebraic structures in mathematical logic. These are special types of lattices. Today's languages and concepts about lattices are formulated by E. Schröder in 1890s.

Let us examine some simple examples to observe the spirit of lattices. Given two natural

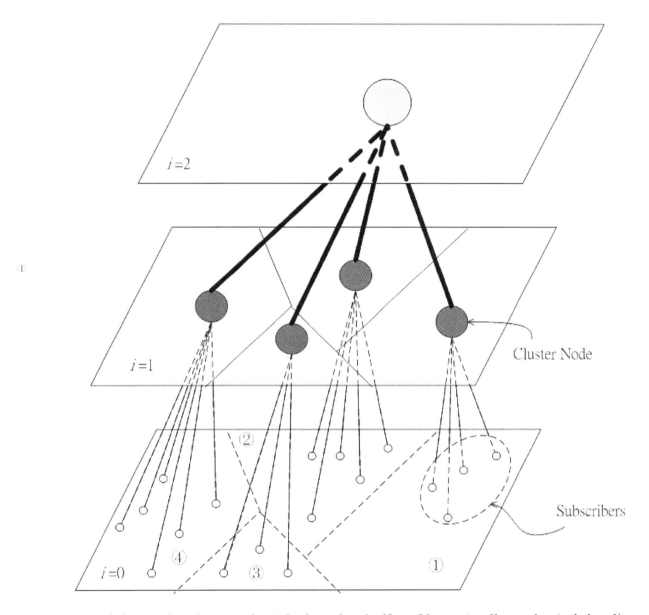

Figure 3.12: A hierarchical network with three levels (four Voronoi cells at the 0-th level). Nodes located within the dashed circle form a peer group.

numbers a and b, there is a largest number, denoted as $\gcd(a,b)$, which divides both a and b. The number $\gcd(a,b)$ is named as the greatest common divisor of a and b. Also, there is a smallest number, denoted as $\operatorname{lcm}(a,b)$, which is multiple of both a and b. The number $\operatorname{lcm}(a,b)$ is called as the smallest common multiple of a and b. Turning to another situation, given two sets A and B. There is a largest set contained in A and B, represented as $A \bigcap B$; and a smallest one containing both A and B, denoted as $A \bigcup B$. From these two examples, the common feature is to study a collection of items which have something like a "greatest lower bound" and a "least upper bound" and we shall call these items as lattices.

An algebraic lattice structure, denoted as $(L, \vee, \wedge)$, is a set L with two binary operations $\vee$ and $\wedge$ [3] which satisfy the following laws for all $a, b, c \in L$.

$$
\begin{aligned}
&\text{commutative law}: a \wedge b = b \wedge a, \quad a \vee b = b \vee a; \\
&\text{associative law}: a \wedge (b \wedge c) = (a \wedge b) \wedge c, \quad a \vee (b \vee c) = (a \vee b) \vee c; \\
&\text{absorption law}: a \wedge (a \vee b) = a, \quad a \vee (a \wedge b) = a; \\
&\text{idempotent law}: a \wedge a = a, \quad a \vee a = a.
\end{aligned} \tag{3.4.1}
$$

Example 11 *Consider a Hasse diagram for poset $\{1, 2, 3\}$. It is easy to check that all elements of lattice (all subsets of set $\{1, 2, 3\}$) satisfy definitions of lattices provided by Eq. (3.4.1) when "belong to" ($\subseteq$) relation is applied.*

In order to define Boolean algebra which will be applied to switching circuits design, two more definitions are required for general lattices. A lattice L is called *distributive* if the following laws are held:

$$
\begin{aligned}
a \vee (b \wedge c) &= (a \vee b) \wedge (a \vee c), \\
a \wedge (b \vee c) &= (a \wedge b) \vee (a \wedge c).
\end{aligned} \tag{3.4.2}
$$

A lattice L with universal upper bound 1, i.e., any element is smaller or equal then 1 and universal lower bound 0, i.e., any element is greater or equal then 0, is called complemented if for each $a \in L$ there is at least one element b such that $a \wedge b = 0$ and $a \vee b = 1$. Each such b is named as a complement of a. A complemented and distributive lattice is called a *Boolean algebra (lattice)*, denoted as $(L, \vee, \wedge, \bar{\ })$ where $\bar{\ }$ represents the complement element of inner component in L.

---

[3] They are also called as intersection or product and union or sum, respectively.

Let $X = \{x_1, x_2, \cdots, x_n\}$ be a set of n symbols which do not include 0 and 1. The *Boolean polynomials* in X are the objects which can be obtained by finitely many 44 successive applications of following two constructions: (1) $x_1, x_2, \cdots, x_n$ and $0, 1$ are Boolean polynomials; (2) if p and q are Boolean polynomials, then so are the formal strings $p \wedge q$, $p \vee q$ and $\bar{p}$. For instances, $x_1 \wedge 1$, $\bar{x}_2 \vee (x_1 \wedge x_2)$ are Boolean polynomials over $\{x_1, x_2\}$. From Boolean polynomials, we then can define *Boolean polynomial function*. Let L be a Boolean algebra, L^n be a set obtained from direct n copies of L and p be a Boolean polynomial in $\{x_1, x_2, \cdots, x_n\}$. Then

$$P_{L,n} : L^n \to L; \quad (a_1, a_2, \cdots, a_n) \to P_{L,n}(a_1, a_2, \cdots, a_n), \tag{3.4.3}$$

where $P_{L,n}$ is called the Boolean polynomial function induced by p and L. The term $P_{L,n}(a_1, a_2, \cdots, a_n)$ is the element in L which is obtained from p by replacing each x_i by $a_i \in L$ for $1 \le i \le n$.

Example 12 *In this example, we will apply Boolean polynomial to simplify the design of switching circuits by preserving the same Boolean polynomial function. Let us begin with some introduction of basic terminologies used in switching circuits. When the switch is in the "off" position we say that there is an* open *circuit between two terminals 1 and 2. Conversely, if the switch is in the "on" position we say that there is a* closed *circuit between two terminals 1 and 2. Common knowledge tell us that we can use an on-off switch to turn on or off an electric appliance.*

No matter how complex of a switching circuit, it is composed by two combinatorial ways of switches: one is parallel *combination and the other is* serial *combination. Based on the following tables, we have a Boolean algebra over set $\{open, closed\}$ and it can be expressed as $(\{open, closed\}, \wedge, \vee, \bar{})$, where $\wedge$ and $\vee$ represent serial and parallel combination of switches. In order to describe the behavior of complex switching networks, we define an algebraic system in Fig. 3.13.*

A light is controlled by the switching circuit shown in Fig. 3.14. Therefore, the Boolean polynomial for such switching circuit is expressed as

$$(x \vee \bar{y} \vee w) \wedge (x \vee y \vee \bar{z}) \wedge (x \vee z \vee w) \wedge y. \tag{3.4.4}$$

By applying Boolean algebra $(\{open, closed\}, \wedge, \vee, \bar{})$ based on relations provided by Tables in Fig. 3.13,

parallel	on	off
on	on	on
off	on	off

serial	on	off
on	on	off
off	off	off

-	on	off
negation	off	on

Figure 3.13: A table for switch on-off relations.

we have following derivations

$$(x \vee \bar{y} \vee w) \wedge (x \vee y \vee \bar{z}) \wedge (x \vee z \vee w) \wedge y$$

$$= \{x \vee [(\bar{y} \vee w) \wedge (y \vee \bar{z})]\} \wedge (x \vee z \vee w) \wedge y$$

$$= x \vee [(\bar{y} \vee w) \wedge (y \vee \bar{z}) \wedge (z \vee w)] \wedge y$$

$$= x \vee [(\bar{y} \wedge \bar{z} \wedge w) \vee (y \wedge z \wedge w) \vee (y \wedge w) \vee (\bar{z} \wedge w)] \wedge y$$

$$= x \vee (y \wedge w) \vee (\bar{z} \wedge w) \wedge y. \tag{3.4.5}$$

Then we can generate the new switching circuit keeping equivalent function for Boolean polynomial given by Eq. (3.4.4). They are shown by Fig. 3.14. As figures show, we implement the same switching circuit function by reducing the number of switches from 10 switches into only 6 switches. The Fig. 3.4.4 indicates

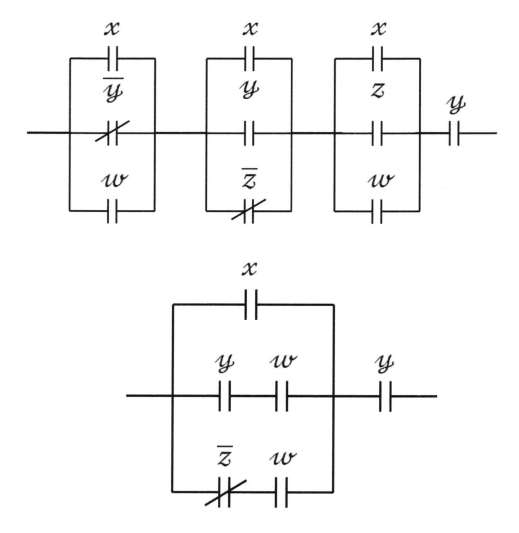

Figure 3.14: Upper part: the original circuit. Lower part: the equivalent new circuit.

3.4.2 Groups

The concept of abstract groups is developed out from several fields of mathematics. In the domain of algebra, the motivation for group theory is the problem for solutions of polynomial equations of degree higher than 4. The 19th-century French mathematician E'variste Galois, extending prior work of Paolo Ruffini and Joseph-Louis Lagrange, gave a condition for the solvability of a particular polynomial equation in terms of the symmetry group of its roots (solutions). The elements of such a Galois group are associated to certain permutations of the roots. More general permutation groups were investigated in particular by Cauchy and Cayley.

The second field contributing to group theory is number theory. Certain abelian group structures had been used in Carl Friedrich Gauss' number-theoretical work Disquisitiones Arithmeticae (1798), and more explicitly by Leopold Kronecker. In 1847, Ernst Kummer applied group theory to describe factorization of a natural number into prime numbers during his attempt to prove Fermat's Last Theorem.

Geometry is the third field in which groups are used systematically, especially symmetry groups as part of Felix Klein's 1872 Erlangen program. Klein used group theory to organize hyperbolic and projective geometry in a more coherent way. By exploiting group ideas further, Sophus Lie founded the study of Lie groups in 1884. In this section, group structure will be defined and two examples about applying group theory will be presented.

A group is a set, G, together with an (only one) operation "+" that combines any two elements a and b to form another element indicated as $a + b$. To qualify as a group, the set and operation, $(G, +)$, must satisfy the following four requirements known as the group axioms:

- Closure: For all a, b in G, the result of the operation $a + b$ is also in G.

- Associativity: For all a, b and c in G, the equation $(a + b) + c = a + (b + c)$ holds.

- Identity: There exists an element e in G, such that for every element a in G, the equation $e + a = a + e = a$ holds.

- Inverse: For each a in G, there exists an element b in G such that $a + b = b + a = e$, where e is the identity element of G.

The order in which the group operation is carried out can be crucial. In other words, the result of combining element a with element b need not yield the same result as combining element b with element a; the equation: $a + b = b + a$, may not always be true. This equation does always hold in the group of integers under addition, because $a+b=b+a$ for any two integers (commutativity of addition). However, it does not always hold in the symmetry group, for example, Dihedral group. Groups for which the equation $a+b=b+a$ always holds are called abelian (in honor of Niels Abel).

One of the most familiar groups is the set of integers Z which consists of the numbers

$$\cdots,-4,-3,-2,-1,0,1,2,3,4,\cdots \tag{3.4.6}$$

The following properties of integer addition serve as a simple example for the abstract group axioms provided in the definition above.

- For any two integers a and b, the sum $a+b$ is also an integer. In other words, the process of adding integers two at a time can never yield a result that is not an integer. This property is known as closure under addition.

- For all integers a, b and c, $(a+b)+c=a+(b+c)$. Expressed in words, adding a to b first, and then adding the result to c gives the same final result as adding a to the sum of b and c, a property known as associativity.

- If a is any integer, then $0+a=a+0=a$. Zero is called the identity element of addition because adding it to any integer returns the same integer.

- For every integer a, there is an integer b such that $a+b=b+a=0$. The integer b is called the inverse element of the integer a and is denoted $-a$.

Example 13 *In this example, we will show that the group theory can be applied to speed up arithmetic addition. The idea is that if we wish to add two natural numbers a and b, the result will be same if we add them as two members of $\mathbb{Z}_n$ where $n > a + b$. Hence, we can replace the addition of large natural numbers by adding a set of small numbers simultaneously and adopt the Chinese Remainder Theorem [19] to get the final addition result.*

Since any natural number n can be decomposed by prime numbers as

$$n=\prod_{i=1}^{k} p_i^{m_i} \tag{3.4.7}$$

where p_i for $1 \leq i \leq k$ are different primes and m_i for $1 \leq i \leq k$ are the multiplicity for the i-th prime number. Then by the Principle Theorem of finite abelian groups, we have

$$\mathbb{Z}_n \cong \bigoplus_{i=1}^{k} \mathbb{Z}_{p_i^{m_i}}, \qquad (3.4.8)$$

where $\bigoplus$ means the direct product and $\cong$ indicates the isomorphism [20], i.e., the algebraic structures of two isomorphic groups are identical. Hence we have

$$a + b = [a]_n + [a]_n \rightarrow$$

$$([a]_{p_1^{m_1}}, [a]_{p_2^{m_2}}, \cdots, [a]_{p_k^{m_k}}) + ([b]_{p_1^{m_1}}, [b]_{p_2^{m_2}}, \cdots, [b]_{p_k^{m_k}})$$

$$([y_1]_{p_1^{m_1}}, [y_2]_{p_2^{m_2}}, \cdots, [y_k]_{p_k^{m_k}}) \qquad (3.4.9)$$

where $[x]_n$ denotes the residue class of x modulo n. Then the final result will be x which satisfies the following set of equations:

$$x \equiv y_1 (\text{mod } p_1^{m_1}), \quad x \equiv y_2 (\text{mod } p_2^{m_2}) \ , \cdots, \quad x \equiv y_k (\text{mod } p_k^{m_k}). \qquad (3.4.10)$$

From the Chinese Remainder Theorem again, we have

$$x = \sum_{i=1}^{k} (y_i \cdot n \cdot p_i^{-m_i} \cdot r_i), \qquad (3.4.11)$$

where r_i is the multiplicative inverse of $np_i^{-m_i}$ in $\mathbb{Z}_{p_i^{m_i}}$.

If we wish to add 37 and 56, we may set $n = 140$. Then we have

$$41 + 56 \ = \ [41]_{140} + [56]_{140} \rightarrow$$

$$([41]_4, [41]_5, [41]_7) + ([56]_4, [56]_5, [56]_7)$$

$$([1]_4, [1]_5, [6]_7) + ([0]_4, [1]_5, [0]_7) = ([1]_4, [2]_5, [6]_7). \qquad (3.4.12)$$

And the final result will be the solution for the following set of equations:

$$x \equiv 1 (\text{mod } 4), \quad x \equiv 2 (\text{mod } 5), \quad x \equiv 6 (\text{mod } 7). \qquad (3.4.13)$$

Therefore, $41 + 56 = 97$.

Let r be the number of input gates in an adding device, then the addition modulo n in binary form consumes $\lceil \log_r (2 \lceil \log_2 n \rceil) \rceil$ time units. However, if the previous addition method is applied, we only need $\lceil \log_r (2 \lceil \log_2 \grave{n} \rceil) \rceil$ time units where $\grave{n}$ is the greatest prime power in the decomposition of the number n. For instance, if $r = 3$ and $n = 2^5 \cdot 3^3 \cdot 5^2 \cdot 7^2 \cdot 13 \cdot 17 \cdot 19 \cdot 23 \cdot 29 \cdot 31 \cdot 37 \cdot 41 \cdot 43 \cdot 47$ which is a natural number with 20 decimal digits, then time units will be reduced from $\lceil \log_3 (2 \lceil \log_2 (3 \cdot 10^{21}) \rceil) \rceil = 5$ to $\lceil \log_3 (2 \lceil \log_2 49 \rceil) \rceil = 3$. Almost 50% reduction!

Example 14 *Suppose we are given a task to design a funny die which allow 3 different symbols at each face. One interesting question raised is to know the number of rotationally distinct symbols of the faces of a cube. According to Burnside's theorem [21], let G be a finite group that acts on a set X. For each g in G let X^g denote the set of elements in X that are fixed by g. Then the number of orbits, denoted $|X/G|$, can be expressed as*

$$|X/G| = \frac{1}{|G|} \sum_{g \in G} |X^g|. \tag{3.4.14}$$

Let X be the set of 3^6 possible face symbol combinations that can be applied to a cube in one particular orientation, and let G be the rotation group acted on the cube with 24 elements. Then two elements of X belong to the same orbit precisely when one is simply a rotation of the other. The number of rotationally distinct symbols is the same as the number of orbits and can be found by counting the sizes of the fixed sets for the 24 elements of G. There are five kinds of rotations in the group G, they are

- *one identity element which leaves all 3^6 elements of X unchanged.*

- *six 90-degree face rotations, each of which leaves 3^3 of the elements of X unchanged.*

- *three 180-degree face rotations, each of which leaves 3^4 of the elements of X unchanged.*

- *eight 120-degree vertex rotations, each of which leaves 3^2 of the elements of X unchanged.*

- *six 180-degree edge rotations, each of which leaves 3^3 of the elements of X unchanged.*

Hence, there are $\frac{1}{24}(3^6 + 6 \cdot 3^3 + 3 \cdot 3^4 + 8 \cdot 3^2 + 6 \cdot 3^3) = 57$ different dies generated.

3.4.3 Rings

A ring is an algebraic structure consisting of a set together with two binary operations (usually called addition and multiplication), where each operation combines two elements to form a third element. To be a ring, the set together with its two operations must satisfy certain conditions, namely, the set must be an abelian group under addition and a monoid under multiplication with multiplication distribution over addition. In this section, ring structure will be defined and two examples about applying ring theory are given.

A ring is a set R equipped with two binary operations $+ : R \times R \to R$ and $\cdot : R \times R \to R$, called addition and multiplication. To be a ring, the set and two operations, represented as

$(R, +, \cdot)$, must satisfy the following requirements known as the ring axioms.

$(R, +, \cdot)$ is required to be an abelian group under addition:

- Closure under addition. For all a, b in R, the result of the operation $a + b$ is also in R.

- Associativity of addition. For all a, b, c in R, the equation $(a + b) + c = a + (b + c)$ holds.

- Existence of additive identity. There exists an element 0 in R, such that for all elements a in R, the equation $0 + a = a + 0 = a$ holds.

- Existence of additive inverse. For each a in R, there exists an element b in R such that $a + b = b + a = 0$.

- Commutativity of addition. For all a, b in R, the equation $a + b = b + a$ holds.

Besides, $(R, +, \cdot)$ is required to be a monoid under multiplication:

- Closure under multiplication. For all a, b in R, the result of the operation $a \cdot b$ is also in R.

- Associativity of multiplication. For all a, b, c in R, the equation $(a \cdot b) \cdot c = a \cdot (b \cdot c)$ holds.

- Existence of multiplicative identity. There exists an element 1 in R, such that for all elements a in R, the equation $1 \cdot a = a \cdot 1 = a$ holds.

Finally, the distributive laws for multiplication with respect to addition have to be satisfied.

- For all a, b and c in R, the equation $a \cdot (b + c) = (a \cdot b) + (a \cdot c)$ holds.

- For all a, b and c in R, the equation $(a + b) \cdot c = (a \cdot c) + (b \cdot c)$ holds.

Example 15 *In this example, we will apply generating multinomial, which has ring structure based on elementary multinomial addition and multiplication, to characterize the energy and delay distribution of transmitting a packet successfully in an IEEE 802.11 wireless network. This example is based on works in [22].*

The wireless networks that we analyze here have the following network layer specifications. First, each station with a fixed position can hear (detect and decode) the transmission of $n - 1$[4] other stations in the network. Second, stations always have a packet ready to transmit. Third,

---

[4]n is the density of stations for each station's neighbor.

each station uses the 802.11 *MAC protocol*. At the PHY layer, a packet of K *information bits is encoded into a packet of N coded symbols. It is assumed that the receivers have no multiple-access capability (i.e., they can only receive one packet at a time) and they cannot transmit and receive simultaneously. The packet error probability depends on the parameters K, N, and E_c/N_0, where E_c is the received coded symbol energy and N_0 is the one-sided power spectral density level of the thermal noise at the receiver.*

In the following we give a brief description of the most salient features of the IEEE 802.11 *MAC protocol. When a station is ready to transmit a packet, it senses the channel for DIFS seconds. If the channel is sensed idle, the transmission station picks a random number j, uniformly distributed in $\{0, 1, \ldots, W_i - 1\}$, where $W_i = 2^i W$ is the contention window (CW) size, i is the contention stage (initially $i = 0$), and W is the minimum CW size. A backoff time counter begins to count down with an initial value j: it decreases by one for every idle slot of duration σ seconds (also referred to as the standard slot) as long as the channel is sensed idle, stops the count down when the channel is sensed busy, and reactivates when the channel is sensed idle again. The station transmits an RTS packet when the counter counts down to zero. After transmitting the RTS packet, the station will wait for a CTS packet from the receiving station. If there is a collision of the RTS packet with other competing stations or a transmission error occurs in the RTS or CTS packet, the transmitting station doubles the CW size (increases the contention stage i by one) and picks another random number j as before. If there are no collisions or errors in the RTS and CTS packets, the station begins to transmit the data packet and waits for an acknowledgment (ACK) packet. However, if the data or the ACK packet is not successfully received, the CW size will also be doubled (the contention stage i will increase by one) and the transmitting station will join the contention period again. The contention stage is reset (i is set to zero) when the transmitting station receives an ACK correctly. It is also noted that there is a maximum CW size (or equivalently, a maximum contention stage, m); when the transmitter is in this maximum stage and needs to join the contention period again, it does not increase further the CW, but picks a random number in $\{0, 1, \ldots, W_m - 1\}$.*

We are ready to analyze the energy and delay characteristics of the wireless networks described above. The delay T_d of each data packet is defined as the time duration from the moment the backoff procedure is initiated until DIFS seconds after the ACK packet is received correctly by the transmitting station, as shown in Fig. 3.15. Similarly, the energy E_t is defined as the energy consumed by both transmitting and receiving stations in the duration of T_d. Without loss of the* generality, for notational simplicity we assume that the propagation loss between transmitter and receiver is one (0 dB). We also assume that the propagation time is negligible. In this paper, we only consider the energy consumption for packet transmission and omit the energy required for signal processing and channel sensing. The system parameter SIFS is defined as the time between the end of a packet reception, say RTS and the beginning of a packet transmission, say CTS. This time includes the time required for decoding a packet and other processing functions at the receiver.

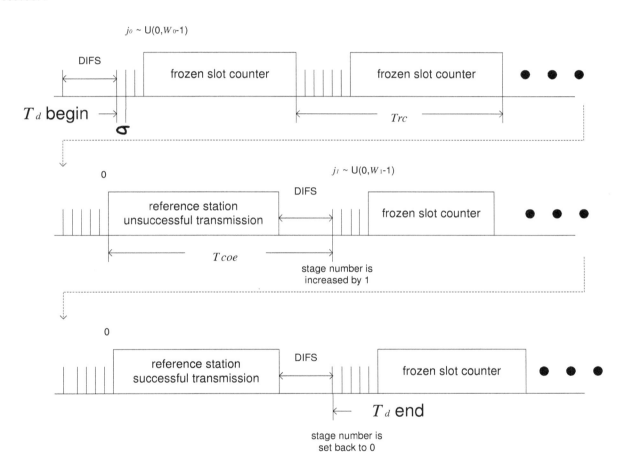

Figure 3.15: Timing diagram to transmit a packet successfully in IEEE 802.11.

In order to analyze energy and delay consumption, we need to evaluate some important probabilities which are crucial in later analysis. By modifying the Markov chain model described above, we can take into account packets errors as shown in Fig. 3.16. We denote the error probability of the four kinds of packets in the system as $P_{e,RTS}$, $P_{e,CTS}$, $P_{e,DT}$ (where DT refers to data packets) and $P_{e,ACK}$. We assume that the channel is memoryless between packets. These probabilities depend on the particular channel, coding, modulation, etc. A successful packet transmission requires that the RTS, CTS, DT, and ACK packets are received correctly. Let p_{ce} denote the probability of the complement of this event, i.e., collision in the RTS packet or error in any of the packets. This is also the transition probability from one contention stage to the next in the two-dimensional Markov chain, as shown in Fig. 3.16. Using similar assumptions as in [23] for the packet collision probability p_c, and since the events of packet collision and packet error are independent, the probability of p_{ce} can be expressed as

$$
\begin{aligned}
p_{ce} \ = \ & p_c + (1 - p_c) \left[P_{e,RTS} + (1 - P_{e,RTS}) P_{e,CTS} \right. \\
& + (1 - P_{e,RTS})(1 - P_{e,CTS}) P_{e,DT} \\
& \left. + (1 - P_{e,RTS})(1 - P_{e,CTS})(1 - P_{e,DT}) P_{e,ACK} \right],
\end{aligned}
\tag{3.4.15}
$$

where p_c is the conditional collision probability. Following the derivation in [23], we can evaluate the stationary probability $P(i, j)$ of each state (i, j) of the Markov chain. Let p_{tx} be the probability of a transmitting station sending an RTS packet during each backoff slots. The transmission probability p_{tx} and the collision probability p_c can be related as in [23]

$$
p_{tx} \triangleq \sum_{i=0}^{m} P(i, 0) = \frac{2(1 - 2p_{ce})}{(1 - 2p_{ce})(W + 1) + p_{ce} W (1 - (2p_{ce})^m)}
\tag{3.4.16}
$$

$$
p_c = 1 - (1 - p_{tx})^{n-1}.
\tag{3.4.17}
$$

From the above three nonlinear equations, (3.4.15)–(3.4.17), the probabilities p_{ce}, p_{tx} and p_c can be evaluated numerically. Another important probability that will be used in our analysis later is the probability of a transmission of an RTS packet from exactly one of the remaining $n - 1$ stations given that at least one of the remaining stations is transmitting. It is denoted by p_{tx_1} and can be expressed as

$$
p_{tx_1} = \frac{(n - 1) p_{tx} (1 - p_{tx})^{n-2}}{p_c}.
\tag{3.4.18}
$$

Our goal is to obtain the joint generating function of energy and delay for a successful data packet transmission, which can be expressed as

$$
G_s(X, Y) \ = \ \sum_{i=0}^{\infty} \sum_{j=0}^{\infty} Pr(T_d = i\Delta_t, E_t = j\Delta_e) X^i Y^j,
\tag{3.4.19}
$$

where Δ_t, Δ_e are parameters that determine the resolution of our analysis (we choose $\Delta_t = T_b$ and $\Delta_e = E_c$ in the remaining part of our analysis). We further define the quantities $N_{SIFS} =$

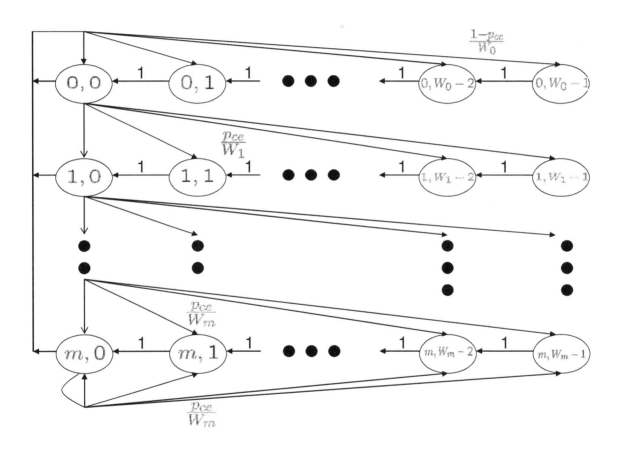

Figure 3.16: Markov chain for backoff counter and contention window stage.

T_{SIFS}/Δ_t, $N_{DIFS} = T_{DIFS}/\Delta_t$, and $N_\sigma = \sigma/\Delta_t$ make the additional assumption that N_{SIFS}, N_{DIFS} and N_σ are integers.

Based on IEEE 802.11 protocol, the state flow diagram shown in Fig. 3.17 can be obtained. Each transition from state A to state B in this diagram is labelled with the conditional joint generating function of the additional energy and delay incurred when the protocol makes a transition from state A to state B. For instance, the generating function G_{rs} corresponding to a channel reservation success is

$$
\begin{aligned}
G_{rs}(X,Y) &= (1-p_c)(1-P_{e,RTS})(1-P_{e,CTS}) \\
&\quad \cdot X^{N_{RTS}+N_{CTS}+2N_{SIFS}} Y^{N_{RTS}+N_{CTS}},
\end{aligned}
\tag{3.4.20}
$$

where $(1-p_c)(1-P_{e,RTS})(1-P_{e,CTS})$ is the probability of not having a collision and having a correct reception of the RTS and CTS packets, $[N_{RTS}+N_{CTS}+N_{SIFS}+T_{DIFS}] \times T_b$ is the delay incurred during this transition, and $[N_{RTS}+N_{CTS}] \times E_c$ is the corresponding energy consumed. Similarly, the generating function G_{ts} corresponding to a data packet transmission success once the channel is reserved can be expressed as

$$
\begin{aligned}
G_{ts}(X,Y) &= (1-P_{e,DT})(1-P_{e,ACK}) \\
&\quad \cdot X^{N_{DT}+N_{ACK}+N_{SIFS}+N_{DIFS}} Y^{N_{DT}+N_{ACK}}.
\end{aligned}
\tag{3.4.21}
$$

The generating functions associated with failure to either reserve a channel or to transmit a data packet are products of two generating functions. Each product contains a factor that is independent of the particular CW stage, and a factor that depends on the contention stage i. We first describe the factors that are independent of the CW stage. The generating function G_{rf}, corresponding to a channel reservation failure is given by

$$
\begin{aligned}
G_{rf}(X,Y) &= [p_c + (1-p_c)P_{e,RTS}]X^{N_{RTS}+N_{DIFS}} Y^{N_{RTS}} \\
&\quad + (1-p_c)(1-P_{e,RTS})P_{e,CTS}X^{N_{RTS}+N_{CTS}+N_{SIFS}+N_{DIFS}} \\
&\quad \cdot Y^{N_{RTS}+N_{CTS}},
\end{aligned}
\tag{3.4.22}
$$

the meaning of which is that a failure can be due to either a collision/RTS transmission error, or a CTS transmission error. Similarly, after reserving the channel, a data packet transmission failure is either due to a data packet transmission error, or an acknowledgement packet transmission

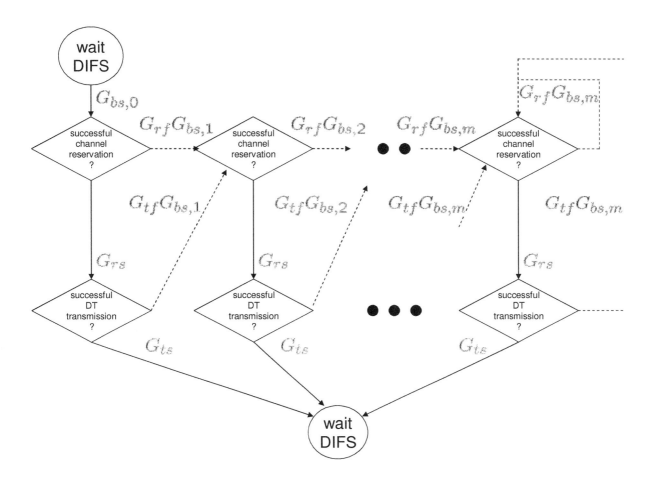

Figure 3.17: State diagram representation of the 802.11 MAC protocol. Transform variables X and Y are omitted for simplicity.

error, which is captured by the generating function G_{tf} as follows

$$
\begin{aligned}
G_{tf}(X,Y) \;=\;& P_{e,DT}X^{N_{DT}+N_{DIFS}}Y^{N_{DT}} \\
&+(1-P_{e,DT})P_{e,ACK}X^{N_{DT}+N_{ACK}+N_{SIFS}+N_{DIFS}} \\
&\cdot Y^{N_{DT}+N_{ACK}}.
\end{aligned}
\tag{3.4.23}
$$

We now evaluate the generating functions denoted by $G_{bs,i}$ of the state diagram. This generating function characterizes the delay for the transmitting station from the instant of starting the backoff procedure to the instant that the backoff counter reaches to zero at stage i. We do not need to consider energy consumption here since the reference station is not transmitting during this period. Thus, $G_{bs,i}$ is not a function of the variable Y. The probability of a busy slot due to the transmission of other stations is p_c and this event is independent and identical for each slot from our previous assumptions. At contention stage i, the range of possible backoff slots is from 1 to 2^iW. Let j be the backoff slot chosen uniformly from the above range. The number of the occupied slots in these j slots is binomialy distributed with parameters (j,p_c). Hence, the generating function, $G_{bs,i}$, is

$$
G_{bs,i}(X) \;=\; \sum_{j=1}^{2^iW}\frac{1}{2^iW}\sum_{k=0}^{j}\binom{j}{k}[(1-p_c)X^{N_\sigma}]^{j-k}(p_cG_{oc}(X))^k.
\tag{3.4.24}
$$

where $G_{oc}(X)$ is the generating function of the delay due to an occupied slot. We define an occupied slot as a slot when the transmitting station senses the channel is busy due to the transmission of one of the $n-1$ remaining stations. In an occupied slot, there are four possible cases. The first case is when two or more RTS packets from the remaining $n-1$ stations collide or have a packet error. The second case is when the RTS packet is correctly received without collision but there is an error in the CTS packet transmission. The third case is when the RTS packet is correctly received without collision and there is no error in the CTS packet but there is an error in the DT packet transmission. The last case is when there is a correct reception of RTS, CTS, and DT and either correct or erroneous reception of the ACK packet. Note that the time duration of successful or unsuccessful ACK transmission are the same. Therefore, the corresponding *generating function is*

$$
\begin{aligned}
G_{oc}(X) &= [(1 - p_{tx_1}) + p_{tx_1}P_{e,RTS}]X^{N_{RTS}+N_{DIFS}} \\
&\quad + p_{tx_1}(1 - P_{e,RTS})P_{e,CTS}X^{N_{RTS}+N_{CTS}+N_{SIFS}+N_{DIFS}} \\
&\quad + p_{tx_1}(1 - P_{e,RTS})(1 - P_{e,CTS})P_{e,DT} \\
&\quad \cdot X^{N_{RTS}+N_{CTS}+N_{DT}+N_{SIFS}+N_{DIFS}} \\
&\quad + p_{tx_1}(1 - P_{e,RTS})(1 - P_{e,CTS})(1 - P_{e,DT}) \\
&\quad \cdot X^{N_{RTS}+N_{CTS}+N_{DT}+N_{ACK}+N_{SIFS}+N_{DIFS}}.
\end{aligned}
$$

$$(3.4.25)$$

From the state diagram and Mason's gain formula [24], we obtain the following backward recursive equations for the generating function $G_s(X,Y)$.

$$
G_s(X,Y) = G_{bs,0}\Bigg\{ 1 + \sum_{j=1}^{m-1}[G_{rf} + G_{rs}G_{tf}]^j \left(\prod_{i=1}^{j} G_{bs,i}\right) + \frac{[G_{rf} + G_{rs}G_{tf}]^m}{1 - [G_{rf} + G_{rs}G_{tf}]G_{bs,m}}\left(\prod_{i=1}^{m} G_{bs,i}\right)\Bigg\}G_{rs}G_{ts}.
$$

$$(3.4.26)$$

where i ($1 \le i \le m$) is the index of the CW stage.

From the joint generating function, the average energy and delay can be easily evaluated as

$$
\overline{T}_d = \Delta_t \frac{\partial G_s}{\partial X}\Big|_{X=Y=1},
$$

$$(3.4.27a)$$

$$
\overline{E}_t = \Delta_e \frac{\partial G_s}{\partial Y}\Big|_{X=Y=1}.
$$

$$(3.4.27b)$$

3.4.4   Fields

Compared to a ring, a field is a ring with multiplicative inverse element. The most familiar field for us may be real numbers in which we can perform addition, subtraction, multiplication and division with those real numbers. A field is a set F that is a set together with two operations, usually called addition and multiplication, and denoted by $+$ and $\cdot$, respectively, such that the following axioms hold. Note that subtraction and division are defined implicitly in terms of the inverse operations of addition and multiplication.

- Closure of F under addition and multiplication. For all a, b in F, both $a + b$ and $a \cdot b$ are in F, where $+$ and $\cdot$ are binary operations on F.

- Associativity of addition and multiplication. For all $a, b,$ and c in F, the following equalities hold: $a + (b + c) = (a + b) + c$ and $a \cdot (b \cdot c) = (a \cdot b) \cdot c$.

- Commutativity of addition and multiplication. For all a and b in F, the following equalities hold: $a + b = b + a$ and $a \cdot b = b \cdot a$.

- Additive and multiplicative identity. There exists an element of F, called the additive identity element and denoted by 0, such that for all a in F, $a + 0 = a$. Likewise, there is an element, called the multiplicative identity element and denoted by 1, such that for all a in F, $a \cdot 1 = a$. The additive identity and the multiplicative identity are required to be distinct.

- Additive and multiplicative inverses. For every a in F, there exists an element $-a$ in F, such that $a + (-a) = 0$. Similarly, for any a in F other than 0, there exists an element a^{-1} in F, such that $a \cdot a^{-1} = 1$.

- Distributivity of multiplication over addition. For all a, b and c in F, the following equality holds: $a \cdot (b + c) = (a \cdot b) + (a \cdot c)$.

The concepts of fields are widely used in number theory, coding theory and combinatorics. Fields of two elements 0 and 1 are useful in computer science. In the following example, we establish an identical field structure relation (isomorphism) to characterize discrete signals and associated Z-transforms, an important and useful tool widely used in signal processing [25]. Based on this result, it is easier for us to manipulate filter design [26].

Example 16 *Some notations have to be setup for this example. A* sequence *is expressed as $\langle a \rangle$ and the corresponding index-n element is represented as $\langle a \rangle_n$ where $n \in \mathbb{Z}$ thereupon.*

In the linear system analysis, the Z-transform converts a discrete-time signal or system, which is a sequence of real or complex numbers, into a complex-valued frequency-domain representation. In this example, we further elaborate the morphism *of the Z-transform (transform a sequence in the Hilbert space into a ring of polynomials or rational functions) which stems from the "generating function method" in the probability theory. There are many advantages for us to apply this abstract algebraic approach for discrete-time systems and signals. We list some of them here: (a) the morphism studies can help to establish an exact representation for a discrete-time signal or system; (b) the morphism studies can help to solve the difference equations* characterizing the linear time-invariant systems and discrete-time signals (sometimes, one may even find a new recurrence relation different from the original difference equation, which provides new insights into the system nature); (c) the morphism studies can help to address the statistical properties of a signal or system (generating functions can lead to extremely quick derivations of various probabilistic aspects associated with the unknown discrete-time signals); (d) the morphism studies can help to manifest the asymptotic behavior or trend of a signal (typically, when one is dealing with a very irregular signal, instead of its exact representation in whatever form, which might be out of the question, we can look for an approximate formula based on the generating function); (e) the morphism studies can help to characterize the variations of a signal, or to infer the rises and falls of its waveform; (f) the morphism studies can help to prove the identities for the essential mathematical operations applied for systems and signals. For example, we have the following identity that

$$\sum_{i=0}^{n} \binom{n}{i} = \binom{2n}{n}, \tag{3.4.28}$$

where $n = 0, 1, 2, \cdots$. It becomes much simpler and more illustrative to prove the above identity through the check of the generating functions associated with the sequences at both sides. In order to present ideas more fluently, we only show theoretical results and all their proofs in this example can be found in [25].

Our discussions will be focused on the stable causal inverse systems (filters) whose impulse responses are causal sequences expressed as

$$\langle a \rangle = (\cdots, 0, 0, \alpha_k, \alpha_{k+1}, \alpha_{k+2}, \cdots), \tag{3.4.29}$$

where $k = ind_l(a) \in \mathbb{Z}$. Without loss of generality, a causal sequence can be denoted as $\langle a \rangle \in \mathcal{S}_C$ or $\langle a \rangle_{n=ind_l(a)}^{+\infty}$ (the filter impulse response sequence $\langle h \rangle$ can also belong to this class of sequences when it is causal). From now on, we treat any impulse response $h[n]$ as a sequence, such that it can also be denoted as $\langle h \rangle$ for our future algebraic manipulation ($\langle h \rangle_n = h[n]$). The causal sequences represent the practical signals and filters. Thus, the (classical) Z-transform of the causal sequence $\langle a \rangle$ is defined as

$$Z(a) \equiv \alpha_k z^{-k} + \alpha_{k+1} z^{-(k+1)}$$
$$+ \alpha_{k+2} z^{-(k+2)} + \cdots \tag{3.4.30}$$

and the power series $Z(a)$ converges under the assumption that

$$\varlimsup_{n \to \infty} |\langle a \rangle_n|^{\frac{1}{n}} = \varlimsup_{n \to \infty} |\alpha_n|^{\frac{1}{n}} < \infty. \tag{3.4.31}$$

Since the sequence $\langle a \rangle$ is causal, there exists an integer $k = ind_l(a)$ such that $\alpha_j = 0$ for $j < k$ and $\alpha_k \neq 0$. Moreover, if $\alpha_{k'} \neq 0$ and $\alpha_j = 0$ for all $j > k' = ind_u(a)$, then such a causal sequence is finite-support. The following lemma characterizes the relationships among $\{ind_l(a*b), ind_u(a*b)\}$ and $\{ind_l(a), ind_u(a), ind_l(b), ind_u(b)\}$ where $*$ denotes the convolutional operation such that

$$\langle c \rangle_n = \langle a \rangle_n * \langle b \rangle_n \equiv \sum_i \langle a \rangle_{n-i} \langle b \rangle_i, \forall n, \tag{3.4.32}$$

where

$$ind_l(c) \equiv ind_l(a * b) \text{ and } ind_u(c) \equiv ind_u(a * b). \tag{3.4.33}$$

In short, Eq. (3.4.32) can be written as $\langle c \rangle = \langle a \rangle * \langle b \rangle$.

Given two sequences $\langle a \rangle$ and $\langle b \rangle$, the addition (subtraction) operation of these two sequence, denoted by $\pm$, results in another sequence $\langle c \rangle$ such that

$$\langle c \rangle \equiv \langle a \rangle \pm \langle b \rangle, \tag{3.4.34}$$

where $\langle c \rangle_n \equiv \langle a \rangle_n \pm \langle b \rangle_n, \forall n$. According to the following theorem, $(\mathcal{S}_\mathcal{C}, +, *)$ forms a field.

Theorem 1 *The set of all causal sequences, $\mathcal{S}_\mathcal{C}$, together with two operations, namely addition $+$ and convolution $*$, form a field $(\mathcal{S}_\mathcal{C}, +, *)$. The addition identity is a zero sequence, i.e., $\langle \mathbf{0} \rangle \equiv (\cdots, 0, \overline{0}, 0, \cdots)$ and the multiplication identity is denoted as $\langle \mathbf{1} \rangle \equiv (\cdots, 0, \overline{1}, 0, \cdots)$ where the overline specifies the 0-th indexed position of a sequence [27].*

Let $\widetilde{M}$ be the function set of $\left\{ f : \exists \langle a \rangle \in \mathcal{S}_\mathcal{C} \text{ such that } f(z) = \sum_{k=-\infty}^{\infty} \langle a \rangle_k z^{-k} \text{ for all } z \in U^*_{R_a}(0) \right\}$, where $U^*_{R_a}(0)$ is the punctured disk (centered at 0) for the convergence region of $\langle a \rangle$ with a convergence radius R_a.

Lemma 1 *$f(z) \in \widetilde{M}$ if and only if there exists $k \in \mathbb{Z}$ such that the function $g(z) \equiv z^{-k} f(z)$ satisfies the following conditions [27]:*

(A) *there exists $\langle b \rangle \in \mathcal{S}_\mathcal{C}$ such that $g(z) = \sum_{k=0}^{\infty} \langle b \rangle_k z^{-k}$ for all $z \in U_{R_b}(0)$, where $U_{R_b}(0)$ is the disk (centered at 0) for the convergence region of $\langle b \rangle$ with a convergence radius R_b;*

(B) *$g(0) = \langle b \rangle_0 \neq 0$.*

According to above Lemmas, we can show that $\widetilde{M}$ forms a field.

Theorem 2 *$(\widetilde{M}, +, \cdot)$ is a field [27].*

Then we are ready to show that the equivalence between causal sequences and z-functions is established by the following field isomorphism between the set of causal sequences and the set of z-functions.

Theorem 3 *The Z-transform, $Z : \mathcal{S}_C \to \widetilde{\mathcal{M}}$, is a field isomorphism [27].*

3.4.5 Linear Algebras

Linear algebra is a branch of mathematics concerned with the study of vector spaces, which are another family of algebraic structures governed by some set of equalities (varieties). An elementary application of linear algebra is to the solution of a systems of linear equations in several unknowns. More advanced applications are widely adopted in various subareas in mathematics, in areas as diverse as abstract algebra and functional analysis. In this section, vector spaces will be defined and matrices concepts are also explored to characterize linear transform between two vector spaces.

Let F be a field, a *vector space over F* is a set V together with an addition operation $V \times V \to V$, denoted as $\vec{x} + \vec{y}$ where $\vec{x}, \vec{y}$ are elements belonged to V, and another operation $F \times V \to V$, represented as $c\vec{x}$ where c is a scaler in F, which also satisfy the following identities:

- (Commutativity) For each $\vec{x}, \vec{y} \in V$, $\vec{x} + \vec{y} = \vec{y} + \vec{x}$.

- (Associativity for Vectors Addition) For each $\vec{x}, \vec{y}, \vec{z} \in V$, $(\vec{x} + \vec{y}) + \vec{w} = \vec{x} + (\vec{y} + \vec{w})$.

- (Associativity for Scalers Multiplication) For each $c, d \in F$ and $\vec{x} \in V$, we have $(cd)\vec{x} = c(d\vec{x})$.

- (Additive Identity) There exist a zero vector in V, denoted as 0, such that $0 + \vec{x} = \vec{x} + 0 = \vec{x}$ for each $\vec{x} \in V$.

- (Additive Inverse) For each $\vec{x} \in V$, there exist $-\vec{x} \in V$ such that $(-\vec{x}) + \vec{x} = 0$.

- (Multiplication Identity) There exist a scaler in F, denoted as 1, such that $1\vec{x} = \vec{x}1 = \vec{x}$

- (Distributivity for Vectors) For each $c \in F$ and $\vec{x}, \vec{y} \in V$, we have $c(\vec{x} + \vec{y}) = c\vec{x} + c\vec{y}$.

- (Distributivity for Scalers) For each $c, d \in F$ and $\vec{x} \in V$, we have $(c + d)\vec{x} = c\vec{x} + d\vec{x}$.

After defining vector spaces, the matrix notions are introduced to describe linear transform between two vector spaces. Let V and W be vector spaces over the same field F, let $\mathfrak{B}_V =$

$\{v_1, v_2, \cdots, v_n\}$ be an basis of V and let $\mathfrak{B}_W = \{w_1, w_2, \cdots, w_m\}$ be an basis of W. The linear transform ϕ from space V to W can be expressed as

$$\phi(v_j) = \sum_{i=1}^{m} \alpha_{i,j} w_j, \qquad (3.4.35)$$

where j ranges from 1 to n. Let $M_{\mathfrak{B}_V}^{\mathfrak{B}_W}(\phi) = \alpha_{i,j} = (a_{i,j})$ be the $m \times n$ matrix whose i, j entry is $\alpha i, j$, i.e., we use the coefficients of the w_i in Eq. (3.4.35) for the j-th column of this matrix. The matrix $M_{\mathfrak{B}_V}^{\mathfrak{B}_W}(\phi)$ is named as the matrix of linear transform ϕ with respect to the bases $\mathfrak{B}_V$ and $\mathfrak{B}_W$. For example, let $V = \mathbb{R}^3$ with basis $\mathfrak{B}_V = \{(1,0,0), (0,1,0), (0,0,1)\}$, $W = \mathbb{R}^2$ with basis $\mathfrak{B}_W = \{(1,0), (0,1)\}$ and let ϕ be the linear transform expressed as $\phi(x, y, z) = (x+3y, x+y+z)$. Since $\phi(1,0,0) = (1,1)$, $\phi(0,1,0) = (3,1)$, $\phi(0,0,1) = (0,1)$, then the matrix $M_{\mathfrak{B}_V}^{\mathfrak{B}_W}(\phi) = \alpha_{i,j}$ becomes $\begin{pmatrix} 1 & 3 & 0 \\ 1 & 1 & 1 \end{pmatrix}$.

Below, two examples are presented about applying linear algebra concepts to design new systems.

Example 17 *Every linear time-invariant system can be described by a set of equations of the following form*

$$\dot{\mathbf{x}}(t) = \mathbf{A}\mathbf{x}(t) + \mathbf{B}\mathbf{u}(t),$$

$$\mathbf{y}(t) = \mathbf{C}\mathbf{x}(t) + \mathbf{D}\mathbf{u}(t), \qquad (3.4.36)$$

where the system is with p inputs expressed by vector $\mathbf{u}(t)$, q outputs indicated by $\mathbf{y}(t)$, and n state variables denoted by $\mathbf{x}(t)$; $\mathbf{A}, \mathbf{B}, \mathbf{C}$ and $\mathbf{D}$ are constant matrices (system description matrices) with size $n \times n$, $n \times p$, $q \times n$ and $q \times p$, respectively. If elements in one of these four matrices $\mathbf{A}, \mathbf{B}, \mathbf{C}$ and $\mathbf{D}$ are time varying, such system is named as a linear time-variant system.

Consider the system illustrated by Fig 2.11 at Book [28]. It consists of two blocks with masses m_1 and m_2, connected by three springs with spring constants k_1 and k_2. We assume that there is no fiction between the blocks and the floor, moreover, blocks 1 and 2 are applied by outer forces u_1 and u_2, respectively. The output to be observed by this system is the displacement of these two blocks. From Newton's laws of motion, we have the following equation for block 1. It is

$$m_1 \ddot{y}_1 + (k_1 + k_2)y_1 - k_2 y_2 = u_1. \qquad (3.4.37)$$

Similarly, we also have the following equation for block 2. It can be written as

$$m_2 \ddot{y}_2 - k_2 y_1 + (k_1 + k_2)y_2 = u_2. \qquad (3.4.38)$$

By defining $x_1 := y_1$, $x_2 := \dot{y}_1$, $x_3 := y_2$ and $x_4 := \dot{y}_2$, we can combine Eqs. (3.4.37) and (3.4.38) jointly as following matrix form:

$$
\begin{bmatrix} \dot{x}_1 \\ \dot{x}_2 \\ \dot{x}_3 \\ \dot{x}_4 \end{bmatrix} = \begin{bmatrix} 0 & 1 & 0 & 0 \\ -\frac{k_1+k_2}{m_1} & 0 & \frac{k_2}{m_1} & 0 \\ 0 & 0 & 0 & 1 \\ \frac{k_2}{m_2} & 0 & -\frac{k_1+k_2}{m_2} & 0 \end{bmatrix} \begin{bmatrix} x_1 \\ x_2 \\ x_3 \\ x_4 \end{bmatrix} + \begin{bmatrix} 0 & 0 \\ \frac{1}{m_1} & 0 \\ 0 & 0 \\ 0 & \frac{1}{m_2} \end{bmatrix} \begin{bmatrix} u_1 \\ u_2 \end{bmatrix}.
\tag{3.4.39}
$$

The output can be related to $\begin{bmatrix} x_1 \\ x_2 \\ x_3 \\ x_4 \end{bmatrix}$ as

$$
\begin{bmatrix} y_1 \\ y_2 \end{bmatrix} = \begin{bmatrix} 1 & 0 & 0 & 0 \\ 0 & 0 & 1 & 0 \end{bmatrix} \begin{bmatrix} x_1 \\ x_2 \\ x_3 \\ x_4 \end{bmatrix}.
\tag{3.4.40}
$$

Hence, we have

$$
\mathbf{A} = \begin{bmatrix} 0 & 1 & 0 & 0 \\ -\frac{k_1+k_2}{m_1} & 0 & \frac{k_2}{m_1} & 0 \\ 0 & 0 & 0 & 1 \\ \frac{k_2}{m_2} & 0 & -\frac{k_1+k_2}{m_2} & 0 \end{bmatrix}, \quad \mathbf{B} = \begin{bmatrix} 0 & 0 \\ \frac{1}{m_1} & 0 \\ 0 & 0 \\ 0 & \frac{1}{m_2} \end{bmatrix},
$$

$$
\mathbf{C} = \begin{bmatrix} 1 & 0 & 0 & 0 \\ 0 & 0 & 1 & 0 \end{bmatrix}, \qquad\qquad \mathbf{D} = [0].
\tag{3.4.41}
$$

The benefits that we formula a linear system by matrices (system description matrices) make us easier to quantify various properties of a control system, for instances, stability, controllability and observability. We said that a system has stability property if it generates bounded outputs whenever bounded inputs are triggered. The condition to have such stability property is to check weather every eigenvalue of matrix $\mathbf{A}$ has a negative real part. For controllability, we define a system is controllable if for any initial state $\mathbf{x}_0$ and any final state $\mathbf{x}_1$, there exists an input that transfer $\mathbf{x}_0$ to $\mathbf{x}_1$ in a finite time. Otherwise, such system is said to be uncontrollable. The condition for the controllability for a linear system described by Eq. (3.4.36) is

$$
\text{Full row rank for the matrix } [\mathbf{B}\mathbf{A}\mathbf{B}\mathbf{A}^2\mathbf{B}\cdots\mathbf{A}^{n-1}\mathbf{B}],
\tag{3.4.42}
$$

where n is the number of states.

The notion of observability is dual to that of controllability and it studies the possibility of estimating the state from the output. The state equation Eq. (3.4.36) is said to be observable if for any unknown initial state $\mathbf{x}_0$, there exists a finite time duration t such that the knowledge of the input $\mathbf{u}$ and the out put $\mathbf{y}$ over $[0, t]$ suffices to determine uniquely the initial state $\mathbf{x}_0$. Otherwise, such system is said to be unobservable. The condition for the observability for a linear system described by Eq. (3.4.36) is

$$\text{Full row rank for the matrix } \int_0^t e^{A^T \tau} C^T C e^{A \tau} d\tau, \tag{3.4.43}$$

where T represents matrix transpose operation. The details about the validation of these conditions can be found at various linear system books, for example [28].

Example 18 *In this example, we will study a reaction network among network components. Such reaction network model can be applied to characterize various systems, such as an organization or a metabolic systems. In Fig. 3.18, we show an example for the reaction network with five units given in.*

Each unit has its own performance, which varies over time. The rate of the performance change is assumed to be proportional to the amount of resources consumed or products (services) generated in all the reactions. The system we discuss here is assumed to have m units with n fluxes of reactions. Let C_i be the performance score of the unit i and v_j be the resources or products flux in reaction j, then

$$\frac{d\mathbf{C}}{dt} = \mathbf{S}\mathbf{v}, \tag{3.4.44}$$

where $\mathbf{C}$ is a $m \times 1$ vector composed by C_i, $\mathbf{v}$ is a $n \times 1$ vector consisted by v_j and $\mathbf{S}$ is a $m \times n$ matrix where $s_{i,j}$ measures the performance score variation of the i-th unit if the j-th reaction flux is applied.

In fact, the reaction equations for system described by Eq. (3.4.44) are nonlinear equations of $\mathbf{C}$ since the fluxes are functions of the performances and some other system parameters. However, we have $\frac{d\mathbf{C}}{dt} = \mathbf{S}\mathbf{v} = 0$ if the equilibrium is achieved. Since all solutions for $\mathbf{v}$ to achieve $\mathbf{S}\mathbf{v} = 0$ form a linear space, denoted as $\mathbf{S}_E$, then we have

$$\mathbf{S}_E = \sum_{i=1}^{l} w_i p_i, \tag{3.4.45}$$

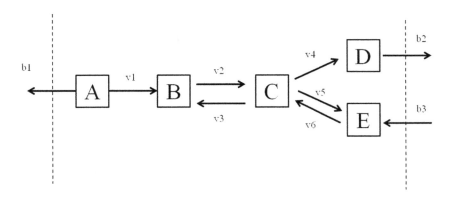

Figure 3.18: A reaction network example

where the set for vectors $p_1, p_2, \cdots, p_l$ are bases for space $\mathbf{S}_E$.

Let $\mathbf{P}$ be a matrix with each column corresponding to a p_i of a given reaction network. Let $\mathbf{Q}$ be the binary representation of $\mathbf{P}$ such that $Q_{i,j} = 1$ if $P_{i,j} \neq 0$ and $Q_{i,j} = 0$ otherwise. Then $(\mathbf{Q}^T \mathbf{Q})_i$ is equal to the lengths of the i-th basis for $\mathbf{S}_E$ and the the element $(\mathbf{Q}^T \mathbf{Q})_{i,j}$ are equal to the number of common reactions in bases i and j. On the other hand, $(\mathbf{Q}\mathbf{Q}^T)_i$ is equal to the number of bases the reactions participate in for the i-th internal as well as external fluxes and the the element $(\mathbf{Q}\mathbf{Q}^T)_{i,j}$ are equal to the number of common reactions participated by the i-th and the j-th internal as well as external fluxes.

3.5 Quasivarieties

A quasivariety is an extension for a variety by allowing those algebraic axioms to be quasiidentities. In order to have more complete mathematical descriptions for invention method, we have to expand the *identical* relation used in characterizing algebraic axioms to the *quasiidentitical* relation. A quasiidentity is an implication of the form

$$\text{Common condition for a list of requirements:} \quad \bigwedge_{i=1}^{n} \alpha_i \rightarrow \beta \tag{3.5.1}$$

where α_i and β are terms built up from variables using the operation symbols of the specified algebraic model. For instance, the class of all torsion-free groups is quasi-variety of groups given by the following infinite set of quasi-identities: $x^p = 1 \rightarrow x = 1$, where p is any prime. In this section, we will introduce two examples about applying quasivarieties in invention procedures.

Example 19 *After some new ideas or products are proposed or generated, we may face the problem about verifying these new things to make sure that the new things satisfied our requirements. We have to test weather the functions possessed by new things achieve our pre-specified requirements or not.*

Suppose the desired (ideal) system S has inputs $x_1, x_2, \cdots, x_n$, and has the corresponding outputs as $y_1, y_2, \cdots, y_n$. Another invented new system S' also has inputs $x_1, x_2, \cdots, x_n$. If, for all possible inputs, one always have the following relations

$$S(x_1) = S'(x_1) = y_1, \; S(x_2) = S'(x_2) = y_2, \; \cdots, S(x_n) = S'(x_n) = y_n \tag{3.5.2}$$

we have both identical system S and S'. Then the new invented system S' have all required functions possessed by the desired system S. The above arguments can be expressed as quasiidentitical *relation as*

$$S(\mathbf{x}) = S'(\mathbf{x}) \ for \ all \ possible \ \mathbf{x} \to S = S'. \tag{3.5.3}$$

The above method can also be named as functional simulation method and has some similarities with the black box *method since both start from the function of system first. In fact, the important step of the method of black box is to apply the functional simulation to build a model. However, the work of method of black box not only understands the overall function of the interesting system but also conjectures the internal structure. Functional simulation focuses on establishing a function which meets the needs of people, and it is not necessary to conjecture the internal structure of the interesting system.*

Example 20 *Graphs are mathematical structures used to model pairwise relations between objects from a certain collection. A "graph" is defined as an ordered pair (V, E), where V is a set of vertices and E is a binary relation on V^2. An edge between vertices a and b is described by the following quasiidentity:*

$$a \bigwedge b \to e_{a,b,*}, \tag{3.5.4}$$

where $e_{a,b,*}$ is an edge connecting vertices a and b with property $*$.

Before performing any invention methods for our interesting things, we have to prepare a clear conceptual representation for our interesting things. There are many insightful motivations for a graph-based approach to such conceptual representation. There are numerous ways existed in diagramming conceptual representation. We can explain these motivations from two perspectives: from a modeling viewpoint and from a computational view point.

From a modeling viewpoint, there are two essential characteristics, objects and reasoning, in diagramming our concepts. The objects are easily comprehensible by users, at least if the graphs are not large in sizes. Note that is is always poassible to split up a large conceptual graph into smaller ones by keeping its semantics. This feature provides the reasons why the success of graphical models, such as entity-relationship model [29], unified modeling language [30], function system chart, etc. Many people are more familiar with kinds of labeled graphs and this property helps persons easier to acquire concepts from graphs. Another important property to adopt graphical representation for concepts is reasoning mechanisms. Two arguments are listed to support such claim. First, homomorphism is a basic step to compare concepts through graph matching and it can be easily visualized. Secondly, the same language (graphical representation) is used at interface and computing manipulation and there is no transformation has to be done on those conceptual components. In summary, as an old adage says "A picture is worth a thousand words". From computational viewpoint, all manipulations on graphs which are corresponding to conceptual processes are not hard to be implemented by computers since graph is a standard data structure in computer science. On the other hand, various mathematical facts about graphs can be applied back to generate new concepts [31].

In software engineering, an entity-relationship model (ERM) is an abstract and conceptual representation of data. Entity-relationship modeling is a database modeling method, used to produce a type of conceptual schema or semantic data model of a system.

There are three building blocks of ERM: entities, relationships and attributes. An entity may be defined as a thing which is recognized as an item capable of an independent existence and which can be uniquely identified. An entity may be a physical object such as a dog or a car, an event such as a dog barking or a car service, or a concept such as a customer transaction or order. Another similar concept related to entity is entity-type, which is a category for a collection of entities. An entity, strictly speaking, is an instance of a given entity-type. Usually, there are many instances of an entity-type. Entities can be associated to nouns from sentence structure perspective. Examples: a computer, an employee, a song, a mathematical theorem.

The second building block for ERM are relationships. A relationship characterizes how two or more entities are related to one another. Relationships can be thought as verbs which link two or more nouns. Examples: an "own" relationship between a company and a employees, a "supervises" relationship between a professor and a group of students, a "performs" relationship between a singer and a song.

The third building block for ERM are attributes, which are used to distinguish among entities and relationships. Entities and relationships can both have attributes. Examples: an student entity might have a student ID number attribute; a car entity might have a plate number attribute. Every entity must have a minimal set of uniquely identifying attributes, which is called the entity's primary key.

Some diagramming conventions are provided below to make ERM more illustrative for users. Entity sets are drawn as rectangles, relationship sets as diamonds. Attributes are drawn as ovals and are connected with a line to exactly one entity or relationship set. Cardinality constraints are expressed as follows:

- *a double line indicates a participation constraint, totality or surjectivity: all entities in the*

110

entity set must participate in at least one relationship in the relationship set;

- *an arrow from entity set to relationship set indicates a key constraint, i.e. injectivity: each entity of the entity set can participate in at most one relationship in the relationship set;*

- *a thick line indicates both, i.e. bijectivity: each entity in the entity set is related in exactly one relationship.*

- *an underlined name of an attribute indicates that it is a key: two different entities or relationships with this attribute always have different values for this attribute.*

In fact, all the above conventional ways to present data in ERM can be changed to other graph symbols under users preferences. In Fig. 3.19, building blocks and their relations for ERM are shown.

After careful understanding to the interesting thing through graphical representation for those concepts and relationships associated to them, then, we are ready to consider and questionable all aspects about the interesting thing, e.g., entities, attributes and relationships in ERM, since all such aspects can be changed , improved, replaced or transformed to create new things. Therefore, many existing methods for creation can be considered as proposing questions with respect to those concepts illustrated by the aforementioned graph model, such as, hopes (or disadvantages) listing method, check-list technique (A. F. Osbern), asking method, and examing-asking method (Arnold). Those questions are raised based on any possible operations on conceptual representation graph, in this example, we will only show those example questions according to algebraic models provided in this section. However, other operations, like association and analog which will be presented at later chapters, can also be applied to manipulate the original conceptual representation graph to invent new things. In general, questions used to excite new inventions can be categorized by the following two kinds:

- *Using* Yes/No Questions *to ask weather we can change any components represented by conceptual graph through operations? For instance, if we wish to improve functions for a pen, we may ask: can the length of pen be increased or decreased (by addition or substraction operation), can the pen be combined with a clock to provide writers time during their work (by product operation), etc.*

- *Using* Wh-Questions *to propose questions from following six issues about the original conceptual representation graph: time (when), space (where), belonging (who, whose, whom),*

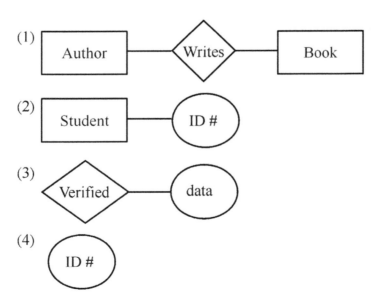

Figure 3.19: (1) Two related entities, (2) An entity with an attribute, (3) A relationship with an attribute, (4) Primary key

causal (why), manner (how), quality and quantity (how much, how many, how often, how far, etc.), compare (which one) and clarification (what). We give an example for asking "why", in order to improve a product, we can ask questions as follows: Why do we improve it? Why do we use such materials in producing this product? Why the cost for making such product is so high? Why this product's performance is unsalable in rainy days? and so on. In questions about issues like causal and compare, we have to collect more useful information as many as possible by associating and analogizing the original conceptual graph to other conceptual graphs.

Final remarks about this example have to be pointed out here. The above two kinds of questions can also be applied to things to be invented which are represented by other mathematical structures.

3.6 Approximation

An approximation is an inexact replacement of something that is still close enough to be useful. The notion about approximation can be found at various areas of science and technology. For examples, we use rational numbers to approximate irrational numbers in dealing with numbers, we approximate the shape of Earth as an exact sphere when we wish to determine satellite orbits and we replace other materials with lower cost for the original product by still keeping satisfactory effects. In computer science and operations research, approximation algorithms are algorithms used to find approximate solutions for optimization problems. Approximation algorithms are often raised when the original problems are hard to solve, i.e., non-polynomial time solvable problems. Mostly, the proposed approximation algorithms can be executed in polynomial time, however, the solutions obtained are not the optimal or exact solution. Approximation algorithms are increasingly being used also for problems where exact polynomial-time algorithms are known but are too expensive due to the input size. The effect of approximation depends on the available resources, the sensitivity of the problem to these available resources, and the savings (usually in time and effort) that can be achieved by approximation. Mathematical parts of this section is based on an excellent textbook [32].

A basic question is raised: what is the exact meaning for an approximation which is *close enough* to the ideal one. A metric concept has to be introduced to quantify the meaning of "close enough". The metric concept can be defined as following:

Definition 1 *A **metric** on a set X is a function.*

$$d : X \times X \to \mathbb{R}$$

having the following properties:

(1) $d(x, y) \geq 0$ for all $x, y \in X$; equality holds if and only if $x = y$.

(2) $d(x, y)$ may not always equal to $d(y, x)$ for all $x, y \in X$.

(3) *(Triangle inequality)* $\rho(d(x, y) + d(y, z)) \geq d(x, z)$ for all $x, y, z \in X$, where $\rho \geq 1$. If $\rho = 1$, it becomes the standard metric definition. If $\rho > 1$, it can be used to measure the difference between two objects in more practical world. For example, such inequalities were introduced to model round-trip delay times in the internet traffic.

The set X in the above definition is the set for all possible or ideal outcomes generated from invention processes (operations). When a metric is defined which satisfies the above three rules, an approximation, denoted as x, which is *close enough* to the ideal one, denoted as y, indicates that the term $d(x, y)$ is smaller or equal then a specified value (tolerable disagreement).

Another situation makes the concept metrizable useful is for *Optimization design method*, which is a method that we adopt the optimization theory in mathematics to solve the engineering design problems. One crucial step in such method is to establish a system optimization mathematical model by specifying restriction conditions and setting system performance measure. The performance measure for systems to be designed has to be a metric on a metrizable space. In later sections, we will have more detail explanations about this method with more advanced algebraic operations.

Several familiar examples about metric spaces are given in the following. (1) The real numbers with the distance function $d(x, y) = |y - x|$ given by the absolute value, and more generally Euclidean n-space with the Euclidean distance, are metric spaces also. (2) If G is an undirected connected graph, then the set V of vertices of G can be turned into a metric space by defining $d(x, y)$ to be the length of the shortest path connecting the vertices x and y. (3) The Levenshtein distance is a measure of the dissimilarity between two strings x and y, defined as the minimal number of character deletions, insertions, or substitutions required to manipulate x into y.

In general, we will embed the metric to measure the difference for things to be invented in real space $\mathbb{R}$ for more convenient computation purpose. Given any countable infinite index set J [5], we wish to show that the product space of real numbers, denoted as $\mathbb{R}^J$, is metrizable with

---

[5]The index set can include various aspects used to characterize invention related things.

114

the product topology by the following lemma.

Lemma 2 *Let $\bar{d}(a,b) = \min\{|a-b|^k, 1\}$ and $\bar{d}(b,a) = \min\{c|a-b|^k, c\}$ be the standard bounded metric on $\mathbb{R}$, which satisfy*

$$\bar{d}(a,b) = \bar{d}(b,a), \quad for\ c = 1;$$

$$\bar{d}(a,b) \geq \bar{d}(b,a), \quad for\ 0 < c < 1;$$

$$\bar{d}(a,b) \leq \bar{d}(b,a), \quad for\ c > 1; \tag{3.6.1}$$

and

$$\bar{d}(a,c) \leq \rho(\bar{d}(a,b) + \bar{d}(b,c)), \tag{3.6.2}$$

where a,b and c are any three real numbers. If $\mathbf{x}$ and $\mathbf{y}$ are two points of $\mathbb{R}^J$, define

$$D(\mathbf{x},\mathbf{y}) = \sup\left[\frac{\bar{d}(x_i, y_i)}{i}\right]. \tag{3.6.3}$$

Then $D(\mathbf{x},\mathbf{y})$ is a metric that induces the product topology on $\mathbb{R}^J$.

PROOF. 1 *In the following proof, we assume that $c \geq 1$. The proof can be applied similarly for $c < 1$. Then we have $\bar{d}(a,b) = \min\{|a-b|^k, 1\} \leq \bar{d}(b,a) = \min\{c|a-b|^k, 1\}$. The property of triangle inequality of $D(\mathbf{x},\mathbf{y})$ can be verified as*

$$\frac{\bar{d}(x_i, z_i)}{i} \leq \rho(\frac{\bar{d}(x_i, y_i)}{i} + \frac{\bar{d}(y_i, z_i)}{i}) \leq \rho(D(\mathbf{x},\mathbf{y}) + D(\mathbf{y},\mathbf{z})), \tag{3.6.4}$$

and we have

$$D(\mathbf{x},\mathbf{z}) = \sup\left\{\frac{\bar{d}(x_i, z_i)}{i}\right\} \leq D(\mathbf{x},\mathbf{y}) + D(\mathbf{y},\mathbf{z}). \tag{3.6.5}$$

Now, we wish to show that the metric $D(\mathbf{x},\mathbf{y})$ gives the product topology. First, let U be open in the metric topology and let $\mathbf{x} \in U$; we find an open set V in the product topology such that $\mathbf{x} \in V \subset U$. Choose an ϵ-ball $B_{D(\mathbf{x},\mathbf{y})}(\mathbf{x}, \epsilon)$ lying in U. Then choose N large enough that $1/N < \epsilon$. Let V be the basis element for the product topology

$$V = (x_1 - \epsilon, x_1 + \epsilon) \times \cdots \times (x_N - \epsilon, x_N + \epsilon) \times \mathbb{R} \times \mathbb{R} \times \cdots. \tag{3.6.6}$$

We claim that $V \subset B_{D(\mathbf{x},\mathbf{y})}(\mathbf{x}, \epsilon)$: Given any $\mathbf{x}$ in $\mathbb{R}^J$,

$$\frac{\bar{d}(x_i, y_i)}{i} \leq \frac{1}{N} \quad for\ i \geq N. \tag{3.6.7}$$

We have,

$$D(\mathbf{x}, \mathbf{y}) \geq \max \left\{ \frac{\bar{d}(x_1, y_1)}{1}, \cdots, \frac{\bar{d}(x_N, y_N)}{N}, \frac{1}{N} \right\}. \tag{3.6.8}$$

If $\mathbf{y}$ is in V, then $V \subset B_{D(\mathbf{x},\mathbf{y})}(\mathbf{x}, \epsilon)$, as desired. If the ϵ-ball is determined based on metric $D(\mathbf{y}, \mathbf{x}$, we choose N large enough that $c/N < \epsilon$. Let V be the basis element for the product topology

$$V = (x_1 - \epsilon, x_1 + \epsilon) \times \cdots \times (x_N - \epsilon, x_N + \epsilon) \times \mathbb{R} \times \mathbb{R} \times \cdots. \tag{3.6.9}$$

We assert that $V \subset B_{D(\mathbf{y},\mathbf{x})}(\mathbf{x}, \epsilon)$: Given any $\mathbf{x}$ in $\mathbb{R}^J$,

$$\frac{\bar{d}(y_i, x_i)}{i} \leq \frac{\epsilon}{N} \quad for \ i \geq N. \tag{3.6.10}$$

We have,

$$D(\mathbf{y}, \mathbf{x}) \geq \max \left\{ \frac{\bar{d}(y_1, x_1)}{1}, \cdots, \frac{\bar{d}(y_N, x_N)}{N}, \frac{c}{N} \right\}. \tag{3.6.11}$$

If $\mathbf{y}$ is in V, then $V \subset B_{D(\mathbf{y},\mathbf{x})}(\mathbf{x}, \epsilon)$ still holds for metric changed as $D(\mathbf{y}, \mathbf{x})$.

Conversely, given metric $D(\mathbf{x}, \mathbf{y})$, we wish to show that $\mathbf{y} \in \prod U_i$, where U_i is open in $\mathbb{R}$ for indices $i = \beta_1, \cdots, \beta_n$ and $U_i = \mathbb{R}$ for all other indices i. Given $\mathbf{x} \in U$, we find an open set V of the metric topology such that $\mathbf{x} \in V \subset U$. Choose an interval $(x_i - \epsilon_i, x_i + \epsilon_i)$ in $\mathbb{R}$ centered about x_i and lying in U_i for $i = \beta_1, \cdots, \beta_n$; choose each $\epsilon_i \leq 1$. Then define

$$\epsilon = \min\{\epsilon_i^k / i \,|\, i = \beta_1, \cdots, \beta_n\}. \tag{3.6.12}$$

We assert that

$$\mathbf{x} \in B_{D(\mathbf{x},\mathbf{y})}(\mathbf{x}, \epsilon) \subset U. \tag{3.6.13}$$

Let $\mathbf{y}$ be a point of $B_{D(\mathbf{x},\mathbf{y})}(\mathbf{x}, \epsilon)$. Then for all i, we have

$$\frac{\bar{d}(x_i, y_i)}{i} \leq D(\mathbf{x}, \mathbf{y}) < \epsilon. \tag{3.6.14}$$

Since $\bar{d}(x_i, y_i) < \epsilon_i^k \leq 1$; it follows that $|x_i - y_i| < \epsilon_i$. Therefore, $\mathbf{y} \in \prod U_i$. For metric $D(\mathbf{y}, \mathbf{x})$, we redefine ϵ as

$$\epsilon = \min\{c\epsilon_i^k / i \,|\, i = \beta_1, \cdots, \beta_n\}. \tag{3.6.15}$$

We claim that

$$\mathbf{x} \in B_{D(\mathbf{y},\mathbf{x})}(\mathbf{x}, \epsilon) \subset U. \tag{3.6.16}$$

Let $\mathbf{y}$ be a point of $B_{D(\mathbf{y},\mathbf{x})}(\mathbf{x},\epsilon)$. Then for all i, we have

$$\frac{\bar{d}(y_i, x_i)}{i} \leq D(\mathbf{y}, \mathbf{x}) < \epsilon. \tag{3.6.17}$$

Since $\bar{d}(y_i, x_i) < c\epsilon_i^k \leq 1$; it follows that $|x_i - y_i| < \epsilon_i$. Again, we also have $\mathbf{y} \in \prod U_i$. $\square$

The following theorem will tell us that what conditions for space X make it metrizable. Two definitions about topological space should be described before stating the following theorem. Regular space means that, given any closed set, H and any point set x that does not belong to the closed set, there exists a neighborhood U of x and a neighborhood V of H that are disjoint. This condition says that x and H can be separated by neighborhoods. A base (or basis) B for a topological space X with topology T is a collection of open sets in T such that every open set in T can be written as a union of elements of B.

Theorem 4 *(Metrization theorem).* *Every regular space X with a countable basis is metrizable.*

PROOF. 2 *We will prove that X is metrizable by imbedding X in a metrizable space $\mathbb{R}^J$; that is, by showing X homeomorphic with a subspace of $\mathbb{R}^J$, which is a metrizable space according to Lemma 2.*

From the consequence of the Urysihn lemma [32], we have the facts. There exists a countable collection of continuous functions $g_n : X \to [0,1]$ having the property that given any point x_0 of X and any neighborhood U of x_0, there exists an index n such that g_n is positive at x_0 and vanishes outside U.

Given the functions g_n obtained from previous step, a map $F : X \to \mathbb{R}^J$ is defined as

$$F(x) = (g_1(x), g_2(x), \cdots).$$

We claim that F is an imbedding. First, F is a continuous map since $\mathbb{R}^J$ has the product topology and each g_n is continuous. Second, F is a one-to-one map because given $x \neq y$, we know there is an index n such that $g_n(x) > 0$ and $g_n(y) = 0$. Finally, we must prove that F is a homeomorphism of X onto its image, the subspace $Z = F(X)$ of $\mathbb{R}^J$. We know that F defines a continuous bijection between X and Z, the condition left to verify that this map is a homeomorphism is to show that for each open set U in X, the set $F(U)$ is open in Z. Let z_0 be a point of $F(U)$. We shall find an open set W of Z such that

$$z_0 \in W \subset F(U).$$

Let x_0 be the point of U such that $F(x_0) = z_0$. Choose an index N for which $g_N(x_0) > 0$ and $g_N(X - U) = \{0\}$. Take the open ray $(0, +\infty)$ in $\mathbb{R}$, and let V be the open set

$$V = \pi_N^{-1}((0, +\infty))$$

of $\mathbb{R}^J$. Let $W = V \cup Z$; then W is open in Z, by definition of the subspace topology. We note that $z_0 \in W \subset F(U)$. First, $z_0 \in W$ because

$$\pi_N(z_0) = \pi_N(F(x_0)) = g_N(x_0) > 0.$$

Second, $W \subset F(U)$. For if $z \in W$, then $z = F(x)$ for some $x \in X$, and $\pi_N(z) \in (0, +\infty)$. Since $\pi_N(z) = \pi_N(F(x)) = g_N(X)$, and g_N vanishes outside U, the point x must be in U. Hence, $z = F(x)$ is in $F(U)$. In conclusion, F is an imbedding of X in $\mathbb{R}^J$. $\square$

In the following, we will provide two examples about approximation which both have metrizable space to measure the disagreement between the approximated approach and the exact one.

Example 21 *Traditional Chinese herbal medicine is widely applied to treat diseases not only in Asia but also in western countries. Traditional Chinese medicine practices include such treatments as Chinese herbal medicine, acupuncture, dietary therapy, and Tui-Na (a kind of massage for medical purpose). Much of the philosophy of traditional Chinese medicine is derived from Tao philosophy, which believes that the life and activity of individual human beings have an intimate relationship with the environment on all aspects.*

The product operation discussed in Sec. 3.2 can be applied to model a treatment for a kind of disease by n different Chinese herbal medicines, it can be formulated as :

$$s_{H,1} \bullet s_{H,2} \bullet \cdots \bullet s_{H,n} \rightarrow$$

Recovery health in D days from a particular disease, \hfill (3.6.18)

where $\bullet$ represents a product operation for combining different Chinese herbal medicines.

Sometimes, patients may not able to acquire all Chinese herbal medicines due to financial problems or ecological protection for some wildlives. Doctors may change the prescription by using other substitutional Chinese herbal medicines to have the same or similar physiological effect. Hence, the algebraic model for this new prescription can be transformed as :

$$\tilde{s}_{H,1} \bullet \tilde{s}_{H,2} \bullet \cdots \bullet \tilde{s}_{H,m} \rightarrow$$

$$\textit{Recovery health in } \tilde{D} \textit{ days from a particular disease,} \qquad (3.6.19)$$

where the total number of different Chinese herbal medicines becomes m and the time required to recover is changed as $\tilde{D}$ days. Since the time duration for recovery (treated as a set $[0, \infty) \in \mathbb{R}$) is a metrizable space, we have the following approximation for the Chinese herbal medical prescription. It is

$$s_{H,1} \bullet s_{H,2} \bullet \cdots \bullet s_{H,n} \approx \tilde{s}_{H,1} \bullet \tilde{s}_{H,2} \bullet \cdots \bullet \tilde{s}_{H,m}, \qquad (3.6.20)$$

under the recovery time changed from D to $\tilde{D}$ days.

Example 22 *A road is a recognizable route, way or path between two places. Many places and roads that connect these places form a road network. Traffic congestion is a condition on road networks that occurs as users increases, and is criticized by slower speeds, longer trip times, and increased queueing length. Several reasons may introduce traffic congestion. The most common reason is the physical use of roads by vehicles. When traffic flow is great enough that the interaction between vehicles slows the speed of the traffic stream, congestion will happen. The second reason is made by car accidents. It has been found that such incidents may cause ripple effects (a cascading failure) which then spread out and create a sustained traffic jam when normal flow might have continued for some period of time. The third reason is road works and/or maintenance since such behaviors on roads will reduce the road capacity and make traffic congestion happen even the users flow is normal. The last factor to cause traffic jam is natural disasters, for examples, earthquakes, thunderstorms, hurricanes or tornados. All these natural disasters will slow down traffic speed and even cause accidents on roads.*

Among various management methods used to avoid traffic congestion, substitutional roads systems make users to reach the same destination, although some extra cost, e.g., time and gas, is needed compared to the original route. The product operation discussed in Sec. 3.2 can also be applied to model the gas consumption from the initial place to the destination place, it can be expressed as :

$$r_1 \bullet r_2 \bullet \cdots \bullet r_n \rightarrow G \textit{ gallons gas consumed,} \qquad (3.6.21)$$

where $\bullet$ represents a product operation for combining different road segments r_i from the initial place to the destination place. Due to the traffic congestion, the driver may select other road segments as :

$$\tilde{r}_1 \bullet \tilde{r}_2 \bullet \cdots \bullet \tilde{r}_m \to \tilde{G} \text{ gallons gas consumed,} \tag{3.6.22}$$

where the total number of road segments becomes m and the gas consumed is modified as $\tilde{G}$ gallons. Since the quantity for gas consumed (treated as a set $[0, \infty) \in \mathbb{R}$) is a metric space, we have the following approximation for using substitutional roads. It is

$$r_1 \bullet r_2 \bullet \cdots \bullet r_n \approx \tilde{r}_1 \bullet \tilde{r}_2 \bullet \cdots \bullet \tilde{r}_m, \tag{3.6.23}$$

under the gas consumption changed from G to $\tilde{G}$ gallons.

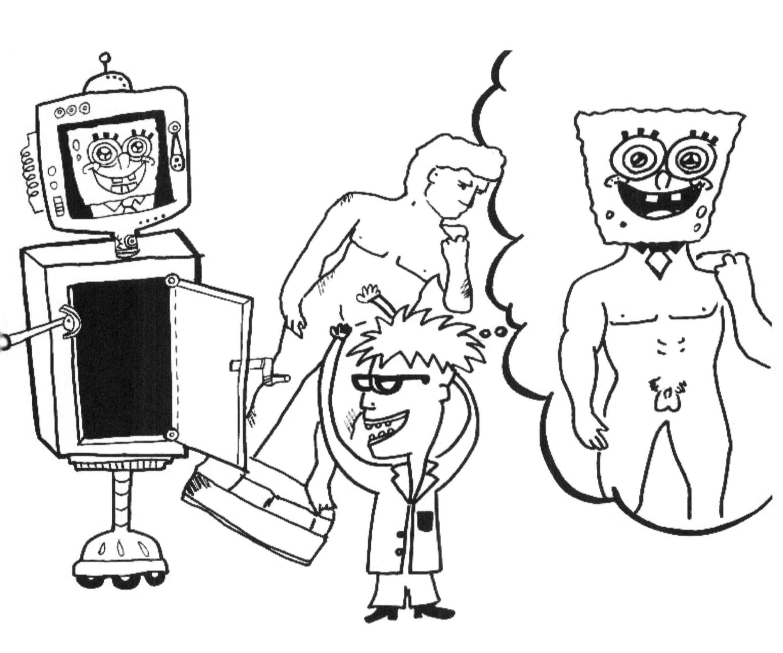

Figure 3.20: Replacement = Subtraction + Addition

Chapter 4

Relations and Actions

Association method is a popular method that applies associative mental mechanism to generate creative ideas. The mental operation of association is try to make conceptual connections among different things; then creative ideas are excited by these connections. The physiological mechanism of association is a temporary connection among neuron models. The more knowledge and experiences one has, the more neuron models his/her brain saves. It becomes much easier to obtain useful ideas through association. The notion of *relation* originated from mathematics is suitable to provide a characterization for association since the concept of a relation adopted in mathematics is to find out the relation (association) between two given sets. In Sec. 4.1, we describe the train of association thoughts and mention the traditional classification for association types. In order to comprehend more associative relations, the notion of relation is defined to provide more powerful association methods for creating new things.

Permutation, which is an ordering of a certain number of elements of a given set, is another important approach used in creating new things and will be discussed in Sec. 4.2. Numerous creations in science and technologies, or even in literature are generated from permutation components in a set, which may be constructed by product operations (combination). For example, Nanotechnology, is the study of the controlling of matter on an atomic and molecular scale. Nanotechnology deals with structures sized between 1 to 100 nanometer in at least one dimension, and involves developing materials or devices within that size. Experts assert that: the core principle of nanotechnology is we can select and permutate those atoms and molecules to create new materials successfully. The applications of nanotechnology are very diverse, those new substances produced by nanotechnology can be used in the textile, food, construction materials, automotive, etc. Such difficult science and technologies are nothing but the permutation and combination of the original substances, incredible! Since the notion about permutation is also used to designate the act of rearranging parts of an object, group actions language borrowing from mathematics can give a precise description of permutation.

4.1 Associations by Relations

Association is a popular mental activity during creation procedures. The main purpose of association is to connect two things with different concepts by figuring out their mutual relation. The train of association thoughts can be classified into two categories: one is *relation-driven* association and the other is *set-driven* association. For relation-driven association, our brains first receive some stimulation and get some concrete concepts in mind, then our brains try to create other things according to any possible relations, which are initiated from those concepts generated from the previous stimulation, recognizable by humans. For set-driven association, our brains first receive two different things in mind and try to create new relation among these two things, instead of associating things from already known relation.

Psychologically, associations can be divided into the following three different types. **Association by Similarity**: When the brain receives some kinds of stimulation, the brain naturally recalls the similar concepts, experiences, actions or things in the space or time. **Association by Contrast**: When the brain receives some kinds of stimulation, the brain recollects the contrary or symmetric concepts, experiences, actions or things. **Association by Causality**: When the brain receives some kinds of stimulation, the brain automatically reminisces the causally related concepts, experiences, actions or things. Unfortunately, these associations types are not enough to characterize all association relations generated during an invention procedure. For example, innovations are created by solving those contradictory relations among existed things, which is one of those basic and important assumptions in TRIZ [33].

4.1.1 Composition of Associations

In our invention procedure, we may not satisfied with only one association outcome. Sometimes, we have to apply a series of associations in order to reach our desired invention. A serious of associations require more rigorous logical thoughts to derive each step of association. For example, the plot of a literature work is composed by a serious of association among scenarios.

From the association pattern and the degree of freedom, we can divide the association into two types: Free Association (FA) and Directional Association (DA). FA is an association without fixed thinking patterns among each association step. In a test related to such kind of association, we can provide testers a word, a concept or other stimulus and ask them to feedback what are those first responsive concepts in their brains. The features of FA are to broaden the mentality, to draw inferences about other cases from one particular instance and to inaugurate a chain reaction of associations. DA is a controlled association. The association patterns and goals are assigned and the association processes only can follow along this pre-specified pattern. In a DA test, there are certain constraints are provided to regulate the stimulus and the responses, such as the synonyms and antonyms of the stimulus. Relation definitions have been given in Chap. II, the concept of *relation composition* will be introduced in this section in order to apply a series of associations for our invention.

Let $X_1, X_2, \cdots, X_l, \; Y_1, Y_2, \cdots, Y_m$, and $Z_1, Z_2, \cdots, Z_n$ are sets and we have the following two multi-ary relations, R and S, based on these sets:

$$R \subseteq X_1 \times X_2 \times \cdots \times X_l \times Y_1 \times Y_2 \times \cdots \times Y_m,$$

$$S \subseteq Y_1 \times Y_2 \times \cdots \times Y_m \times Z_1 \times Z_2 \times \cdots \times Z_n, \qquad (4.1.1)$$

where R and S are $(l+m)$-ary and $(m+n)$-ary relations, respectively. Then their composition (concatenation of association) is the $l+n$ relation written as

$$
\begin{aligned}
S \circ R \;=\; & \{(x_1, x_2, \cdots, x_l, z_1, z_2, \cdots, z_n) \in \\
& X_1 \times X_2 \times \cdots \times X_l \times Z_1 \times Z_2 \times \cdots \times Z_n | \exists (y_1, y_2, \cdots, y_m) \in \\
& Y_1 \times Y_2 \times \cdots \times Y_m \text{ such that } (x_1, x_2, \cdots, x_l, y_1, y_2, \cdots, y_m) \in \\
& R \text{ and } (y_1, y_2, \cdots, y_m, z_1, z_2, \cdots, z_n) \in S\}.
\end{aligned}
\qquad (4.1.2)
$$

According to the formulation of Eq. (4.1.2), we can apply it consecutively by associating a series of components for our invention.

4.1.2 Associations by Functions

The concept of function is defined as a special kind of binary relation. One precise definition of a function is that it consists of an ordered triple of sets, which may be written as (X, Y, F). X is the domain of the function, Y is the codomain (or called as range or image), and F is a set of ordered pairs. In each of these ordered pairs (x, y), the first element x is from the domain, the second element y is from the codomain, and every element in the domain is the first element in one and only one ordered pair. The set of all y is known as the image of the function.

A function is a "well-behaved" relation since, given a starting point, we know exactly where to go; given an x, we get only and exactly one y. The pairing of names and heights for students in a class is a relation. Let us suppose that the domain is the set of everybody's heights and there is a cake-delivery guy waiting in the hallway. And all the delivery guy knows is that the cake is for the student in classroom whose height is six feet. Now let the delivery guy in. Who does he go to? What if nobody is six feet? What if there are seven students in the room that are six feet? Do they all have to pay? What if you are six feet but you do not have enough to pay? What a mess! The relation "height indicates name" is not well-behaved since it is not a function due to that many students who may share the same heights. Given the relationship $(x, y) =$ (six feet person, name), there might be seven different possibilities for $y =$ name. For a relation to be a function, there must be only and exactly one y that corresponds to a given x.

Since functions are well-behaved relations, we will introduce a way to decompose any relation with finite corresponding elements in range for a given element in domain. Any relation R over sets $X_1, X_2, \cdots, X_k$ is a subset of their Cartesian product, written as $R \subset X_1 \times X_2 \times \cdots \times X_k$. Suppose we partition these k sets into two two groups and treat the sets at the first (second) group as the input (output) of this relation, respectively. Let $X_{I,1}, X_{I,2}, \cdots, X_{I,m}$ be those sets at the input group and $X_{O,1}, X_{O,2}, \cdots, X_{O,k-m}$ be another group of sets at the output group. By transforming the product operation for sets $X_{I,1}, X_{I,2}, \cdots X_{I,m}$ into one set, denoted as $\mathbb{X}$, and the product operation for sets $X_{O,1}, X_{O,2}, \cdots X_{O,k-m}$ into another set, denoted as $\mathbb{Y}$, then we can have a binary relation, represented as $\tilde{R}_{\mathbb{X},\mathbb{Y}}$, induced by R with respect to these input and output groups of sets. This binary relation can be expressed as $\mathbb{X}\tilde{R}_{\mathbb{X},\mathbb{Y}}\mathbb{Y}$.

For each m-tuples element in the set $\mathbb{X}$, we order those relations to the $(k-m)$-tuples elements in the set $\mathbb{Y}$ with respect to such m-tuples element in the set $\mathbb{X}$. Since each relation between sets $\mathbb{X}$ and $\mathbb{Y}$ at some particular order is a function relation due to one and only one mapped element in the range for each domain element, we can decompose the relation $\mathbb{X}\tilde{R}_{\mathbb{X},\mathbb{Y}}\mathbb{Y}$ in terms of functions by these ordered relations

$$\mathbb{X}\tilde{R}_{\mathbb{X},\mathbb{Y}}\mathbb{Y} = F_1(\mathbf{X}_1, \mathbf{Y}_1) \bowtie F_2(\mathbf{X}_2, \mathbf{Y}_2) \bowtie \cdots \bowtie F_n(\mathbf{X}_n, \mathbf{Y}_n), \tag{4.1.3}$$

where $\mathbf{X}_i$ and $\mathbf{Y}_i$ for $1 \le i \le n$ are domains and ranges with respect to the i-th function relation after ordering. The number n is finite since we assume that there are finite $(k-m)$-tuples elements in the set $\mathbb{Y}$ for each given domain element in the set $\mathbb{X}$. Following example is given to illustrate such decomposition.

Example 23 *There are two investment banks named as B_1 and B_2. The investment bank B_1 investigates three companies C_1, C_2 and C_3 and the investment bank B_2 investigates two companies C_2 and C_3. These two investment banks B_1 and B_2 form a set $\mathbb{X}$ and those three companies C_1, C_2 and C_3 investigated by these two banks form another set $\mathbb{Y}$. For each bank, we order their investigation relations to these three companies according to $C_1 > C_2 > C_3$. Hence, we have following order $(B_1, C_1) > (B_1, C_2) > (B_1, C_3)$ for those three companies investigated by B_1, and the following order $(B_2, C_2) > (B_2, C_3)$ for those two companies investigated by B_2. Based on these relations (functions) order, the sets for $\mathbf{X}_1$ and $\mathbf{Y}_1$ with respect to the first order function relation are $\mathbf{X}_1 = \{B_1, B_2\}$ and $\mathbf{Y}_1 = \{C_1, C_2\}$. The sets for $\mathbf{X}_2$ and $\mathbf{Y}_2$ with respect to the second order function relation are $\mathbf{X}_2 = \{B_1, B_2\}$ and $\mathbf{Y}_2 = \{C_2, C_3\}$. Finally, the sets for $\mathbf{X}_3$ and $\mathbf{Y}_3$ with respect to the third order function relation are $\mathbf{X}_3 = \{B_1\}$ and $\mathbf{Y}_2 = \{C_3\}$.*

At this state, we are ready to decompose the investigation relations between $\mathbb{X}$ and $\mathbb{Y}$ as

$$\mathbb{X}\tilde{R}_{\mathbb{X},\mathbb{Y}}\mathbb{Y} = F_1(\mathbf{X}_1, \mathbf{Y}_1) \bowtie F_2(\mathbf{X}_2, \mathbf{Y}_2) \bowtie F_3(\mathbf{X}_3, \mathbf{Y}_3). \tag{4.1.4}$$

Following figure is provided to illustrate the concept of decomposition for the investigation relation mentioned in this example. In Fig. 4.1, we show how a relation is decomposed by functions for this investment example.

4.1.3 Association Examples

In this section, we will provide some existing creation ways based on association. All association involved in these existing methods can be enhanced by contents mentioned in Sec. 1.1 and 1.2. By relational (functional) perspective, one can include more various association relations besides similarity, contrast and causality. Further, the composition of relations (functions) enables one to expand the knowledge domains for problem solving. Finally, the property of decomposition of a n-ary relation by functions is easier for us to manipulate relation operation by computing machines.

Example 24 *William J. J. Gordon was an American inventor and psychologist. He is recognized as the creator of a problem solving method called* synectics, *which he developed while working in the Invention Design Group of Arthur D. Little. The basic steps to process such method are*

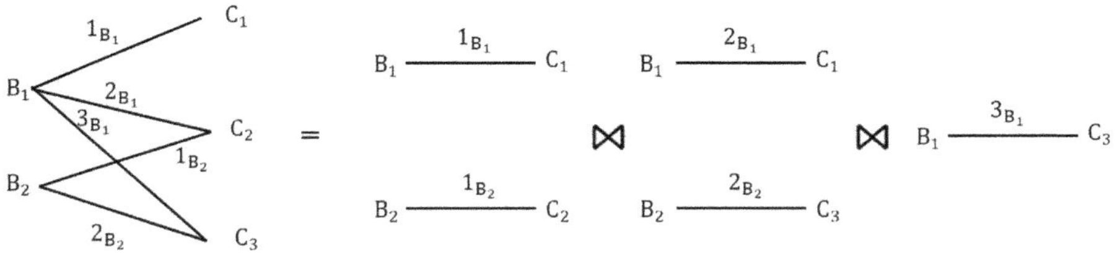

Figure 4.1: A relation decomposition example.

described by the following four steps. (1) Abstracting out those nouns, verbs, adjectives and adverbs which can reflect the basic functions or properties of the desired invention. (2) Using association to find a serious of related terms. For example, one can utilize a synonym dictionary or an antonym dictionary to obtain abundant synonym (Association by Similarity) or antonym terms (Association by Contrast) with respect to those terms abstracted out from the first step. (3) Finding out those existing entities which can also be described by those terms collected at the Step (2). (4) Inspiring ideas for invention from those entities obtained from the Step (3).

Suppose we are given a task to develop a new stroller. We may choose the term movement to indicate the property of such invention. By looking up a synonym dictionary under the term movement, following similar terms can be found: pull, push, roll, shift, collide, etc. When we read these terms, then we can be inspired by many existing facilities which can be moved by ways suggested by those terms found out in a synonym dictionary.

Example 25 *One difficulty to generate new idea is that peoples' thoughts are used to adopt known knowledge and habits. In order to overcome such restriction, an American psychologist C. S. Hvard proposed a creative way called as* compulsory association. *This method tries to list a sequence of concepts or items which are not directly related to the invention goals at the beginning, then one enforces himself/herself to associate the invention goals with these concepts or items through a succession of compositions. Hence, compulsory association is belonged to the set-driven association since our brains first receive two different things in mind and try to create new relations among these two things, instead of associating things from already known relations.*

The substantial steps to process compulsory association are described by the following four steps. (1) Confirming invention goals or problems to be solved. (2) Listing as much as concepts or things even they are not directly related to those invention goals or problems. (3) Performing a sequence of relational (functional) compositions to link those concepts or things generated from the Step (1) and the Step (2). (4) Selecting the most proper or satisfied association relations in Step (3). Otherwise, backing to the Step (2) again.

For example, if we face a problem to invent a new telephone. Then the telephone will be our invention goal. We list some unrelated things to telephone, for instance, light bulb, rubber, clock, etc. If the light bulb is selected for compulsory association, then many properties about a light bulb can be utilized to invent a new telephone, such as round shape, radiation of light, glass, transparent, etc. By compulsory association, we may have ideas to invent a telephone with round shape, a telephone which can radiate different colors of light, a telephone made by glass or *a telephone made by some limpid materials, etc.*

Example 26 *Input-Output technique is a method to invent new ideas through control theory by controlling association procedures, which is also called I/O method for short and first provided by General Electric, an American company. The method is to treat the initial states of problems such as the stimuli which are acceptable by creators as inputs, and to treat the intended goals or functions as outputs. The requirements to achieve these goals or functions are put as constraints. Based on such model, creators can consider the object of creation as a* black box *with input-output properties. Through performing a series of free associations and evaluations, one may translate the black box into a* white box *step by step and forms ideas to achieve desired invention goals.*

The operational steps of Input-Output technique are described as following: First, one defines the input and output properties for the object to be invented, then determines the black box properties with required constraints. Second, if one cannot figure out the clear relation between the input and output, one begins to perform association by thinking what are possible outputs based on current inputs and what are possible inputs to generate such desired outputs. Third, we evaluate all outcomes of association thinking and exclude inadequate ideas according to the requirements of output and the constraints. Fourth, we take the reserved idea as a new start point and execute previous steps until we can find out the optimal or satisfied association relations between the inputs and the outputs.

Example 27 *Zero waste is a philosophy that encourages to reuse all trash, hence, there are nothing sent to landfills. Association is a way to realize such ideal world. We can proceed the following steps to reuse or even create new values from trash.*

First, one selects an explicit topic about trash to be sent to landfills originally and also picks out a circumstance or an object to be applied by such trash. The topic has to be with proper range size and, if the topic range is too broad, we carry out hierarchical decomposition of the topic into several smaller topics. Second, we list and analyze each component part of trash and its corresponding attributes. Generally speaking, the object attributes can be classified into four categories as: noun attributes, adjective attributes, adverb attributes and verb attributes. Third, each attribute has to be considered as improvable and replaceable, then we can utilize association (or a series of associations by relational composition operations) to connect trash and the circumstance (or an object). In this step, both set-driven and relation-driven techniques could be applied. Fourth, we compare and evaluate the proposed ideas and select one with high innovation level and good practicability.

Empty cans are a kind of trash which are easy to be generated from a military camp. At the first step, we choose empty cans and a military camp as our starting points of later association. From the purpose of cans, we may think about filling other tiny things into empty cans, e.g., sands, rubble, etc(first association from cans' original function). After an empty can filled with something, we may think about using it as a bell, a siren or any things which capable to generate sounds after shaking it (second association from the sound property of a can filled with something). Note the composition operation is applied here to enable us to associate an empty can to an instrument.

We also may begin our association thought from a military camp. If we analyze possible components required to constitute a military camp, we may think about tents, logistical facilities and goods, weapons and ammunition, siren systems to guard the military camp, etc (first association from constitutional components of a military camp). If we wish to find out something installed at a siren systems which can generate sounds when intrusion events happen, then rings, bells or any instruments which can generate sounds from disturbance may served as candidates (second association from possible objects used by siren systems). The composition operation is applied again here to associate a military camp to instruments. At this status, we are ready to use an empty can with rubble inside as bells of a siren system since instruments which can generate sounds after disturbing are common elements obtained from two association thoughts with respect to an empty can and a military camp.

Remarks for Association

The psychology studies have shown that associations have the best stable area. When it deviates from the area, it leads to unwanted results. If associations are too stable, the thinking inertia will increase. It becomes difficult to get rid of existing thought models. Nevertheless, if associations are too free and flexible, the thinking becomes messy and jumpy. It will affect the thinking agility. In order to form the best stable area of associations in the brain and to develop the maximum of creativity, the first thing is to form the best dynamic knowledge structure. Therefore, one try to make his/her thinking by keeping the necessary tensity between logic and intuition, rationality and irrationality. Association method can not only be applied in the science, technology and creative arts, but also form some concrete normative creativity methods based on it.

4.2 Permutations by Actions

From previous chapters, we have recognized that the combination design method is an important technique in creating new things. However, the combination method dose not provide complete information about mutual order relations among constitutional components of things to be invented in space, time or other parameter spaces. Besides, permutation concept is also crucial in management science since one can allocate most resources to the most important factor in order to get most significant products improvement,e.g., Pareto Diagram. Ordering those factors based on appearance frequencies or other measures is the key step to perform such management method. After abstracting out those components for things to be invented, we then collect these components into a set, named as B. According to Theorem 5 which will be presented in Sec. 4.2.1, we can apply a group to act the set B by permuting the mutual order of elements in B.

The concept of permutation is used in various subjects of sciences and technologies, all related to the act of permuting (rearranging by some ordered) objects or values. Basically, a permutation of a set of values is an arrangement of those values into a particular order. Thus there are six arrangement results of the set $\{1, 2, 3\}$, namely $[1, 2, 3], [1, 3, 2], [2, 1, 3], [2, 3, 1], [3, 1, 2]$, and $[3, 2, 1]$. In mathematics, a *group action* is a way of describing mutual orders (symmetries) of objects using groups. We can utilize the language of group to interpret permutation.

4.2.1 Group Actions

A group action of a group G on a set B is a map from $G \times B$ to B, expressed as $g \cdot b$ for all $g \in G$ and $b \in B$ satisfying the following two properties:

(1) $g_1 \cdot (g_2 \cdot b) = (g_1 \cdot g_2) \cdot b$ for all $g_1, g_2 \in G$ and $b \in B$;

(2) $1 \cdot b = b$ for all $b \in B$.

Intuitively, a group action G on a set B just indicates that every element $g \in G$ acts as a permutation on elements in B. Let us formulate this fact formally by the following theorem.

Theorem 5 *We define a map from B to B with respect to $g \in G$ as σ_g by sending element $b \in B$ to $g \cdot b \in B$. Then, for each element $g \in G$, σ_g is a permutation of B. Moreover, the map from G to permutation group S_B defined by $g \mapsto \sigma_g$ is a homomorphism.*

PROOF. 3 *To show σ_g is a permutation of B is equivalent to show that σ_g is a bijection map between B and B. We first show that $\sigma_{g^{-1}}$ is a left-inverse of σ_g. For all $b \in B$, we have*

$$(\sigma_{g^{-1}} \circ \sigma_g)(b) = \sigma_{g^{-1}}(\sigma_g(b)) = g^{-1} \cdot (g \cdot b) = (g^{-1} \cdot g) \cdot b = b,$$

where $\circ$ represents the composition operation between two maps σ_g for $g \in G$. Similarly, we also can show that $\sigma_{g^{-1}}$ is a right-inverse of σ_g. For all $b \in B$, we have

$$(\sigma_g \circ \sigma_{g^{-1}})(b) = \sigma_g(\sigma_{g^{-1}}(b)) = g \cdot (g^{-1} \cdot b) = (g \cdot g^{-1}) \cdot b = b.$$

Thus, σ_g induces a bijection (permutation) of set B.

If we name the map from G to S_B as ϕ, the homomorphism of ϕ is to verify $\phi(g_1 g_2) = \phi(g_1)\phi(g_2)$. The permutations $\phi(g_1 g_2)$ and $\phi(g_1)\phi(g_2)$ are equal if their values agree on every element of $b \in B$. For all $b \in B$,

$$\phi(g_1 g_2)(b) = \sigma_{g_1 g_2}(b) = (g_1 g_2) \cdot b = \sigma_{g_1}(\sigma_{g_2}(b)) = (\phi(g_1)\phi(g_2))(b). \tag{4.2.1}$$

Hence, the homomorphism is proved.

For a given $b \in B$, the set $\{gb\}$, is called the group orbit of b. The subgroup of G which fixes b is called *isotropy group* or *stabilizer* of b, denoted as G_b. For example, the group $Z_2 = [0], [1]$ acts on the real numbers x by multiplication by $(-1)^n$. The identity leaves everything fixed, while $[1]$ sends x to $-x$. Note that $[1]P[1] = [0]$, which corresponds to $-(-x) = x$. For $x = 0$, the orbit of x is $x, -x$, and the isotropy subgroup is trivial, $[0]$. The only group fixed point of this action is $x = 0$. The *kernel* of the action is the set of elements of G that act trivially on every element of B: $\{g \in G | g \cdot b = b \text{ for all } b \in B\}$. An action is *faithful* if its kernel is the identity. Let n be a positive integer. The group $G = S_n$ acts on the set $B = \{1, 2, \ldots, n\}$ by $\sigma \cdot i = \sigma(i)$ for all $\in \{1, \ldots, n\}$. The permutation representation associated to this action is the identity map $\phi : S_n \to S_n$. This action is faithful and for each $i \in \{1, \ldots, n\}$ the stabilizer G_i (the subgroup of all permutations fixing i) is isomorphic to S_{n-1}.

4.2.2   Permutation Representations of Groups

In this section, we wish to apply group action concept to show that every group G is isomorphic to a subgroup of the permutation (symmetric) group on G. This theorem helps us to embed any given group into a subgroup of the permutation group. Hence, we can study any groups by an unified language. This theorem is due to Cayley.

Theorem 6 *Every group G is isomorphic to a subgroup of the permutation group on G.*

PROOF. **4** *For any $g \in G$, we define a function F_g from G to G as $F_g(x) = g \cdot x$, where x is any element in G and $\cdot$ is the group operation in G. The set $K = \{F_g : g \in G\}$ is a subgroup of permutation group of G, denoted as S_G. Our goal is to show that K is isomorphic to G. By defining the function $T : G \to S_G$ with $T(g) = F_g$ for every g in G, then T is a group homomorphism since*

$$T(g) * T(h) = F_g * F_h = F_{g \cdot h} = T(g \cdot h), \qquad (4.2.2)$$

where $*$ is the operation in permutation group S_G and g, h are group elements in G. The homomorphism of T is also injective since $T(g) = Id$ (the identity element of S_G) implies that $g \cdot x = x$ for all x in G, and taking x to be the identity element of G, represented as e, yields $g = g \cdot e = e$. Surjective of T to K is obvious. Thus G is isomorphic to the image of T, which is the subgroup K.

4.2.3   Permutation Invention Examples

In this section, several well-known invention techniques using permutation skills are presented.

Example 28 *Inverse thinking method is a thinking method which inverses routine thoughts to find out solutions. By using inverse thinking method, the thoughts of creators will be changed from the original approach. For example, one may reconsider the invention from the invention goal instead of the approach or vice versa. If inventors try to get solutions from the invention goals directly, inventors are eager to move obstacles in the way to achieve desired goals and they do not limit themselves in already existing concepts, methods and thinking modes. Hence, if people can not solve problems or generate creative ideas efficiently by routine thoughts, they have to change their concepts or thoughts inversely by taking indirect approaches to get creative objectives.*

In general, there are three possible situations to be applied by inverse thinking methods: structure inverse, function inverse and causal inverse. Structure inverse means that one applies group S_2 (permutation group with order two) to the structural (geometrical) aspects of things to be invented. For instance, one can investigate from the outside of things to the inside of things, form the macro of things to the micro of things or from the parts of things to the whole things. Moreover, we can inverse our thought process by examining things to be invented, in other words, one can study from the inside of things to the outside of things, form the micro of things to the macro *of things or from the whole things to the parts of things. In technical creations and arts, people are able to conceive variations of structures or mutual order relations of objects by applying more complicated groups to obtain more complex permutations.*

Function inverse indicates that the inventor applies group S_2 to the functional aspects of things to be invented. Then, creators could directly inverse some functions of any interesting objects or are inspired by opposite functions on existing objects. The effects of inverse thinking for technical creation are outstanding. For instance, the work about a new resource reservation protocol introduced by [34] achieve great success by changing the traditional role of controlling the quality of service (QoS) from data transmitters to the data receivers. This new protocol can provide the following benefits compared to the previous ones: (1) It provides receiver oriented reservations to accommodate heterogeneity among receivers as well as dynamic membership changes. (2) It supports a dynamic and robust multi-terminals to multi-terminals communication model by taking a soft-state approach in maintaining resource reservations. (3) Finally, it decouples the reservation and routing functions and thus can take advantage of any multicast routing protocols.

Causal inverse demonstrates that the inventor applies group S_2 to the components of causes and components of consequences with respect to a causal relation for things to be invented. The inventor can deduce consequences from causes and find out possible causes from consequences. In addition, inventors can generate more valuable ideas by applying causal inverse thoughts.

Example 29 *Morphological analysis, which is proposed by professor F. Zwicky in California Institute of Technology, is a method that utilizes combination and the permutation to generate new technological ideas. He applied this method to study the project of rocket structure, totally, there are 576 new technological inventions feasible based on the technological levels at the time. From the following explanations, we can observe that the permutation operation is a crucial step in adopting morphological analysis.*

The steps to perform morphological analysis are summarized as follows. (1) Determining all possible constitutional elements for things to be invented. (2) Enumerating all possible solutions for the technological aspects (technological systems, technological units or technological processes) of constitutional elements. (3) Using morphological analysis matrixes to perform the combination and the permutation operation with respect to solutions obtained from the Step (2). (4) Comparing all possible approaches generated from the Step (3) through theoretical analysis and (or) practical experiments to select the best approach.

For example, if one wish to invent a new transportation system. The first step may help us to figure out three constitutional elements (subsystems), such as the loading subsystem, the transmission subsystem and power source subsystem. If we consider the inter-operation between the new transportation system and the environment, we may separate a new transportation system into four subsystems as the structure support subsystem, the navigation subsystem, the control subsystem and the stability subsystem. In Step (2), the possible solutions for the loading subsystem include cars, conveyer belts, containers, crane ladles, etc. The possible solutions for the transmitting subsystem may have water, air, tracks, pipes and ground, etc. The possible solutions for the power source subsystem may have steam, electrical motors, internal combustion engines, electromagnetic forces, atomic energy and solar energy, etc. Based on the basic constituent rules of the technological system categories, we execute permutation and combination on the solutions of each constituent element and list all possible solutions. Finally, we pick the best one among reserved solutions and finally form the most satisfied technological solution.

In conclusion, the main advantage of morphological method is easy to attain amount of ideas. It can be applied not only in technological innovation, but also in management science.

Figure 4.2: Permuation: Warrior or Coward

Chapter 5

Plurioperad

From discussions in previous chapters, the input sets in the algebraic model of invenrelation form a finite sequence, i.e., a one dimensional array. In order to process more complicated invention procedure, we have to propose more delicate algebraic operations for inputs which form as some higher dimensional geometrical objects, e.g., grids, trees or pasting structures. In Sec. 5.1, we will introduce several motivations of plurioperads. The definitions about plurioperads are provided in Sec. 5.2. Not every algebraic operation proposed to model invention procedures is plurioperadic, the conditions for an algebraic operation to be a plurioperad are introduced in Sec. 5.3. Finally, many invention examples generated by plurioperads are illustrated in Sec. 5.4.

5.1 Motivations of Plurioperad

In this section, we will introduce three motivations for us to propose the plurioperad - a new algebraic model. The first is the capability for this new algebraic model to infer new things from known facts which share common rules. The second is the capability for the plurioperad to have the function to compose consecutively since we may require many steps in order to achieve our invention goals. Lastly, we wish plurioperad can enlarge traditional inputs structures by encoding more geometrical information, which is a desired property for us to manipulate many knowledge (ontology) systems represented by diagrams.

In "Analects of Confucius", the greatest teacher and scholar in Chinese had mentioned his methods and attitudes about how to teach students. Confucius paid much attention to learning motivations and inspirations by asking his students to think initiatively instead of following or cramming up knowledge passively. He said: "I will not to enlighten my students if they do not think first in order to seek understanding. I will not to inspire my students if they do not think deeply in order to overcome knowledge difficulties. If I take a square as an example and also prompt a corner to a student, I will not teach him further in case that he can not response other three corners to me." In this talks, Confucius emphasized the importance of active learning and thinking skills. If one lacks of active learning and thinking skills, he/she could only blindly accept the claims of others but not inference by himself/herslef, which makes the obtained knowledge weekly. Hence, a good teacher has to focus on heuristic education, then students not only learn initiatively but also develop the capability to reason similar things from analogy.

A famous idiom in Chinese, to deduce many things from one case, is based on the talk of Confucius presented above. This idiom indicates that one should be able to draw inferences about other cases from one instance in order to generate new things. Hence, the proposed new algebraic model, plurioperad, has to be able to summarize out a rule for a set of operations which share some common properties.

In a thinking procedure, we often need to use the results obtained from the previous thoughts as the inputs (materials) for the next thinking action. The concepts of *composition* utilized extensively in mathematics have to be borrowed by us to build a new algebraic model, plurioperad, since the composition operation in mathematics enable one can process previous results by new mathematical objects, for instance, composition of functions and composition of relations. Composition operation also make us to create a new function (or relation) between two sets which are unrelated at the beginning.

Since the composition of functions (or relation) is always associative, there is no distinction between the choices of placement of parentheses. Therefore, if f, g, and h are three functions (or relation) with suitably chosen domains and codomains, then we have $f \circ (g \circ h) = (f \circ g) \circ h$ where $\circ$ indicates the composition operation. The proposed plurioperads will also possess such property in order to model multi-steps invention procedures.

Diagram-based conceptual representations have appeared in the human history for a long time, e.g., using blueprints to represent technical structures, using a tree structure to represent kin relations of a family, etc. Using diagrams to represent concepts has the following three advantages: (1) It can have a denotational semantic system formally. (2) It will be logically founded. (3) It allows for a structured representation of concepts. Therefore, we have to develop a new algebraic system which can have inputs as structural objects instead of numbers in order to manipulate these diagram algebraically.

5.2 Definition of Plurioperad

The definition of plurioperad is given in this section. A plurioperad with multiple outputs, denoted as $\mathcal{P}$, is the data consisted by a sequence $(P(n))_{n \in \mathbb{N}}$ of sets, whose elements can be decomposed by n-ary operations, i.e.,

$P(n) = \bowtie_{i=1}^{I_n} P_i(n)$ where I_n is the number of possible outcomes and $P_i(n)$ is the i-th operation with only one outcome. The composition maps for each $n, k_1, \cdots, k_n \in \mathbb{N}$ such that the output of $P_{i_{k_j}}$ is the j-th $(1 \leq j \leq n)$ input of P_{i_n} can be expressed as

$$\zeta_{\mathcal{I}} : P_{i_n}(n) \times P_{i_{k_1}}(k_1) \times \cdots \times P_{i_{k_n}}(k_n) \longrightarrow P_{i_{(k_1+\cdots+k_n)}}(k_1 + \cdots + k_n), \tag{5.2.1}$$

where $\mathcal{I}$ indicates order indices of $i_n, i_{k_1}, \cdots, i_{k_n}$ and $i_{(k_1+\cdots+k_n)}$.

These data have to satisfy the following conditions:

1. (right identity) $P_i(n) \times Id \times \cdots \times Id \longrightarrow P_i(\overbrace{1 + \cdots + 1}^{n \text{ terms}}) = P_i(n)$, where Id is the identity operation with respect to the identity input and $1 \leq i \leq I_n$.

2. (left identity) $Id \times P_i(n) \longrightarrow P_i(n)$, where $1 \leq i \leq I_n$.

3. (associativity) Given order indices $\mathcal{I}, \mathcal{I}_1, \cdots, \mathcal{I}_n, \mathcal{I}_{1,1}, \cdots, \mathcal{I}_{1,m_1}, \cdots, \mathcal{I}_{n,1}, \cdots, \mathcal{I}_{n,m_1}$ for compositions, we have

$$\zeta_{\mathcal{I}} \circ (\zeta_{\mathcal{I}_1} \circ (\zeta_{\mathcal{I}_{1,1}}, \cdots \zeta_{\mathcal{I}_{1,m_1}}), \cdots \zeta_{\mathcal{I}_n} \circ (\zeta_{\mathcal{I}_{n,1}}, \cdots \zeta_{\mathcal{I}_{n,m_n}})) =$$

$$(\zeta_{\mathcal{I}} \circ (\zeta_{\mathcal{I}_1}, \cdots, \zeta_{\mathcal{I}_n})) \circ (\zeta_{\mathcal{I}_{1,1}}, \cdots \zeta_{\mathcal{I}_{1,m_1}}, \cdots, \zeta_{\mathcal{I}_{n,1}}, \cdots \zeta_{\mathcal{I}_{n,m_n}}),$$

where $\circ$ denotes for composition.

A map $f : P \longrightarrow Q$ of plurioperads with multiple outputs consists of a family $f_{i,n} : P_i(n) \longrightarrow Q_i(n)$ for all $n \in \mathbb{N}$ which preserve compositions and identities with respect to all order indices $i \in \mathcal{I}$.

If I_n is always equal to one, the definition of plurioperad is reduced as the definition of operad. We then have composition maps for each $n, k_1, \cdots, k_n \in \mathbb{N}$ as

$$\zeta : P(n) \times P(k_1) \times \cdots \times P(k_n) \longrightarrow P(k_1 + \cdots + k_n). \tag{5.2.2}$$

These data have to satisfy the following conditions:

1. (right identity) $P(n) \times P(1) \times \cdots \times P(1) \longrightarrow P(\overbrace{1 + \cdots + 1}^{n \text{ terms}}) = P(n)$, where $P(1)$ becomes the identity operation with respect to the identity input.

2. (left identity) $P(1) \times P(n) \longrightarrow P(n)$.

3. (associativity)

$$\zeta \circ (\zeta_1 \circ (\zeta_{1,1}, \cdots \zeta_{1,m_1}), \cdots \zeta_n \circ (\zeta_{n,1}, \cdots \zeta_{n,m_n})) =$$

$$(\zeta \circ (\zeta_1, \cdots, \zeta_n)) \circ (\zeta_{1,1}, \cdots \zeta_{1,m_1}, \cdots, \zeta_{n,1}, \cdots \zeta_{n,m_n}),$$

where $\circ$ denotes for composition.

A map $f : P \longrightarrow Q$ of plurioperads consists of a family $f_n : P(n) \longrightarrow Q(n)$ for all $n \in \mathbb{N}$ which preserve compositions and identities.

5.3 Existence of Plurioperads

In this section, we will consider the existence for an algebraic system to be plurioperadic. In Sec. 5.3.1, the concept of regular equations is introduced, which will be used to describe the condition for the existence of an algebraic system. In Sec. 5.3.2, free structures are introduced to represent derived operations from primitive operations. In Sec. 5.3.3, the conditions for an algebraic system to be plurioperadic are given and proved.

5.3.1 Regular Algebraic Systems

An algebraic system used to model the invention process is called as a **regular algebraic system** if it can be presented by operations and regular equations. An equation (made up by variables and finitary operation symbols) is a **regular equation** if the same variables appear in the same order, without repetition, on each side of identities. For example, we have following regular equations: $(x \cdot y) \cdot z = x \cdot (y \cdot z)$, $x \cdot 1 = x$, $(x^y)^z = x^{y \cdot z}$. Following are not regular equations: $x \cdot y = y \cdot x$, $x \cdot (y + z) = x \cdot y + x \cdot z$.

5.3.2 Free Plurioperads Construction

Free plurioperads structure enables us to construct algebraic structure by encoding geometric information. A plurioperad with multiple outputs, denoted as $\mathcal{P}$, is composed by a set A, a set of operations $P_{i_n}(n) : a_1, \cdots, a_n \to a_{i_n}$ where $a_{i_n}, a_1, \cdots, a_n \in A$ for each mapping order $i_n \in I_n$ with respect to inputs $a_1, \cdots, a_n$ and $n \in \mathbb{N}$.

The free pluriopeards structure on $\mathcal{P}$, indicated by $\mathcal{FP}$, has the same set for constitutional objects as $\mathcal{P}$. The elements of $\mathcal{FP}$ are expressed as $FP_{\underline{i}_n}(n)$ if there are n inputs and the order indices used by operations to construct $FP_{\underline{i}_n}(n)$ are described by the vector $\underline{i}_n$. The $\mathcal{FP}$ is constructed recursively based on the following rules:

(1) If $a \in A$, then $1_a \in FP_{\underline{i}_1}(1)$, where 1_a is the identity map for a.

(2) If $\zeta \in P_{i_n}(n)$ and $\theta_1 \in FP_{\underline{i}_{k_1}}(k_1), \cdots, \theta_n \in FP_{\underline{i}_{k_n}}(k_n)$,

$$\text{then} \zeta \circ (\theta_1, \cdots, \theta_n) \in FP_{\underline{i}_{k_1 + \cdots + k_n}}(k_1 + \cdots + k_n). \tag{5.3.1}$$

A typical example for $FP_{\underline{i}_8}(8)$ is expressed as

$$\theta_1 \circ (\theta_2 \circ (1_{a_3}, 1_{a_4}), \theta_3 \circ (\theta_4 \circ (1_{a_{11}}, 1_{a_{12}}), \theta_5 \circ (1_{a_8}, 1_{a_9}, 1_{a_{10}})), 1_{a_{11}}), \tag{5.3.2}$$

where $\theta_1 \in P_2(3)$, $\theta_2 \in P_1(2)$, $\theta_3 \in P_2(2)$, $\theta_4 \in P_1(2)$ and $\theta_5 \in P_2(3)$. The components of $\underline{i}_8$ is $[2, 1, 2, 1, 2]$, which are mapping orders for operations $\theta_1, \theta_2, \theta_3, \theta_4$ and θ_5, respectively. We also depict such free plurioperad structure in Fig. 5.1.

5.3.3 The Existence Theorem of Plurioperads

The main purpose of this section is to demonstrate that the regular algebraic systems are plurioperadic. We begin by setting up notations used during our proof. A plurioperad with multiple outputs, denoted as $\mathcal{P}$, is composed by a set A, a set of n-ary operations $P_{i_n}(n) : a_1, \cdots, a_n \to a_{i_n}$ where $a_{i_n}, a_1, \cdots, a_n \in A$ for each mapping order $i_n \in I_n$ with respect to inputs $a_1, \cdots, a_n$ and $n \in \mathbb{N}$. The free pluriopeards structure on $\mathcal{P}$ constructed according to Sec. 5.3.2, indicated by $\mathcal{FP}$, has the same set for constitutional objects as $\mathcal{P}$. The elements of $\mathcal{FP}$ are expressed as $FP_{\underline{i}_n}(n)$ if there are n inputs and the order indices used by operations to construct $FP_{\underline{i}_n}(n)$ are described by the vector $\underline{i}_n$. A system of equations $\mathcal{E}$ composed by a family of $E_{\underline{i}_n}(n)$ with respect to each $n \in \mathbb{N}$ and order indices $\underline{i}_n$. The terms $E_{\underline{i}_n}(n)$ are in the product space of $FP_{\underline{i}_n}(n)$, i.e., $FP_{\underline{i}_n}(n) \times FP_{\underline{i}_n}(n)$. The purpose for us to introduce $\mathcal{E}$ is to identify out algebraic systems with regular properties introduced in Sec. 5.3.1.

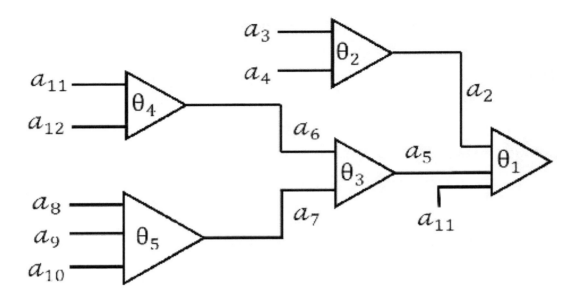

Figure 5.1: A plurioperad example.

Let us present a simple example to illustrate these notations. A monoid is a set, S, together with a binary operation $\cdot$ that satisfies the following three axioms:

- Closure: For all a, b in S, the result of the operation $a \cdot b$ is also in S.

- Associativity: For all a, b and c in S, the equation $(a \cdot b) \cdot c = a \cdot (b \cdot c)$ holds.

- Identity: There exists an element e in S, such that for all elements a in S, the equation $e \cdot a = a \cdot e = a$ holds.

The parameters $\mathcal{P}$ and $\mathcal{E}$ for monoid will be

$$P(n) = \begin{cases} \{\cdot\}, & \text{if } n = 2; \\ \emptyset, & \text{otherwise.} \end{cases}$$

$$E_n = \begin{cases} \{\cdot(\cdot,\ e), \cdot(e,\ \cdot)\}, & \text{if } n = 3; \\ \emptyset, & \text{otherwise.} \end{cases} \tag{5.3.3}$$

The equation E_3 in monoid represents the associativity property (regular) of monoid. We have to note that all order indices are omitted due to functional mapping (only one output given any input) for $\cdot$ operation in a monoid.

By disjoint union of a sequence of elements $FP_{\underline{i}_n}(n)$, we have the following algebraic system operating at the set A

$$T_{\mathcal{FP},\underline{I}}A = \coprod_{n \in \mathbb{N}} FP_{\underline{i}_n}(n) \times A^n, \tag{5.3.4}$$

where $\underline{I} = \bigcup_{n \in \mathbb{N}} \underline{i}_n$. The following two mappings are related to $T_{\mathcal{FP}}$ as

$$\mu_{\mathcal{FP},\underline{I}} \; : \; Id \to T_{\mathcal{FP},\underline{I}},$$
$$\eta_{\mathcal{FP},\underline{I}} \; : \; T_{\mathcal{FP},\underline{I}} \circ T_{\mathcal{FP},\underline{I}} \to T_{\mathcal{FP},\underline{I}}; \tag{5.3.5}$$

which satisfy

$$\mu_{\mathcal{FP},\underline{I}} \circ T_{\mathcal{FP},\underline{I}} \mu_{\mathcal{FP},\underline{I}} \;=\; \mu_{\mathcal{FP},\underline{I}} \circ \mu_{\mathcal{FP},\underline{I}} T_{\mathcal{FP},\underline{I}},$$
$$\mu_{\mathcal{FP},\underline{I}} \circ T_{\mathcal{FP},\underline{I}} \eta_{\mathcal{FP},\underline{I}} \;=\; \mu_{\mathcal{FP},\underline{I}} \circ \eta_{\mathcal{FP},\underline{I}} T_{\mathcal{FP},\underline{I}} = Id. \tag{5.3.6}$$

We will define another algebraic system, denoted as $T_{\mathcal{P},\mathcal{E},\underline{I}}A$, by quotient out the equivalent relation of A, a subset of A, from $T_{\mathcal{FP},\underline{I}}A$. The term $T_{\mathcal{P},\mathcal{E},\underline{I}}A$ can be expressed as

$$T_{\mathcal{P},\mathcal{E},\underline{I}}A = T_{\mathcal{FP},\underline{I}}A/\sim_{\mathrm{A}}. \tag{5.3.7}$$

Moreover, if the equivalent relation $\sim$ A has the following two properties, then the algebraic system $T_{\mathcal{P},\mathcal{E},\underline{I}}A$ is called a regular algebraic system. They are

- If $\sigma \in P_{\underline{i}_n}(n)$, $\tau_j \in FP_{\underline{i}_{k_j}}(k_j)$, $\acute{\tau}_j \in FP_{\acute{\underline{i}}_{k_j}}(\acute{k}_j)$ and

$$\tau_j(a_{j,1}, \cdots, a_{j,k_j}) \sim_{\mathrm{A}} \acute{\tau}_j(\acute{a}_{j,1}, \cdots, \acute{a}_{j,k_j}), \quad \text{for } 1 \leq j \leq n,$$

we have

$$\sigma \circ (\tau_1, \cdots, \tau_n)(a_{1,1}, \cdots, a_{1,k_1}, a_{2,1}, \cdots, a_{2,k_2}, \cdots, a_{n,1}, \cdots, a_{n,k_n}) \sim_{\mathrm{A}}$$
$$\sigma \circ (\acute{\tau}_1, \cdots, \acute{\tau}_n)(\acute{a}_{1,1}, \cdots, \acute{a}_{1,k_1}, \acute{a}_{2,1}, \cdots, \acute{a}_{2,k_2}, \cdots, \acute{a}_{n,1}, \cdots, \acute{a}_{n,k_n}) \tag{5.3.8}$$

- If $(\tau, \acute{\tau}) \in E_{\underline{i}_n}(n)$ and $\tau_j \in FP_{\underline{i}_{k_j}}(k_j)$ for $1 \leq j \leq n$, then

$$\tau \circ (\tau_1, \cdots, \tau_n)(a_{1,1}, \cdots, a_{1,k_1}, a_{2,1}, \cdots, a_{2,k_2}, \cdots, a_{n,1}, \cdots, a_{n,k_n}) \sim_{\mathrm{A}}$$
$$\acute{\tau} \circ (\tau_1, \cdots, \tau_n)(\acute{a}_{1,1}, \cdots, \acute{a}_{1,k_1}, \acute{a}_{2,1}, \cdots, \acute{a}_{2,k_2}, \cdots, \acute{a}_{n,1}, \cdots, \acute{a}_{n,k_n}) \tag{5.3.9}$$

Now, we are ready to prove that a regular algebraic system is plurioperadic. The first step of the proof is to reduce an algebraic regular system which is obtained by quotient set A into an algebraic system which is obtained by quotient e, the unit element of A. Then we further show that the reduced algebraic system has desired properties of a plurioperad. The following lemma is given to show the correspondence between the $T_{\mathcal{P},\mathcal{E},\underline{I}}A$ and the reduced algebraic system.

Lemma 3 *For any set A and the quotient set* A *reduced as the identity element of the set A, denoted as id, we have the following bijection map*

$$\coprod_{n \in \mathbb{N}} (F\mathcal{P}_{\underline{i}_n}(n)/ \sim_{id}) \times A^n \to T_{\mathcal{P},\mathcal{E},\underline{I}}A. \tag{5.3.10}$$

PROOF. 5 *We have to demonstrate the following two facts in order to show the bijection relation stated in Eq. (5.3.10).*

  1. If $\tau \sim_{id} \acute{\tau}$ and $n = \acute{n}$ then $\tau(a_1, \cdots, a_n) \sim_A \acute{\tau}(a_1, \cdots, a_n)$ for all $a_1, \cdots, a_n \in A$.

  2. If $\tau(a_1, \cdots, a_n) \sim_A \acute{\tau}(\acute{a}_1, \cdots, \acute{a}_{\acute{n}})$ then $n = \acute{n}, a_1 = \acute{a}_1, \cdots, a_n = \acute{a}_{\acute{n}}$, and $\tau \sim_{id} \acute{\tau}$.

For $\tau \in F\mathcal{P}_{\underline{i}_n}(n)$, $\acute{\tau} \in F\mathcal{P}_{\underline{i}_{\acute{n}}}(\acute{n})$ and all $a_1, \cdots, a_n \in A$, we define a new relation, denoted as $\approx$, on $T_{\mathcal{F}\mathcal{P},\underline{I}}A$ as

$$\tau \approx \acute{\tau} \Leftrightarrow n = \acute{n} \text{ and } \tau(a_1, \cdots, a_n) \sim_A \acute{\tau}(a_1, \cdots, a_n). \tag{5.3.11}$$

We then claim $\sim_{id} \in \approx$ by showing that the new equivalent relation $\approx$ also satisfies the two requirements provided by Eqs. (5.3.8) and (5.3.9) to construct a regular algebraic system.

  If $\sigma \in P_{\underline{i}_n}(n)$ and $\tau_j \approx \acute{\tau}_j$ for $1 \leq j \leq n$, then we have $\tau_j(a_{j,1}, \cdots, a_{j,k_j}) \sim_A \acute{\tau}_j(a_{j,1}, \cdots, a_{j,k_j})$ from the definition of $\approx$. From the congruence relation provided by Eq. (5.3.8), it implies that

$$\sigma \circ (\tau_1, \cdots, \tau_n)(a_{1,1}, \cdots, a_{1,k_1}, a_{2,1}, \cdots, a_{2,k_2}, \cdots, a_{n,1}, \cdots, a_{n,k_n}) \sim_A$$

$$\sigma \circ (\acute{\tau}_1, \cdots, \acute{\tau}_n)(a_{1,1}, \cdots, a_{1,k_1}, a_{2,1}, \cdots, a_{2,k_2}, \cdots, a_{n,1}, \cdots, a_{n,k_n}).$$

We can conclude that $\sigma \circ (\tau_1, \cdots, \tau_n) = \sigma \circ (\acute{\tau}_1, \cdots, \acute{\tau}_n)$ (First requirement of a regular algebraic system). If $(\tau, \acute{\tau}) \in E_{\underline{i}_n}(n)$ and $\tau_i = Id$ for $1 \leq i \leq n$, we have $\tau(a_1, \cdots, a_n) \sim_A \acute{\tau}(a_1, \cdots, a_n)$ (Second requirement of a regular algebraic system). Therefore, the first fact is proved. The second fact can be verified similarly. Hence, we have the bijection between $\coprod_{n \in \mathbb{N}} (F\mathcal{P}_{\underline{i}_n}(n)/ \sim_{id}) \times A^n$ and $T_{\mathcal{P},\mathcal{E},\underline{I}}$.

The following lemma is provided to show that $\sim_{id}$ has congruence property.

Lemma 4 *If* $\tau, \acute{\tau} \in FP_{\underline{i}_n}(n)$ *with* $\tau \sim_{id} \acute{\tau}$ *, and* $\tau_j, \acute{\tau}_j \in FP_{\underline{i}_{k_j}}(k_j)$ *with* $\tau_j \sim_{id} \acute{\tau}_j$ *for each* $1 \leq j \leq n$, *then* $\tau \circ (\tau_1, \cdots, \tau_n) \sim_{id} \acute{\tau} \circ (\acute{\tau}_1, \cdots, \acute{\tau}_n)$.

PROOF. 6 *For* $\tau \in FP_{\underline{i}_n}(n)$ *and* $\acute{\tau} \in FP_{\underline{i}_{\acute{n}}}(\acute{n})$, *we define a new relation, denoted as* $\approx$, *on* $\coprod_{n \in \mathbb{N}} FP_{\underline{i}_n}(n)$ *as*

$$\tau \approx \acute{\tau} \Leftrightarrow n = \acute{n} \text{ and } \tau(\tau_1, \cdots, \tau_n) \sim_{id} \acute{\tau}(\acute{\tau}_1, \cdots, \acute{\tau}_{\acute{n}}), \tag{5.3.12}$$

where $\tau_j \sim_{id} \acute{\tau}_j$. *Then we can show that* $\sim_{id} \subseteq \approx$ *in the same way as Lemma 3.*

Lemma 4 tells us that there is an unique plurioperad structure on $\coprod_{n \in \mathbb{N}} (FP_{\underline{i}_n}(n) / \sim_{id})$, an algebraic system can be induced based on such plurioperad which has similar properties regulated by Eq. (5.3.6), denoted as $T_{\mathcal{P}, id, \underline{I}}$.

Now, we are ready to present the following theorem which indicates that any regular algebraic system is plurioperadic with respect to given order indices.

Theorem 7 *We have the following isomorphism between* $T_{\mathcal{P}, id, \underline{I}}$ *and* $T_{\mathcal{P}, \mathcal{E}, \underline{I}}$. *Therefore, any regular algebraic system is plurioperadic with respect to given order indices.*

PROOF. 7 *From Lemma 3, we have an isomorphism between* $T_{\mathcal{P}, id, \underline{I}}$ *and* $T_{\mathcal{P}, \mathcal{E}, \underline{I}}$, *which makes the following mapping structure diagram,*

$$
\begin{array}{c}
T_{\mathcal{FP}, \underline{I}} \\[2pt]
\overset{\sim_{id}}{\frown} \quad \overset{\sim_A}{\frown} \\[2pt]
\swarrow \qquad \searrow \\[4pt]
T_{\mathcal{P}, id, \underline{I}} \longrightarrow T_{\mathcal{P}, \mathcal{E}, \underline{I}}.
\end{array}
\tag{5.3.13}
$$

The left-hand map is obtained by quotient out $A = id$ *and the right-hand map is obtained by quotient out any* $A \in A$.

From Eqs. (5.3.5), (5.3.6) and (5.3.7), we also have the following mapping structure diagram

$$
\begin{array}{ccc}
T_{\mathcal{FP}, \underline{I}} \circ T_{\mathcal{FP}, \underline{I}} A \overset{\eta_{\mathcal{FP}, \underline{I}}}{\rightrightarrows} T_{\mathcal{FP}, \underline{I}} A \overset{\mu_{\mathcal{FP}, \underline{I}}}{\leftharpoondown} A \\[4pt]
\downarrow (\sim_A)^2 \qquad\quad \downarrow \sim_A \qquad\quad \| \\[4pt]
T_{\mathcal{P}, \mathcal{E}, \underline{I}} \circ T_{\mathcal{P}, \mathcal{E}, \underline{I}} A \overset{\eta_{\mathcal{P}, \mathcal{E}, \underline{I}}}{\rightrightarrows} T_{\mathcal{P}, \mathcal{E}, \underline{I}} A \overset{\mu_{\mathcal{P}, \mathcal{E}, \underline{I}}}{\leftharpoondown} A,
\end{array}
\tag{5.3.14}
$$

where the mappings $\eta_{\mathcal{P}, \mathcal{E}, \underline{I}}$ *and* $\mu_{\mathcal{P}, \mathcal{E}, \underline{I}}$ *also satisfy relations provided by Eq. (5.3.6).*

The multiplication operation, denoted as $\eta_{\mathcal{P},id,\underline{I}}$, of the algebraic system $T_{\mathcal{P},id,\underline{I}}$ comes via the quotient map from composition in the plurioperad $F\mathcal{P}_{\underline{i}_n}(n)$, so it follows from diagram shown by Eq. (5.3.14) that $\eta_{\mathcal{P},id,\underline{I}}$ corresponds to $\eta_{\mathcal{P},\mathcal{E},\underline{I}}$ under the isomorphism. The same argument is also applicable to identity operation, denoted as $\mu_{\mathcal{P},id,\underline{I}}$, of the algebraic system $T_{\mathcal{P},id,\underline{I}}$.

On the other hand, we wish to show that any plurioperadic algebraic system is regular with respect to given order indices. One important notion, namely *universal map*, has to be introduced for maps between two plurioperads.

A plurioperadic map $\epsilon : \mathcal{FP}_{\underline{I}} \to (\mathcal{P}, id, \underline{I})$ with respect to the order indices $\underline{I}$ is called an universal map if $\delta : \mathcal{FP}_{\underline{I}} \to Q_{\underline{I}}$ is a map from $\mathcal{FP}_{\underline{I}}$ to any plurioperad $Q_{\underline{I}}$ with order indices $Q_{\underline{I}}$ satisfying $\delta(\tau)$ and $\delta(\acute{\tau})$ for all $(\tau, \acute{\tau}) \in \mathcal{E}$, then there is an unique plurioperad map $\overline{\delta} : (\mathcal{P}, id, \underline{I}) \to Q_{\underline{I}}$ such that $\overline{\delta} \circ \epsilon = \delta$. Following two lemmas are provided to prepare the required facts for proving that any plurioperadic algebraic system is regular with respect to given order indices.

Lemma 5 *If $(\mathcal{P}, \mathcal{E}, \underline{I})$ is a regular algebraic system, then the quotient map $\epsilon : \mathcal{FP}_{\underline{I}} \to (\mathcal{P}, id, \underline{I})$ with respect to order indices $\underline{I}$ with the property that $\epsilon(\tau)$ and $\epsilon(\acute{\tau})$ for all $(\tau, \acute{\tau}) \in \mathcal{E}$.*

PROOF. 8 *Because $\sim_{id}$ is the smallest equivalence relation on $\coprod\limits_{n \in \mathbb{N}} FP_{\underline{i}_n}(n)$, which satisfies the conditions given by Lemma 4 and satisfies $\tau \sim_{id} \acute{\tau}$ for all $(\tau, \acute{\tau}) \in \mathcal{E}$. Hence, this lemma is valid by checking the universal map conditions.*

By fixing the plurioperad $Q_{\underline{i}}$ with respect to the order indices $\underline{i}$, we define $\mathcal{P}_{Q_{\underline{i}}}$ as a plurioperad with multiple outputs induced by members from the plurioperad $Q_{\underline{i}}$ and $\mathcal{E}_{Q_{\underline{i}}}$ as a system of equations generated by members from the plurioperad $Q_{\underline{i}}$. Following lemma about the universal map related to the pluriperad $\mathcal{P}_{Q_{\underline{i}}}$ is provided.

Lemma 6 *$\epsilon : \mathcal{FP}_{Q_{\underline{i}}} \to Q_{\underline{i}}$ is the universal plurioperad map with the property that $\epsilon(\tau) = \epsilon(\acute{\tau})$ for all $(\tau, \acute{\tau}) \in \mathcal{E}_{Q_{\underline{i}}}$.*

PROOF. 9 *$\epsilon(\tau)$ is equal to $\epsilon(\acute{\tau})$ due to the congruence relations provided by Eqs. (5.3.8) and (5.3.9).*

For universality, we consider a map $\delta : \mathcal{FP}_{\underline{I}} \to R_{\underline{j}}$ of plurioperads such that $\delta(\tau) = \delta(\acute{\tau})$ for all $(\tau, \acute{\tau}) \in \mathcal{E}_{Q_{\underline{i}}}$. We wish that there to be an unique plurioperad map $\overline{\delta} : Q_{\underline{i}} \to R_{\underline{j}}$ such that $\overline{\delta} \circ \epsilon = \delta$. Let σ_θ be free structure composed by any $\theta \in Q_{\underline{i}}$ and we have $\epsilon(\sigma_\theta) = \theta$ for all $\theta \in Q_{\underline{i}}$,

146

then σ_θ will be the only argument make $\bar{\delta} \circ \epsilon = \delta$ hold. Hence, the condition of the universal map ϵ is established.

At this stage, we are ready to present the following theorem that any plurioperadic algebraic system is regular with respect to given order indices.

Theorem 8 *There is an isomorphism of $T_{(\mathcal{P}_{Q_i}, \mathcal{E}_{Q_i}, \underline{I})} \cong T_{Q_i}$. Hence, any plurioperadic algebraic system is regular with specific order indices.*

PROOF. 10 *From Lemmas 5 and 6, there is an isomorphism between plurioperads $(\mathcal{P}_{Q_i}, \mathcal{E}_{Q_i}, \underline{I})$ and Q_i. Hence, we have $T_{(\mathcal{P}_{Q_i}, \mathcal{E}_{Q_i}, \underline{I})} \cong T_{Q_i}$ and the result follows.*

5.3.4 Differential Rules for Plurioperads

In this section, we discuss the derivative of plurioperads and present several rules about the derivative of plurioperads. The general definition of derivative is provided first. Such general definition allow us to consider various types of infinitesimal variation for various objects used in invention procedures, e.g., ordinary derivation where the infinitesimal variation is a number and topological derivative where the infinitesimal variation is a ball [35].

Definition 2 *Let F be a field and f be a function from the set of interesting objects, denoted as X, to F. The set Δ is a partial order set with an unique infimum element, denoted as $\delta_{\inf}$, composed by all elements which can be used to construct a new element $x' \in X$ from other $x \in X$ by some pre-determined method, e.g., if X and Δ both are a real number set then the new real number x' can be obtained from any other real number x by adding $(x' - x)$. We also have following two families of functions $\{g_i\}$ and $\{h_i\}$, where each g_i is a function with two variables from $F \times \Delta$ to F and each h_i is a function used to measure with one variable from Δ to F. The function g_i is used to measure the displacement for the i-th derivative contributed by the element of Δ at an object of X. On the other hand, the function h_i is used to measure the cost required to construct a new element for the i-th derivative by an element in Δ. Then the first derivative at the object x is defined as:*

$$f^{(1)}_{g_1, h_1, \gamma_1}(x) = \lim_{\delta_1 \overset{\gamma_1}{\rightarrow} \delta_{\inf}} \frac{g_1(f(x, \delta_1), f(x), \delta_1)}{h_1(\delta_1)}, \tag{5.3.15}$$

where $\delta_1 \in \Delta$ and γ_1 is the path index for path trace from the value δ_1 to δ_{inf}. For higher order derivatives, we have following recursion:

$$f^{(n+1)}_{g_{n+1},h_{n+1},\gamma_{n+1}}(x) =$$
$$\lim_{\substack{\gamma_{n+1} \\ \delta_{n+1} \xrightarrow{\frown} \delta_{\text{inf}}}} \frac{g_{n+1}(f^{(n)}_{g_n,h_n,j_n}(x,\delta_{n+1}), f^{(n)}_{g_n,h_n,j_n}(x), \delta_{n+1})}{h_{n+1}(\delta_{n+1})}, \tag{5.3.16}$$

where $\delta_{n+1} \in \Delta$ and γ_{n+1} is the path index for path trace from the value δ_{n+1} to δ_{inf}.

For example, if we set $g_1(f(x,\delta_1), f(x), \delta_1) = (f(x+\delta_1) - f(x))/f(x)$ (normalization error), $h_1(\delta_1) = \delta_1$, $f(x) = x^n$ and $\gamma_1 = \delta_1 \to 0$, we have following formula for the derivative in normalization error sense:

$$\lim_{\delta_1 \to 0} \frac{\frac{(x+\delta_1)^n - x^n}{x^n}}{\delta_1} = \frac{n}{x}. \tag{5.3.17}$$

From the above definition, the traditional derivative is the special case of ours by treating Δ, X and F as real number sets. The function g_1 becomes $f(x+\delta_1) - f(x)$ and the function $h_1(\delta_1)$ will be δ_1. Moreover, we say that the derivative at x_0 exists if that the value of $f^{(1)}_{g_1,h_1,\gamma_1}(x)$ dose not alter for any path from $\delta + x_0$ approaching to x_0. The topological derivative is formed by treating Δ, F as real number sets and X as an open set in $\mathbb{R}^N$ for some N. The function g_1 becomes $f(\Omega \backslash B_{\delta_1}(x)) - f(\Omega)$, where Ω is a region in $\mathbb{R}^N$ and the function $h_1(\delta_1)$ will be $B_{\delta_1}(x)$, the N-dimensional ball with radius δ_1 at the center x.

A partial derivative of a function with several variables is its derivative with respect to one of those variables, with the others held constant. Partial derivatives are widely used in vector calculus and differential geometry. Let F be a field and f be a function with several variables from the set of interesting objects, denoted as X, to F. The set Δ is a partial order set with an unique infimum element, denoted as δ_{inf}, composed by all elements which can be used to construct a new element $x' \in X$ from other $x \in X$ by some pre-determined method. We also have following two families of functions $\{g_{i,k}\}$ and $\{h_{i,k}\}$, where each $g_{i,k}$ is a function with two variables from $F \times \Delta$ to F and each $h_{i,k}$ is a function used to measure with one variable from Δ to F. The function $g_{i,k}$ is used to measure the displacement contributed by the element for the k-th derivative of Δ at the i-th variable. On the other hand, the function $h_{i,k}$ is used to measure the cost required to construct a new element for the k-th derivative at the i-th variable. Then the first partial derivative with respect to the i-th variable is defined as:

$$\frac{\partial_{g_{i,1},h_{i,1},\gamma_{i,1}} f(x_1, x_2, \cdots, x_n)}{\partial x_i} =$$
$$\lim_{\substack{\gamma_{i,1} \\ \delta_i \overset{\frown}{\to} \delta_{\inf}}} \frac{g_{i,1}(f(x_1, x_2, \cdots, x_n, \delta_i), f(x_1, x_2, \cdots, x_n), \delta_i)}{h_{i,1}(\delta_i)}, \qquad (5.3.18)$$

where $\delta_i \in \Delta$ and γ_1 is the path index for path trace from the value δ_i to $\delta_{\inf}$. For the second order derivatives, we have :

$$\frac{\partial_{g_{j,1},h_{j,1},\gamma_{j,1}} \partial_{g_{i,1},h_{i,1},\gamma_{i,1}} f(x_1, x_2, \cdots, x_n)}{\partial x_j \partial x_i} =$$
$$\lim_{\substack{\gamma_{j,1} \\ \delta_j \overset{\frown}{\to} \delta_{\inf}}} \frac{g_{j,1}(f'_{x_i}(x_1, x_2, \cdots, x_n, \delta_j), f'_{x_i}(x_1, x_2, \cdots, x_n), \delta_j)}{h_{j,1}(\delta_j)}, \qquad (5.3.19)$$

where $f'_{x_i}(x_1, x_2, \cdots, x_n) = \frac{\partial_{g_{i,1},h_{i,1},\gamma_{i,1}} f(x_1, x_2, \cdots, x_n)}{\partial x_i}$, $\delta_j \in \Delta$ and $\gamma_{j,1}$ is the path index for path trace from the value δ_j to $\delta_{\inf}$.

Based on this definition, we have following rules about derivative of plurioperads.

- Addition/Substraction : $\frac{\partial_{g_{k,1},h_{k,1},\gamma_{k,1}}(P(n)\pm P(m))}{\partial x_k} = \frac{\partial_{g_{k,1},h_{k,1},\gamma_{k,1}} P(n)}{\partial x_k} \pm \frac{\partial_{g_{k,1},h_{k,1},\gamma_{k,1}} P(m)}{\partial x_k}$, where $1 \le m, n$.

- Multiplication : $\frac{\partial_{g_{k,1},h_{k,1},\gamma_{k,1}}(P(n)P(m))}{\partial x_k} =$
  $\frac{\partial_{g_{k,1},h_{k,1},\gamma_{k,1}} P(n)}{\partial x_k} P(m) + P(n) \frac{\partial_{g_{k,1},h_{k,1},\gamma_{k,1}} P(m)}{\partial x_k}$, where $1 \le m, n$.

- Composition, I: $\frac{\partial_{g_{l,1},h_{l,1},\gamma_{l,1}}(P(n)\circ_k P(m))}{\partial x_l} = \frac{\partial_{g_{l,1},h_{l,1},\gamma_{l,1}} P(n)}{\partial x_l}\Big|_{x_k=P(m)}$, if x_l is a variable of $P_i(n)$ and $l \ne k$.

- Composition, II: $\frac{\partial_{g_{l,1},h_{l,1},\gamma_{l,1}}(P(n)\circ_k P(m))}{\partial x_l} =$
  $\left(\frac{\partial_{g_{k,1},h_{k,1},\gamma_{k,1}} P(n)}{\partial x_k}\Big|_{x_k=P(m)}\right) \frac{\partial_{g_{l,1},h_{l,1},\gamma_{l,1}} P(m)}{\partial x_l}$, if x_l is a variable of $P(m)$.

Remarks:

The proposed new definition of derivative introduced in this section has many theoretical problems to be investigated further. For example, what are corresponding definitions for integral and their fundamental theorems of calculus? How do we modify the traditional theorems of Gradient, Green, Stokes and Divergence with respect to functions $\{g_i\}$ and $\{h_i\}$ in vector calculus? Ordinary and partial differential equations have to be re-examined for those existing comprehensive results based on such new derivative definitions.

5.4   Invention Examples Rooted From Plurioperads

In this section, we will provide invention examples by applying techniques from plurioperads. The main feature of plurioperadic operations is permitting any number of similar invention components to form a new things according to some specific rules. This feature is attractable! Because every one's ideas and imaginations can contribute as invention components and these components can be composed by some rules to generate new things which reflect every one's creations. One significant example is YouTube. Deepak Thomas and Vineet Buch wrote an interesting article about the success of YouTube (http://www.startup-review.com/blog/youtube-case- study-widget-marketing-comes-of-age.php) and claimed that "Widget marketing comes of age". They explain the following key factors that assured YouTube's success:

- Online video definitely has existed before YouTube came into vogue. However, uploading videos, sharing and watching them is not easy to operate before the platform like YouTube. Video files are too large to be e-mailed. Users would, in general, need to wait for the entire video to download before they could start watching it. This problem not just exists at peer-to-peer video sharing. Most professional websites with video content also have similar problem. Downloading the video is just half of the task. Users are required to install the appropriate video player, but the free versions of which often behave like "spyware".

- Distributing popular and hard-to-find video clips is another success factor. Clips of the popular, long-running television show, Saturday Night Live were significant examples.

- YouTube allows users to embed any hosted videos on web pages or blogs easily. This becomes to be particularly popular with social-networking websites, especially MySpace.

- While the technology platform used by YouTube may not be very remarkable, it is designed to solve the problem at hand. The technology concept is to encode videos in the Macromedia Flash format and takes advantage of the millions of computers which already have the Flash player installed on it.

- YouTube was launched when social networks started to become popular due to cheaper bandwidth and more convenient computing machines.

In summary, YouTube is success due to every one can have an intensive interaction with many others by the mature of network technologies. Moreover, this interaction becomes more influential if more users join YouTube.

There are three invention examples about applying plurioperads provide by this section. The first example is about art pattern design. The second example is about Fast Fourier Transform (FFT), which is an efficient algorithm to compute the discrete Fourier transform (DFT) and its inverse. The last example is about fault tree analysis.

Example 30 *A pattern, is a type of motif of recurring events or objects, sometimes referred to as elements of a set. These elements repeat in a predictable manner by pre-specific templates or models. These templates or models can be used to generate new things, especially if the created things have enough parts in common to be inferred by templates or models.*

Without any doubt, patterns play an important role in design, art and architecture. For example, firms which produce patterned wallpapers to suit their clients' desires and offer personal items instead of woodfiber paper are enjoying increasing market. Artists are discovering the principle of patterns again, while renowned New York galleries do not hesitate, after many years of temperance, to show the early work of a pioneer of optical art like Victor Vasarely. In the realm of architecture, we are meeting decorations and patterns at various places: in interiors, on exterior facades and even at constructional principles.

From the turn of the century, the revival of patterns design would, all the same, like many ephemeral trends, which will soon have passed its peak and then be faded away. But people who value only the brief optical attraction in patterns and expect from a system of decor nothing more than a colorful rejuvenation of their own living-space. Patterns are above all one thing: shape-transforming. They appear ubiquitously at our daily life, in biology and information science as in philosophy and behavioral science, in the past as much as in the present. Hence, whoever works with patterns is close to be free from any limits. As Gregory Bateson [1] proposed a third scientific methodology (except from induction and deduction), abduction, which was central to Gregory Bateson's holistic and qualitative approac. Gregory Bateson mentioned the importance of studying and comparing patterns of relationship and their symmetry or asymmetry, especially in complex organic (or mental) systems.

Below, we provide an illustration for new patterns design from each individual pattern design. Let $n \in \mathbb{N}$ and let G be the group of transformations α of $\mathbb{R}^n$ with the form $\alpha(x) = a + \lambda x$, with $a \in \mathbb{R}^n$ and $\lambda > 0$. Denote by $D(a, \lambda)$ the closed ball in $\mathbb{R}^n$ with center a and radius λ. Then

---

[1]Gregory Bateson (9 May 1904 - 4 July 1980) was a great British anthropologist, social scientist, linguist, visual anthropologist, semiotician and cyberneticist whose work intersected that of many other fields.

$(G^k)_{k\in\mathbb{N}}$ *is a plurioperad, since*

$$(\alpha_1, \cdots, \alpha_k) \circ ((\alpha_1^1, \cdots, \alpha_1^{j_1}), \cdots, (\alpha_k^1, \cdots, \alpha_k^{j_k})$$

$$= (\alpha_1\alpha_1^1, \cdots, \alpha_1\alpha_1^{j_1}, \cdots, \alpha_k\alpha_k^1, ..., \alpha_k\alpha_k^{j_k}), \tag{5.4.1}$$

where α_i, α_i^l have same form with $\alpha(\boldsymbol{x}) = \boldsymbol{a} + \lambda\boldsymbol{x}$. We then define $\boldsymbol{D}_n(k)$, n-balls plurioperad, as

$$\boldsymbol{D}_n(k) = \{(\alpha_1, \cdots, \alpha_k) \in G^k \mid \text{the images of } D(\boldsymbol{0}, 1) \text{ under } \alpha_1, \cdots, \alpha_k \}. \tag{5.4.2}$$

Since G acts freely and transitively on the set $\{D(\boldsymbol{a}, \lambda) | \boldsymbol{a} \in \mathbb{R}^n, \lambda > 0\}$ of balls, $\boldsymbol{D}_n(k)$ may be identified with the set of configurations of n ordered disjoint smaller balls inside the unit ball: the i-th small ball is $\alpha_i D(\boldsymbol{0}, 1)$. The left hand side of Fig. 5.2 shows an example of composition (laugh face)

$$\boldsymbol{D}_2(3) \times (\boldsymbol{D}_2(4) \times \boldsymbol{D}_{2, smile}(6) \times \boldsymbol{D}_2(4)) \to \boldsymbol{D}_2(14). \tag{5.4.3}$$

If we consider another component (sad mouth) for mouth part of the new face, the right hand side of Fig. 5.2 provides an example of composition (cry face)

$$\boldsymbol{D}_2(3) \times (\boldsymbol{D}_2(4) \times \boldsymbol{D}_{2, sad}(6) \times \boldsymbol{D}_2(4)) \to \boldsymbol{D}_2(14) \tag{5.4.4}$$

The same can be done with cubes instead of balls; this leaves the homotopy type of $\boldsymbol{D}_d(k)$ unchanged.

Example 31 *A fast Fourier transform (FFT) is an efficient algorithm to evaluate the discrete Fourier transform (DFT) and its inverse. There are many distinct FFT algorithms involving a wide range of mathematics and engineering applications, from simple complex-number arithmetic to group theory, digital signal processing and number theory. FFT algorithms can be defined whenever the total transform length N can be factorized as $N = N_1 N_2 \cdots N_k$, where the factors N_i are integers. Although there are many variants of these algorithms, they fall into two basic categories: those based on the prime factor algorithm (PFA) of Good [36] , which are only applicable if the factors N_i are mutually prime, and those modified from Cooley-Tukey algorithm, named after J.W. Cooley and John Tukey, for which the most familiar case is $N_i = 2$ for all i.*

The sequence $(S_n)_{n\in\mathbb{N}}$ consisting of the underlying sets of the symmetric groups is a plurioperad. Such plurioperad is named as symmetric plurioperad with respect to S. *In Fig. 5.3, we*

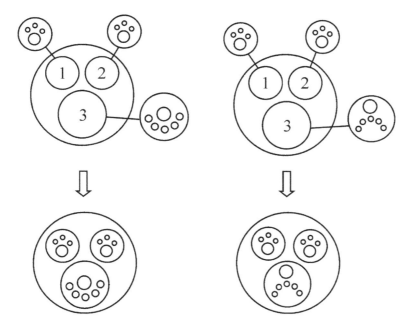

Figure 5.2: Laugh and cry face made by plurioperads

show an example of the composition in symmetry plurioperads.

$$S_3 \times (S_2 \times S_4 \times S_5) \quad \rightarrow \quad S_{11},$$

$$(\sigma, \rho_1, \rho_2, \rho_3) \quad \longmapsto \quad \sigma \circ (\rho_1, \rho_2, \rho_3), \tag{5.4.5}$$

where

$$\sigma = \begin{pmatrix} 1 & 2 & 3 \\ 2 & 3 & 1 \end{pmatrix},$$

$$\rho_1 = \begin{pmatrix} 1 & 2 \\ 2 & 1 \end{pmatrix}, \quad \rho_2 = \begin{pmatrix} 1 & 2 & 3 \\ 1 & 2 & 3 \end{pmatrix}, \quad \rho_3 = \begin{pmatrix} 1 & 2 & 3 & 4 \\ 1 & 4 & 2 & 3 \end{pmatrix}$$

; and

$$\sigma \circ (\rho_1, \rho_2, \rho_3) = \begin{pmatrix} 1 & 2 & 3 & 4 & 5 & 6 & 7 & 8 & 9 \\ 6 & 5 & 7 & 8 & 9 & 1 & 4 & 2 & 3 \end{pmatrix}$$

In general, let $\sigma \in S_n, \rho_1 \in S_{k_1}, \cdots, \rho_n \in S_{k_n}$, we have the following relation for any element in S_n after the operation of $\sigma \circ (\rho_1, ..., \rho_n)$,

$$\sigma \circ (\rho_1, ..., \rho_n)(k_1 + ... + k_{i-1} + j)$$

$$= k_{\sigma^{-1}(1)} + ... + k_{\sigma^{-1}(i-1)} + \rho_i(j), \tag{5.4.6}$$

where $1 \leq i \leq n$, $1 \leq j \leq k_i$ and k_0 assumed to be 0.

From the construction of the symmetric operad with respect to S, if $\sigma_2 = \begin{pmatrix} 1 & 2 \\ 2 & 1 \end{pmatrix}$, Cooley-Tukey FFT algorithm for signal inputs directed to the order different from the origianl one can be written as

$$\sigma_2(\sigma_{2^{n-1}}, \sigma_{2^{n-1}}) = \sigma_{2^n}, \tag{5.4.7}$$

where n can be any natural number and the value of n depends on the size of signals to be transformed by DFT.

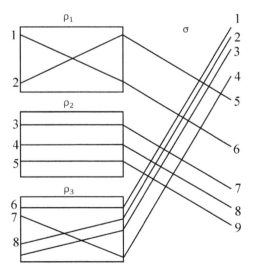

Figure 5.3: Composition example of symmetric plurioperads.

Example 32 *Fault tree analysis (FTA) is a failure analysis where an error state of a system is analyzed using boolean logic to combine a series of lower-level events. This analysis method is mainly used in the field of safety engineering to quantify possible risks. Basically, following steps will be required for FTA analysis.*

- *Understanding of the system.*

- *Define the error event to study.*

- *Construct the fault tree by logical causing effects.*

- *Evaluate the fault tree by providing a measure for the error event.*

- *Analyzing how each factor affects the error event.*

A fault tree can be characterized by a planar rooted tree, which is a tree with a distinguished vertex of degree one (the root) together with an embedding in the plane. Other vertices of degree one are called leaves. Given a set F to represent all possible factors to introduce the interesting error event, the fault tree TF can be described logically by

- *If $f \in F$ then $f \in TF$.*

- *If $t_1, \cdots, t_n \in TF$ then $(t_1, \cdots, t_n) \in TF$.*

For instance, $((f_1, f_2), f_3, (f_4, f_5)) \in TF$ is drawn as

Figure 5.4: Example for $((f_1, f_2), f_3, (f_4, f_5))$.

And the composition is given by grafting of leaves with roots, for example,

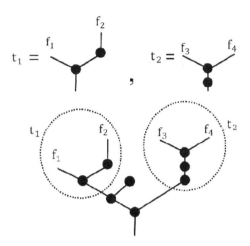

Figure 5.5: Fault tree modules.

The example fault tree shown in Fig. 5.5 consists of several independent modules. There are two issues to be considered. First, how dose the system reliability depend on each of the modules? Second, how do we combine the sensitivity analysis of the separate modules into system-level reliable measures?

Suppose there are k modules at the first level, and that there are m_t components in the subtree t, for $t = 1, 2, \cdots, k$. Since each component can only be in a specific module, $m_1, m_2, \cdots, m_k$ should sum up to m. Let us suppose that component i is an element of module j. Let y_j denote the reliability of module j. The system reliability, denoted as $\Phi(\mathbf{Y})$, can be represented as follows

$$\Phi(\mathbf{Y}) = \Phi(y_1, y_2, \cdots, y_k) \tag{5.4.8}$$

where $\Phi(\mathbf{Y})$ is the system reliability function in term of $y_1, y_2, \cdots, y_k$, and $\mathbf{Y}$ is the vector of $\{y_1, y_2, \cdots, y_k\}$. Then the important sensitivity measure of the component i with respect to failure probability, denoted as $I(i)$, is

$$
\begin{aligned}
I(i) &= \frac{\partial \Phi(\mathbf{Y})}{\partial p_i} \\
&= \sum_{l=1}^{k} \frac{\partial \Phi(\mathbf{Y})}{\partial y_l} \cdot \frac{\partial y_l}{\partial p_i}
\end{aligned}
\tag{5.4.9}
$$

where p_i is the failure probability of the i-th component and $i = 1, 2, \cdots, m$.

Since the component i is only in module j, the reliability change of the component i will only affect reliability change of the module j.

$$\frac{\partial y_t}{\partial p_i} = 0, \quad t = 1, 2, \cdots, k \ \ but \ t \neq j. \tag{5.4.10}$$

Hence, we have

$$I(i) = \frac{\partial \Phi(\mathbf{Y})}{\partial y_j} \cdot \frac{\partial y_j}{\partial p_i} \quad i = 1, 2, \cdots, m \tag{5.4.11}$$

In the expression (5.4.11), $\frac{\partial y_j}{\partial p_i}$ indicates the importance of the component i with respect to the module j, and $\frac{\partial \Phi(\mathbf{Y})}{\partial y_j}$ demonstrates the importance of module j with respect to the whole system. The term $I_{System}(i)$ denotes the importance of component i with respect to the whole system, $I_{j\text{-th module}}(i)$ indicates the importance of the component i with respect to the module j, and $I_{System}(j\text{-th module})$ represents the importance of the module j with respect to the whole system. The relationship among $I_{System}(i)$, $I_{System}(j\text{-th module})$ and $I_{j\text{-th module}}(i)$ can be expressed as

$$I_{System}(i) = I_{System}(j\text{-th module}) \cdot I_{j\text{-th module}}(i) \tag{5.4.12}$$

We can adopt the proposed generalized derivative and the chain-rule approach to calculate sensitivity measures for the separate modules, and combine them hierarchically for higher-level results.

Figure 5.6: Snowman from various snowballs

Chapter 6

Analogy by Invengory

Analogy has been claimed as the core for invention. The purpose of this section is to describe a mathematical language to describe an analogical invention procedure. In Sec. 6.1, the concept about *analogy* is introduced. The mathematical language used to emulate such analogical procedure is provided by Sec. 6.2. Finally, some examples about applying learning and creating new things according to analogy are presented in Sec. 6.3.

6.1   Analogy

Analogy is a logical method which enables one to infer other features among two categories of things according to compare those existing features between such two categories of things. In ancient Greek, the word $\alpha\nu\alpha\lambda o\gamma\iota\alpha$ (analogia) originally meant proportionality. Later on, more broader meanings about analogy from various aspects of science and technologies are derived, for example, association, comparison, correspondence, mathematical and morphological homology, homomorphism, iconicity, isomorphism, metaphor, resemblance, and similarity. The procedure of analogical inference is, firstly, to compare compare those existing features between two interesting categories of things by finding out their identical or similar features. Secondly, one tries to transfer attributes and relations obtained from the previous step to other categories of things under investigation in order to get inspirations.

Analogy method is based on attributes of things and their relations. There are various types of relations among things. We can classify those types into the following four classes.

(1) Coexistence analogy: Objects a and b have coexistence relation in the category A. In the

160

category B, one finds that the object b' has similar properties to the object b. Then we infer that the object a' which has similar properties to the object a may coexist with b' in the category B.

(2) Causal analogy: Objects a and b have causal relation in the category A. In the category B, one finds that the object b' has similar properties to the object b. Then we infer that the object a' which has similar properties to the object a may have causal relation with b' in the category B.

(3) Symmetry analogy: Objects a and b share symmetry relation in the category A. In the category B, one finds that the object b' has similar properties to the object b. Then we infer that the object a' which has similar properties to the object a may have symmetry relation with b' in the category B.

(4) Covariant analogy: Objects a and b have functional relation in the category A, say $f(a) = b$. In the category B, one finds that the object b' has similar properties to the object b. Then we infer that the object a' which has similar properties to the object a may also have the functional relation, $f(a') = b'$, in the category B.

The significant characteristic of analogy method is to enable one to image and observe creatively under the condition of insufficient knowledge or experiences. Following issues have to be carefully treated in performing analogy approach. (1) One has to select proper objects and their category for comparison in an analogical method, i.e., objects and other objects to be explained have to find out more regular and intrinsic relations among them. (2) We have to collect more and more relations between objects and other objects to be explained. (3) The results obtained from analogy method have to be verified carefully by other observational or experimental approaches.

6.2 A Mathematical Language for Analogy

In this section, we will present a mathematical language to describe an analogical invention method.

6.2.1 Invengory Definition

From the previous discussions, we have to collect a set of objects with specific relations among them to form an invengory before our comparison for analogy. An invengory is defined below to characterize these features (objects and their relations in an invengory) mathematically.

Definition 3 *An invengory **C** consists of:*

1. *A collection of objects;*

2. *A collection of relations;*

3. *Operations assigning to each relation F an object $domF$, its domain, and an object $ranF$, its range (we write $F : A \to B$ to show that $domF = A$ and $ranF = B$; the collection of all relations with domain A and range B is written as $\mathbf{C}(A, B)$);*

4. *The relations F, G and H can be decomposed by functions as $F = \bowtie_{i=1}^{I_F} f_i, G = \bowtie_{j=1}^{I_G} g_j$ and $H = \bowtie_{k=1}^{I_H} h_k$, where each f_i, g_j and h_k is a function. A composition operator assigning to each pair of functions f_i and g_j, with $ranf_i = domg_j$ for some indices $i \in I_F$ and $j \in I_G$, respectively. A composite function $g_j \circ f_i : domf_i \to rang_j$, satisfying the following associative law:*

   For any relations $F : A \to B, G : B \to C$, and $H : C \to D$ where $A, B, C,$ and D are not necessarily distinct, we always have

   $$h_k \circ (g_j \circ f_i) = (h_k \circ g_j) \circ f_i, \tag{6.2.1}$$

   where indices i, j and k satisfy $ran\ f_i = dom\ g_j$ and $ran\ g_j = dom\ h_k$.

5. *For each object A, an identity relation $id_A : A \to A$ satisfies the following identity law with respect to any $F : A \to B$ and each index i:*

   $$id_B \circ f_i = f_i, \text{ and } f_i \circ id_A = f_i, \tag{6.2.2}$$

   where $F = \bowtie_{i=1}^{I_F} f_i$.

The invengory of **Set** is the most basic and important invengory to understand since we often transform complicated invengories into **Set** invengories in order to study their structure. The invengory of **Set** has sets as objects and set relations between sets. Hence, the **Set** invengory is defined by the following terms.

1. An object in **Set** is a set;

2. A relation $F : A \to B$ in **Set** is a set relation from set A to B;

3. For each relation F with domain A and range B, we have *dom* $F = A$, *ran* $F = B$ and $F \in \mathbf{Set}(A, B)$;

4. For set relations $F : A \to B, G : B \to C$, and $H : C \to D$, we have

$$h_k \circ (g_j \circ f_i) = (h_k \circ g_j) \circ f_i, \qquad (6.2.3)$$

where indices i, j and k satisfy *ran* $f_i = dom$ g_j and *ran* $g_j = dom$ h_k.

5. For each set A, an identity relation $id_A : A \to A$ satisfies the following identity law:

$$id_b \circ f_i = f_i, \text{and } f_i \circ id_a = f_i, \qquad (6.2.4)$$

where $F : A \to B$ and $F = \bowtie_{i=1}^{I_F} f_i$.

A special case of invengories is an invengory where all relations in such invengory are functions. Let us see another invengory example, the invengory of **Poset**, where all its relations are functions. We begin by introducing some notions before defining such **Poset** invengory. A *partial ordering* $\leq_P$ on a set P is a reflexive, transitive, and antisymmetric relation on the elements of P, i.e., (1) $p \leq_P p$, (2) $p \leq_P q \leq_P r$ implies $p \leq_P r$, and (3) $p \leq_P q$ and $q \leq_P p$ imply $p = q$ for all p, q, r. An order-preserving function F from P to Q has the following property : if $p \leq_P q$ then $F(p) \leq_Q F(q)$. The invengory **Poset** has objects as partial-ordered sets with relations as order-preserving functions. The invengory **Poset** compromises:

1. An object in **Poset** is a set P with a reflexive, transitive and antisymmetric relation $\leq_P$ on the elements of P, denoted as $(P, \leq_P)$;

2. A relation $F : (P, \leq_P) \to (Q, \leq_Q)$ in **Poset** is a function preserving the ordering on P, i.e, if $p \leq_P q$ then $F(p) \leq_Q F(q)$;

3. For each function F with domain P and range Q, we have *dom* $F = P$, *ran* $F = Q$ and $F \in \mathbf{Poset}(P, Q)$;

163

4. The composition of two order-preserving functions $F : P \to Q$ and $G : Q \to R$ is a function $G \circ F$ from P to R. If $p \leq_P q$, then $F(p) \leq_Q F(q)$ since F preserves order in elements of P. Moreover, we also have $G(F(p)) \leq_R G(F(q))$ since G preserves order in elements of R. Hence, $G \circ F$ is order-preserving. Composition of order-preserving functions is associative because each order-preserving function on partially-ordered sets is a function on sets and composition of functions on sets is associative.

5. For each object $(P, \leq_P)$, the identity function preserves the ordering on P and such identity function satisfies the equations of identity law.

In Chapter III, we discussed about various basic algebraic structures which help us to model invention process. Generally, algebraic structures could be classified by the following three kinds: arithmetics, varieties and quasivarieties. Abstractly, many of these algebraic structures can be restated by the Ω-algebra (will be defined soon) by specifying operations for operators in the set Ω. Then we can form the invengory Ω-**Alg** in order to manipulate analogy invention procedure related to aforementioned basic algebraic structures.

Let Ω be a set of operator symbols, associated with a function α from elements of Ω to natural numbers. For each $\omega \in \Omega$, $\alpha(\omega)$ is the arity of ω. An Ω-algebra is a set of variables, denoted as X, and a function $a_\omega : X^{\alpha(\omega)} \to X$ for each operator ω. An Ω-homomorphism from an Ω-algebra A to an Ω-algebra B is a function $h : A \to B$ such that for each operator $\omega \in \Omega$ and $\alpha(\omega)$-tuples of elements $x_1, x_2, \cdots, x_{\alpha(\omega)}$, we have the following equation:

$$h(a_\omega(x_1, x_2, \cdots, x_{\alpha(\omega)})) = b_\omega(h(x_1), h(x_2), \cdots, h(x_{\alpha(\omega)})), \tag{6.2.5}$$

where b_ω is the function associated to the operator ω in the Ω-algebra B. The invengory Ω-**Alg** is composed by Ω-algebras as objects and Ω-homomorphisms as relations. For instance, if following parameters are provided,

- $\Omega = \{id, \cdot\}$;

- $\alpha(\cdot) = 2$;

- $\alpha(id) = 0$;

- $E = \{(x \cdot y) \cdot z = x \cdot (y \cdot z), \ id \cdot x = x \cdot id = x, \ \forall x, \text{ we always have } y \in X \text{ such that } x \cdot y = y \cdot x = id \}$;

164

then such Ω-algebra is a group.

Besides obtaining invengories from mathematical objects directly, several ways to build invengories from other invengories are discussed here.

For each invengory $\mathbf{C}$, the objects of the *dual invengory*, denote as $\mathbf{C}^{op}$, are the same as those of $\mathbf{C}$; the relations in $\mathbf{C}^{op}$ are relations in $\mathbf{C}$ by inverting their domains and ranges. That is, if $F: A \to B$ is a relation in $\mathbf{C}$ then $F^{op}: B \to A$ is a relation in $\mathbf{C}^{op}$ corresponding to F.

For any pair of invengories $\mathbf{C}$ and $\mathbf{D}$, the product invengory $\mathbf{C} \times \mathbf{D}$ has object (C, D) where C is a $\mathbf{C}$ object and D is a $\mathbf{D}$ object. The relation in $\mathbf{C} \times \mathbf{D}$ is (F, G) where F is a relation in $\mathbf{C}$ and G is a relation in $\mathbf{D}$. Composition and identity laws are defined pairwise: $(F, G) \circ (F', G') = (F \circ F', G \circ G')$ and $id_{\mathbf{C} \times \mathbf{D}} = (id_{\mathbf{C}}, id_{\mathbf{D}})$.

A invengory $\mathbf{D}$ is a *subinvengory* of a invengory $\mathbf{C}$ if

1. each object of $\mathbf{D}$ is an object of $\mathbf{C}$;

2. For all $\mathbf{D}$-objects D and D', $\mathbf{D}(D, D') \in \mathbf{C}(D, D')$;

3. composition and identity laws are the same in $\mathbf{D}$ as in $\mathbf{C}$.

6.2.2   Relations in an Invengory

When we manipulate sets and functions, we are often interested in functions with nice properties such as being surjective (onto), injective (one-to-one), or even bijective (isomorphism). Analogical concepts can be applied at invengorical reasoning.

We begin by introducing the concept of *monic* relations which is similar to the concept of injective functions.

Definition 4 *A relation $F: B \to C$ ($F = \bowtie_{i=1}^{I_F} f_i$) in an invengory $\mathbf{C}$ is* monic *if, for any of $\mathbf{C}$-relations $G: A \to B$ ($G = \bowtie_{j=1}^{I_G} g_j$) and $H: A \to B$ ($H = \bowtie_{k=1}^{I_H} h_k$), the identities $f_i \circ g_j = f_i \circ h_k$ for all i, j, k implies $G = H$.*

Theorem 9 *In* **Set** *invengory with relations as functions, the monics are injective functions.*

PROOF. 11 *Let $F: B \to C$ be an injective function, and let G, H be functions from A to B such that $F \circ G = F \circ H$. If we assume that $G \neq H$, there exists at least an element $a \in A$ for which $G(a) \neq H(a)$. Since F is an injective function, we have $F(G(a)) \neq F(H(a))$, which contradicts the assumption $F \circ G = G \circ F$. Hence, F is a monic.*

Conversely, let $F : B \to C$ be a monic. If F is not injective, then we have $F(b) = F(b')$. Also, let a be an element in A such that $G(a) = b$ and $H(a) = b'$. Then $F(G(a)) = F(H(a))$, which contradicts the assumption of monic.

The other relations in an invengory which is similar to the concept of surjective functions are *epic* relations.

Definition 5 *A relation* $F : A \to B$ *(*$F = \bowtie_{i=1}^{I_F} f_i$*) in an invengory* **C** *is epic if, for any of* **C***-relations* $G : B \to C$ *(*$G = \bowtie_{j=1}^{I_G} g_j$*) and* $H : B \to C$ *(*$H = \bowtie_{k=1}^{I_H} h_k$*), the identities* $g_j \circ f_i = h_k \circ f_i$ *for all* i, j, k *implies* $G = H$.

Theorem 10 *In* **Set** *invengory with relations as functions, the epics are surjective functions.*

PROOF. 12 *Let* $F : A \to B$ *be an surjective function, and let* G, H *be functions from* B *to* C *such that* $G \circ F = H \circ F$. *If we assume that* $G \neq H$, *there exists at least an element* $b \in B$ *for which* $G(b) \neq H(b)$. *Since* F *is an surjective function, we have an element* $a \in A$ *such that* $F(a) = b$. *Hence,* $G(F(a)) \neq H(F(a))$, *which contradicts the assumption* $G \circ F = H \circ F$. *Hence,* F *is a epic.*

Conversely, let $F : A \to B$ *be a epic. If* F *is not surjective, then we have some element* $b \in B$ *which can not find any element* $a \in A$ *such that* $F(a) = b$. *Since we do not have* $G(F(a)) = H(F(a))$, *which contradicts the assumption of epic. Therefore,* F *is surjective.*

Definition 6 *A relation* $F : A \to B$ *in an invengory* **C** *is isomorphism if there is an inverse relation from* B *to* A, *denoted as* F^{-1}, *such that* $F^{-1} \circ F = id_A$ *and* $F \circ F^{-1} = id_B$. *Two objects* A *and* B *are said to be isomorphic if there is an isomorphism between them.*

6.2.3 Objects Constructions

In this section, we will discuss several constructions in invengories.

Initial and Terminal Objects

The basic ones are concepts of *initial object* and *terminal object*.

The definition about an *initial object* is provided as:

Definition 7 *An object* $\mathfrak{I}$ *is called an* initial object *if, for every object* a, *there is exactly one relation from* $\mathfrak{I}$ *to* a.

Dually, we also have the following definition about a *terminal object*.

Definition 8 *An object $\mathfrak{T}$ is called a* terminal object *if, for every object a, there is exactly one relation from a to $\mathfrak{T}$.*

In **Set**, the empty set $\emptyset$ is the only initial object. Since the empty relation is the unique relation from $\emptyset$ to S, a set in **Set**. Each one element set is a terminal object since there is a relation from S to any one element set in **Set**. Terminal objects can also be used to provide relational representations for objects in an invengory. Considering the invengory **Set** with functional relations as an example, the relations from a singleton set to a set S are in one-to-one correspondence with the elements of S. Furthermore, let s be an element of S and we have a relation from some one-element terminal object to the set S, denoted as $\tilde{s}$. If F is a relation from S to T, then the element $F(s)$ is the unique element of T that is in the image of the composite function $F \circ \tilde{s}$. Such relation from a terminal object to an object S is called a *global element*. Hence, we can treat elements as relations from a terminal object.

Products and Co-products

We have discussed the definition of the cartesian product of two sets A and B at Chap. III in order to compute a combinatorial invention procedure. From the discussion at the end of Sec. 6.2.3, we can define an invengorical product construction with global elements. This helps us abstract from elements used in invention procedures by focusing at the properties of relations between objects. Hence, we have to redefine the product operation by relational characterization.

Definition 9 *A product of two objects A and B is an object $A \times B$ with two* projection functions $\pi_1 : A \times B \to A$ and $\pi_2 : A \times B \to B$, *such that for any object C and pair of relations $F : C \to A$ $(F = \bowtie_{i=1}^{I_F} f_i)$ and $G : C \to B$ $(G = \bowtie_{j=1}^{I_G} g_j)$ there is exactly one function $(f_i, g_j) : C \to A \times B$ for each index i and j making the diagram (shown by Fig. 6.1) commute, that is $\pi_1 \circ (f_i, g_j) = f_i$ and $\pi_2 \circ (f_i, g_j) = g_j$.*

From the above definition, we find that three tuples $(A \times B, \pi_1, \pi_2)$ (set, relation, relation) is the optimal representative of any three tuples (X, f_1, f_2) which have properties $f_1 : X \to A$ and $f_2 : X \to B$. Since for some set C, there are two relations $F : C \to A$ and $G : C \to B$. We define a product relation as $(F, G)(x) = (F(x), G(x))$. The relations F and G can be rebuilt from (F, G) by setting $F = \pi_1 \circ (F, G)$ and $G = \pi_2 \circ (F, G)$. Also, the relation (F, G) is the

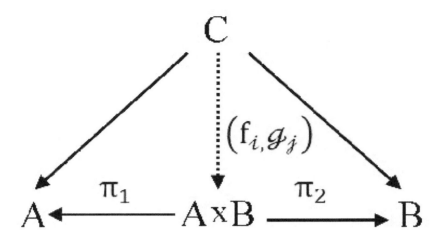

Figure 6.1: Product of Invengory.

only function from C to $A \times B$ with such property. However, one may question that the three tuples $(A \times B, \pi_1, \pi_2)$ is not the only representative of the set of three tuples (X, f_1, f_2) which have properties $f_1 : X \to A$ and $f_2 : X \to B$. For instance, $(B \times A, \pi_2, \pi_1)$ is also optimal since it also can be used to reconstruct relations F and G from (F, G) by setting $F = \pi_1 \circ (F, G)$ and $G = \pi_2 \circ (F, G)$. In invengorical language, we can treat $A \times B$ as $B \times A$ since there is a one-to-one correspondence between them which makes them have exact identical relational characterizations in terms of analogy.

By reversing roles of domains and ranges of all relations in the product definition, the dual concept for product operation is introduced below, namely *co-product*.

Definition 10 *A co-product of two objects A and B is an object $A + B$ with two injection functions $\iota_1 : A \to A + B$ and $\iota_2 : B \to A + B$, such that for any object C and pair of relations $F : A \to C$ ($F = \bowtie_{i=1}^{I_F} f_i$) and $G : B \to C$ ($G = \bowtie_{j=1}^{I_G} g_j$) there is exactly one function $[f_i, g_j] : A + B \to C$ for each index i and j making the diagram (shown by Fig. 6.2) commute, that is $[f_i, g_j] \circ \iota_1 = f_i$ and $[f_i, g_j] \circ \iota_2 = g_j$.*

A product of a family $(A_i)_{i \in I}$ of objects indexed by a set I consists of an object $\prod_{i \in I} A_i$ and a family of projection functions $\pi_i : \prod_{i \in I} A_i \to A_i$ such that for each object C and family of relations $(F_i : C \to A_i)_{i \in I}$ ($F_i = \bowtie_{j_i=1}^{I_{F_i}} f_{j_i}$) there is a unique function $(f_{j_i})_{i \in I} : C \to \prod_{i \in I} A_i$ for each index j_i such that the following diagram commutes for all $i \in I$. See Fig. 6.3.

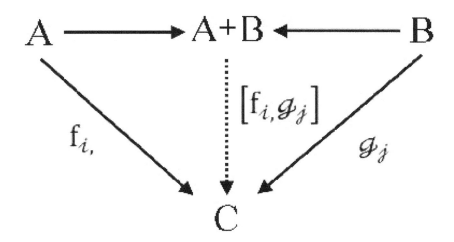

Figure 6.2: Co-product of Invengory.

Similarly, the co-product for a family $(A_i)_{i \in I}$ of objects indexed by a set I can also be defined by just reversing roles of domains and ranges of all relations in the product definition of a family $(A_i)_{i \in I}$ of objects.

Pullbacks and Pushouts

Analog to intersection and union operations of sets, *pullbacks* and *pushouts* are two operations in an invengory in order to construct a new object. We begin by defining the pullback operation.

Definition 11 *A pullback of the pair of relations* $F : A \to C$ *(*$F = \bowtie_{i=1}^{I_F} f_i$*) and* $G : B \to C$ *(*$G = \bowtie_{j=1}^{I_G} g_j$*) is an object* P *and a pair of relations* $G' : P \to A$ *(*$G' = \bowtie_{k=1}^{I_{G'}} g'_k$*) and* $F' : P \to B$ *(*$F' = \bowtie_{l=1}^{I_{F'}} f'_l$*) such that*

$$f_i \circ g'_k = g_j \circ f'_l, \qquad (6.2.6)$$

for all i, j, k *and* l*. Moreover, if for another object* X *and two relations* $E : X \to A$ *(*$E = \bowtie_{m=1}^{I_E} e_m$*) and* $H : X \to B$ *(*$H = \bowtie_{n=1}^{I_H} h_n$*) with*

$$f_i \circ e_m = g_j \circ h_n \qquad (6.2.7)$$

for all i, j, m *and* n*, then there is a unique function* $\beta_{k,l,m,n}$ *from* X *to* P *with respect to indices* (k, l, m, n) *such that* $e_m = g'_k \circ \beta_{k,l,m,n}$ *and* $h_n = f'_l \circ \beta_{k,l,m,n}$*. It can be shown as Fig. 6.4.*

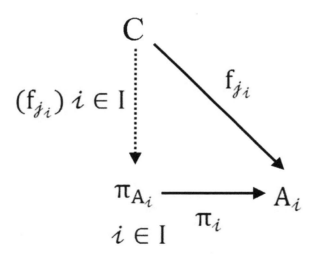

Figure 6.3: Multiple product diagram.

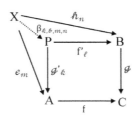

Figure 6.4: Pull back definition.

Let us examine two examples about pullbacks. In invengory **Set** with only functional relations between each pair of objects, Let $F : A \to B$ be a function in **Set** and let $C \subseteq B$. Then the pullback is the set $F^{-1}(C)$ with the following two functions: inclusion function $F^{-1}(C) \hookrightarrow C$ and $F|_{F^{-1}(C)} : F^{-1}(C) \to C$. In summary, we have the following diagram to show such pullback example. See Fig. 6.5.

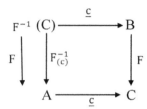

Figure 6.5: Pull back example 1.

If A and B are subsets of S, then the pullback is the set $A \bigcap B$ with the following two functions: inclusion function $A \bigcap B \hookrightarrow A$ and $A \bigcap B \hookrightarrow B$. In summary, we have the following diagram to show such pullback example. See Fig. 6.6.

The definition of a pushout is provided below.

Definition 12 *A pushout of the pair of relations* $F : C \to A$ *(F* $= \bowtie_{i=1}^{I_F} f_i$*) and* $G : C \to B$ *(G* $= \bowtie_{j=1}^{I_G} g_j$*) is an object* P *and a pair of relations* $G' : A \to P$ *(G'* $= \bowtie_{k=1}^{I_{G'}} g'_k$*) and* $F' : B \to P$ *(F'* $= \bowtie_{l=1}^{I_{F'}} f'_l$*) such that*

$$g'_k \circ f_i = f'_l \circ g_j, \tag{6.2.8}$$

for all i, j, k *and* l. *Moreover, if for another object* X *and two relations* $E : A \to X$ *(E* $= \bowtie_{m=1}^{I_E} e_m$*) and* $H : B \to X$ *(H* $= \bowtie_{n=1}^{I_H} h_n$*) with*

$$e_m \circ f_i = h_n \circ g_j \tag{6.2.9}$$

for all i, j, m *and* n, *then there is a unique function* $\beta_{k,l,m,n}$ *from* P *to* X *with respect to indices* (k, l, m, n) *such that* $e_m = \beta_{k,l,m,n} \circ g'_k$ *and* $h_n = \beta_{k,l,m,n} \circ f'_l$. *It can be shown as Fig. 6.7.*

172

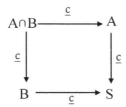

Figure 6.6: Pull back example 2.

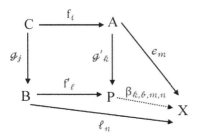

Figure 6.7: Push out definition.

Let us examine two examples about pushouts. In invengory **Set**, suppose that A and B are two sets. Then if we write C for their intersection, there are functions $F : C \to A$ and $G : C \to B$

173

given by inclusion. The pushout of F and G is the union of A and B together with the inclusion functions from A and B. See Fig. 6.8.

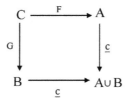

Figure 6.8: Push out example.

The construction of adjunction spaces by identifying is an example of pushouts in the invengory of geometrical spaces. More precisely, if C is a subspace of B and $G : C \to B$ is the inclusion map we can glue B to another space A along C using an attaching map $F : C \to A$. The result is the adjunction space $A \cup_F B$ which is just the pushout of F and G. More generally, all identification spaces can be treated as pushouts in this way.

Limits and Co-limits

Initial and terminal objects, products and co-products, pullbacks and pushouts are special cases of the more general constructions, *limits* and *co-limits*. We begin by defining the notion of *cone* in order to define a limit.

Definition 13 *Let $\boldsymbol{C}$ be an invengory and $\boldsymbol{D}$ a diagram in $\boldsymbol{C}$. A cone for $\boldsymbol{D}$ is an object X in $\boldsymbol{C}$ and relations $F_i : X \to D_i$ (one for each object D_i in $\boldsymbol{D}$), we have $F_j = G \circ F_i$ for each relation G in $\boldsymbol{D}$. The notation for cones is denoted as $\{F_i : X \to D_i\}$.*

Then the limit for a diagram $\boldsymbol{D}$ is defined as follows.

Definition 14 *A limit for a diagram $\boldsymbol{D}$ is a cone $\{F_i : X \to D_i\}$ ($F_i = \bowtie_{j_i=1}^{I_i} f_{j_i}$) with the property that if $\{F_i' : X' \to D_i\}$ ($F_i' = \bowtie_{j_i'=1}^{I_i'} f_{j_i'}'$) is another cone for $\boldsymbol{D}$ then there is a unique function $\beta_{j_i,j_i'} : X' \to X$ such that $F_i' = F_i \circ \beta_{j_i,j_i'}$ with respect to every D_i and functions f_{j_i} and $f_{j_i'}'$ in $\boldsymbol{D}$.*

Two constructions for new objects that we mentioned previously, product and pullback, can be regarded as limits for two special diagrams. Let $\boldsymbol{D}$ be the diagram with only two objects A and B without any relations on these two objects. A cone for this diagram is an object X with two relations $F : X \to A$ and $G : X \to B$. If the limit for such cone exists, it is the product of objects A and B.

Let $\boldsymbol{D}$ be the diagram

$$B$$
$$\downarrow G$$
$$A \xrightarrow{F} C$$

with three objects A, B and C and two relations $F : A \to C$ and $G : B \to C$. A cone for $\boldsymbol{D}$ is an object P with two relations $F' : P \to B$ and $G' : P \to A$ which make the following diagram commutes:

$$P \xrightarrow{F'} B$$

$$G' \downarrow \qquad \downarrow G$$

$$A \xrightarrow{F} C \qquad\qquad\qquad (6.2.10)$$

If the object P and relations $F' = \bowtie_{k=1}^{I_{F'}} f_k'$ and $G' = \bowtie_{l=1}^{I_{G'}} f_l'$ form a limit, given any other object P' with relations $F'' = \bowtie_{m=1}^{I_{F''}} f_m''$ and $G'' = \bowtie_{n=1}^{I_{G''}} g_n''$, there will be a unique function $\beta_{k,l,m,n}$ from P' to P with respect to indices (k, l, m, n) such that $f_m'' = f_k' \circ \beta_{k,l,m,n}$ and $g_n'' = g_l' \circ \beta_{k,l,m,n}$. This shows that a limit of $\mathbf{D}$ is a pullback of F and G.

Dually, we also have definitions for a co-cone and a co-limit.

Definition 15 *Let $\mathbf{C}$ be an invengory and $\mathbf{D}$ a diagram in $\mathbf{C}$. A co-cone for $\mathbf{D}$ is an object X in $\mathbf{C}$ and relations $F_i : D_i \to X$ (one for each object D_i in $\mathbf{D}$), we have $F_j = F_i \circ G$ for each relation G in $\mathbf{D}$. The notation for co-cones is denoted as $\{F_i : D_i \to X\}$.*

Then the co-limit for a diagram $\mathbf{D}$ is defined as follows.

Definition 16 *A co-limit for a diagram $\mathbf{D}$ is a co-cone $\{F_i : D_i \to X\}$ ($F_i = \bowtie_{j_i=1}^{I_i} f_{j_i}$) with the property that if $\{F_i' : D_i \to X'\}$ ($F_i' = \bowtie_{j_i'=1}^{I_i'} f_{j_i'}'$) is another cone for $\mathbf{D}$ then there is a unique function $\beta_{j_i,j_i'} : X \to X'$ such that $F_i' = \beta_{j_i,j_i'} \circ F_i$ with respect to every D_i and functions f_{j_i} and $f_{j_i'}'$ in $\mathbf{D}$.*

We have to note that not all diagrams have limits. For example, the empty diagram in an invengory with no terminal object has no limit. The following theorem is provided to give conditions for an invengory to have a limit for a diagram $\mathbf{D}$ in such invengory.

Theorem 11 *Let $\mathbf{D}$ be a diagram in an invengory $\mathbf{C}$. If every family of objects in $\mathbf{C}$ has a product and every pair of relations in $\mathbf{C}$ has an equalizer [1], then $\mathbf{D}$ has a limit.*

PROOF. 13 *Let objects in $\mathbf{D}$ form a set V with index v to represent each object in $\mathbf{D}$. Also, relations between each pair of objects in $\mathbf{D}$ form another set E with index e to represent each relation in $\mathbf{D}$.*

A possible candidate for the limit object would be the product $\prod_{v \in V} D_v$. However, this will not work always because the relations from the product do not always form commuting diagrams with

---

[1] An equalizer is a limit for a diagram with two relations from the same domain to the same range.

the relations D_e. Hence, we have to construct another product with respect to each relation in E as $\prod\limits_{(v \to v') \in E} D_{v'}$. The relations between the product $\prod\limits_{v \in V} D_v$ and the product $\prod\limits_{(v \to v') \in E} D_{v'}$ can be expressed by the following diagram:

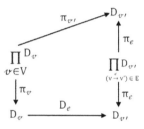

Figure 6.9: The relations between the product $\prod\limits_{v \in V} D_v$ and the product $\prod\limits_{(v \to v') \in E} D_{v'}$.

For each $D_{v'}$ at the upper half of the diagram, there is a projection function $\pi_{v'} : \prod_{v \in V} D_v \to D_{v'}$. By the universal property of the product, there exists an unique function $p : \prod_{v \in V} D_v \to \prod_{(v \to v') \in E} D_{v'}$ such that $\pi_e \circ p = \pi_{v'}$ for each relation $e : v \to v'$. On the other hand, for each $D_{v'}$ at the lower half of the diagram, there is a function $D_e \circ \pi_v : \prod_{v \in V} D_v \to D_{v'}$, which implies the existence of an unique relation $p : \prod_{v \in V} D_v \to \prod_{(v \to v') \in E} D_{v'}$ such that $\pi_e \circ q = D_e \circ \pi_v$ for each relation $e : v \to v'$. See Fig. 6.10.

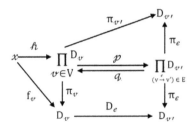

Figure 6.10: Diagram of uniqueness.

Let h be an equalizer of functions p, q and define relations F_v as $\pi_v \circ h$ for each $v \in V$. Note that $F_v = \bowtie_{i_v=1}^{I_{F_v}} f_{i_v}$. Actually, the cone $\{F_v : X \to D_v\}$ is a limit for $\mathbf{D}$. We have to verify two facts about such claim; the first is to show that $\{F_v : X \to D_v\}$ is really a cone and the second is to verify its universal among all cones for $\mathbf{D}$. Because we have

$$D_e \circ F_v = D_e \circ \pi_v \circ h = \pi_e \circ q \circ h = \pi_e \circ p \circ h = \pi_{v'} \circ h = F_{v'}, \tag{6.2.11}$$

the term $\{F_v : X \to D_v\}$ is a cone for $\mathbf{D}$.

The next goal is to show the universal property of such cone. Assume that $\{\acute{F}_v : \acute{X} \to D_v\}$ is a cone for $\mathbf{D}$. By the universal property of products, there is a unique relation $\acute{h} : \acute{X} \to \prod_{v \in V} D_v$ such that $\pi_v \circ \acute{h} = \acute{F}_v$ for each $v \in V$. Because $\pi_e \circ p \circ \acute{h} = \pi_{v'} \circ \acute{h} = \acute{F}_{v'} = D_e \circ \pi_v \circ \acute{h} = \pi_e \circ q \circ \acute{h}$, the following commutative diagram can be established as :

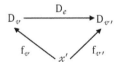

Figure 6.11: Commutative diagram.

which implies that $p \circ \acute{h} = q \circ \acute{h}$ and this shows that $\acute{h}$ is also an equalizer for p and q. From the universal property of equalizers, there is a unique relation $k : \acute{X} \to X$ such that $F_v \circ k = \pi_v \circ h \circ k = \pi_v \circ h' = \acute{F}_v$. As desired.

6.2.4   Functors and Their Transformations

A *functor* is a structure-preserving of analogical relations between two invengories. Given two invengories **C** and **D**, a functor **F** from **C** to **D** can be treated of as an analogy relation between **C** and **D**, because **F** has to map objects of **C** to objects of **D** and relations of **C** to relations of **D** by preserving the compositional structure of these two invengories. Hence, we define a functor as:

Definition 17 *Let **C** and **D** be two invengories. A functor $\mathbf{F} : \mathbf{C} \to \mathbf{D}$ is a map taking each **C**-object A to a **D**-object $F(A)$ and each **C**-relation $F : A \to B$ to a **D**-relation $\mathbf{F}(F) : F(A) \to F(B)$ such that*

$$
\begin{aligned}
\mathbf{F}(id_A) &= id_{\mathbf{F}(A)}, \\
\mathbf{F}(g_j \circ_C f_i) &= \mathbf{F}(g_j) \circ_D \mathbf{F}(f_i)
\end{aligned}
\tag{6.2.12}
$$

*for all **C**-objects A, all composable **C**-relations $F = \bowtie_{i=1}^{I_F} f_i$ and $G = \bowtie_{j=1}^{I_G} g_j$ (a relation from the object B to the object C), and all functions f_i and g_j.*

Let us examine two examples about functors. In invengogy **Set**, we can form the set $FL(S)$ (object) of finite lists with elements selected from S. The function from $f : S \to S'$ is mapped to a function $FL(f) : FL(S) \to FL(S')$. Given a list $L = [s_1, s_2, \cdots, s_n]$, maps f over the elements of L as: $FL(f)(L) = [f(s_1), f(s_2), \cdots, f(s_n)]$. The power set functor $\mathbf{F}: \mathbf{Set} \to \mathbf{Set}$ maps each set to its power set and each function $f : X \to Y$ to the function which sends $U \subseteq X$ to its image $f(U) \subseteq Y$.

In the following, we classify functors according to their mapping properties.

- A functor $\mathbf{F}: \mathbf{C} \to \mathbf{D}$ is called *faithful* if it maps any relation in **C** to **D** injectively.

- A functor $\mathbf{F}: \mathbf{C} \to \mathbf{D}$ is called *full* if it maps any relation in **C** to **D** surjectively.

- A functor $\mathbf{F}: \mathbf{C} \to \mathbf{D}$ is called *dense* if each object D in **D** is isomorphic with some $\mathbf{F}(A)$ for an object A in **C**.

- A *forgetful* functor (also called underlying functor) is defined from an invengory of algebraic gadgets (groups, modules, rings, vector spaces, etc.) to the invengory of sets. A forgetful functor leaves the objects and the relations as they are, except for the fact they are finally considered only as sets and relations by omitting their algebraic properties.

Different types of functors will preserve various relational structures. We have to define *analogical property* first in order for us to figure out the relations between different types of functors and preserved relational structures. We name $AP(A, \cdots; F, \cdots)$ an analogical property when $A, \cdots$ and $F, \cdots$ are notations standing for objects and relations and AP is some expression involving such objects and relations that is meaningful (that is true or false) in any invengory. For instance, (A is an terminal object), or (F is an epic relation). Given a functor $\mathbf{F} \colon \mathbf{C} \to \mathbf{D}$, we say that $\mathbf{F}$ *preserves* the property $AP(A, \cdots; F, \cdots)$ if, given any set of objects $(A, \cdots)$ and relations $(F, \cdots)$ from $\mathbf{C}$ in the meaningful relation $AP(A, \cdots; F, \cdots)$, always implies that $AP(\mathbf{F}(A), \cdots; \mathbf{F}(F), \cdots)$ is true (or false) if the expression $AP(A, \cdots; F, \cdots)$ is true (or false). Moreover, we say that $\mathbf{F}$ *reflects* the property $AP(A, \cdots; F, \cdots)$ if, given any set of objects $(A, \cdots)$ and relations $(F, \cdots)$ from $\mathbf{C}$ in the meaningful relation $AP(\mathbf{F}(A), \cdots; \mathbf{F}(F), \cdots)$, always implies that $AP(A, \cdots; F, \cdots)$ is true (or false) if the expression $AP(\mathbf{F}(A), \cdots; \mathbf{F}(F), \cdots)$ is true (or false). The following theorem is provided to characterize the relations between different types of functors and preserved relational structures.

Theorem 12 *(1) Any functor $\mathbf{F} \colon \mathbf{C} \to \mathbf{D}$ preserves identities, isomorphisms, and commutativity of a triangular diagram.*

(2) A faithful functor $\mathbf{F} \colon \mathbf{C} \to \mathbf{D}$ reflects monic, epic relations and commutativity of a triangular diagram.

(3) A full and faithful functor $\mathbf{F} \colon \mathbf{C} \to \mathbf{D}$ reflects isomorphisms.

(4) A full, faithful and dense functor $\mathbf{F} \colon \mathbf{C} \to \mathbf{D}$ preserves monic and epic relations.

PROOF. 14 *(1) From the definition of a functor which requires that $\mathbf{F}(id_A) = id_{\mathbf{F}(A)}$ for any object A in $\mathbf{C}$, the functor $\mathbf{F}$ preserves identities.*

For a given relation $F \colon A \to B$ in the invengory $\mathbf{C}$, the existence of another relation $G \colon B \to A$ in the invengory $\mathbf{C}$ with $G \circ F = id_A$ indicates that there is an $\mathbf{F}(G) \colon \mathbf{F}(B) \to \mathbf{F}(A)$ for $\mathbf{F}(F) \colon \mathbf{F}(A) \to \mathbf{F}(B)$ satisfying $\mathbf{F}(G) \circ \mathbf{F}(F) = \mathbf{F}(G \circ F) = \mathbf{F}(id_A) = id_{\mathbf{F}(A)}$. On the other hand, for a given relation $F \colon A \to B$ in the invengory $\mathbf{C}$, the existence of another relation $G \colon B \to A$ in the invengory $\mathbf{C}$ with $F \circ G = id_A$ would mean that there is an $\mathbf{F}(G) \colon \mathbf{F}(B) \to \mathbf{F}(A)$

for $\mathbf{F}(F) : \mathbf{F}(A) \to \mathbf{F}(B)$ *satisfying* $\mathbf{F}(F) \circ \mathbf{F}(G) = \mathbf{F}(F \circ G) = \mathbf{F}(id_A) = id_{\mathbf{F}(A)}$. *Hence, any functor preserves isomorphisms.*

When three relations F, G and H form a commutative triangle in $\boldsymbol{C}$ with $F = G \circ H$, we have $\mathbf{F}(F) = \mathbf{F}(G \circ H) = \mathbf{F}(G) \circ \mathbf{F}(H)$. Hence, $\mathbf{F}(F), \mathbf{F}(G)$ and $\mathbf{F}(H)$ also forms a commutative triangle.

(2)Given the relation $F : A \to B$, and two relations G, H from the object C to the object A in $\boldsymbol{C}$, if $\mathbf{F}(F)$ is a monic relation, then $F \circ G = F \circ H$ implies $\mathbf{F}(F) \circ \mathbf{F}(G) = \mathbf{F}(F) \circ \mathbf{F}(H) \Rightarrow \mathbf{F}(G) = \mathbf{F}(H)$. Since $\mathbf{F}$ is a faithful functor, we have $G = H$. On the other hand, given the relation $F : A \to B$, and two relations G, H from the object B to the object C in $\boldsymbol{C}$, if $\mathbf{F}(F)$ is a epic relation, then $G \circ F = H \circ F$ implies $\mathbf{F}(G) \circ \mathbf{F}(F) = \mathbf{F}(H) \circ \mathbf{F}(F) \Rightarrow \mathbf{F}(G) = \mathbf{F}(H)$. Since $\mathbf{F}$ is a faithful functor, we also have $G = H$.

When three relations F, G and H form a commutative triangle in $\boldsymbol{D}$ with $\mathbf{F}(F) = \mathbf{F}(G) \circ \mathbf{F}(H)$, we have $F = G \circ H$ in $\boldsymbol{C}$. Therefore, $\mathbf{F}$ reflects a commutative triangle.

(3) A relation F is given from the object A to B with left inverse for $\mathbf{F}(F)$, then there is a relation G' from the object $\mathbf{F}(B)$ to the $\mathbf{F}(A)$ with $G' \circ \mathbf{F}(F) = id_{\mathbf{F}(A)} = \mathbf{F}(id_A)$. Since the functor $\boldsymbol{F}$ is full, there is a relation G from object B to A such that $\mathbf{F}(G) = G'$. We then have $\mathbf{G} \circ \mathbf{F} = \mathbf{F}(id_A)$, which implies $G \circ F = id_A$ due to the faithful functor $\boldsymbol{F}$. Therefore, the functor preserves the left inverse for the relation F.

On the other hand, if a relation F is given from the object A to B with right inverse for $\mathbf{F}(F)$, then there is a relation G' from the object $\mathbf{F}(B)$ to the $\mathbf{F}(A)$ with $\mathbf{F}(F) \circ G' = id_{\mathbf{F}(B)} = \mathbf{F}(id_B)$. Since the functor $\boldsymbol{F}$ is full, there is a relation G from object B to A such that $\mathbf{F}(G) = G'$. We then have $\mathbf{F} \circ \mathbf{G} = \mathbf{F}(id_B)$, which implies $F \circ G = id_B$ because of the faithful functor $\boldsymbol{F}$. Hence, the functor also preserves the right inverse for the relation F. In conclusion, the functor $\boldsymbol{F}$ reflects the isomorphic relations.

(4)Let $F : A \to B$ and G', H' be two relations from an object D in the invengory $\boldsymbol{D}$ to the object $\mathbf{F}(A)$. Since the functor $\boldsymbol{F}$ is dense, we always can find an object C in the invengory $\boldsymbol{C}$ and an isomorphism $J : \mathbf{F}(C) \to D$ in $\boldsymbol{D}$. Hence, we can obtain G, H from the object C to the object A in $\boldsymbol{C}$ with $\mathbf{F}(G) = G' \circ J$ and $\mathbf{F}(H) = H' \circ J$.

Let us assume that F is a monic relation in C, since we have

$$\mathbf{F}(F) \circ G' = \mathbf{F}(F) \circ H'$$

$$\Rightarrow \mathbf{F}(F) \circ G' \circ J = \mathbf{F}(F) \circ H' \circ J$$

$$\Rightarrow \mathbf{F}(F) \circ \mathbf{F}(G) = \mathbf{F}(F) \circ \mathbf{F}(H) \text{(From above paragraph.)}$$

$$\Rightarrow F \circ G = F \circ H \text{(From faithful functor.)}$$

$$\Rightarrow G = H \text{(From monic relation of } F.)$$

$$\Rightarrow G' \circ J = \mathbf{F}(G) = \mathbf{F}(H) = H' \circ J$$

$$\Rightarrow G' = H' \quad\quad\quad (6.2.13)$$

Hence, $\mathbf{F}$ preserves monic relations. On the other hand, if we assume that F is a epic relation in C, then we have

$$G' \circ \mathbf{F}(F) = H' \circ \mathbf{F}(F)$$

$$\Rightarrow J \circ G' \circ \mathbf{F}(F) = J \circ H' \circ \mathbf{F}(F)$$

$$\Rightarrow \mathbf{F}(G) \circ \mathbf{F}(F) = \mathbf{F}(H) \circ \mathbf{F}(F) \text{(From the duality.)}$$

$$\Rightarrow G \circ F = H \circ F \text{(From faithful functor.)}$$

$$\Rightarrow G = H \text{(From epic relation of } F.)$$

$$\Rightarrow J \circ G' = \mathbf{F}(G) = \mathbf{F}(H) = J \circ H'$$

$$\Rightarrow G' = H' \quad\quad\quad (6.2.14)$$

Therefore, $\mathbf{F}$ also preserves epic relations.

At this status, we move our attention to a structure-preserving relation between functors. Given two functors $\mathbf{F} : \mathbf{C} \to \mathbf{D}$ and $\mathbf{G} : \mathbf{C} \to \mathbf{D}$, we define a relation Ψ_A from the object $\mathbf{F}(A)$ to the object $\mathbf{G}(A)$ with respect to the object A in the invengory $\mathbf{C}$. To ensure that the structure of functor $\mathbf{F}$ is preserved by this map, we need that, for each relation $F : A \to B$ in $\mathbf{C}$, the transformations Ψ_A and Ψ_B take the endpoints of the relation $\mathbf{F}(F)$ to the endpoints of the relation $\mathbf{G}(F)$. The definition of a *natural transformation* (a structure-preserving relation between functors) is provided as:

Definition 18 *Let $\mathbf{C}$ and $\mathbf{D}$ be invengories and let $\mathbf{F}$ and $\mathbf{G}$ be two functors from $\mathbf{C}$ to $\mathbf{D}$. A natural transformation Ψ from the functor $\mathbf{F}$ to the functor $\mathbf{G}$ is a relation that assigns to* *every **C**-object A a **D**-relation Ψ_A ($\Psi_A = \bowtie_{i=1}^{I_A} \psi_{A,i}$ if such relation can be by several but finite functions.) such that for any **C**-relation $F : A \to B (F = \bowtie_{k=1}^{I_F} f_k)$ the following diagram commutes in **D** with respect to all indices i, j and k when codomain $\psi_{A,i}$ equals to the domain $\mathbf{G}(f_k)$ and codomain $\mathbf{F}(f_k)$ equals to the domain $\psi_{B,j}$:*

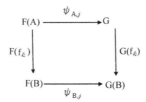

Figure 6.12: The diagram commutes in **D** with respect to all indices i, j and k.

*Moreover, if Ψ_A is an isomorphic relation in **D** for every object A, then Ψ is called a natural isomorphism.*

For any functor **F**, the elements of the identify natural transformation ι are the identity relations of the objects in the range of **F**, that is, $\iota_A = id_{\mathbf{F}(A)}$. Actually, ι is a natural isomorphism. Facts like "Every group is naturally isomorphic to its opposite group" teem in mathematics. We will explain such similar facts by the natural isomorphism of group functors. Consider the invengory **Grp** of all groups with group homomorphisms as relations. If $(G, *)$ is a group, we define its opposite group $(G^{op}, *^{op})$ as follows: G^{op} is the same set as G, and the operation $*^{op}$ is defined as $a *^{op} b = b * a$. Forming the opposite group is a functor from **Grp** to **Grp** by defining $f^{op} = f$, where $f : G \to H$. Note that f^{op} is indeed a group homomorphism from G^{op} to H^{op} since $f^{op}(a *^{op} b) = f(b * a) = f(b) * f(a) = f^{op}(a) *^{op} f^{op}(b)$. By setting the isomorphism $\psi_G : G \to G^{op}$ for every group G and $\psi_G(a) = a^{-1}$, we have $\psi_G(a * b) = a^{-1} *^{op} a^{-1} = \psi_G(a) *^{op} \psi_G(b)$. Hence, the function ψ_G is a homomorphism. Moreover, given an element a in G and the isomorphism $\psi_H : H \to H^{op}$, we have $(f(a))^{-1} = f(a^{-1}) = f^{op}(a^{-1})$, i.e., $\psi_H \circ f = f^{op} \circ \psi_G$. This shows that the identity functor $\mathbf{Id_{Grp}} : \mathbf{Grp} \to \mathbf{Grp}$ is naturally isomorphic to the opposite functor $\mathbf{Op_{Grp}} : \mathbf{Grp} \to \mathbf{Grp}$.

Let $\mathcal{R}_S$ be the function that reverses a finite list $FL(S)$. For instance, $\mathcal{R}_S[2, 3, 4] = [4, 3, 2]$. For a set homomorphism $f : S \to T$, we have $\mathcal{R}_T \circ FL(f) = FL(f) \circ \mathcal{R}_S$. This shows that $\mathcal{R}$ is a natural transformation for functors between two invengories of **Set**.

6.2.5 Set-Valued Functor

We have discussed issues about invention approaches by actions in Chap. IV. In this section, we will show that actions can be interpreted by invengorical language through *set-valued functor*-the main topic of this section. The advantage of using set-valued functors to describe actions is that one can consider more structure on sets to be acted. Let a set-valued functor as $\mathbf{F} : \mathbf{C} \to \mathbf{Set}$, the objects of $\mathbf{C}$ form a space, called a *perspective space*, for the variation of the set being acted. We can think that each object of $\mathbf{C}$ is a perspective, that the set being acted will be different from different perspectives, and the relations of $\mathbf{C}$ are changes in perspectives.

Another reason for us to study set-valued functors is enable us to understand structure of an abstract invengory. A *representable functor* is a special functor from an arbitrary invengory into the invengory of sets. Such functors give representations of an abstract invengory in terms of familiar structures, sets and functions between sets.

Finite State Machines: Set-Valued Functors from Monoidal Invengory

In this section, we will describe finite state machines (FSM) in terms of set-valued functors. We begin by defining an algebraic structure, *monoid*. A monoid is a set, M, together with a binary operation $\cdot$ that satisfies the following three rules:

- Closure: For all a, b in M, the result of the operation $a \cdot b$ is also in M.

- Associativity: For all a, b and c in M, the equation $(a \cdot b) \cdot c = a \cdot (b \cdot c)$ holds.

- Identity element: There exists an element id in M, such that for all elements a in M, the equation $id \cdot a = a \cdot id = a$ holds.

Let M be a monoid with identity id and let S be a set. A monoid action of M on S is a function $\omega : M \times S \to S$ for which

- Identity action: $\omega(id, s) = s$ for all $s \in S$.

- Compositive action: $\omega(mn, s) = \omega(m, \omega(n, s))$ for all $m, n \in M$ and $s \in S$.

Finite state machines (FSM) are adopted to solve a large number of problems in science and engineering. For instance, electronic design automation, communication protocol design, programming language parsing design and other engineering applications. In biology and artificial intelligence research, FSM are also used to describe neurological systems and logical thinking procedure. By corresponding the set M as the set of tokens or action behaviors and the set S as the set of states, the monid action is a finite state machine with the transition function $\omega : M \times S \to S$. By treating a monoid M as an invengory, denoted as $\mathbf{C}_M$, through setting the only object as M and relations of $\mathbf{C}_M$ as the elements of M, the monoid action ω can induce a functor $\mathbf{F}_\omega : \mathbf{C}_M \to \mathbf{Set}$ satisfying:

- $\mathbf{F}_\omega(M) = S$.

- $\mathbf{F}_\omega(m) = (s \to \omega(m, s))$ for $m \in M$ and $s \in S$.

This interpretation by functors will allow us to generalize actions by monoids to actions by invengories.

Generalized Finite State Machine: Set-Valued Functors from Observable Invengory

In addition to the state space S, there is an observation space which characterizes measurable or observable properties of each state. A generalized FSM consists of an observable space $\mathbf{O}$ with a function, denoted as ω, from $\mathbf{O}$ to the state space S satisfying $\omega(o) = s$, and for each mapping relation $f : o \to o$ for $o, o' \in \mathbf{O}$, there is a function $\omega(o) \to \omega(o')$ corresponding to $\omega(f)$.

For instance, a hidden Markov model (HMM) is a statistical Markov model where the system being modeled is assumed to be a Markov process with unobserved (hidden) states [37]. In a normal Markov model, the state is directly visible to the observer, and therefore the state transition probabilities are the only parameters. In a hidden Markov model, the state is not directly observable, but the output which depends on the state is observable. Since each state has a probability distribution over the possible output tokens, the sequence of tokens generated by an HMM provides some information about the sequence of states. Hidden Markov models are especially proper to be applied in temporal pattern recognition such as speech, handwriting, gesture recognition, musical score following, partial discharges and bioinformatics.

If the action m acts on three observations, we then replace m by three elements, one for each observation. We can have two indicator functions, namely $\mathfrak{M}$ and $\mathfrak{OU}$, to represent input and output functions from the set M to the set $\mathbf{O}$ for which $\mathfrak{M}(m)$ are the observable elements that m acts and $\mathfrak{OU}(m)$ are the observable elements of $m(s)$ for s with the observable elements $\mathfrak{M}(m)$.

The set $\mathbf{O}$ is composed by observable elements and we define an invengory $\mathbf{C}$ with objects as elements of $\mathbf{O}$ and relations as actions, collected by the set M, to the observable element. We then define a set-valued functor $\mathbf{F} \colon \mathbf{C} \to \mathbf{Set}$ (sets of state spaces) as $\mathbf{F}(o) = \{s \in S | \text{The observation of } s \text{ is } t\}$. If m is a function of M with input and output observable elements o and o', respectively. Then we have $\mathbf{F}(m)$ as mapping relation $\mathbf{F}(o) \to \mathbf{F}(o')$. Suppose $s \in S$ has observable element t and $m, m' \in M$ have input observable elements o, o', respectively, and output observable elements o', o'', respectively, then we have $m'(m(s)) = (m' \circ m)(s)$ and $id_{\mathbf{O}}(s) = s$. Hence, the functor $\mathbf{F}$ preserves composition and identity. The above statements about the set-valued functor $\mathbf{F} \colon \mathbf{C} \to \mathbf{Set}$ are exact about the principle of a generalized FSM.

Representable functors

For an arbitrary invengory $\mathbf{C}$, the functors from $\mathbf{C}$ to $\mathbf{Set}$ are crucial because the hom functors $\mathbf{Hom}(C, -)$ (will be introduced soon) for each object C in $\mathbf{C}$ are set-valued functor. The concept of using representable functors to study a general invengory by set-valued functors is the main theme of this section. The definition about hom functors will come first.

Let $\mathbf{C}$ be an invengory with object C and relation $F \colon A \to B$. The relation from $\mathbf{Hom}(C, A)$ (all relations from the objects C to A) to $\mathbf{Hom}(C, B)$ (all relations from the objects C to B) is defined as $\mathbf{Hom}(C, F)$ by

$\mathbf{Hom}(C, F)(G) = F \circ G$ for $\forall G \in \mathbf{Hom}(C, A)$. Such relation enables us to define the *hom* functor with respect to the object C, denoted by $\mathbf{Hom}(C, -) \colon \mathbf{C} \to \mathbf{Set}$, as follows:

- Objects mapping: $\mathbf{Hom}(C, -)(A) = \mathbf{Hom}(C, A)$ for each object A of $\mathbf{C}$.

- Relations mapping: $\mathbf{Hom}(C, -)(F) = \mathbf{Hom}(C, F) \colon \mathbf{Hom}(C, A), \to \mathbf{Hom}(C, B)$ for each relation $F \colon A \to B$ in the invengory $\mathbf{C}$.

For an object A, $\mathbf{Hom}(C, id_A) \colon \mathbf{Hom}(C, A) \to \mathbf{Hom}(C, A)$ takes identity relation $F \colon A \to A$ to $id_A \circ F = F$. Moreover, given two relations $F \colon A \to B$ ($F = \bowtie_{i=1}^{I_F} f_i$) and $G \colon B \to C$ ($G = \bowtie_{j=1}^{I_G} g_j$), we have following derivations for any relation $H \colon C \to A$ ($H = \bowtie_{k=1}^{I_H} h_k$)

$$
\begin{aligned}
(\mathbf{Hom}(C, g_j) \circ \mathbf{Hom}(C, f_i))(h_k) &= \mathbf{Hom}(C, g_j)(\mathbf{Hom}(C, f_i)(h_k)) \\
&= \mathbf{Hom}(C, g_j)(f_i \circ h_k) \\
&= g_j \circ (f_i \circ h_k) \\
&= (g_j \circ f_i) \circ h_k, \text{association of relations composition} \\
&= \mathbf{Hom}(C, g_j \circ f_i)(h_k), \qquad\qquad (6.2.15)
\end{aligned}
$$

with respect to all indices i, j and k. Therefore, $\mathbf{Hom}(C, -)$ is a functor.

A functor from an invengory **C** to the invengory **Set** is said to be *representable* if it is naturally isomorphic to a hom functor. A functor is naturally isomorphic to **Hom**$(C, -)$ for some object C in **C**. We say that C *represents* the functor. Let us consider a simple example about representing the set-of-nodes functor by the graph with one node and no edges.

Example 33 *Let **Graph** be the invengory of graphs and **F** be a functor from **Graph** to **Set**. We also take a simple graph with one node $\mathfrak{N}$ without any edges and call such graph as G_1. Let V defined as **Hom**$(G_1, -)$ be a hom functor based on the invengory **Graph**. Then we can define a mapping α between functors **F** and **V** as*

$$\alpha : \mathcal{G}(f) \to f_0(\mathfrak{N}), \tag{6.2.16}$$

*where $\mathcal{G}$ is any graph in **Graph**, f is a graph homomorphism from G_1 to $\mathcal{G}$ and f_0 is the homomorphism for sets (nodes) from G_1 to $\mathcal{G}$. We claim that α is a natural transformation. For each graph homomorphism $g : \mathcal{G}_1 \to \mathcal{G}_2$, the following diagram*

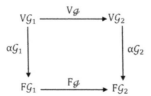

Figure 6.13: Commutative diagram.

commutes. This is true since

$$(\alpha\mathcal{G}_2 \circ \mathbf{Hom}(G_1, g))(f) = \alpha\mathcal{G}_2(g \circ f) = (g \circ f)_0(G_1) = g_0(f_0(\mathfrak{N}))$$

$$= \mathbf{F}g(f_0(\mathfrak{N})) = (\mathbf{F}g \circ \alpha\mathcal{G}_1)(f). \tag{6.2.17}$$

This example shows that a graph homomorphism from the graph G_1 to an arbitrary graph $\mathcal{G}$ is determined by the image of G_1 to any node of $\mathcal{G}$. Hence, nodes of $\mathcal{G}$ are exact the same things to graph homomorphisms from G_1 to $\mathcal{G}$.

Let $\mathbf{C}$ be an invengory, we define a functor $\mathbf{\Upsilon}$ from the invengory $\mathbf{C}^{op}$ to the invengory of set-valued functors $\mathbf{SVF}\ (\mathbf{C}, \mathbf{Set})$ as follows

- For an object C in $\mathbf{C}$, $\mathbf{\Upsilon}(C) = \mathbf{Hom}(C, -)$.

- For a relation $F : C \to D$ in $\mathbf{C}$, $\mathbf{\Upsilon}(F) : \mathbf{Hom}(D, -) \to \mathbf{Hom}(C, -)$. If we have another relation $G : D \to A$ in $\mathbf{C}$, following conditions should be satisfied for all indices i and j:

$$[\mathbf{\Upsilon}(f_i)A](g_j) = g_j \circ f_i, \tag{6.2.18}$$

where $F = \bowtie_{i=1}^{I_F} f_i$ and $G = \bowtie_{j=1}^{I_G} g_j$.

Actually, $\mathbf{\Upsilon}(F)$ is a natural transformation by verifying the commutativity for every relation $G : A \to B(G = \bowtie_{j=1}^{I_G} g_j)$ of the following diagram:

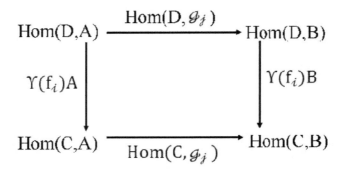

Figure 6.14: Commutative diagram.

For any relation $H : D \to A(H = \bowtie_{k=1}^{I_H} h_k)$ at the upper-left corner, the upper-right route has $(g_j \circ h_k) \circ f_i$. Moreover, the lower-left route has $g_j \circ (h_k \circ f_i)$. Since $(g_j \circ h_k) \circ f_i = g_j \circ (h_k \circ f_i)$ for all indices i, j and k due to associativity, $\mathbf{\Upsilon}(F)$ is a natural transformation.

Following theorem is provided about the functor $\mathbf{\Upsilon}$.

Theorem 13 *The functor* $\mathbf{\Upsilon} : \mathbf{C} \to \mathbf{SVF}(\mathbf{C}, \mathbf{Set})$ *is a full and faithful functor.*

PROOF. 15 *For* $\mathbf{\Upsilon}(F)D : \mathbf{Hom}(D, D) \to \mathbf{Hom}(C, D)$, *it takes* id_D *to* F. *Similarly, for another relation* $G : C \to D$, *the natural transformation* $\mathbf{\Upsilon}(G)$ *at* D *will bring* id_D *to* G. *If* $F \neq G$, *we must have* $\mathbf{\Upsilon}(F)D \neq \mathbf{\Upsilon}(G)D$. *Hence,* $\mathbf{\Upsilon}(F) \neq \mathbf{\Upsilon}(G)$, *which shows the faithfulness of* $\mathbf{\Upsilon}$.

Given $\alpha : \mathbf{Hom}(D, -) \to \mathbf{Hom}(C, -)$, *we define the relation at* $\mathbf{C}$ *from the object* C *to the object* D *as* $F = \alpha D(id_D)$, *where* $\alpha D : \mathbf{Hom}(D, D) \to \mathbf{Hom}(C, D)$. *Moreover, if* $H : D \to A$ *is an relation in* $\mathbf{C}$, *then we have* $\alpha A(H) = H \circ F$ *as a relation from the object* C *to the object* A *due to the naturality of* α. *This shows the fullness of the functor* $\mathbf{\Upsilon}$.

Given a set-valued functor $\mathbf{F} : \mathbf{C} \to \mathbf{Set}$ and a $\mathbf{C}$-object C, an element at the set $\mathbf{F}(C)$, denoted as $\hat{c}$, can induce a natural transformation from the functor $\mathbf{Hom}(C, -)$ to the functor $\mathbf{F}$ by

$$F \to \mathbf{F}(F)(\hat{c}). \tag{6.2.19}$$

The following theorem is provided to construct the correspondence relation between elements of $\mathbf{F}(C)$ and natural transformations from the functor $\mathbf{Hom}(C, -)$ to the functor $\mathbf{F}$.

Theorem 14 *There is a bijective correspondence between natural transformation $\alpha : \mathbf{Hom}(C, -) \to$ $\mathbf{SVF}(\mathbf{C}, \mathbf{Set})$ and elements of $\mathbf{F}(C)$ if following conditions are satisfied: for any two relation $F : X \to Y (F =\bowtie_{i=1}^{I_F} f_i)$ and $G : C \to X (G =\bowtie_{j=1}^{I_G} g_j)$ we have*

$$\mathbf{F}(f_i \circ_{\mathbf{C}} g_j) = \mathbf{F}(f_i) \circ_{\mathbf{Set}} \mathbf{F}(g_j) \tag{6.2.20}$$

PROOF. 16 *We define a transformation between the functor $\mathbf{Hom}(C, -)$ and the functor $\mathbf{F}$ associated at $\hat{c}$, an element of $\mathbf{F}(C)$, by*

$$\Phi_X(\hat{c})(G) : \mathbf{Hom}(C, X) \to \mathbf{F}(G)(\hat{c}), \text{where } G \in \mathbf{Hom}(C, X) . \tag{6.2.21}$$

For two relations F and G as $F : X \to Y (F =\bowtie_{i=1}^{I_F} f_i)$ and $G : C \to X (G =\bowtie_{j=1}^{I_G} g_j)$, then we have the following diagram with respect to each indices i and j

$$
\begin{array}{ccc}
& \mathbf{Hom}(C, f_i) & \\
\mathbf{Hom}(C, X) & \rightrightarrows & \mathbf{Hom}(C, Y) \\
\Phi_X(\hat{c}) \downarrow & & \Phi_Y(\hat{c}) \downarrow \\
\mathbf{F}(X) & \underset{\mathbf{F}(f_i)}{\longrightarrow} & \mathbf{F}(Y)
\end{array}
\tag{6.2.22}
$$

By starting at the upper-left side of the diagram, we have

$$
\begin{aligned}
\Phi_Y(\hat{c})(\mathbf{Hom}(C, f_i)(g_j)) &= \Phi_Y(\hat{c})(f_i \circ_{\mathbf{C}} g_j) \\
&= \mathbf{F}(f_i \circ_{\mathbf{C}} g_j)(\hat{c}) \\
&= \mathbf{F}(f_i) \circ_{\mathbf{Set}} \mathbf{F}(g_j) \quad \textit{From Eq. (6.2.20)} \\
&= \mathbf{F}(f_i)(\mathbf{F}(g_j)(\hat{c})) \\
&= \mathbf{F}(f_i)(\Phi_X(\hat{c})(g_j)).
\end{aligned}
\tag{6.2.23}
$$

This shows the commutativity of the diagram provided by Eq. (6.2.22). Hence, the transformation $\Phi(\hat{c})$ is natural.

To show the bijective correspondence, we have to show that $\Phi_X(\alpha(id_C)) = \alpha_X$, where $\alpha_X :$ $\mathbf{Hom}(C, X) \to \mathbf{SVF}(\mathbf{C}, \mathbf{Set})$. From the naturality of α, we have the following diagram with *respect to each index i:*

$$\mathbf{Hom}(C,C) \overset{\mathbf{Hom}(C,g_j)}{\Longrightarrow} \mathbf{Hom}(C,X)$$

$$\alpha_C \downarrow \qquad\qquad \alpha_X \downarrow$$

$$\mathbf{F}(C) \underset{\mathbf{F}(g_j)}{\overrightarrow{}} \mathbf{F}(X) \qquad\qquad (6.2.24)$$

Then, we have

$$
\begin{aligned}
(\Phi_X(\alpha(id_C)))(g_j) &= \mathbf{F}(g_j)(\alpha_C(id_C)) \\
&= (\mathbf{F}(g_j)\alpha_C)(id_C) \\
&= (\alpha_X \mathbf{Hom}(C,g_j))(id_C) \\
&= \alpha_X(g_j). \qquad\qquad (6.2.25)
\end{aligned}
$$

Therefore, the bijective correspondence is proved.

6.2.6 Universal Property

An *universal construction* indicates a class of objects and relations that share a common property and selects out the objects that are terminal (or initial) when this class is considered as an invengory. Universal properties occur ubiquitously at various branches in mathematics. By understanding their abstract properties, one obtains information about all these constructions and can save time in performing each individual instance with the same invengorical structure. The other motivation for us to study universal properties is to construct *adjoint functors*, that is the main topic to be discussed at the next section.

Given two invengories $\mathbf{C}$ and $\mathbf{D}$ and a functor $\mathbf{F}$ from the invengory $\mathbf{C}$ to the invengory $\mathbf{D}$, an *initial relation* from X (an object of $\mathbf{D}$) to the functor $\mathbf{F}$ is an initial object in the invengory of relations from X to $\mathbf{F}$. More precisely, it consists of a pair (A, Φ), where A is an object of $\mathbf{C}$ and $\Phi(\Phi = \bowtie_{k=1}^{I_\Phi} \phi_k))$ is a relation in $\mathbf{D}$, such that the following *initial property* is satisfied: For any $\mathbf{C}$-object Y and $\mathbf{D}$-relation $G : X \to \mathbf{F}(Y)(G = \bowtie_{i=1}^{I_G} g_i)$, then there exists an unique relation $H : A \to Y(H = \bowtie_{i=1}^{I_H} h_j)$ such that the following diagram commutes with respect to each indices i, j and k:

$$X \overset{\phi_k}{\Longrightarrow} \mathbf{F}(A)$$

$$g_i \searrow \quad \downarrow \mathbf{F}(h_j)$$

$$\mathbf{F}(Y) \qquad\qquad (6.2.26)$$

Similarly, we also can define a *terminal relation* and its *terminal property*. Given two in-vengories $\mathbf{C}$ and $\mathbf{D}$ and a functor $\mathbf{F}$ from the invengory $\mathbf{C}$ to the invengory $\mathbf{D}$, an *terminal relation* from the functor $\mathbf{F}$ to X (an object of $\mathbf{D}$) is a terminal object in the invengory of relations from $\mathbf{F}$ to X. More precisely, it consists of a pair (A, Φ), where A is an object of $\mathbf{C}$ and $\Phi(\Phi =\bowtie_{k=1}^{I_\Phi} \phi_k))$ is a relation in $\mathbf{D}$, such that the following *terminal property* is satisfied: For any $\mathbf{C}$-object Y and $\mathbf{D}$-relation $G : \mathbf{F}(Y) \to X(G =\bowtie_{i=1}^{I_G} g_i)$, then there exists an unique relation $H : Y \to A(H =\bowtie_{i=1}^{I_H} h_j)$ such that the following diagram commutes with respect to each indices i, j and k:

$$
\begin{array}{c}
\mathbf{F}(Y) \\[4pt]
\mathbf{F}(h_j) \downarrow \quad \searrow g_i \\[4pt]
\mathbf{F}(A) \overset{\phi_k}{\Longrightarrow} X
\end{array}
\qquad (6.2.27)
$$

The term *universal relation* indicates either to an initial relation or a terminal relation, and the term *universal property* refers either to an initial property or a terminal property.

Let us consider an example about the product operation of two objects. Given two objects A and B in the invengory $\mathbf{C}$, we define three tuples (X, f_1, f_2), where $f_1 : X \to A$ and $f_2 : X \to B$, as an object. Then we define a mapping, denoted as g, from the object (X, f_1, f_2) to the object (X', f_1', f_2') such that $f_1 = f_1' \circ g$ and $f_2 = f_2' \circ g$. It is easy to verify that objects with the form (X, f_1, f_2) and mappings between such objects with the conditions that g have form an invengory. A terminal object in such invengory, say $(A \times B, \pi_1, \pi_2)$, is one with unique mapping to it from each object (X, f_1, f_2) other then the object $(A \times B, \pi_1, \pi_2)$.

We also can characterize the product operation in terms of terminal properties. By defining the diagonal functor $\Delta : \mathbf{C} \to \mathbf{C} \times \mathbf{C}$ as $\Delta(A) = (A, A)$ and $\Delta(F : A \to B) = (F, F)$, the terminal relation $(A \times B, \pi_1, \pi_2)$ is a mapping from Δ to the object (A, B) of $\mathbf{C} \times \mathbf{C}$.

6.2.7 Adjoints

In mathematics, adjoint functors are pairs of functors which share a particular relationship, named as *adjunction*, with one another. The notion about adjunction exists everywhere in mathematics, as it rigorously reflects the intuition of efficiency and optimization. An adjoint functor is a way of providing the most efficient construction to some problem via a method which is formulaic, where the meaning of *the most efficient* way is to build a desired construction with no unnecessary extra components. The notion of universal property discussed at the previous chapter is the most proper and rigorous tool to describe this issue. From the optimization perspective, the concept that the functor $\mathbf{F}$ is the most efficient solution to the problem related by the functor $\mathbf{G}$ is equivalent to the notion that $\mathbf{G}$ poses the most difficult problem which $\mathbf{F}$ solves. Based on this fact, we often solve our original optimization problems in their dual forms.

From concepts about universal properties, we can define *adjoint functors*, a pair of functor which satisfy adjunction relation. Suppose (A_1, Φ_1), where $\Phi_1 = \bowtie_{k_1=1}^{I_{\Phi_1}} \phi_{1,k_1}$, is an initial relation from X_1 to the functor $\mathbf{F}$ and (A_2, Φ_2), where $\Phi_2 = \bowtie_{k_2=1}^{I_{\Phi_2}} \phi_{2,k_2}$, is an initial relation from X_2 to the functor $\mathbf{F}$. By the initial property, given any relation $F : X_1 \to X_2 (F = \bowtie_{i=1}^{I_F} f_i)$, there exists a unique relation $G : A_1 \to A_2 (G = \bowtie_{j=1}^{I_G} g_j)$ such that the following diagram commutes with respect to indices k_1, k_2, i and j:

$$
\begin{array}{ccc}
 & \phi_{1,k_1} & \\
X_1 & \Longrightarrow & \mathbf{F}(A_1) \\
f_i \downarrow & & \downarrow \ \mathbf{F}(g_j) \\
 & \phi_{2,k_2} & \\
X_2 & \Longrightarrow & \mathbf{F}(A_2)
\end{array}
\tag{6.2.28}
$$

If every object X_i of $\mathbf{C}$ has an initial relation to $\mathbf{F}$, then the assignment $X_i \to A_i$ and $F \to G$ defines a functor $\mathbf{G}$ from the invengory $\mathbf{C}$ to the invengory $\mathbf{D}$. The pair of functors $(\mathbf{F}, \mathbf{G})$ are then a pair of adjoint functors, with $\mathbf{G}$ left-adjoint to $\mathbf{F}$ and $\mathbf{F}$ right-adjoint to $\mathbf{G}$.

Formally, the left-adjoint and the right-adjoint functors are defined as follows:

Definition 19 *A functor* $\mathbf{F} : \mathbf{C} \longleftarrow \mathbf{D}$ *is a left adjoint functor if for each object* X *in* $\mathbf{C}$, *there exists a terminal relation from* $\mathbf{F}$ *to* X. *Similarly, a functor* $\mathbf{G} : \mathbf{C} \longrightarrow \mathbf{D}$ *is a right adjoint functor if for each object* Y *in* $\mathbf{D}$, *there exists an initial morphism from* Y *to* $\mathbf{G}$.

Following example is given to illustrate the notions about adjoint functors. Let **Integer** and **Real** are two order invengories with respect to integers and real numbers. The inclusion from the invengory **Integer** to the invengory **Real** forms a functor, denoted as $\mathbf{F}$. The ceiling functor, denoted as $\mathbf{G}$, which takes each real number $r \in \mathbb{R}$ to the smallest integer greater than or equal to r. Since the universal property of $\mathbf{F}(\lceil r \rceil)$ in the diagram of Eq. (6.2.26) corresponds to the "smallest integer" definition of a ceiling function, the functor $\mathbf{F}$ and the functor $\mathbf{G}$ are adjoint functors.

In the rest part of this section, we will discuss the relationship between the knowledge development or representation and machines to implement such knowledge development or representation. By applying the language of invengory, we show that any knowledge development or representation described a directed graph can be implemented by a minimal finite state machine (FSM). The meaning of " *minimal*" is a way of providing the construction of a FSM with no unnecessary extra components but with desired behaviors. Such construction is characterized by the adjunction relation between the invengory of knowledge development or representation and the invengory of FSMs.

Various directed-graph models have been suggested to describe the specification and analysis of computer systems or knowledge structures in terms of both hardware and software [38]. A directed graph DG is a set V of vertices and a set E of edges (f) with a pair of functions $E \rightrightarrows V$ such that

$$E \overset{\partial_d}{\underset{\partial_c}{\rightrightarrows}} V, \tag{6.2.29}$$

where the $\partial_d f$ = initial vertex of f and the $\partial_c f$ = final vertex of f. A morphism $\zeta : DG \to DG'$ of graphs is a pair of functions $\zeta_V : V \to V'$ and $\zeta_E : E \to E'$ such that

$$\zeta_V \partial_d f = \partial_d \zeta_E f, \text{ and } \zeta_V \partial_c f = \partial_c \zeta_E f. \tag{6.2.30}$$

These functions, with their composition, and these objects (vertices of a directed graph) form an invengory of directed graph, denoted as **D-Graph**.

Behaviors can be defined as the actions of a system or organism, usually in relation to its environment, which includes the other systems or organisms. Behaviors are the response of the system or organism to various stimuli or inputs, whether internal or external, conscious or subconscious, and voluntary or involuntary. Behaviors can be associated to conceptual structures characterized by directed graphs according to ontological perspectives.

In the sequel, we will construct an invengory of behaviors. A *behavior* is defined as a surjective relation $F : \Sigma^* \to \Gamma$ (object), where Σ and Γ represent the input set and output set, respectively, and Σ^* is the free monoid generated by Σ. The relation of behaviors $F \to F'$ is a pair of relation $[A, C]$, where $A : \Sigma \to \Sigma'$ and $C : \Gamma \to \Gamma'$, such that we have the following commutative diagram:

$$
\begin{array}{ccc}
\Sigma^* & \overset{F}{\rightsquigarrow} & \Gamma \\
\downarrow A^* & & \downarrow C \\
\Sigma'^* & \overset{F'}{\rightsquigarrow} & \Gamma'
\end{array}
\tag{6.2.31}
$$

Behaviors and their relations form an invengory under component-wise composition, denoted as **Behaviors**.

A finite state machine, denoted as FSM, is a six-tuples $\langle \Sigma, S, \Gamma, \delta, \lambda, s_0 \rangle$, where Σ, S and Γ are input, state and output sets, respectively. $\delta : \Sigma \times S \to S$ and $\lambda : S \to \Gamma$ represent transition and output functions. $s_0 \in S$ is the initial state. Moreover, we also require that the relation $\bar{\delta} : \Sigma^* \to S$ is a surjective relation. A relation $FSM \to FSM'$ of finite state machines is a triple $[A, B, C]$ of relations, $A : \Sigma \to \Sigma$, $B : S \to S'$, and $C : \Gamma \to \Gamma'$ such that $B(s_0) = s_0'$, and the following commutative diagrams:

$$
\begin{array}{ccc}
\Sigma \times S & \overset{\delta}{\Longrightarrow} & S \\
A \times B \downarrow & & \downarrow \\
\Sigma' \times S' & \overset{\delta'}{\Longrightarrow} & S'
\end{array}
\tag{6.2.32}
$$

and

$$
\begin{array}{ccc}
S & \overset{\lambda}{\Longrightarrow} & \Gamma \\
B \downarrow & & \downarrow C \\
S' & \overset{\lambda'}{\Longrightarrow} & \Gamma'
\end{array}
\tag{6.2.33}
$$

If objects are composed by FSM and relations are $FSM \to FSM'$, then we have an invengory of finite state machines, denoted as **FSM**, under component-wise composition of $[A, B, C]$.

When three invengories **D-Graph**, **Behaviors** and **FSM** are defined, we have the following theorem about realizing concept structures described by directed graphs through a minimal FSM. The proof of this theorem is based on the condition that all relations are functions, however, the proof procedure can be extended easily by considering relations instead of functions.

Theorem 15 *Any directed conceptual graph can be minimal realized by a FSM, i.e., there exist an adjoint pair of functors between the invengory **D-Graph** and the invengory **FSM**.*

PROOF. 17 *The proof consists of three parts: the first part is to show the adjoint functors exist between invengories **D-Graph** and **Behaviors**; the second part is to show the adjoint functors exist between invengories **Behaviors** and **FSM**; the last part is to show the composition of adjoint functors is still an adjoint functor pair. We begin by the first part.*

*Every invengory **Behaviors** determines an underling directed graph invengory **D-Graph** by treating objects in **Behaviors** as vertices in **D-Graph** and forgetting (omitting) those relations in **Behaviors** which are identities and composites. Such determination by forgetting some existing* mathematical structures can be characterized by a special functor, named as a forgetful functor. On the other hand, any directed graph can be used to generate an invengory **Behaviors** on the same set of V of objects; the relations of this invengory will be the strings of composable functions of **D-Graph**. Therefore, a relation of **Behaviors** from the object A to the object B can be delineated by a path from A to B, consisting of successive functions (arrows) of **D-Graph**. Such **Behaviors** invengory is generated by the directed graph freely.

Let $DG = \{E \rightrightarrows V\}$ be a directed graph, then there is an invengory **Behaviors** with V as set of behaviors (objects) and a morphism $P : DG \to U_{\textbf{Behaviors}}$ of graphs, where $U_{\textbf{Behaviors}}$ is the underlying graph of the invengory **Behaviors**. We claim that the morphism P satisfies the following property. Given any invengory $\textbf{C}$ and any graph morphism $\mu : DG \to U_{\textbf{C}}$, there is an unique functor $\mu' : \textbf{Behaviors} \to \textbf{C}$ with $U_{\mu'} \circ P = \mu$, where $U_{\mu'}$ is the graph morphism from the underlying directed graph $U_{\textbf{Behaviors}}$ to the underlying directed graph $U_{\textbf{C}}$.

We treat the objects of **Behaviors** to be those vertices of DG and the arrows of **Behaviors** to be the finite paths:

$$F_1 \overset{f_1}{\Longrightarrow} F_2 \overset{f_2}{\Longrightarrow} F_3 \longrightarrow \cdots \overset{f_{n-1}}{\Longrightarrow} F_n \tag{6.2.34}$$

composed of n objects (behaviors) of DG connected by $n-1$ arrows $f_i : F_i \longrightarrow F_{i+1}$ of DG. For each such finite length path as an arrow

$\langle F_1, f_1, \cdots, f_{n-1}, F_n \rangle : F_1 \to F_n$ in **Behaviors**, the composition of two paths is defined as juxtaposition by identifying the common end. This composition is associative and every path of length $n > 1$ is a composite of strings of length 2. The morphism $P : DG \to U_{\textbf{Behaviors}}$ of directed graphs sends each arrow $f_1 : F_1 \to F_2$ of the given graph DG to the path $\langle F_1, f_1, F_2 \rangle$ of length 2. If the functor μ' is defined as $\mu'(F) = \mu(F)$ on objects and $\mu'\langle F_1, f_1, F_2 \rangle = \mu f_1$ on arrows, then we have

$$\mu'\langle F_1, f_1, F_2, \cdots, f_{n-1}, F_n \rangle = \mu f_1 \circ \cdots \mu f_{n-1}. \tag{6.2.35}$$

Moreover, such definition of μ' makes the identity $U_{\mu'} \circ P = \mu$ hold. Since the morphism P satisfies universal property discussed in Sec. 6.2.6, we have functor $\textbf{F}_{Behaviors} : \textbf{D-Graph} \to \textbf{Behaviors}$ which is left adjoint to the forgetful functor $\textbf{U} : \textbf{Behaviors} \to \textbf{D-Graph}$.

We will begin to present the adjointness for functors between invengories **Behaviors** and **FSM**.

Given FSM and morphism $[A, B, C]$ from FSM to FSM', we define a mapping from the invengory **FSM** to the invengory **Behaviors** by mapping each object FSM to the behavior F :

$\Sigma^* \to \Gamma$ and mapping each morphism $[A, B, C]$ to $[A, C]$, i.e., $\mathbf{F}_{MB}([A, B, C]) = [A, C]$. Such mapping is a functor since this preserves the composition from concatenation of commutative square in Eq. (6.2.31). This functor is denoted as $\mathbf{F}_{M,B}$.

We first define an equivalence relation for inputs $w, v \in \Sigma^*$ with respect to the behavior F, denoted as $w \equiv_F v$, if $F(uw) = F(uv)$ for all $u \in \Sigma^*$. A new state space S_F is defined as $\Sigma^* / \equiv_F$, where elements of S_F are equivalent classes $[w]_F$ for $w \in \Sigma^*$. The new transition and output functions related to S_F, renamed as δ_F and λ_F, become $\delta_F(x, [w]_F) = [wx]_F$ and $\lambda_F([w]_F) = F(w)$. Then we can define a mapping from the invengory **Behaviors** to the invengory **FSM** by mapping each behavior $F : \Sigma^* \to \Gamma$ (object) to the finite state machine $FSM : \langle \Sigma, S_F, \Gamma, \delta_F, \lambda_F, s_{F,0} \rangle$, where $s_{F,0}$ is the equivalent class for the empty word. For morphism $[A, C] : F \to F'$, it is mapped to $[A, B, C]$ by setting $B[w]_F = [A^*(w)]'_F$. Since $B(s_{F,0}) = s_{F',0}$, $B \circ \delta_F = \delta_{F'} \circ (A \times B)$ and $C \circ \lambda_F = \lambda_{F'} \circ B$, the morphism $[A, B, C]$ is a morphism between two FSMs. From the component-wise of compositions with respect to A, B and C, the above mapping from the invengory **Behaviors** to the invengory **FSM** is a functor, denoted as $\mathbf{F}_{B,M}$.

Let $1_{\mathbf{FSM}}$ be the identity functor of the invengory **FSM**, we claim that the transformation, denoted as η_{BM}, from the functor $1_{\mathbf{FSM}}$ to the functor $\mathbf{F}_{B,M}\mathbf{F}_{M,B}$ is natural. This is to show that the

$$
\begin{array}{ccc}
& \eta_{BM}FSM & \\
FSM & \overset{}{\rightrightarrows} & \mathbf{F}_{B,M}\mathbf{F}_{M,B}(FSM) \\
[A, B, C] \downarrow & & \downarrow \mathbf{F}_{B,M}\mathbf{F}_{M,B}([A, B, C]) \\
& \eta_{BM}FSM' & \\
FSM' & \overset{}{\rightrightarrows} & \mathbf{F}_{B,M}\mathbf{F}_{M,B}(FSM')
\end{array}
\tag{6.2.36}
$$

commutes. Since the input and output components are not changed by $\mathbf{F}_{B,M}$ and $\mathbf{F}_{M,B}$, we only need to verify that the diagram

$$
\begin{array}{ccc}
& /\equiv_F & \\
S & \overset{}{\rightrightarrows} & S_F \\
B \downarrow & & \downarrow B' \\
& /\equiv_{F'} & \\
S' & \overset{}{\rightrightarrows} & S_{F'}
\end{array}
\tag{6.2.37}
$$

commutes. However, this is true due to $B'[w]_F = [A^*(w)]'_F$ from the definition of mapping $\mathbf{F}_{B,M}([A, C]) = [A, B, C]$. This shows that the transformation η is natural. From Theorem 14, we have $\eta_{BM}(FSM)$ universal with respect to each FSM in **FSM** from FSM to $\mathbf{F}_{B,M}$. Hence, the functor $\mathbf{F}_{B,M}$ and the functor $\mathbf{F}_{M,B}$ are an adjoint pair.

From previous two constructed adjunctions:

$$\langle \mathbf{F}_{Behaviors}, \mathbf{U}, \eta_{DB}, \epsilon_{DB} \rangle : \textbf{\textit{D-Graph}} \rightarrow \textbf{\textit{Behaviors}}$$

$$\langle \mathbf{F}_{B,M}, \mathbf{F}_{M,B}, \eta_{BM}, \epsilon_{BM} \rangle : \textbf{\textit{Behaviors}} \rightarrow \textbf{\textit{FSM}} \tag{6.2.38}$$

*where η_{DB} and ϵ_{DB} are unit and co-unit for the adjoint functors $\mathbf{F}_{Behaviors}$ and $\mathbf{U}$, similarly., η_{BM} and ϵ_{BM} are unit and co-unit for the adjoint functors $\mathbf{F}_{B,M}$ and $\mathbf{F}_{M,B}$. By the functors composition, such two adjunctions have the following isomorphic relations for $DG \in$ **D-Graph** and $FSM \in$ **FSM***

$$\textbf{\textit{D-Graph}}(DG, \mathbf{U} \circ \mathbf{F}_{M,B}(FSM)) \cong$$

$$\textbf{\textit{Behaviors}}(\mathbf{F}_{Behaviors}(DG), \mathbf{F}_{M,B}(FSM)) \cong$$

$$\textbf{\textit{FSM}}(\mathbf{F}_{B,M} \circ \mathbf{F}_{Behaviors}(DG), FSM). \tag{6.2.39}$$

This makes the composite functor $\mathbf{F}_{B,M} \circ \mathbf{F}_{Behaviors}$ left adjoint to the composite functor $\mathbf{U} \circ \mathbf{F}_{M,B}$. From the following composite relation

$$DG \overset{\eta_{DB}(DG)}{\Longrightarrow} \mathbf{U} \circ \mathbf{F}_{Behaviors}(DG) \overset{\mathbf{U} \circ \eta_{BM} \circ \mathbf{F}_{Behaviors}(DG)}{\Longrightarrow}$$

$$\mathbf{U} \circ \mathbf{F}_{M,B} \circ \mathbf{F}_{B,M} \circ \mathbf{F}_{Behaviors}(DG), \tag{6.2.40}$$

we have unit $\mathbf{U} \circ \eta_{BM} \circ \mathbf{F}_{Behaviors} \circ \eta_{DB}$ for the adjoint functors $\mathbf{F}_{B,M} \circ \mathbf{F}_{Behaviors}$ and $\mathbf{U} \circ \mathbf{F}_{M,B}$. Dually, the co-unit for the adjoint functors $\mathbf{F}_{B,M} \circ \mathbf{F}_{Behaviors}$ and $\mathbf{U} \circ \mathbf{F}_{M,B}$ will be $\epsilon_{BM} \circ \mathbf{F}_{B,M} \circ \epsilon_{DB} \circ \mathbf{F}_{M,B}$.

*Since we have found an adjoint pair of functors between the invengory **D-Graph** and the invengory **FSM**, any directed conceptual graph can be minimal realized by a FSM.*

6.3 Examples of Analogies

Example 34 *Utilizing analogy is helpful for us to understand other abstract concepts from known knowledge and familiar experiences. Hence, it has been proved that adopting analogy in science eduction will obtain great learning effects [39].*

For elementary students, it is not easy for them to acquire the notion about electricity. However, it is easier for elementary students to see pumpers to pump water and feel the strength of water current. The functor to analog the objects and relations of the invengory of an electricity system to the objects and relations of the invengory of a water pumping system. The following table is presented to characterize such functor.

an electricity system (invengory)	a water pumping system (invengory)
electric current	water current
cables	water pipes
batteries (voltages)	pumpers (kgw/m^2)
bulbs (brightness)	mill wheels (Revolutions Per Minute, RPM)
batteries connected to cables	pumpers connected to water pipes
bulbs connected to cables	mill wheels connected to water pipes

The second to the fifth rows indicate the objects correspondence between the invengory of an electricity system and the invengory of a water pumping system. The last two rows show the relations among objects.

From Table 34, various electrical concepts can be understood from a water pumping system. We list some of them below.

- If pumpers are arranged serially, the water pressure becomes larger and it makes the water current larger and mill wheels with higher RPM. $\implies$ If batteries are arranged serially, the voltage becomes larger and it makes the electric current larger and bubbles more bright.

- If pumpers are arranged parallelly, the water pressure is not changed and it makes the water current and RPM of mill wheels stay the same. $\implies$ If batteries are arranged parallelly, the voltage is not changed and it makes the electric current and bubbles' brightness stay the same.

- If water mills are arranged serially, the water pressure becomes smaller at each water mill and it makes the water current smaller and mill wheels with lower RPM. $\implies$ If light bulbs are arranged serially, the voltage becomes smaller at each light bulb and it makes the electric current smaller and bubbles less bright.

- If water mills are arranged parallelly, the water pressure is the same at each water mill and it makes the water current be the same at each water mill with same RPM. $\implies$ If light bulbs are arranged parallelly, the voltage is the same at each light bulb and it makes the electric current be the same at each light bulb with same brightness.

- *If water pipes are arranged parallelly, the water current can still exist if any one of these parallel pipes get stuck. $\implies$ If cables are arranged parallelly, the electric current can still exist if any one of these parallel cables get broken.*

- *If water pipes are arranged serially, there is no water current if any one of these serial pipes get stuck. $\implies$ If cables are arranged serially, there is no electric current if any one of these serial cables get broken.*

Fig. 6.15 shows the analog correspondence between water system and electricity for series connection.

Figure 6.15: Analog comparison between lamps and waterwheels for series connection.

Example 35 *There are finite number of regulations, however, there are infinite personal matters. It is quite impossible to have statue laws that can govern all personal matters. A legal loophole is a weakness or exception that allows a law system to be circumvented without the explanations and validation from current laws. Loopholes are searched for and used strategically by persons with evil intentions in a variety of circumstances, including taxes, business, politics, the criminal justice system, or in breaches of security. Once a legal loophole is discovered, one has to complement such legal loophole. The most popular way to complement a legal loophole is through analogy by reasoning out the law effect from known cases. Different from criminal laws, in which crimes are defined by statue laws, civil laws focus at regulating private legal relations. Hence, judges have some rights to complement legal loopholes in dealing with civil cases.*

The operation of analogy in legal cases may involve the following steps: The first step is to find out weather there are common constitutive requirements existing in current laws and the arguing case. If the arguing case has common and (or) similar constitutive requirements with current laws, then we apply related articles to deal such arguing cases. If there are no common and (or) similar constitutive requirements between current laws and the arguing case, then we may try to legislate some articles about this arguing case according to equitable principle.

We can model an arguing case (or current articles related to such case) by an invengory. An invengory **C** *consists of*

- *a class of constitutive requirements (objects);*

- *a class of relations between constitutive requirements;*

- *for every three constitutive requirements a, b and c with relations $f : a \longrightarrow b$ and $g : b \longrightarrow c$, a composition of relations, denoted as $g \circ f$, which associates the constitutive requirement a to the constitutive requirement c;*

such that the associativity and identity axioms hold. Based on such invengorical structure, the logical structure about applying analogy in law can be described as:

1. $\exists\, S\ (M_1, M_2, \cdots, M_n; f_1, f_2, \cdots, f_k) \vdash \{L_i\}$;

2. $\exists\, T\ (M_1', M_2', \cdots, M_n'; f_1', f_2', \cdots, f_k')$;

3. $\because F(M_j) = M_j'$, for $1 \leq j \leq n$ and $F(f_j) = f_j'$, for $1 \leq j \leq k$;

4. $\therefore \exists\, T\ (M_1', M_2', \cdots, M_n'; f_1', f_2', \cdots, f_k') \vdash \{L_i\}$.

The corresponding explanations for above logical structure are: 1. An existing case S is composed by n legal elements $M_1, M_2, \cdots, M_n$ with k relations among these n legal elements. Such case has been dealt with or judged according to a set of articles $\{L_i\}$. 2. We assume that the arguing case T is composed by n legal elements $M'_1, M'_2, \cdots, M'_n$ with k relations among these n legal elements. 3. We find an identical or similar correspondence between the invengory for the case S and the invengory for the case T through the functor F. 4. Therefore, the arguing case T can also be regulated by articles $\{L_i\}$.

In this arguing case, the contractor has right to demand a part of the remuneration that corresponds to the work performed and reimbursement of those expenses if the work is destroyed or becomes impracticable as the result of a defect in the materials supplied by the customer or as the result of an instruction given by the customer for the carrying out of the work before acceptance without a circumstance for which the contractor is responsible contributing to this. This argument is based on the section 645 of German civil code.

The Section 645 of German civil code is regulated as: (1) If the work, before acceptance, is destroyed or deteriorates or becomes impracticable as the result of a defect in the materials supplied by the customer or as the result of an instruction given by the customer for the carrying out of the work, without a circumstance for which the contractor is responsible contributing to this, then the contractor may demand a part of the remuneration that corresponds to the work performed and reimbursement of those expenses not included in the remuneration. The same applies if the contract is canceled under section 643. (2) A more extensive liability of the customer for fault is unaffected.

We provided the following two examples, adopted from [40], about applying analogy to judge new cases with respect to the occurrence time of events. The first case is about the accused asked the plaintiff to build a granary on the farm belonged to the accused. However, the accused moved some fodder into the granary before the complete construction of the granary and this fodder introduced a fire to burn and destroy the whole granary because such fodder was not sun-baked carefully. The plaintiff then initiated a lawsuit to request reimbursement of those expenses used for the partial construction of the granary. BGH judged this case by asking the accused to responsible for those expenses used for the construction of the granary according to the Section 645. Because the accused moved incomplete dried fodder into the granary before the complete construction of the granary and such behavior is belonged to the case that the work, before acceptance, is destroyed as the result of an instruction given by the customer for the carrying out of the work through the analogical inference from the first part of the Section 645.

The second case is about divorce due to one party of a couple betraying his (her) country. According to the Article 1052 of Taiwan civil code, one reason for the husband or the wife to request the court for a judical decree of divorce is that he or she abuses the other party as to render common living intolerable. The meaning for "intolerable common living" indicates that the husband or the wife cannot tolerate the pain physically and (or) psychologically. According to legal precedents No. 7545 at AC. 1948 and No. 1433 at AC. 1956, they both considered that the collaboration with the enemy by one party of a couple will induce intolerable common living conditions. Hence, the other parties of couples in legal precedents are allowed to request the court for a judical decree of divorce based on analogy from the Article 1052.

Whenever legal loopholes are found, a sound legal system has to complete such legal loopholes. Analogy, limit of purpose, extension of purpose and establishment new laws are basic ways to complete legal loopholes. Analogy, limit of purpose and extension of purpose are three methods to complete loopholes in current stature laws and legal precedents. To establish new laws is a way to complete loopholes by preparing new legal articles since the arguing case cannot be judged from current stature laws and legal precedents through analogy, restriction of purpose and extension of purpose. According to the number of legal precedents, analogy can also be classified as single-analogy if there is only one legal precedent used for analogy and multiple-analogy if there are many legal precedents used for analogy. The single-analogy uses only one legal precedent to derive the law effect for the arguing case analogically. Such operation likes the functor operation of an ordinary invengory (the main content of this chapter). The multiple-analogy utilizes many legal principles to derive the law effect for the arguing case from many precedents. Such operation will like the functor operation of multi-invengory, the main topic of next chapter.

The law is a kind of culture phenomenon. O. W. Holmes believed that judges cannot derive the final law effect logically without assessing various values from current social scenarios [41]. Although analogy itself has strict logical steps to derive out the law effect of the arguing case, we expect that the derivation procedure and the final legal results can match social experiences more tightly. When legislators try to legislate new laws or judges want to find out proper laws to administer justice, those legal results prepared by them are not just the results from their logical concepts but the results from their social and culture experiments. We may say that the law is a kind of social evaluation model utilized to realize social equity developed from social cultures. Analogy is a method, which is belonged to a procedure of legal evaluation, adopted by judges to complete legal loopholes. Hence, the operation of analogy requires the judge to access the similarity between precedents and the arguing case for constitutive requirements based on his (or her) personal experiences and feelings.

In order to complete legal loopholes, analogy is applied to provide legal effects for new arguing cases. Since the judge has to use his (or her) personal experiences to derive out legal effects for new arguing cases by evaluating the similarities between the precedents and the arguing cases, we may consider analogy is a kind of creative recognition activity. Rights will possess their own lives and spirits from a healthy legal system. Analogy is a way to make a legal system more complete by removing legal loopholes according to new recognition from judges.

Figure 6.16: Analogy

Chapter 7

Multi-Analogy by Multi-Invengory

The analogical invention procedure discussed at Chap. VI is named as *single analogy invention* since an analogical relation is constructed with one and exactly one source of objects. Most previous theories about analogy treat single analogy. One most well known type of analogy is the *proportional* analogy introduced by Aristotle, where analogies are indicated in terms of proportions $A : B :: C : D$, or "A is to B as C is to D" in English. For example, the solution for the question about "A rectangle is to a square as an oval is to *what*" is "a circle" under proportional analogy.

However, analogies can be extended to contain more than one analogical sources. A multi-invengory (will be defined formally at Sec. 7.1 later) consists of objects $a_1, a_2, \cdots$, relations $\theta, \phi, \cdots$, a composition operation, and identities, just as the invengory that we introduced at Chap. VI, the difference being that the domain of a relation is not just a single object but a finite sequence of objects. A relation is therefore drawn as

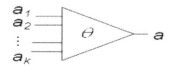

where $k \in \mathbb{N}$, and composition turns a tree of relations into a single relation. For instance, vector spaces and linear maps form an invengory; vector spaces and multi-linear maps form a multi-invengory.

A finite sequence can be treated as a 1-dimensional entity. However, one can consider more complicated structure about objects of sources by forming the input of a relation into a higher-dimensional shape, e.g., a tree, a grid or a composable structure. For each choice of input structure

Γ, there is a class of Γ-**multi-invengories**. A Γ-**multi-invengory** consists of a family of relations whose inputs are of the specified type Γ, together with a rule for composition. Fig. 7.1 shows θ relation for three different Γ input types. If all objects involved in input type Γ are identical, then the Γ-**multi-invengory** becomes a Γ-**plurioperad**.

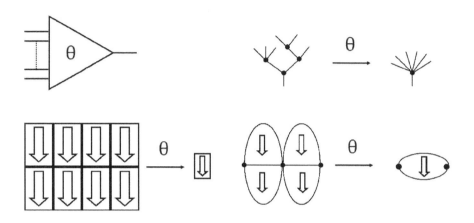

Figure 7.1: Different types of relations.

In Sec. 7.1, concepts about *multiple analogy* and the corresponding mathematical language used to describe multiple analogy are introduced. In Sec. 7.2, we consider the relations between relations, which enable us to characterize the evolution of train of thoughts. The other reason for us to consider relations between relations, or even relations between higher order relations, is that the relation-set between objects A and B has richer mathematical properties. Such mathematical properties help us to classify our creation thoughts geometrically. For instance, if $\mathbf{C}$ is an invengory of chain complexes, then $\mathbf{C}(A, B)$ is an abelian group for chain complexes A and B. Finally, some examples about creating new things according to multiple analogy are presented by Sec. 7.3. We have to show our appreciation to Tom Leinster because his book [42] inspired our works at this Chapter.

7.1   Multi-invengory

In Chap. VI, all relations involved in an invengory are one dimensional arrows from a geometrical perspective, such as

$$A \rightarrow B \rightarrow C \rightarrow D, \tag{7.1.1}$$

209

where A, B, C and D are objects in an invengory. One can image more complex structure for a relation with multiple inputs and outputs, for example,

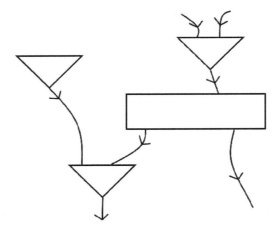

Figure 7.2: More complex input and output relation.

Think of such relation as a box with n inputs and m outputs, where n and m are any two natural numbers. An invengorical structure with relations like this is called a multi-invengory. A very familiar example: the input objects are vector spaces, and the relation are multilinear maps with multiple input vector spaces. The special case of a multi-invengory where there is only one object is called a plurioperad; for a basic example, fix a vector space X and define a mapping with n inputs to be a continuous map $X^n \to X$.

We start with the most simple case of multi-invengories, plain multi-invengory, in Sec. 7.1.1. The multi-invengory with more complicated structure for inputs is discussed in Sec. 7.1.2.

7.1.1 Plain Invengory

We will begin this section by providing the definition about a multi-invengory used to model a multi-analogy thought.

Definition 20 *A multi-invengory* $\mathbf{C}$ *consists of:*

1. *a class* $\mathbf{C}_0$, *whose elements are called the objects of* $\mathbf{C}$.

2. *for each* $n \in \mathbb{N}$ *and* $a_1, \cdots, a_n, a, \in \mathbf{C}_0$, *a set* $\mathbf{C}(a_1, \cdots, a_n; a)$, *whose elements* F *are called relations expressed as*

$$a_1, \cdots, a_n \xrightarrow{F} a$$

3. *for each* $n, i_1, \cdots, i_n \in \mathbb{N}$ *and* $a, a_j, a_{j,k} \in \mathbf{C}_0$, *a function*

$$\mathbf{C}(a_1, \cdots, a_n; a) \times \mathbf{C}(a_{1,1}, \cdots, a_{1,i_1}; a_1) \times \cdots \times \mathbf{C}(a_{n,1}, \cdots, a_{n,i_n}; a_n)$$

$$\longrightarrow \mathbf{C}(a_{1,1}, \cdots, a_{1,i_1}, \cdots, a_{n,1}, \cdots, a_{n,i_n}; a), \qquad (7.1.2)$$

called composition and written as

$$(F, F_1, \cdots, F_n) \longrightarrow F \circ (F_1, \cdots, F_n) \qquad (7.1.3)$$

4. *Associativity. For relations* $F, F_i, F_{i,j} \in \mathbf{C}(a_1, \cdots, a_n; a)$ *decomposed by functions as* $F = \bowtie_{l=1}^{I_F} f_{;l}$, $F_i = \bowtie_{l_i=1}^{I_{F_i}} f_{i;l_i}$, *and* $F_{i,j} = \bowtie_{l_{i,j}=1}^{I_{F_{i,j}}} f_{i,j;l_{i,j}}$, *respectively, they have to satisfy*

$$f_{;l} \circ (f_{1;l_1} \circ (f_{1,1;l_{1,1}}, \cdots, f_{1,i_1;l_{1,i_1}}), \cdots, f_{n;l_n} \circ (f_{n,1;l_{n,1}}, \cdots, f_{n,i_n;l_{n,i_n}})$$

$$= (f_{;l} \circ (f_{1;l_1}, \cdots, f_{n;l_n})) \circ (f_{1,1;l_{1,1}}, \cdots, f_{1,i_1;l_{1,i_1}}, \cdots, f_{n,1;l_{n,1}}, \cdots, f_{n,i_n;l_{n,i_n}}) \qquad (7.1.4)$$

with respect to all indices l, l_i *and* $l_{i,j}$ *such that* dom $f_{;l} = \{ran\ f_{1;l_1}, \cdots, ran\ f_{n;l_n}\}$ *and* dom $f_{k;l_k} = \{ran\ f_{k,1;l_{k,1}}, \cdots, ran\ f_{k,i_k;l_{k,i_k}}\}$ *for* $1 \le k \le n$.

5. *For each object a, an identity relation $id_a : a \to a$ satisfying the following identity law with respect to each index i:*

$$f_i \circ (id_{a_1}, \cdots, id_{a_n}) = f_i = id_a \circ f_i, \tag{7.1.5}$$

where $F : a_1, a_2, \cdots, a_n \to a$ and $F = \bowtie_{i=1}^{I_F} f_i$.

Let us provide the following example about multi-invengory.

Example 36 *This example shows how to compose a beautiful pattern from various regular polygons. If $\mathbf{A}$ is an invengory with finite co-products, then there is a multi-invengory $\mathbf{C}$ with the same objects as $\mathbf{A}$ made by*

$$\mathbf{C}(a_1, \cdots, a_n; a) = A(a_1, a) \times \cdots \times A(a_n, a), \tag{7.1.6}$$

where $a_1, \cdots, a_n, a$ are objects of $\mathbf{A}$. The composition is given by

$$(f_1, \cdots, f_n) \circ ((f_{1,1}, \cdots, f_{1,k_1}), \cdots, (f_{1,n}, \cdots, f_{n,k_n}))$$
$$= (f_1 \circ f_{1,1}, \cdots, f_1 \circ f_{1,k_1}, \cdots, f_n \circ f_{n,1}, \cdots, f_n \circ f_{n,k_n}) \tag{7.1.7}$$

where f_i is a mapping in $\mathbf{A}$ from the object a_i to a and $f_{i,j}$ is also a mapping in $\mathbf{A}$ from the object $a_{i,j}$ to a_i.

For each $d \in \mathbb{N}$, let $B^{[d]} = \{ \mathbf{x} \in \mathbb{R}^\infty | \sum\limits_{n=1}^{\infty} |x_n| \leq 1, \text{ and } x_n \geq 0 \text{ for all } n > d\}$. Moreover, let G be the group of bijections on $\mathbb{R}^2$ of the form $\mathbf{x} \longmapsto \mathbf{b} + \lambda \mathbf{x}$ for some $\mathbf{b} \in \mathbb{R}^2$ and $\lambda > 0$. Then, we have an invengory $\mathbf{A}$ in which the objects are those regular polygons, each object constituted by d-sides regular polygons indicates by the natural number d. The map between the object represented by d' and the object represented by d is an element $\alpha \in G$ such that $\alpha B^{[d']} \subseteq B^{[d]}$

By the constructions for multi-invengory from ordinary invengory suggested by Eqs. (7.1.6) and (7.1.7), there arises a multi-invengory $\mathbf{C}$ with

$$C(d_1, \cdots, d_k; d) = A(d_1, d) \times \cdots \times A(d_k, d). \tag{7.1.8}$$

The desired multi-invengory consisting of the same objects of $\mathbf{C}$ but only those relations $(\alpha_1, \cdots, \alpha_k) \in \mathbf{C}(d_1, \cdots, d_k; d)$ for which the images $\alpha_i B^{[d_i]}$ and $\alpha_j B^{[d_j]}$ are disjoint whenever $i \neq j$. The Fig. 7.3 is an example for map

$$(1, 2, 2, 3) \longrightarrow 1, \tag{7.1.9}$$

where there are one half-pyramid, two pyramids, one octahedron mapped inside a half-pyramid. Note that the four little fractions of regular polygons are disjoint.

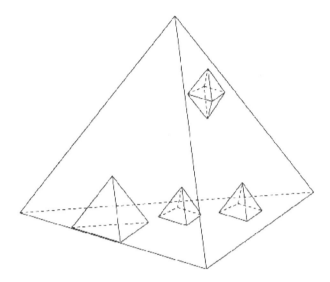

Figure 7.3: The example for map $(1, 2, 2, 3) \longrightarrow 1$.

A *functor* is a structure-preserving of analogical relations between two invengories. By coping similar ideas from functor between two invengories, we define a **multi-functor** for mapping between two multi-invengories as:

Definition 21 *Let* **C** *and* **D** *be two multi-invengories. A* multi-functor $\mathbf{F} : \mathbf{C} \to \mathbf{D}$ *is a map taking each* **C**-*object* a *to a* **D**-*object* $\mathbf{F}(a)$ *and each* **C**-*relation* $F : a_1, \cdots, a_n \to a$, *where* $a_1, \cdots, a_n, a$ *are objects of* **C**, *to a* **D**-*relation* $\mathbf{F}(F) : F(a_1), \cdots, F(a_n) \to F(a)$ *such that*

$$\mathbf{F}(id_a) = id_{\mathbf{F}(a)},$$

$$\mathbf{F}(g_j \circ_{\mathbf{C}} (f_{1;k_1}, \cdots, f_{n;k_n})) = \mathbf{F}(g_j) \circ_{\mathbf{D}} (\mathbf{F}(f_{1,k_1}), \cdots, \mathbf{F}(f_{n,k_n})) \qquad (7.1.10)$$

for all **C**-*objects* $a_1, \cdots, a_n, a$, *all composable* **C**-*relations* $G = \bowtie_{j=1}^{I_G} g_j$ *and* $F_i = \bowtie_{k_i=1}^{I_{F_i}} f_{i;k_i}$ *for* $1 \leq i \leq n$, *and all functions indices* j *and* k_i.

Hence, we can form an invengory of multi-invengories according to multi-functors defined by the above definition.

Monoidal Invengories with One Multiplication

In order to have analogy relations from more than one sources, the most intuitive way is to combine multiple sources of objects. Monoidal invengories play roles with such spirit. A monoidal

213

invengory is an invengory $\mathbf{C}$ equipped with a bi-functor

$$\otimes : \mathbf{C} \times \mathbf{C} \to \mathbf{C} \tag{7.1.11}$$

which is associative and an unit object which is both a left and right identity for $\otimes$. The associative isomorphisms are subject to certain coherence conditions which ensure that any two ways of removing brackets are equal. The ordinary tensor product between vector spaces, abelian groups can be put into the framework of monoidal invengories. Monoidal invengories can be seen as a generalization of these examples.

The definition of a basic monoidal invengory (two invengories at input) is described below.

Definition 22 *A basic monoidal invengory is an invengory $\mathbf{C}$ equipped with a functor $\otimes : \mathbf{C} \times \mathbf{C} \to \mathbf{C}$, an unit object $Id \in \mathbf{C}$, and following isomorphisms*

$$(A \otimes B) \otimes C \overset{\alpha_{A,B,C}}{\Longrightarrow} A \otimes (B \otimes C),$$
$$Id \otimes A \overset{\rho_A}{\Longrightarrow} A,$$
$$A \otimes Id \overset{\lambda_A}{\Longrightarrow} A, \tag{7.1.12}$$

natural with respect to all objects $A, B, C \in \mathbf{C}$.

Moreover, we have following diagrams commutes for all $A, B, C, D \in \mathbf{C}$:

$$((A \otimes B) \otimes C) \otimes D \overset{\alpha_{A \otimes B,C,D}}{\Longrightarrow} (A \otimes B) \otimes (C \otimes D) \overset{\alpha_{A,B,C \otimes D}}{\Longrightarrow} A \otimes (B \otimes (C \otimes D))$$

$$\alpha_{A,B,C} \otimes Id_D \downarrow \qquad\qquad\qquad\qquad\qquad \uparrow Id_A \otimes \alpha_{B,C,D}$$

$$(A \otimes (B \otimes C)) \otimes D \overset{\alpha_{A,B \otimes C,D}}{\Longrightarrow} A \otimes ((B \otimes C) \otimes D)$$

$$(A \otimes Id) \otimes B \overset{\alpha_{A,Id,B}}{\Longrightarrow} A \otimes (Id \otimes B)$$

$$\lambda_A \otimes Id_B \searrow \qquad \swarrow Id_A \otimes \rho_B$$

$$A \otimes B \tag{7.1.13}$$

For maps between basic monoidal invengories, we have the following definition.

Definition 23 *Let $\mathbf{C}$ and $\mathbf{C}'$ be monoidal invengories, a monoidal functor is composed by two elements : a functor $\mathbf{F}$ from $\mathbf{C}$ to $\mathbf{C}'$ and a coherence map ϕ in $\mathbf{C}'$ such that*

$$\mathbf{F}A \otimes' \mathbf{F}B \overset{\phi_{A,B}}{\Longrightarrow} \mathbf{F}(A \otimes B), \quad \phi(Id_{\mathbf{C}'}) = \mathbf{F}(Id_{\mathbf{C}}) \tag{7.1.14}$$

where $\otimes$ and $\otimes'$ are multiplication operations related to invengories $\mathbf{C}$ and $\mathbf{C}'$, respectively.

We also have following diagrams commute for all objects $A, B, C \in \mathbf{C}$.

$$
\begin{array}{ccc}
(\mathbf{F}A \otimes' \mathbf{F}B) \otimes' \mathbf{F}C & \overset{\phi_{A,B} \otimes' Id_{\mathbf{F}C}}{\Longrightarrow} \mathbf{F}(A \otimes B) \otimes' \mathbf{F}C \overset{\phi_{A \otimes B, C}}{\Longrightarrow} \mathbf{F}((A \otimes B) \otimes C) \\
\alpha'_{\mathbf{F}A, \mathbf{F}B, \mathbf{F}C} \downarrow & \downarrow \mathbf{F}\alpha_{A,B,C} \\
\mathbf{F}A \otimes' (\mathbf{F}B \otimes' \mathbf{F}C) & \overset{Id_{\mathbf{F}A} \phi_{B,C}}{\Longrightarrow} \mathbf{F}A \otimes' \mathbf{F}(B \otimes C) \overset{\phi_{A, B \otimes C}}{\Longrightarrow} \mathbf{F}(A \otimes (B \otimes C)) \quad (7.1.15)
\end{array}
$$

$$
\begin{array}{ccc}
\mathbf{F}A \otimes' Id_{\mathbf{C}'} & \overset{Id_{\mathbf{F}A} \otimes' \phi}{\Longrightarrow} \mathbf{F}A \otimes' \mathbf{F}(Id_{\mathbf{C}}) \overset{\phi_{A, Id_{\mathbf{C}}}}{\Longrightarrow} \mathbf{F}(A \otimes Id_{\mathbf{C}}) \\
\lambda_{\mathbf{F}A} \downarrow & \downarrow \mathbf{F}\lambda_A \\
\mathbf{F}A & = & \mathbf{F}A \quad (7.1.16)
\end{array}
$$

$$
\begin{array}{ccc}
Id_{\mathbf{C}'} \otimes' \mathbf{F}A & \overset{\phi \otimes' Id_{\mathbf{F}A}}{\Longrightarrow} \mathbf{F}(Id_{\mathbf{C}}) \otimes' \mathbf{F}A \overset{\phi_{Id_{\mathbf{C}}, A}}{\Longrightarrow} \mathbf{F}(Id_{\mathbf{C}} \otimes A) \\
\rho_{\mathbf{F}A} \downarrow & \downarrow \mathbf{F}\rho_A \\
\mathbf{F}A & = & \mathbf{F}A \quad (7.1.17)
\end{array}
$$

From Definitions 22 and 23, we can form an invengory of basic monoidal invengories, denoted as **2-MonInv**.

The number of input invengories of a basic monoidal invengory is two. The following two definitions are presented to construct a monoidal invengory with n input invengories.

Definition 24 *A n-monoidal invengory* $\mathbf{C}$ *consists of*

- *an invengory* $\mathbf{C}$ *and a functor* $\mathbf{F}_n : \mathbf{C}^n \to \mathbf{C}$ *with respect to each integer* $n \in \mathbb{N}$.

- *For each* $n, p_1, \cdots, p_n \in \mathbb{N}$ *and two-folds sequence* $((a_{1,1}, \cdots, a_{1,p_1}), \cdots, (a_{n,1}, \cdots, a_{n,p_n}))$ *of objects of* $\mathbf{C}$, *we have a map*

$$
\alpha_{((a_{1,1}, \cdots, a_{1,p_1}), \cdots, (a_{n,1}, \cdots, a_{n,p_n}))} : ((a_{1,1} \otimes, \cdots, \otimes a_{1,p_1}) \otimes, \cdots, \otimes (a_{n,1}, \cdots, \otimes a_{n,p_n}))
$$
$$
\longrightarrow (a_{1,1} \otimes, \cdots, \otimes a_{1,p_1} \otimes, \cdots, \otimes a_{n,1} \otimes, \cdots, \otimes a_{n,p_n}). \quad (7.1.18)
$$

The above mappings satisfy the following properties:

- $\alpha_{((a_{1,1}, \cdots, a_{1,p_1}), \cdots, (a_{n,1}, \cdots, a_{n,p_n}))}$ *is natural with respect to each* $a_{i,j}$.

- *associativity: for any $n, l_i, m_{i,j} \in \mathbb{N}$ and three-folds of objects $(((a_{i,k,k})_{k=1}^{m_{i,j}})_{j=1}^{l_i})_{i=1}^n$, we have following commutative diagram*

$$
\begin{array}{ccc}
\mathfrak{A} & \overset{\alpha_D}{\rightrightarrows} & \mathfrak{C} \\
{\scriptstyle \alpha_{D_1} \otimes \cdots \otimes \alpha_{D_n}} \downarrow & & \downarrow {\scriptstyle \alpha_{D'}} \\
\mathfrak{B} & \overset{\alpha_{D''}}{\rightrightarrows} & \mathfrak{D}
\end{array}
\tag{7.1.19}
$$

where

$$
\begin{aligned}
\mathfrak{A} &\triangleq (((a_{1,1,1} \otimes \cdots \otimes a_{1,1,m_{1,1}}) \otimes \cdots \otimes (a_{1,l_1,1} \otimes \cdots \otimes a_{1,l_1,m_{1,l_1}})) \otimes \\
&\quad \cdots \otimes ((a_{n,1,1} \otimes \cdots \otimes a_{n,1,m_{n,1}}) \otimes \cdots \otimes (a_{n,l_n,1} \otimes \cdots \otimes a_{n,l_n,m_{n,l_n}}))) \\
\mathfrak{B} &\triangleq ((a_{1,1,1} \otimes \cdots \otimes a_{1,m_1,m_{1,m_1}}) \otimes \cdots \otimes (a_{n,l_1,1} \otimes \cdots \otimes a_{n,l_n,m_{n,l_n}}) \\
\mathfrak{C} &\triangleq (a_{1,1,1} \otimes \cdots \otimes a_{1,1,m_{1,1}}) \otimes \cdots \otimes (a_{n,l_n,1} \otimes \cdots \otimes a_{n,l_n,m_{n,l_n}}) \\
\mathfrak{D} &\triangleq (a_{1,1,1} \otimes \cdots \otimes a_{n,l_n,m_{n,l_n}}),
\end{aligned}
$$

and two-folds sequences

$$
\begin{aligned}
D &\triangleq (((a_{1,1,1}, \cdots, a_{1,1,m_{1,1}}), \cdots, (a_{1,l_1,1}, \cdots, a_{1,l_1,m_{1,l_1}})), \\
&\quad \cdots, ((a_{n,1,1}, \cdots, a_{n,1,m_{n,1}}), \cdots, (a_{n,l_n,1}, \cdots, a_{n,l_n,m_{n,l_n}}))) \\
D' &\triangleq (a_{1,1,1}, \cdots, a_{1,1,m_{1,1}}), \cdots, (a_{n,l_n,1}, \cdots, a_{n,l_n,m_{n,l_n}}) \\
D'' &\triangleq ((a_{1,1,1}, \cdots, a_{1,m_1,m_{1,m_1}}), \cdots, (a_{n,l_1,1}, \cdots, a_{n,l_n,m_{n,l_n}}) \\
D_r &\triangleq ((a_{r,1,1}, \cdots, a_{r,1,m_{r,1}}), \cdots, (a_{r,l_r,1}, \cdots, a_{r,l_r,m_{r,l_r}})) \text{ for } 1 \leq r \leq n.
\end{aligned}
$$

- *identity: for each $n \in \mathbf{N}$ and sequence $(a_1, \cdots, a_n)$ of objects, the following diagrams*

$$
\begin{array}{ccc}
(a_1 \otimes \cdots \otimes a_n) & \overset{Id_{a_1} \otimes \cdots \otimes Id_{a_n}}{\rightrightarrows} & ((a_1) \otimes \cdots \otimes (a_n)) \\
{\scriptstyle =} \downarrow & & \swarrow {\scriptstyle \alpha_{((a_1), \cdots, (a_n))}} \\
(a_1 \otimes \cdots \otimes a_n) & &
\end{array}
\tag{7.1.20}
$$

and

$$
\begin{array}{ccc}
((a_1 \otimes \cdots \otimes a_n)) & \overset{Id_{a_1} \otimes \cdots \otimes a_n}{\leftleftarrows} & (a_1 \otimes \cdots \otimes a_n) \\
{\scriptstyle \alpha_{((a_1, \cdots, a_n))}} \downarrow & & \swarrow {\scriptstyle =} \\
(a_1 \otimes \cdots \otimes a_n) & &
\end{array}
\tag{7.1.21}
$$

commute.

For maps between monoidal invengories with n input invengories, we have the following definition about functors between two monoidal invengories with n input invengories.

Definition 25 *A functor between two monoidal invengories with n input invengories, denoted as $(\mathbf{F}, \phi)$, consists of*

- *a functor $\mathbf{F} : \mathbf{C} \longrightarrow \mathbf{C}'$.*

- *for each $n \in mathbbN$ and sequence $a_1, \cdots, a_n$ of objects of $\mathbf{C}$, we have a map*

$$\phi_{a_1, \cdots, a_n} : (\mathbf{F}a_1 \otimes' \cdots \otimes' \mathbf{F}a_n) \longrightarrow \mathbf{F}(a_1 \otimes \cdots \otimes a_n) \tag{7.1.22}$$

satisfying :

- $\phi_{a_1, \cdots, a_n}$ *is natural in each a_i.*

- *For each $n, p_1, \cdots, p_n \in \mathbb{N}$ and two-folds sequence $((a_{1,1}, \cdots, a_{1,p_1}), \cdots, (a_{n,1}, \cdots, a_{n,p_n}))$ of objects of $\mathbf{C}$, we have the diagram*

$$((\mathbf{F}a_{1,1} \otimes' \cdots \mathbf{F}a_{1,p_1}) \otimes' \cdots (\mathbf{F}a_{n,1} \otimes' \cdots \mathbf{F}a_{n,p_n})) \overset{\alpha_D}{\Longrightarrow} (\mathbf{F}a_{1,1} \otimes' \cdots \mathbf{F}a_{n,p_n})$$

$$\phi_{a_{1,1}, \cdots, a_{1,p_1}} \otimes' \cdots \phi_{a_{n,1}, \cdots, a_{n,p_n}} \downarrow \qquad\qquad \downarrow \phi_{a_{1,1}, \cdots, a_{n,p_n}}$$

$$(\mathbf{F}(a_{1,1} \otimes \cdots a_{1,p_1}) \otimes' \cdots \mathbf{F}(a_{n,1} \otimes \cdots a_{n,p_n}))$$

$$\phi_{((a_{1,1} \otimes, \cdots, a_{1,p_1}), \cdots, (a_{n,1} \otimes, \cdots, a_{n,p_n}))} \downarrow$$

$$\mathbf{F}((a_{1,1} \otimes \cdots a_{1,p_1}) \otimes \cdots (a_{n,1} \otimes \cdots a_{n,p_n})) \quad \overset{\mathbf{F}\alpha_{D'}}{\Longrightarrow} \quad \mathbf{F}(a_{1,1} \otimes \cdots a_{n,p_n}) \tag{7.1.23}$$

commutes, where $D = ((\mathbf{F}a_{1,1}, \cdots \mathbf{F}a_{1,p_1}), \cdots, (\mathbf{F}a_{n,1}, \cdots \mathbf{F}a_{n,p_n}))$ and $D' = ((a_{1,1}, \cdots, a_{1,p_1}), \cdots, (a_{n,1}, \cdots, a_{n,p_n}))$.

From Definitions 24 and 25, we can form a monoidal invengory with n input invengories, denoted as n-**MonInv**.

Monoidal Invengories with m Multiplications

In order to handle more complicated multi-analogy relation for invention, we consider monoidal invengories with multiple multiplication operations. The following definitions are provided to regulate a basic monoidal invengory with m multiplication operations.

Definition 26 *A basic monoidal invengory with m multiplication operations is an invengory* **C** *with the following structure:*

- *There are m distinct multiplications*

$$\circ_1, \circ_2, \cdots, \circ_m : \mathbf{C} \times \mathbf{C} \longrightarrow \mathbf{C} \tag{7.1.24}$$

which are associative and has an object, denoted as 0, which is a unit for all the multiplications.

- *For each pair (i, j, k) such that $1 \leq i < j < k \leq m$, there is a natural transformation*

$$\alpha^{i;j,k}_{A,B,C,D} : (A \circ_i B) \circ_j (C \circ_k D) \longrightarrow (A \circ_j C) \circ_i (B \circ_j D) \tag{7.1.25}$$

where A, B, C, D are objects in **C**. *If we use backward operation to link brackets, there is another natural transformation*

$$\beta^{i;j,k}_{A,B,C,D} : (A \circ_k B) \circ_j (C \circ_i D) \longrightarrow (A \circ_j C) \circ_i (B \circ_j D) \tag{7.1.26}$$

The natural transformations $\alpha^{i;j,k}_{A,B,C,D}$ are subject to the following conditions

- *unit conditions:* $\alpha^{i;j,k}_{A,B,0,0} = \alpha^{i;j,k}_{0,0,A,B} = Id_{A \circ_i B}$, $\alpha^{i;j,k}_{A,0,B,0} = \alpha^{i;j,k}_{0,A,0,B} = Id_{A \circ_j B}$

- *associativity condition I: The following diagram commutes:*

$$
\begin{array}{ccc}
(U \circ_1 V) \circ_2 (W \circ_3 X) \circ_4 (Y \circ_5 Z) & \overset{\alpha^{1;2,3}_{U,V,W,X} \circ_4 Id_{Y \circ_5 Z}}{\Longrightarrow} & ((U \circ_2 W) \circ_1 (V \circ_2 X)) \circ_4 (Y \circ_5 Z) \\
Id_{U \circ_1 V} \circ_2 \alpha^{3;4,5}_{W,X,Y,Z} \downarrow & & \downarrow \alpha^{1;4,5}_{U \circ_2 W, V \circ_2 X, Y, Z} \\
(U \circ_1 V) \circ_2 ((W \circ_4 Y) \circ_3 (X \circ_4 Z)) & \overset{\alpha^{1;2,3}_{U,V,W \circ_4 Y, X \circ_4 Z}}{\Longrightarrow} & (U \circ_2 W \circ_4 Y) \circ_1 (V \circ_2 X \circ_4 Z)
\end{array}
$$

$$\tag{7.1.27}$$

- *associativity condition II: The following diagram commutes:*

$$
\begin{array}{ccc}
(U \circ_1 V \circ_2 W) \circ_3 (X \circ_4 Y \circ_5 Z) & \overset{\alpha^{2;3,5}_{U \circ_1 V, W, X \circ_4 Y, Z}}{\Longrightarrow} & ((U \circ_1 V) \circ_3 (X \circ_4 Y)) \circ_2 (W \circ_3 Z) \\
\alpha^{1;3,4}_{U, V \circ_2 W, X, Y \circ_5 Z} \downarrow & & \downarrow \alpha^{1;3,4}_{U,V,X,Y} \circ_2 Id_{W \circ_3 Z} \\
(U \circ_3 X) \circ_1 ((V \circ_2 W) \circ_3 (Y \circ_5 Z)) & \overset{Id_{U \circ_3 X} \circ_1 \alpha^{2;3,5}_{V,W,Y,Z}}{\Longrightarrow} & (U \circ_3 X) \circ_1 (V \circ_3 Y) \circ_2 (W \circ_3 Z)
\end{array}
$$

$$\tag{7.1.28}$$

The natural transformations $\beta^{i;j,k}_{A,B,C,D}$ are subject to the following conditions

- unit conditions: $\beta^{i;j,k}_{A,B,0,0} = \beta^{i;j,k}_{0,0,A,B} = Id_{A\circ_i B}$, $\beta^{i;j,k}_{A,0,B,0} = \beta^{i;j,k}_{0,A,0,B} = Id_{A\circ_j B}$

- associativity condition I: The following diagram commutes:

$$(U \circ_1 V) \circ_2 (W \circ_3 X) \circ_4 (Y \circ_5 Z) \quad \overset{\beta^{3;1,2}_{U,V,W,X}\circ_4 Id_{Y\circ_5 Z}}{\Longrightarrow} \quad ((U \circ_2 W) \circ_3 (V \circ_2 X)) \circ_4 (Y \circ_5 Z)$$

$$Id_{U\circ_1 V} \circ_2 \beta^{5;4,3}_{W,X,Y,Z} \downarrow \qquad\qquad \downarrow \beta^{5;4,3}_{U\circ_2 W, V\circ_2 X, Y, Z}$$

$$(U \circ_1 V) \circ_2 ((W \circ_4 Y) \circ_5 (X \circ_4 Z)) \quad \overset{\beta^{5;2,1}_{U,V,W\circ_4 Y, X\circ_4 Z}}{\Longrightarrow} \quad (U \circ_2 W \circ_4 Y) \circ_5 (V \circ_2 X \circ_4 Z)$$

$$(7.1.29)$$

- associativity condition II: The following diagram commutes:

$$(U \circ_1 V \circ_2 W) \circ_3 (X \circ_4 Y \circ_5 Z) \quad \overset{\beta^{5;3,2}_{U\circ_1 V, W, X\circ_4 Y, Z}}{\Longrightarrow} \quad ((U \circ_1 V) \circ_3 (X \circ_4 Y)) \circ_5 (W \circ_3 Z)$$

$$\beta^{1;3,4}_{U,V\circ_2 W, X, Y\circ_5 Z} \downarrow \qquad\qquad \downarrow \beta^{4;3,1}_{U,V,X,Y} \circ_5 Id_{W\circ_3 Z}$$

$$(U \circ_3 X) \circ_4 ((V \circ_2 W) \circ_3 (Y \circ_5 Z)) \quad \overset{Id_{U\circ_3 X}\circ_4 \beta^{5;3,2}_{V,W,Y,Z}}{\Longrightarrow} \quad (U \circ_3 X) \circ_4 (V \circ_3 Y) \circ_5 (W \circ_3 Z)$$

$$(7.1.30)$$

The map between two basic monoidal invengories with m multiplication operations is defined as:

Definition 27 *A monoidal functor* $(\mathbf{F}, \lambda_1, \cdots, \lambda_m) : \mathbf{C} \to \mathbf{C}'$ *between two basic monoidal invengories with m multiplication operations consists of a functor* $\mathbf{F} : \mathbf{C} \to \mathbf{C}'$ *such that* $\mathbf{F}(Id_{\mathbf{C}}) = Id_{\mathbf{C}'}$ *together with the following natural transformations with respect to each* $1 \leq i \leq m$

$$\lambda_{i;A,B} : \mathbf{F}(A) \circ_i' \mathbf{F}(B) \longrightarrow \mathbf{F}(A \circ_i B), \qquad (7.1.31)$$

which satisfy the same associativity and unit conditions presented at Definition 26. In addition, the following diagram commutes with respect to $\alpha^{i;j,k}_{A,B,C,D}$

$$(\mathbf{F}(A) \circ_i' \mathbf{F}(B)) \circ_j' (\mathbf{F}(C) \circ_k' \mathbf{F}(D)) \quad \overset{\alpha^{i;j,k}_{\mathbf{F}(A),\mathbf{F}(B),\mathbf{F}(C),\mathbf{F}(D)}}{\Longrightarrow} \quad (\mathbf{F}(A) \circ_j' \mathbf{F}(C)) \circ_i' (\mathbf{F}(B) \circ_j' \mathbf{F}(D))$$

$$\lambda_{i;A,B} \circ_j' \lambda_{k;C,D} \downarrow \qquad\qquad \downarrow \lambda_{j;A,C} \circ_i' \lambda_{j;B,D}$$

$$\mathbf{F}(A \circ_i B) \circ_j' \mathbf{F}(C \circ_k D) \qquad\qquad \mathbf{F}(A \circ_j C) \circ_i' \mathbf{F}(B \circ_j D)$$

$$\lambda_{j;A\circ_i B, C\circ_k D} \downarrow \qquad\qquad \downarrow \lambda_{i;A\circ_j C, B\circ_j D}$$

$$\mathbf{F}((A \circ_i B) \circ j(C \circ_k D)) \quad \overset{\mathbf{F}(\alpha^{i;j,k}_{A,B,C,D})}{\Longrightarrow} \quad \mathbf{F}((A \circ_j C) \circ_i (B \circ_j D)) \quad (7.1.32)$$

Similarly, the following diagram commutes with respect to $\beta^{i;j,k}_{A,B,C,D}$

$$
\begin{array}{ccc}
(\mathbf{F}(A) \circ'_i \mathbf{F}(B)) \circ'_j (\mathbf{F}(C) \circ'_k \mathbf{F}(D)) & \xrightarrow{\beta^{k;j,i}_{\mathbf{F}(A),\mathbf{F}(B),\mathbf{F}(C),\mathbf{F}(D)}} & (\mathbf{F}(A) \circ'_j \mathbf{F}(C)) \circ'_k (\mathbf{F}(B) \circ'_j \mathbf{F}(D)) \\[4pt]
\lambda_{i;A,B} \circ'_j \lambda_{k;C,D} \downarrow & & \downarrow \lambda_{j;A,C} \circ'_k \lambda_{j;B,D} \\[4pt]
\mathbf{F}(A \circ_i B) \circ'_j \mathbf{F}(C \circ_k D) & & \mathbf{F}(A \circ_j C) \circ'_k \mathbf{F}(B \circ_j D) \\[4pt]
\lambda_{j;A \circ_i B, C \circ_k D} \downarrow & & \downarrow \lambda_{i;A \circ_j C, B \circ_j D} \\[4pt]
\mathbf{F}((A \circ_i B) \circ j(C \circ_k D)) & \xrightarrow{\mathbf{F}(\beta^{k;j,i}_{A,B,C,D})} & \mathbf{F}((A \circ_j C) \circ_k (B \circ_j D))
\end{array}
\tag{7.1.33}
$$

From Definitions 26 and 27, we can form an invengory composed by basic monidal invengories with m multiplication operations. We denote such invengory as **2-MonInv-m**

The following definitions are provided to extend a monoidal invengory **2-MonInv-m** with n input invengories and with m multiplication operations.

Definition 28 *A monoidal invengory with n input invengories and with m multiplication operations, represented as* $(\mathbf{C}, \alpha^{i_p;i_1,\cdots,i_n,j})$, *is an invengory $\mathbf{C}$ with the following structure:*

- *There are m distinct multiplications*

$$
\circ_1, \circ_2, \cdots, \circ_m : \mathbf{C}^n \longrightarrow \mathbf{C} \tag{7.1.34}
$$

  which are associative and has an object, denoted as 0, which is a unit for all the multiplications.

- *For each pair $(i_1, \cdots, i_n, j)$ such that $i_1, \cdots, i_n, j$ between 1 and m, there is a natural transformation*

$$
\alpha^{i_p;i_1,\cdots,i_n,j}_{(A_{1,1},\cdots,A_{1,n}),\cdots,(A_{n,1},\cdots,A_{n,n})} : (A_{1,1} \circ_{i_1} \cdots A_{1,n}) \circ_j \cdots (A_{n,1} \circ_{i_n} \cdots, A_{n,n})
$$
$$
\longrightarrow (A_{1,1} \circ_j \cdots A_{n,1}) \circ_{i_p} \cdots (A_{1,n} \circ_j \cdots A_{n,n}) \tag{7.1.35}
$$

  where $A_{i,j}$ are objects in $\mathbf{C}$.

The natural transformations $\alpha^{i_p;i_1,\cdots,i_n,j}_{(A_{1,1},\cdots,A_{1,n}),\cdots,(A_{n,1},\cdots,A_{n,n})}$ *are subject to the following conditions*

- *unit conditions:* $\alpha^{i_p;i_1,\cdots,i_n,j}_{(0,\cdots,0),\cdots,(A_{i_p,1},\cdots,A_{i_p,n}),\cdots,(0,\cdots,0)} = Id_{A_{i_p,1} \circ_{i_p} \cdots, A_{i_p,n}}$ *for any $i_p \in \{1, 2, \cdots, m\}$.*
  $\alpha^{i_p;i_1,\cdots,i_n,j}_{(0,\cdots,A_{1,i_p},\cdots,0),\cdots,(0,\cdots,A_{n,i_p},\cdots,0)} = Id_{A_{1,i_p} \circ_j,\cdots,A_{n,i_p}}$ *for any $i_p \in \{1, 2, \cdots, m\}$.*

- *associativity condition I: The following diagram commutes with respect to $q, r \in \{1, 2, \cdots, m\}$ and i_p (used to link brackets after interchange):*

$$\begin{array}{ccc} & \Theta_{1,1} & \\ \Phi_1 & \Longrightarrow & \Phi_{2,q} \\ & & \\ \Theta_{1,3} \downarrow & & \downarrow \Theta_{2,4} \\ & \Theta_{3,4} & \\ \Phi_{3,r} & \Longrightarrow & \Phi_4 \end{array} \qquad (7.1.36)$$

where

$$\Phi_1 = (A_{1,1} \circ_{i_1} \cdots A_{1,n}) \circ_j \cdots (A_{2n-1,1} \circ_{i_{2n-1}} \cdots A_{2n-1,n}),$$

$$\Phi_{2,q} = (A_{1,1} \circ_{i_1} \cdots A_{1,n}) \circ_j \cdots (A_{q-1,1} \circ_{i_{q-1}} \cdots A_{q-1,n}) \circ_j$$

$$((A_{1,q} \circ_j \cdots A_{n,q}) \circ_{i_p} \cdots (A_{1,n+q-1} \circ_j \cdots A_{n,n+q-1}))$$

$$\circ_j (A_{n+q,1} \circ_{i_{n+q}} \cdots A_{n+q,n}) \circ_j \cdots (A_{2n-1,1} \circ_{i_{2n-1}} \cdots A_{2n-1,n}),$$

$$\Phi_{3,r} = (A_{1,1} \circ_{i_1} \cdots A_{1,n}) \circ_j \cdots (A_{r-1,1} \circ_{i_{r-1}} \cdots A_{r-1,n}) \circ_j$$

$$((A_{1,r} \circ_j \cdots A_{n,r}) \circ_{i_p} \cdots (A_{1,n+r-1} \circ_j \cdots A_{n,n+r-1}))$$

$$\circ_j (A_{n+r,1} \circ_{i_{n+r}} \cdots A_{n+r,n}) \circ_j \cdots (A_{2n-1,1} \circ_{i_{2n-1}} \cdots A_{2n-1,n}),$$

$$\Phi_4 = (A_{1,1} \circ_j \cdots A_{2n-1,1}) \circ_{i_p} \cdots (A_{1,2n-1} \circ_j \cdots A_{2n-1,2n-1}),$$

and

$$\Theta_{1,2} = Id_{(A_{1,1} \circ_{i_1} \cdots A_{1,n}) \circ_j \cdots (A_{q-1,1} \circ_{i_{q-1}} \cdots A_{q-1,n})} \circ_j \alpha^{i_p; i_q, \cdots, i_{n+q-1}, j}_{(A_{q,1}, \cdots, A_{q,n}), \cdots, (A_{n+q-1,1}, \cdots, A_{n+q-1,n})}$$

$$\circ_j Id_{(A_{n+q,1} \circ_{i_{n+q}} \cdots A_{n+q,n}) \circ_j \cdots (A_{2n-1,1} \circ_{i_{2n-1}} \cdots A_{2n-1,n})},$$

$$\Theta_{1,3} = Id_{(A_{1,1} \circ_{i_1} \cdots A_{1,n}) \circ_j \cdots (A_{r-1,1} \circ_{i_{r-1}} \cdots A_{r-1,n})} \circ_j \alpha^{i_p; i_r, \cdots, i_{n+r-1}, j}_{(A_{r,1}, \cdots, A_{r,n}), \cdots, (A_{n+r-1,1}, \cdots, A_{n+r-1,n})}$$

$$\circ_j Id_{(A_{n+r,1} \circ_{i_{n+r}} \cdots A_{n+r,n}) \circ_j \cdots (A_{2n-1,1} \circ_{i_{2n-1}} \cdots A_{2n-1,n})},$$

$$\Theta_{2,4} = \alpha^{i_p; i_1, \cdots, i_{2n-1}, j}_{(A_{1,1}, \cdots, A_{1,n}), \cdots, ((A_{1,q} \circ_j \cdots A_{n,q}), \cdots, (A_{1,n+q-1} \circ_j \cdots A_{n,n+q-1})), \cdots, (A_{2n+1,1}, \cdots, A_{2n+1,n})},$$

$$\Theta_{3,4} = \alpha^{i_p; i_1, \cdots, i_{2n-1}, j}_{(A_{1,1}, \cdots, A_{1,n}), \cdots, ((A_{1,r} \circ_j \cdots A_{n,r}), \cdots, (A_{1,n+r-1} \circ_j \cdots A_{n,n+r-1})), \cdots, (A_{2n+1,1}, \cdots, A_{2n+1,n})}.$$

- *associativity condition II: The following diagram commutes with respect to $q, r \in \{1, 2, \cdots, m\}$ and i_p (used to link brackets after interchange):*

$$
\begin{array}{ccc}
& \Theta_{1,2} & \\
\Phi_1 & \overset{\Theta_{1,2}}{\Longrightarrow} & \Phi_{2,q} \\
\Theta_{1,3} \downarrow & & \downarrow \Theta_{2,4} \\
& \Theta_{3,4} & \\
\Phi_{3,r} & \overset{\Theta_{3,4}}{\Longrightarrow} & \Phi_4
\end{array}
\tag{7.1.37}
$$

where

$$
\Phi_1 = (A_{1,1} \circ_{i_1} \cdots A_{1,2n-1}) \circ_j \cdots (A_{n,1} \circ_{i_n} \cdots A_{n,2n-1}),
$$

$$
\Phi_{2,q} = (A_{1,1} \circ_j \cdots A_{1,n}) \circ_{i_p} \cdots (A_{q-1,1} \circ_j \cdots A_{q-1,n}) \circ_{i_p}
$$
$$
((A_{q,1} \circ_{i_q} \cdots A_{q,n}) \circ_j \cdots (A_{n+q-1,1} \circ_{i_{n+q-1}} \cdots A_{n+q-1,n}))
$$
$$
\circ_{i_p} (A_{n+q,1} \circ_j \cdots A_{n+q,n}) \circ_{i_p} \cdots (A_{2n-1,1} \circ_j \cdots A_{2n-1,n}),
$$

$$
\Phi_{3,r} = (A_{1,1} \circ_j \cdots A_{1,n}) \circ_{i_p} \cdots (A_{r-1,1} \circ_j \cdots A_{r-1,n}) \circ_{i_p}
$$
$$
((A_{r,1} \circ_{i_r} \cdots A_{r,n}) \circ_j \cdots (A_{n+r-1,1} \circ_{i_{n+r-1}} \cdots A_{n+r-1,n}))
$$
$$
\circ_{i_p} (A_{n+r,1} \circ_j \cdots A_{n+r,n}) \circ_{i_p} \cdots (A_{2n-1,1} \circ_j \cdots A_{2n-1,n}),
$$

$$
\Phi_4 = (A_{1,1} \circ_j \cdots A_{1,n}) \circ_{i_p} \cdots (A_{2n-1,1} \circ_j \cdots A_{2n-1,n}),
$$

and

$$
\Theta_{1,2} = \alpha^{i_p; i_1, \cdots, i_n, j}
$$
$$
(A_{1,1}, \cdots, A_{1,n}), \cdots, (A_{q-1,1}, \cdots, A_{q-1,n}), ((A_{q,1} \circ_{i_q} \cdots A_{q,n}), \cdots,
$$
$$
(A_{n+q-1,1} \circ_{i_{n+q-1}} \cdots A_{n+q-1,n})), \cdots, (A_{2n-1,1}, \cdots, A_{2n-1,n})
$$

$$
\Theta_{1,3} = \alpha^{i_p; i_1, \cdots, i_n, j}
$$
$$
(A_{1,1}, \cdots, A_{1,n}), \cdots, (A_{r-1,1}, \cdots, A_{r-1,n}), ((A_{r,1} \circ_{i_r} \cdots A_{r,n}), \cdots,
$$
$$
(A_{n+r-1,1} \circ_{i_{n+r-1}} \cdots A_{n+r-1,n})), \cdots, (A_{2n-1,1}, \cdots, A_{2n-1,n})
$$

$$
\Theta_{2,4} = Id_{(A_{1,1} \circ_j \cdots A_{1,n}) \circ_{i_p} \cdots (A_{q-1,1} \circ_j \cdots A_{q-1,n})} \circ_j \alpha^{i_p; i_q, \cdots, i_{n+q-1}, j}_{(A_{q,1}, \cdots, A_{q,n}), \cdots, (A_{n+q-1,1}, \cdots, A_{n+q-1,n})}
$$
$$
\circ_j Id_{(A_{n+q,1} \circ_j \cdots A_{n+q,n}) \circ_{i_p} \cdots (A_{2n-1,1} \circ_j \cdots A_{2n-1,n})},
$$

$$
\Theta_{3,4} = Id_{(A_{1,1} \circ_j \cdots A_{1,n}) \circ_{i_p} \cdots (A_{r-1,1} \circ_j \cdots A_{r-1,n})} \circ_j \alpha^{i_p; i_r, \cdots, i_{n+r-1}, j}_{(A_{r,1}, \cdots, A_{r,n}), \cdots, (A_{n+r-1,1}, \cdots, A_{n+r-1,n})}
$$
$$
\circ_j Id_{(A_{n+r,1} \circ_j \cdots A_{n+r,n}) \circ_{i_p} \cdots (A_{2n-1,1} \circ_j \cdots A_{2n-1,n})}.
$$

The map between two n-inputs monoidal invengories with m multiplication operations is defined as:

Definition 29 *A monoidal functor* $(\mathbf{F}, \lambda_1, \cdots, \lambda_m) : \mathbf{C} \to \mathbf{C}'$ *between two n-inputs monoidal invengories with m multiplication operations consists of a functor* $\mathbf{F} : \mathbf{C} \to \mathbf{C}'$ *such that* $\mathbf{F}(Id_{\mathbf{C}}) = Id_{\mathbf{C}'}$ *together with the following natural transformations with respect to each* $1 \leq i \leq m$

$$\lambda_{i;A_1,\cdots,A_n} : \mathbf{F}(A_1) \circ_i' \cdots \mathbf{F}(A_n) \longrightarrow \mathbf{F}(A_1 \circ_i \cdots A_n), \tag{7.1.38}$$

which satisfy the same associativity and unit conditions presented at Definition 28. In addition, the following diagram commutes with respect to $\alpha^{i_p;i_1,\cdots,i_n,j}_{(A_{1,1},\cdots A_{1,n})\cdots(A_{n,1},\cdots A_{n,n})}$

$$
\begin{array}{ccc}
 & \Theta_{1,2} & \\
\Phi_1 & \Longrightarrow & \Phi_2 \\
\Theta_{1,3} \downarrow & & \downarrow \Theta_{2,4} \\
\Phi_3 & & \Phi_4 \\
\Theta_{3,5} \downarrow & & \downarrow \Theta_{4,6} \\
 & \Theta_{5,6} & \\
\Phi_5 & \Longrightarrow & \Phi_6
\end{array}
\tag{7.1.39}
$$

$$\Phi_1 = (\mathbf{F}(A_{1,1}) \circ_{i_1}' \cdots \mathbf{F}(A_{1,n})) \circ_j' \cdots (\mathbf{F}(A_{n,1}) \circ_{i_n}' \cdots \mathbf{F}(A_{n,n})),$$

$$\Phi_2 = (\mathbf{F}(A_{1,1}) \circ_j' \cdots \mathbf{F}(A_{n,1})) \circ_{i_p}' \cdots (\mathbf{F}(A_{1,n}) \circ_j' \cdots \mathbf{F}(A_{n,n})),$$

$$\Phi_3 = \mathbf{F}(A_{1,1} \circ_{i_1} \cdots A_{1,n}) \circ_j' \cdots \mathbf{F}(A_{n,1} \circ_{i_n} \cdots A_{n,n}),$$

$$\Phi_4 = \mathbf{F}(A_{1,1} \circ_j \cdots A_{n,1}) \circ_{i_p}' \cdots \mathbf{F}(A_{1,n} \circ_j \cdots A_{n,n}),$$

$$\Phi_5 = \mathbf{F}((A_{1,1} \circ_{i_1} \cdots A_{1,n}) \circ_j \cdots (A_{n,1} \circ_{i_n} \cdots A_{n,n})),$$

$$\Phi_6 = \mathbf{F}((A_{1,1} \circ_j \cdots A_{n,1})) \circ_{i_p} \cdots ((A_{1,n} \circ_j \cdots A_{n,n})),$$

and

$$\Theta_{1,2} = \alpha^{i_p;i_1,\cdots i_n,j}_{(\mathbf{F}(A_{1,1}),\cdots \mathbf{F}(A_{1,n}))\cdots(\mathbf{F}(A_{n,1}),\cdots \mathbf{F}(A_{n,n}))},$$

$$\Theta_{1,3} = \lambda_{i_1, A_{1,1}, \cdots, A_{1,n}} \circ'_j \cdots \lambda_{i_n, A_{n,1}, \cdots, A_{n,n}},$$

$$\Theta_{2,4} = \lambda_{j, A_{1,1}, \cdots, A_{n,1}} \circ'_{i_p} \cdots \lambda_{j, A_{1,n}, \cdots, A_{n,n}},$$

$$\Theta_{3,5} = \lambda_{j, (A_{1,1} \circ_{i_1} \cdots, A_{1,n}), \cdots (A_{n,1} \circ_{i_n} \cdots A_{n,n})},$$

$$\Theta_{4,6} = \lambda_{i_p, (A_{1,1} \circ_j \cdots, A_{1,n}), \cdots (A_{n,1} \circ_j \cdots A_{n,n})},$$

$$\Theta_{5,6} = \mathbf{F}(\alpha^{i_p; i_1, \cdots i_n, j}_{((A_{1,1}), \cdots (A_{1,n})) \cdots ((A_{n,1}), \cdots (A_{n,n}))}).$$

From definitions 28 and 29, we can form an invengory composed by basic monidal invengories with m multiplication operations. We denote such invengory as **n-MonInv-m**

Multi-analogy Realization by Single Analogy

In this section, we will demonstrate that a multi-invengory (multi-analogy) can be constructed from a traditional invengory with the same set of objects if such invengory can form a *monoidal* invengory. We extend basic monoidal invengory definition by allowing more multiplication operations among invengories.

Let Ω be a set of multiplication operations of invengories and $F\Omega(l)$, where l is any nonnegative integer, be a set composed by free composition of trees such that each internal node denotes a multiplication operation in Ω and the final composed tree has l leaves. For example, $F\Omega(3)$ will be

-

, if there is one 3-inputs multiplication operation and one with cascades of 2-inputs multiplication operation.

In the sequel, we will define a Ω-monoidal invengory which is composed by free construction of objects in **n-MonInv-m**. In order to define a Ω-monoidal invengory, we have to present the structure about free multi-invengories. Free structures are the formal origin of various mathematical structure used in invention modeling. A directed multi-graph is a set X_0 together with a relation set $X(a_1, \cdots, a_n; a)$ for each $n \in \mathbb{N}$ and $a_1, \cdots, a_n, a \in X_0$. By forgetting composition and identities, we have a forgetful functor $\mathbf{U}$: multi-invengory $\longrightarrow$ multi-graph. This induces a left adjoint $\mathbf{F}$, the free multi-invengory functor, which can be constructed as follows similar to the relation between a traditional invengory and a directed graph. Let X be a directed multi-graph. The free multi-invengory FX on X has the same objects: $(FX)_0 = X_0$. Its relations are obtained by concatenating of relations (arrows) of X, that is, the relations of FX are generated recursively by the following two rules:

- if $a \in X_0$ then $Id_a \in FX(a; a)$.

- if $\theta \in X(a_1, \cdots, a_n; a)$ and $\theta_1 \in FX(a_{1,1}, \cdots, a^{1,k_1}; a_1), \cdots, \theta_n \in FX(a_{n,1}, \cdots, a^{n,k_n}; a_n)$ then $\theta \circ (\theta_1, \cdots, \theta_n) \in FX(a_{1,1}, \cdots, a_{n,k_n}; a)$.

For instance, the free multi-invengory on the terminal object with n objects is denoted as $\mathrm{TR}(n)$, which is generated recursively by

- $\mathrm{TR}(1)$ has an element $|$.

- if $n, k_1, \cdots, k_n \in \mathbb{N}$ and $\theta_1 \in \mathrm{TR}(k_1), \cdots, \theta_n \in \mathrm{TR}(k_n)$, then $\mathrm{TR}(k_1 + \cdots + k_n)$ has an element $\theta \circ (\theta_1, \cdots, \theta_n)$.

Definition 30 *A Ω-monoidal invengory, represented as $(\mathbf{C}, \mathbf{F}_\tau, \delta)$, consists of*

- *an invengory $\mathbf{C}$*

- *a functor $\mathbf{F}_\tau : \mathbf{C}^l \longrightarrow \mathbf{C}$ for each n and $\tau \in F\Omega(l)$*

- *a natural isomorphism in $\mathbf{C}$*

$$\delta_{\tau,\tau';a_1,\cdots,a_l} : \mathbf{F}_\tau(a_1, \cdots, a_l) \cong \mathbf{F}'_\tau(a_1, \cdots, a_l), \qquad (7.1.40)$$

where $\tau, \tau' \in F\Omega(l)$ and $a_i \in \mathbf{C}$. Such isomorphism satisfies

- $\delta_{\tau',\tau'';a_1,\cdots,a_l} \circ \delta_{\tau,\tau';a_1,\cdots,a_l} = \delta_{\tau,\tau'';a_1,\cdots,a_l}$ *for each* n *and* $\tau,\tau',\tau'' \in F\Omega(l)$

- $\mathbf{F}_{\tau\circ}(\tau_1,\cdots,\tau_l) = (\mathbf{C}^{k_1+\cdots+k_l} \xrightarrow{\mathbf{F}_{\tau_1}\cdots\mathbf{F}_{\tau_l}} \mathbf{C}^l \xrightarrow{\mathbf{F}_{\tau}} \mathbf{C})$ *for all* $l, k_i \in \mathbb{N}, \tau \in F\Omega(l), \tau_i \in$ $F\Omega(k_i)$ *and* $Id_{\mathbf{C}} = \mathbf{F}_|$

- *the diagram*

$$\mathbf{F}_{\tau}(\mathbf{F}_{\tau_1}(a_{1,1},\cdots,a_{1,k_1}),\cdots,\mathbf{F}_{\tau_l}(a_{l,1},\cdots,a_{l,k_l})) = \mathbf{F}_{\tau\circ(\tau_1,\cdots,\tau_l)}(a_{1,1},\cdots,a_{l,k_l})$$

$$\mathbf{F}_{\tau}(\delta_{\tau_1,\tau_1'},\cdots,\delta_{\tau_l,\tau_l'}) \downarrow \qquad\qquad\qquad \downarrow \delta_{\tau\circ(\tau_1,\cdots,\tau_l),\tau'\circ(\tau_1',\cdots,\tau_l')}$$

$$\mathbf{F}_{\tau}(\mathbf{F}_{\tau_1'}(a_{1,1},\cdots,a_{1,k_1}),\cdots,\mathbf{F}_{\tau_l'}(a_{l,1},\cdots,a_{l,k_l}))$$

$$\delta_{\tau,\tau'} \downarrow$$

$$\mathbf{F}_{\tau'}(\mathbf{F}_{\tau_1'}(a_{1,1},\cdots,a_{1,k_1}),\cdots,\mathbf{F}_{\tau_l'}(a_{l,1},\cdots,a_{l,k_l})) = \mathbf{F}_{\tau'\circ(\tau_1',\cdots,\tau_l')}(a_{1,1},\cdots,a_{l,k_l})$$

commutes, for all $l, k_i \in \mathbb{N}, \tau,\tau' \in F\Omega(l), \tau_i,\tau_i' \in F\Omega(k_i)$ *and* $a_{i,j} \in \mathbf{C}$.

A functor between two Ω-monoidal invengories $(\mathbf{G},\pi) : (\mathbf{C},\mathbf{F}_{\tau},\delta) \longrightarrow (\mathbf{C}',\mathbf{F}_{\tau}',\delta)$ is defined as:

Definition 31 *A functor between two* Ω*-monoidal invengories, represented as* $(\mathbf{G},\pi)$*, consists of*

- *a functor* $\mathbf{G} : \mathbf{C} \longrightarrow \mathbf{C}'$

- *a natural map*

$$\pi_{\tau;a_1,\cdots,a_l} : \mathbf{F}_{\tau}'(\mathbf{G}(a_1),\cdots,\mathbf{G}(a_l)) \longrightarrow \mathbf{G}(\mathbf{F}_{\tau}(a_1,\cdots,a_n)), \qquad (7.1.41)$$

for each $l \in \mathbb{N}, \tau \in F\Omega(l), a_i \in \mathbf{C}$ *satisfying*

- *the diagram*

$$\mathbf{F}_{\tau}'(\mathbf{G}(a_1),\cdots,\mathbf{G}(a_l)) \xrightarrow{\delta_{\tau,\tau'}} \mathbf{F}_{\tau'}'(\mathbf{G}(a_1),\cdots,\mathbf{G}(a_l))$$

$$\pi_{\tau;a_1,\cdots,a_l} \downarrow \qquad\qquad \downarrow \pi_{\tau';a_1,\cdots,a_l}$$

$$\mathbf{G}_{\tau}(\mathbf{F}(a_1,\cdots,a_l)) \xrightarrow{\mathbf{G}(\delta_{\tau,\tau'})} \mathbf{G}_{\tau'}(\mathbf{F}(a_1,\cdots,a_l)) \qquad (7.1.42)$$

commutes, for all $l \in \mathbb{N}, \tau,\tau' \in F\Omega(l), a_i \in \mathbf{C}$

− the diagram

$$\mathbf{F}'_\tau(\mathbf{F}'_{\tau_1}(\mathbf{G}(a_{1,1}),.,\mathbf{G}(a_{1,k_1})),.,\mathbf{F}'_{\tau_l}(\mathbf{G}(a_{l,1}),.,\mathbf{G}(a_{l,k_l}))) = \mathbf{F}'_{\tau\circ(\tau_1,.,\tau_l)}(\mathbf{G}(a_{1,1}),.,\mathbf{G}(a_{l,k_l}))$$

$$\mathbf{F}'_\tau(\pi_{\tau_1;a_{1,1},.a_{1,l}},\cdots,\pi_{\tau_n;a_{n,1},.a_{n,l}}) \downarrow \qquad\qquad\qquad\qquad\qquad \downarrow \pi_{\tau\circ(\tau_1,\cdots,\tau_l)}$$

$$\mathbf{F}'_\tau(\mathbf{G}(\mathbf{F}_{\tau_1}(a_{1,1},.a_{1,k_1})),.,\mathbf{G}(\mathbf{F}_{\tau_l}(a_{l,1},.a_{l,k_l})))$$

$$\pi_{\tau;\mathbf{F}_{\tau_1}(a_{1,1},.,a_{1,k_1}),.\mathbf{F}_{\tau_l}(a_{l,1},.,a_{l,k_l})} \downarrow$$

$$\mathbf{G}(\mathbf{F}_\tau(\mathbf{F}_{\tau_1}(a_{1,1},.,a_{1,k_1}),.,\mathbf{F}_{\tau_l}(a_{l,1},.,a_{l,k_l}))) \;=\; \mathbf{G}(\mathbf{F}_{\tau\circ(\tau_1,.,\tau_l)})(a_{1,1},.,a_{l,k_l})$$

commutes, for all $l, k_i \in \mathbb{N}, \tau, \tau' \in F\Omega(l), \tau_i, \tau_i' \in F\Omega(k_i)$ and $a_{i,j} \in \mathbf{C}$.

From definitions 30 and 31, we can form an invengory composed by n-**MonInv**-m freely. We denote such invengory as $\Omega_{n,m}$-**MonInv**. The following theorem is provided to show the equivalence between the invengory $\Omega_{n,m}$-**MonInv** and the invengory n-**MonInv**-m. Hence, any multi-analogy relation with $\Omega_{n,m}$-**MonInv** structure can be constructed from a monoidal invengory n-**MonInv**-m, which is obtained from combining n single-analogy relations by m multiplications.

Theorem 16 *The invengory $\Omega_{n,m}$-**MonInv** is equivalent to the invengory n-**MonInv**-m for $n \geq 2$ and $m \geq 1$.*

PROOF. 18 *A functor $\mathbf{H}$ is defined from the invengory $\Omega_{n,m}$-**MonInv** to the invengory n-**MonInv**-m*

*The first task is to define a functor $\mathbf{H}$ from the invengory $\Omega_{n,m}$-**MonInv**, denoted as $(\mathbf{C},\mathbf{F}_\tau,\delta)$, to the invengory n-**MonInv**-m, denoted as $(\mathbf{C},\alpha^{i_p;i_1,\cdots,i_n,j})$, i.e., $\mathbf{H}: (\mathbf{C},\mathbf{F}_\tau,\delta) \longrightarrow (\mathbf{C},\alpha^{i_p;i_1,\cdots,i_n,j})$.*

*On objects Let $(\mathbf{C},\mathbf{F}_\tau,\delta)$ be an object of $\Omega_{n,m}$-**MonInv**. The invengory n-**MonInv**-m is given by taking the underlying invengory to be $\mathbf{C}$, the n-fold tensor $\mathbf{F}_{\tau_{\circ_k;n}} : \mathbf{C}^n \longrightarrow \mathbf{C}$ to be $\circ_k$, where $\tau_{\circ_k;n}$ is the multiplication structure of n identical invengory $\mathbf{C}$ by the multiplication operation $\circ_k$, and the coherence maps to be*

$$\alpha^{i_p;i_1,\cdots,i_n,j}_{(a_{1,1},.,a_{1,n}),.,(a_{n,1},.,a_{n,n})} = \delta_{\tau_{\circ_j;n}\circ_j(\tau_{\circ_{i_1};n},.,\tau_{\circ_{i_n};n}),\tau_{\circ_j;n}\circ_{i_p}(\tau_{\circ_j;n},.,\tau_{\circ_j;n})}$$

$$: (a_{1,1}\circ_{i_1}\cdots a_{1,n})\circ_j\cdots(a_{n,1}\circ_{i_n}\cdots,a_{n,n}) \longrightarrow$$

$$(a_{1,1}\circ_j\cdots a_{n,1})\circ_{i_p}\cdots(a_{1,n}\circ_j\cdots a_{n,n}). \qquad (7.1.43)$$

*On maps Let $(\mathbf{G},\pi): (\mathbf{C},\mathbf{F}_\tau,\delta) \longrightarrow (\mathbf{C}',\mathbf{F}'_\tau,\delta)$ be a map in $\Omega_{n,m}$-**MonInv**. The functor $\mathbf{H}(\mathbf{G},\pi): \mathbf{H}(\mathbf{C}) \longrightarrow \mathbf{H}(\mathbf{C}')$ is given by taking the same underlying functor $\mathbf{H}$, and by taking the* *coherence map*

$$\pi_{\tau_{\circ_i};n;a_1,\ldots,a_n} : (\mathbf{G}(a_1)\circ_i,\cdots,\circ_i\mathbf{G}(a_n)) \longrightarrow \mathbf{G}(a_1,\cdots,a_n). \qquad (7.1.44)$$

The definitions of invengory $\mathbf{H}(\mathbf{C},\mathbf{F}_\tau,\delta)$ *and functors* $\mathbf{H}(\mathbf{G},\pi)$ *provided by Definitions 28 and 29 can be verified from the Definitions 30 and 31.*

The functor $\mathbf{H}$ **is dense.**

Take an invengory n-$\mathbf{MonInv}$-m $(\mathbf{C},\alpha^{i_p;i_1,\cdots,i_n,j})$. *We try to define an invengory* $(\mathbf{C},\mathbf{F}_\tau,\delta)$ *in* $\Omega_{n,m}$-$\mathbf{MonInv}$ *such that* $\mathbf{H}(\mathbf{C},\mathbf{F}_\tau,\delta) = (\mathbf{C},\alpha^{i_p;i_1,\cdots,i_n,j})$ *as follows :*

- *The underlying invengory* $\mathbf{C}$ *is the same.*

- *The tensor* $\mathbf{F}_\tau : \mathbf{C}^l \longrightarrow \mathbf{C}$, *for* $\tau \in F\Omega(l)$, *is defined inductively on* τ *by* $\mathbf{F}_| = Id_\mathbf{C}$ *and*
  $$\mathbf{F}_{\tau_{\circ_k};n(\tau_1,\ldots,\tau_n)} = (\mathbf{C}^{p_1+\cdots+p_n} \xrightarrow{\mathbf{F}_{\tau_1}\circ_k\cdots\mathbf{F}_{\tau_n}} \mathbf{C}^n \xrightarrow{\tau_{\circ_k};n} \mathbf{C}).$$

- *The coherence isomorphisms* $\delta_{\tau,\tau'}$ *are defined from each operation of 2-folds objects* $(a_{1,1}\circ_{i_1} \cdots a_{1,n})\circ_j \cdots (a_{n,1}\circ_{i_n}\cdots,a_{n,n})$ *by* $\alpha^{i_p;i_1,\cdots,i_n,j}$.

- *The term* $\mathbf{C}^n \xrightarrow{\circ_k} \mathbf{C}$ *is equal to* $\mathbf{F}_{\tau_{\circ_k},n}$.

- $\alpha^{i_p;i_1,\cdots,i_n,j}_{(a_{1,1},\cdots,a_{1,n}),\cdots,(a_{n,1},\cdots,a_{n,n})}$ *is equal to* $\delta_{\tau_{\circ_j};n\circ(\tau_{\circ_{i_1}};n,\ldots,\tau_{\circ_{i_n}};n),\tau'_{\circ_j};n\circ(\tau'_{\circ_{i_1}};n,\ldots,\tau'_{\circ_{i_n}};n)}$.

Because we have $\mathbf{F}_| = Id_\mathbf{C}$ *and the following diagram*

$$\mathbf{F}_{\tau_{\circ_j};n}(\mathbf{F}_{\tau_{\circ_{i_1}};n}(a_{1,1},\cdots,a_{1,n}),\cdots,\mathbf{F}_{\tau_{\circ_{i_n}};n}(a_{n,1},\cdots,a_{n,n})) = \mathbf{F}_{\tau_{\circ_j};n\circ(\tau_{\circ_{i_1}};n,\cdots,\tau_{\circ_{i_n}};n)}(a_{1,1},\cdots,a_{n,n})$$

$$\mathbf{F}_{\tau_{\circ_j};n}(\delta_{\tau_{\circ_{i_1}};n,\tau'_{\circ_{i_1}};n},\cdots,\delta_{\tau_{\circ_{i_n}};n,\tau'_{\circ_{i_n}};n})\downarrow \qquad\qquad \downarrow\delta_{\tau_{\circ_j};n\circ(\tau_{\circ_{i_1}};n,\ldots,\tau_{\circ_{i_n}};n),\tau'_{\circ_j};n\circ(\tau'_{\circ_{i_1}};n,\ldots,\tau'_{\circ_{i_n}};n)}$$

$$\mathbf{F}_{\tau_{\circ_j};n}(\mathbf{F}_{\tau'_{\circ_{i_1}};n}(a_{1,1},\cdots,a_{1,n}),\cdots,\mathbf{F}_{\tau'_{\circ_{i_n}};n}(a_{n,1},\cdots,a_{n,n}))$$

$$\delta_{\tau_{\circ_j};n,\tau'_{\circ_j};n}\downarrow$$

$$\mathbf{F}_{\tau'_{\circ_j};n}(\mathbf{F}_{\tau'_{\circ_{i_1}};n}(a_{1,1},\cdots,a_{1,n}),\cdots,\mathbf{F}_{\tau'_{\circ_{i_n}};n}(a_{n,1},\cdots,a_{n,n})) = \mathbf{F}_{\tau'_{\circ_j};n\circ(\tau'_{\circ_{i_1}};n,\cdots,\tau'_{\circ_{i_n}};n)}(a_{1,1},\cdots,a_{n,n})$$

commutes with respect to all $\tau_{\circ_j};n, \tau_{\circ_{i_p}};n \in F\Omega(n)$ *and* $a_{i,j} \in \mathbf{C}$. *Then the conditions about natural isomorphism given in Definition 30 can be established from the mathematical induction with respect to the free structure* τ. *Hence, the functor* $\mathbf{H}$ *is dense.*

full and faithful of functor $\mathbf{H}$

Given two functors $\mathbf{C} \xrightarrow{(\mathbf{G},\pi)} \mathbf{C}'$ *and* $\mathbf{C} \xrightarrow{(\tilde{\mathbf{G}},\tilde\pi)} \mathbf{C}'$ *with* $\mathbf{H}(\mathbf{G},\pi) = \mathbf{H}(\tilde{\mathbf{G}},\tilde\pi)$, *then we have to show that* $\mathbf{G} = \tilde{\mathbf{G}}$ *and* $\pi_\tau = \tilde\pi_\tau$. *The functor* $\mathbf{G}$ *is equal to the functor* $\mathbf{G}'$ *since the objects are both from* $\mathbf{C}$.

If $\mathbf{F}_{|}(\mathbf{G}(Id_{\mathbf{C}})) = \mathbf{G}(\mathbf{F}(Id_{\mathbf{C}})) = \tilde{\mathbf{G}}(\mathbf{F}(Id_{\mathbf{C}})) = \mathbf{F}_{|}(\tilde{\mathbf{G}}(Id_{\mathbf{C}}))$ *and*

$$\mathbf{F}_{\tau_{\circ_j};n\circ(\tau_{\circ_{i_1}};n,\cdots,\tau_{\circ_{i_n}};n)}(\mathbf{G}(a_{1,1}),\cdots,\mathbf{G}(a_{n,n}))$$

$$= \mathbf{G}_{\tau_{\circ_j};n\circ(\tau_{\circ_{i_1}};n,\cdots,\tau_{\circ_{i_n}};n)}(\mathbf{F}(a_{1,1}),\cdots,\mathbf{F}(a_{n,n}))$$

$$= \tilde{\mathbf{G}}_{\tau_{\circ_j};n\circ(\tau_{\circ_{i_1}};n,\cdots,\tau_{\circ_{i_n}};n)}(\mathbf{F}(a_{1,1}),\cdots,\mathbf{F}(a_{n,n}))$$

$$= \mathbf{F}_{\tau_{\circ_j};n\circ(\tau_{\circ_{i_1}};n,\cdots,\tau_{\circ_{i_n}};n)}(\tilde{\mathbf{G}}(a_{1,1}),\cdots,\tilde{\mathbf{G}}(a_{n,n}))$$

with respect to all object $a_{i,j} \in \mathbf{C}$, *then we have* $\pi_\tau = \tilde{\pi}_\tau$ *by the mathematical induction with respect to any free structure* $\tau \in F\Omega(l)$. *Therefore, the functor* $\mathbf{H}$ *is a faithful functor.*

Let $\mathbf{C}, \mathbf{C}' \in \Omega_{n,m}\text{-}\boldsymbol{MonInv}$ *and let* $\mathbf{H}(\mathbf{C}) \overset{(\mathbf{G},\varpi)}{\longrightarrow} \mathbf{H}(\mathbf{C}')$ *be a map in* $n\text{-}\boldsymbol{MonInv}\text{-}m$. *We will define a map* $\mathbf{C} \overset{(\mathbf{F},\pi)}{\longrightarrow} \mathbf{C}'$ *in* $\Omega_{n,m}\text{-}\boldsymbol{MonInv}$ *as follows:*

- *The functor* $\mathbf{F}$ *is set as* $\mathbf{G}$.

- *The coherence maps* π_τ *are defined by induction on* τ. *We take* $\pi_{|} = Id_{\mathbf{C}}$ *and take*

$$\mathbf{F}'_{\tau_1}(\mathbf{G}(a_{1,1}),.,\mathbf{G}(a_{1,k_1})) \circ_j \cdots \circ_j \mathbf{F}'_{\tau_n}(\mathbf{G}(a_{n,1}),.,\mathbf{G}(a_{n,k_n}))$$

$$\overset{\pi_{\tau_1}\circ_j\cdots\circ_j\pi_{\tau_n}}{\longrightarrow} \mathbf{G}(\mathbf{F}_{\tau_1}(a_{1,1},.,a_{1,k_1})) \circ_j \cdots \circ_j \mathbf{G}(\mathbf{F}_{\tau_n}(a_{n,1},.,a_{n,k_n}))$$

$$\overset{\pi_{\mathbf{F}_{\tau_1}(a_{1,1},.,a_{1,k_1}),.,\mathbf{F}_{\tau_n}(a_{n,1},.,a_{n,k_n})}}{\longrightarrow} \mathbf{G}(\mathbf{F}_{\tau_1}(a_{1,1},.,a_{1,k_1}) \circ_j \cdots \circ_j \mathbf{F}_{\tau_n}(a_{n,1},.,a_{n,k_n}))$$

Since

$$\mathbf{F}'_{\tau_{\circ_p};n}(\mathbf{G}(a_1),\cdots,\mathbf{G}(a_n)) \overset{\delta_{\tau_{\circ_p};n,\tau'_{\circ_p};n}}{\longrightarrow} \mathbf{F}'_{\tau'_{\circ_p};n}(\mathbf{G}(a_1),\cdots,\mathbf{G}(a_l))$$

$$\pi_{\tau;a_1,\cdots,a_l} \downarrow \qquad\qquad\qquad \downarrow \pi_{\tau'_{\circ_p};n;a_1,\cdots,a_l}$$

$$\mathbf{G}_{\tau_{\circ_p};n}(\mathbf{F}(a_1,\cdots,a_l)) \overset{\mathbf{G}(\delta_{\tau_{\circ_p};n,\tau'_{\circ_p};n})}{\longrightarrow} \mathbf{G}_{\tau'_{\circ_p};n}(\mathbf{F}(a_1,\cdots,a_l)) \qquad (7.1.45)$$

commutes for all multiplication operations $\circ_p$, *then we can extend Eq. (7.1.45) as (7.1.42) by other integer* l *through mathematical induction.*

Similarly, because we have

$$\mathbf{F}'_{\tau_{\circ_p};n}(\mathbf{F}'_{\tau_{\circ_{i_1}};n}(\mathbf{G}(a_{1,1}),.,\mathbf{G}(a_{1,n})),.,$$

$$\mathbf{F}'_{\tau_{\circ_{i_n}};n}(\mathbf{G}(a_{n,1}),.,\mathbf{G}(a_{n,n}))) = \mathbf{F}'_{\tau_{\circ_p};n\circ(\tau_{\circ_{i_1}};n,.,\tau_{\circ_{i_n}};n)}(\mathbf{G}(a_{1,1}),.,\mathbf{G}(a_{n,n}))$$

$$\mathbf{F}'_{\tau_{\circ_p};n}(\pi_{\tau_{\circ_{i_1}};n;a_{1,1},.a_{1,l}},\cdots,\pi_{\tau_{\circ_{i_n}};n;a_{n,1},.a_{n,l}}) \downarrow \qquad\qquad \downarrow \pi_{\tau_{\circ_p};n\circ(\tau_{\circ_{i_1}};n,\cdots,\tau_{\circ_{i_n}};n)}$$

$$\mathbf{F}'_{\tau_{\circ_p};n}(\mathbf{G}(\mathbf{F}_{\tau_{\circ_{i_1}};n}(a_{1,1},.a_{1,n})),.,\mathbf{G}(\mathbf{F}_{\tau_{\circ_{i_n}};n}(a_{n,1},.a_{n,n})))$$

$$\pi_{\tau_{\circ_p};n;\mathbf{F}_{\tau_1}(a_{1,1},.,a_{1,n}),.\mathbf{F}_{\tau_l}(a_{n,1},.,a_{n,n})} \downarrow$$

$$\mathbf{G}(\mathbf{F}_{\tau_{\circ_p};n}(\mathbf{F}_{\tau_{\circ_{i_1}};n}(a_{1,1},.,a_{1,n}),.,\mathbf{F}_{\tau_{\circ_{i_n}};n}(a_{n,1},.,a_{n,n}))) = \mathbf{G}(\mathbf{F}_{\tau_{\circ_p};n\circ(\tau_{\circ_{i_1}};n,.,\tau_{\circ_{i_n}};n)}(a_{1,1},.,a_{n,n})$$

commutes, for all multiplication operations $\circ_{i_1}, \cdots, \circ_{i_n}, \circ_p$ *and* $a_{i,j} \in \mathbf{C}$. *Then we can extend Eq. (7.1.46) as (7.1.43) by other integer l through mathematical induction. These components satisfy the requirement for a functor between objects in* $\Omega_{n,m}$-**MonInv**. *Therefore, the functor* **H** *is a full functor.*

Because the functor **H** *is dense, faithful and full, the invengory* $\Omega_{n,m}$-**MonInv** *is equivalent to the invengory n-**MonInv**-m.*

Multiple-input and Multiple-output, MIMO-invengory

In this section, we will utilize monoidal structure to construct an invengory with multiple input objects and multiple output objects. Given a multi-invengory **C** and a functor **F** from **Multi-inv** to n-**MonInv**, the objects (respectively, relations) of **F(C)** are finite ordered sequences of objects (respectively, relations) of **C**, and the multiplication operation in **F(C)** is concatenation of sequences. So a typical relation is $(a_1, a_2, a_3, a_4, a_5, a_6, a_7) \longrightarrow (b_1, b_2, b_3)$ in **F(C)** looks like

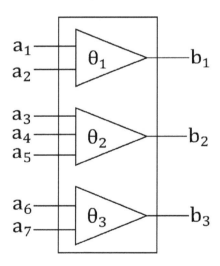

Figure 7.4: MIMO invengoty example.

230

where $\theta_1 : a_1, a_2 \longrightarrow b_1$, $\theta_2 : a_3, a_4, a_5 \longrightarrow b_2$ and $\theta_3 : a_6, a_7 \longrightarrow b_3$ in $\mathbf{C}$.

Let $\mathbf{C}_{n,m}$ be a $\Omega_{n,m}$-**MonInv** monoidal invengory; a MIMO-invengory is constructed by the finite product of invengories $\Omega_{n,m}$-**MonInv** as

$$\prod_i^I \mathbf{C}_{n_i, m_i}, \tag{7.1.47}$$

where the number of output components is I and the total number of input components is the summation of the input number with respect to each invengory $\mathbf{C}_{n_i, m_i}$. The MIMO-invengory shown by Fig. **Ref: Figure to show MIMO: 2,3,2 to 3** has 8 inputs and 3 outputs. The maps between two MIMO-invengories is the product of $(\mathbf{G}_i, \pi_i)$, the functor between two invengories in Ω_{n_i, m_i}-**MonInv**. The invengory form by MIMO-invengories is denoted as **MIMO-Inv**.

Algebra for Multi-invengory

In Chap VI, we discussed about set-valued functors which enable us to study any unfamiliar invengories through set invengories-the most familiar invengories. Generalized Finite State Machine (FSM) is also developed based on the structure of a set-valued functor.

Let $\mathbf{C}$ be a multi-invengory, an algebra for $\mathbf{C}$ is a set-valued functor from $\mathbf{C}$ into the multi-invengory **Set**. Such functor, denoted as $\mathbf{F}$, consists of

- for each object a of $\mathbf{C}$, a set $\mathbf{F}(a)$;

- for each map $\theta : a_1, \cdots, a_n \longrightarrow a$ in $\mathbf{C}$, a function $\mathbf{F}(\theta) : \mathbf{F}(a_1) \times \cdots \times \mathbf{F}(a_n) \longrightarrow \mathbf{F}(a)$,

which satisfy axioms of the associativity and the identity axioms in multi-invengory Definition 20. A map between two $\mathbf{C}$-algebras, $\alpha : \mathbf{F} \longrightarrow \mathbf{G}$, should be defined as a family of functions $(\mathbf{F}(a) \xrightarrow{\alpha_a} \mathbf{G}(a))$ for each object $a \in \mathbf{C}$, which satisfy

$$\alpha_a \circ (\mathbf{F}(\theta)) = \mathbf{G}(\theta) \circ (\alpha_{a_1}, \cdots, \alpha_{a_n}), \tag{7.1.48}$$

for every map $a_1, \cdots, a_n \longrightarrow a$ in $\mathbf{C}$.

7.1.2 Structure Invengory

In an invengory, a relation has a single object as its domain and a single object as its codomain. In a multi-invengory, a relation has a finite sequence of objects as its domain and a single object as its codomain. Could we have a tree or a multi-dimensional structure of objects as the input type of a domain in order to manipulate more complicated components of an invention procedure mathematically? We will try to answer these questions in this section. We formalize the structure of an input type, and for each input type we define a corresponding theory of operads and multi-invengories. Such multi-invengory is named as *structured multi-invengory*. For example, if the input type is finite sequences, then this is about the theory of plain multi-invengories discussed in Sec. 7.1.1.

In Sec. 7.1.2, the definition about structured multi-invengories is provided. Next (Sec. 7.1.2) are the definitions of algebra for a structured multi-invengory. Since any directed graph freely generates an invengory, parallelly, we extend this spirit to structured multi-invengories in Sec. 7.1.2. Finally, we discuss how to transform between two structured multi-invengories with different input structures in Sec. 7.1.2.

Structured Multi-invengory Definition

The purpose of this section is to define a structured multi-invengory. We begin by introducing *monad*, a special functor on an invengory characterizing computation.

Definition 32 *A monad on an invengory* **C** *composed by a functor* $T : \mathbf{C} \longrightarrow \mathbf{C}$ *together with natural transformations*

$$\mu : T \circ T \longrightarrow T, \quad \eta : Id_{\mathbf{C}} \longrightarrow T, \tag{7.1.49}$$

named as multiplication and unit respectively, such that the following diagrams commute. The

left (right) diagram of the above figure corresponds to the associativity (unit) laws.

Any adjunction : $\mathbf{D} \underset{F}{\overset{G}{\rightleftarrows}} \mathbf{C}$, where $\mathbf{C}, \mathbf{D}$ are invengories and F, G are functors, will induces a monad (T, μ, η) on $\mathbf{C}$ by taking $T = G \circ F$, $\mu = G \circ \epsilon \circ F$ (ϵ is the unit of adjunction) and η as the unit of adjunction. For instance, by taking the free forgetful adjunction between the invengory of sets and the invengory of monoids through $T\mathbf{C}$, the set of finite sequences of elements of the set $\mathbf{C}$, we have $T \circ (T\mathbf{C}) \xrightarrow{\mu} T\mathbf{C}$ as

$$((a_{1,1}, \cdots, a_{1,k_1}), \cdots, (a_{n,1}, \cdots, a_{n,k_n})) \longrightarrow$$
$$(a_{1,1}, \cdots, a_{1,k_1}, \cdots, a_{n,1}, \cdots, a_{n,k_n}) \tag{7.1.50}$$

where $n, k_i \in \mathbb{N}$ and $a_{i,j} \in \mathbf{C}$. The unit η forms sequences of length 1 $\mathbf{C} \xrightarrow{\eta} T\mathbf{C}$ as $a \longrightarrow (a)$.

In the sequel, we discuss cartesian conditions required for a monad T in order to define a T-structured multi-invengory. An invengory is *cartesian* if it has all pullbacks. A functor is *cartesian* if it preserves pullbacks. A natural transformation $\alpha : F \longrightarrow G$, where F, G are functors from the invengory $\mathbf{C}$ to the invengory $\mathbf{D}$, is *cartesian* if for each map $A \xrightarrow{h} B$ in $\mathbf{C}$, the following square

$$\begin{array}{ccc} F(A) & \xrightarrow{F(h)} & F(B) \\ \alpha_A \downarrow & & \downarrow \alpha_B \\ G(A) & \xrightarrow{G(h)} & G(B) \end{array} \tag{7.1.51}$$

is a pullback. Finally, a monad (T, μ, η) on an invengory $\mathbf{C}$ is cartesian if the invengory $\mathbf{C}$, the functor T, and the natural transformations μ, η are all cartesian.

Example 37 *Let T be a monoid monad arising from the adjunction* **Monoids** $\rightleftarrows$ **Sets** *and $A =$ **Sets**, we want to show that it is a cartesian monad. The invengory A is cartesian. For unit natural transformation η, we have the following pullback square*

$$\begin{array}{ccc} (a_1) & \xrightarrow{\eta_{a_1}} & (a_1, \cdots, a_n) \\ f \downarrow & & \downarrow T(f) \\ 1 & \xrightarrow{\mu_1} & \mathbb{N} \end{array}$$

For multiplication natural transformation μ, we also have the following pullback square

$$\begin{array}{ccc} ((a_{1,1}, \cdots, a_{1,k_1}), \cdots, (a_{n,1}, \cdots, a_{n,k_n})) & \xrightarrow{\mu_A} & (a_1, \cdots, a_{k_1+\cdots+k_n}) \\ T(T(f)) \downarrow & & \downarrow T(f) \\ T(\mathbb{N}) & \xrightarrow{\mu_1} & \mathbb{N} \end{array}$$

where μ_1 is $(k_1, \cdots, k_n) \longrightarrow k_1 + \cdots + k_n$.

Finally, given

$$W \longrightarrow Y$$
$$\downarrow \qquad \downarrow g$$
$$X \xrightarrow{f} Z$$

we have

$$
\begin{aligned}
T(X) \times_{T(Z)} T(Y) &= \{(x_1, \cdots, x_n), (y_1, \cdots, y_m) | (f(x_1), \cdots, f(x_n)) = (g(y_1), \cdots, g(y_m))\} \\
&\equiv \{(x_1, y_1), \cdots, (x_n, y_n) \mid f(x_i) = g(y_i) \text{ for each } i\} = T(W).
\end{aligned}
$$

Hence, the pullback is preserved by the functor T.

For a cartesian monad (T, μ, η) on an invengory $\mathbf{C}$, the induced generalized bi-invengory is defined as

Definition 33 • **0-cells** *are objects of* $\mathbf{C}$

- **1-cells** , *denoted as* (F, D, Ω), *are expressed as*

$$(F, D, \Omega) = \bowtie_{i=1}^{I_F} (Tc_i \xleftarrow{d_i} f_i \xrightarrow{\omega_i} c_i')$$

where $F = \{f_i\}$, $D = \{d_i\}$, $\Omega = \{\omega_i\}$ and c_i, c_i' are objects of $\mathbf{C}$. Hence, the one cell is a relation between the multiple input objects and the multiple output objects.

- **2-cells** , *denoted as* $\mathcal{A} : (F, D, \Omega) \longrightarrow (G, P, Q)$, *are maps satisfying the following commutative diagram*

$$
\begin{array}{ccc}
Tc_i \xleftarrow{d_i} f_i \xrightarrow{\omega_i} c_i' \\
\| \qquad \downarrow \alpha_{i,j} \quad \| \\
Tc_j \xleftarrow{p_j} g_j \xrightarrow{q_j} c_j'
\end{array}
\tag{7.1.52}
$$

*with respect to each i, j and $\mathcal{A} = \bowtie_{i,j}$ **and** $Tc_i = Tc_j, c_i' = c_j'$ $\alpha_{i,j}$.*

- **1-cell composition** *is the composition of two 1-cells* $(F, D, \Omega) = \bowtie_{i=1}^{I_F} (Tc_i \xleftarrow{d_i} f_i \xrightarrow{\omega_i} c_i')$ *and* $(G, P, Q) = \bowtie_{j=1}^{I_G} (Tc_j \xleftarrow{p_j} g_j \xrightarrow{q_j} c_j')$. *It is expressed as*

$$(G, P, Q) \circ (F, D, \Omega) =$$
$$\bowtie_{i,j=1}^{I_F \circ G} {}_{\textbf{and } Tc_i' = Tc_j} (Tc_i \xleftarrow{\pi_{Tf_i} \circ Td_i \circ \mu} f_i \circ g_j \xrightarrow{\pi_{g_j} q_j} c_j'),
\tag{7.1.53}$$

234

where $I_{F \circ G} = I_G \cdot I_F$, π_{Tf_i} and π_{g_j} are mappings for the following pullback diagram:

$$f_i \circ g_j \xrightarrow{\pi_{g_j}} g_j$$

$$\pi_{Tf_i} \downarrow \qquad \downarrow q_j$$

$$Tf_i \xrightarrow{T\omega_i} (Tc_i' = Tc_j) \tag{7.1.54}$$

- **1-cell identity** is $Tc \xleftarrow{\eta_c} c \xrightarrow{Id} c$.

- **2-cell compositions** is the composition of two 2-cells $(F_1, D_1, \Omega_1) \xrightarrow{\mathcal{A} = \bowtie_{i,j} \alpha_{i,j}} (F_2, D_2, \Omega_2)$ and $(F_2, D_2, \Omega_2) \xrightarrow{\mathcal{B} = \bowtie_{j,k} \beta_{j,k}} (F_3, D_3, \Omega_3)$, denoted as $\mathcal{B} \circ \mathcal{A}$, and $\mathcal{B} \circ \mathcal{A}$ is expressed as

$$\mathcal{A} \circ \mathcal{B} = \bowtie_{i,j,k} \beta_{j,k} \circ \alpha_{i,j}, \tag{7.1.55}$$

where the indices are considered with respect to i, j, k such that $Tc_i = Tc_j, c_i' = c_j'$ and $Tc_j = Tc_k, c_j' = c_k'$.

- **2-cell identity** is $(F, D, \Omega) \xrightarrow{\mathcal{ID}} (F, D, \Omega)$.

- **associativity coherence**, for each triple $A \xrightarrow{(F_1, D_1, \Omega_1)} B \xrightarrow{(F_2, D_2, \Omega_2)} C \xrightarrow{(F_3, D_3, \Omega_3)} D$ of 1-cells, we have an isomorphism as $(F_3 \circ F_2) \circ F_1 \xrightarrow{\mathcal{A}_{F_1, F_2, F_3}} F_3 \circ (F_2 \circ F_1)$, where F_i is the abbreviation for (F_i, D_i, Ω_i).

- **unit coherence**, for each 1-cell $A \xrightarrow{(F, D, \Omega)} B$, we have following two isomorphisms as $Id_B \circ F \xrightarrow{\rho_F} F$ and $F \circ Id_A \xrightarrow{\lambda_F} F$.

At this point, we are ready to define a $(T, \mathbf{C})$-structured multi-invengory, which is a monad in the generalized bi-invengory provided by Definition 33. A functor $\mathbf{F}$ between two $(T, \mathbf{C})$-structured multi-invengories, say $\mathbf{D}$ and $\mathbf{D}'$, is a map composed by a pair of functions (F_0, F_1) such that F_0 is a function between objects (0-cells) of $\mathbf{D}$ and $\mathbf{D}'$ and F_1 is a function between relations (1-cells) of $\mathbf{D}$ and $\mathbf{D}'$. The functions F_0 and F_1 make the following two diagrams commute. The first diagram about identity is

$$D_0 \xrightarrow{Id} D_1$$

$$F_0 \downarrow \qquad \downarrow F_1$$

$$D_0' \xrightarrow{Id} D_1' \tag{7.1.56}$$

where $D_0(D_0')$ and $D_1(D_1')$ are 0-cell and 1-cell of the $(T, \mathbf{C})$-structured multi-invengory $\mathbf{D}(\mathbf{D}')$. The second diagram about composition is

$$
\begin{array}{ccc}
D_1 \circ D_1 & \xrightarrow{\textbf{composition}} & D_1 \\
F_1 \circ F_1 \downarrow & & \downarrow F_1 \\
D_1' \circ D_1' & \xrightarrow{\textbf{composition}} & D_1'
\end{array}
\tag{7.1.57}
$$

In Sec. 7.3, several invention examples about multiple analogy can be characterized by $(T, \mathbf{C})$-structured multi-invengory with respect to different monad T and the base invengory $\mathbf{C}$.

Algebras of Structured Multi-invengories

In ordinary invengory, we have set-valued functor used to study the structure of an unfamiliar invengory through the study of a set invengory, which is a familiar invengory. Under this spirit, we wish to study the algebra (set-valued functor) for a $(T, \mathbf{C})$-structured multi-invengory in this section.

For a traditional invengory $\mathbf{C}$, the functor invengory from $\mathbf{C}$ to the invengory of $\mathbf{Set}$ is equivalent to the invengory of discrete op-fibrations over $\mathbf{C}$. Given a functor from $\mathbf{C}$ to $\mathbf{Set}$, the op-fiberations over $\mathbf{C}$ can be formulated by another way through the pullback of the following diagram

$$
\begin{array}{ccc}
\mathbf{Set}_0 & \xleftarrow{\textbf{domain}} & \mathbf{Set}_1 \\
F_0 \downarrow & & \downarrow F_1 \\
\mathbf{C}_0 & \xleftarrow{\textbf{domain}} & \mathbf{C}_1
\end{array}
\tag{7.1.58}
$$

where $\mathbf{Set}_0(\mathbf{C}_0)$ and $\mathbf{Set}_1(\mathbf{C}_1)$ are objects and relations of the invengory $\mathbf{Set}(\mathbf{C})$, respectively. Generalizing this to $(T, \mathbf{C})$-structured multi-invengories, we said that a functor among two $(T, \mathbf{C})$-structured multi-invengories, denoted as F, from the invengory $\mathbf{Set}_{T,\mathbf{C}}$ to the invengory $\mathbf{E}_{T,\mathbf{C}}$ is a *discrete op-fibration* if the following diagram

$$
\begin{array}{ccc}
TX_i & \xleftarrow{i\text{--th domain}} & g_i \\
TF_0 \downarrow & & \downarrow F_{1;i,j} \\
Te_j & \xleftarrow{j\text{--th domain}} & f_j
\end{array}
\tag{7.1.59}
$$

is a pullback with respect to each i and j, where g_i and f_i are one mappings among 1-cell of $\mathbf{Set}_{T,\mathbf{C}}$ and $\mathbf{E}_{T,\mathbf{C}}$, respectively. Then, we obtain, for any $(T, \mathbf{C})$-structured multi-invengories $\mathbf{E}$, the discrete op-fibration invengory over $\mathbf{E}$, denoted as $\mathbf{DOPFib}_{T,\mathbf{C}}(\mathbf{E})$. The object is a discrete op-fibration with codomain $\mathbf{E}$, and a map from the object $(\mathbf{Set}_{T,\mathbf{C}} \xrightarrow{F} \mathbf{E}_{T,\mathbf{C}})$ to $(\mathbf{Set}'_{T,\mathbf{C}} \xrightarrow{F'} \mathbf{E}_{T,\mathbf{C}})$ is a map $\mathbf{Set}_{T,\mathbf{C}} \xrightarrow{G} \mathbf{Set}'_{T,\mathbf{C}}$ of $(T,\mathbf{C})$-structured multi-invengories such that $F' \circ G = F$.

An $\mathbf{E}$-algebra for the $(T,\mathbf{C})$-structured multi-invengory $\mathbf{E}$ consists by the following two family of maps $X_i \xrightarrow{p_i} \mathbf{E}_0$ where X_i is a set associated to the i-th mapping of 1-cell (Recall a 1-cell is $\bowtie_{i=1}^{I_F} (Tc_i \xleftarrow{d_i} f_i \xrightarrow{\omega_i} c'_i)$ and $h_i : T_{\mathbf{E}} X_i \longrightarrow X_i$. The h_i is determined by the following pullback diagram

$$
\begin{array}{ccc}
T_{\mathbf{E}} X_i & \xrightarrow{\pi_{1,i}} & f_i \\
\pi_{0,i} \downarrow & & \downarrow d_i \\
T X_i & \xrightarrow{T p_i} & T e_i
\end{array}
\tag{7.1.60}
$$

Then the invengory of algebras for $\mathbf{E}$ is the invengory of $\mathbf{E}$-algebra, denoted as $\mathbf{Alg}_{T,\mathbf{C}}(\mathbf{E})$. From Eqs. (7.1.59) and (7.1.60), we can conclude that there is an equivalence of invengories between $\mathbf{DOPFib}_{T,\mathbf{C}}(\mathbf{D})$ and $\mathbf{Alg}_{T,\mathbf{C}}(\mathbf{D})$ by corresponding F_0 as each p_i and $F_{1;i,i}$ as $\pi_{1,i}$.

Free Structured Multi-invengories

From the discussion about traditional invengory at previous chapter, we understand that any directed graph freely generates an invengory by assigning objects as vertices and relations as chains of edges. If we generalize the meaning of edge by allowing an edge with a finite sequence of inputs and a single output, then such generalized graph freely generates a plain multi-invengory. In this section, we wish to extend this idea to $(T,\mathbf{C})$-structured multi-invengories.

Following theorem states the relation between $(T,\mathbf{C})$-structured multi-invengories and $(T,\mathbf{C})$-structured graph.

Theorem 17 *Let T be a cartesian monad on a cartesian invengory $\mathbf{C}$. Then the forgetful functor*

$$
(T,\mathbf{C}) - \mathbf{Multicat} \xrightarrow{U} (T,\mathbf{C}) - \textbf{\textit{Graph}}
\tag{7.1.61}
$$

has a left adjoint. Hence, the invengories of $(T,\mathbf{C}) - \mathbf{Multicat}$ and $(T,\mathbf{C}) - \mathbf{Graph}$ are adjoint pair.

PROOF. 19 *Our first task is to construct a functor $F : (T,\mathbf{C}) - \textbf{\textit{Graph}} \longrightarrow (T,\mathbf{C}) - \mathbf{Multicat}$. Let X be a $(T,\mathbf{C})$-graph, then X_1 and X_0 represent an edge and a vertex of the $(T,\mathbf{C})$-graph X.*

For a $(T, \mathbf{C})$-graph composed by n edges, denoted as $X_1^{(n)}$, we represent this as

$$X_1^{(n)} = \bowtie_{I_n} (TX_0 \xleftarrow{d_{I_n}} X_1^{I_n} \xrightarrow{\omega_{I_n}} X_0), \qquad (7.1.62)$$

where I_n is an index set with n indices and each index represents the component used to form such n edges $(T, \mathbf{C})$-graph. I_0 is set as 0. The n edges graph $X_1^{I_n}$ is constructed recursively by

$$X_1^{I_{n+1}} = X_0 + X_1^{I_1} \circ X_1^{I_n}, \qquad (7.1.63)$$

where $\circ$ is the 1-cell composition provided by Definition 33 $X_1^{(0)} = X_0$, $d_0 = \eta_{X_0}$, and $\omega_0 = Id$. Then the $(T, \mathbf{C})$-structured multi-invengory corresponding to X, denoted as FX, is

$$FX = \bowtie_{\mathcal{I}} (TX_0 \xleftarrow{d_{\mathcal{I}}} X_1^{\mathcal{I}} \xrightarrow{\omega_{\mathcal{I}}} X_0), \qquad (7.1.64)$$

where $X_1^{\mathcal{I}}$ the co-limit of the sequence $X_1^{I_0} \longrightarrow X_1^{I_1} \longrightarrow X_1^{I_2}, \cdots$. For mapping from a $(T, \mathbf{C})$-graph X to another $(T, \mathbf{C})$-graph Y, $F(X \longrightarrow Y)$ is composed by mappings from $TX_0 \xleftarrow{d_{\mathcal{I}_X}} X_1^{\mathcal{I}} \xrightarrow{\omega_{\mathcal{I}_X}} X_0$ to $TY_0 \xleftarrow{d_{\mathcal{I}_Y}} Y_1^{\mathcal{I}} \xrightarrow{\omega_{\mathcal{I}_Y}} Y_0$, again from 1-cell mapping given in Definition 33. Hence, we construct a functor $F : (T, \mathbf{C}) - \mathbf{Graph} \longrightarrow (T, \mathbf{C}) - \mathbf{Multicat}$.

The next task is to show the adjunction between the functor F and U. We do this by constructing unit and co-unit transformations with respect to each $\mathcal{I}$ and verifying the triangle identities required by an adjunction pair. For the unit $\eta_X^{\mathcal{I}} : X_1^{I_1} \longrightarrow X_1^{\mathcal{I}}$ with respect to the indices set $\mathcal{I}$ and $(T, \mathbf{C})$-structured graph X, it is formed by the following mapping:

$$X_1^{I_1} \xrightarrow{co\text{-}limit} X_1^{\mathcal{I}}. \qquad (7.1.65)$$

For the co-unit $\epsilon_{\mathbf{E}}^{\mathcal{I}} : X_1^{\mathcal{I}} \longrightarrow \mathbf{E}_1$ [1] with respect to the indices set $\mathcal{I}$ and the $(T, \mathbf{C})$-structured multi-invengory $\mathbf{E}$, it is formed by the co-limit of $\epsilon_{\mathbf{E}}^{I_n}$, where $\epsilon_{\mathbf{E}}^{I_n}$ is constructed by

$$\epsilon_{\mathbf{E}}^{I_{n+1}} = (\mathbf{E}_0 + \mathbf{E}_1 \circ X_1^{I_n} \xrightarrow{Id + (Id \circ \epsilon_{\mathbf{E}}^{I_n})} \mathbf{E}_0 + \mathbf{E}_1 \circ \mathbf{E}_1 \xrightarrow{\pi_{\mathbf{E}_1}} \mathbf{E}_1) \qquad (7.1.66)$$

recursively. Verification of the triangle identities is straightforward.

Change of Structure

In order to compare methods to higher analogy structure using different shapes (or dimensions) as inputs, we have to consider the map between two different structured inputs of structured

---

[1] We do 1-cells only since 0-cells are same.

238

multi-invengory. Let two input structures be $(T, \mathbf{C})$ and $(T', \mathbf{C}')$, a map of input structures $(T, \mathbf{C}) \longrightarrow (T', \mathbf{C}')$ is a functor $Q : \mathbf{C} \longrightarrow \mathbf{C}'$ with a natural transformation

$$
\begin{array}{ccc}
\mathbf{C} & \xrightarrow{T} & \mathbf{C} \\
Q \downarrow \nearrow \phi & & \downarrow Q \\
\mathbf{C}' & \xrightarrow{T'} & \mathbf{C}'
\end{array}
\tag{7.1.67}
$$

making the following diagrams

$$
\begin{array}{ccc}
T'^2 Q \xrightarrow{T'\phi} T'QT \xrightarrow{\phi T} QT^2 \\
\mu' Q \downarrow \qquad\qquad\qquad \downarrow Q\mu \\
T'Q \qquad \xrightarrow{\psi} \qquad QT
\end{array}
\tag{7.1.68}
$$

and

$$
\begin{array}{ccc}
Q & = & Q \\
\eta' Q \downarrow & & \downarrow Q\eta \\
T'Q & \xrightarrow{\phi} & QT
\end{array}
\tag{7.1.69}
$$

commutes.

The algebras associated to two different input structures can be related by a functor. Since $(Q, \phi) : (T, \mathbf{C}) \longrightarrow (T', \mathbf{C}')$, then there is an induced functor $\tilde{Q}$ from the $(T, \mathbf{C})$-structured multi-invengory to the $(T', \mathbf{C}')$-structured multi-invengory, where the underlying relation (graph) is given by $\bowtie_{i=1}^{I_F} T'Qc_i \xleftarrow{\pi_1} (\tilde{Q}f)_i \xrightarrow{Q\omega_i \circ \pi_2} Qc_i'$. The terms π_1, π_2 and $(\tilde{Q}f)_i$ are determined by the following pullback diagram with respect to Qf_i and $T'Qc_i$

$$
\begin{array}{ccc}
(\tilde{Q}f)_i & \xrightarrow{\pi_2} Qf_i \xrightarrow{Q\omega_i} Qc_i' \\
\pi_1 \downarrow & \downarrow Qd_i \\
T'Qc_i & \xrightarrow{\phi} QTc_i
\end{array}
\tag{7.1.70}
$$

The following theorem is ready to present the relation between the algebra variation from the $(T, \mathbf{C})$ structure to the $(T', \mathbf{C}')$ structure.

Theorem 18 *The functor from the algebra* $\mathbf{Alg}_{T,\mathbf{C}}(\mathbf{D})$ *to the algebra* $\mathbf{Alg}_{T',\mathbf{C}'}(\mathbf{D})$ *is made by*

- *the object X_i is mapped to the object QX_i, where X_i is the set used at $\mathbf{Alg}_{T,\mathbf{C}}(\mathbf{D})$ for the i-th component of a relation.*

- the map h_i in the algebra $\mathbf{Alg}_{T,\mathbf{C}}(\mathbf{D})$ is mapped to $\phi_{\mathbf{D}}(Qh_i)$

where $h_i : T_{\mathbf{D}}X_i \longrightarrow X_i$ and $\phi_{\mathbf{D}}$ is the natural transformation between monad maps $(T_{\mathbf{D}}, \mathbf{C}/\mathbf{D}_0) \longrightarrow (T'_{\tilde{Q}\mathbf{D}}, \mathbf{C}'/Q\mathbf{D}_0)$.

PROOF. 20 *For objects part is clearly, we will concentrate at the relations.*

For algebra $\mathbf{Alg}_{T,\mathbf{C}}(\mathbf{D})$, *it is the invengory for the monad* $T_{\mathbf{D}}$ *on* $\mathbf{C}/\mathbf{D}_0$. *By the functor* $\tilde{Q}$, *the algebra for the* $(T', \mathbf{C}')$-*structure multi-invengory has the invengory for the monad* $T'_{\tilde{Q}\mathbf{D}}$ *on* $\mathbf{C}'/Q\mathbf{D}_0$. *Hence, we have the following diagram for monad maps between* $(T_{\mathbf{D}}, \mathbf{C}/\mathbf{D}_0) \longrightarrow (T'_{\tilde{Q}\mathbf{D}}, \mathbf{C}'/Q\mathbf{D}_0)$, *it is*

$$
\begin{array}{ccc}
\mathbf{C}/\mathbf{D}_0 & \xrightarrow{T_{\mathbf{D}}} & \mathbf{C}/\mathbf{D}_0 \\
Q\downarrow & \nearrow \phi_{\mathbf{D}} & \downarrow Q \\
\mathbf{C}'/Q\mathbf{D}_0 & \xrightarrow{T'_{\tilde{Q}\mathbf{D}}} & \mathbf{C}'/Q\mathbf{D}_0
\end{array}
\tag{7.1.71}
$$

where $\phi_{\mathbf{D}}$ *is the natural transformation between the functor* $\mathbf{C}/\mathbf{D}_0$ *and the functor* $\mathbf{C}'/Q\mathbf{D}_0$.

Since we have $T'_{\tilde{Q}\mathbf{D}}QX_i \xrightarrow{\phi_{\mathbf{D}}} QT_C X_i \xrightarrow{Qh_i} QX_i$, *the corresponding map for* h_i *in the algebra* $\mathbf{Alg}_{T',\mathbf{C}'}(\mathbf{D})$ *becomes*

$$
T'_{\tilde{Q}\mathbf{D}}QX_i \xrightarrow{\phi_{\mathbf{D}}(Qh_i)} QX_i,
\tag{7.1.72}
$$

which is the desired functor map (algebra map) between the algebra $\mathbf{Alg}_{T,\mathbf{C}}(\mathbf{D})$ *and the algebra* $\mathbf{Alg}_{T',\mathbf{C}'}(\mathbf{D})$.

Let T and T' be monads on the same invengory. We said that these two monads are *interchangeable* if the map $\lambda : T \circ T' \longrightarrow T' \circ T$ is a natural transformation such that (T', λ) is a lax map of monads $T \longrightarrow T$ and (T, λ) is a co-lax map of monads $T' \longrightarrow T'$. Following theorem is a special case for Theorem 18 when two monads are interchangeable.

Theorem 19 *If all monads on the invengory* $\mathbf{D}$ *are interchangeable, there is an universal algebra on* $\mathbf{D}$, *i.e., the functor from the algebra* $\mathbf{Alg}_{T,\mathbf{C}}(\mathbf{D})$ *to the algebra* $\mathbf{Alg}_{T',\mathbf{C}}(\mathbf{D})$ *is an isomorphism if* T *and* T' *are interchangeable.*

PROOF. 21 *From Eq.* (7.1.72), *the functor* Q *becomes identical functor since all interchangeable monads operate at the same invengory.*

Since T and T' are interchangeable monads on the invengory $\mathbf{C}$ and let $\widehat{T}$ be the corresponding monad on $\mathbf{C}^T$. Then there is a canonical natural transformation

$$\mathbf{C}^T \xrightarrow{\widehat{T}} \mathbf{C}^T$$

$$U \downarrow \quad \nearrow \phi \quad \downarrow U$$

$$\mathbf{C} \xrightarrow{T' \circ T} \mathbf{C} \tag{7.1.73}$$

This induces an isomorphic functor between $(\mathbf{C}^T)^{\widehat{T}}$ and $\mathbf{C}^{T' \circ T}$. Hence, the term $\phi_{\mathbf{D}}$ provided by Eq. (7.1.72) is an identity map.

Therefore, the functor from the algebra $\mathbf{Alg}_{T,\mathbf{C}}(\mathbf{D})$ to the algebra $\mathbf{Alg}_{T',\mathbf{C}}(\mathbf{D})$ is an isomorphism.

Remark The definition 33 can be further generalized by

$$(F, D, \Omega) = \bowtie_{i=1}^{I_F} \left(T_i c_i \xleftarrow{d_i} f_i \xrightarrow{\omega_i} c'_i \right)$$

where the monad T_i is different.

7.2 n-fold Invengory

In Sec. 7.1.2, we discussed about bi-invengories in Definition 33. In this section, we wish to generalize bi-invengories by considering maps between two 2-cells and so on. Such invengory is named as *n-fold invengory* if we consider maps up to n folds for maps between maps. A *n*-fold invengory have following components :

- **0-cells (objects)**: $A, B, \cdots$

- **1-cells (relations, morphisms)**: $A \xrightarrow{f} B$

- **2-cells (relations between relations, morphisms between morphisms)**:

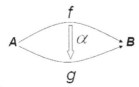

- **3-cells (relations between relations obtained from 2-cells, morphisms between morphisms obtained from 2-cells)**:

241

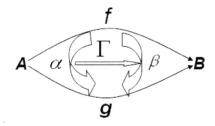

- ...up to n-cells

- various kinds of composition

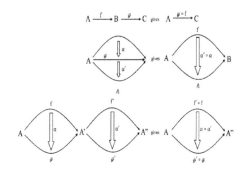

In the sequel, we will provide a definition about n-fold invengory. Recall the definition of a traditional invengory $\mathbf{C}$, it consists of:

1. A collection of objects;

2. A collection of relations;

3. Operations assigning to each relation F an object $domF$, its domain, and an object $ranF$, its range (we write $F : A \to B$ to show that $domF = A$ and $ranF = B$; the collection of all relations with domain A and range B is written as $\mathbf{C}(A, B)$);

4. The relations F, G and H can be decomposed by functions as $F = \bowtie_{i=1}^{I_F} f_i, g = \bowtie_{j=1}^{I_G} g_j$ and $H = \bowtie_{k=1}^{I_H} h_k$, where each f_i, g_j and h_k is a function. A composition operator assigning to each pair of functions f_i and g_j, with $ranf_i = domg_j$ for some indices $i \in I_F$ and $j \in I_G$, respectively. A composite function $g_j \circ f_i : domf_i \to rang_j$, satisfying the following associative law:

   For any relations $F : A \to B, G : B \to C$, and $H : C \to D$ where A, B, C, and D are not necessarily distinct, we always have

$$h_k \circ (g_j \circ f_i) = (h_k \circ g_j) \circ f_i, \qquad (7.2.1)$$

where indices i, j and k satisfy $ran\ f_i = dom\ g_j$ and $ran\ g_j = dom\ h_k$.

5. For each object A, an identity relation $id_A : A \to A$ satisfying the following identity law with respect to each index i:

$$id_B \circ f_i = f_i, \text{and } f_i \circ id_A = f_i, \qquad (7.2.2)$$

where $F : A \to B$ and $F = \bowtie_{i=1}^{I_F} f_i$.

We can restate the definition of a traditional invengory $\mathbf{C}$ by specifying source objects and target objects of each relation (morphism) in the invengory $\mathbf{C}$. An invengory for $\mathbf{C} = (\mathcal{R}, s, t, *)$ consists of a relation (morphism) set $\mathcal{R}$, functions $s, t : \mathcal{R} \longrightarrow \mathcal{R}$ which represent sources and targets, satisfying the equations $s \circ s = t \circ s = s$ and $t \circ t = s \circ t = t$ and a function $* : \{(A, B) \in \mathcal{R} \times \mathcal{R} | s(A) = t(B)\} \longrightarrow \mathcal{R}$, such that $s(A * B) = s(B)$ and $t(A * B) = t(A)$. Moreover, we also have

$$\text{if } s(a_i) = t(v) = v, \text{ then } a_i * v = a_i \text{ where } A = \bowtie_{i=1}^{I_A} a_i;$$

$$\text{if } s(u) = t(a_i) = u, \text{ then } u * a_i = a_i;$$

$$\text{if } s(a_i) = t(b_j), s(b_j) = t(c_k), \text{ then } a_i * (b_j * c_k) = (a_i * b_j) * c_k$$

$$\text{where } A = \bowtie_{i=1}^{I_A} a_i, B = \bowtie_{j=1}^{I_B} b_j \text{ and } C = \bowtie_{k=1}^{I_C} c_k. \quad (associativity) \tag{7.2.3}$$

For a $(T, \mathbf{C})$-structured multi-invengory $\mathbf{D}$, it is represented by $(\mathcal{R}, s, t, *)$ [2] which consists of a $(T, \mathbf{C})$-structured relation (morphism) set $\mathcal{R}$, functions $s, t : \mathcal{R} \longrightarrow \mathcal{R}$ satisfying the equations $s \circ s = t \circ s = s$ and $t \circ t = s \circ t = t$ and a function $* : \{(A, B_1, \cdots, B_n) \in \overbrace{\mathcal{R} \times \cdots \times \mathcal{R}}^{(n+1) \text{ product sets}} \mid s(A) = \bigcup_{i=1}^{n} t(B_i) \text{ and } t(B_i) \cap t(B_j) = \emptyset \text{ for any } i, j \text{ and } i \neq j\} \longrightarrow \mathcal{R}, \text{ such that } s(A * (B_1, \cdots, B_n)) = \bigcup_{i=1}^{n} s(B_i) \text{ and } t(A * (B_1, \cdots, B_n)) = t(A)$. We also have

- if $s(a_{i;l}) = t(v_l) = v_l$, then $a_i * (v_1, \cdots, v_n) = a_i$ where $A = \bowtie_{i=1}^{I_A} a_i$ and $a_{i;l}$ represents the relation for the l-th input and the i-th component of the relation A;

- if $s(u) = t(a_i) = u$, then $u * a_i = a_i$;

- For relations $F, F_i, F_{i,j} \in \mathbf{C}(a_1, \cdots, a_n; a)$ decomposed by functions as $F = \bowtie_{l=1}^{I_F} f_{;l}$, $F_i = \bowtie_{l_i=1}^{I_{F_i}} f_{i;l_i}$, and $F_{i,j} = \bowtie_{l_{i,j}=1}^{I_{F_{i,j}}} f_{i,j;l_{i,j}}$ respectively, furthermore, we have $s(f_{;l}) = \bigcup_i t(f_{i,l_i})$ and $s(f_{i;l_i}) = \bigcup_j t(f_{i,j;l_{i,j}})$, then these relations have to satisfy

$$f_{;l} * (f_{1;l_1} * (f_{1,1;l_{1,1}}, \cdots, f_{1,i_1;l_{1,i_1}}), \cdots, f_{n;l_n} * (f_{n,1;l_{n,1}}, \cdots, f_{n,i_n;l_{n,i_n}}))$$

$$= (f_{;l} * (f_{1;l_1}, \cdots, f_{n;l_n})) * (f_{1,1;l_{1,1}}, \cdots, f_{1,i_1;l_{1,i_1}}, \cdots, f_{n,1;l_{n,1}}, \cdots, f_{n,i_n;l_{n,i_n}}) \tag{7.2.4}$$

with respect to all indices l, l_i and $l_{i,j}$. (associativity)

A 2-invengory $(\mathcal{R}, s_0, t_0, *_0, s_1, t_1, *_1)$ consists of $(\mathcal{R}, s_0, t_0, *_0)$ for 1-cell composition and $(\mathcal{R}, s_1, t_1, *_1)$ for 2-cell composition with respect to the $(T, \mathbf{C})$-structured multi-invengory satisfying the following requirements:

- $s_0 \circ s_1 = s_0 \circ t_1 = s_0$, $t_0 \circ s_1 = t_0 \circ t_1 = t_0$;

- if $s_0(A) = \bigcup_{i=1}^{n} t_0(B_i)$, where n is a positive integer depending on the input number of the relation A, then $s_1(A *_0 (B_1, \cdots, B_n)) = s_1(A) *_0 (s_1(B_1), \cdots, s_1(B_n))$ and $t_1(A *_0 (B_1, \cdots, B_n)) = t_1(A) *_0 (t_1(B_1), \cdots, t_1(B_n))$;

---

[2] The composition operation $*$ is the composition under the $(T, \mathbf{C})$-structured multi-invengory.

- if $s_1(A) = t_1(B)$, $s_1(A') = t_1(B')$, $s_0(A) = \bigcup_{i=1}^{n} t_0(A'_i)$, then $(A *_1 B) *_0 (A'_1 *_1 B', \cdots, A'_n *_1 B') = (A *_0 (A'_1, \cdots, A'_n)) *_1 (B *_0 (B', \cdots, B'))$.

Let infinite ordinal set as $\aleph$, where $\aleph = \{0, 1, 2, 3, \cdots\}$. Then, we define $\aleph$-invengory $(\mathcal{R}, (s_n, t_n, *_n)_{n \in \aleph})$ by consisting of invengories $(\mathcal{R}, s_n, t_n, *_n)$ for each $n \in \aleph$ such that $(\mathcal{R}, s_m, t_m, *_m, s_n, t_n, *_n)$ is a 2-invengory for all $m < n$. The identities for $*_n$ are called n-cells. For $m \in \aleph$, an m-invengory is an $\aleph$-invengory for which all elements are m-cells. An $\aleph$-functor $F : (\mathcal{R}, (s_n, t_n, *_n)_{n \in \aleph}) \longrightarrow (\mathcal{R}', (s'_n, t'_n, *'_n)_{n \in \aleph})$ is a function $F : \mathcal{R} \longrightarrow \mathcal{R}'$ such that $Fs_n = s'_n F, Ft_n = t'_n F$ and $s_n(A) = \bigcup_{i=1}^{l} t_n(B_i)$ implies $F(A *_n (B_1, \cdots, B_1)) = F(A) *'_n (F(B_1), \cdots, F(B_1))$, for all $n \in \aleph$.

7.3 Examples of Multiple Analogies

The first example is about applying $(T, \mathbf{C})$-structured multi-invengory with tree-like structure to the design of organizations for enterprises. Organization design is a crucial problem for managers. What is the more proper structure for the organization? What are the criteria for selecting the most proper structure? What symptoms indicate that the existing structure may not be appropriate to current tasks and environments? Basically, an organization structure has to achieve following objectives: (1) it coordinates organization components properly for dealing with suffered problems. (2) it assists the information exchange effectively within the organization. (3) it is able to allocate tasks and responsibilities equitable based on components' resources, or at least no conflict. Although there are different kinds of organization structures that managers can select. Here, we present a tree structure for managers to select the appropriate structure according to requirements of the environment.

7.3.1 Organization Design

We first show how to construct a tree-like $(T, \mathbf{C})$-structured multi-invengory, then we will use this tree to form a decision tree by considering environmental factors which enables us to manipulate the most proper organization structure for a enterprise.

By taking $\mathbf{C}$ as a **Set** invengory and monad T as finitary free tree [3] for a $(T, \mathbf{C})$-structured multi-invengory $\mathbf{D}$, it consists of a set $\mathbf{D}_0$ of objects and relation sets like

---
[3]Given a set S, the set TA can be obtained inductively within finite steps by (1) if $s \in S$, then $a \in TS$; (2) if $t_1, \cdots, t_n \in TS$, then $(t_1, \cdots, t_n) \in TS$.

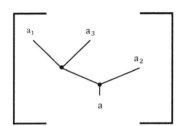

$(a_1, a_2, a \in \mathbf{D}_0)$, together with an identity

$$\mathbf{1}_a \in C \left[\begin{array}{c} a \\ | \\ a \end{array} \right]$$

for each $a \in C_0$ and composition functions like

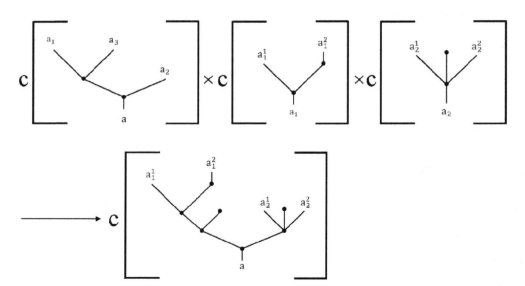

where $(a_{i,j}, a_i, a \in \mathbf{D}_0)$. The above $(T, \mathbf{C})$-structured multi-invengory can be also be explained as a plain multi-invengory in which the relations sets are graded by trees: to each $a_1, \cdots, a_n, a \in \mathbf{D}_0$ and n-leaves tree $\tau \in mathbftr(n)$, there is associated a relation $\mathbf{D}_\tau(a_1, \cdots, a_n; a)$ in $\mathbf{D}$, composition consists of functions

$$\mathbf{D}_\tau(a_1, \cdots, a_n; a) \times \mathbf{D}_{\tau_1}(a_{1,1}, \cdots, a_{1,k_1}; a_1) \times \cdots \times \mathbf{D}_{\tau_n}(a_{n,1}, \cdots, a_{n,k_n}; a_n)$$

$$\longrightarrow \mathbf{D}_{\tau \circ (\tau_1, \cdots, \tau_n)}(a_{1,1}, \cdots, a_{n,k_n}; a). \qquad (7.3.1)$$

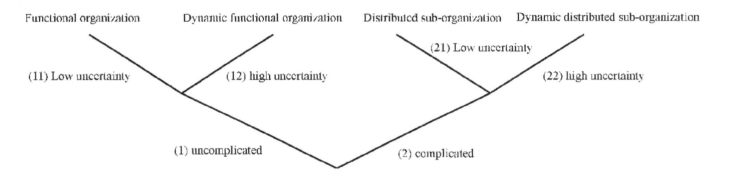

Figure 7.5: Organization design by decision tree.

The Fig. 7.5 presents a decision tree analysis for selecting either the functional or decentralized organization structure. The objects ($\mathbf{D}_0$) used in this tree are complicated, uncomplicated, decomposable, indecomposable, low uncertainty, and high uncertainty. The first question is weather that the surrounding environment is complex enough for the manager to partition the organization into distributed sub-organizations. If the environment is recognized as simple, the next question focuses on whether the environmental factors are with low uncertainty, that keeps the same over time, or are with high uncertainty, that keeps changing over time. If we recognize the environment as low uncertainty, there is likely to be little uncertainty associated with decision making. In turn, information requirements for decision making are low. In this uncomplicated environment with low uncertainty, the functional organization is the most efficient. If the environment is complex, we consider whether it is possible to decompose the organization. This phenomenon is indicated by objects : decomposable and indecomposable. Of course, we can select other design criterions as objects ($\mathbf{D_0}$) to decide out the most proper organization with respect to environments and tasks faced by the manager.

7.3.2 Puzzle Design

The second example is about puzzle design. A puzzle is a problem that challenges the ingenuity of the solver. In a basic puzzle, one is intended to arrange pieces in a logical way in order to come up with the desired solution. Puzzles are often design as a form of entertainment, but background reasons to get the desired solution often stem from deep mathematical or logistical problems-their successful answer can be a significant contribution to mathematical research.

We consider to design a puzzle which is composed by a class of planar geometric objects. The definition of a rectangular puzzle is provided first.

Definition 34 *A rectangular puzzle $\mathcal{E}$ consists of :*

- *a closed rectangle $R = [a, b] \times [c, d]$ in the Euclidean plane,*

- *a finite set P of points in R,*

- *a finite set V of vertical edges,*

- *a finite set H of horizontal edges*

satisfying the following conditions;

- *the end points of each vertical and horizontal edge are points in P,*

- *every point on the boundary of R lies on some vertical or horizontal edge,*

- *any vertex on the vertical boundary of R is the end point of an edge in H,*

- *any vertex on the horizontal boundary of R is the end point of an edge in V,*

- *any two edges are disjoint or intersect only at endpoints.*

A simple example about rectangular puzzle is provided by Fig. 7.6 to show a rectangular puzzle with 13 vertices, 7 horizontal edges and 8 vertical ones. If the top boundary of a rectangular puzzle $\mathcal{E}$ matches the bottom boundary of another $\mathcal{E}'$, we can paste them together vertically and erase the common boundary to get another rectangular puzzle $\mathcal{E} \circ_v \mathcal{E}'$. Similarly, we can paste

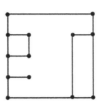

Figure 7.6: A simple example about rectangular puzzle.

two puzzles horizontally if the right boundary of the first puzzle matches the left boundary of the second puzzle.

A double graph is a graph object with the following diagram of sets

$$C_{1,1} \longrightarrow C_{0,1}$$
$$\downarrow \qquad \downarrow$$
$$C_{1,0} \longrightarrow C_{0,0}, \tag{7.3.2}$$

where the set $C_{0,0}$ is composed by objects, $C_{0,1}$ the vertical relations, $C_{1,0}$ the horizontal relations, and $C_{1,1}$ the cells. The free double invengory generated by 7.3.2, denoted as $\mathbf{C}$, has objects as $C_{0,0}$ with two kinds of relations-the horizontal and vertical relations, where the horizontal relation is composed by $C_{1,0} \longrightarrow C_{0,0}$ freely and the vertical relation is composed by $C_{0,1} \longrightarrow C_{0,0}$ freely.

By considering the homotopy classes of puzzles, they form a double invengory of rectangular puzzles, indicated as $\mathbf{RP}$, and there exists a double functor $F : \mathbf{RP} \longrightarrow \mathbf{C}$ such that

$$F(\mathcal{E}) = (F(e_{1,1}) \circ_v \cdots \circ_v F(e_{1,m})) \circ_h \cdots \circ_h (F(e_{n,1}) \circ_v \cdots \circ_v F(e_{n,m})) \tag{7.3.3}$$

where $e_{i,j}$ are basic complexes used to construct any rectangular puzzle given by Definition 34. There are 19 formats for $e_{i,j}$, they are

One advantage of using double invengory language to describe rectangular puzzles is to check the equivalence of two serious of operations through the mapping relation in the double invengory.

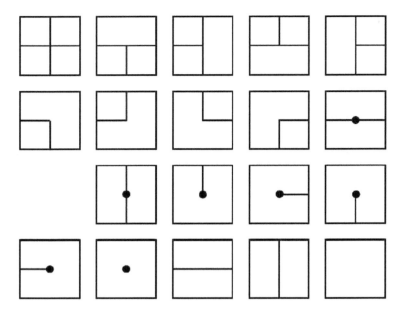

Since two paths of operations $\{c_i\}$ and $\{d_j\}$ represent equal relation in the invengory $\mathcal{E}$ if and only if there is a 2-cell α in the free double invengory. Such cell is expressed as

$$C \xrightarrow{c_1} C_1 \xrightarrow{c_2} \cdots \xrightarrow{c_m} D$$
$$\| \qquad\qquad \alpha \qquad\qquad \|$$
$$C \xrightarrow{d_1} D_1 \xrightarrow{d_2} \cdots \xrightarrow{d_m} D. \tag{7.3.4}$$

7.3.3 Flow Chart Design

The third example is about the manipulation of flowcharts through various compositions. Flowcharts are a modeling technique introduced around the Second World War and popularized for structured development in the 1970s as well as business modeling. With more usage of information related devices around our life, it has focused upon the necessity for an orderly representation of information flow. The order in which operations are to be executed should be precisely stated. A flowchart is a diagram that shows operations performed in an information processing system and the order in which the operations are performed. The data and the sequence of operations to be performed upon the data together constitute a flowchart. Flowchart symbols are used to represent the operations and sequence of operations. There are three basic symbols on this flowchart: Squares which represent activities or tasks, diamonds which represent decision points, arrows which represent flow of control and double-arrows which indicate the variation between arrows.

Abstractly, there are three parts of flowcharts. The first part is composed by states involved in a procedure which are often represented as circles, ovals or rounded rectangles to indicate the meaning of "Start", "End", "Inputs (Outputs)", "Conditions" or "Decisions". The second part is composed by arrows (process directions between states). An arrow coming from one state and ending at another state represents that control passes to the state that the arrow points to. The third part consists of arrow-relations between two arrows. An arrow-relations coming from one arrow and ending at another arrow where these two arrows share the same initial and ending states. In Fig. 7.7, we depict a flowchart for the registration procedure in an university.

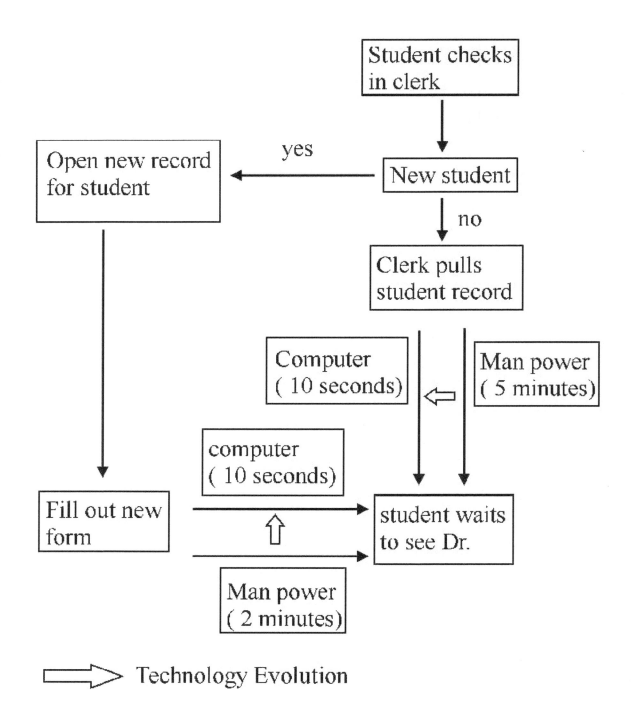

Figure 7.7: A flowchart for the registration procedure in an university.

Following figure is an example about composing flowcharts into a larger one.

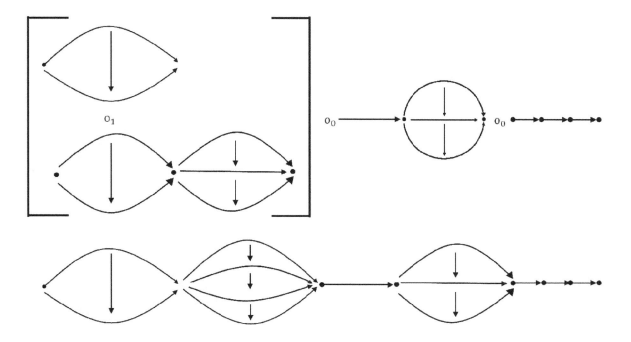

Figure 7.8: The symbols $\circ_1$ and $\circ_0$ represent flowcharts attach along to a one dimensional (arrow) object and a zero dimensional (dot) object, respectively.

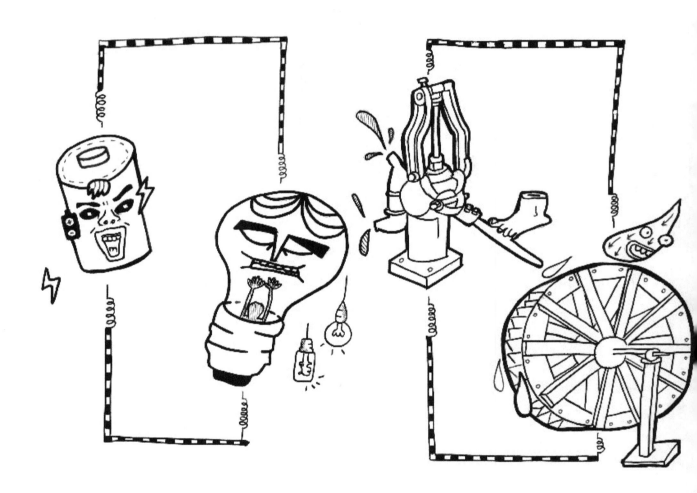

Figure 7.9: Multi−Analogy

Chapter 8

Evaluation Invenrelational Process Equationally

The main goal of this chapter is to apply oriented complexes [1] to evaluate invenrelational processes equationally. We begin by introducing the motivation behind modelling invenrelational processes through gluing cells formed by n-fold invengory in Sec. 8.1. In Sec. 8.2, we discuss the conditions required for objects in n-fold invengory to be defined equationally. The definition of oriented Complexes and their construction rules are provided in Sec. 8.3. The main theorem in this chapter about evaluating gluing design equationally is established in Sec. 8.4. Finally, some examples about characterizing invenrelational evolution processes (IEPs) are provided in Sec. 8.5.

8.1   Motivation of Gluing Design for Invenrelational Process

Until so far, various invention processes have been introduced to create new things from basic components, e.g., arithmetic, analogy, etc. We often meet the situation where there are basic components, processes inventing new things from basic components, meta-processes [2] taking one process to another, meta-meta-process, and so on.

Let us consider a very simple invention process with just one interesting process, denoted as C:

$$C : x \xrightarrow{f} y. \tag{8.1.1}$$

---

[1] A notion modified from cell complexes in Algebraic Topology.

[2] The process of constructing process models is a meta-process, it is the process behind the process used to construct processes for building new products.

The meta-process relation, denoted as F, sends objects to objects, processes to processes by preserving structure. It can be expressed as

$$x \xrightarrow{f} y \xrightarrow{F} F(x) \xrightarrow{F(f)} F(y) \qquad (8.1.2)$$

The meta process for F, which can be interpreted as changing perspectives from the relation F to the relation G, is written as

$$
\begin{array}{ccc}
x \xrightarrow{f} y \xrightarrow{F} & F(x) \xrightarrow{F(f)} F(y) \\[4pt]
& A(x) \downarrow \qquad \downarrow A(y) \\[4pt]
x \xrightarrow{f} y \xrightarrow{G} & G(x) \xrightarrow{G(f)} G(y) \quad ,
\end{array}
\qquad (8.1.3)
$$

where $F \xrightarrow{A} G$. Such "meta-" operation for process can be continued further, moreover, we observe that the space for relations is increased by one if we perform "meta-" operation for new processes obtained from the previous "meta-" operation.

Below, we provide another example about perception evolution. Around 2500 years ago, the Greek philosopher Heraclitus, observing that the world was in eternal flux, said "No man ever step in the same river twice". The perception at each time instant, place or any parametricable context can be modeled as flux on a manifold [43]. Similar idea can be applied to model an invenrelation space by manifold. By using the concept of the boundary between two manifolds, we can characterize the evolution between two invenrelation spaces.

Fig. 8.1 shows a two-folds evolution and we can analyze this evolution by 2-invengory.

The notion about n-fold invengories discussed at Chap. VII provides us an excellent tool to evaluate above examples if we assign our interesting things or processes involved in creation to cells in a n-fold invengory with various dimensions. The manipulation of gluing among different dimensional cells is a valuable tool for working with several different compositions in n-fold invengories discussed at Chap. VII. Such gluing among different dimensional cells is named as a *gluing design*, which is an algebraic expression with inventors-defined elements which can be evaluated as soon as we have associated to these inventors-defined elements in those cells of an n-invengory. If we construct a gluing design according to some rules, for instance, product and join, and all 0-cells involved in such construction are equations definable objects, then gluing design can be mapped to an associated n-invengory for evaluation equationally. This is the main topic we wish to present at this chapter.

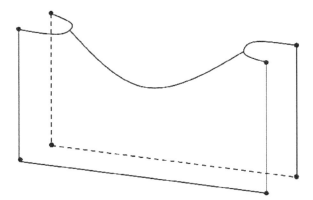

L = ● ● , L' = ● ● , M = ⌣⌣ M' = | |
⌢

Figure 8.1: A two-folds evolution of invenrelation spaces composed by parts L, L' and M, M'.

8.2 Equations Definable Objects

In this section, we will present conditions for objects in an n-fold invengory to be definable by equations (identities). For instance, a group is definable by following three identities; $(a \cdot b) \cdot c = a \cdot (b \cdot c)$(Associativity), $a \cdot e = e \cdot a = a$ (Identity element) and, for each a, there exists b such that $a \cdot b = b \cdot a = e$ (Inverse element).

8.2.1 One-Sorted Representation of Many-Sorted Algebras

The purpose of this section is to provide a constructive theorem to establish the equivalence between many-sorted algebras and one-sorted algebras based on works [44]. In Chap. II, we presented the algebraic system for invention. Let us recall this system for later theory. There are two family of sets in this algebraic model, denoted as $\mathbb{S}$ and $\mathbb{F}$. The family $\mathbb{S}$ is composed by sets S_i where i is the index for sets in $\mathbb{S}$. The index i belongs to the index set I (or called by proper names). The family $\mathbb{F}$ is made up by relations f_ω where ω is the index for different relation. The index ω belongs to the index set Ω (or called by appropriate names). For each ω, the relation f_ω is a $n(\omega) + 1$-ary relation where $n(\omega)$ is an positive integer depending on the index ω. Let

$S_{i_{1,\omega}}, S_{i_{2,\omega}}, \cdots, S_{i_{n(\omega),\omega}}$ be those $n(\omega)$ sets at the input of the relation f_ω and the set $S_{i_{n(\omega)+1,\omega}}$ is the output of the relation f_ω, then f_ω can be expressed as

$$f_\omega : S_{i_{1,\omega}} \times S_{i_{2,\omega}} \times \cdots \times S_{i_{n(\omega),\omega}} \to S_{i_{n(\omega)+1,\omega}}, \tag{8.2.1}$$

in which $i_{j,\omega}$ is the corresponding index with respect to the index set of $\mathbb{S}$ (I) for the j-th set associated with $n(\omega) + 1$-ary relation f_ω. The family $\mathbb{S}$ is produced by collecting constitutive elements followed by classifying them into different sets S_i based on their attributes. After figuring out relations among sets in $\mathbb{S}$, the family $\mathbb{F}$ can also be determined. Briefly, we use the notation $\langle \mathbb{S}, I, \mathbb{F}, \Omega \rangle$ to represent such algebraic system. If all S_i are same in $\mathbb{S}$, this is named as a one-sorted algebra; otherwise, this is called as a many-sorted algebra.

Lemma 7 *The invengory of $\langle \mathbb{S}, I, \mathbb{F}, \Omega \rangle$-algebras is isomorphic to an invengory of algebraic structures with cartesian products indexed by I with respect to each decomposed function.*

PROOF. 22 *For any relation $f_\omega : S_{i_1} \times S_{i_2} \times \cdots \times S_{i_n} \longrightarrow S_j$, we can decompose f_ω as finite functions as $f_\omega \bowtie_m f_{\omega,m}$, where each $f_{\omega,m}$ is a function, i.e., $f_{\omega,m} : S_{i_1} \times S_{i_2} \times \cdots \times S_{i_n} \longrightarrow S_j$. The following proof is based on $f_{\omega,m}$ but it is obvious to consider other decomposed function from f_ω.*

Let us define two invengories: $\mathbf{EXT}_{f_{\omega,m}}$ and $\mathbf{PROD}_\omega$. For the invengory $\mathbf{EXT}_{f_{\omega,m}}$, objects are sets $\{S_l : l \in I\}$ with a function $f_{\omega,m}$. A morphism from one object $\{S_l : l \in I\}$ to another object $\{T_l : l \in I\}$ is a set of functions $\{h_l : l \in I\}$ where $h_l : S_l \longrightarrow T_l$ such that

$$h_j(f_{\omega,m}(s_{i_1}, \cdots, s_{i_n})) = f_{\omega,m}(g_{i_1}(s_{i_1}), \cdots, g_{i_n}(s_{i_n})), \tag{8.2.2}$$

where s_{i_k} is the element of the set S_{i_k} for $1 \leq k \leq n$.

Recall that $\omega(i_1, \cdots, i_n) = j$. The objects of the invengory $\mathbf{PROD}_\omega$ are cartesian products of sets $\{S_l\}$, denoted as $\prod_{l \in I} S_l$, with an n-ary operation of tuples $\widetilde{\omega}$ such that, for $l \neq j$, the l-th component of $\widetilde{\omega}((s_{i_1,l})_{l \in I}, (s_{i_2,l})_{l \in I}, \cdots, (s_{i_n,l})_{l \in I}) = s_{i_n,l}$, where $s_{i_k,l}$ is the l-th component of tuples selected from the set S_{i_k} indexed by I, i.e., $(s_{i_k,1}, s_{i_k,2}, \cdots, s_{i_k,l}, \cdots)$. For $l = j$, the j-th component of $\widetilde{\omega}((s_{i_1,l})_{l \in I}, (s_{i_2,l})_{l \in I}, \cdots, (s_{i_n,l})_{l \in I})$ and $\widetilde{\omega}((t_{i_1,l})_{l \in I}, (t_{i_2,l})_{l \in I}, \cdots, (t_{i_n,l})_{l \in I})$ is the same if $(s_{i_k,l})_{l \in I} = (t_{i_k,l})_{l \in I}$ for $1 \leq k \leq n$. A morphism from the object $\prod_{l \in I} S_l$ to another object $\prod_{l \in I} T_l$ is a tuple of functions indexed by I, i.e., $(h_l)_{l \in I}$ where $h_l : S_l \longrightarrow T_l$ such that

$$\widetilde{\omega}((h_l(s_{i_1,l}))_{l \in I}, (h_l(s_{i_2,l}))_{l \in I}, \cdots, (h_l(s_{i_n,l}))_{l \in I}) = (h_l(s_{i_n,l}))_{l \in I}, \tag{8.2.3}$$

where s_{i_k} is the element of the set S_{i_k} for $1 \leq k \leq n$.

We claim that the invengories $\mathbf{EXT}_{f_{\omega,m}}$ and $\mathbf{PROD}_\omega$ are isomorphic. Define the functor $\mathbf{F}$ from $\mathbf{EXT}_{f_{\omega,m}}$ to $\mathbf{PROD}_\omega$ as

$$\mathbf{F}(\{S_l : l \in I\}, f_{\omega,m}) = (\prod_{l \in I} S_l, \widetilde{\omega}) \tag{8.2.4}$$

such that

$$\widetilde{\omega}((s_{i_1,l})_{l \in I}, (s_{i_2,l})_{l \in I}, \cdots, (s_{i_n,l})_{l \in I}) =$$
$$\begin{cases} s_{i_n,l} \text{ for the } l\text{-th component and } l \neq j, \text{ where } l \in I; \\ f(s_{i_1}, s_{i_2}, \cdots, s_{i_n}) \text{ for the } l\text{-th component and } l = j. \end{cases}$$
$$\tag{8.2.5}$$

For map of morphisms, we have $\mathbf{F}(\{h_l : l \in I\}) = (h_l)_{l \in I}$.

On the other hand, we also define a functor $\mathbf{G}$ from $\mathbf{PROD}_\omega$ to $\mathbf{EXT}_{f_{\omega,m}}$ as

$$\mathbf{G}(\prod_{l \in I} S_l, \widetilde{\omega}) = (\{S_l : l \in I\}, f_{\omega,m}) \tag{8.2.6}$$

such that $f_{\omega,m}(s_{i_1}, s_{i_2}, \cdots, s_{i_n})$ is the j-th component of any $\widetilde{\omega}((t_{i_1,l})_{l \in I}, (t_{i_2,l})_{l \in I}, \cdots, (t_{i_n,l})_{l \in I})$, where $(s_{i_k,l})_{l \in I} = (t_{i_k,l})_{l \in I}$ for $1 \leq k \leq n$. For map of morphisms, we have $\mathbf{G}((h_l)_{l \in I}) = (\{h_l : l \in I\})$.

For objects $\{S_l : l \in I\}$ acted by the composed functor $\mathbf{G}(\mathbf{F})$, we have

$$f_{\omega,m}(s_{i_1}, s_{i_2}, \cdots, s_{i,n}) = \text{the } j\text{-th component of any}$$
$$\widetilde{\omega}((t_{i_1,l})_{l \in I}, (t_{i_2,l})_{l \in I}, \cdots, (t_{i_n,l})_{l \in I}),$$
$$\text{where } (s_{i_k,l})_{l \in I} = (t_{i_k,l})_{l \in I} \text{ for } 1 \leq k \leq n.$$
$$= f_{\omega,m}(s_{i_1}, s_{i_2}, \cdots, s_{i,n}). \tag{8.2.7}$$

Moreover, for objects $\prod_{l \text{ in} I} S_l$ acted by the functor $\mathbf{F}(\mathbf{G})$, we have

$$\widetilde{\omega}((s_{i_1,l})_{l \in I}, (s_{i_2,l})_{l \in I}, \cdots, (s_{i_n,l})_{l \in I}) =$$
$$\begin{cases} s_{i_n,l} \text{ for the } l\text{-th component and } l \neq j, \text{ where } l \in I; \\ f_{\omega,m}(s_{i_1}, s_{i_2}, \cdots, s_{i_n}) \text{ for the } l\text{-th component and } l = j. \end{cases}$$
$$\tag{8.2.8}$$

Then all components obtained from $\mathbf{F}(\mathbf{G})(\prod_{l \text{ in} I} S_l)$ and $\prod_{l \text{ in} I} S_l$ are same no matter $l \neq j$ or $l = j$. It is easy to see that the functors $\mathbf{F}$ and $\mathbf{G}$ are mutually inverse on morphisms. Therefore, our claim that the invengories $\mathbf{EXT}_f$ and $\mathbf{PROD}_\omega$ are isomorphic is valid.

Actually, the above arguments can be extended to any other relations similar to f_ω which are mapped from finite collection of sets to an individual set. Hence, the theorem is proved.

The next phase is to obtain the equivalence between the invengory of $\langle \mathbb{S}, I, \mathbb{F}, \Omega \rangle$-algebras and the invengory of one-sorted algebras. We have to introduce the notion about [45], which provides an one-set representation of cartesian products.

A diagonal algebra is an algebra with a single operation d satisfying the following two postulates:

- $d(x, x, \cdots, x) = x$

- $d(d(x_{1,1}, x_{1,2}, \cdots, x_{1,n}), d(x_{2,1}, x_{2,2}, \cdots, x_{2,n}), \cdots, d(x_{n,1}, x_{n,2}, \cdots, x_{n,n})) = d(x_{1,1}, x_{2,2}, \cdots, x_{n,n})$

Theorem 20 *For finite I, every variety of $\langle \mathbb{S}, I, \mathbb{F}, \Omega \rangle$-algebras is equivalent to a variety of one-sorted algebras.*

PROOF. 23 *From the language of diagonal algebras and same $\omega(i_1, i_2, \cdots, i_n) = j$ relation, the first condition about $\mathbf{PROD}_\omega$ when $l \neq j$:*

$$\text{the } l\text{-th component of } \widetilde{\omega}((s_{i_1,l})_{l\in I}, (s_{i_2,l})_{l\in I}, \cdots, (s_{i_n,l})_{l\in I}) \text{ is } s_{i_n,l} \tag{8.2.9}$$

can be expressed as

$$\widetilde{\omega}((s_{i_1,l})_{l\in I}, (s_{i_2,l})_{l\in I}, \cdots, (s_{i_n,l})_{l\in I}) =$$
$$d\left(\overbrace{(s_{i_n,l})_{l\in I}, \cdots, (s_{i_n,l})_{l\in I}}^{j-1}, \widetilde{\omega}((s_{i_1,l})_{l\in I}, (s_{i_2,l})_{l\in I}, \cdots, (s_{i_n,l})_{l\in I}),\right.$$
$$\left. (s_{i_n,l})_{l\in I}, \cdots, (s_{i_n,l})_{l\in I} \right) \tag{8.2.10}$$

The second condition about $\mathbf{PROD}_\omega$ when $l = j$:

$$\text{the } j\text{-th component of } \widetilde{\omega}((t_{i_1,l})_{l\in I}, (t_{i_2,l})_{l\in I}, \cdots, (t_{i_n,l})_{l\in I})$$
$$\text{and } \widetilde{\omega}((s_{i_1,l})_{l\in I}, (s_{i_2,l})_{l\in I}, \cdots, (s_{i_n,l})_{l\in I}) \text{ are same,}$$
$$\text{whenever } (s_{i_k,l})_{l\in I} = (t_{i_k,l})_{l\in I} \text{ for } 1 \leq k \leq n \tag{8.2.11}$$

can be expressed as $a = d(\overbrace{a, \cdots, a}^{j-1}, b, a, \cdots, a)$, where $a = \widetilde{\omega}((s_{i_1,l})_{l\in I}, (s_{i_2,l})_{l\in I}, \cdots, (s_{i_n,l})_{l\in I})$ and *b is*

$$b = \widetilde{\omega} \, [d(\overbrace{(t_{i_1,l})_{l \in I}, \cdots, (t_{i_1,l})_{l \in I}}^{i_1-1}, (s_{i_1,l})_{l \in I}, (t_{i_1,l})_{l \in I}, \cdots, (t_{i_1,l})_{l \in I}),$$

$$d(\overbrace{(t_{i_2,l})_{l \in I}, \cdots, (t_{i_2,l})_{l \in I}}^{i_2-1}, (s_{i_2,l})_{l \in I}, (t_{i_2,l})_{l \in I}, \cdots, (t_{i_2,l})_{l \in I}), \cdots,$$

$$d(\overbrace{(t_{i_n,l})_{l \in I}, \cdots, (t_{i_n,l})_{l \in I}}^{i_n-1}, (s_{i_n,l})_{l \in I}, (t_{i_n,l})_{l \in I}, \cdots, (t_{i_n,l})_{l \in I}), \,] \tag{8.2.12}$$

Thus, the invengory of $\langle \mathbb{S}, I, \mathbb{F}, \Omega \rangle$-algebras is equivalent to an invengory of one-sorted algebras since each term related to $\mathbf{PROD}_\omega$ is expressed by elements with form $(\ )_{l \in I}$ (one-sort). As proof in the previous lemma, there is no difference when the single relation f_ω is replaced by a set of relations.

A variety of $\langle \mathbb{S}, I, \mathbb{F}, \Omega \rangle$-algebras, which are equivalent to one-sorted algebras, is a class whose members are all those $\langle \mathbb{S}, I, \mathbb{F}, \Omega \rangle$-algebras in which a given collection of relations holds identically. Hence, the theorem is proved.

Theorem 20 also holds for quasi-varieties since a quasi-variety of $\langle \mathbb{S}, I, \mathbb{F}, \Omega \rangle$-algebras, which are equivalent to one-sorted algebras, is a class whose collection of relations holds implicitly.

Example 38 *Given three sets S_1, S_2 and S_3 and three additions $+_1, +_2$ and $+_3$ with respect to S_1, S_2 and S_3, we assume that*

$$(s_1, s_2, s_3) +_1 (s_1', s_2', s_3') = (s_1 +_1 s_1', s_2', s_3')$$
$$(s_1, s_2, s_3) +_2 (s_1', s_2', s_3') = (s_1', s_2 +_2 s_2', s_3')$$
$$(s_1, s_2, s_3) +_3 (s_1', s_2', s_3') = (s_1', s_2', s_3 +_3 s_3'). \tag{8.2.13}$$

Next, we define $+$ on $S_1 \times S_2 \times S_3$ by

$$(s_1, s_2, s_3) + (s_1', s_2', s_3') = (s_1 +_1 s_1', s_2 +_2 s_2', s_3 +_3 s_3'). \tag{8.2.14}$$

Because

$$(s_1, s_2, s_3) +_1 (s_1', s_2', s_3') = (s_1 +_1 s_1', s_2', s_3')$$
$$= [(s_1, s_2, s_3) + (s_1', s_2', s_3')] \circ (s_1', s_2', s_3') \circ (s_1', s_2', s_3');$$
$$(s_1, s_2, s_3) +_2 (s_1', s_2', s_3') = (s_1', s_2 +_2 s_2', s_3')$$
$$= (s_1', s_2', s_3') \circ [(s_1, s_2, s_3) + (s_1', s_2', s_3')] \circ (s_1', s_2', s_3');$$
$$(s_1, s_2, s_3) +_3 (s_1', s_2', s_3') = (s_1', s_2', s_3 +_3 s_3')$$
$$= (s_1', s_2', s_3') \circ (s_1', s_2', s_3') \circ [(s_1, s_2, s_3) + (s_1', s_2', s_3')], \tag{8.2.15}$$

where ∘ is the 3-ary operation of a diagonal algebra. Hence, any addition in sets S_1, S_2 and S_3 can be expressed by a single addition of product sets with several 3-ary operations of a diagonal algebra.

8.2.2 Infinite Algebraic Systems

The main goal of this section is to consider underlying sets of Eq. (8.2.1) with infinite elements. We want to prove that many-sorted algebras is a variety (equalities or in-equalities definable) if and only if it is closed under the formation of homomorphic images, subalgebras and products. Furthermore, we also prove that many-sorted algebras is a quasi-variety (implications definable) if and only if it is closed under subalgebras and products.

Continuous Algebras

In this section, we will introduce *continuous algebras* in order to consider algebraic systems which allow equalities and (or) inequalities to present terms for computation.

Given a partial order set P, a *subset system* Z is a method assigning to each partial order set P a collection of subsets of P, denoted as $Z(P)$, such that $A \in Z(P)$ implies $f(A) \in Z(Q)$ for any order-preserving map f. A partial order set P is ♠-complete, where ♠ denotes for any set operation which acts on a family of sets, if the operation ♠A_i exists for every $A_i \in Z(P)$. An order-preserving map $f : P \to Q$ is ♠-continuous if it preserves the operation of ♠, i.e., $f(♠A_i) = ♠f(A_i)$ whenever $A_i \in Z(P)$.

Definition 35 *A ♠-continuous algebra is a ♠-complete partial order set A with the operation $\omega : A^n \to A$, where ω is any n-ary operation of Ω (the set of all invention operations), satisfying following conditions:*

- *All $\omega \in \Omega$ preserve set operation ♠ from $Z(A^n)$ to A.*

- *Subalgebra of ♠-continuous algebra is preserved, i.e., for any partial order set $B \subseteq A$ which is closed under the $\omega \in \Omega$ and ♠.*

- *A homomorphic image of a ♠-continuous algebra is a ♠-continuous algebra if there is a homomorphism from partial order set A to B.*

- *The cartesian product of a family $(A_l)_{l \in I}$ of ♠-continuous algebras which both the operations and the ordering are defined componentwise is also a ♠-continuous algebra.*

If the operation ♠ is $\bigvee$, then continuous algebras reduce as Z-continuous. Further details about Z-continuous algebras can be found in cite: **Free Z-continuous algebras by E. Nelson**.

At this stage, we are ready to define varieties, i.e., equationally defined classes, of ♠-continuous algebras. The meaning of *equationally defined* of a class should be recognized as any one of the following three aspects:

1. the class of all ♠-continuous algebras satisfying a collection of equalities.

2. the class of all ♠-continuous algebras satisfying a collection of inequalities.

3. the class of all ♠-continuous algebras satisfying a collection of terms defined iteratively.

The following definition is provided to characterize the notion about terms.

Definition 36 *Given a partial order set P and a set of invention operations Ω, the set $T(X)$ of terms in variables from the set X is defined iteratively as follows:*

$$T(X) = \bigcup_{i=0}^{\widetilde{X}} T_i(X), \tag{8.2.16}$$

where $\widetilde{X}$ is the least cardinal number larger than $2^{\max(|X|,|\Omega|,\aleph_0)}$. The expression $T_0(X)$ is the ordinary free algebra of type Ω over X. The expression $T_{i+1}(X)$ can be related as $T_i(X)$ by

$$T_{i+1}(X) = \spadesuit_{p \in P} t_p, \tag{8.2.17}$$

where $t_p \in T_i(X)$ for all $p \in P$. Finally, $T_i(X) = \bigcup_{j<i} T_j(X)$ for each limit ordinal i.

Definition 37 *For each ♠-continuous algebra A and each map $\gamma : X \longrightarrow A$ (valuation), we define the map $\gamma^* : T(X) \longrightarrow A$ as $\gamma^* = \bigcup_{i<\widetilde{X}} \gamma_i$, where $\gamma_i : T_i(X) \longrightarrow A$ satisfying*

- *γ_0 is the Ω-homomorphism extended from γ.*

- *$\gamma_i(t_p) \leq \gamma_i(t_q)$ if $p \leq q$ in P.*

- *$\gamma_{i+1}(t) = \spadesuit_{p \in P} \gamma_i(t_p)$.*

- *$\{\gamma_i(t_p) | p \in P\} \in Z(A)$.*

- *For a limit ordinal i, γ_i is set as $\bigcup_{j<i} \gamma_j$.*

And we say that a term $t \in T(X)$ is definable in A if γ^* is defined for every map $\gamma : X \longrightarrow A$.

Theorem 21 *For a ♠-continuous homomorphism $f : A \longrightarrow B$ and any map $\gamma : X \longrightarrow A$ and $t \in T(X)$, if $\gamma^*(t)$ is defined then so is $(f\gamma)^*(t)$, and $(f\gamma)^*(t) = f(\gamma^*(t))$.*

PROOF. 24 *The proof is based on the induction for $(f\gamma)_i(t) = f(\gamma_i(t))$ with respect to $i < \widetilde{X}$. When $i = 0$, this is true from homomorphism map of free algebras. For other i, we have*

$$(f\gamma)_i(t_p) = f(\gamma_i(t_p)) \leq f(\gamma_i(t_q)) = (f\gamma)_i(t_q), \tag{8.2.18}$$

since $\gamma_i(t_p) \leq \gamma_i(t_q)$ if $p \leq q$ in P. Therefore,

$$
\begin{aligned}
(f\gamma)_{i+1}(t) &= \spadesuit_{p \in P}(f\gamma)_i(t_p) \quad \text{by definition} \\
&= \spadesuit_{p \in P} f(\gamma_i(t_p)) \quad \text{by induction hypothesis} \\
&= f(\spadesuit_{p \in P}\gamma_i(t_p)) \quad \text{by the continuity of } f \\
&= f(\gamma_{i+1}(t)), \tag{8.2.19}
\end{aligned}
$$

the theorem is proved.

Variety

The purpose of this section is to show that many-sorted ♠-continuous algebras is a variety (equationally or in-equationally definable) if and only if it is closed under the homomorphic images, subalgebras and products. We begin by several lemmas required for later proof of the main theorem.

Lemma 8 *For any set X and a class of ♠-continuous algebras which is closed under subalgebras and products, denoted as $\mathbf{A}_{SP}$, the map $\alpha_X^* : T(X) \longrightarrow F_{\mathbf{A}_{SP}}(X)$ is surjective, where $F_{\mathbf{A}_{SP}}(X)$ is the subalgebra of the cartesian product of ♠-continuous algebras generated by X.*

PROOF. 25 *We wish to show that the map α^* is closed under ♠ and any ω for $\omega \in \Omega$.*

Given $P \in Z(F_{\mathbf{A}_{SP}}(X))$ as a sub-partial order set of $F_{\mathbf{A}_{SP}}(X)$, there exists $t_p \in T(X)$ such that $\alpha_X^*(t_p) = p$ for each $p \in P$. Since $t = \spadesuit_{p \in P} t_p \in T(X)$ and $\alpha_X^*(t_p) \leq \alpha_X^*(t_q)$ for $p \leq q$ in P, $\alpha_X^*(t)$ is defined and equals to $\spadesuit_{p \in P}\alpha_X^*(t_p) = \spadesuit_{p \in P} p$. Hence, the operation ♠ is preserved.

The next step is to prove that α_X^* preserves any ω for $\omega \in \Omega$. For each n-ary operation $\omega : F_{\mathbf{A}_{SP}}(X) \times F_{\mathbf{A}_{SP}}(X), \cdots, \times F_{\mathbf{A}_{SP}}(X) \longrightarrow F_{\mathbf{A}_{SP}}(X)$ at partial order set $F_{\mathbf{A}_{SP}}(X)$, we assume, for the i-th step, that

$$\omega(y_0, y_1, \cdots, y_{i-1}, z_i, z_{i+1}, \cdots, z_{n-1}) \in \alpha_X^*(T(X)) \tag{8.2.20}$$

if $y_0, y_1, \cdots, y_{i-1} \in \alpha_X^*(T(X))$ and $z_i, z_{i+1}, \cdots, z_{n-1} \in \alpha_X^*(T_0(X))$. If $i = 0$, it is true since α_X^* is a Ω-homomorphism on $T_0(X)$. Define another map g between $F_{\mathbf{A}_{SP}}(X)$ as

$$g(y) = \omega(y_0, y_1, \cdots, y_{i-1}, y, z_{i+1}, \cdots, z_{n-1}). \tag{8.2.21}$$

Since $F_{\mathbf{A}_{SP}}(X)$ is $\spadesuit$-continuous, the map g preserves $\spadesuit$ operation of sets in $Z(P)$ and all elements of $g(\alpha_X^*(T(X)))$ are obtained from those $g(\alpha_X^*(T_0(X)))$ by successive $\spadesuit$ operations. From the induction hypothesis and closed $\spadesuit$ operations in $F_{\mathbf{A}_{SP}}(X)$, we have $g(\alpha_X^*(T(X))) \subseteq \alpha_X^*(T(X))$, which finish induction proof. Therefore, $\alpha_X^*(T(X))$ is a subalgebra of $F_{\mathbf{A}_{SP}}(X)$ and the map α_X^* is surjective.

The following lemma is provided to indicate the existence of unique extension from the map $\gamma : X \longrightarrow A$ to the map $\breve{\gamma} : F_{\mathbf{A}_{SP}}(X) \longrightarrow A$.

Lemma 9 Let $\mathbf{A}_{SP}$ be the class of $\spadesuit$-continuous algebras which is closed under subalgebras and products and A be any $\spadesuit$-continuous algebra such that every term definable in $\mathbf{A}_{SP}$ is also definable in A. Then every map $\gamma : X \longrightarrow A$ has an extension to a homomorphic map $\breve{\gamma} : F_{\mathbf{A}_{SP}}(X) \longrightarrow A$.

PROOF. 26 We define $\breve{\gamma} : F_{\mathbf{A}_{SP}}(X) \longrightarrow A$ as $\breve{\gamma}(\alpha_X^*(t)) = \gamma^*(t)$ due to the surjective of map α_X^*. We first show that the map $\breve{\gamma}$ is well-defined and order-preserving. If $t_0, t_1 \in T(X)$ are terms such that $\alpha_X^*(t_0) \leq \alpha_X^*(t_1)$, we have $\gamma^*(t_0)$ and $\gamma^*(t_1)$ defined from Theorem 21 with $\gamma^*(t_0) \leq \gamma^*(t_1)$. Hence, the map $\breve{\gamma}$ is well-defined and order-preserving.

Given $P \in Z(F_{\mathbf{A}_{SP}}(X))$, then there exists $t_p \in T(X)$ such that $p = \alpha_X^*(t_p)$ for each $p \in P$. From $\alpha_X^*(\spadesuit_{p \in P} t_p) = \spadesuit_{p \in P} p$, we have

$$
\begin{aligned}
\breve{\gamma}(\spadesuit_{p \in P} p) &= \breve{\gamma}(\alpha_X^*(t)) \\
&= \gamma^*(t) = \spadesuit_{p \in P} \gamma^*(t_p) \\
&= \spadesuit_{p \in P} \breve{\gamma}(p),
\end{aligned}
\tag{8.2.22}
$$

which indicates that the map $\breve{\gamma}$ is $\spadesuit$-continuous.

For homomorphism of the map $\breve{\gamma}$, the proof is proceeded by induction argument with respect to the entry index for the operation $\omega : F_{\mathbf{A}_{SP}}(X) \times F_{\mathbf{A}_{SP}}(X), \cdots, \times F_{\mathbf{A}_{SP}}(X) \longrightarrow F_{\mathbf{A}_{SP}}(X)$. Suppose we have

$$\breve{\gamma}(\omega(y_0, y_1, \cdots, y_{i-1}, z_i, \cdots, z_{n-1})) = \omega(\breve{\gamma}(y_0), \breve{\gamma}(y_1), \cdots, \breve{\gamma}(y_{i-1}), \breve{\gamma}(z_i), \cdots, \breve{\gamma}(z_{n-1})), \tag{8.2.23}$$

for all $y_0, y_1, \cdots, y_{i-1} \in F_{\mathbf{A}_{SP}}(X)$ and $z_i, \cdots, z_{n-1} \in \alpha_X^*(T_0(X))$.

The case for $i = 0$ at Eq. (8.2.23) is valid since α_X^* and γ^* are homomorphisms on $T_0(X)$ and $\breve{\gamma}\alpha_X^* = \gamma^*$ from our definition of $\breve{\gamma}$. For the induction step, we have to prove that

$$F_{\mathbf{A}_{SP}}(X) = \{y \in F_{\mathbf{A}_{SP}}(X) | \breve{\gamma}(\omega(y_0, y_1, \cdots, y_{i-1}, y, z_{i+1}, \cdots, z_{n-1})) =$$
$$\omega(\breve{\gamma}(y_0), \breve{\gamma}(y_1), \cdots, \breve{\gamma}(y_{i-1}), \breve{\gamma}(y), \breve{\gamma}(z_{i+1}), \cdots, \breve{\gamma}(z_{n-1}))\}. \qquad (8.2.24)$$

By the induction hypothesis, the set $\alpha_X^*(T_0(X))$ belongs to the set

$$\{y \in F_{\mathbf{A}_{SP}}(X) | \breve{\gamma}(\omega(y_0, y_1, \cdots, y_{i-1}, y, z_{i+1}, \cdots, z_{n-1})) =$$
$$\omega(\breve{\gamma}(y_0), \breve{\gamma}(y_1), \cdots, \breve{\gamma}(y_{i-1}), \breve{\gamma}(y), \breve{\gamma}(z_{i+1}), \cdots, \breve{\gamma}(z_{n-1}))\}. \qquad (8.2.25)$$

Moreover, the set given by Eq. (8.2.25) is closed under all ♠ operations. Hence, the condition provided by Eq. (8.2.24) is true because $F_{\mathbf{A}_{SP}}(X)$ can be obtained from $\alpha_X^*(T_0(X))$ by successive ♠ operation from the surjective map of α_X^*.

In conclusion, such constructed map about $\breve{\gamma}$ is an extension from the homomorphic map $\gamma : X \longrightarrow A$.

We are ready to state and prove the main theorem at this section.

Theorem 22 *A class of many-sorted ♠-continuous algebras is a variety (equationally or in-equationally definable) if and only if it is closed under the homomorphic images, subalgebras and products.*

PROOF. 27 *The proof can be divided into two parts. The first part of this proof is to show that the many-sorted variety K is closed under homomorphic images, subalgebras and products. The second part of this proof is to prove the converse direction: if a class of algebras satisfies the closure property with respect to the homomorphic images, subalgebras and products, such class of algebras is definable by equalities or in-equalities. From Theorem 20, since the many-sorted variety K is equivalent to another one-sorted variety, it is enough to prove this theorem under one-sorted algebras. We use K' to represent the equivalent class for one-sorted algebras for the original many-sorted variety K.*

Suppose K' is a variety (one-sorted) definable by equalities or in-equalities. We shows that K' is closed under homomorphic images first. Let $A, B \in K'$ and $f : A \longrightarrow B$ be a surjective ♠-continuous homomorphism. Then we can find an inverse map for f, denoted as $f^{-1} : B \longrightarrow A$, such that $f(f^{-1}(b)) = b$ for all b in B. Because $(f^{-1}\gamma)^*(t)$ is defined in A, we have $\gamma^*(t)$ defined in B from $f(f^{-1}\gamma)^*(t) = (ff^{-1}\gamma)^*(t) = \gamma^*(t)$ (see Theorem 21). Since $\gamma^*(t)$ is defined for each map $\gamma : X \longrightarrow B$ whenever t is a term definable in A, k' is closed under homomorphic image.

Now, we show that K' is closed under subalgebras. Given a subalgebra B of A with inclusion homomorphism $\iota : B \longrightarrow A$. For each map $\gamma : X \longrightarrow B$, we wish to prove that $\gamma_i(t)$ is defined in B with respect to each i if $(\iota\gamma)_i(t)$ is defined in A for $t \in T_i(X)$. The cases for $i = 0$ and limit ordinals are obvious true.

From Theorem 21, we have

$$\gamma_i(t_p) = \iota\gamma_i(t_p) = (\iota\gamma)_i(t_p), \tag{8.2.26}$$

where $p \in P$. Then, $\spadesuit_{p \in P}(\iota\gamma)_i(t_p) = (\iota\gamma)_{i+1}(t)$ implies that $\gamma_{i+1}(t)$ is defined in B.

The last step of the proof in the first part is to show that K' is closed under products. Let $B = \prod A_j$ be a product of algebras $A_j \in K'$ with projection $\pi_j B \longrightarrow A_j$. We still apply induction argument for i with respect to every term $t \in T_i(X)$ definable by every A_j and each map $\gamma : X \longrightarrow B$. Hence, we can assume that $t \in T_{i+1}(X)$ with $t = \spadesuit_{p \in P} t_p$, where $t_p \in T_i(X)$ for all $p \in P$, and $\gamma_i(t)$ is defined in B. Given $p \leq q$ in P, we have

$$\begin{aligned} \pi_j\gamma_i(t_p) &= (\pi_j\gamma)_i(t_p) \\ &\leq (\pi_j\gamma)_i(t_q) = \pi_j\gamma_i(t_q) \end{aligned} \tag{8.2.27}$$

from Theorem 21. Since any j-th component for $\gamma_{i+1}(t)$ is $\spadesuit_{p \in P}\pi_j\gamma_i(t_p)$, which is defined in B, we conclude that $\gamma_{i+1}(t)$ is defined in B.

The second part of this proof is to prove the converse direction. Suppose K' is any class of $\spadesuit$-continuous algebras satisfies the closure property with respect to the homomorphic images, subalgebras and products. We will prove that $A \in K'$ if and only if each $t \in T(X)$ is definable in A. The direction of "only if" is obvious. For the "if" direction, we define an identity map from X to A as $\beta : X \longrightarrow A$. From Lemma 9, the map β has an extension to a surjective homomorphism $\breve{\beta} : F_{K'}(X) \longrightarrow A$. Since $F_{K'}(X) \in K'$ and K' is closed under homomorphic images, subalgebras and products, we have $A \in K'$ as desired.

Quasi-variety

The purpose of this section is to show that many-sorted $\spadesuit$-continuous algebras is a quasi-variety (implication definable by equalities or inequalities) if and only if it is closed under the subalgebras and products. We begin by several definitions about "implication" and "quasi-variety".

267

Definition 38 *An* implication *for terms generated from the set X, indicated as*

$$t_i \leq t'_i \text{ for } i \in I \implies t \leq t', \tag{8.2.28}$$

is meant a collection of inequalities $t_i \leq t'_i$ for $i \in I$ together with a single inequality $t \leq t'$. We say that a ♠-continuous algebra A satisfies such implication if, given a map $\gamma : X \longrightarrow A$ with $\gamma^*(t_i) \leq \gamma^*(t'_i)$ for all $i \in I$, we have $\gamma^*(t) \leq \gamma^*(t')$.

From Definition 38, a quasi-variety of ♠-continuous algebras is a class expressed by a collection of implications. The main theorem at this section is presented below.

Theorem 23 *A class of many-sorted ♠-continuous algebras is a quasi-variety (implication definable by equalities or inequalities) if and only if it is closed under subalgebras and products.*

PROOF. 28 *From Theorem 20, K' is used to represent the equivalent class for one-sorted algebras for the original many-sorted variety K which is closed under subalgebras and products. We will prove that K' is the quasi-variety expressed by the collection of all implications satisfied by all K'-algebras. It is equivalent to show $A \in K'$ for any ♠-continuous algebra A satisfying all implications.*

Given a map $f : A \longrightarrow B$, let $\overline{A}$ be the least subalgebra of B containing $f(A)$, then f is decomposed as the restriction $f_0 : A \longrightarrow \overline{A}$, which generates $\overline{A}$, followed by the inclusion map $\iota : \overline{A} \to B$. If each map $f : A \longrightarrow B$ in K' has such decomposition, K' is said to have reflective property. For an algebra K' which is closed under subalgebras and products, it can be shown that K' has reflective property from basic category theory. Therefore, if we can confirm that the reflective property of map $\iota : A \longrightarrow \overline{A}$ in K' is an embedding of a subalgebra, then $\overline{A} \in K'$ implies $A \in K'$.

For each $B \in K'$ and the map $f : A \longrightarrow B$, we prove first that there is ♠-continuous homomorphism $\overline{f} : \overline{A} \longrightarrow B$ with $f = \overline{f}\iota$. Given $P \in Z(A)$, we have a term $t = \spadesuit_{p \in P} t_p \in T(X)$. The map f is a ♠-continuous map from the following relation:

$$f(\spadesuit_{p \in P} t_p) = f(\gamma^*(t)) = f^*(t) = \spadesuit_{p \in P} f(t_p), \tag{8.2.29}$$

where $\gamma^* = \bigcup_{i < \widetilde{X}} \gamma_i$ and each $\gamma_i : T_i(X) \longrightarrow A$ satisfies the same rules as before (See Theorem 21). Next we show that the map f is a homomorphism. From Lemma 9, the map $\gamma : X \longrightarrow A$ can be extended to a ♠-continuous homomorphism $\breve{\gamma} : F_{\mathbf{A}_{SP}}(X) \longrightarrow A$. Since $\gamma^*(t) = \breve{\gamma}\alpha_X^*(t)$, we have $f\breve{\gamma} = \breve{f}$ from Lemma 8. Because $\breve{f}$ is a homomorphism and $\breve{\gamma}$ is a surjective homomorphism, *it follows that f is a homomorphism. Hence, there is a unique ♠-continuous homomorphism $\overline{f} : \overline{A} \longrightarrow B$ with $f = \overline{f}\iota$ from the reflexive property of the variety K'.*

Next we show that ι is order preserving, i.e., $\iota(x) \leq \iota(y)$ implies that $x \leq y$ for $x, y \in A$. We define two maps about terms algebra. The first map $\gamma^*_{A,B} : T(A) \longrightarrow B$ is defined as $\gamma^*_{A,B} = \bigcup_{i < \widetilde{A}} \gamma_{A,B;i}$, where $\gamma_{A,B;i} : T_i(A) \longrightarrow B$ satisfying same rules about terms required by Definition 37. The second map $\gamma^*_{A,A} : T(A) \longrightarrow A$ is defined as $\gamma^*_{A,A} = \bigcup_{i < \widetilde{A}} \gamma_{A,A;i}$, where $\gamma_{A,A;i} : T_i(A) \longrightarrow A$ satisfying same rules about terms required by Definition 37. Given a map $f : A \longrightarrow B$ with $\gamma^*_{A,B}(t) = \gamma^*_{A,B}(t')$ for all $t, t' \in \ker \gamma^*_{A,A}$, we have $\gamma^*_{A,B}(x) \leq \gamma^*_{A,B}(y)$ since $\iota(x) \leq \iota(y)$ and $f = \overline{f}\iota$ (reflexive property of the variety K'). Hence, the following implication is valid with respect to each algebra $B \in K'$: $t = t'$ for all $t, t' \in \ker \gamma^*_{A,A}$ and $\iota(x) \leq \iota(y) \implies x \leq y$ in B. By applying above argument with respect to the map $h : A \longrightarrow A$, we have $\gamma^*_{A,A}(x) \leq \gamma^*_{A,A}(y)$, which implies that $x \leq y$ in A.

The last portion left to prove that the map $\iota(A)$ is a subalgebra of $\overline{A}$ is to show that $\iota(A)$ is closed under ♠ operations. Let $P \subseteq A$ be a set with $\iota(P) \in Z(\overline{A})$, then we show that $P \in Z(A)$. Given a map $f : A \longrightarrow B$ with $\gamma^*_{A,B}(t) = \gamma^*_{A,B}(t')$ for all $t, t' \in \ker \gamma^*_{A,A}$ and reflectivity, we have

$$f(P) = \overline{f}(\iota(P)) \in Z(B). \tag{8.2.30}$$

Hence, $\gamma^*_{A,B}$ is defined at the term $♠_{p \in P} p$. By applying above argument to the the map $h : A \longrightarrow A$, we have $\gamma^*_{A,A}$ is defined at the term $♠_{p \in P} p$. Therefore, $P = \gamma^*_{A,A}(♠_{p \in P} p) \in Z(A)$. This concludes that $\iota(A)$ is a subalgebra of $\overline{A}$ and $A \in K'$.

8.2.3 Finite Algebraic Systems

The purpose of this section is to consider underlying sets of Eq. (8.2.1) with finite elements. We adopt non-standard approach (see [46])to prove that finite many-sorted algebras is a variety (equalities or in-equalities definable) if and only if it is closed under the formation of homomorphic images, subalgebras and products. Moreover, we show that finite many-sorted algebras is a quasi-variety (implications definable) if and only if it is closed under subalgebras and products.

Non-stand Analysis

This section will introduce non-standard analysis briefly and present several lemmas required for later proof about characterizing many-sorted algebras by homomorphic images, subalgebras and products.

The notion about non-standard analysis was first proposed by Abraham Robinson in the early 1960s. There are two reasons to support the importance of non-standard analysis: educational and technical purposes. In the early development of calculus, Newton and Leibniz utilized the concept about infinitesimal widely in establishing various basic facts in calculus. These formulations were criticized seriously by some mathematicians, for example, George Berkeley. Although Cauchy suggested *"epsilon-delta"* approach to make Newton and Leibniz formulations rigorously, most educators feel that the use of infinitesimals is more intuitive and more easily comprehended by students than the so-called epsilon-delta approach to analytic concepts. Non-standard analysis provides a rigorous language to formulate the notion about infinitesimal by keeping the intuition about infinitesimal. For technical reasons, some recent works about statistics and mathematical physics utilized non-standard analysis in investigating limiting processes of sequences or functions.

The main idea of non-standard analysis is to embed every set S from the universal set U in an extension $\tilde{S}$ from the non-standard universal set $\tilde{U}$ such that the following axiom hold:

- (Transfer Principle) For every $S_1, \cdots, S_n \in U$ and every bounded quantifier [3] statement $\phi(x_1, \cdots, x_n)$, the condition $\phi(S_1, \cdots, S_n)$ holds in U if and only if $\phi(\tilde{S}_1, \cdots, \tilde{S}_n)$ holds in $\tilde{U}$.

- (Idealization Principle) The set $\{\tilde{s} : s \in S\}$ is a proper subset of $\tilde{S}$ if and only if S is infinite.

A set S is named as *internal* if $S \in \tilde{U}$ and external of $S = \tilde{T}$ for some $T \in U$. Let us consider a short example about non-standard extension of natural numbers. Let $\mathbb{N}$ be the linearly ordered semigroup of natural numbers. Then by the transfer principle, the extension of $\mathbb{N}$ is a linearly ordered semigroup too. From idealization principle, we have $\mathbb{N} \neq \tilde{\mathbb{N}}$. Hence, there are elements $\mathcal{N} \in \tilde{\mathbb{N}} \backslash \mathbb{N}$, which are *infinite* numbers. More details about non-stand analysis can be found at [46]

Let $\langle \mathbb{S}, I, \mathbb{F}, \Omega \rangle$ denote algebraic systems for invention and let $\mathfrak{F}$ be the class of all finite algebraic $\langle \mathbb{S}, I, \mathbb{F}, \Omega \rangle$ systems. The usual algebraic terms of the lower predicate language over the alphabet set X form a set, denoted as $T(X)$, which is constructed by Definition 36. Hence, *non-standard* terms of the non-standard formal language, which is the non-standard generalization of the lower predicate language, as elements of the non-standard extension for the set $T(X)$, represented as $\tilde{T}(X)$. Expressions with the form $t_1 = t_2$ and $\omega(t_1, \cdots, t_n)$ are called *non-standard identities*, where $t_1, \cdots, t_n \in \tilde{T}(X)$ and ω is an n-ary relation symbol of $\langle \mathbb{S}, I, \mathbb{F}, \Omega \rangle$.

---

[3] A bounded quantifier statement is a statement that can be made using only the propositional connectives and bounded quantifiers, for example, $\forall$ or $\exists$.

Let A be a finite algebraic system with type $\langle \mathbb{S}, I, \mathbb{F}, \Omega \rangle$. The functional and predicate constants of the non-standard formal language are interpreted as elements and relations from the algebraic system A. The non-standard variables are interpreted with a mapping $\gamma : X \longrightarrow A$, which is a non-standard extendsion to the mapping $\tilde{\gamma}^* = \bigcup_{i < \overline{X}} \tilde{\gamma}_i$ and each $\tilde{\gamma}_i : \tilde{T}_i(X) \longrightarrow A$. The set of formulas is inductively defined by the following rules:

- Relation symbols: If ω is an n-ary relation symbol and $t_1, \cdots, t_n$ are terms then $\omega(t_1, \cdots, t_n)$ is a formula.

- Equality: If the equality symbol is considered part of logic and t_1, t_2 are terms, then $t_1 = t_2$ is a formula.

- Negation. If ϕ is a formula, then $\neg\phi$ is also a formula.

- Binary connection: If ϕ and ψ are formulas, then (ϕ logical connectives ψ) is a formula.

- Quantifiers. If ϕ is a formula and y is a variable, then $\forall y \phi$ and $\exists y \phi$ are formulas.

Hence, every formula ϕ of the non-standard formal language under this interpretation becomes a statement which is either true or false. For instance, a formula $t_1 = t_2$ is true, if the images $\tilde{\gamma}^*(t_1), \tilde{\gamma}^*(t_2)$ are equal in the algebraic system A. This truth can be represented as $A \models_\gamma t_1 = t_2$. Similarly, a formula $\omega(t_1, \cdots, t_n)$ is true if $(\tilde{\gamma}^*(t_1), \cdots, \tilde{\gamma}^*(t_n))$ belongs to the corresponding relation ω of the algebraic system A. This truth is indicated as $A \models_\gamma \omega(t_1, \cdots, t_n)$.

Let A be a finite algebraic with type $\langle \mathbb{S}, I, \mathbb{F}, \Omega \rangle$. We use symbol $\eta_{A,\gamma}$ to represent the kernel for the mapping $\tilde{\gamma}^* : \tilde{T}(X) \longrightarrow A$ and symbol $\mathfrak{M}(X, A)$ to denote the set of all mappings from X to A. Then following four terms are defined

$$
\begin{aligned}
\mathfrak{K}_X(A) &\triangleq \bigcap \{\eta_{A,\gamma} : \gamma \in \mathfrak{M}(X, A)\}; \\
\mathfrak{K}_X(\mathfrak{F}) &\triangleq \bigcap \{\eta_{A,\gamma} : A \in \mathfrak{F} \text{ and } \gamma \in \mathfrak{M}(X, A)\}; \\
\mathfrak{K}_X(A, \omega) &\triangleq \bigcap \{(\tilde{\gamma}^*)^{-n} \circ \omega \circ (\tilde{\gamma}^*)^n : \gamma \in \mathfrak{M}(X, A)\}; \\
\mathfrak{K}_X(\mathfrak{F}, \omega) &\triangleq \bigcap \{(\tilde{\gamma}^*)^{-n} \circ \omega \circ (\tilde{\gamma}^*)^n : A \in \mathfrak{F} \text{ and } \gamma \in \mathfrak{M}(X, A)\}, \quad (8.2.31)
\end{aligned}
$$

where the symbol ω involved at the last two definitions is any n-ary relation symbol in $\langle \mathbb{S}, I, \mathbb{F}, \Omega \rangle$. The set of non-standard identities which hold in A with the form $t_1 = t_2$ is denoted as $ID_X(A, =)$ and the set of non-standard identities which hold in A with the form $\omega(t_1, \cdots, t_n)$ is denoted as $ID_X(A, \omega)$. The set of non-standard identities which hold in $\mathfrak{F}$ with the form $t_1 = t_2$ is denoted as $ID_X(\mathfrak{F}, =)$ and the set of non-standard identities which hold in A with the form $\omega(t_1, \cdots, t_n)$ is denoted as $ID_X(\mathfrak{F}, \omega)$. For conditions about in-equalities, the set of non-standard in-equalities which hold in A with the form $t_1 \leq t_2$ is denoted as $ID_X(A, \leq)$ and the set of non-standard in-equalities which hold in A with the form $\omega_\leq(t_1, \cdots, t_n)$ is denoted as $ID_X(A, \omega_\leq)$, where $\omega_\leq$ is the in-equality relation for terms $t_1, \cdots, t_n$. The set of non-standard in-equalities which hold in $\mathfrak{F}$ with the form $t_1 = t_2$ is denoted as $ID_X(\mathfrak{F}, \leq)$ and the set of non-standard in-equalities which hold in A with the form $\omega_\leq(t_1, \cdots, t_n)$ is denoted as $ID_X(\mathfrak{F}, \omega_\leq)$.

Then we have the following lemma.

Lemma 10 *Let A be a finite algebraic system with type $\langle \mathbb{S}, I, \mathbb{F}, \Omega \rangle$, $\mathfrak{F}$ a class of finite algebraic system with type $\langle \mathbb{S}, I, \mathbb{F}, \Omega \rangle$, $\mathfrak{F}$ and ω be an n-ary relation symbol of $\langle \mathbb{S}, I, \mathbb{F}, \Omega \rangle$, $\mathfrak{F}$. Then*

$$ID_X(A, =) = \{t_1 = t_2 : (t_1, t_2) \in \mathfrak{K}_X(A)\};$$

$$ID_X(A, \leq) = \{t_1 \leq t_2 : (t_1, t_2) \in \mathfrak{K}_X(A)\};$$

$$ID_X(\mathfrak{F}, =) = \{t_1 = t_2 : (t_1, t_2) \in \mathfrak{K}_X(\mathfrak{F})\};$$

$$ID_X(\mathfrak{F}, \leq) = \{t_1 \leq t_2 : (t_1, t_2) \in \mathfrak{K}_X(\mathfrak{F})\};$$

$$ID_X(A, \omega) = \{\omega(t_1, \cdots, t_n) : (t_1, \cdots, t_n) \in \mathfrak{K}_X(A, \omega)\};$$

$$ID_X(A, \omega_\leq) = \{\omega_\leq(t_1, \cdots, t_n) : (t_1, \cdots, t_n) \in \mathfrak{K}_X(A, \omega_\leq)\};$$

$$ID_X(\mathfrak{F}, \omega) = \{\omega(t_1, \cdots, t_n) : (t_1, \cdots, t_n) \in \mathfrak{K}_X(\mathfrak{F}, \omega)\};$$

$$ID_X(\mathfrak{F}, \omega_\leq) = \{\omega_\leq(t_1, \cdots, t_n) : (t_1, \cdots, t_n) \in \mathfrak{K}_X(\mathfrak{F}, \omega_\leq)\}. \tag{8.2.32}$$

PROOF. 29 *Given any mapping $\gamma : X \longrightarrow A$, the condition $t_1 = t_2 \in \mathfrak{K}_X(A)$ means $A \models_\gamma t_1 = t_2$ and the condition $(t_1, \cdots, t_n) \in \mathfrak{K}_X(A, \omega)$ indicates $A \models_\gamma \omega(t_1, \cdots, t_n)$. Similarly, the condition $t_1 \leq t_2 \in \mathfrak{K}_X(A)$ means $A \models_\gamma t_1 \leq t_2$ and the condition $(t_1, \cdots, t_n) \in \mathfrak{K}_X(A, \omega_\leq)$ indicates $A \models_\gamma \omega_\leq(t_1, \cdots, t_n)$. This argument can be applied to $\mathfrak{F}$. Then this lemma is proved through checking definitions of $ID_X(A, =)$, $ID_X(A, \leq)$, $ID_X(A, \omega)$, $ID_X(A, \omega_\leq)$, $ID_X(\mathfrak{F}, =)$, $ID_X(\mathfrak{F}, \leq)$, $ID_X(\mathfrak{F}, \omega)$ and $ID_X(\mathfrak{F}, \omega_\leq)$.*

Given a class of non-standard formulas, named as Σ, the class of all algebraic system with type $\langle \mathbb{S}, I, \mathbb{F}, \Omega \rangle$ in which all formulas of Σ are true is denoted as $\mathbf{Mod}_\Omega(\Sigma)$. These algebraic systems are referred as the *models* for the class Σ. Therefore, the non-standard variety and the non-standard quasi-variety can be defined.

Definition 39 *Each class $\mathbf{Mod}_\Omega(\Sigma)$ of models for formulas class Σ of non-standard identities is referred as a non-standard variety of algebraic systems with type $\langle \mathbb{S}, I, \mathbb{F}, \Omega \rangle$. Similarly, each* class $\mathbf{Mod}_\Omega(\Sigma)$ of models for formulas class Σ of non-standard quasi-identities is referred as a non-standard quasi-variety of algebraic systems with type $\langle \mathbb{S}, I, \mathbb{F}, \Omega \rangle$.

Following lemmas are about the stability property of non-standard identities and non-standard quasi-identities with respect to actions of subalgebra, homomorphic images and Cartesian products of algebraic systems.

Lemma 11 *Non-standard identities and non-standard quasi-identities are stable with respect to the action of subalgebras.*

PROOF. 30 *If B is a sub-algebraic system of A with type $\langle \mathbb{S}, I, \mathbb{F}, \Omega \rangle$ and $\gamma : X \longrightarrow A$, we have*

$$\eta_{A,\gamma} = \eta_{B,\gamma};$$
$$(\tilde{\gamma^*})^{-n} \circ \omega_A \circ (\tilde{\gamma^*})^n = (\tilde{\gamma^*})^{-n} \circ \omega_B \circ (\tilde{\gamma^*})^n; \tag{8.2.33}$$

where ω_A and ω_B are n-ary operations in Ω. Hence, the validity of a non-standard identity (or quasi-identity) in the algebraic system B under $\gamma : X \longrightarrow B$ is equivalent to the validity of a non-standard identity (or quasi-identity) in the algebraic system A under $\gamma : X \longrightarrow A$.

Lemma 12 *Non-standard identities are stable with respect to homomorphisms.*

PROOF. 31 *Let A, B be two finite algebraic systems with type $\langle \mathbb{S}, I, \mathbb{F}, \Omega \rangle$ and f be a homomorphism from A to B. If the mappings $\gamma_A : X \longrightarrow A$ and $\gamma_B : X \longrightarrow B$ satisfy $\gamma_B = f \circ \gamma_A$, then*

$$\eta_{A,\gamma_A} = \widetilde{\gamma_A^{-1} \circ \gamma_A} \subset \gamma_A^{-1} \circ \widetilde{f^{-1} \circ f} \circ \gamma_A = \widetilde{\gamma_B^{-1} \circ \gamma_B} = \eta_{B,\gamma_B}; \tag{8.2.34}$$

and

$$\widetilde{\gamma_A^{-n}} \circ \omega_A \circ \widetilde{\gamma_A^n} \subset \widetilde{\gamma_A^{-n}} \circ f^{-n} \circ \omega_B \circ f^n \circ \widetilde{\gamma_A^n} = \widetilde{\gamma_B^{-n}} \circ \omega_B \circ \widetilde{\gamma_B^n}. \tag{8.2.35}$$

From Lemma 10, the relation $\eta_{A,\gamma_A} \subset \eta_{B,\gamma_B}$ and the relation $\widetilde{\gamma_A^{-n}} \circ \omega_A \circ \widetilde{\gamma_A^n} \subset \widetilde{\gamma_B^{-n}} \circ \omega_B \circ \widetilde{\gamma_B^n}$, we can concluded that $A \models \phi$ implies $B \models \phi$ for any non-standard identity ϕ.

Lemma 13 *Non-standard identities and non-standard quasi-identities are stable with respect to the action of finite Cartesian products.*

PROOF. 32 *Let A be an algebraic system with type $\langle \mathbb{S}, I, \mathbb{F}, \Omega \rangle$ and be the direct product of a finite family of A_i with same type through project $\pi_i : A \longrightarrow A_i$. We claim the following two identities for any mapping $\gamma : X \longrightarrow A$ and the composites $\gamma_i = \pi \circ \gamma$:*

$$\eta_{A,\gamma} = \bigcap_{i \in I} \eta_{A_i, \gamma_i};$$
(8.2.36)

and

$$\widetilde{\gamma^{-n}} \circ \omega_A \circ \widetilde{\gamma^n} = \bigcap_{i \in I} (\widetilde{\gamma_i^{-n}} \circ \omega_{A_i} \circ \widetilde{\gamma_i^n}),$$
(8.2.37)

with respect to any n-ary relation $\omega \in \Omega$.

From proof in Lemma 12, we have

$$\eta_{A,\gamma} \subset \bigcap_{i \in I} \eta_{A_i, \gamma_i};$$
(8.2.38)

and

$$\widetilde{\gamma^{-n}} \circ \omega_A \circ \widetilde{\gamma^n} \subset \bigcap_{i \in I} (\widetilde{\gamma_i^{-n}} \circ \omega_{A_i} \circ \widetilde{\gamma_i^n}).$$
(8.2.39)

For the inverse inclusion, we note that

$$\bigcap_{i \in I} \eta_{A_i, \gamma_i} = \bigcap_{i \in I} \widetilde{\gamma_i^{-1} \circ \gamma_i} \subset \widetilde{\gamma^{-1}} \circ \bigcap_{i \in I} \widetilde{\ker \pi_i} \circ \widetilde{\gamma} = \eta_{A,\gamma};$$
(8.2.40)

and

$$\bigcap_{i \in I} (\widetilde{\gamma_i^{-n}} \circ \omega_{A_i} \circ \widetilde{\gamma_i^n}) \subset \widetilde{\gamma^{-n}} \circ \bigcap_{i \in I} (\pi_i^{-n} \circ \omega_{A_i} \circ \pi_i^n) = \widetilde{\gamma^{-n}} \circ \omega_A \circ \widetilde{\gamma^n}.$$
(8.2.41)

Hence, claims for two identities presented by Eqs. (8.2.36) and (8.2.37) is valid.

For any non-standard identity (or quasi-identity) ϕ and a family of algebraic systems with type $\langle \mathbb{S}, I, \mathbb{F}, \Omega \rangle$, the conditions $A_i \models \phi$ for $i \in I$ imply that $\prod_{i \in I} A_i \models \phi$. Therefore, non-standard identities and non-standard quasi-identities are stable with respect to taking of finite Cartesian products.

Finite Varieties

In this section, we want to prove a Birkhoff-like theorem (Theorem 24) for a many-sorted finite variety from non-standard techniques. Partial contents about this section are modified from [47].

Theorem 24 *A class of many-sorted finite algebraic system with type $\langle \mathbb{S}, I, \mathbb{F}, \Omega \rangle$, represented by $\mathfrak{F}$, and finite number of relation symbols in Ω is a non-standard variety if and only if it is closed under the homomorphic images, subalgebras and finite Cartesian products.*

PROOF. 33 *From Theorem 20, since the many-sorted variety $\mathfrak{F}$ is equivalent to another one-sorted variety, it is enough to prove this theorem under one-sorted algebras. We use $\mathfrak{F}'$ to represent the equivalent class for one-sorted algebras for the original many-sorted variety $\mathfrak{F}$. The proof can be divided into two parts. The first part of this proof is to show that the many-sorted finite variety $\mathfrak{F}'$ is closed under homomorphic images, subalgebras and products. This part is verified through Lemmas 11, 12, 13.*

The second part of this proof is to prove the converse direction: if a class of one-sorted algebras with type $\langle \mathbb{S}', I', \mathbb{F}', \Omega' \rangle$, denoted as $\mathfrak{F}'$, satisfies the closure property with respect to the homomorphic images, subalgebras and products, such class of algebras, then it is definable by equalities or in-equalities. Let $\Sigma = ID(\mathfrak{F}', =) \bigcup ID(\mathfrak{F}', \leq) \bigcup ID(\mathfrak{F}', \omega) \bigcup ID(\mathfrak{F}', \omega_\leq)$, the converse direction is valid if $\mathfrak{F}' = \mathbf{Mod}_{\Omega'}(\Sigma)$. It is obvious that $\mathfrak{F}' \subset \mathbf{Mod}_{\Omega'}(\Sigma)$. We have to show that $\mathbf{Mod}_{\Omega'}(\Sigma) \subset \mathfrak{F}'$.

Given an arbitrary finite algebraic system with type $\langle \mathbb{S}', I', \mathbb{F}', \Omega' \rangle$, represented as A, in the class $\mathbf{Mod}_{\Omega'}(\Sigma)$, there is a mapping γ from any set X (with size greater then $|A|$) to A. Since Σ belongs to the set of all non-standard identities which hold in A, the set $ID_X(\mathfrak{F}', =)$ also belongs to the set $ID_X(A, =)$. From Lemma 10, we have $\mathfrak{K}_X(\mathfrak{F}') \subset \mathfrak{K}_X(A) \subset \eta_{A,\gamma}$. Consider any finite collection of algebras $B_j \in \mathfrak{F}'$ indexed by a finite set J with $\theta_j : X \longrightarrow B_j (j \in J)$, the direct product $B = \prod_{j \in J} B_j$ belongs to $\mathfrak{F}'$ from our assumption. Let θ be the production of functions θ_j, we have the family of directed sets $\{\eta_{B_j, \theta_j} : B_j \in \mathfrak{F}' \text{ and } \theta_j \in \mathfrak{M}(X, B_j)\}$ and $\eta_{B,\theta} = \bigcap_{i \in I} \eta_{B_j, \theta_j}$ from Eqs. (8.2.36) and (8.2.37). By saturation principle of non-standard analysis, the condition $\bigcap_{j \in J} \{\eta_{B_j, \theta_j} : B_j \in \mathfrak{F}' \text{ and } \theta_j \in \mathfrak{M}(X, B_j)\} \subset \eta_{A, \theta_j}$ concludes that

$$\eta_{B_n, \theta_n} \subset \eta_{A, \gamma}, \tag{8.2.42}$$

for some $B_n \in \mathfrak{F}'$ and $\theta_n : X \longrightarrow B_n$.

Consider an n-ary relation symbol $\omega \in \Omega$. The inclusion $\mathfrak{K}_X(\mathfrak{F}', \omega) \subset \mathfrak{K}_X(A, \omega)$ and Lemma 10 imply that the condition $ID_X(\mathfrak{F}', \omega) \in ID_X(A, \omega) \in \widetilde{\gamma^{-n}} \circ \omega_A \circ \widetilde{\gamma^n}$, where ω_A is the n-ary relation symbol acting on the algebra A. Consider any finite collection of algebras $B_k \in \mathfrak{F}'$ indexed by a finite set K with $\theta_k : X \longrightarrow B_k (k \in K)$, the direct product $B = \prod_{k \in K} B_k$, again, belongs to $\mathfrak{F}'$

from our assumption. Let θ be the production of functions θ_k, we have the family of directed sets $\widetilde{\theta^{-n}} \circ \omega_B \circ \widetilde{\theta^n} = \bigcup_{k \in K} (\widetilde{\theta_k^{-n}} \circ \omega_{B_k} \circ \widetilde{\theta_k^n})$ from Eqs. (8.2.36) and (8.2.37). By saturation principle of non-standard analysis, the condition $\bigcap_{k \in K} \{\widetilde{\theta_k^{-n}} \circ \omega_{B_k} \circ \widetilde{\theta_k^n} : B_k \in \mathfrak{F}'$ and $\theta_k \in \mathfrak{M}(X, B_k)\} \subset \widetilde{\gamma^{-n}} \circ \omega_A \circ \widetilde{\gamma^n}$ concludes that

$$\widetilde{\theta_\omega^{-n}} \circ \omega_{B_\omega} \circ \widetilde{\theta_\omega^n} \subset \widetilde{\gamma^{-n}} \circ \omega_A \circ \widetilde{\gamma^n}, \tag{8.2.43}$$

for some $B_\omega \in \mathfrak{F}'$ and $\theta_\omega : X \longrightarrow B_\omega$.

Let C be the algebraic system obtained by the product of B_n and B_ω with mapping $\theta_C = \theta_n \times \theta_\omega$ from X to C. From Eqs. (8.2.36), (8.2.37) and conditions (8.2.42), (8.2.43), it follows that

$$\eta_{C,\theta_C} \subset \eta_{A,\gamma},$$
$$\widetilde{\theta_C^{-n}} \circ \omega_C \circ \widetilde{\theta_C^n} \subset \widetilde{\gamma^{-n}} \circ \omega_A \circ \widetilde{\gamma^n}, \tag{8.2.44}$$

for all relation symbols $\omega \in \Omega$. For any n-ary relation symbol $\omega \in \Omega$ and the composition $f = \gamma \circ \theta_C^{-1}$, the relations provided by Eq. (8.2.44) imply that

$$f^n \circ \omega_B \circ f^{-n} \subset \gamma^n \circ \gamma^{-n} \circ \omega_A \circ \gamma^n \circ \gamma^{-n} \omega_A. \tag{8.2.45}$$

Therefore, f is a homomorphism of the algebraic system C with type $\langle \mathbb{S}', I', \mathbb{F}', \Omega' \rangle$ onto the algebraic system A with same type. We have $\mathbf{Mod}_{\Omega'}(\Sigma) \subset \mathfrak{F}'$, which is $\mathfrak{F}' = \mathbf{Mod}_{\Omega'}(\Sigma)$.

Finite Quasi-varieties

In this section, we wish to show a Birkhoff-like theorem (Theorem 25) for a many-sorted finite quasi-variety from non-standard techniques.

Theorem 25 *A class of many-sorted finite algebraic system with type $\langle \mathbb{S}, I, \mathbb{F}, \Omega \rangle$, represented by $\mathfrak{F}$, and finite number of relation symbols in Ω is a non-standard finite quasi-variety if and only if it is closed under subalgebras and finite Cartesian products.*

PROOF. 34 *From Theorem 20, since the many-sorted variety $\mathfrak{F}$ is equivalent to another one-sorted variety, it is enough to prove this theorem under one-sorted algebras. We use $\mathfrak{F}'$ to represent the equivalent class for one-sorted algebras for the original many-sorted variety $\mathfrak{F}$. The proof can be divided into two parts. The necessary part of this proof is to done by Lemmas 11 and 13.*

To prove the sufficient part, we assume that $\mathfrak{F}'$ is a class of one-sorted finite algebras with type $\langle \mathbb{S}', I', \mathbb{F}', \Omega' \rangle$ which is closed under subalgebras and finite Cartesian products. Let Σ be the *class of all non-standard quasi-identities, the sufficient part is proved if $\mathfrak{F}' = \mathbf{Mod}_{\Omega'}(\Sigma)$. It is obvious that $\mathfrak{F}' \subset \mathbf{Mod}_{\Omega'}(\Sigma)$. We have to show that $\mathbf{Mod}_{\Omega'}(\Sigma) \subset \mathfrak{F}'$.*

Given an arbitrary finite algebraic system A with type $\langle \mathbb{S}', I', \mathbb{F}', \Omega' \rangle$ in the class $\mathbf{Mod}_{\Omega'}(\Sigma)$, there is a mapping γ from any set X (with size greater then $|A|$) to A. Consider any finite collection of algebras $B_j \in \mathfrak{F}'$ indexed by a finite set J with $\theta_j : X \longrightarrow B_j (j \in J)$, the direct product $B = \prod\limits_{j \in J} B_j$ belongs to $\mathfrak{F}'$ from our assumption. Let θ be the production of functions θ_j, we have the family of directed sets $\{\eta_{B_j,\theta_j} : B_j \in \mathfrak{F}' \text{ and } \theta_j \in \mathfrak{M}(X, B_j)\}$ which have $\bigcap\limits_{j \in J} \{\eta_{B_j,\theta_j} : B_j \in \mathfrak{F}' \text{ and } \theta_j \in \mathfrak{M}(X, B_j)\} \subset \eta_{A,\theta_j}$ from Eqs. (8.2.36) and (8.2.37). Since Σ belongs to the set of all non-standard quasi-identities which hold in A, the condition $\bigcap\limits_{j \in J} \{\eta_{B_j,\theta_j} : B_j \in \mathfrak{F}' \text{ and } \theta_j \in \mathfrak{M}(X, B_j)\} \subset \eta_{A,\theta_j}$ concludes that

$$\eta_{B_n,\theta_n} \subset \eta_{A,\gamma}, \tag{8.2.46}$$

for some algebraic system $B_n \in \mathfrak{F}'$ and some mapping $\theta_n : X \longrightarrow B_n$.

Let $\widetilde{W}$ be the non-standard extension of the words set generated by elements in X freely, then there is a mapping from $\widetilde{W}/\eta_{B_n,\theta_n}$ onto $\widetilde{W}/\eta_{A,\gamma}$ according to the transfer principle. Since the set $\widetilde{B_n}$ is equal to B_n due to their finite property, the finite index for equivalent classes of $\widetilde{W}/\eta_{B_n,\theta_n}$ implies that the set of equivalent classes obtained by $\widetilde{W}/\eta_{A,\gamma}$ forms a finite transversal T in $\widetilde{W}$.

We define a new algebraic system on T from the signature Ω', denoted as (T, Ω_T), as follows: Given a n-ary relation symbol $\omega \in \Omega'$ and terms $t_1, \cdots, t_n \in T$, we set $(t_1, \cdots, t_n) \in \omega_T$, where ω_T is a n-ary relation symbol in Ω_T, if $A \models_\gamma \omega(t_1, \cdots, t_n)$. Moreover, given a n-ary function symbol f associated with Ω' and terms $t_1, \cdots, t_n, t_{n+1} \in T$, we say $f_T(t_1, \cdots, t_n) = t_{n+1}$, where f_T is a n-ary function symbol associated with relations in Ω_T, if $A \models_\gamma f(t_1, \cdots, t_n) = t_{n+1}$. Then we have an algebraic system on T with the signature Ω_T and a one-to-one mapping from T onto A.

Let Φ be the set of all formulas with the following types: $t_1 = t_2$, $f(t_1, \cdots, t_n) = t_{n+1}$ and $\omega(t_1, \cdots, t_n)$, where $t_1, \cdots, t_n, t_{n+1} \in T$, f is a n-ary function symbol and ω is a n-ary relation symbol. The set Φ is finite from the finiteness of the sets T and Ω. Given $\gamma : X \longrightarrow A$, the set Φ can be decomposed as two disjoint sets $\Phi_{\gamma,v}$ and $\Phi_{\gamma,a}$, where $\Phi_{\gamma,v}$ is the set of all formulas in Φ that are valid in A under γ and $\Phi_{\gamma,a}$ is the set of all formulas in Φ that are invalid in A under γ. By collecting conjunction of all formulas in $\Phi_{\gamma,v}$, we get a set Q and have a quasi-identity $Q \Longrightarrow \psi$ with respect to each formula $\psi \in \Phi_{\gamma,a}$. Since all non-standard quasi-identities true in $\mathfrak{F}'$ are also true in A, there is an algebraic system, denoted as (B_ψ, Ω), in $\mathfrak{F}'$ such that the formula

$(Q \implies \psi)$ *is false in* (B_ψ, Ω) *under some valuation* $\theta_\psi : X \longrightarrow B_\psi$.

Let (B, Ω) be the Cartesian product of algebraic systems (B_ψ, Ω) with respect to all $\phi \in \Phi_{\gamma,a}$ and θ be the product of all mappings θ_ψ with respect to all $\phi \in \Phi_{\gamma,a}$. The restriction of the extended mapping $\tilde{\theta}$ to the set T is a one-to-one mapping from T to B since, for any distinct terms $t_1, t_2 \in T$, we have $t_1 = t_2$ belongs to $\Phi_{\gamma,a}$, which implies $\tilde{\theta}(t_1) \neq \tilde{\theta}(t_2)$. Such restriction mapping is represented as θ_T.

If $A \models_\gamma \omega(t_1, \cdots, t_n)$ for any $\omega \in \Omega'$, the formula $\omega(t_1, \cdots, t_n)$ belongs to $\Phi_{\gamma,v}$ and $B \models_\theta \omega_T(t_1, \cdots, t_n)$. For function symbol $f_T(t_1, \cdots . t_n) = t_{n+1}$, the formula $f(t_1, \cdots, t_n) = t_{n+1}$ belongs to $\Phi_{\gamma,v}$ and this implies that $B \models_\theta f(t_1, \cdots, t_n) = t_{n+1}$. We have

$$\theta_T(f_T(t_1, \cdots, t_n)) = \widetilde{\theta(t_{n+1})} = f_B(\theta_T(t_1), \cdots, \theta_T(t_n)). \tag{8.2.47}$$

We also note that if $A \nvDash_\gamma \omega(t_1, \cdots, t_n)$, then the formula $\omega(t_1, \cdots, t_n)$ belongs to $\Phi_{\gamma,a}$ and $B \nvDash_\theta \omega(t_1, \cdots, t_n)$. Therefore, θ_T is an isomorphism from the algebraic system (T, Ω_T) to (B, Ω). We conclude that the algebraic system A, which is isomorphism to T, is isomorphic to a subalgebra of B. Hence, $A \in \mathfrak{F}'$ and $\mathfrak{F}' = \mathbf{Mod}_{\Omega'}(\Sigma)$.

8.3 Closed Construction for Oriented Complexes

The goal of this section is to figure out what constructing methods will preserve the classes of oriented complexes; these are cell complexes used to build gluing designs with positive or negative signs on each cell and will be defined exactly later. Since gluing designs are geometrical objects, the existence and configuration of fixed-point sets obtained by group action on gluing designs are also discussed.

8.3.1 Construction Methods of Oriented Complexes

In this section, we will define *oriented complexes* and construction methods based on them. Although our definitions are based on simplicial complexes [4], they can be extended to a broader sense of complexes-cell complex [48]. We begin by defining *prime components* of a simplicial complex K. The approached adopted in this subsection is based on [49], however, the reduction way to generate a new oriented complex is not addressed there.

---

[4] a simplicial complex is a topological space, constructed by "attaching together" points, line segments, triangles, and any n-dimensional objects

Definition 40 (Prime Components Definition) *Given a simplicial complex K, there are three associated functions dm, ∂^+ and ∂^- defined on K; such that, for each simplex $\sigma \in K$,*

- *$dm(\sigma)$ is a non-negative integer, the dimension of σ,*

- *∂^+ and ∂^- are subsets of K consisting of elements of dimension $dm(\sigma) - 1$.*

A simplicial complex K with such extra mathematical structure is called as a partial oriented complex, *denoted as $\mathcal{K}$. A subset x of $\mathcal{K}$ is closed if $\partial^+(\sigma) \subset x$ and $\partial^-(\sigma) \subset x$ for every $\sigma \in x$. The closure of a simplex σ, denoted as $\overline{\sigma}$, is defined as a* prime component.

A component x with dimension n if $\max_{\sigma \in x} dm(\sigma) = n$, where $\overline{\sigma}$ is a prime component.

The following definition is about the set of boundaries with dimension n for a subset of $\mathcal{K}$.

Definition 41 (n-boundary Definition) *Let x be a subset of $\mathcal{K}$ and n be an integer, the term $d_n^+(x)$ represents a set of boundary elements $\varsigma \in x$ such that*

- *$dm(\varsigma) \leq n$,*

- *when τ is a $n+1$-dimensional element of x with $\varsigma \in \overline{\tau}$, we have ς in the closure of $\partial^+(\tau)$.*

Similarly, the term $d_n^-(x)$ represents a set of boundary elements ς such that

- *$dm(\varsigma) \leq n$,*

- *when τ is a $n+1$-dimensional element of x with $\varsigma \in \overline{\tau}$, we have ς in the closure of $\partial^-(\tau)$.*

Then the composition between two components with dimension n can be regulated by the following definition.

Definition 42 (n-composition Definition) *The composition operation for two components x and y with $d_n^+(x) = d_n^-(y)$, denoted as $x \circ_n y$, is defined to be the union of x and y along $d_n^+(x)(d_n^-(y))$ and one has $x \bigcap y = d_n^+(x) = d_n^-(y)$.*

At this point, we are ready to define an oriented complex.

Definition 43 (Oriented Complex Definition) *An oriented complex induced by $\mathcal{K}$, denoted as $\overrightarrow{\mathcal{K}}$, is a partial oriented complex in which, for every atom $\overline{\sigma} \in \mathcal{K}$ with $dm(\overline{\sigma}) = n$, we have*

- *$d_{n-1}^+(\overline{\sigma})$ and $d_{n-1}^-(\overline{\sigma})$ are generated by prime components with composition operations $\circ_n$ for $n = 0, 1, 2, \cdots$;*

- $d_m^{\zeta_m}(d_n^{\zeta_n}(\overline{\sigma})) = d_m^{\zeta_m}(\overline{\sigma})$ *for* $m \le n$, *where* ζ_m *and* ζ_n *can be set as* $+$ *or* $-$ *signs.*

The class $Q(\overrightarrow{\mathcal{K}})$ in $\overrightarrow{\mathcal{K}}$ is named as a *gluing design* consists of sets $x \in \overrightarrow{\mathcal{K}}$ such that

- $x, d_n^-(x)$ and $d_n^+(x)$ are closed,

- $d_m^{\zeta_m}(d_n^{\zeta_n}(x)) = d_m^{\zeta_m}(x)$ for $m \le n$, where ζ_m and ζ_n can be set as $+$ or $-$ signs.

Following simple example is given to illustrate the meaning of oriented complexes.

Example 39 *Oriented complexes of dimension 1 turn out to be directed graphs: if x is an edge, then $d_0^+ x$ is its head and $d_0^- x$ is its tail. For a higher-dimensional oriented complex, consider a simplicial complex where the set of vertices is totally ordered. An n-simplex x with vertices $V_0, \cdots, V_n$ in order has boundary consisting of the $(n-1)$-simplexes $\partial_i x (0 < i < n)$, where $\partial_i x$ has vertices $V_0, \cdots, V_{i-1}, V_{i+l}, \cdots, V_n$. By following the conventions of homological algebra, the set $d_{n_l}^+ x$ is consisted by $\partial_i x$ for even i and the set $d_{n_l}^- x$ is consisted by $\partial_i x$ for odd i.*

Product of Oriented Complexes

Given two oriented complexes $\overrightarrow{\mathcal{K}}$ and $\overrightarrow{\mathcal{L}}$, the atom of the *product* complex $\overrightarrow{\mathcal{K}} \times \overrightarrow{\mathcal{L}}$ is defined as $\overline{\sigma} \times \overline{\tau}$, where $\overline{\sigma}$ and $\overline{\tau}$ are atoms of complexes $\overrightarrow{\mathcal{K}}$ and $\overrightarrow{\mathcal{L}}$, respectively. Then such atom at the product complex is denoted as $\overline{(\sigma, \tau)}$. The boundary operator for the product complex is defined as

$$d_n^+(x \times y) = \bigcup_{0 \le i \le n} d_i^+(x) \times d_{n-i}^{(-1)^i +}(y),$$
$$d_n^-(x \times y) = \bigcup_{0 \le i \le n} d_i^-(x) \times d_{n-i}^{(-1)^i -}(y). \tag{8.3.1}$$

Join of Oriented Complexes

Given two oriented complexes $\overrightarrow{\mathcal{K}}$ and $\overrightarrow{\mathcal{L}}$, the atom of the *join* complex $\overrightarrow{\mathcal{K}} * \overrightarrow{\mathcal{L}}$ is defined as $\overline{\sigma \times \tau}^J$, where σ is the atom in the suspension of $\mathcal{K}$ and τ is the atom in the suspension of $\mathcal{L}$, respectively, and J indicates the whole line segment with ending points as σ and τ. Let z be a subset of the product of two suspended oriented complexes $\overrightarrow{\mathcal{K}}$ and $\overrightarrow{\mathcal{L}}$, we have expression z^J for the set $\{x^J \in \overrightarrow{\mathcal{K}} * \overrightarrow{\mathcal{L}} : x \in z\}$. Hence, the boundary operator for the join complex is defined as

$$d_n^+(z^J) = (d_{n+1}^+(z))^J,$$
$$d_n^-(z^J) = (d_{n+1}^-(z))^J. \tag{8.3.2}$$

Combinatorial Reduction of Oriented Complexes

Let $V_{F,(\overrightarrow{\mathcal{K}})_0}$ be a vector space with bases as 0-dimensional components of the oriented complex $\overrightarrow{\mathcal{K}}$ and the field F, the exterior algebra of the vector space $V_{F,(\overrightarrow{\mathcal{K}})_0}$ is denoted as $\Lambda(V_{F,(\overrightarrow{\mathcal{K}})_0})$. The exterior algebra $\Lambda(V_{F,(\overrightarrow{\mathcal{K}})_0})$ has a F-vector space basis consisting of all the monomials v^S defined as $v_{i_1} \wedge v_{i_2} \cdots , \wedge v_{i_n}$ where $S = \{v_{i_1}, v_{i_2}, \cdots , v_{i_n}\} \subset (\overrightarrow{\mathcal{K}})_0$. Let I_{NOC} be the ideal of $\Lambda(V_{F,(\overrightarrow{\mathcal{K}})_0})$ generated by all $\{v^S\}$ such that all components in S can not form an oriented complex. The quotient algebra $\Lambda[\overrightarrow{\mathcal{K}}]$ defined as $\Lambda(V_{F,(\overrightarrow{\mathcal{K}})_0})/I_{NOC}$ has F-vector space bases as the set of all v^S such that S forms an oriented complex. Then we define a map $f : \Lambda[\overrightarrow{\mathcal{K}}] \longrightarrow \Lambda[\overrightarrow{\mathcal{K}}]$ as $f(y) = y \wedge (v_1 + v_2 + \cdots + v_N)$ for $y \in \Lambda[\overrightarrow{\mathcal{K}}]$, where N is the total number of 0-dimensional components of the oriented complex $\overrightarrow{\mathcal{K}}$.

We define the lexicographic ordering $\leq_D$ on k subsets of $(\overrightarrow{\mathcal{K}})_0$ as follows. Given the ordering $\{v_1 \leq v_2 \leq \cdots \leq v_N\}$, denoted as $\mathcal{O}_N$, of all 0-dimensional components of the oriented complex $\overrightarrow{\mathcal{K}}$, we say $S = \{v_{i_1} \leq \cdots \leq v_{i_k}\} \leq_D T = \{v_{j_1} \leq \cdots \leq v_{j_k}\}$ if, for some p, we have $i_p \leq j_p$ and $i_q = j_q$ for $q < p$. The *combinatorial reduction* for the oriented complex $\overrightarrow{\mathcal{K}}$ with respect to the ordering $\mathcal{O}_N$ is defined as $\overrightarrow{\mathcal{K}_{R,\mathcal{O}_N}} = \{S : v^S \in L\}$, where L be the set of those least bases of the quotient space $\Lambda[\overrightarrow{\mathcal{K}}]/\ker f$ with respect to the lexicographic ordering $\leq_D$ and $\mathcal{O}_N$.

8.3.2 Closed Construction Theorem

We introduce three construction methods for oriented complexes: product, join and combinatorial reduction. The goal of this section is to show that these three construction methods preserve the classes of oriented complexes.

Lemma 14 *Let $\overrightarrow{\mathcal{K}}$ and $\overrightarrow{\mathcal{L}}$ be oriented complexes. Then $\overrightarrow{\mathcal{K}} \times \overrightarrow{\mathcal{L}}$ is an oriented complex.*

PROOF. 35 *If any prime component $\overline{\sigma} \times \overline{\tau}$ with $dm(\overline{\sigma} \times \overline{\tau}) = n$ of a closed subset, say D, of $\overrightarrow{\mathcal{K}} \times \overrightarrow{\mathcal{L}}$ satisfies the condition that $d_{n-1}^+(\overline{\sigma} \times \overline{\tau})$ and $d_{n-1}^-(\overline{\sigma} \times \overline{\tau})$ are generated by prime components with composition operations, we claim that D is an oriented complex. [Claim 1]*

We first prove the following relation

$$d_m^{\zeta_m} d_n^{\zeta_n}(x \times y) = d_m^{\zeta_m}(x \times y), \tag{8.3.3}$$

where x, y are closed subsets and $m < n$. This procedure is based on the induction on $n - m$. For cases $m = n-1$ and $\zeta_m = \zeta_n$, we have $d_{n-1}^{\zeta_n}(x \times y) \subset d_{n-1}^{\zeta_n}(d_n^{\zeta_n}(x \times y))$ since $d_{n-1}^{\zeta_n}(x \times y) \subset d_n^{\zeta_n}(x \times y)$ and the fact $a \bigcap d_k^{\zeta_k}(b) \subset d_k^{\zeta_k}(a \bigcap b)$ for any closed sets a, b and integer k. On the other hand,

281

given $(\sigma, \tau) \in d_{n-1}^{\zeta_n}(d_n^{\zeta_n}(x \times y))$, we have $(\sigma, \tau) \in d_{n-1}^{\zeta_n}(d_j^{\zeta_n}(x) \times d_{n-j}^{(-1)^j \zeta_n}(y))$ where j is the minimal dimension such that $\sigma \in d_j^{\zeta_n}(x)$. Since j is minimal, $(\sigma, \tau) \in d_j^{\zeta_n}(d_j^{\zeta_n}(x)) \times d_{n-1-j}^{(-1)^j \zeta_n}(d_{n-j}^{(-1)^j \zeta_n}(y)) \subset d_{n-1}^{\zeta_n}(x \times y)$. Hence, $d_m^{\zeta_m} d_n^{\zeta_n}(x \times y) = d_m^{\zeta_m}(x \times y)$ for $m = n - 1$ and $\zeta_m = \zeta_n$.

For cases $m = n-1$ and $\zeta_m = -\zeta_n$, we have $d_{n-1}^{-\zeta_n}(x \times y) \subset d_{n-1}^{-\zeta_n}(d_n^{\zeta_n}(x \times y))$ since $d_{n-1}^{-\zeta_n}(x \times y) \subset d_n^{\zeta_n}(x \times y)$ and the fact $a \bigcap d_k^{\zeta_k}(b) \subset d_k^{\zeta_k}(a \bigcap b)$ for any closed sets a, b and integer k. Conversely, given $(\sigma, \tau) \in d_{n-1}^{-\zeta_n}(d_n^{\zeta_n}(x \times y))$, we have $(\sigma, \tau) \in d_{n-1}^{-\zeta_n}(d_{n-j}^{\zeta_n}(x) \times d_j^{(-1)^{n-j} \zeta_n}(y))$ where j is the minimal dimension such that $\tau \in d_j^{(-1)^{n-j} \zeta_n}(y)$. Since j is minimal, $(\sigma, \tau) \in d_{n-1-j}^{\zeta_m}(d_{n-j}^{\zeta_m}(x)) \times d_j^{(-1)^{n-j} \zeta_n}(d_j^{(-1)^{n-j} \zeta_n}(y)) \subset d_{n-1}^{\zeta_m}(x \times y)$. Hence, $d_m^{\zeta_m} d_n^{-\zeta_n}(x \times y) = d_m^{\zeta_m}(x \times y)$ for $m = n - 1$ and $\zeta_m = -\zeta_n$.

Finally, if $m < n-1$, we have $d_m^{\zeta_m}(x \times y) \subset d_m^{\zeta_m}(d_n^{\zeta_n}(x \times y))$ from $d_m^{\zeta_m}(x \times y) \subset d_n^{\zeta_n}(x \times y)$ and the fact $a \bigcap d_k^{\zeta_k}(b) \subset d_k^{\zeta_k}(a \bigcap b)$ for any closed sets a, b and integer k. The inductive hypothesis gives $d_m^{\zeta_m}(d_j^{\zeta_n}(x) \times d_{n-j}^{(-1)^j \zeta_n}(y)) \subset d_{n-1}^{\zeta_m}(d_j^{\zeta_n}(x) \times d_{n-j}^{(-1)^j \zeta_n}(y))$ for each j which implies $d_m^{\zeta_m}(d_n^{\zeta_n}(x \times y)) \subset d_{n-1}^{\zeta_m}(d_n^{\zeta_n}(x \times y))$, hence, we have $d_m^{\zeta_m}(d_n^{\zeta_n}(x \times y)) \subset d_m^{\zeta_m}(d_{n-1}^{\zeta_m}(d_n^{\zeta_n}(x \times y))) \subset d_m^{\zeta_m}(x \times y)$.

From Definition 43 and the relation (8.3.3), the object D is an oriented complex. [Claim 1] is proved.

Let $\overrightarrow{\mathcal{K}^{(p)}}$ be $\{\sigma \in \overrightarrow{\mathcal{K}} : dm(\sigma) \leq p\}$ and $\overrightarrow{\mathcal{L}^{(q)}}$ be $\{\tau \in \overrightarrow{\mathcal{K}} : dm(\tau) \leq q\}$, the term $C_{\overrightarrow{\mathcal{K}};p,q}(x)$ represents the class generated by the composition operations from the set $d_i^+(x) \times \overline{\tau}$ or $d_i^-(x) \times \overline{\tau}$, where x is a p-dimensional component in $\overrightarrow{\mathcal{K}}$ (can be a prime or a non-prime element) and $\overline{\tau}$ is an atom in $\overrightarrow{\mathcal{L}^{(q)}}$. Similarly, $C_{\overrightarrow{\mathcal{L}};p,q}(y)$ is the class generated by the composition operations from the set $\overline{\sigma} \times d_i^+(y)$ or $\overline{\sigma} \times d_i^-(y)$, where y is a q-dimensional component (can be a prime or a non-prime element) in $\overrightarrow{\mathcal{L}}$ and $\overline{\sigma}$ is an atom in $\overrightarrow{\mathcal{K}^{(p)}}$. If a is a member of $C_{\overrightarrow{\mathcal{K}};p-1,q}(d_{p-1}^- x)$, we define three closed subsets of $\overrightarrow{\mathcal{K}} \times \overrightarrow{\mathcal{L}}$ as

$$
\begin{aligned}
\psi(a) &= \{a \bigcap [(d_{p-1}^-(x) \bigcup d_{p-1}^+(x)) \times \overrightarrow{\mathcal{L}}]\} \bigcup \\
&\quad (x \times \{\tau \in \overrightarrow{\mathcal{L}} : d_{p-1}^-(x) \times \{\tau\} \subset a\}); \\
\phi_s^+(a) &= \{a \bigcap [(d_{p-1}^-(x) \bigcup d_{p-1}^+(x)) \times \overrightarrow{\mathcal{L}}]\} \bigcup \\
&\quad (d_{p-1}^+(x) \times \{\tau \in \overrightarrow{\mathcal{L}} : d_{p-1}^-(x) \times \{\tau\} \subset a\}) \bigcup \\
&\quad (x \times \{\tau \in \overrightarrow{\mathcal{L}} : d_{p-1}^-(x) \times \{\tau\} \subset d_s^-(a)\}); \\
\phi_s^-(a) &= \{a \bigcap [(d_{p-1}^-(x) \bigcup d_{p-1}^+(x)) \times \overrightarrow{\mathcal{L}}]\} \bigcup \\
&\quad (d_{p-1}^-(x) \times \{\tau \in \overrightarrow{\mathcal{L}} : d_{p-1}^-(x) \times \{\tau\} \subset a\}) \bigcup \\
&\quad (x \times \{\tau \in \overrightarrow{\mathcal{L}} : d_{p-1}^-(x) \times \{\tau\} \subset d_s^+(a)\}),
\end{aligned}
\tag{8.3.4}
$$

where s is an integer greater or equal to zero.

We claim that the member $a \in C_{\vec{\mathcal{K}};p-1,q}(d_{p-1}^- x)$ has the properties: [Claim 2]

- *$\psi(a)$, $\phi_s^+(a)$ and $\phi_s^-(a)$ are oriented complexes for $s \geq 0$,*

- *$\psi(a)$, $\phi_s^+(a)$ and $\phi_s^-(a)$ belong to $C_{\vec{\mathcal{K}};p,q}(x)$ and are generated by prime components for $s \geq 0$;*

if following conditions hold for a given non-negative integer t:

$$
\begin{aligned}
d_s^{\zeta_s}(\psi(a)) &= \phi_s^{\zeta_s}(d_s^{\zeta_s}(a)) \text{ for } s \geq 0, \\
d_s^{\zeta_s}(\phi_t^{\zeta_t}(a)) &= \phi_s^{\zeta_s}(d_s^{\zeta_s}(a)) \text{ for } 0 \leq s \leq t, \\
d_s^{\zeta_s}(\phi_t^{\zeta_t}(a)) &= \phi_t^{\zeta_t}(d_s^{\zeta_s}(a)) \text{ for } t < s.
\end{aligned}
\tag{8.3.5}
$$

Let b be the set of $\psi(a)$ or $\phi_s^{\zeta_s}(a)$, our goal is to show that b is an oriented complex. For any atom $\overline{\sigma} \times \overline{\tau}$ with dimension $p + q$ in b, we have

$$
\begin{aligned}
d_{p+q-1}^+(\overline{\sigma} \times \overline{\tau}) &= d_{p+q-1}^+(\psi(d_{p-1}^-(x) \times \overline{\tau})) \\
&= \phi_{p+q-1}^+(d_{p+q-1}^+(d_{p-1}^-(x) \times \overline{\tau})) \\
&= \phi_{p+q-1}^+(d_{p-1}^-(x) \times \overline{\tau}),
\end{aligned}
\tag{8.3.6}
$$

and

$$
\begin{aligned}
d_{p+q-1}^-(\overline{\sigma} \times \overline{\tau}) &= d_{p+q-1}^-(\psi(d_{p-1}^-(x) \times \overline{\tau})) \\
&= \phi_{p+q-1}^-(d_{p+q-1}^-(d_{p-1}^-(x) \times \overline{\tau})) \\
&= \phi_{p+q-1}^-(d_{p-1}^-(x) \times \overline{\tau}).
\end{aligned}
\tag{8.3.7}
$$

Since the set $d_{p+q-1}^+(\overline{\sigma} \times \overline{\tau})$ (or $d_{p+q-1}^-(\overline{\sigma} \times \overline{\tau})$) is generated by prime components, the set b is an oriented complex from [Claim 1] and the induction argument over $p + q$.

Next, we show that b belong to $C_{\vec{\mathcal{K}};p,q}(x)$ and are generated by prime components. There are four situations about the formation of b:

- *If $b = \psi(a), b = \phi_0^+(a)$ or $\phi_0^-(a)$ and a is generated from the set $d_{p-1}^-(x) \times \overline{\tau}$, then $b = d_j^{\zeta_j}(x) \times \overline{\tau}$ for some j and sign ζ_j. Hence, b belongs to $C_{\vec{\mathcal{K}};p,q}(x)$ and is generated by prime components.*

- If $b = \psi(a)$ and a is equal to a proper composition $a_1 \circ_n a_2$, then we have a decomposition for b into proper subsets as $b = \psi(a_1 \circ_n a_2) = \psi(a_1) \circ_{n+1} \psi(a_2)$. Hence, b belongs to $\mathcal{C}_{\overrightarrow{\mathcal{K}};p,q}(x)$ and is generated by prime components from iterative decomposition of a into a serious of proper composition from the set $d_{p-1}^-(x) \times \overline{\tau}$ and induction arguments.

- If $b = \phi_s^{\zeta_s}(a)$, then we have a decomposition for b as $b = \phi_s^+(a) = \phi_{s-1}^+(a) \circ_{s-1} \psi(d_{s-2}^-(a))$ or $b = \phi_s^-(a) = \phi_{s-1}^-(a) \circ_{s-1} \psi(d_{s-2}^+(a))$. Hence, b belongs to $\mathcal{C}_{\overrightarrow{\mathcal{K}};p,q}(x)$ and is generated by prime components from induction arguments.

- If $b = \phi_0^{\zeta_0}(a)$ and a is equal to a proper composition $a_1 \circ_n a_2$, then we have a decomposition for $b = \phi_0^+(a) = \phi_0^+(a_1) \circ_n \phi_0^+(a_2)$ or $b = \phi_0^-(a) = \phi_0^-(a_1) \circ_n \phi_0^-(a_2)$. b belongs to $\mathcal{C}_{\overrightarrow{\mathcal{K}};p,q}(x)$ and is generated by prime components from iterative decomposition of a into a serious of proper composition from the set $d_{p-1}^-(x) \times \overline{\tau}$ and induction arguments.

Therefore, the [Claim 2] is established.

If c is a member of $\mathcal{C}_{\overrightarrow{\mathcal{K}};p,q}(x)$, then we claim that c is a component generated by prime components of $\mathcal{C}_{\overrightarrow{\mathcal{K}};p,q}(x)$, $d_i^+(c)($ or $d_i^-(c)) \in \mathcal{C}_{\overrightarrow{\mathcal{K}};p,q}(x)$ for $i \geq 0$ and $x \times d \in \mathcal{C}_{\overrightarrow{\mathcal{K}};p,q}(x)$ if d is a component generated by prime components of $\overrightarrow{\mathcal{L}^{(q)}}$. [Claim 3]

Let g be a generator of $\mathcal{C}_{\overrightarrow{\mathcal{K}};p,q}(x)$, then

$$
\begin{aligned}
g &= \phi_0^{\zeta_0}(d_i^{\zeta_0}(x) \times \overline{\tau}) \text{ for } i < p-1, \\
g &= \phi_0^{\zeta_0}(d_{p-1}^-(x) \times \overline{\tau}) \text{ for } i = p-1, \\
g &= \psi(d_{p-1}^-(x) \times \overline{\tau}) \text{ for } i \geq p.
\end{aligned}
\tag{8.3.8}
$$

From [Claim 2], g can be generated by prime components of $\mathcal{C}_{\overrightarrow{\mathcal{K}};p,q}(x)$ and $d_i^+(g)($ or $d_i^-(g)) \in \mathcal{C}_{\overrightarrow{\mathcal{K}};p,q}(x)$ for $i \geq 0$. Since the member c of $\mathcal{C}_{\overrightarrow{\mathcal{K}};p,q}(x)$ can be obtained from g, the set c can be generated by prime components of $\mathcal{C}_{\overrightarrow{\mathcal{K}};p,q}(x)$. The function d_s^+ (or d_s^-) maps $\mathcal{C}_{\overrightarrow{\mathcal{K}};p,q}(x)$ into itself since $d_s^+(g)$ (or $d_s^-(g)$) belongs to $\mathcal{C}_{\overrightarrow{\mathcal{K}};p,q}(x)$ for each generator g. If d is a component generated by prime components of $\overrightarrow{\mathcal{L}^{(q)}}$, then $d_{p-1}^- x \times d \in \mathcal{C}_{\overrightarrow{\mathcal{K}};p-1,q}(d_{p-1}^- x)$ from inductive hypothesis, therefore, $x \times d = \psi(d_{p-1}^- x \times d) \in \mathcal{C}_{\overrightarrow{\mathcal{K}};p,q}(x)$. [Claim 3] is proved.

Let a' be a member of $\mathcal{C}_{\overrightarrow{\mathcal{L}};p,q-1}(d_{q-1}^-(y))$, we define three closed subsets of $\overrightarrow{\mathcal{K}} \times \overrightarrow{\mathcal{L}}$ as

$$
\begin{aligned}
\psi'(a') &= \{a' \textstyle\bigcap [\overrightarrow{\mathcal{K}} \times (d_{p-1}^-(y) \textstyle\bigcup d_{p-1}^+(y))]\} \textstyle\bigcup \\
&\quad (\{\sigma \in \overrightarrow{\mathcal{K}} : \{\sigma\} \times d_{q-1}^-(y) \subset a'\} \times y); \\
\phi_s^{+'}(a') &= \{a' \textstyle\bigcap [\overrightarrow{\mathcal{K}} \times (d_{p-1}^-(y) \textstyle\bigcup d_{p-1}^+(y))]\} \textstyle\bigcup \\
&\quad (\{\sigma \in \overrightarrow{\mathcal{K}} : \{\sigma\} \times d_{q-1}^-(y) \subset a'\} \times d_{q-1}^{(-1)^{s-q+1}}(y)) \textstyle\bigcup \\
&\quad (\{\sigma \in \overrightarrow{\mathcal{K}} : \{\sigma\} \times d_{q-1}^-(y) \subset d_s^-(a')\} \times y); \\
\phi_s^{-'}(a') &= \{a' \textstyle\bigcap [\overrightarrow{\mathcal{K}} \times (d_{p-1}^-(y) \textstyle\bigcup d_{p-1}^+(y))]\} \textstyle\bigcup \\
&\quad (\{\sigma \in \overrightarrow{\mathcal{K}} : \{\sigma\} \times d_{q-1}^-(y) \subset a'\} \times d_{q-1}^{(-1)^{s-q+1}}(y)) \textstyle\bigcup \\
&\quad (\{\sigma \in \overrightarrow{\mathcal{K}} : \{\sigma\} \times d_{q-1}^-(y) \subset d_s^+(a')\} \times y). \qquad (8.3.9)
\end{aligned}
$$

We claim that the member $a' \in \mathcal{C}_{\overrightarrow{\mathcal{L}};p,q-1}(d_{q-1}^-(y))$ has the properties for $s \geq 0$: [Claim 4]

- $\psi'(a')$, $\phi_s^{+'}(a')$ and $\phi_s^{-'}(a')$ are oriented complexes,

- $\psi'(a')$, $\phi_s^{+'}(a')$ and $\phi_s^{-'}(a')$ belong to $\mathcal{C}_{\overrightarrow{\mathcal{L}};p,q}(y)$ and are generated by prime components;

if following conditions hold given a non-negative integer t:

$$
\begin{aligned}
d_s^{\zeta_s}(\psi'(a')) &= \phi_s^{\zeta_s'}(d_s^{\zeta_s}(a')) \text{ for } s \geq 0, \\
d_s^{\zeta_s}(\phi_t^{\zeta_t'}(a')) &= \phi_s^{\zeta_s'}(d_s^{\zeta_s}(a')) \text{ for } 0 \leq s \leq t, \\
d_s^{\zeta_s}(\phi_t^{\zeta_t'}(a')) &= \phi_t^{\zeta_t'}(d_s^{\zeta_s}(a')) \text{ for } t < s. \qquad (8.3.10)
\end{aligned}
$$

Let b' be the set of $\psi'(a')$ or $\phi_s^{\zeta_s'}(a')$, we want to show that b' is an oriented complex. For any atom $\overline{\sigma} \times \overline{\tau}$ with dimension $p+q$ in b', we have

$$
\begin{aligned}
d_{p+q-1}^+(\overline{\sigma} \times \overline{\tau}) &= d_{p+q-1}^+(\psi'(\overline{\sigma} \times d_{q-1}^-(y))) \\
&= \phi_{p+q-1}^{+'}(d_{p+q-1}^+(\overline{\sigma} \times d_{q-1}^-(y))) \\
&= \phi_{p+q-1}^{+'}(\overline{\sigma} \times d_{q-1}^-(y)), \qquad (8.3.11)
\end{aligned}
$$

and

$$
\begin{aligned}
d_{p+q-1}^-(\overline{\sigma} \times \overline{\tau}) &= d_{p+q-1}^-(\psi'(\overline{\sigma} \times d_{q-1}^-(y))) \\
&= \phi_{p+q-1}^{-'}(d_{p+q-1}^-(\overline{\sigma} \times d_{q-1}^-(y))) \\
&= \phi_{p+q-1}^{-'}(\overline{\sigma} \times d_{q-1}^-(y)). \qquad (8.3.12)
\end{aligned}
$$

Since the set $d_{p+q-1}^+(\overline{\sigma} \times \overline{\tau})$ (or $d_{p+q-1}^-(\overline{\sigma} \times \overline{\tau})$) is generated by prime components, the set b' is an oriented complex from [Claim 1] and the induction argument over $p + q$.

Next, we show that b' belong to $C_{\overrightarrow{\mathcal{L}};p,q}(y)$ and are generated by prime components. There are four situations about the formation of b':

- If $b' = \psi(a'), b' = \phi_0^{+'}(a')$ or $\phi_0^{-'}(a')$ and a' is generated from the set $\overline{\sigma} \times d_{q-1}^-(y)$, then $b' = \overline{\sigma} \times d_j^{\zeta_j}(y)$ for some j and sign ζ_j. Hence, b' belongs to $C_{\overrightarrow{\mathcal{L}};p,q}(y)$ and is generated by prime components.

- If $b' = \psi'(a')$ and a' is equal to a proper composition $a_1' \circ_n a_2'$, then we have a decomposition for b' into proper subsets as $b' = \psi'(a_1' \circ_n a_2') = \psi'(a_1') \circ_{n+1} \psi'(a_2')$. Hence, b' belongs to $C_{\overrightarrow{\mathcal{L}};p,q}(y)$ and is generated by prime components from induction arguments.

- If $b' = \phi_s^{\zeta_s'}(a')$, then we have a decomposition for b' as $b' = \phi_s^{+'}(a') = \phi_{s-1}^{+'}(a') \circ_{s-1} \psi'(d_{s-2}^{-'}(a'))$ or $b' = \phi_s^{-'}(a') = \phi_{s-1}^{-'}(a') \circ_{s-1} \psi'(d_{s-2}^{+'}(a'))$. Hence, b' belongs to $C_{\overrightarrow{\mathcal{L}};p,q}(x)$ and is generated by prime components from induction arguments.

- If $b' = \phi_0^{\zeta_0}(a')$ and a' is equal to a proper composition $a_1' \circ_n a_2'$, then we have a decomposition for $b' = \phi_0^{+'}(a') = \phi_0^{+'}(a_1') \circ_n \phi_0^{+'}(a_2')$ or $b' = \phi_0^{-'}(a') = \phi_0^{-'}(a_1') \circ_n \phi_0^{-'}(a_2')$. Hence, b' belongs to $C_{\overrightarrow{\mathcal{L}};p,q}(y)$ and is generated by prime components.

Then [Claim 4] is proved.

If c' is a member of $C_{\overrightarrow{\mathcal{L}};p,q}(y)$, then we claim that c' is a component generated by prime components of $C_{\overrightarrow{\mathcal{L}};p,q}(y)$, $d_i^+(c')$ (or $d_i^-(c')$) $\in C_{\overrightarrow{\mathcal{L}};p,q}(y)$ for $i \geq 0$ and $d' \times y \in C_{\overrightarrow{\mathcal{L}};p,q}(y)$ if d' is a component generated by prime components of $\mathcal{K}^{(p)}$. [Claim 5]

Let g' be a generator of $C_{\overrightarrow{\mathcal{L}};p,q}(y)$, then

$$g' = \phi_0^{\zeta_0'}(\overline{\sigma} \times d_i^{\zeta_0}y) \text{ for } i < q - 1,$$
$$g' = \phi_0^{\zeta_0'}(\overline{\sigma} \times d_{q-1}^- y) \text{ for } i = q - 1,$$
$$g' = \psi'(\overline{\sigma} \times d_{p-1}^{-'}y) \text{ for } i \geq q. \tag{8.3.13}$$

From [Claim 4], g' can be generated by prime components of $C_{\overrightarrow{\mathcal{L}};p,q}(y)$ and $d_i^+(g')$ (or $d_i^-(g')$) $\in C_{\overrightarrow{\mathcal{L}};p,q}(y)$ for $i \geq 0$. Since the member c' of $C_{\overrightarrow{\mathcal{L}};p,q}(y)$ can be obtained from g', the set c' can be generated by prime components of $C_{\overrightarrow{\mathcal{L}};p,q}(y)$. The function d_s^+ (or d_s^-) maps $C_{\overrightarrow{\mathcal{L}};p,q}(y)$ into itself since $d_s^+(g')$ (or $d_s^-(g')$) belongs to $C_{\overrightarrow{\mathcal{L}};p,q}(y)$ for each generator g. If d' is a component generated

286

by prime components of $\overrightarrow{\mathcal{K}^{(p)}}$, *then* $d' \times d_{q-1}^-(y) \in \mathcal{C}_{\overrightarrow{\mathcal{L}};p,q-1}(d_{p-1}^-(y))$ *from inductive hypothesis,* *therefore,* $d' \times y = \psi(d' \times d_{q-1}^-(y)) \in \mathcal{C}_{\overrightarrow{\mathcal{L}};p,q}(q)$. *[Claim 5] is proved.*

From [Claim 1] to [Claim 5], we proved that the product of two oriented complexes is an oriented complex.

Lemma 15 *Let* $\overrightarrow{\mathcal{K}}$ *and* $\overrightarrow{\mathcal{L}}$ *be oriented complexes. Then* $\overrightarrow{\mathcal{K}} * \overrightarrow{\mathcal{L}}$ *is an oriented complex.*

PROOF. 36 *From boundary operators defined by Eq. (8.3.15), for subsets* z, w *in the product of the suspension of we have*

$$(z \circ_n w)^J \;\; = \;\; z^J \circ_{n-1} w^J, \tag{8.3.14}$$

and

Given two oriented complexes $\overrightarrow{\mathcal{K}}$ and $\overrightarrow{\mathcal{L}}$, the atom of the join complex $\overrightarrow{\mathcal{K}} * \overrightarrow{\mathcal{L}}$ is defined as $\overline{\sigma \times \tau}^J$, where σ is the atom in the suspension of $\mathcal{K}$ and τ is the atom in the suspension of $\mathcal{L}$, respectively, and J indicates the whole line segment with ending points as σ and τ. Let z be a subset of the product of two suspended oriented complexes $\overrightarrow{\mathcal{K}}$ and $\overrightarrow{\mathcal{L}}$, we have expression z^J for the set $\{x^J \in \overrightarrow{\mathcal{K}} * \overrightarrow{\mathcal{L}} : x \in z\}$. Hence, the boundary operator for the join complex is defined as

$$d_n^+(z^J) = (d_{n+1}^+(z))^J,$$
$$d_n^-(z^J) = (d_{n+1}^-(z))^J. \tag{8.3.15}$$

Lemma 16 *Let* $\overrightarrow{\mathcal{K}}$ *be an oriented complexes. Then* $\overrightarrow{\mathcal{K}_{R,\mathcal{O}_N}}$ *is an oriented complex.*

PROOF. 37 *Let* L *be the set of those least bases of the quotient space* $\Lambda[\overrightarrow{\mathcal{K}}]/\ker f$, *where* $f : \Lambda[\overrightarrow{\mathcal{K}}] \longrightarrow \Lambda[\overrightarrow{\mathcal{K}}]$, *with respect to the lexicographic ordering* $\leq_D$ *and* $\mathcal{O}_N$. *If* $S \in \overrightarrow{\mathcal{K}}$, *then* $x^S \notin L$ *when*

$$v^S = a_1 v^{S_1} + \cdots + a_i v^{S_i} + b \tag{8.3.16}$$

where $b \in \ker f$, $a_j \in F$, $S_j \in \overrightarrow{\mathcal{K}}$ *and* $S_j \leq_D S$ *for each* $j \in \{1, 2, \cdots, i\}$. *Since* $v^S \notin L$ *and we assume that* $S \subset T$ *for some face* T *in* $\overrightarrow{\mathcal{K}}$, *we want to prove that* $\overrightarrow{\mathcal{K}_{R,\mathcal{O}_N}}$ *is an oriented complex again by showing* $v^T \notin L$.

By multiplying v^{S-T} on left hand side of Eq. (8.3.16), we have $v^{S-T} \bigwedge v^{S_i} = \pm v^{(S-T) \bigcup S_i}$ in $\Lambda[\overrightarrow{\mathcal{K}}]$. Then we obtain an expression for v^S as a linear combination of monomials $v^{(S-T) \bigcup S_i}$ and $(S-T) \bigcup S_i \leq_D (S-T) \bigcup S = S$, which gives $v^T \notin L$.

Theorem 26 *The constructions of product, join and combinatorial reduction preserve the classes of oriented complexes.*

PROOF. 38 *From Lemmas 14, 15 and 16, this theorem is proved.*

8.3.3 Constructions from Group Actions

In this section, we provide another construction method to obtain other oriented complexes given a finite oriented complex through groups actions. Let G be a finite group not of p-power order and $\overrightarrow{\mathcal{K}}$ be an oriented complex satisfying some geometrical requirements, then a construction method is proposed to build a finite $\mathbb{Z}_p$-acyclic oriented complex which has fixed-point set as $\overrightarrow{\mathcal{K}}$ under the action of G.

A Characterization of Oriented Complexes

We consider a finite oriented complex $\overrightarrow{\mathcal{K}}$, writing $(\overrightarrow{\mathcal{K}})_i$ for its i-dimensional objects where $0 \leq i \leq dm(\overrightarrow{\mathcal{K}})$ and, when a, b are i-dimensional objects, $\mathcal{K}(a, b)$ for the set of maps from a to b.

Definition 44 *We use $\Upsilon_i(\overrightarrow{\mathcal{K}})$ to represent the $\mathbb{Q}$-algebra functions $(\overrightarrow{\mathcal{K}})_i \times (\overrightarrow{\mathcal{K}})_i \longrightarrow \mathbb{Q}$, with pointwise addition and scaler multiplication, multiplication defined by*

$$(fg)(a, c) = \sum_{b \in (\overrightarrow{\mathcal{K}})_i} f(a, b)g(b, c) \tag{8.3.17}$$

where $f, g \in \Upsilon_i(\overrightarrow{\mathcal{K}})$ and $a, c \in (\overrightarrow{\mathcal{K}})_i$. The unit is Kronecker delta function.

The zeta function associated to the i-dimensional objects, denoted as ζ_i, is defined by $\zeta_i(a, b) = |\mathcal{K}(a, b)|$ (cardinality for the set $\mathcal{K}(a, b)$). If ζ_i is invertible in $\Upsilon_i(\overrightarrow{\mathcal{K}})$ then $\overrightarrow{\mathcal{K}}$ is said to have *inversion* and its inversion is denoted as $\mu_i (= \zeta_i^{-1})$.

Definition 45 *Let $\overrightarrow{\mathcal{K}}$ be an finite oriented complex, a spectrum on $(\overrightarrow{\mathcal{K}})_i$ is a function, denoted as $\mathcal{F}_i$, from domain as objects in $(\overrightarrow{\mathcal{K}})_i$ to $\mathbb{Q}$ such that for all $a \in (\overrightarrow{\mathcal{K}})_i$,*

$$\sum_b \zeta_i(a, b)\mathcal{F}_i(b) = 1. \tag{8.3.18}$$

The characteristic for $\overrightarrow{\mathcal{K}}$ is composed by $dm(\overrightarrow{\mathcal{K}})$ rational numbers, denoted by a vector $\vec{\chi}_{\overrightarrow{\mathcal{K}}}$, such that the i-th component for $i-1$-dimensional objects and their mappings is

$$\chi_i(\overrightarrow{\mathcal{K}}) = \sum_{a \in (\overrightarrow{\mathcal{K}})_i} \mathcal{F}_i(a), \tag{8.3.19}$$

288

where $1 \leq i \leq dm(\overrightarrow{\mathcal{K}})$.

Example 40 *If $\overrightarrow{\mathcal{K}}$ is a finite oriented complex with only 0-dimensional components, then $\vec{\chi}_{\overrightarrow{\mathcal{K}}} = [\chi_1] = [|(\overrightarrow{\mathcal{K}})_0|]$.*

Example 41 *If G is a finite group, then $\vec{\chi}_G = [\chi_1] = [\frac{1}{|G|}]$ if the group is treated as an oriented complex based on group elements and their relations by the group definition. If G acts freely on a contractible space X with dimension 1 which has characteristic $[1]$, then the quotient space X/G has characteristic $[\frac{1}{|G|}]$. One has*

$$\chi_i(\overrightarrow{\mathcal{K}}) + (p-1)\chi_i((\overrightarrow{\mathcal{K}})^{\mathbb{Z}_p}) = p\chi_i(\overrightarrow{\mathcal{K}}/\mathbb{Z}_p), \tag{8.3.20}$$

given $\overrightarrow{\mathcal{K}}$ acted by $\mathbb{Z}_p$. Hence, $\chi_i((\overrightarrow{\mathcal{K}})^H) = \frac{1}{|(\overrightarrow{\mathcal{K}})_i|}$ if H has normal subgroups with p-power order for $1 \leq i \leq dm(\overrightarrow{\mathcal{K}})$.

Dissolution Functions

In this section, a lemma is provided to record actions of a group on acyclic spaces terms of characteristics of the fixed point sets of subgroups by *dissolution functions*. For a finite group H, $\mathcal{S}(H)$ will denote the set of subgroups of H.

Lemma 17 *Let H be a group acting on the finite oriented complex X with dimension $dm(X)$. For each i, where $1 \leq i \leq dm(X)$, we have following facts:*
(1) There is a unique function $\phi_i : \mathcal{S}(H) \longrightarrow \mathbb{Q}$ such that

$$\chi_i(X^G) = \frac{1}{|(X)_{i-1}|} + \sum_{K \supset G} \phi_i(K) \tag{8.3.21}$$

for all $G \subset H$.

(2) If $\mathcal{G}$ is any non-empty subset with the maximality condition, i.e., $G \in \mathcal{G}$ and $G \subseteq K \subseteq H$ imply $K \in \mathcal{G}$, then

$$\chi_i(\bigcup_{G \in \mathcal{G}} X^G) = \frac{1}{|(X)_{i-1}|} + \sum_{G \in \mathcal{G}} \phi_i(G). \tag{8.3.22}$$

(3) ϕ_i is constant on conjugacy classes of subgroups and

$$\chi_i(X^G \backslash \bigcup_{K \supsetneq G} X^K) - \frac{1}{|(X)_{i-1}|} = n \times |N(G)/G|, \tag{8.3.23}$$

for some integer n where $N(G)$ is the normal subgroup of G.

PROOF. 39 *Choose an inclusion ordering for $\mathcal{S}(H) = \{G_0, G_1, \cdots, G_m\}$ such that $G_j \subseteq G_k$ when $j \geq k$. Then the condition*

$$\phi_i(G) = \chi_i(X^{G_j}) - \sum_{G_k \supsetneq G_j} \phi(G_k) - \frac{1}{|(X)_{i-1}|}, \tag{8.3.24}$$

for all G_j is a necessary and sufficient condition for Eq. (8.3.21) to hold. And ϕ can be defined uniquely for $j = 0, 1, \cdots, m$ successively.

If we assume that Eq. (8.3.22) holds for all proper subsets of $\mathcal{G}$ and G_0 is the minimal set in $\mathcal{G}$, we set $\mathcal{G}_1$ as $\mathcal{G} - \{G_0\}$ and $\mathcal{G}_2$ as $\{K : G_0 \subseteq K \subseteq H\}$.

For the case $\mathcal{G}_2 = \mathcal{G}$, we have

$$\chi_i(\bigcup_{G \in \mathcal{G}} X^G) = \chi_i(X^{G_0}) = \frac{1}{|(X)_{i-1}|} + \sum_{G \supset G_0} \phi_i(G) = \frac{1}{|(X)_{i-1}|} + \sum_{G \subset \mathcal{G}} \phi_i(G). \tag{8.3.25}$$

Otherwise, since Eq. (8.3.22) holds for the sets $\mathcal{G}_1$, $\mathcal{G}_2$ and $\mathcal{G}_1 \bigcap \mathcal{G}_1$, we have

$$
\begin{aligned}
\chi_i(\bigcup_{G \in \mathcal{G}} X^G) &= \chi_i(\bigcup_{G \in \mathcal{G}_1} X^G) + \chi_i(\bigcup_{G \in \mathcal{G}_2} X^G) - \chi_i(\bigcup_{G \in \mathcal{G}_1 \bigcap \mathcal{G}_2} X^G) \\
&= \frac{1}{|(X)_{i-1}|} + \sum_{G \subset \mathcal{G}_1} \phi_i(G) + \sum_{G \subset \mathcal{G}_2} \phi_i(G) - \sum_{G \subset \mathcal{G}_1 \bigcap \mathcal{G}_2} \phi_i(G) \\
&= \frac{1}{|(X)_{i-1}|} + \sum_{G \subset \mathcal{G}} \phi_i(G). \tag{8.3.26}
\end{aligned}
$$

The action of an element $h \in H$ takes the pair $(X^G, \bigcup_{K \supsetneq G} X^K)$ homeomorphically to the pair $(X^{hGh^{-1}}, \bigcup_{K \supsetneq hGh^{-1}} X^K)$, hence $\phi_i(G) = \phi_i(hGh^{-1})$. Since the group $N(G)/G$ acts semi-freely on $X^G \backslash \bigcup_{K \supsetneq G} X^K$ with one fixed point, from Example 41, we have

$$\chi_i(X^G \backslash \bigcup_{K \supsetneq G} X^K) - \frac{1}{|(X)_{i-1}|} = n \times |N(G)/G|, \tag{8.3.27}$$

for some integer n.

A mod p *dissolution function* for group H is defined as any function $\phi : \mathcal{S}(H) \longrightarrow \mathbb{Q}$ such that

- ϕ is constant on conjugacy classes of subgroups.

- For any $G \subseteq H$ and G that has normal subgroup with p-power order, $\sum\limits_{K \subseteq G} \phi(K) = 0$.

Construction Theorem from Dissolution Functions

The basic idea will be to use the dissolution function as a pattern for constructing an oriented space X acted by H, such that $\chi_i(X^G) = \frac{1}{|(X)_{i-1}|} + \sum\limits_{K \subseteq H} (K)$ for all $G \subseteq H$. Following lemma will first be required.

Lemma 18 *If X is an n-dimensional $(n-1)$-connected finite oriented complex with an action of some cyclic group $\mathbb{Z}_m$ such that $\chi_i(X^G) = \frac{1}{|(X)_{i-1}|}$ for all $0 \neq G \subseteq \mathbb{Z}_m$ and $1 \leq i \leq n$, then $H_n(X;R)$ is a free $R[\mathbb{Z}_m]$-module for $R = \mathbb{Z}_p (p \nmid m)$ or $R = \mathbb{Q}$.*

PROOF. 40 *Let $\phi_i : S(\mathbb{Z}_m) \longrightarrow \mathbb{Z}$ be defined by $\phi_i(0) = \chi_i(X) - \frac{1}{|(X)_{i-1}|}$ and $\phi(G) = 0$ for all subgroups $G \neq 0$. Then ϕ_i satisfies the condition $\chi_i(X^G) = \frac{1}{|(X)_{i-1}|} + \sum\limits_{K \supseteq G} \phi_i(K)$ for all $G \subseteq \mathbb{Z}_m$. By Lemma 17, we have $\chi_i(X^G) = \chi_i(\bigcup\limits_{K \supsetneq G} X^K)$ for all $0 \neq G \subsetneq H$. It follows that $\chi_{i,\mathbb{Z}_m}(X^G) = \chi_{i,\mathbb{Z}_m}(\bigcup\limits_{K \supsetneq G} X^K) = [R]$ for all $0 \neq G \subsetneq H$, where $\chi_{i,\mathbb{Z}_m}$ is the χ_i characteristic taking values in the group ring $R(\mathbb{Z}_m)$.*

Therefore, we have

$$(-1)^n [H_n(X;R)] = \chi_{i,\mathbb{Z}_m}(X) - [R] \equiv \chi_{i,\mathbb{Z}_m}(\bigcup\limits_{0 \neq G \supsetneq \mathbb{Z}_m} X^G) - [R]$$
$$= 0 \ (\mod [R[\mathbb{Z}_m]]), \qquad (8.3.28)$$

and $H_n(X;R)$ becomes a free $R[\mathbb{Z}_m]$-module since $R[\mathbb{Z}_m]$ is semi-simple.

The construction theorem is then ready to be formulated.

Theorem 27 *Let F be an finite oriented complex with dimension $dm(F)$, H be a finite group not of p-power of order, and ϕ_i be a $\mod p$ dissolution function for H and $1 \leq i \leq dm(F)$. F is the fixed-point set of an action of H on some finite $\mathbb{Z}_p$-acyclic oriented complex if $\chi_i(F) = \frac{1}{|(F)_{i-1}|} + \phi_i(H)$.*

PROOF. 41 *The purpose is to embed F as the fixed-point set of some space, say X, acted by H such that (1) $\chi_i(X^G) = \frac{1}{|(X^G)_{i-1}|} + \sum\limits_{K \supsetneq G} \phi_i(K)$ for all $G \subseteq H$ and i, and (2) X^G is $\mathbb{Z}_p$-acyclic if G is of p-power order. This is valid for X^H. By induction, we assume that the oriented complex*

X_0 has been constructed with H-action such that the above two requirements hold for all $G \supsetneq G_0$ for some fixed $G_0 \subseteq H$. Oriented complexes must be added in orbits of type H/G_0 until the fixed-point set of G_0 satisfies conditions (1) and (2) and all conjugate subgroups will be built up at the same time to meed these conditions.

From Lemma 17 and $\chi_i(X_0^G) = \frac{1}{|(X_0^G)_{i-1}|} + \sum_{K \supseteq G} \phi_i(K)$, one has

$$\chi_i(X_0^{G_0}) \equiv \chi_i(\bigcup_{G \supsetneq G_0} X_0^G) \equiv \frac{1}{|(X_0^G)_{i-1}|} + \sum_{G \subsetneq G_0} \phi_i(G)(\mod |N(G_0)/G_0|). \qquad (8.3.29)$$

There are two cases for group G_0. If G_0 is not of p-power order, orbits of oriented cells of type $N(G_0)/G_0$ can be added to $X_0^{G_0}$ to produce an oriented complex with the desired characteristic. If G_0 is of p-power order, we can add orbits of cells of type $N(G_0)/G_0$ to $X_0^{G_0}$ to generate a space Z which is n-dimensional and $(n-1)$-connected for some n larger than the dimension of $X_0^{G_0}$ for any $G \supsetneq G_0$. Since $H_n(Y; \mathbb{Z}_p)$ is a projective $\mathbb{Z}_p[T]$ module for a p-Sylow subgroup T of $N(G_0)/G_0$, $H_n(Y; \mathbb{Z}_p)$ is also a projective $\mathbb{Z}_p[N(G_0)/G_0]$-module.

Let $\tilde{K} = K/G_0 \subseteq N(G_0)/G_0$ be any non-zero cyclic subgroup, then $\chi_i(Y^{\tilde{K}}) = \frac{1}{Y^{\tilde{K}}} + \sum_{G \supseteq K} \phi_i(G) = \frac{1}{Y^{\tilde{K}}}$. From Lemma 18, $H_n(Y; \mathbb{Z}_p)$ is a free $\mathbb{Z}_p[\tilde{K}]$-module for all cyclic subgroups $\tilde{K}$ with order prime to p. Therefore, orbits of $(n+1)$-dimensional oriented cells of type $N(G_0)/G_0$ can be added to Y to make it $\mathbb{Z}_p$-acyclic.

8.4 Evaluation Gluing Design Equationally

The main goal of this section is to give conditions for evaluatio gluing design equationally.

8.4.1 Definition of Generalized ω-Invengories

A generalized ω-invengory is provided by the following definition.

Definition 46 *A generalized ω-invengory is a set X together with unary operations d_n^+ and d_n^-, binary operations $\circ_n$ for $n = 0, 1, 2, \cdots$ and multi-nary operations $\#_n$ for $n = 0, 1, 2, \cdots$, such that the following properties hold:*

(1) For any signs of ζ_m and ζ_n, $d_m^{\zeta_m} d_n^{\zeta_n}(x) = d_m^{\zeta_m}(x)$ if $m < n$ and $d_m^{\zeta_m} d_n^{\zeta_n}(x) = d_n^{\zeta_n}(x)$ if $m \geq n$.

(2) $x \circ_n y$ is defined whenever $d_n^+(x) = d_n^-(y)$ (target-source composition). Moreover,

- $d_n^-(x \circ_n y) = d_n^-(x)$ and $d_n^+(x \circ_n y) = d_n^+(y)$.

- $d_m^{\zeta_m}(x \circ_n y) = d_m^{\zeta_m}(x) = d_m^{\zeta_m}(y) = d_m^{\zeta_m}(x) \circ_n d_m^{\zeta_m}(y)$ for $m < n$.

- $d_m^{\zeta_m}(x \circ_n y) = d_m^{\zeta_m}(x) \circ_n d_m^{\zeta_m}(y)$ for $m \geq n$.

(3) $x_1 \#_n x_2 \#_n \cdots \#_n x_k$ *is defined whenever* $d_n^+ x_1 = d_n^+ x_2 = \cdots = d_n^+ x_k$ *and* $d_n^- x_1 = d_n^- x_2 = \cdots = d_n^- x_k$ *(target-target composition). Moreover,*

- $d_n^-(x_i) = d_n^-(x_j)$ and $d_n^+(x_i) = d_n^+(x_j)$ for any i, j in $[1, 2, \cdots, k]$.

- $d_m^{\zeta_m}(x_1 \#_n x_2 \#_n \cdots \#_n x_k) = d_m^{\zeta_m}(x_i)$ for any $1 \leq i \leq k$ and $m < n$.

- $d_m^{\zeta_m}(x_1 \#_n x_2 \#_n \cdots \#_n x_k) = d_m^{\zeta_m}(x_1) \#_n d_m^{\zeta_m}(x_2) \#_n \cdots d_m^{\zeta_m}(x_k)$ for $m \geq n$.

(4) $(x \circ_n y) \circ_n z = x \circ_n (y \circ_n z)$.

(5) $(x_1 \#_n \cdots \#_n x_k) \#_n x_{k+1} \#_n \cdots \#_n x_{2k-1} = x_1 \#_n (x_2 \#_n \cdots \#_n x_{k+1}) \#_n x_{k+2} \#_n \cdots \#_n x_{2k-1} = \cdots = x_1 \#_n \cdots \#_n x_{k-1} \#_n (x_k \#_n \cdots \#_n x_{2k-1})$.

(6) $(x \circ_n y) \circ_m (z \circ_n w) = (x \circ_m z) \circ_n (y \circ_m w)$ if $m < n$.

(7) $(x_{1,1} \#_n \cdots \#_n x_{1,k_1}) \#_m (x_{2,1} \#_n \cdots \#_n x_{2,k_1}) \cdots \#_m (x_{k_2,1} \#_n \cdots \#_n x_{k_2,k_1})$
$= (x_{1,1} \#_m \cdots \#_n x_{k_2,1}) \#_n (x_{1,2} \#_m \cdots \#_m x_{k_2,2}) \cdots \#_n (x_{1,k_1} \#_m \cdots \#_m x_{k_2,k_1})$

(8) $(x_{1,1} \#_n x_{1,2} \#_n \cdots \#_n x_{1,k}) \circ_m (x_{2,1} \#_n x_{2,2} \#_n \cdots \#_n x_{2,k})$
$= (x_{1,1} \circ_m x_{2,1}) \#_n (x_{1,2} \circ_m x_{2,2}) \#_n \cdots \#_n (x_{1,k} \circ_m x_{2,k})$.

An example is shown at Fig. 8.2 for various compositions in generalized ω-invengory.

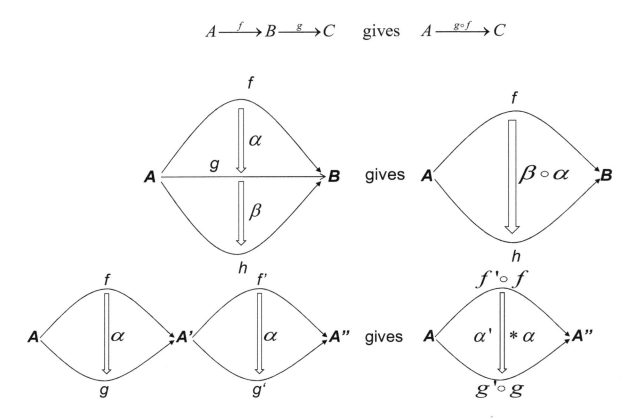

Figure 8.2: Examples of generalized ω-invengory: (a) $f \circ_0 g$, (b) $f\#_0 g\#_0 h$, (c) $(f\#_0 g) \circ_0$ $(f'\#_0 g')$

8.4.2 Gluing Design Evaluation Theorem

The main purpose of this section is to give conditions for evaluation gluing design equationally. We first define a morphism between oriented complexes (Definition 43) and generalized ω-invengories (Definition 46).

Definition 47 *The class of oriented cells made by oriented complex $\overrightarrow{\mathcal{K}}$, e.g., gluing design $Q(\overrightarrow{\mathcal{K}})$, is composed by a serious of graphs $G_0, G_1, \cdots, G_{dm(\overrightarrow{\mathcal{K}})}$, represented as $[G_i]$, such that G_i is the graph consisted by i-dimensional objects of $\overrightarrow{\mathcal{K}}$. The generalized ω-invengory X is also composed by a serious of graphs $H_0, H_1, \cdots, H_{dm(\overrightarrow{\mathcal{K}})}$, represented as $[H_j]$, such that H_i is the graph consisted by i-dimensional objects of X.*

An evaluation morphism *from $([G_i], d_i^+, d_i^-)$ for $0 \le i \le dm(\overrightarrow{\mathcal{K}})$ to $([H_j], d_j^+, d_j^-)$ for $0 \le j \le$*

$dm(\overrightarrow{\mathcal{K}})$ consists of a set of functions $[f_k] = [G_k \longrightarrow H_k]$ for $0 \leq k \leq dm(\overrightarrow{\mathcal{K}})$ such that

$$
\begin{aligned}
d_j^- \circ f_{i+1} &= f_i \circ d_j^-; \\
d_j^+ \circ f_{i+1} &= f_i \circ d_j^+,
\end{aligned}
\tag{8.4.1}
$$

for any i, j in $[0, 1, 2, \cdots, dm(\overrightarrow{\mathcal{K}})]$. We say that an oriented complex evalutable if an evaluation morphism exists between such oriented complex and a generalized ω-invengory.

The following theorem is about the gluing design evaluation theorem.

Theorem 28 (1) Any gluing design made by product, join and combinatorial reduction of other existing oriented complexes can be evaluated equationally by a generalized ω-invengory if its 0-dimensional objects are closed under the homomorphic images, subalgebras and products (objects as varieties).

(2) Any gluing design made by product, join and combinatorial reduction of other existing oriented complexes can be evaluated implicationally by a generalized ω-invengory if its 0-dimensional objects are closed under the subalgebras and products (objects as quasi-varieties).

PROOF. 42 If $\overrightarrow{\mathcal{K}}$ is made by product, join and combinatorial reduction of other existing oriented complexes, then it is oriented complex again by Theorem 26. Hence, we can construct a generalized ω-invengory based on $\overrightarrow{\mathcal{K}}$, denoted as $B(\overrightarrow{\mathcal{K}})$. The elements of $B(\overrightarrow{\mathcal{K}})$ are double infinite sequences

$$
\mathcal{B} = \{B_n^+ \bigcup B_n^- \text{ for } n = 0, 1, 2, \cdots \},
\tag{8.4.2}
$$

where B_n^+ (or B_n^-) are subsets of $\overrightarrow{\mathcal{K}}$ such that $B_m^{\zeta_m} \subset B_n^{\zeta_n}$ for $m < n$ and for any signs of ζ_m and ζ_n. With the following structures, one can verifies that $B(\overrightarrow{\mathcal{K}})$ is a generalized ω-invengory:

$$
(d_n^{\zeta_n} B)_m^{\zeta_m} =
\begin{cases}
B_m^{\zeta_m} \text{ for } m < n, \\
B_n^{\zeta_n} \text{ for } m \geq n;
\end{cases}
\tag{8.4.3}
$$

and

$$
(B_1 \circ_n B_2)_m^{\zeta_m} = (B_1)_m^{\zeta_m} \bigcup (B_2)_m^{\zeta_m}, \text{ for } d_n^+ B_1 = d_n^- B_2;
\tag{8.4.4}
$$

and

$$
(B_1 \#_n B_2 \#_n \cdots \#_n B_k)_m^{\zeta_m} = (B_1)_m^{\zeta_m} \#_n (B_2)_m^{\zeta_m} \#_n \cdots \#_n (B_k)_m^{\zeta_m},
\tag{8.4.5}
$$

Therefore, the gluing design $Q(\vec{\mathcal{K}})$ can be evaluated by $B(\vec{\mathcal{K}})$ through the evaluation morphism $x \longmapsto d_n^{\zeta_n} x$ for any element $x \in Q(\vec{\mathcal{K}})$ and sign ζ_n. From Theorems 22 and 24, the class $Q(\vec{\mathcal{K}})$ can be evaluated equationally by a generalized ω-invengory since its 0-dimensional objects are closed under the homomorphic images, subalgebras and products (objects as varieties). Hence, part (1) of this theorem proved. Similarly, from Theorems 23 and 25, $Q(\vec{\mathcal{K}})$ can be evaluated implicationally by a generalized ω-invengory since its 0-dimensional objects are closed under the subalgebras and products (objects as quasi-varieties). Hence, part (2) of this theorem proved.

We have to note that the gluing design is not the only class of oriented cells made by oriented complexes which can be evaluated equationally (or implicationally). Any class of oriented cells made by oriented complexes can be evaluated equationally (or implicationally) if an evaluation morphism can be found between an oriented class to a generalized ω-invengory with varieties (or quasi-varieties) as 0-dimensional objects. Hence, the statement in Theorem 28 can be transformed as group action language based on results from Theorem 27.

8.5 Example: Invenrelation Evolution Characterization

In this section, a concrete example about characterizing invenrelation evolution processes (IEPs) based on Theorem 28 is provided. The idea is to treat invenrelation spaces as 0-dimensional components of oriented complexes; the evolution processes between creation spaces are treated as 1-dimensional components of oriented complexes; the evolution processes between *the evolution processes between invenrelation spaces* are treated as 2-dimensional components of oriented complexes, etc. Then, we try to find out a mapping from the category of IEPs to the category composed by objects which are varieties. From theorem 28, we can evaluate IEPs equationally to classify and decompose IEPs.

8.5.1 Cobordism Model for Invenrelation Evolution Processes

The term "visual design" is referred to any invenrelation made in respect of the shape, pattern, color, or combination thereof of an article through eye appeal. Some designs are originated from and similar to his/her original design, called as "associated design". To precisely characterize the variability of associated designs and their original designs, it is essential to take a mathematical approach.

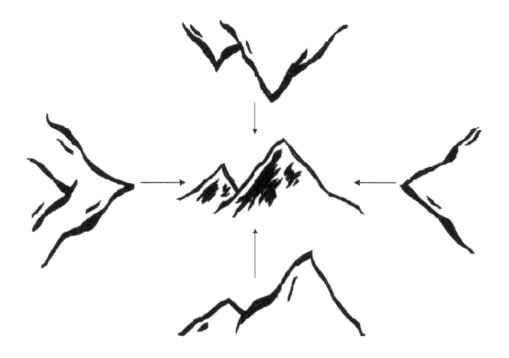

Figure 8.3: Different views from different observation positions.

Now consider an example of picture (two-dimensions) variability between the original design and associated designs, the set P of all pictures generated by varying the orientation of the original picture, see Fig. 8.3. The set to parameterize the figure rotation forms a curve because it is generated by varying a single degree of freedom, the angle of rotation. In other words, P is intrinsically one-dimensional, although a two-dimensional picture is embedded in image space, which has a high dimensionality equal to the number of image pixels. If we were to allow other types of picture transformations to generate other similar associated designs, such as scaling and translation, then the dimensionality of P would increase, but would still remain much less than that of the image space. In this generalized case, P is said to be a manifold embedded in the image space. In mathematics, a manifold is a topological space that is like an Euclidean space of a particular dimension, named as the dimension of the manifold. For instances, a plane and sphere (the surface of a ball) are two-dimensional manifolds, and so on into high-dimensional space. More formally, every point of an n-dimensional manifold has a neighborhood homeomorphic to an open subset of the space $\mathbb{R}^n$. Hence, we can adopt a manifold to model a parameters space (invenrelation space) which describes the variation between the original design and associated designs.

The invenrelation space for visual design may evolve due to marketing preference and this may introduce a new fashion. *Cobordism* is a proper mathematical tool to study the evolution relation between two invenrelation spaces (manifolds). Two manifolds are cobordant if their disjoint union is the boundary of a manifold one dimension higher. Rigorously, an $d+1$-dimensional cobordism is a quintuple $(B; M, N, \iota_M, \iota_N)$ consisting of an $d+1$-dimensional manifold with boundary ∂B, closed d-dimensional manifolds M, N and embeddings $\iota_M : M \hookrightarrow \partial B$, $\iota_N : N \hookrightarrow \partial B$ with disjoint images such that

$$\partial B = \iota_M(M) \bigcup \iota_N(N). \tag{8.5.1}$$

All invenrelation spaces with same dimension d and have morphisms among them can form a CEP 1-category, named as $1 - \mathcal{C}(d)$. It has objects as closed, oriented, d-dimensional smooth manifolds. A morphism with domain (manifold) M_1 and codomain M_2, called a cobordism from M_1 to M_2, is an oriented, closed d-dimensional manifold with boundary $M_1 \bigcup M_2$. If we wish to consider evolution processes between the evolution processes between invenrelation spaces, we can extend invengory $\mathcal{C}_1(d)$ as a 2-invengory, denoted as $\mathcal{C}_2(d)$ and this procedure can be iterated if higher level evolution processes are considered.

8.5.2 Vector Spaces Assignment

In this section, vector spaces are assigned to invenrelation spaces (manifolds) according to some rules which reflect the evolutional properties among invenrelation spaces. Such assignment will enable us to evaluate IEPs through vector spaces equationally. We use the symbols E and M to refer manifolds of codimension 1 (evolution space) and 0 (invenrelation space) with respect to the dimension of invenrelation space under consideration. For instance, if the dimension of a invenrelation space M is d, then the dimension of its evolution space is $d + 1$. This assignment will include the following elements:

A A vector space is assigned to every d-dimensional invenrelation space, denoted as $\mathcal{V}(M)$.

B A vector $\mathcal{V}(E) \in \mathcal{V}(\partial E)$ to every $d + 1$-dimensional evolution space E (with boundary).

These elements are subject to the following rules:

1. (Duality) $\mathcal{V}(M^*) = \mathcal{V}(M)^*$, where M^* is M with opposite orientation and $\mathcal{V}(M)^*$ represents the dual vector space of $\mathcal{V}(M)$.

2. (Multiplicativity) $\mathcal{V}(M_1 \bigsqcup M_2) = \mathcal{V}(M_1) \bigotimes \mathcal{V}(M_2)$, where $\bigsqcup$ denotes for the disjoin union.

3. (Pasting) If $\partial E_1 = M_1 \bigsqcup M_3$, $\partial E_2 = M_2 \bigsqcup M_3^*$ and $E = E_1 \bigcup_{M_3} E_2$ is the evolution space obtained by pasting together along the common component M_3, then we have

$$
\begin{aligned}
\mathcal{V}(E) &= \mathcal{V}(E_1) \bigotimes \mathcal{V}(E_2) \\
&= \mathcal{V}(M_1) \bigotimes \mathcal{V}(M_3) \bigotimes \mathcal{V}(M_3^*) \bigotimes \mathcal{V}(M_2), \\
&= \mathcal{V}(M_1) \bigotimes \mathcal{V}(M_2).
\end{aligned}
\tag{8.5.2}
$$

4. (Functionality) Any diffeomorphism $f : M \longrightarrow N$ induces an isomorphism $\mathcal{V}(f) : \mathcal{V}(M) \longrightarrow \mathcal{V}(N)$ such that $\mathcal{V}(g \circ f) = \mathcal{V}(g) \circ \mathcal{V}(f)$ for all $g : N \longrightarrow L$.

Under above assignment of vector spaces to invenrelation spaces, invenrelation evolution characterization can be treated as a functor $\mathcal{V}$ of tensor categories from the category $\mathcal{C}_1(d)$ to the category $(\mathbb{F})$, a category of vector space over field $\mathbb{F}$. Fig. 8.4 shows an example of the pasting of cobordisms along boundaries.

We are ready to classify $\mathcal{E}$ through vector spaces assignment to creation spaces provided in Sec. .

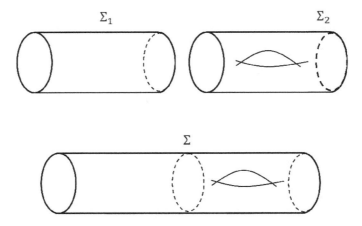

Figure 8.4: Pasting of cobordisms along boundaries.

We will focus at 2-dimensional creation evolution spaces E. Since any 2-dimensional compact orientable manifolds with boundary can be constructed by gluing together copies of a disc and a trinion along boundary circles. Therefore, any such manifolds can be obtained by gluing together copies of the three elementary pieces as indicated in Fig. 8.5.

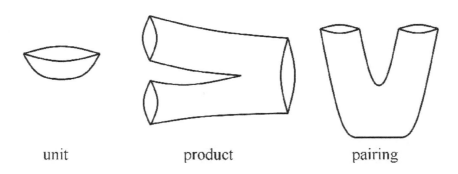

unit   product   pairing

Figure 8.5: Elementary 2 dimensional pieces

By $\mathcal{V}$, these elementary pieces map to vector spaces made by V which are denoted as $1 \in V$, $p \in V^* \bigotimes V^* \bigotimes V^*$ and $r \in V^* \bigotimes V^*$, respectively. If V is finite dimensional with orthogonal basis $\{b_i\}$, then the unit is $1 = \sum_i b_i$ and $p = \sum_i (r(b_i \otimes b_i))^{-2} b_i \otimes b_i \otimes b_i$. A manifold E of genus g

and with k boundary components can be separated into $2g - 2 + k$ trinions by $3g - 3 + k$ interior curves. Hence, we can classify $\mathcal{E}$ by bases $\{b_i\}$ as

$$\mathcal{V}(E) \;=\; \sum_i (r(b_i \otimes b_i))^{1-g-r} b_i^{\otimes r}. \tag{8.5.3}$$

Chapter 9

Derivability

The main goal of Chap 8. is to provide conditions for evaluating gluing design equationally. In order to solve invention problems through mathematical calculation systematically, it is more convenient to introduce variables to represent components of things to be invented first and one, then, can perform computation over these variables. The purpose of this chapter is to answer the basic question about derivability between terms related to variables.

This chapter is organized as follows. In Sec. 9.1, we will review many-sorted algebras (MSA) and introduce rules of deduction for MSA equations with variables. Conditions for derivability between terms in one invengory of MSA are provided in Sec. 9.2. In Sec. 9.3, we propose a generalized invenrelation process which enables us to associate one invengory of MSA to the other invengory of MSA with more flexible relations by considering structural associations among relations. Finally, conditions for derivability between algebraic invention terms in different invengory of MSA are provided in Sec. 9.4. Finally, we discuss the problem about derivation complexity in algebraic invenrelation systems in Sec. 9.5.

9.1   Rules of Equational Deduction

Notions about a many-sorted algebra (MSA) which represents an algebraic system for invention are reviewed. Algebraic terms which involve variables are defined recursively based on ground MSA. These are main topics covered by Sec. 9.1.1. MSA would be very impoverished without equations indicated by an example in Sec. 9.1.2. In Sec. 9.1.3, we define equations with variables of MSA and rules required to derive many-sorted equations.

9.1.1 Many-Sorted Algebras and Terms

In Chap. II, we presented the algebraic system for invention. Let us review this algebraic system for later theory. Let $(\mathcal{S}, \mathcal{R})$ be a many-sorted signature. A many-sorted $(\mathcal{S}, \mathcal{R})$-algebra, denoted as $\mathcal{A}$, is a family $\{A_s | s \in \mathcal{S}\}$ of sets named as *carriers* of $\mathcal{A}$, together with a family of relations $\{R_{\overline{w};s} \in \mathcal{R}\}$ such that

$$R_{\overline{w};s} \quad : \quad A_{\overline{w}} \longrightarrow A_s, \tag{9.1.1}$$

where $A_{\overline{w}} = A_{s_1} \times A_{s_2} \times \cdots \times A_{s_n}$ and $s_1, s_2, \cdots, s_n \in \mathcal{S}$. Note that the relation $R_{\overline{w};s}$ can be decomposed by functions as $R_{\overline{w};s} = \bowtie_{i=1}^{I_{\overline{w};s}} r_{i|\overline{w};s}$, where $I_{\overline{w};s}$ is a finite inter and $r_{i|\overline{w};s}$ is a function from the domain $A_{\overline{w}}$ to the codomain A_s. A two-sorted algebra, i.e., a many-sorted algebra when $|\mathcal{S}| = 2$, is provided by the following example.

Example 42 *A semiautomaton is basically an automaton without specified sets of starting and terminal states. Formally, a semiautomaton $\mathcal{A}$ is a triple (S, Σ, δ) where*

- *S is a non-empty set whose elements are called* states *(first sort).*

- *Σ is a non-empty set whose elements are called* input symbols *(second sort).*

- *δ is a* transition function *that assigns each pair (s, σ) of the state s and the input symbol σ a subset, denoted as $\delta(s, a)$, of states in S*

Let $(\mathcal{S}, \mathcal{R})$ be a many-sorted signature, and let $\mathcal{A}$ and $\mathcal{B}$ be $(\mathcal{S}, \mathcal{R})$-algebras. Then an $(\mathcal{S}, \mathcal{R})$-homomorphism-relation $H : \mathcal{A} \longrightarrow \mathcal{B}$ is composed by a family of functions, i.e., $H = \bowtie_{i=1}^{I_H} h_i$ and $h_i = \{h_{i;s} : A_s \longrightarrow B_s | s \in \mathcal{S}\}$ satisfying the following homomorphism conditions

$$h_{i;s}(r_{j|\overline{w};s}(a_1, a_2, \cdots, a_n)) \quad = \quad r_{j|\overline{w};s}(h_{i;s}(a_1), h_{i;s}(a_2), \cdots, h_{i;s}(a_n))$$

$$\text{for each } i, j, s \text{ and } a_1, a_2, \cdots, a_n \in A_{\overline{w}}, \tag{9.1.2}$$

where $\overline{w} = s_1 s_2 \cdots s_n$. The special case of $(\mathcal{S}, \mathcal{R})$-homomorphism-relation $H : \mathcal{A} \longrightarrow \mathcal{B}$ is that $I_H = 1$ and $h = \{h_s : A_s \longrightarrow B_s | s \in \mathcal{S}\}$ satisfying the following homomorphism conditions

$$h_s(r_{j|\overline{w};s}(a_1, a_2, \cdots, a_n)) \quad = \quad r_{j|\overline{w};s}(h_s(a_1), h_s(a_2), \cdots, h_s(a_n))$$

$$\text{for each } s, j \text{ and } a_1, a_2, \cdots, a_n \in A_{\overline{w}}. \tag{9.1.3}$$

Such special $(\mathcal{S}, \mathcal{R})$-homomorphism-relation is named as $(\mathcal{S}, \mathcal{R})$-homomorphism.

Algebraic terms made by $(\mathcal{S}, \mathcal{R})$-MSA with carrier sets A_s can be defined recursively. The expression $T_{\mathcal{R},s}$ is used to represent all algebraic terms made by $(\mathcal{S}, \mathcal{R})$-MSA of the sort with index s. Then $T_{\mathcal{R},s}$ can be defined as :

- $R_{\lambda;s} \in T_{\mathcal{R},s}$, where $R_{\lambda;s}$ represents constant relations.

- if $R_{\overline{w};s} \in \mathcal{R}$ and $t_i \in T_{\mathcal{R},s_i}$ for $1 \leq i \leq n$, then $R_{\overline{w};s}(t_1, t_2, \cdots, t_n) \in T_{\mathcal{R},s}$

Two basic concepts should be introduced about the relation between the MSA $\mathcal{A}$ and the term algebra $T_{\mathcal{R}} = \bigcup_{s \in \mathcal{S}} T_{\mathcal{R},s}$. If the $\mathcal{R}$-homomorphism $H : T_{\mathcal{R}} \longrightarrow \mathcal{A}$ is injective, i.e, each h_s is injective, then the data interpretation $\mathcal{A}$ by $T_{\mathcal{R}}$ has *no ambiguity*. Moreover, if the $\mathcal{R}$-homomorphism $H : T_{\mathcal{R}} \longrightarrow \mathcal{A}$ is surjective, i.e., each h_s is surjective, then the MSA $\mathcal{A}$ is the *minimal* representation for $T_{\mathcal{R}}$. The following theorem is provided to describe that it is enough to consider an invengory of many-sorted $(\mathcal{S}, \mathcal{R})$-algebra only by its corresponding term algebra $T_{\mathcal{R}}$.

Theorem 29 *For each $(\mathcal{S}, \mathcal{R})$-algebra $\mathcal{A}$, there is one $(\mathcal{S}, \mathcal{R})$-homomorphism-relation from $T_{\mathcal{R}}$ to $\mathcal{A}$. If $I_H = 1$, then there is one and only one $(\mathcal{S}, \mathcal{R})$-homomorphism. Moreover, $\mathcal{A}$ is isomorphic to $T_{\mathcal{R}}$ if the MSA $\mathcal{A}$ is minimal with no ambiguity.*

PROOF. 43 *We first express $T_{\mathcal{R}}$ by a countable union of hierarchical term sets with respect to different construction levels. It is*

$$T_{\mathcal{R}} = \bigcup_n T_{\mathcal{R}}^{(n)}, \tag{9.1.4}$$

where $T_{\mathcal{R}}^{(0)} = \{R_{\lambda;s} | s \in \mathcal{S}\}$ and

$$T_{\mathcal{R}}^{(n+1)} = T_{\mathcal{R}}^{(n)} \bigcup \{R_{\overline{w};s}(t_1, \cdots, t_n) | t_i \in T_{\mathcal{R}}^{(n)}\}. \tag{9.1.5}$$

The proof is based on induction arguments. For each index i, s and j, we define $h_{i;s} : T_{\mathcal{R}} \longrightarrow \mathcal{A}$ on $T_{\mathcal{R}}^{(0)}$ as

$$h_{i;s}(r_{j|\lambda;s}) = r_{j|\lambda;s}. \tag{9.1.6}$$

Then the $(\mathcal{S}, \mathcal{R})$-homomorphism-relation H becomes

$$H = \bowtie_{i=1}^{I_H} h_i = \bowtie_{i=1}^{I_H} \bigcup_{s \in \mathcal{S}} \{h_{i;s}\}. \tag{9.1.7}$$

The following rule is adopted to construct $T_{\mathcal{R}}^{(n+1)}$ from $T_{\mathcal{R}}^{(n)}$

$$h_{i;s}(r_{j|\overline{w};s}(t_1, t_2, \cdots, t_n)) = r_{j|\overline{w};s}(h_{i;s}(t_1), h_{i;s}(t_2), \cdots, h_{i;s}(t_n)), \tag{9.1.8}$$

for each i, s, j and $a_1, a_2, \cdots, a_n \in A_{\overline{w}}$. Eq. 9.1.7 is then applied to get H on $T_{\mathcal{R}}^{(n+1)}$. By induction, H is defined on all of $T_{\mathcal{R}}$ if H is already defined on $T_{\mathcal{R}}^{(n)}$. Hence, there is one $(\mathcal{S}, \mathcal{R})$-homomorphism-relation from $T_{\mathcal{R}}$ to $\mathcal{A}$.

If $I_H = 1$, we wish to show that there is one and only one $(\mathcal{S}, \mathcal{R})$-homomorphism. For existence, we define h_s as

$$h_s(r_{j|\lambda;s}) = r_{j|\lambda;s}, \tag{9.1.9}$$

and the $(\mathcal{S}, \mathcal{R})$-homomorphism H becomes

$$H = \bigcup_{s \in \mathcal{S}} \{h_s\}. \tag{9.1.10}$$

The following rule is used to construct $T_{\mathcal{R}}^{(n+1)}$ from $T_{\mathcal{R}}^{(n)}$

$$h_s(r_{j|\overline{w};s}(t_1, t_2, \cdots, t_n)) = r_{j|\overline{w};s}(h_s(t_1), h_s(t_2), \cdots, h_s(t_n)), \tag{9.1.11}$$

for each s, j and $a_1, a_2, \cdots, a_n \in A_{\overline{w}}$. Eq. 9.1.10 is then applied to get H on $T_{\mathcal{R}}^{(n+1)}$. By induction, H is defined on all of $T_{\mathcal{R}}$ if H is already defined on $T_{\mathcal{R}}^{(n)}$. Hence, there is one $(\mathcal{S}, \mathcal{R})$-homomorphism from $T_{\mathcal{R}}$ to $\mathcal{A}$.

For uniqueness, suppose that h_s, h'_s are two identical homomorphisms from $T_{\mathcal{R}}$ to $\mathcal{A}$ on $T_{\mathcal{R}}^{(0)}$. Then they are identical on $T_{\mathcal{R}}^{(0)}$ since

$$h_s(r_{j|\lambda;s}) = h'_s(r_{j|\overline{w};s}) = r_{j|\overline{w};s}. \tag{9.1.12}$$

Because we have

$$\begin{aligned} h_s(r_{j|\overline{w};s}(t_1, t_2, \cdots, t_n)) &= r_{j|\overline{w};s}(h_s(t_1), h_s(t_2), \cdots, h_s(t_n)) \\ &= r_{j|\overline{w};s}(h'_s(t_1), h'_s(t_2), \cdots, h'_s(t_n)) \\ &= h'_s(r_{j|\overline{w};s}(t_1, t_2, \cdots, t_n)), \end{aligned} \tag{9.1.13}$$

the identical relation between h_s and h'_s on $T_{\mathcal{R}}^{(n)}$ implies the identical relation between h_s and h'_s on $T_{\mathcal{R}}^{(n+1)}$. Therefore, functions h_s and h'_s are identical on all $T_{\mathcal{R}}$, which demonstrates the uniqueness.

Finally, the uniqueness of $(\mathcal{S}, \mathcal{R})$-homomorphism from $T_{\mathcal{R}}$ to $\mathcal{A}$ is bijective if and only if it is surjective and injective. Consequently, $\mathcal{A}$ is isomorphic to $T_{\mathcal{R}}$ if the MSA $\mathcal{A}$ is minimal with no ambiguity.

305

9.1.2 Equations of MSA

We first give an invenrelation example of what equations can do, and then we give the formal definitions.

Why Music Design

It is well known that our moods are affected by music deeply. Bad music, for example, induced by traffic noise or mechanical vibration, is harmful to human physically and psychologically. Conversely, good music possesses functions to purify souls and civilize society. In recent years, scientist from many countries are more active in exploring the effects of health care contributed by religion music, like European Medieval music and Eastern Buddhism music.

The concept of Yin-Yang and Five-Elements is the universe view of the ancient Chinese which also affects the Chinese philosophy of life. Yin and Yang indicates that all things in the universe are consisted by things with relative properties, for instance, the world we live is composed by day and night (time), cold and hot (temperature), male and female (humans), and so on. Compared to Yin-Yang, Five-Elements classifies individual attributes of everything in the universe into five types. Therefore, Five-Elements (metal, wood, water, fire and earth) is not to identify out five specific substances according to modern science classification, instead, it describes five characteristics or functions in nature. For instance, "metal" refers to things with solid and rigid properties and "metal" possesses the function to clean, eliminate and converge; "wood" refers to things with original property and "wood" possesses the function to grow up; "water" refers to things with damp and downward properties and "water" possesses the function to circulate; "fire" refers to things with warm and ascensive properties and "fire" possesses the function to heat; "soil" represents the earth itself with the capability to stabilize, load and pregnant all things on earth.

Five notes of ancient Chinese music [gong, shang, jiao, zhe, yu](Chinese pronunciation) are obtained from five natural types of sounds, which correspond roughly to do, re, mi, sol, la (modern musical notes). In Chinese medicine psychology, music can infect, adjust emotions and even affect human bodies. During the process of listening music, it resonates with tunes, moods and organs which achieves health goals by circulating blood and inspiring the spirit. The characteristics of these five Chinese musical notes are corresponding to the five properties of Five-Elements. For example, the sound of "gong" makes people feel steady and this function, which is beneficial to human spleen, is possessed by soil; the sound of "shang" makes people feel cool and respectful and this function, which is beneficial to human lung, is possessed by metal; the sound of "jiao" makes people feel vigor and this function, which is beneficial to human liver, is possessed by wood; the sound of "zhe" makes people feel happy and this function, which is beneficial to human heart, is possessed by fire; finally, the sound of "yu" makes people feel tender and this function, which is beneficial to human kidney, is possessed by water.

According to our health condition, one can design the proportion of each note in a melody in order to achieve curative effects. Even for the same melody, a musical therapist could use different instruments, orchestration, rhythm, intensity, harmony, etc., to enhance treatment. Therefore, it is desirable to *design music*.

Music Definition

A *musical alphabet* is a finite set whose elements are musical notes. Musical alphabets are denoted by capital letters: $A, B, \cdots$ and musical notes by lower case letters, for instance, Do-Re-Mi-Fa-So-La-Ti represented by C, D, E, F, G, A, B. A musical composition (over the musical alphabet A) is a finite sequence $(a_1, a_2, \cdots, a_n)$ of letters of A, where n is an integer representing the length of the musical composition. The empty composition, which is the unique word of length 0, is denoted by 1. Given an musical note a, the number of occurrences of a in a music μ is denoted by $\#_\mu(a)$. For instance, $\#_{abababa}(a) = 4$ and $\#_{abababa}(b) = 3$.

The concatenation (product) of two music compositions
$\mu = (a_1, a_2, \cdots, a_m)$ and $\nu = (b_1, b_2, \cdots, b_n)$ is the music composition $\mu\nu = a_1, a_2, \cdots, a_m, b_1, b_2, \cdots, b_n$. The product is an associative operation on compositions. The set of all compositions on the alphabet A is denoted by A^*. The set of non-empty compositions is denoted by A^+; it is the free semigroup on the set A. The composition *implementable* by a finite automata $\mathcal{A}$, represented by $M^*(\mathcal{A})$, is the set of all successful paths of $\mathcal{A}$.

Musical Design by Systems of Equations over Semigroups

In this part, we try to provide a more algebraic definition of the implementable compositions by using semigroups with automata. Although this definition is more abstract than the definition using automata, it is more convenient to formulate systems of equations over semigroups for musical design.

Let $\mathcal{AU} = (S, A, E, I, T)$ be an automata where S is the set of states, A is the set of musical notes, E is a subset of relations $S \times A \longrightarrow S$ representing transitions and I and T are the set of initial and final states. For each $\mu \in A^+$, there corresponds a boolean square matrix of size $|S|$, denoted by $U(\mu)$, and defined as $U(\mu)_{i,j} = 1$ if there exists a path from the state i to the state

j with label μ and $U(\mu)_{i,j} = 0$, otherwise. For instance, the following automata has $S = \{1,2\}$, $A = \{a,b\}$, $I = \{1\}$, $T = \{2\}$ and $E = \{(1,a,2),(2,b,1)\}$, where

$$U(a) = \begin{pmatrix} 0 & 1 \\ 0 & 0 \end{pmatrix}, U(b) = \begin{pmatrix} 0 & 0 \\ 1 & 0 \end{pmatrix}, U(ab) = \begin{pmatrix} 1 & 0 \\ 0 & 0 \end{pmatrix}, U(ba) = \begin{pmatrix} 0 & 0 \\ 0 & 1 \end{pmatrix}.$$

It is not hard to check that U is a semigroup morphism from A^+ into the multiplicative semigroup of square bool⟨⟩ ata example.

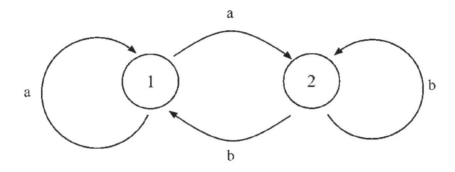

Figure 9.1: A semigroup example, automata.

At this circumstance, musical design can be transformed as solving a set of equations. For example, if we wish to design a composition with N sections $(\mu_1, \mu_2, \cdots, \mu_N)$, the relation of these N sections can be formulated by the following system of equations:

$$
\begin{aligned}
U(\mu_i)U(\mu_{i+1}) &= \begin{pmatrix} 0 & 1 \\ 0 & 0 \end{pmatrix}, \text{ (tune constraints)} \\
\#_{\mu_i}(a) + \#_{\mu_i}(b) &= n_i, \text{ (length constraints)} \\
m_i \#_{\mu_i}(a) &= \#_{\mu_i}(b), \text{ (proportion constraints)}
\end{aligned}
\tag{9.1.14}
$$

where $1 \le i \le N$ and n_i, m_i are positive integers. Several related works have been provided to discuss the solvability and complexity of a system of equations over semigroup, see [50] and references therein.

We now define a $(\mathcal{S}, \mathcal{R})$-*equation* to be a triple $\langle X, t_1, t_2 \rangle$, where X is a finite $\mathcal{S}$-indexed set and t_1, t_2 are in $T_{\mathcal{R}}(X)$ (term algebra with one more set constituted by variables). Given a $(\mathcal{S}, \mathcal{R})$-algebra $\mathcal{A}$, let us now define an *assignment* from X to $\mathcal{A}$ to be a mapping $f: X \longrightarrow \mathcal{A}$. Then there is a unique $(\mathcal{S}, \mathcal{R})$-homomorphism from $T_{\mathcal{R}}(X)$ to A, i.e., a unique $(\mathcal{S}, \mathcal{R})$-homomorphism

$T_{\mathcal{R}}(X) \longrightarrow A$ extending f, denoted as f^*. We say that a $(\mathcal{S}, \mathcal{R})$-algebra A *satisfies* the $(\mathcal{S}, \mathcal{R})$-equation $\langle X, t_1, t_2 \rangle$ if and only if we have $f^*(t_1) = f^*(t_2)$ for every assignment.

9.1.3   Rules of MSA Deduction

In this section, we will provide rules of deduction for MSA. Given a many-sorted signature $\mathcal{R}$ and a set $\mathcal{E}$ of $(\mathcal{S}, \mathcal{R})$ equations, we consider each equation in $\mathcal{E}$ to be derivable. The following rules allow allow us to derive further equations from the MSA $(\mathcal{S}_1, \mathcal{R}_1)$ to the MSA $(\mathcal{S}_2, \mathcal{R}_2)$ in one invengory. They are :

1. *Reflexivity.* Each equation of the form $(\forall X)\ t = t'$ is derivable.

2. *Symmetry.* If $(\forall X)\ t = t'$ is derivable, then so is $(\forall X)\ t' = t$.

3. *Transitivity.* If the equations $(\forall X)\ t = t'$ and $(\forall X)\ t' = t''$ are derivable, then so is $(\forall X)\ t = t''$.

4. *Substitutivity.* If $(\forall X)\ t = t'$ is in $\mathcal{E}$, and if $\phi : X \longrightarrow T_{\mathcal{R}}(Y)$ is a substitution, then $(\forall Y)\ \phi(t) = \phi(t')$ is derivable.

5. *Congruence* If $\phi, \phi' : X \longrightarrow T_{\mathcal{R}}(Y)$ are substitutions such that for each $x \in X$, the equation $(\forall Y)\ \phi(x) = \phi'(x)$ is derivable, then given $t \in T_{\mathcal{R}}(X)$, the equation $(\forall Y)\ \phi(t) = \phi'(t)$ is also derivable.

9.2   Derivability in One Invengory

The purpose of this section is to show derivability for algebraic invenrelation terms in the MSA $(\mathcal{S}_1, \mathcal{R}_1)$ to the MSA $(\mathcal{S}_2, \mathcal{R}_2)$, which is in the same invengory of the MSA $(\mathcal{S}_1, \mathcal{R}_1)$. We say that MSAs with type $(\mathcal{S}, \mathcal{R})$ in the same invengory if there is an unique MSA homomorphism-relation from $T_{\mathcal{R}}$ to any other MSAs with type $(\mathcal{S}, \mathcal{R})$. Following theorem is provided to describe conditions for derivability in the same invengory.

Theorem 30 $(\mathcal{S}_1, \mathcal{R}_1)$ *and* $(\mathcal{S}_2, \mathcal{R}_2)$ *are two MSAs which are in the same invengory with respect to* $T_{\mathcal{R}}$. *Given terms* t *and* t' *in* $(\mathcal{S}_1, \mathcal{R}_1)$ *and* $(\mathcal{S}_2, \mathcal{R}_2)$, *respectively, such that there exist isomorphic homomorphisms* $f_1 : T_{\mathcal{R}} \longrightarrow (\mathcal{S}_1, \mathcal{R}_1)$ *and* $f_2 : T_{\mathcal{R}} \longrightarrow (\mathcal{S}_2, \mathcal{R}_2)$. *If* $(\forall X) f_1^{-1}(t) = f_2^{-1}(t')$ *(inverse* *exists due to isomorphic homomorphism of f_1 or f_2) is satisfied by every many-sorted $(\mathcal{S}, \mathcal{R})$-algebra that satisfies $\mathcal{E}$ (a set of $(\mathcal{S}, \mathcal{R})$ equations), then algebraic terms t and t' can be derived from each other using rules mentioned in Sec. 9.1.3 and f_1, f_2.*

PROOF. 44 *From first three rules mentioned in Sec. 9.1.3, we have an equivalence relation on $T_\mathcal{R}(X)$ with respect to $\mathcal{E}$, denoted as $\sim_\mathcal{E}$. Such equivalence relation is also a many-sorted $(\mathcal{S}, \mathcal{R})$-congruence. Then, we can construct a new many-sorted algebra by taking quotient of $T_\mathcal{R}(X)$ by $\sim_\mathcal{E}$, named as $T_{\mathcal{R}/\mathcal{E}}(X)$. We adopt $[\tau]$ for the equivalence invengory with respect to $\sim_\mathcal{E}$ of term τ in $T_\mathcal{R}(X)$.*

By the construction of $T_{\mathcal{R}/\mathcal{E}}(X)$, for each $f_1^{-1}(t), f_2^{-1}(t') \in T_\mathcal{R}(X)$ we have

$$[f_1^{-1}(t)] = [f_2^{-1}(t')] \text{ in } T_{\mathcal{R}/\mathcal{E}}(X) \tag{9.2.1}$$

if and only if $(\forall X)\ f_1^{-1}(t) = f_2^{-1}(t')$ is derivable from $\mathcal{E}$ using those rules in Sec. 9.1.3. By inclusion map $i_X : X \longrightarrow T_{\mathcal{R}/\mathcal{E}}(X)$ which sends x to $[x]$, the condition $(\forall X)\ f_1^{-1}(t) = f_2^{-1}(t')$ satisfied in $T_{\mathcal{R}/\mathcal{E}}(X)$ implies that $(\forall X)\ f_1^{-1}(t) = f_2^{-1}(t')$ is derivable from $\mathcal{E}$ using those rules in Sec. 9.1.3.

Next, we show that $T_{\mathcal{R}/\mathcal{E}}(X)$ satisfies $\mathcal{E}$. We consider the case where there is a set of conditional equations, denoted as $\mathfrak{C}$, in $\mathcal{E}$ first. Let $(\forall Y)\ f_1^{-1}(t) = f_2^{-1}(t')$ if $\mathfrak{C}$ be a conditional equation in $\mathcal{E}$, and let $\theta : Y \longrightarrow T_{\mathcal{R}/\mathcal{E}}(X)$ be a $(\mathcal{S}, \mathcal{R})$-homomorphism-relation such that $\theta(u) = \theta(v)$ for each $u = v$ in $\mathfrak{C}$. Let $\phi : Y \longrightarrow T_\mathcal{R}(X)$ be the substitution, we have $\theta(\tau) = [\phi(\tau)]$ in $T_{\mathcal{R}/\mathcal{E}}(X)$ for any $\tau \in T_\mathcal{R}(Y)$ by the freeness of $T_\mathcal{R}(Y)$ over Y. Let us present the following mapping diagram:

$$
\begin{array}{ccc}
Y & \xrightarrow{\phi} & T_\mathcal{R}(X) \\
& \searrow{\theta} \quad \downarrow{[-]} & \\
& T_{\mathcal{R}/\mathcal{E}}(X) &
\end{array}
\tag{9.2.2}
$$

Since $[\phi(u)] = [\phi(v)]$ holds in $T_{\mathcal{R}/\mathcal{E}}(X)$, the equation $(\forall X)\ \phi(f_1^{-1}(t)) = \phi(f_2^{-1}(t'))$ is derivable from $\mathcal{E}$ by the rule of substitutivity. Therefore, the conditional equation $(\forall Y)\ f_1^{-1}(t) = f_2^{-1}(t')$ is satisfied if $\mathfrak{C}$ holds in $T_{\mathcal{R}/\mathcal{E}}(X)$. Because an unconditional equation is a special case of conditional equation whose set $\mathfrak{C}$ of conditions is empty, the algebra $T_{\mathcal{R}/\mathcal{E}}(X)$ satisfies $\mathcal{E}$ for the case with unconditional equations.

At this state, we have shown that $(\forall X)\ f_1^{-1}(t) = f_2^{-1}(t')$ is derivable from $\mathcal{E}$ using rules in Sec. 9.1.3. Then algebraic terms t and t' can be derived from each other using rules mentioned *in Sec. 9.1.3 by isomorphic homomorphisms f_1 and f_2 through $f_2(f_1^{-1}(t)) = f_2(f_2^{-1}(t')) = t'$ or $f_1(f_2^{-1}(t')) = f_1(f_1^{-1}(t)) = t$.*

9.3 Generalized Invenrelation Processes

During a traditional invenrelation process, one may adopt arithmetic operations over components sets to derive new things at beginning; then analog method (meta-process taking arithmetic processes from one invengory of invenrelation algebra to arithmetic processes in another invengory of invenrelation algebra) can be applied to derive new things at other invengory. However, such process can be generalized by considering meta-processes of analog relations to create new analog relations, and so on. In Example 43, we can observe that an invenrelation procedure cannot be achieved from the original invengory of invenrelation algebra to the terminal invengory of invenrelation algebra based on a traditional invenrelation process but can be achieved from a generalized invenrelation process which adopts multiple folds of meta-processes. Theorem 31 will provide conditions for the existence of such generalized invenrelation process. We begin by several definitions which are modified from [49].

Definition 48 *Let x be a finite closed set in a partial oriented complex $\mathcal{K}$, the neighbor dimension of x, represented as $dim_{NB}(x)$, is defined as $\max_{i,j} dm(\overline{\sigma}_i \cap \overline{\sigma}_j)$, where $dm(\cdot)$ is the dimension function and indices i, j run over pairs of distinct maximal prime components $\overline{\sigma}_i$ and $\overline{\sigma}_j$ in x.*

The Fig. 9.2 shows a set of oriented complexes with neighbor dimension 1.

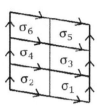

Figure 9.2: Oriented complexes with neighbor dimension 1.

Definition 49 *The invengory $E(\overrightarrow{\mathcal{K}})$ of* composable *subsets of an oriented complex $\overrightarrow{\mathcal{K}}$ consists of sets x satisfies:*

- *x is finite and closed;*

- *$\partial^+(\sigma)$ and $\partial^-(\sigma)$ are disjoint for each element σ of x;*

- *x can be obtained by an iterated process of compositions of prime components using operations $\circ_n$, where $n \leq dim_{NB}(x)$.*

Following definition is provided to characterize generalized invenrelation processes which adopt multiple folds of meta-processes.

Definition 50 *Let $\overrightarrow{\mathcal{K}}$ be an oriented complex and let n be a non-negative integer. An $[l_1, l_2, \cdots, l_m]$-invenrelation process, where $l_1, l_2, \cdots, l_m$ are m non-negative integers, is a sequence of elements $\sigma_0, \sigma_1, \cdots, \sigma_m$ of $\overrightarrow{\mathcal{K}}$ (invenrelation objects and relations) such that*

$$dm(\sigma_{i-1}) \leq l_i, \ \ dm(\sigma_i) > l_i, \ \ \overline{\sigma}_{i-1} \in \partial_{l_i}^-(\overline{\sigma}_i) \backslash (\partial_{l_i-1}^-(\overline{\sigma}_i) \bigcap \partial_{l_i-1}^+(\overline{\sigma}_i))$$

$$for \ 1 \leq i \leq m; \tag{9.3.1}$$

or

$$dm(\sigma_{i-1}) > l_i, \ \ dm(\sigma_i) \leq l_i,$$

$$\overline{\sigma}_{i-1} \in \partial_{l_i}^+(\overline{\sigma}_{i-1}) \backslash (\partial_{l_i-1}^-(\overline{\sigma}_{i-1}) \bigcap \partial_{l_i-1}^+(\overline{\sigma}_{i-1})) \ for \ 1 \leq i \leq m; \tag{9.3.2}$$

We require two lemmas below in order to prove our main result in this section.

Lemma 19 *Let x be a composable set in an oriented complex such that $dim_{NB}(x) \leq r < dm(x)$, where r is a non-negative integer. Then there exists a decomposition $x = x_1 \circ_r x_2 \cdots \circ_r x_m$ of x into composable sets such that each x_i has a unique maximal prime component of dimension greater than r.*

PROOF. 45 *The proof is based on inductive argument. If x is a prime component, then the result is valid obviously. For the case that x is not a prime component, there is a proper decomposition $x = y \circ_q z$ for some integer $q \leq r$. Since $dim_{NB}(y) \leq r$ and $dim_{NB}(z) \leq r$, we have decompositions for y and z as (by induction)*

$$y = y_1 \circ_r y_2 \circ_r \cdots \circ_r y_j \circ_r \overbrace{\partial_r^+(y) \circ_r \cdots \circ_r \partial_r^+(y)}^{(m-j) \ copies \ \partial_r^+(y)},$$

and

$$z = \overbrace{\partial_r^-(z) \circ_r \cdots \circ_r \partial_r^-(z)}^{j \ copies \ \partial_r^-(z)} \circ_r z_{j+1} \circ_r z_{j+2} \circ_r \cdots \circ_r z_m,$$

where y_i, z_i are unique maximal prime components with dimension greater than r.

  Hence, we have the required decomposition of x as

$$
\begin{aligned}
x &= y \circ_q z = (y_1 \circ_r y_2 \circ_r \cdots \circ_r y_j \circ_r \overbrace{\partial_r^+(y) \circ_r \cdots \circ_r \partial_r^+(y)}^{(m-j) \ copies \ \partial_r^+(y)}) \circ_q \\
&\quad (\overbrace{\partial_r^-(z) \circ_r \cdots \circ_r \partial_r^-(z)}^{j \ copies \ \partial_r^-(z)} \circ_r z_{j+1} \circ_r z_{j+2} \circ_r \cdots \circ_r z_m) \\
&= (y_1 \circ_q \partial_r^-(z)) \circ_r \cdots \circ_r (y_j \circ_q \partial_r^-(z)) \circ_r (\partial_r^+(y) \circ_q z_{j+1}) \circ_r \cdots \circ_r (\partial_r^+(y) \circ_q z_m). (9.3.3)
\end{aligned}
$$

Lemma 20 *Let x be a composable set in an oriented complex with $dim_{NB}(x) = r$. Let $\overline{\sigma}$ be a maximal prime component in x with dimension greater than r such that there is no $[r, r, \cdots, r]$-invenrelation process in x from τ to σ, where $\overline{\tau}$ is any other prime component in x with dimension greater than r. Then there exists a decomposition $x = x' \circ_r x''$ such that $\overline{\sigma}$ is the maximal prime component in x' with dimension greater than r.*

PROOF. 46 *From Lemma 19, there exists a decomposition $x = x_1 \circ_r \cdots, \circ_r x_m$ such that each x_i has an unique maximal prime component $\overline{\sigma}_i$ of dimension greater than r. Hence, $\overline{\sigma}_1, \cdots, \overline{\sigma}_m$ is a list of the maximal prime components in x with dimension grater than r. Suppose $\overline{\sigma} = \overline{\sigma}_i$ for* some $i > 1$, then we can group the factors of $x_1, \cdots, x_m$ properly to have factorization $x = z' \circ_s z''$ according to Lemma 19 such that $\overline{\sigma}$ is only belonged to z' and other $\overline{\sigma}_j$ for $(j \neq i)$ are belonged to z'', where s is the neighbor dimension of $z' \circ_r z''$.

Note that the value of s is smaller than r since there are no $[r, r, \cdots, r]$-invenrelation process in x from τ to σ. Therefore,

$$
\begin{aligned}
x &= z' \circ_s z'' = (\partial_r^-(z') \circ_r z') \circ_s (z'' \circ_r \partial_r^+(z'')) \\
&= (\partial_r^-(z') \circ_s z'') \circ_r (z' \circ_s \partial_r^+(z'')) = x' \circ_r x'',
\end{aligned}
\tag{9.3.4}
$$

where $\overline{\sigma}$ is the maximal prime component in x' with dimension greater than r.

The main theorem in this section is to show conditions for the existence of an $[\overbrace{r_1, \cdots, r_1}^{m_1 \text{ copies}}, \overbrace{r_2, \cdots, r_2}^{m_2 \text{ copies}}, \cdots, \overbrace{r_k, \cdots, r_k}^{m_k \text{ copies}}]$-invenrelation process in an oriented complex, where r_i are non-negative integers and m_i are positive integers.

Theorem 31 *Let $\sigma_0, \sigma_1, \cdots, \sigma_k$ be elements of a composable set x in an oriented complex such that, for $1 \leq i \leq k$, $x_{\sigma_{i-1}, \sigma_i}$ are also composable sets in x which include σ_{i-1} and σ_i. If following conditions holds for $1 \leq i \leq k$:*

- *$dim_{NB}(x_{\sigma_i, \sigma_{i+1}}) = r_i$;*

- *$x_{\sigma_{i-1}, \sigma_i}$ can be decomposed as $x_{i,1} \circ_{r_i} x_{i,2} \circ_{r_i} \cdots \circ_{r_i} x_{i, m_i - 1}$ such that each $x_{i,j}$ has a unique maximal prime component of dimension greater than r_i (Lemma 19),*

then we have an $[\overbrace{r_1, \cdots, r_1}^{m_1 \text{ copies}}, \overbrace{r_2, \cdots, r_2}^{m_2 \text{ copies}}, \cdots, \overbrace{r_k, \cdots, r_k}^{m_k \text{ copies}}]$-invenrelation process from σ_0 to σ_k through σ_i sequentially.

PROOF. 47 *From Lemma 19, there is a decomposition $x_{\sigma_{i-1}, \sigma_i} = x_{i,1} \circ_{r_i} x_{i,2} \circ_{r_i} \cdots \circ_{r_i} x_{i, m_i - 1}$ such that each $x_{i,j}$ has a unique maximal prime component $\overline{\tau}_{i,j}$ of dimension greater than r_i, we will show that there is an $[\overbrace{r_i, \cdots, r_i}^{m_i \text{ copies}}]$-invenrelation process with length m_i from σ_{i-1} to $\tau_{i,1}$, $\tau_{i,1}$ to $\tau_{i, m_i - 1}$ and $\tau_{i, m_i - 1}$ to σ_i.*

First we show that there is an $[r_i]$-invenrelation process (length 1) from σ_{i-1} to $\tau_{i,1}$. This is obvious true for $\sigma_{i-1} = \tau_{i,1}$. Let us assume that $\sigma_{i-1} \neq \tau_{i,1}$, where $dm(\overline{\tau_{i,1}}) = p$. We claim that

314

$p = r_i + 1$. If $p > r_1 + 1$, we have

$$
\begin{aligned}
x_{\sigma_{i-1},\sigma_i} &= x_{i,1} \circ_{r_i} (x_{i,2} \circ_{r_i} \cdots \circ_{r_i} x_{i,m_i-1}) \\
&= [\partial^-_{p-1}(x_{i,1}) \circ_{p-1} x_{i,1}] \circ_{r_i} [(x_{i,2} \circ_{r_i} \cdots \circ_{r_i} x_{i,m_i-1}) \circ_{p-1} \\
&\quad \partial^+_{p-1}(x_{i,2} \circ_{r_i} \cdots \circ_{r_i} x_{i,m_i-1})] \\
&= [\partial^-_{p-1}(x_{i,1}) \circ_{r_i} (x_{i,2} \circ_{r_i} \cdots \circ_{r_i} x_{i,m_i-1})] \circ_{p-1} [x_{i,1} \circ_{r_i} \\
&\quad \partial^+_{p-1}(x_{i,2} \circ_{r_i} \cdots \circ_{r_i} x_{i,m_i-1})],
\end{aligned}
$$

and this shows that $\partial^-_{p-1}(x_{i,1}) \circ_{r_i} (x_{i,2} \circ_{r_i} \cdots \circ_{r_i} x_{i,m_i-1})$ is composable containing σ_{i-1} and σ_i contrary to the minimal hypothesis. Hence, the value of p will be $r_i + 1$. Since σ_{i-1} belongs to $\partial^-_{r_i}(\overline{\tau_{i,1}}) \backslash \partial^+_{r_i}(\overline{\tau_{i,1}})$ or $\partial^+_{r_i}(\overline{\tau_{i,1}}) \backslash \partial^-_{r_i}(\overline{\tau_{i,1}})$, then there is an $[r_i]$-invenrelation process with length 1. Similarly, there is an $[r_i]$-invenrelation process with length 1 from τ_{i,m_i-1} to σ_i.

We now show that there is an $[\overbrace{r_i, \cdots, r_i}^{m_i-2 \ copies}]$-invenrelation process with length $m_i - 2$ from $\tau_{i,1}$ to τ_{i,m_i-1}. Suppose that $m_i - 1 > 2$, we claim that there are $[r_i, \cdots, r_i]$-invenrelation processes with some lengths from $\tau_{i,1}$ to $\tau_{i,2}$ and from $\tau_{i,2}$ to τ_{i,m_i-1}. If there is no such invenrelation process in $x_{\sigma_{i-1},\sigma_i}$ from $\tau_{i,1}$ to $\tau_{i,2}$, then, by Lemma 20, there is a decomposition $x_{\sigma_{i-1},\sigma_i} = x' \circ_{r_i} x''$ such that $\overline{\tau_{i,2}}$ is the only maximal prime component of dimension greater than r_i in x', contrary to the minimal hypothesis. Hence, there are $[r_i, \cdots, r_i]$-invenrelation processes with some lengths from $\tau_{i,1}$ to $\tau_{i,2}$ and from $\tau_{i,2}$ to τ_{i,m_i-1} (recurrent relation among $\tau_{i,j}$).

If $m_i - 1 = 2$, we have $dm(\overline{\tau_{i,1}} \bigcap \overline{\tau_{i,2}}) = r_i$ since $dim_{NB}(x_{\sigma_i,\sigma_{i+1}}) = r_i$. Let ρ be an r_i dimensional element of $\overline{\tau_{i,1}} \bigcap \overline{\tau_{i,2}}$, then $\rho \in \partial^+_{r_i}(\overline{\tau_{i,1}}) \bigcap \partial^-_{r_i}(\overline{\tau_{i,2}})$. Hence, there is an $[r_i]$-invenrelation process from $\tau_{i,1}$ to $\tau_{i,2}$ with length 1. From recurrent relation among $\tau_{i,j}$ and induction argument, we have an $[\overbrace{r_i, \cdots, r_i}^{(m_i-2) \ copies}]$-invenrelation processes with length $m_i - 2$ from $\tau_{i,1}$ to τ_{i,m_i-1}. Finally, there is an $[\overbrace{r_i, \cdots, r_i}^{m_i \ copies}]$-invenrelation process with length m_i from σ_{i-1} to $\tau_{i,1}$, $\tau_{i,1}$ to τ_{i,m_i-1} and τ_{i,m_i-1} to σ_i $(1 + (m_i - 2) + 1) = m_i$ for $1 \leq i \leq k$.

Example 43 *If we are given an invenrelation procedure presented by Fig. 9.3, we find that there is no $[0, 0, \cdots, 0]$ (no matter how many finite copies of 0)-invenrelation process from the original invengory of invenrelation algebra to the terminal invengory. However, if we are allowed to adopt oriented components with dimension 1 in such invenrelation procedure. We have, for example, an $[1, 0, 1, 1]$-invenrelation process $\rho, \sigma_1, \sigma_4, \sigma_6, \rho'$ as indicated by subpart of Fig. 9.3*

$(\rho, \sigma_1, \sigma_4, \sigma_6, \rho')$ from the original invengory of invenrelation algebra to the terminal invengory.

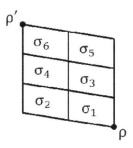

Figure 9.3: Oriented complex for an invenrelation procedure.

9.4 n-Invengory Derivability

In Sec. 9.2, we consider derivability for algebraic terms in the MSA $(\mathcal{S}_1, \mathcal{R}_1)$ to the MSA $(\mathcal{S}_2, \mathcal{R}_2)$, which is in the same invengory of the MSA $(\mathcal{S}_1, \mathcal{R}_1)$. In this section, we consider one more step further by discussing derivability for algebraic invenrelation terms in the MSA $(\mathcal{S}_1, \mathcal{R}_1)$ to the MSA $(\mathcal{S}_2, \mathcal{R}_2)$, which is *not* in the same invengory of the MSA $(\mathcal{S}_1, \mathcal{R}_1)$.

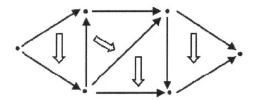

Figure 9.4: Meta-procedures.

As we explain in Sec. 9.3, meta-procedures can be applied repeatedly to derive new things at other invengory. Fig. 9.4 illustrates an example of a serious meta-procedures among invengories with dimension 2 (two folds meta-procedures), where vertices are different invengories of algebraic invenrelation systems. The notion about generalized n-invengories defined at Sec. IV in Chap. VIII provides us a proper tool to derive invenrelation outcomes for those meta-procedures among various classes. In Sec. 9.4.1, relations between two MSA invengories considered in generalized n-invengories are single-input and single-output (SISO). We generalize relations as multiple-input and multiple-output (MIMO) relations among two groups of MSA invengories in Sec. 9.4.2.

9.4.1 Derivability : SISO Invenrelation Steps

The goal of this section is to show derivability for algebraic invenrelation terms from the MSA $(\mathcal{S}_1, \mathcal{R}_1)$ to the MSA $(\mathcal{S}_2, \mathcal{R}_2)$, which is not in the same invengory of the MSA $(\mathcal{S}_1, \mathcal{R}_1)$. Comparing to Sec. 9.2 (same invengory case), we have to adopt more techniques about generalized n-invengories (n can be any positive integer) to show the existence of compositions of relations from the invengory which MSA $(\mathcal{S}_1, \mathcal{R}_1)$ belongs to the invengory which MSA $(\mathcal{S}_2, \mathcal{R}_2)$ is within.

We begin by a lemma which shows that for any n-gluing design $Q(\overrightarrow{\mathcal{K}})$ (defined in Sec. III A at Chap. VIII), there is at least one $[n, n, \cdots, n]$-invenrelation process from σ_0 to σ_1, where $\sigma_0 = \partial_n^-(Q(\overrightarrow{\mathcal{K}}))$ and $\sigma_1 = \partial_n^+(Q(\overrightarrow{\mathcal{K}}))$. That will be used to show that every evaluation morphism for a gluing design has at least one composite.

Lemma 21 *For any gluing design $Q(\overrightarrow{\mathcal{K}})$, where $\overrightarrow{\mathcal{K}}$ is a composable oriented complex with neighbor dimension n, then there exists an $[\overbrace{n, n, \cdots, n}^{m-copies}]$-invenrelation process from σ_0 to σ_1, where $\sigma_0 = \partial_n^-(Q(\overrightarrow{\mathcal{K}}))$, $\sigma_1 = \partial_n^+(Q(\overrightarrow{\mathcal{K}}))$ and m is the number of elements, which have unique maximal prime components in each of these elements, in the decomposition of $Q(\overrightarrow{\mathcal{K}})$ by $\circ_n$.*

PROOF. 48 *If we set $k = 1$, $\sigma_0 = \partial_n^-(Q(\overrightarrow{\mathcal{K}}))$ and $\sigma_1 = \partial_n^+(Q(\overrightarrow{\mathcal{K}}))$ in Theorem 31, this lemma holds from Theorem 31.*

The next goal is to show Lemma 23 which helps us to prove the uniqueness of compositions from the invengory which MSA $(\mathcal{S}_1, \mathcal{R}_1)$ belongs to the invengory which MSA $(\mathcal{S}_2, \mathcal{R}_2)$ is within. Several definitions are provided below before Lemma 23.

Definition 51 *A top composition in an $(n+1)$-invengory is exactly an n-composition.*

Definition 52 *A non-top composition in an $(n+1)$-invengory consists of all compositions except n-compositions.*

Definition 53 *An* $(n+1)$-*unicellular is an gluing design with dimension* $(n+1)$ *that contains exactly one prime component with dimension* $(n+1)$.

Definition 54 *An* assignment *of a gluing design* $Q(\overrightarrow{\mathcal{K}})$ *with dimension* $(n+1)$ *in an* $(n+1)$-*invengory* **A** *is an evaluation morphism from* $Q(\overrightarrow{\mathcal{K}})$ *to* **A**. *An assigned* gluing design, *say* $Q(\overrightarrow{\mathcal{K}})$, *in an* $(n+1)$-*invengory* **A** *is denoted as* $Q_{\mathbf{A}}(\overrightarrow{\mathcal{K}})$.

Definition 55 *A* strong composition *of an assigned gluing design* $Q_{\mathbf{A}}(\overrightarrow{\mathcal{K}})$ *with dimension* $(n+1)$ *is the top composition of the compositions of assigned unicellular determined by any* $[n, \cdots, n]$-*invenrelation process of* $Q(\overrightarrow{\mathcal{K}})$.

Monads give us a way of free construction of various "algebraic theories", for examples, groups, rings and n-invengories. Following lemma is provided to show the interchange law for monad in top composition and monads in non-top compositions.

Lemma 22 *Let* $T_0, \cdots, T_n$ *be monads on a* n-*invengory, equipped with*

- *for all* $i > j$, *an interchange law* $\chi_{i,j} : T_i T_j \Rightarrow T_j T_i$;

- $\mu^{T_i} : T_i T_i \Rightarrow T_i$;

- *for all* $i > j > k$, *following diagram holds for commutativity:*

$$
\begin{array}{ccc}
T_j T_i T_k & \xrightarrow{T_j \chi_{i,k}} & T_j T_k T_i \\[4pt]
\chi_{i,j} T_k \uparrow & & \downarrow \chi_{j,k} T_i \\[4pt]
T_i T_j T_k & & T_k T_j T_i \\[4pt]
T_i \chi_{j,k} \downarrow & & \uparrow T_k \chi_{i,j} \\[4pt]
T_i T_k T_j & \xrightarrow{\chi_{i,k} T_j} & T_k T_i T_j
\end{array}
\tag{9.4.1}
$$

Then for all $0 \leq i < n$ *we have monads* $T_0 T_1 \cdots T_i$ *and* $T_{i+1} \cdots T_n$ *with interchange law as*

$$
(T_{i+1} \cdots T_n)(T_0 T_1 \cdots T_i) \quad \Rightarrow \quad (T_0 T_1 \cdots T_i)(T_{i+1} \cdots T_n). \tag{9.4.2}
$$

PROOF. 49 *The proof is based on induction with respect to* n [1]. *We begin with the simplest*

---

[1]The proof is modified from the work *Iterated distributive laws* by Eugenia Cheng at 2007 (http://arxiv.org/pdf/0710.1120.pdf).

case when $n = 3$. Given interchange laws

$$\chi_{1,0} : T_1 T_0 \Rightarrow T_0 T_1$$

$$\chi_{2,0} : T_2 T_0 \Rightarrow T_0 T_2$$

$$\chi_{2,1} : T_2 T_1 \Rightarrow T_1 T_2,$$

$$(9.4.3)$$

we will verify the following interchange law

$$T_1 T_2 T_0 \xrightarrow{T_1 \chi_{2,0}} T_1 T_0 T_2 \xrightarrow{\chi_{2,1} T_2} T_0 T_1 T_2. \qquad (9.4.4)$$

When there are four monads constructed from each T_0, T_1 and T_2, we have following commutative diagrams [2] to show the interchange law of $T_1 T_2 T_0 \xrightarrow{T_1 \chi_{2,0}} T_1 T_0 T_2 \xrightarrow{\chi_{2,1} T_2} T_0 T_1 T_2$.

$$T_1 T_2 T_0 T_0 \xrightarrow{T_1 \chi_{2,0} T_0} T_1 T_0 T_2 T_0 \xrightarrow{\chi_{1,0} T_2 T_0} T_0 T_1 T_2 T_0 \xrightarrow{T_0 T_1 \chi_{2,0}} T_0 T_1 T_0 T_2 \xrightarrow{T_0 \chi_{1,0} T_2} T_0 T_0 T_1 T_2$$

$$T_1 T_0 \chi_{2,0} \searrow \qquad\qquad \nearrow \chi_{1,0} T_0 T_2$$

$$\downarrow T_1 T_2 \mu^{T_0} \qquad\qquad\qquad T_1 T_0 T_0 T_2 \qquad\qquad\qquad \downarrow \mu^{T_0} T_1 T_2$$

$$\downarrow T_1 \mu^{T_0} T_2$$

$$T_1 T_2 T_0 \xrightarrow{\quad T_1 \chi_{2,0} \quad} T_1 T_0 T_2 \xrightarrow{\quad \chi_{1,0} T_2 \quad} T_0 T_1 T_2$$

When there are five monads constructed from each T_0, T_1 and T_2, we have following commutative diagrams [3] to show the interchange law of $T_1 T_2 T_0 \xrightarrow{T_1 \chi_{2,0}} T_1 T_0 T_2 \xrightarrow{\chi_{2,1} T_2} T_0 T_1 T_2$.

$$T_1 T_2 T_1 T_2 T_0 \xrightarrow{T_1 T_2 T_1 \chi_{2,0}} T_1 T_2 T_1 T_0 T_2 \xrightarrow{T_1 T_2 \chi_{1,0} T_2} T_1 T_2 T_0 T_1 T_2 \xrightarrow{T_1 \chi_{2,0} T_1 T_2} T_1 T_0 T_2 T_1 T_2 \xrightarrow{\chi_{1,0} T_2 T_1 T_2} T_0 T_1 T_2 T_1 T_2$$

$$\downarrow T_1 \chi_{2,1} T_2 T_0 \qquad \downarrow T_1 \chi_{2,1} T_0 T_2 \qquad\quad By \ (9.4.1) \qquad\quad \downarrow T_1 T_0 \chi_{2,1} T_2 \qquad \downarrow T_0 T_1 \chi_{2,1} T_2$$

$$T_1 T_1 T_2 T_2 T_0 \xrightarrow{T_1 T_1 T_2 \chi_{2,0}} T_1 T_1 T_2 T_0 T_2 \xrightarrow{T_1 T_1 \chi_{2,0} T_2} T_1 T_1 T_0 T_2 T_2 \xrightarrow{T_1 \chi_{1,0} T_2 T_2} T_1 T_0 T_1 T_2 T_2 \xrightarrow{\chi_{1,0} T_1 T_2 T_2} T_0 T_1 T_1 T_2 T_2$$

$$\downarrow \mu^{T_1} T_2 T_2 T_0 \qquad \downarrow \mu^{T_1} T_2 T_0 T_2 \mu^{T_1} T_0 T_2 T_2 \swarrow \searrow T_1 T_1 T_0 \mu^{T_1} \qquad \downarrow T_1 T_0 T_1 \mu^{T_2} \qquad \downarrow T_0 T_1 T_1 \mu^{T_2}$$

$$T_1 T_2 T_2 T_0 \xrightarrow{T_1 T_2 \chi_{2,0}} T_1 T_2 T_0 T_2 \xrightarrow{T_1 \chi_{2,0} T_2} T_1 T_0 T_2 T_2 \qquad T_1 T_1 T_0 T_2 \xrightarrow{T_1 \chi_{1,0} T_2} T_1 T_0 T_1 T_2 \xrightarrow{\chi_{1,0} T_1 T_2} T_0 T_1 T_1 T_2$$

$$\downarrow T_1 \mu^{T_2} T_0 \qquad\qquad T_1 T_0 \mu^{T_2} \searrow \quad \swarrow \mu^{T_1} T_0 T_2 \qquad\qquad\qquad \downarrow T_0 \mu^{T_1} T_2$$

$$T_1 T_2 T_0 \xrightarrow{\quad T_1 \chi_{2,0} \quad} T_1 T_2 T_0 T_2 \qquad\qquad T_1 T_0 T_2 \qquad\qquad \xrightarrow{\quad \chi_{1,0} T_2 \quad} T_0 T_1 T_2$$

Results for the other interchange laws follow similarly. For cases that there are more than five monads constructed from each T_0, T_1 and T_2, they can always be reduced as four or five monads cases through applying $\chi_{i,j}$ and μ^{T_i} repeatedly.

---

[2] Without lose of generality, we assume that T_0 is adopted twice in these four monads.

[3] Without lose of generality, we assume that T_1 and T_2 are adopted twice in these five monads.

Now, we consider cases for $n > 2$. By defining a new set of monads S_i as $S_i = T_i$ for $0 \leq i \leq n - 2$ and $S_{n-1} = T_{n-1}T_n$, we wish to show interchange laws for $(S_{i+1} \cdots S_{n-1})(S_0 S_1 \cdots S_i) \Rightarrow (S_0 S_1 \cdots S_i)(S_{i+1} \cdots S_{n-1})$, that is $(T_{i+1} \cdots T_n)(T_0 T_1 \cdots T_i) \Rightarrow (T_0 T_1 \cdots T_i)(T_{i+1} \cdots T_n)$.

For all $i > j$ and $i < n - 1$, we have $\chi_{i,j} : S_i S_j \Rightarrow S_j S_i$. For all $i > j$ and $i = n - 1$, we also have interchange law $\chi'_{i,j} : S_{n-1}S_j \Rightarrow S_j S_{n-1}$ from three monads case T_j, T_{n-1}, T_n provided in the previous arguments.

For commutativity of S_i, S_j and S_k [4], we immediate have all cases valid for $i < (n-1)$ since these cases are commutativity requirements for T_i, T_j and T_k. For the case that $i = (n-1)$, we have to check the commutativity for S_{n-1}, T_j and T_k. This is true based on the following diagram:

$$
\begin{array}{ccccc}
T_k\underline{T_{n-1}T_n}T_j & \longrightarrow & T_kT_{n-1}T_jT_n & \longrightarrow & T_kT_j\underline{T_{n-1}T_n} \\
\uparrow & & \uparrow & & \downarrow \\
T_{n-1}T_kT_nT_j & \longrightarrow & T_{n-1}T_kT_jT_n & I & T_jT_k\underline{T_{n-1}T_n} \\
\uparrow & & \downarrow & & \uparrow \\
\underline{T_{n-1}T_n}T_kT_j & II & T_{n-1}T_jT_kT_n & \longrightarrow & T_jT_{n-1}T_kT_n \\
\downarrow & & \uparrow & & \uparrow \\
\underline{T_{n-1}T_n}T_jT_k & \longrightarrow & T_{n-1}T_jT_nT_k & \longrightarrow & T_j\underline{T_{n-1}T_n}T_k,
\end{array}
$$

$$\text{(9.4.5)}$$

where I and II are based on commutativity diagram by Eq. (9.4.1). Hence, by the induction results for previous $(n-1)$ cases, we have

$$(S_{i+1} \cdots S_{n-1})(S_0 S_1 \cdots S_i) \Rightarrow (S_0 S_1 \cdots S_i)(S_{i+1} \cdots S_{n-1}). \tag{9.4.6}$$

Lemma 23 *Every assigned gluing design in an n-invengory $\mathbf{A}$ has a strong composition.*

PROOF. 50 *Given two assigned unicellulars $Q_{\mathbf{A}_1}(\overrightarrow{\mathcal{K}_1})$ and $Q_{\mathbf{A}_2}(\overrightarrow{\mathcal{K}_2})$ containing $(n+1)$-prime components σ_1 and σ_2 respectively, such that $\partial^-(\overrightarrow{\mathcal{K}_2}) = \partial^+(\overrightarrow{\mathcal{K}_1})$, $\partial^-(\sigma_2) = \partial^+(\sigma_1)$ and $\overrightarrow{\mathcal{K}_1}, \overrightarrow{\mathcal{K}_2}$ disjoint at other components. Our first claim (First Claim) is that the top composition of the compositions of the assigned unicellulars equals to the composition of the assigned unicellulars provided by the top composition of σ_1 and σ_2.*

Since the i-sources and i-targets of $a_1(\sigma_1)$ (objects and relations in $\mathbf{A}_1$ assigned by σ_1) and $a_2(\sigma_2)$ (objects and relations in $\mathbf{A}_2$ assigned by σ_2) agree for $0 \leq i \leq n - 1$, it follows from the

---
[4]Without lose of generality, we assume that $i > j > k$.

interchange laws, by Lemma 22, between monads T_n and $T_{j_0}T_{j_1}\cdots T_{j_{n-1}}$ where $\{j_0, j_1, \cdots, j_{n-1}\}$ are distinct and selected from $\{0, 1, 2, \cdots, n-1\}$ that the top composition of these expressions equals to the composition determined by replacing $a_1(\sigma_1)$ in the original expression by the top composition of $a_1(\sigma_1)$ and $a_2(\sigma_2)$, as claimed.

Let $Q_{\mathbf{A}}(\overrightarrow{\mathcal{K}})$ be an assigned gluing design made by non-top compositions, and assume that $\overrightarrow{\mathcal{K}}$ contains at least one $(n+1)$-prime component. We claim (Second Claim) that the non-top composition for $Q_{\mathbf{A}}(\overrightarrow{\mathcal{K}})$ is formed by the top composition of assigned unicellulars with any order. This argument is verified by induction on the number of $(n+1)$-prime components in $\overrightarrow{\mathcal{K}}$. If $\overrightarrow{\mathcal{K}}$ has one $(n+1)$-prime component, the result is trivial. If $\overrightarrow{\mathcal{K}}$ has $(k+1)$ $(n+1)$-prime components, one choose any two of them, say σ_1 and σ_2. By considering the top composition of $\overrightarrow{\mathcal{K}_1}$ and $\overrightarrow{\mathcal{K}_2}$, where $\overrightarrow{\mathcal{K}_1}$ is given by removing $\partial^-(\sigma_1)$ from $\overrightarrow{\mathcal{K}}$ and replacing it by $\partial^+(\sigma_1)$ and $\overrightarrow{\mathcal{K}_2}$ is obtained similarly by removing $\partial^-(\sigma_2)$ from $\overrightarrow{\mathcal{K}}$ and replacing it by $\partial^+(\sigma_2)$, we have the result due to the First Claim and the number of $(n+1)$-prime components in the oriented complex $\overrightarrow{\mathcal{K}_2}$ (become k).

At this status, we are ready to prove our lemma. If $n=1$, the result is obvious. We assume that the statement in lemma is true for n-invengory and wish to prove $(n+1)$-invengory. Existence is true since every $(n+1)$-gluing design has an $[n, n, \cdots, n]$-invenrelation process by Lemma 21 and every assigned unicellular has a unique composition. For uniqueness, If the gluing design $\overrightarrow{\mathcal{K}}$ contains at most one $(n+l)$ prime component, unicity holds by induction on n and by the definition of the composition of an assigned unicellular. If $\overrightarrow{\mathcal{K}}$ has $k+l$ $(n+l)$ prime components, suppose we have two $[n, n, \cdots, n]$-invenrelation process in $\overrightarrow{\mathcal{K}}$. Either they commence with the same $(n+l)$ prime component, in which case we have proved it by induction, or they commence with different $(n+l)$ prime components. In the latter case, the result follows by induction and the Second Claim.

Before stating our main theorem, we have several definitions about the decomposition of a gluing design.

Definition 56 *An $(n+1)$-gluing design, $\overrightarrow{\mathcal{K}}$, is called* indecomposable *if $\overrightarrow{\mathcal{K}}$ consists of one k-prime component and its domain and codomain for some $k \leq n$.*

Definition 57 *If an $(n+1)$-gluing design, $\overrightarrow{\mathcal{K}}$, is not indecomposable, then its decomposition consists of two sub $(n+1)$-gluing design $\overrightarrow{\mathcal{K}_1}$ and $\overrightarrow{\mathcal{K}_2}$ such that*

- *$\partial_k^-(\overrightarrow{\mathcal{K}_2}) = \partial_k^+(\overrightarrow{\mathcal{K}_1})$ for some $k \leq n$;*

- $\vec{\mathcal{K}_1}$ and $\vec{\mathcal{K}_2}$ are disjoint except common parts at the first item;

- $\vec{\mathcal{K}} = \vec{\mathcal{K}_1} \bigcup \vec{\mathcal{K}_2}$;

- neither $\vec{\mathcal{K}_1}$ nor $\vec{\mathcal{K}_2}$ is a sub gluing design of the other.

Definition 58 *An $(n+1)$-gluing composition of an assigned $(n+1)$-gluing design $Q_{\mathbf{A}}(\vec{\mathcal{K}})$ consists of evaluation in $\mathbf{A}$ for all decompositions $\vec{\mathcal{K}} = \vec{\mathcal{K}_1} \bigcup_k \vec{\mathcal{K}_2}$, where $\bigcup_k$ indicates k-composition and $0 \leq k \leq n$.*

Now, we have prepared enough tools to establish the main theorem of this Chapter about derivability for algebraic invenrelation terms between two different invengories of MSA associated by n-ingengories.

Theorem 32 *The MSA $(\mathcal{S}_i, \mathcal{R}_i)$ is the i-th object in the MSA invengory with the initial object $T_{\mathcal{R}}$, denoted as $\mathbf{C}_{\mathcal{R}}$, and $t^{(i)}$ is used to represent an algebraic term made from $(\mathcal{S}_i, \mathcal{R}_i)$. Similarly, the MSA $(\mathcal{S}'_k, \mathcal{R}'_k)$ is the k-th object in the MSA invengory with the initial object $T_{\mathcal{R}'}$, indicated as $\mathbf{C}_{\mathcal{R}'}$, and $t'^{(k)}$ is used to represent an algebraic term made from $(\mathcal{S}'_k, \mathcal{R}'_k)$. If following conditions hold:*

- *there is an assigned gluing design $Q_{\mathbf{A}}(\vec{\mathcal{K}})$ such that $\mathbf{C}_{\mathcal{R}}$ and $\mathbf{C}_{\mathcal{R}'}$ are 0-dimensional objects of n-invengory $\mathbf{A}$;*

- *there are isomorphic homomorphisms $f_i : T_{\mathcal{R}} \longrightarrow (\mathcal{S}_i, \mathcal{R}_i)$, $f'_j : T_{\mathcal{R}'} \longrightarrow (\mathcal{S}'_j, \mathcal{R}'_j)$ and $f'_k : T_{\mathcal{R}'} \longrightarrow (\mathcal{S}'_k, \mathcal{R}'_k)$ for each i, j and k (objects indices);*

- *given any object in the invengory $\mathbf{C}_{\mathcal{R}'}$, represented as $(\mathcal{S}'_j, \mathcal{R}'_j)$, there exists a function $\mathbf{I}_j$ such that terms in $T_{\mathcal{R}}$ can be mapped as terms in $(\mathcal{S}'_j, \mathcal{R}'_j)$ with respect to $\mathbf{A}$;*

then algebraic invenrelation terms $t^{(i)}$ and $t'^{(k)}$ can be derived from each other using rules mentioned in Sec. 9.1.3 and relations between objects and invengories, for instances, functions and functors.

PROOF. 51 *We first show that there exists an unique n-gluing composition in $Q_{\mathbf{A}}(\vec{\mathcal{K}})$ for every positive natural number n. The proof is based on induction for n. The case for $n = 1$ is true by associativity of composition in the n-invengory $\mathbf{A}$.*

Let us assume that the result true for n and we wish to prove it for $n + 1$. If $\vec{\mathcal{K}}$ has at most one $(n + 1)$-prime component, then there exists an n-gluing composition in $Q_{\mathbf{A}}(\vec{\mathcal{K}})$ by the *definition of strong composition. If $\overrightarrow{\mathcal{K}}$ has more than one $(n+1)$-prime components, then a strong composition is a top composition of unicellulars, each containing fewer prime components than $\overrightarrow{\mathcal{K}}$ and there still exists an n-gluing composition in $Q_{\mathbf{A}}(\overrightarrow{\mathcal{K}})$ by induction. Hence, we have existence by Lemma 23.*

For uniqueness, if $\overrightarrow{\mathcal{K}}$ is indecomposable, then the result is obvious. If the gluing design $\overrightarrow{\mathcal{K}}$ is a top composition of the $(n+1)$-gluing composition of $\overrightarrow{\mathcal{K}_1}$ and $\overrightarrow{\mathcal{K}_2}$, then by induction, one takes the unique n-gluing composition of $\overrightarrow{\mathcal{K}_1}$ followed by the unique n-gluing composition of $\overrightarrow{\mathcal{K}_2}$ to get the uniqueness of n-gluing composition in $Q_{\mathbf{A}}(\overrightarrow{\mathcal{K}})$.

Since there is an n-gluing composition in $Q_{\mathbf{A}}(\overrightarrow{\mathcal{K}})$, the index j in $\mathbf{I}_j(\tau)$ can be determined through the functor from the invengory $\mathbf{C}_{\mathcal{R}}$ to the invengory $\mathbf{C}_{\mathcal{R}'}$ for terms τ in $T_{\mathcal{R}}$. By Theorem 30 and previous arguments, we have

$$t^{(i)} \xrightarrow{f_i^{-1}} \tau_1 = f_i^{-1}(t^{(i)}) \xrightarrow{The. \ 2} \tau_2 \xrightarrow{\mathbf{I}_j,\mathbf{A}} t'^{(j)} \xrightarrow{f_j'^{-1}} \zeta_1 = f_j'^{-1}(t'^{(j)}) \xrightarrow{The. \ 2} \zeta_2 \xrightarrow{f_k'} t'^{(k)},$$

where $\tau_1, \tau_2 \in T_{\mathcal{R}}$ and $\zeta_1, \zeta_2 \in T_{\mathcal{R}'}$.

In Fig. 9.5, we illustrate those objects and relations involved in this theorem.

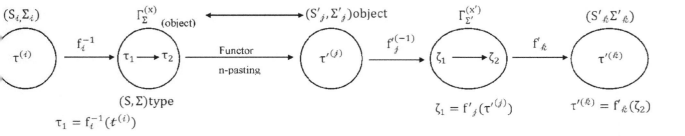

Figure 9.5: Derivability of a SISO system.

The following corollary is the special case of Theorem 32 when the j-th object is the object $T_{\mathcal{R}'}$ itself.

Corollary 1 *The MSA $(\mathcal{S}_i, \mathcal{R}_i)$ is the i-th object in the MSA invengory with the initial object $T_{\mathcal{R}}$, denoted as $\mathbf{C}_{\mathcal{R}}$, and $t^{(i)}$ is used to represent an algebraic term made from $(\mathcal{S}_i, \mathcal{R}_i)$. Similarly, the MSA $(\mathcal{S}_k', \mathcal{R}_k')$ is the k-th object in the MSA invengory with the initial object $T_{\mathcal{R}'}$, indicated as*

$\mathbf{C}_{\mathcal{R}'}$, and $t'^{(k)}$ is used to represent an algebraic term made from $(\mathcal{S}_k', \mathcal{R}_k')$. If following conditions hold:

- there is an assigned gluing design $Q_{\mathbf{A}}(\overrightarrow{\mathcal{K}})$ such that $\mathbf{C}_{\mathcal{R}}$ and $\mathbf{C}_{\mathcal{R}'}$ are objects of n-invengory $\mathbf{A}$;

- there are isomorphic homomorphisms $f_i : T_{\mathcal{R}} \longrightarrow (\mathcal{S}_i, \mathcal{R}_i)$ and $f_k' : T_{\mathcal{R}'} \longrightarrow (\mathcal{S}_k', \mathcal{R}_k')$ for each i and k;

- given any object in the invengory $\mathbf{C}_{\mathcal{R}'}$, represented as $(\mathcal{S}_j', \mathcal{R}_j')$, there exists a function $\mathbf{I}_j$ such that terms in $T_{\mathcal{R}}$ can be mapped as terms in $(\mathcal{S}_j', \mathcal{R}_j')$ with respect to $\mathbf{A}$;

then algebraic invenrelation terms $t^{(i)}$ and $t'^{(k)}$ can be derived from each other using rules mentioned in Sec. 9.1.3 and relations between objects and invengories, for instances, functions and functors.

PROOF. **52** *Since we have*

$$t^{(i)} \xrightarrow{f_i^{-1}} \tau_1 = f_i^{-1}(t^{(i)}) \xrightarrow{The.\ 2} \tau_2 \xrightarrow{\mathbf{I}_j, \mathbf{A}} \zeta_1 \xrightarrow{The.\ 2} \zeta_2 \xrightarrow{f_k'} t'^{(k)},$$

where $\tau_1, \tau_2 \in T_{\mathcal{R}}$ *and* $\zeta_1, \zeta_2 \in T_{\mathcal{R}'}$.

Example 44 *Relation modeling is a crucial step in the product creation process. This example suggests an inductive approach to create a common design language, named as* relational language, *for use with relational models, focusing mainly on electromechanical systems. Two key terms are required to define for such language usage:*

- *Relation: a description of an operation to be acted by a device or artifact;*

- *Object : a set which consists of variations of materials, energy or signal involved in the discussed system.*

Several reasons motivate the creation of a relational language for electromechanical design.

- Criterions Determination. *An important aspect of creating product is to formulate objective measures for benchmarking and quality criterions. Relational language can greatly enhance methods, such as Quality Function Development, by identifying and choosing proper metrics.*

- Comparison. *Actually, very few product designs are really original. Instead, most product designs stem from previous designs. If products are expressed by relational language through relations and objects, one can build a data base for searching products with similar functions.*

- Products Architecture. *Products expressed by relational language enable us to construct products structure according to their functionalities.*

- Processing Design Information. *A relational model is a good way to record and communication design information. To achieve this consistently, a common set of relations and objects with clear (and timeless) expressions is necessary.*

- Creativity generation. *Relational language will help us to design out new products automatically through computers.*

Objects

A basic component of any relational modeling approach is the representation of inputs and outputs by quantities relations. These quantities (or entities) are known as objects. Energy, material and information are three fundamental classes in product creation problems. Following table is provided to show most popular design objects from these three classes.

Class	Object
Material	Woods, Metal, etc.
Information	Visual, Auditory, etc.
Energy	Thermal, Chemical, Electromagnetic, etc.

Relations

As with objects, relations are formalized through a study of past methods, in addition to the patents and other literature. Through these studies, the relations have been used to represent hundreds of products, both redesigns and original developments. Relations can be divided as the following classes with respect their attributes: divide (to cause a material or energy to separate), connect (to cause a material or energy to combine), placement (to cause a material or energy to move from one location to another location), guide (to direct the course of an energy or material along a determined path), transform (to change from one form of energy or material to another), provision (to accumulate or provide material or energy) and signal (to provide information). Following table is provided to show most popular design relations according to relational classes.

Class	*Object*
divide	*separate, cut, etc.*
connect	*couple, mix, etc.*
placement	*import, export, etc.*
guide	*rotate, transport, etc.*
transform	*energy type transformation, etc.*
provision	*store, supply, etc.*
signal	*sense, display, etc.*

Relational Model Derivation

There are three steps involved to derive a relational model using objects and relations.

- *Generate one unit of relational model. This step associates the customer requirements to the relational model and one has to identify several input or output objects and their relation for one component of the product as shown by Fig. 9.6.*

- *Create Relation Chains for Each Input Object. This step develops a chain of one unit relations that operate on the object. There are two types of relation chains: sequential relation chains and parallel relation chains. In sequential relation chains, the relations must be performed in a specific order to generate the desired result. Parallel relation chains consist of sets of sequential relation chains sharing one or more common objects. Fig. 9.7 demonstrates sequential relation chains and parallel relation chains for electric razor.*

- *Assemble Relation Chains Into a Relational Model. The final step of relational model derivation is to aggregate all of the function chains from previous step into a single model. It may be necessary to connect the distinct relation chains together as illustrated by Fig. 9.8.*

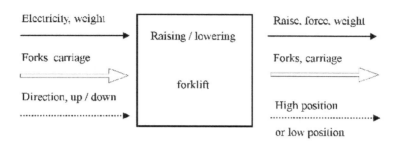

Figure 9.6: Relation for one component.

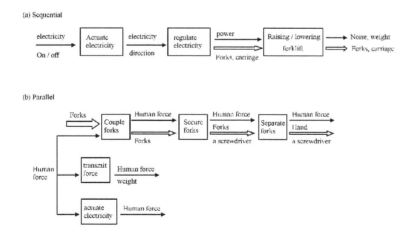

Figure 9.7: Sequential and parallel relation chains.

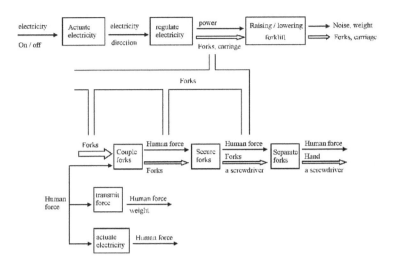

Figure 9.8: Assemble relation chains.

A double invengory **D** *which consists objects, vertical morphisms (the morphisms of parallel objects), horizontal morphisms (the morphisms of sequential objects), and double morphisms (the morphisms of vertical or horizontal morphisms). A double morphism has a horizontal domain and codomain, and a vertical domain and codomain. It can be expressed as*

$$
\begin{array}{ccc}
A & \xrightarrow{f} & B \\
l\downarrow & \alpha & \downarrow l' \\
C & \xrightarrow{f'} & D
\end{array}
$$

or simply denoted as

$$
\begin{array}{ccc}
\bullet & \longrightarrow & \bullet \\
\downarrow & \alpha & \downarrow \\
\bullet & \longrightarrow & \bullet
\end{array}
$$

Then horizontal pasting (corresponding to sequential relation chains) of two double morphisms α *and* β *is represented* $\alpha \circ_h \beta$ *and pictured as*

$$
\begin{array}{ccccc}
\bullet & \longrightarrow & \bullet & \longrightarrow & \bullet \\
\downarrow & \alpha & \downarrow & \beta & \downarrow \\
\bullet & \longrightarrow & \bullet & \longrightarrow & \bullet
\end{array}
$$

Similarly, vertical pasting (corresponding to parallel relation chains) of two double morphisms α and β is represented $\alpha \circ_v \beta$ and pictured as

$$
\begin{array}{ccc}
\bullet & \longrightarrow & \bullet \\
\downarrow & \alpha & \downarrow \\
\bullet & \longrightarrow & \bullet \\
\downarrow & \beta & \downarrow \\
\bullet & \longrightarrow & \bullet
\end{array}
$$

A natural question is weather an arrangement of double cells stemmed from sequential and (or) parallel relation chains in a double invengory has a unique composition, independent of the order in which the operations of horizontal and vertical composition are taken. Consider the following arrangement of double cells:

$$
\begin{array}{ccccc}
\bullet & \longrightarrow & \bullet & \longrightarrow & \bullet \\
\downarrow & \alpha & \downarrow & \gamma & \downarrow \\
\bullet & \longrightarrow & \bullet & \longrightarrow & \bullet \\
\downarrow & \beta & \downarrow & \delta & \downarrow \\
\bullet & \longrightarrow & \bullet & \longrightarrow & \bullet
\end{array}
$$

We can evaluate this either as

$$(\alpha \circ_h \gamma) \circ_v (\beta \circ_h \delta) = (\alpha \circ_v \beta) \circ_h (\gamma \circ_v \delta). \tag{9.4.7}$$

Let $\mathcal{D}$ be a deign of a system (arrangement of double cells), composable in two different ways, giving $\varepsilon_h(\mathcal{D}) = \varepsilon_v(\mathcal{D})$ where ε is a value determined by order of the cells operations (horizontal or vertical pasting). Then we have $\varepsilon_h(\mathcal{D}) = \varepsilon_h(\mathcal{D}_{h,1}) \circ_h \varepsilon_h(\mathcal{D}_{h,2})$ and $\varepsilon_v(\mathcal{D}) = \varepsilon_v(\mathcal{D}_{h,1}) \circ_v \varepsilon_h(\mathcal{D}_{v,2})$. Also, let $\mathcal{D}'_{i,j} = \mathcal{D}_{h,i} \bigcap \mathcal{D}_{v,j}$. Since each $\mathcal{D}'_{i,j}$ is unique composable by induction, we have following desire identity for Fig. 9.9.

$$
\begin{aligned}
\varepsilon_h(\mathcal{D}) &= \varepsilon_h(\mathcal{D}_{h,1}) \circ_h \varepsilon_h(\mathcal{D}_{h,1}) \\
&= (\varepsilon(\mathcal{D}'_{1,1}) \circ_v \varepsilon(\mathcal{D}'_{1,2})) \circ_h (\varepsilon(\mathcal{D}'_{2,1}) \circ_v \varepsilon(\mathcal{D}'_{2,2})) \\
&= \varepsilon_v(\mathcal{D}_{v,1}) \circ_v \varepsilon_v(\mathcal{D}_{v,2}) \\
&= \varepsilon_v(\mathcal{D}),
\end{aligned}
\tag{9.4.8}
$$

which shows that two different composition ways sharing the same result.

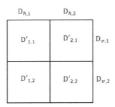

Figure 9.9: General association identity.

9.4.2 Derivability : MIMO Invenrelation Steps

The purpose of this section is to discuss derivability for algebraic invenrelation terms from several initial MSA invengories $(\mathcal{S}_i, \mathcal{R}_i)$ indexed by i to several terminal MSA invengories $(\mathcal{S}_j, \mathcal{R}_j)$ indexed by j, which are different from initial MSA invengories $(\mathcal{S}_i, \mathcal{R}_i)$. Comparing to Sec. 9.4.1 (SISO invenrelation step), we consider n-invengories that have multiple inputs and multiple outputs (MIMO) as 1-dimensional arrows between 0-dimensional objects, i,e, invengories of MSA. The motivation and definition for such n-invengory with MIMO invenrelation steps is introduced first at Sec. 9.4.2. Then, a new class of oriented complexes is built for such n-invengory with MIMO invenrelation steps, main content in Sec. 9.4.2. Finally, derivability theorem for MIMO n-invengory is provided in Sec. 9.4.2.

n-Invengory with MIMO Invenrelation Steps

In invenrelation processes, we may derive new things via analogy from many sources. This motives us to consider n-invengories that have multiple inputs with single output, or even multiple inputs with multiple outputs (MIMO), as 1-dimensional arrows between 0-dimensional objects. The central idea is to have a space of operations (1-dimensional arrows) with n inputs and m outputs such that the n inputs have 0-dimensional objects $c_1, \cdots, c_n$ (MSA invengories), and the m outputs have 0-dimensional objects $d_1, \cdots, d_m$ (MSA invengories). The later definition about our n-invengory with MIMO invention steps is based on colored PROPs from [51].

Let $\mathfrak{M}$ be a non-empty set with elements as MSA invengories. Also let $\mathcal{P}(\mathfrak{M})$ denote the invengory whose objects, named as $\mathfrak{M}$-profiles, are finite non-empty sequences of elements in $\mathfrak{M}$. If $\underline{c} = [c_1, c_2, \cdots, c_n] \in \mathcal{P}(\mathfrak{M})$, we express $|\underline{c}| = n$. Morphisms of the invengory $\mathcal{P}(\mathfrak{M})$ are permutations for objects $\underline{c} \in \mathcal{P}(\mathfrak{M})$ such that $\sigma(\underline{c}) = \underline{d} \in \mathcal{P}(\mathfrak{M})$. The functor,

$$P : \mathcal{P}(\mathfrak{M}) \times \mathcal{P}(\mathfrak{M}) \longrightarrow \mathbf{Set}, \tag{9.4.9}$$

is defined to satisfy

- (1) For any $\mathfrak{M}$-profiles $\underline{c}, \underline{d} \in \mathcal{P}(\mathfrak{M})$, it has a set $P \begin{pmatrix} d_1 & \cdots & d_m \\ c_1 & \cdots & c_n \end{pmatrix}$.

- (2) For any permutations σ (acted to m elements) and τ (acted to n elements), it has a map $(\sigma, \tau) : P \begin{pmatrix} \underline{d} \\ \underline{c} \end{pmatrix} \longrightarrow P \begin{pmatrix} \sigma\underline{d} \\ \underline{c}\tau \end{pmatrix}$ such that $(\sigma'\sigma; \tau\tau') = (\sigma'; \tau')(\sigma; \tau)$.

- (3) For a morphism $f : P \begin{pmatrix} \underline{d} \\ \underline{c} \end{pmatrix} \longrightarrow Q \begin{pmatrix} \underline{d} \\ \underline{c} \end{pmatrix}$ and permutations σ, τ, we have the commutative square

$$
\begin{array}{ccc}
P \begin{pmatrix} \underline{d} \\ \underline{c} \end{pmatrix} & \xrightarrow{f} & Q \begin{pmatrix} \underline{d} \\ \underline{c} \end{pmatrix} \\
(\sigma, \tau) \downarrow & & \downarrow (\sigma, \tau) \\
P \begin{pmatrix} \sigma\underline{d} \\ \underline{c}\tau \end{pmatrix} & \xrightarrow{f} & Q \begin{pmatrix} \sigma\underline{d} \\ \underline{c}\tau \end{pmatrix}
\end{array}
\tag{9.4.10}
$$

Hence, we define a $\mathfrak{M}$-*profiled MIMO P* consisting of functor P defined by Eq. (9.4.9) with following extra structures:

- (1) The *joint composition* operation between $P \begin{pmatrix} \underline{d} \\ \underline{c} \end{pmatrix}$ and $P \begin{pmatrix} \underline{c} \\ \underline{b} \end{pmatrix}$ is defined as

$$P \begin{pmatrix} \underline{d} \\ \underline{c} \end{pmatrix} \circ P \begin{pmatrix} \underline{c} \\ \underline{b} \end{pmatrix} \longrightarrow P \begin{pmatrix} \underline{d} \\ \underline{b} \end{pmatrix}, \tag{9.4.11}$$

which satisfies

$$
\begin{array}{ccc}
P \begin{pmatrix} \underline{d} \\ \underline{c} \end{pmatrix} \circ P \begin{pmatrix} \underline{c} \\ \underline{b} \end{pmatrix} & \longrightarrow & P \begin{pmatrix} \underline{d} \\ \underline{b} \end{pmatrix} \\
\downarrow (\sigma; 1) \times (1; \mu) & & \downarrow (\sigma; \mu) \\
P \begin{pmatrix} \sigma\underline{d} \\ \underline{c} \end{pmatrix} \circ P \begin{pmatrix} \underline{c} \\ \underline{b}\mu \end{pmatrix} & \longrightarrow & P \begin{pmatrix} \sigma\underline{d} \\ \underline{b}\mu \end{pmatrix}
\end{array}
\tag{9.4.12}
$$

- (2) The *parallel composition* operation between $P\begin{pmatrix} \underline{d_1} \\ \underline{c_1} \end{pmatrix}$ and $P\begin{pmatrix} \underline{d_2} \\ \underline{c_2} \end{pmatrix}$ is defined as

$$P\begin{pmatrix} \underline{d_1} \\ \underline{c_1} \end{pmatrix} \otimes P\begin{pmatrix} \underline{d_2} \\ \underline{c_2} \end{pmatrix} \longrightarrow P\begin{pmatrix} \underline{d_1}, \underline{d_2} \\ \underline{c_1}, \underline{c_2} \end{pmatrix} \tag{9.4.13}$$

which satisfies

$$
\begin{array}{ccc}
P\begin{pmatrix} \underline{d_1} \\ \underline{c_1} \end{pmatrix} \otimes P\begin{pmatrix} \underline{d_2} \\ \underline{c_2} \end{pmatrix} & \longrightarrow & P\begin{pmatrix} \underline{d_1}, \underline{d_2} \\ \underline{c_1}, \underline{c_2} \end{pmatrix} \\
\downarrow (\sigma_1; \tau_1) \times (\sigma_2; \tau_2) & & \downarrow (\sigma_1 \times \sigma_2; \tau_1 \times \tau_2) \\
P\begin{pmatrix} \sigma_1 \underline{d_1} \\ \underline{c_1} \tau_1 \end{pmatrix} \otimes P\begin{pmatrix} \sigma_2 \underline{d_2} \\ \underline{c_2} \tau_2 \end{pmatrix} & \longrightarrow & P\begin{pmatrix} \sigma_1 \underline{d_1}, \sigma_2 \underline{d_2} \\ \underline{c_1} \tau_1, \underline{c_2} \tau_2 \end{pmatrix}
\end{array}
\tag{9.4.14}
$$

- For each invengory c in $\mathfrak{M}$, it has an unit $1_c \in P\begin{pmatrix} c \\ c \end{pmatrix}$ such that for $\underline{c} = [c_1, c_2, \cdots, c_n]$, the

parallel composition $1_{c_1} \otimes \cdots \otimes 1_{c_n} \in P\begin{pmatrix} \underline{c} \\ \underline{c} \end{pmatrix}$ is the two-sided unit for joint compositions.

We have to define a special class of directed graphs that serve as the gluing design for higher dimensional $\mathfrak{M}$-profiled MIMO P.

Definition 59 *For $m, n \geq 1$, an (m, n)-graph is a non-empty, finite directed graph G satisfying the following requirements:*

- *(1) There are exactly n edges, called inputs, that do not have an initial vertex.*

- *(2) There are exactly m edges, called outputs, that do not have an terminal vertex.*

- *(3) Each vertex in G has at least one incoming edge and at least one outgoing edge.*

- *(4) There are no directed cycles in G.*

- *(5) Each connected component in G has at least one vertex (and hence at least one input and one output).*

- *(6) If a graph G has l connected components, then we write $G = G_1 \bigsqcup \cdots \bigsqcup G_l$.*

Before constructing sliced $\mathfrak{M}$-profiled MIMO P, we have to introduce *decoration* and *evaluation* of G.

Definition 60 *A P-decorated graph consists*

- *An (m, n)-graph;*

- *A decoration function*

$$\delta : v(G) \bigsqcup e(G) \longrightarrow \bigsqcup_{\overline{d}, \overline{c}} P \begin{pmatrix} \underline{d} \\ \underline{c} \end{pmatrix} \bigsqcup \mathfrak{M} \qquad (9.4.15)$$

where $V(G)$ is the vertex set of the graph G, $E(G)$ is the edge set of the graph G and $\bigsqcup_{\overline{d}, \overline{c}}$ is the disjoint union over all the pairs $(\overline{d}, \overline{c})$ of $\mathfrak{M}$-profile. The function δ should satisfy

$$\delta(v) \in P \begin{pmatrix} \delta(v_{O,1}), & \cdots, & \delta(v_{O,s}) \\ \delta(v_{I,1}), & \cdots, & \delta(v_{I,r}) \end{pmatrix} \text{ for every } v \in V(G) \text{ with } r \text{ incoming and } s \text{ outgoing}$$

edges , where $v_{I,i}$ and $v_{O,j}$ are the i-th incoming edge and the j-th outgoing edge of v.

- *For each decorated graph (G, δ), there is an evaluation of (G, δ), denoted as $\epsilon(G, \delta)$, which is obtained from the composition of $\delta(v)$ for $v \in V(G)$ according to the graph G.*

Slice Construction

Now we define the slice construction for $\mathfrak{M}$-profiled MIMO P, denoted as P^+.

Given that $\alpha_i (1 \leq i \leq k)$ and $\beta_j (1 \leq j \leq l)$ are elements in P with a partition of the number k by l positive integers:

$$k_1 + \cdots + k_l = k, \qquad (9.4.16)$$

one define $\overline{P}^+_{k_1, \cdots, k_l}(\beta_1, \cdots, \beta_l; \alpha_1, \cdots, \alpha_k)$ to be the set of P-decorated graphs (G, δ) such that

- $G = G_1 \bigsqcup \cdots \bigsqcup G_l$ and each connected component has k_j vertices.

- for $1 \leq j \leq l$ and $1 \leq r \leq k_j$, one has $\delta(v_{j,r}) = \alpha_{k_1 + \cdots + k_{j-1} + r}$ and $\epsilon((G_j, \delta_j)) = \beta_j$.

- $\epsilon((G, \delta)) = \beta_1 \otimes \cdots \otimes \beta_l$ for each $(G, \delta) \in \overline{P}^+_{k_1, \cdots, k_l}(\beta_1, \cdots, \beta_l; \alpha_1, \cdots, \alpha_k)$.

Suppose that α_i and β are elements in P. Define the set $\overline{P}^+ \begin{pmatrix} \beta \\ \alpha_1, \cdots, \alpha_k \end{pmatrix}$ as

$$\overline{P}^+ \begin{pmatrix} \beta \\ \alpha_1, \cdots, \alpha_k \end{pmatrix} = \bigsqcup_{\substack{k = k_1 + \cdots + k_l \\ \beta = \beta_1 \otimes \cdots \otimes \beta_l}} \overline{P}^+_{k_1, \cdots, k_l}(\beta_1, \cdots, \beta_l; \alpha_1, \cdots, \alpha_k), \qquad (9.4.17)$$

333

where disjoint union is taken over all integers $l \geq 1$, all possible partitions $k = k_1 + \cdots + k_l$ and all possible decompositions of $\beta = \beta_1 \otimes \cdots \otimes \beta_l$. Then $P^+ \begin{pmatrix} \beta_1, \cdots, \beta_r \\ \alpha_1, \cdots, \alpha_s \end{pmatrix}$ is defined as

$$
P^+ \begin{pmatrix} \beta_1, \cdots, \beta_r \\ \alpha_1, \cdots, \alpha_s \end{pmatrix} = \bigsqcup_{\substack{s = s_1 + \cdots + s_r \\ \sigma, \tau}} \overline{P}^+ \begin{pmatrix} \beta_{\sigma(1)} \\ \alpha_{\tau^{-1}(1)}, \cdots, \alpha_{\tau^{-1}(s_1)} \end{pmatrix} \times \cdots
$$

$$
\times \overline{P}^+ \begin{pmatrix} \beta_{\sigma(r)} \\ \alpha_{\tau^{-1}(s_1 + \cdots + s_{r-1} + 1)}, \cdots, \alpha_{\tau^{-1}(s)} \end{pmatrix}, \quad (9.4.18)
$$

where disjoint union is taken over all possible partitions $s = s_1 + \cdots + s_r$ and all possible permutations σ for r elements and τ for s elements.

P-propertopes

Since we can apply the slice MIMO construction to get P^+ repeatedly, P^{n+} is defined inductively as $(P^{(n-1)+})^+$. The invengory of P-propertopes, denoted $\mathbf{P}(P)$, has the n-dimensional P-propertopes as objects. Its morphisms have to be defined based on face maps.

Suppose that υ is an n-dimensional P-propertope and α is an $(n-1)$-dimensional P-propertope. To every input α and output

$\upsilon \in P^{(n-1)+} \begin{pmatrix} \beta_1, \cdots, \beta_s \\ \alpha_1, \cdots, \alpha_r \end{pmatrix}$, there is exactly one morphism $\upsilon \to \alpha$ for every $\beta_i = \alpha$ or $\alpha_j = \alpha$.

A morphism of the form

$$
g_j : \upsilon \to \beta_j, \quad (9.4.19)
$$

is called an *out-face* map, where $1 \leq j \leq s$. Similarly, a morphism of the form

$$
f_i : \upsilon \to \alpha_i, \quad (9.4.20)
$$

is called an *in-face* map, where $1 \leq i \leq r$. A face map is either an in-face map or an out-face map. The face maps will generate all the morphisms in $\mathbf{P}(P)$ subject to four consistency conditions below.

Given that υ is an n-dimensional P-propertope and α is a k-dimensional P-propertope. We have following two cases:

(1) If $k \geq n$, then $\mathbf{P}(P)(\upsilon, \alpha) = 1_\upsilon$ when $\upsilon = \alpha$ and $\mathbf{P}(P)(\upsilon, \alpha) = \emptyset$ when $\upsilon \neq \alpha$.

(2) If $k < n$, then the morphism from υ to α, denoted as $\mathbf{P}(P)(\upsilon, \alpha)$, is a sequence

$$
\upsilon = \alpha_n \xrightarrow{h_n} \alpha_{n-1} \xrightarrow{h_{n-1}} \cdots \xrightarrow{h_{k+1}} \alpha_{k+1} = \alpha, \quad (9.4.21)
$$

where each $h_j : \alpha_j \to \alpha_{j-1}$ is a face map.

These morphisms are subject to the following consistency conditions:

- *Joint Consistency Conditions*: For $n \geq 2$ with two $(n-1)$-dimensional P-propertopes $\alpha = P^{(n-2)+}\begin{pmatrix} \varepsilon \\ \underline{\theta} \end{pmatrix}$ and $\beta = P^{(n-2)+}\begin{pmatrix} \theta \\ \underline{\gamma} \end{pmatrix}$, all the joint consistency diagrams of face maps

$$\alpha \xleftarrow{\text{in}} G_{\alpha\circ\beta} \xrightarrow{\text{in}} \beta$$

$$\text{out} \downarrow \quad \text{out} \downarrow \quad \text{in} \downarrow$$

$$\varepsilon_i \xleftarrow{\text{out}} \alpha \circ \beta \xrightarrow{\text{in}} \gamma_j \qquad (9.4.22)$$

are commutative, where $G_{\alpha\circ\beta} \in P^{(n-1)+}\begin{pmatrix} \alpha \circ \beta \\ \alpha, \beta \end{pmatrix}$.

- *Parallel Consistency Conditions*: For $n \geq 2$ with two $(n-1)$-dimensional P-propertopes $\alpha = P^{(n-2)+}\begin{pmatrix} \varepsilon \\ \underline{\theta} \end{pmatrix}$ and $\beta = P^{(n-2)+}\begin{pmatrix} \varepsilon' \\ \underline{\theta}' \end{pmatrix}$, all the joint consistency diagrams of face maps

$$\alpha \xleftarrow{\text{in}} G_{\alpha\circ\beta} \xrightarrow{\text{in}} \beta$$

$$\text{in} \downarrow \quad \text{out} \downarrow \quad \text{in} \downarrow$$

$$\theta_i \xleftarrow{\text{in}} \alpha \otimes \beta \xrightarrow{\text{in}} \theta'_j \qquad (9.4.23)$$

and

$$\alpha \xleftarrow{\text{in}} G_{\alpha\circ\beta} \xrightarrow{\text{in}} \beta$$

$$\text{out} \downarrow \quad \text{out} \downarrow \quad \text{out} \downarrow$$

$$\varepsilon_k \xleftarrow{\text{out}} \alpha \otimes \beta \xrightarrow{\text{out}} \varepsilon'_l \qquad (9.4.24)$$

are commutative, where $G_{\alpha\otimes\beta} \in P^{(n-1)+}\begin{pmatrix} \alpha \circ \beta \\ \alpha, \beta \end{pmatrix}$.

- *Unity Consistency Condition*: For $n \geq 1$ and $(n-1)$-dimensional P-propertopes $\alpha_i (1 \leq i \leq l)$, all the unity consistency diagrams

$$1_{\alpha_1} \otimes \cdots \otimes 1_{\alpha_l} \quad = \quad 1_{\alpha_1} \otimes \cdots \otimes 1_{\alpha_l}$$

$$i\text{-th in} \downarrow \qquad\qquad i\text{-th out} \downarrow$$

$$\alpha_i \qquad = \qquad \alpha_i \qquad (9.4.25)$$

are commutative, where 1_{α_i} is the unit for MSA invengory α_i.

- *Equivariance Consistency Condition*: For $n \geq 1$, an n-dimensional P-propertope $\gamma \in$ $P^{(n-1)+}\begin{pmatrix} \beta_1, \cdots, \beta_s \\ \alpha_1, \cdots, \alpha_r \end{pmatrix}$ and permutations σ, τ, all equivariance consistency diagrams of face maps

$$\sigma 1_\gamma \tau \xrightarrow{\ out\ } \sigma \gamma \tau$$

$$\text{in} \downarrow \qquad \downarrow \sigma^{-1} j\text{-th out}$$

$$\gamma \xrightarrow{\ j\text{-th out}\ } \beta_j \qquad\qquad (9.4.26)$$

are commutative, where $\sigma 1_\gamma \tau \in P^{n+}\begin{pmatrix} \sigma\gamma\tau \\ \gamma \end{pmatrix}$.

- *Interchange Consistency Condition*: For $n \geq 2$ with four $(n-1)$-dimensional P-propertopes $\alpha_1 = P^{(n-2)+}\begin{pmatrix} \underline{d}_1 \\ \underline{b}_1 \end{pmatrix}$, $\alpha_2 = P^{(n-2)+}\begin{pmatrix} \underline{d}_2 \\ \underline{b}_2 \end{pmatrix}$, $\alpha_3 = P^{(n-2)+}\begin{pmatrix} \underline{d}_3 \\ \underline{b}_3 \end{pmatrix}$ and $\alpha_4 = P^{(n-2)+}\begin{pmatrix} \underline{d}_4 \\ \underline{b}_4 \end{pmatrix}$, the interchange consistency diagrams

$$[\alpha_1 \otimes \alpha_2] \circ [\alpha_3 \otimes \alpha_4] \xrightarrow{\ switch\ } [\alpha_1 \circ \alpha_3] \otimes [\alpha_2 \circ \alpha_4]$$

$$(\otimes, \otimes) \downarrow \qquad\qquad\qquad \downarrow (\circ, \circ)$$

$$P^{(n-2)+}\begin{pmatrix} \underline{d}_1, \underline{d}_2 \\ \underline{b}_1, \underline{b}_2 \end{pmatrix} \circ P^{(n-2)+}\begin{pmatrix} \underline{b}_1, \underline{b}_2 \\ \underline{c}_1, \underline{c}_2 \end{pmatrix} \qquad P^{(n-2)+}\begin{pmatrix} \underline{d}_1 \\ \underline{c}_1 \end{pmatrix} \otimes P^{(n-2)+}\begin{pmatrix} \underline{d}_2 \\ \underline{c}_2 \end{pmatrix}$$

$$\circ \downarrow \qquad\qquad\qquad\qquad \downarrow \otimes$$

$$P^{(n-2)+}\begin{pmatrix} \underline{d}_1, \underline{d}_2 \\ \underline{c}_1, \underline{c}_2 \end{pmatrix} \qquad = \qquad P^{(n-2)+}\begin{pmatrix} \underline{d}_1, \underline{d}_2 \\ \underline{c}_1, \underline{c}_2 \end{pmatrix}$$

are commutative.

We are ready to define a MIMO n-invengory. A MIMO n-invengory X with $1 \leq n < \infty$: (1) There is a set X_k of k-cells for each k in the range $0 \leq k \leq n$, where X_k is

$$X_k = \bigsqcup_{\alpha \in \bigsqcup_{\underline{d};\underline{c}} P^{(k-1)+}\begin{pmatrix} \underline{d} \\ \underline{c} \end{pmatrix}} X(\alpha). \qquad\qquad (9.4.27)$$

(2) For $0 \leq k \leq n$, the composition of k-cells is a multi-valued function defined by Eq. (9.4.29) below satisfying consistency conditions ((9.4.22) - (9.4.27)). If $\alpha \in P^{(k-1)+}\begin{pmatrix} \varepsilon_1, \cdots, \varepsilon_s \\ \gamma_1, \cdots, \gamma_s \end{pmatrix}$ is a

k-dimensional P-propertope, then its in-face and out-face maps are

$$X(\alpha)$$

$$(X(f_1), \cdots, X(f_r)) \swarrow \text{in} \qquad \text{out} \searrow (X(g_1), \cdots, X(g_s))$$

$$X(\gamma_1) \times \cdots \times X(\gamma_r) \qquad\qquad X(\varepsilon_1) \times \cdots \times X(\varepsilon_s). \qquad (9.4.28)$$

Thus, we have a multi-valued composition function of $(k-1)$-cells

$$\alpha : X(\gamma_1) \times \cdots \times X(\gamma_r) \longrightarrow X(\varepsilon_1) \times \cdots \times X(\varepsilon_s), \qquad (9.4.29)$$

such that the image of a sequence $\underline{y} \in \prod X(\gamma_i)$ of $(k-1)$-cells under multi-valued composition function α is

$$\alpha(\underline{y}) = \{(X(g_1), \cdots, X(g_s))(x) : x \in X(\alpha), (X(f_1), \cdots, X(f_r))(x) = \underline{y}\}. \qquad (9.4.30)$$

Oriented Complexes for MIMO n-Invengory

In this section, we give a combinatorial treatment for MIMO n-invengory by using oriented complex language as we adopted in Chap. VIII. Several definitions will be provided first to prove the main theorem (Theorem 33) of this section.

Definition 61 *Given a simplicial complex K, there are three associated functions dm, $\partial_{\mathbf{M}}^+$ and $\partial_{\mathbf{M}}^-$ defined on K; such that, for each simplex $\sigma \in \mathcal{K}$,*

- *$dm(\sigma)$ is a non-negative integer, the dimension of σ,*

- *$\partial_{\mathbf{M}}^+$ and $\partial_{\mathbf{M}}^-$ are subsets of K consisting of elements of dimension $dm(\sigma) - 1$.*

A simplicial complex K with such extra mathematical structure is called as a partial oriented *MIMO complex, denoted as $\mathcal{K}_{\mathbf{M}}$. A subset x of $\mathcal{K}_{\mathbf{M}}$ is closed if $\partial_{\mathbf{M}}^+(\sigma) \subset x$ and $\partial_{\mathbf{M}}^-(\sigma) \subset x$ for every $\sigma \in x$. The closure of a MIMO simplex σ, denoted as $\overline{\sigma}$, is defined as a prime MIMO component.*

A component x with dimension n if $\max_{\sigma \in x} dm(\overline{\sigma}) = n$, where $\overline{\sigma}$ is a prime MIMO component.

The following definition is about the set of boundaries with dimension n for a subset of $\mathcal{K}_{\mathbf{M}}$.

Definition 62 *(n-boundary Definition for MIMO) Let x be a subset of $\mathcal{K}_{\mathbf{M}}$ and n be an integer, the term $d_{\mathbf{M},n}^+(x)$ represents a set of boundary elements $\varsigma \in x$ such that*

- $dm(\varsigma) \le n$,

- when τ is a $(n+1)$-dimensional element of x with $\varsigma \in \overline{\tau}$, we have ς in the closure of $\partial_{\mathbf{M}}^{+}(\tau)$.

Similarly, the term $d_{\mathbf{M},n}^{-}(x)$ represents a set of boundary elements ς such that

- $dm(\varsigma) \le n$,

- when τ is a $(n+1)$-dimensional element of x with $\varsigma \in \overline{\tau}$, we have ς in the closure of $\partial_{\mathbf{M}}^{-}(\tau)$.

Then the composition between two components with dimension n can be regulated by the following definition.

Definition 63 (n-MIMO composition Definition) *The joint n-MIMO composition for the component of x's n dimensional boundary and the component of y's n dimensional boundary such that $d_{\mathbf{M},n}^{+}(x) = d_{\mathbf{M},n}^{-}(y)$, denoted as $x \circ_n y$, is defined to be the union of x and y along the boundary with dimension n and one has $x \bigcap y = d_{\mathbf{M},n}^{+}(x) = d_{\mathbf{M},n}^{-}(y)$.*

The parallel n-MIMO composition for two components x and y, denoted as $x \otimes_n y$, is defined to be $d_{\mathbf{M},n}^{+}(x \otimes_n y) = d_{\mathbf{M},n}^{+}(x) \bigsqcup d_{\mathbf{M},n}^{+}(y)$, and $d_{\mathbf{M},n}^{-}(x \otimes_n y) = d_{\mathbf{M},n}^{-}(x) \bigsqcup d_{\mathbf{M},n}^{-}(y)$, where $\bigsqcup$ indicates disjoint union. n-MIMO-invengory is made by joint n-MIMO composition and parallel n-MIMO composition.

At this point, we are ready to define an oriented complex.

Definition 64 (Oriented MIMO Complex Definition) *An oriented complex induced by $\mathcal{K}_{\mathbf{M}}$, denoted as $\overrightarrow{\mathcal{K}_{\mathbf{M}}}$, is a partial oriented complex in which, for every atom $\overline{\sigma} \in \mathcal{K}$ with $dm(\overline{\sigma}) = n$, we have*

- $d_{n-1}^{+}(\overline{\sigma})$ and $d_{n-1}^{-}(\overline{\sigma})$ are generated by prime MIMO components with composition operations $\circ_n$ for $n = 0, 1, 2, \cdots$;

- $d_m^{\zeta_m}(d_n^{\zeta_n}(\overline{\sigma})) = d_m^{\zeta_m}(\overline{\sigma})$ for $m \le n$, where ζ_m and ζ_n can be set as $+$ or $-$ signs.

The class $Q(\overrightarrow{\mathcal{K}_{\mathbf{M}}})$ in $\overrightarrow{\mathcal{K}_{\mathbf{M}}}$ is named as a *gluing MIMO design* consists of sets $x \in \overrightarrow{\mathcal{K}_{\mathbf{M}}}$ such that

- $x, d_n^{-}(x)$ and $d_n^{+}(x)$ are closed,

- $d_m^{\zeta_m}(d_n^{\zeta_n}(x) = d_m^{\zeta_m}(x)$ for $m \le n$, where ζ_m and ζ_n can be set as $+$ or $-$ signs.

A MIMO n-invengory is provided by the following definition.

Definition 65 *A MIMO n-invengory is a set X together with unary operations $d_{\mathbf{M},n}^{+}$ and $d_{\mathbf{M},n}^{-}$, binary operations $\circ_n$ (joint composition) for $n = 0, 1, 2, \cdots$, and binary operations $\otimes_n$ (parallel composition) for $n = 0, 1, 2, \cdots$, such that the following properties hold:*

(1) For any signs of ζ_m and ζ_n, $d_{\mathbf{M},m}^{\zeta_m} d_{\mathbf{M},n}^{\zeta_n}(x) = d_{\mathbf{M},m}^{\zeta_m}(x)$ if $m < n$ and $d_{\mathbf{M},m}^{\zeta_m} d_{\mathbf{M},n}^{\zeta_n}(x) = d_{\mathbf{M},n}^{\zeta_n}(x)$ if $m \geq n$.

(2) $x \circ_n y$ is defined if $d_{\mathbf{M},n}^{+}(x) = d_{\mathbf{M},n}^{-}(y)$ is the i-th composition realization at the dimension n. Moreover,

- $d_{\mathbf{M},n}^{-}(x \circ_n y) = d_{\mathbf{M},n}^{-}(x)$ *and* $d_{\mathbf{M},n}^{+}(x \circ_n y) = d_{\mathbf{M},n}^{+}(y)$.

- $d_{\mathbf{M},m}^{\zeta_m}(x \circ_n y) = d_{\mathbf{M},m}^{\zeta_m}(x) = d_{\mathbf{M},m}^{\zeta_m}(y) = d_{\mathbf{M},m}^{\zeta_m}(x) \circ_n d_{\mathbf{M},m}^{\zeta_m}(y)$ *for* $m < n$.

- $d_{\mathbf{M},m}^{\zeta_m}(x \circ_n y) = d_{\mathbf{M},m}^{\zeta_m}(x) \circ_n d_{\mathbf{M},m}^{\zeta_m}(y)$ *for* $m \geq n$.

(3) $x \otimes_n y$ is defined whenever $dm(x) \geq n$ and $dm(y) \geq n$. Moreover,

- $d_{\mathbf{M},m}^{\zeta_m}(x \otimes_n y) = d_{\mathbf{M},m}^{\zeta_m}(x) \otimes_n d_{\mathbf{M},m}^{\zeta_m}(y)$ *for* $m \geq n$.

- $d_{\mathbf{M},m}^{\zeta_m}(x \otimes_n y) = d_{\mathbf{M},m}^{\zeta_m}(x) \bigsqcup d_{\mathbf{M},m}^{\zeta_m}(y)$ *for* $m < n$.

(4) $(x \circ_n y) \circ_n z = x \circ_n (y \circ_n z)$.

(5) $(x \otimes_n y) \otimes_n z = x \otimes_n (y \otimes_n z)$.

(6) $(x \circ_n y) \otimes_m (z \circ_n w) = (x \otimes_m z) \circ_n (y \otimes_m w)$ if $m \leq n$.

(7) $(x \circ_n y) \circ_m (z \circ_n w) = (x \circ_m z) \circ_n (y \circ_m w)$ if $m \leq n$.

The following definition is about neighbor dimension of a partial oriented MIMO complex.

Definition 66 *Let x be a finite closed set in a partial oriented MIMO complex $\mathcal{K}_{\mathbf{M}}$, the MIMO neighbor dimension of x, represented as $dim_{\mathbf{M},NB}(x)$, is defined as $\max\limits_{i,j} dm(\overline{\sigma}_i \bigcap \overline{\sigma}_j)$, where $dm(\cdot)$ is the dimension function and indices i, j run over pairs of distinct maximal prime MIMO components $\overline{\sigma}_i$ and $\overline{\sigma}_j$ in x.*

Definition 67 *The class of MIMO composable subsets of an oriented complex $\overrightarrow{\mathcal{K}}$ consists of sets x satisfies:*

- *x is finite and closed;*

- *$\partial_{\mathbf{M}}^{+}(\sigma)$ and $\partial_{\mathbf{M}}^{-}(\sigma)$ are disjoint for each element σ of x;*

- *x can be obtained by an iterated process of compositions of prime MIMO components using operations $\circ_n$, where $n \leq dim_{NB}(x)$.*

Following definition is provided to characterize generalized invenrelation processes with MIMO invenrelation steps.

Definition 68 *Let $\overrightarrow{\mathcal{K}_{\mathbf{M}}}$ be an oriented MIMO complex and let n be a non-negative integer. An $[l_1, l_2, \cdots, l_m]$-invenrelation process, where $l_1, l_2, \cdots, l_m$ are m non-negative integers, is a sequence of elements $\sigma_0, \sigma_1, \cdots, \sigma_m$ of $\overrightarrow{\mathcal{K}_{\mathbf{M}}}$ (invenrelation objects and relations) such that*

$$dm(\sigma_{i-1}) \leq l_i, \quad dm(\sigma_i) > l_i, \quad \overline{\sigma}_{i-1} \in \partial_{\mathbf{M},l_i}^{-}(\overline{\sigma}_i) \backslash (\partial_{\mathbf{M},(l_i-1)}^{-}(\overline{\sigma}_i)$$
$$\bigcap \partial_{\mathbf{M},(l_i-1)}^{+}(\overline{\sigma}_i)), \quad \text{for } 1 \leq i \leq m; \tag{9.4.31}$$

or

$$dm(\sigma_{i-1}) > l_i, \quad dm(\sigma_i) \leq l_i, \quad \overline{\sigma}_{i-1} \in \partial_{\mathbf{M},l_i}^{+}(\overline{\sigma}_{i-1}) \backslash (\partial_{\mathbf{M},(l_i-1)}^{-}(\overline{\sigma}_{i-1})$$
$$\bigcap \partial_{\mathbf{M},(l_i-1)}^{+}(\overline{\sigma}_{i-1})), \quad \text{for } 1 \leq i \leq m. \tag{9.4.32}$$

Following two lemmas are needed in order to prove our main result in this section.

Lemma 24 *Let x be a MIMO composable set in an oriented MIMO complex such that $dim_{\mathbf{M},NB}(x) \leq r < dm(x)$, where r is a non-negative integer. Then there exists a decomposition $x = x_1 \circ_r x_2 \cdots \circ_r x_m$ of x into composable sets such that each x_i has a unique maximal prime component of dimension greater than r with some $m - 1$ composition realizations $i_1, i_2, \cdots, i_{m-1}$, where $\{i_1, i_2, \cdots, i_{m-1}\} \in I_r$.*

PROOF. 53 *The proof is based on inductive argument. If x is a prime component, then the result is valid obviously. For the case that x is not a prime MIMO component, there is a proper decomposition $x = y \circ_q z$ for some integer $q \leq r$ and i'-th composition realization. Since $dim_{\mathbf{M},NB}(y) \leq r$ and $dim_{\mathbf{M},NB}(z) \leq r$, we have decompositions for y and z as (by induction)*

$$y = y_1 \circ_r y_2 \circ_r \cdots \circ_r y_j \circ_r \overbrace{\partial^+_{\mathbf{M},r}(y) \circ_r \cdots \circ_r \partial^+_{\mathbf{M},r}(y)}^{m-j \ copies \ \partial^+_{\mathbf{M},r}(y)},$$

and

$$z = \overbrace{\partial^-_{\mathbf{M},r}(z) \circ_r \cdots \circ_r \partial^-_{\mathbf{M},r}(z)}^{j \ copies \ \partial^-_r(z)} \circ_r z_{j+1} \circ_r z_{j+2} \circ_r \cdots \circ_r z_m,$$

where y_i, z_i are unique maximal prime MIMO components with dimension greater than r.

Hence, we have the required decomposition of x as

$$
\begin{aligned}
x &= y \circ_q z = (y_1 \circ_r y_2 \circ_r \cdots \circ_r y_j \circ_r \overbrace{\partial^+_{\mathbf{M},r}(y) \circ_r \cdots \circ_r \partial^+_{\mathbf{M},r}(y)}^{m-j \ copies \ \partial^+_{\mathbf{M},r}(y)}) \circ_q \\
&\quad \overbrace{(\partial^-_{\mathbf{M},r}(z) \circ_r \cdots \circ_r \partial^-_{\mathbf{M},r}(z)}^{j \ copies \ \partial^-_{\mathbf{M},r}(z)} \circ_r z_{j+1} \circ_r z_{j+2} \circ_r \cdots \circ_r z_m) \\
&= (y_1 \circ_q \partial^-_{\mathbf{M},r}(z)) \circ_r \cdots \circ_r (y_j \circ_q \partial^-_{\mathbf{M},r}(z)) \circ_r \\
&\quad (\partial^+_{\mathbf{M},r}(y) \circ_q z_{j+1}) \circ_r \cdots \circ_r (\partial^+_{\mathbf{M},r}(y) \circ_q z_m). \quad (9.4.33)
\end{aligned}
$$

Lemma 25 *Let x be a composable set in an oriented MIMO complex with $dim_{\mathbf{M},NB}(x) = r$. Let $\bar{\sigma}$ be a maximal prime MIMO component in x with dimension greater than r such that there is no $[r, r, \cdots, r]$-invenrelation process in x from τ to σ, where $\bar{\tau}$ is any other prime MIMO component in x with dimension greater than r. Then there exists a decomposition $x = x' \circ_r x''$ for some j' such that $\bar{\sigma}$ is the maximal prime MIMO component in x' with dimension greater than r.*

PROOF. 54 *From Lemma 24, there exists a decomposition $x = x_1 \circ_r \cdots, \circ_r x_m$ such that each x_i has an unique maximal prime component $\bar{\sigma}_i$ of dimension greater than r. Hence, $\bar{\sigma}_1, \cdots, \bar{\sigma}_m$ is a list of the maximal prime components in x with dimension grater than r. Suppose $\bar{\sigma} = \bar{\sigma}_i$ for some $i > 1$, then we can group the factors of $x_1, \cdots, x_m$ properly to have factorization $x = z' \circ_s z''$ according to Lemma 24 such that $\bar{\sigma}$ is only belonged to z' and other $\bar{\sigma}_j$ for $(j \neq i)$ are belonged to z'', where s is the neighbor dimension of $z' \circ_r z''$.*

341

Note that the value of s is smaller than r since there are no $[r, r, \cdots, r]$-invenrelation process in x from τ to σ. Therefore,

$$
\begin{aligned}
x &= z' \circ_s z'' = (\partial^-_{\mathbf{M},r}(z') \circ_r z') \circ_s (z'' \circ_r \partial^+_{\mathbf{M},r}(z'')) \\
&= (\partial^-_{\mathbf{M},r}(z') \circ_s z'') \circ_r (z' \circ_s \partial^+_{\mathbf{M},r}(z'')) = x' \circ_r x'', \tag{9.4.34}
\end{aligned}
$$

where j' is determined by l', l'', k and $\bar{\sigma}$ is the maximal prime component in x' with dimension greater than r.

The main theorem in this section is to show conditions for the existence of an $[\overbrace{r_1, \cdots, r_1}^{m_1 \text{ copies}}, \overbrace{r_2, \cdots, r_2}^{m_2 \text{ copies}}, \cdots, \overbrace{r_k, \cdots, r_k}^{m_k \text{ copies}}]$-invenrelation process in an oriented MIMO complex, where r_i are non-negative integers and m_i are positive integers.

Theorem 33 *Let $\sigma_0, \sigma_1, \cdots, \sigma_k$ be elements of a composable set x in an oriented MIMO complex such that, for $1 \leq i \leq k$, $x_{\sigma_{i-1}, \sigma_i}$ are also composable sets in x which include σ_{i-1} and σ_i. If following conditions holds for $1 \leq i \leq k$:*

- *$dim_{\mathbf{M}, NB}(x_{\sigma_i, \sigma_{i+1}}) = r_i$;*

- *$x_{\sigma_{i-1}, \sigma_i}$ can be decomposed as $x_{i,1} \circ_{r_i} x_{i,2} \circ_{r_i} \cdots \circ_{r_i} x_{i, m_i - 1}$ for some $j_1, j_2, \cdots, j_{m_i - 2}$ composition realizations such that each $x_{i,j}$ has a unique maximal prime MIMO component of dimension greater than r_i (Lemma 24),*

then we have an $[\overbrace{r_1, \cdots, r_1}^{m_1 \text{ copies}}, \overbrace{r_2, \cdots, r_2}^{m_2 \text{ copies}}, \cdots, \overbrace{r_k, \cdots, r_k}^{m_k \text{ copies}}]$-invenrelation process from σ_0 to σ_k through σ_i sequentially.

PROOF. 55 *From Lemma 24, there is a decomposition $x_{\sigma_{i-1}, \sigma_i} = x_{i,1} \circ_{r_i} x_{i,2} \circ_{r_i} \cdots \circ_{r_i} x_{i, m_i - 1}$ such that each $x_{i,j}$ has a unique maximal prime component $\bar{\tau}_{i,j}$ of dimension greater than r_i, we will show that there is an $[\overbrace{r_i, \cdots, r_i}^{m_i \text{ copies}}]$-invenrelation process with length m_i from σ_{i-1} to $\tau_{i,1}$, $\tau_{i,1}$ to $\tau_{i, m_i - 1}$ and $\tau_{i, m_i - 1}$ to σ_i.*

First we show that there is an $[r_i]$-invenrelation process (length 1) from σ_{i-1} to $\tau_{i,1}$. This is obvious true for $\sigma_{i-1} = \tau_{i,1}$. Let us assume that $\sigma_{i-1} \neq \tau_{i,1}$, where $dm(\overline{\tau_{i,1}}) = p$. We claim that

$p = r_i + 1$. *If $p > r_1 + 1$, we have*

$$
\begin{aligned}
x_{\sigma_{i-1},\sigma_i} &= x_{i,1} \circ_{r_i} \left(x_{i,2} \circ_{r_i} \cdots \circ_{r_i} x_{i,m_i-1}\right) \\
&= \left[\partial^-_{\mathbf{M},p-1}(x_{i,1}) \circ_{p-1} x_{i,1}\right] \circ_{r_i} \left[\left(x_{i,2} \circ_{r_i} \cdots \circ_{r_i} x_{i,m_i-1}\right) \circ_{p-1} \right.\\
&\qquad \left. \partial^+_{\mathbf{M},p-1}(x_{i,2} \circ_{r_i} \cdots \circ_{r_i} x_{i,m_i-1})\right] \\
&= \left[\partial^-_{\mathbf{M},p-1}(x_{i,1}) \circ_{r_i} \left(x_{i,2} \circ_{r_i} \cdots \circ_{r_i} x_{i,m_i-1}\right)\right] \circ_{p-1} \left[x_{i,1} \circ_{r_i} \right.\\
&\qquad \left. \partial^+_{\mathbf{M},p-1}(x_{i,2} \circ_{r_i} \cdots \circ_{r_i} x_{i,m_i-1})\right],
\end{aligned}
$$

and this shows that $\partial^-_{\mathbf{M},p-1}(x_{i,1}) \circ_{r_i} (x_{i,2} \circ_{r_i} \cdots \circ_{r_i} x_{i,m_i-1})$ is composable containing σ_{i-1} and σ_i contrary to the minimal hypothesis. Hence, the value of p will be $r_i + 1$. Since σ_{i-1} belongs to $\partial^-_{r_i}(\overline{\tau_{i,1}}) \backslash \partial^+_{r_i}(\overline{\tau_{i,1}})$ or $\partial^+_{r_i}(\overline{\tau_{i,1}}) \backslash \partial^-_{r_i}(\overline{\tau_{i,1}})$, then there is an $[r_i]$-invenrelation process with length 1. Similarly, there is an $[r_i]$-invenrelation process with length 1 from τ_{i,m_i-1} to σ_i.

We now show that there is an $[\overbrace{r_i, \cdots, r_i}^{m_i-2 \text{ copies}}]$-invenrelation process with length $m_i - 2$ from $\tau_{i,1}$ to τ_{i,m_i-1}. Suppose that $m_i - 1 > 2$, we claim that there are $[r_i, \cdots, r_i]$-invenrelation processes with some lengths from $\tau_{i,1}$ to $\tau_{i,2}$ and from $\tau_{i,2}$ to τ_{i,m_i-1}. If there is no such invenrelation process in $x_{\sigma_{i-1},\sigma_i}$ from $\tau_{i,1}$ to $\tau_{i,2}$, then, by Lemma 25, there is a decomposition $x_{\sigma_{i-1},\sigma_i} = x' \circ_{r_i} x''$ such that $\overline{\tau_{i,2}}$ is the only maximal prime component of dimension greater than r_i in x', contrary to the minimal hypothesis. Hence, there are $[r_i, \cdots, r_i]$-invenrelation processes with some lengths from $\tau_{i,1}$ to $\tau_{i,2}$ and from $\tau_{i,2}$ to τ_{i,m_i-1} (recurrent relation among $\tau_{i,j}$).

If $m_i - 1 = 2$, we have $dm(\overline{\tau_{i,1}} \cap \overline{\tau_{i,2}}) = r_i$ since $dim_{NB}(x_{\sigma_i,\sigma_{i+1}}) = r_i$. Let ρ be an r_i dimensional element of $\overline{\tau_{i,1}} \cap \overline{\tau_{i,2}}$, then $\rho \in \partial^+_{r_i}(\overline{\tau_{i,1}}) \cap \partial^-_{r_i}(\overline{\tau_{i,2}})$. Hence, there is an $[r_i]$-invenrelation process from $\tau_{i,1}$ to $\tau_{i,2}$ with length 1. From recurrent relation among $\tau_{i,j}$ and induction argument, we have an $[\overbrace{r_i, \cdots, r_i}^{(m_i-2) \text{ copies}}]$-invenrelation processes with length $m_i - 2$ from $\tau_{i,1}$ to τ_{i,m_i-1}. Finally, there is an $[\overbrace{r_i, \cdots, r_i}^{m_i \text{ copies}}]$-invenrelation process with length m_i from σ_{i-1} to $\tau_{i,1}$, $\tau_{i,1}$ to τ_{i,m_i-1} and τ_{i,m_i-1} to σ_i $(1 + (m_i - 2) + 1) = m_i$ for $1 \le i \le k$.

Derivability Theorem for MIMO n-Invengory

The goal of this section is to show derivability for algebraic invenrelation terms from source with n_s MSAs to terminal with n_t MSAs through n-MIMO compositions. Comparing to Sec. 9.4.1, we allow MIMO arrows instead of SISO arrows in invenrelation processes.

We begin by a lemma which shows that for any n-gluing MIMO design $Q(\overrightarrow{\mathcal{K}_{\mathbf{M}}})$, there is at least one $[n, n, \cdots, n]$-invenrelation process from σ_0 to σ_1, where $\sigma_0 = \partial^-_{\mathbf{M},n}(Q(\overrightarrow{\mathcal{K}_{\mathbf{M}}}))$ and

$\sigma_1 = \partial^+_{\mathbf{M},n}(Q(\overrightarrow{\mathcal{K}_{\mathbf{M}}}))$. That will be used to show that every evaluation morphism for a gluing MIMO design has at least one composite.

Lemma 26 *For any gluing MIMO design $Q(\overrightarrow{\mathcal{K}_{\mathbf{M}}})$, where $\overrightarrow{\mathcal{K}_{\mathbf{M}}}$ is a composable oriented complex*

$$\overbrace{[n, n, \cdots, n]}^{m-copies}$$

with neighbor dimension n, then there exists an $[\overbrace{n, n, \cdots, n}^{m-copies}]$-invenrelation process from σ_0 to σ_1, where $\sigma_0 = \partial^-_{\mathbf{M},n}(Q(\overrightarrow{\mathcal{K}_{\mathbf{M}}}))$, $\sigma_1 = \partial^+_{\mathbf{M},n}(Q(\overrightarrow{\mathcal{K}_{\mathbf{M}}}))$ and m is the number of elements, which have unique maximal prime MIMO components in each of these elements, in the decomposition of $Q(\overrightarrow{\mathcal{K}_{\mathbf{M}}})$ by $\circ_n$.

PROOF. 56 *If we set $k = 1$, $\sigma_0 = \partial^-_{\mathbf{M},n}(Q(\overrightarrow{\mathcal{K}_{\mathbf{M}}}))$ and $\sigma_1 = \partial^+_{\mathbf{M},n}(Q(\overrightarrow{\mathcal{K}_{\mathbf{M}}}))$ in Theorem 33, this lemma holds from Theorem 33.*

The next goal is to show Lemma 28 which helps us to prove the uniqueness of joint compositions from invengories $\{(\mathcal{S}_{sr,1}, \mathcal{R}_{sr,1}), \cdots, (\mathcal{S}_{sr,n_s}, \mathcal{R}_{sr,n_s})\}$ to invengories $\{(\mathcal{S}_{tr,1}, \mathcal{R}_{tr,1}), \cdots, (\mathcal{S}_{tr,n_t}, \mathcal{R}_{tr,n_t})\}$. Several definitions are provided below before Lemma 28.

Definition 69 *A top MIMO joint composition in an $(n+1)$-invengory is exactly an n-MIMO joint composition. A top MIMO parallel composition in an $(n+1)$-invengory is exactly an n-MIMO parallel composition.*

Definition 70 *A non-top MIMO joint composition in an $(n+1)$-invengory consists of all joint compositions except n-MIMO joint compositions. A non-top MIMO parallel composition in an $(n+1)$-invengory consists of all parallel compositions except n-MIMO parallel compositions.*

Definition 71 *An $(n+1)$-MIMO unicellular is an gluing MIMO design with dimension $(n+1)$ that contains exactly one prime MIMO component with dimension $(n+1)$.*

Definition 72 *An assignment of a gluing MIMO design $Q(\overrightarrow{\mathcal{K}_{\mathbf{M}}})$ with dimension $(n+1)$ in an $(n+1)$-MIMO invengory $\mathbf{A}$ is an evaluation morphism from $Q(\overrightarrow{\mathcal{K}_{\mathbf{M}}})$ to $\mathbf{A}$. An assigned gluing MIMO design in an $(n+1)$-MIMO invengory $\mathbf{A}$ is denoted as $Q_{\mathbf{A}}(\overrightarrow{\mathcal{K}_{\mathbf{M}}})$.*

Definition 73 *A strong MIMO joint composition of an assigned gluing MIMO design $Q_{\mathbf{A}}(\overrightarrow{\mathcal{K}_{\mathbf{M}}})$ with dimension $(n+1)$ is the top MIMO joint composition of assigned MIMO unicellulars determined by any $[n, \cdots, n]$-invenrelation process of $Q_{\mathbf{A}}(\overrightarrow{\mathcal{K}_{\mathbf{M}}})$.*

Following lemma is provided to show the interchange law for monad in top MIMO composition and monads in non-top MIMO compositions.

Lemma 27 *Let $T_{0,\underline{I}_0}, \cdots, T_{n,\underline{I}_n}$ be monads on an n-MIMO invengory, where $\underline{I}_i$ is the set of joint composition realizations at the dimension i. These monads are equipped with*

- *for all $i > j$, an interchange law $\chi_{i,j} : T_{i,\underline{I}_i} T_{j,\underline{I}_j} \Rightarrow T_{j,\underline{I}_j} T_{i,\underline{I}_i}$;*

- *$\mu^{T_{i,\underline{I}_i}} : T_{i,\underline{I}_i} T_{i,\underline{I}_i} \Rightarrow T_{i,\underline{I}_i}$;*

- *for all $i > j > k$ and $\underline{I}_i, \underline{I}_j, \underline{I}_k$, following diagram holds for commutativity:*

$$
\begin{array}{ccc}
T_{j,\underline{I}_j} T_{i,\underline{I}_i} T_{k,\underline{I}_k} & \overset{T_{j,\underline{I}_j}\chi_{i,k}}{\longrightarrow} & T_{j,\underline{I}_j} T_{k,\underline{I}_k} T_{i,\underline{I}_i} \\
\chi_{i,j}T_{k,\underline{I}_k} \uparrow & & \downarrow \chi_{j,k}T_{i,\underline{I}_i} \\
T_{i,\underline{I}_i} T_{j,\underline{I}_j} T_{k,\underline{I}_k} & & T_{k,\underline{I}_k} T_{j,\underline{I}_j} T_{i,\underline{I}_i} \\
T_{i,\underline{I}_i}\chi_{j,k} \downarrow & & \uparrow T_{k,\underline{I}_k}\chi_{i,j} \\
T_{i,\underline{I}_i} T_{k,\underline{I}_k} T_{j,\underline{I}_j} & \overset{\chi_{i,k}T_{j,\underline{I}_j}}{\longrightarrow} & T_{k,\underline{I}_k} T_{i,\underline{I}_i} T_{j,\underline{I}_j}
\end{array}
\tag{9.4.35}
$$

Then for all $0 \leq i < n$ we have monads $T_{0,\underline{I}_0} T_{1,\underline{I}_1} \cdots T_{i,\underline{I}_i}$ and $T_{i+1,\underline{I}_{i+1}} \cdots T_{n,\underline{I}_n}$ with interchange law as

$$
(T_{i+1,\underline{I}_{i+1}} \cdots T_{n,\underline{I}_n})(T_{0,\underline{I}_0} T_{1,\underline{I}_1} \cdots T_{i,\underline{I}_i}) \Rightarrow
$$
$$
(T_{0,\underline{I}_0} T_{1,\underline{I}_1} \cdots T_{i,\underline{I}_i})(T_{i+1,\underline{I}_{i+1}} \cdots T_{n,\underline{I}_n}),
\tag{9.4.36}
$$

with respect to each composition realizations $\underline{I}_0, \underline{I}_1, \cdots, \underline{I}_n$.

PROOF. 57 *The proof is based on induction with respect to n. We begin with the simplest case when $n = 3$. Given interchange laws*

$$
\chi_{1,0} : T_{1,\underline{I}_1} T_{0,\underline{I}_0} \Rightarrow T_{0,\underline{I}_0} T_{1,\underline{I}_1}
$$
$$
\chi_{2,0} : T_{2,\underline{I}_2} T_{0,\underline{I}_0} \Rightarrow T_{0,\underline{I}_0} T_{2,\underline{I}_2}
$$
$$
\chi_{2,1} : T_{2,\underline{I}_2} T_{1,\underline{I}_1} \Rightarrow T_{1,\underline{I}_1} T_{2,\underline{I}_2},
$$

$$
\tag{9.4.37}
$$

we will verify the following interchange law

$$
T_{1,\underline{I}_1} T_{2,\underline{I}_2} T_{0,\underline{I}_0} \overset{T_{1,\underline{I}_1}\chi_{2,0}}{\longrightarrow} T_{1,\underline{I}_1} T_{0,\underline{I}_0} T_{2,\underline{I}_2} \overset{\chi_{2,1}T_{2,\underline{I}_2}}{\longrightarrow} T_{0,\underline{I}_0} T_{1,\underline{I}_1} T_{2,\underline{I}_2}.
\tag{9.4.38}
$$

When there are four monads constructed from each $T_{0,\underline{I}_0}, T_{1,\underline{I}_1}$ and $T_{2,\underline{I}_2}$, we have following commutative diagrams [5] to show the interchange law of $T_{1,\underline{I}_1} T_{2,\underline{I}_2} T_{0,\underline{I}_0} \overset{T_{1,\underline{I}_1}\chi_{2,0}}{\longrightarrow} T_{1,\underline{I}_1} T_{0,\underline{I}_0} T_{2,\underline{I}_2} \overset{\chi_{2,1}T_{2,\underline{I}_2}}{\longrightarrow}$ $T_{0,\underline{I}_0} T_{1,\underline{I}_1} T_{2,\underline{I}_2}$. We have similar relations as Eq. (9.4.5) by replacing T_i as $T_{i,\underline{I}_i}$ for $0 \leq i \leq 2$.

---

[5]Without lose of generality, we assume that $T_{0,\underline{I}_0}$ is adopted twice in these four monads.

When there are five monads constructed from each $T_{0,\underline{L}_0}, T_{1,\underline{L}_1}$ and $T_{2,\underline{L}_2}$, we have following commutative diagrams [6] to show the interchange law of $T_{1,\underline{L}_1} T_{2,\underline{L}_2} T_{0,\underline{L}_0} \xrightarrow{T_{1,\underline{L}_1} \chi_{2,0}} T_{1,\underline{L}_1} T_{0,\underline{L}_0} T_{2,\underline{L}_2} \xrightarrow{\chi_{2,1} T_{2,\underline{L}_2}} T_{0,\underline{L}_0} T_{1,\underline{L}_1} T_{2,\underline{L}_2}$. We also have similar relations as Eq. (9.4.5) by replacing T_i as $T_{i,\underline{L}_i}$ for $0 \leq i \leq 2$.

Results for the other interchange laws follow similarly. For cases that there are more than five monads constructed from each $T_{0,\underline{L}_0}, T_{1,\underline{L}_1}$ and $T_{2,\underline{L}_2}$, they can always be reduced as four or five monads cases through applying $\chi_{i,j}$ and μ^{T_i} repeatedly.

At this moment, we consider cases for $n > 2$. By defining a new set of monads $S_{i,\underline{L}_i}$ as $S_{i,\underline{L}_i} = T_{i,\underline{L}_i}$ for $0 \leq i \leq n-2$ and $S_{n-1,\underline{L}_{n-1}} = T_{n-1,\underline{L}_{n-1}} T_{n,\underline{L}_n}$, we wish to show interchange laws for $(S_{i+1,\underline{L}_{i+1}} \cdots S_{n-1,\underline{L}_{n-1}})(S_{0,\underline{L}_0} S_{1,\underline{L}_1} \cdots S_{i,\underline{L}_i})$

$\Rightarrow (S_{0,\underline{L}_0} S_{1,\underline{L}_1} \cdots S_{i,\underline{L}_i})(S_{i+1,\underline{L}_{i+1}} \cdots S_{n-1,\underline{L}_{n-1}})$, that is

$(T_{i+1,\underline{L}_{i+1}} \cdots T_{n,\underline{L}_n})(T_{0,\underline{L}_0} T_{1,\underline{L}_1} \cdots T_i) \Rightarrow (T_{0,\underline{L}_0} T_{1,\underline{L}_1} \cdots T_{i,\underline{L}_i})(T_{i+1,\underline{L}_{i+1}} \cdots T_{n,\underline{L}_n})$.

For all $i > j$ and $i < n-1$, we have $\chi_{i,j} : S_{i,\underline{L}_i} S_{j,\underline{L}_j} \Rightarrow S_{j,\underline{L}_j} S_{i,\underline{L}_i}$. For all $i > j$ and $i = n-1$, we also have interchange law $\chi'_{i,j} : S_{n-1,\underline{L}_{n-1}} S_{j,\underline{L}_j} \Rightarrow S_{j,\underline{L}_j} S_{n-1,\underline{L}_{n-1}}$ from three monads case $T_{j,\underline{L}_j}, T_{n-1,\underline{L}_{n-1}}, T_{n,\underline{L}_n}$ provided in the previous arguments.

For commutativity of $S_{i,\underline{L}_i}, S_{j,\underline{L}_j}$ and $S_{k,\underline{L}_k}$ [7], we immediate have all cases valid for $i < (n-1)$ since these cases are commutativity requirements for $T_{i,\underline{L}_i}, T_{j,\underline{L}_j}$ and $T_{k,\underline{L}_k}$. For the case that $i = (n-1)$, we have to check the commutativity for $S_{n-1,\underline{L}_{n-1}}, T_{j,\underline{L}_j}$ and $T_{k,\underline{L}_k}$. This is true based on the following diagram:

$$
\begin{array}{ccccc}
\underline{T_{k,\underline{L}_k} T_{n-1,\underline{L}_{n-1}} T_{n,\underline{L}_n}} T_{j,\underline{L}_j} & \longrightarrow & T_{k,\underline{L}_k} T_{n-1,\underline{L}_{n-1}} T_{j,\underline{L}_j} T_{n,\underline{L}_n} & \longrightarrow & T_{k,\underline{L}_k} T_{j,\underline{L}_j} \underline{T_{n-1,\underline{L}_{n-1}} T_{n,\underline{L}_n}} \\
\uparrow & & \uparrow & & \downarrow \\
T_{n-1,\underline{L}_{n-1}} T_{k,\underline{L}_k} T_{n,\underline{L}_n} T_{j,\underline{L}_j} & \longrightarrow & T_{n-1,\underline{L}_{n-1}} T_{k,\underline{L}_k} T_{j,\underline{L}_j} T_{n,\underline{L}_n} & I & T_{j,\underline{L}_j} T_{k,\underline{L}_k} \underline{T_{n-1,\underline{L}_{n-1}} T_{n,\underline{L}_n}} \\
\uparrow & & \downarrow & & \uparrow \\
\underline{T_{n-1,\underline{L}_{n-1}} T_{n,\underline{L}_n}} T_{k,\underline{L}_k} T_{j,\underline{L}_j} & II & T_{n-1,\underline{L}_{n-1}} T_{j,\underline{L}_j} T_{k,\underline{L}_k} T_{n,\underline{L}_n} & \longrightarrow & T_{j,\underline{L}_j} T_{n-1,\underline{L}_{n-1}} T_{k,\underline{L}_k} T_{n,\underline{L}_n} \\
\downarrow & & \uparrow & & \uparrow \\
\underline{T_{n-1,\underline{L}_{n-1}} T_{n,\underline{L}_n}} T_{j,\underline{L}_j} T_{k,\underline{L}_k} & \longrightarrow & T_{n-1,\underline{L}_{n-1}} T_{j,\underline{L}_j} T_{n,\underline{L}_n} T_{k,\underline{L}_k} & \longrightarrow & T_{j,\underline{L}_j} \underline{T_{n-1,\underline{L}_{n-1}} T_{n,\underline{L}_n}} T_{k,\underline{L}_k},
\end{array}
$$

where I and II are based on commutativity diagram by Eq. (9.4.35). Hence, by the induction

---

[6] Without lose of generality, we assume that $T_{1,\underline{L}_1}$ and $T_{2,\underline{L}_2}$ are adopted twice in these five monads.

[7] Without lose of generality, we assume that $i > j > k$.

results for previous $(n-1)$ cases, we have

$$(S_{i+1,\underline{I}_{i+1}} \cdots S_{n-1,\underline{I}_{n-1}})(S_{0,\underline{I}_0} S_{1,\underline{I}_1} \cdots S_{i,\underline{I}_i}) \Rightarrow$$

$$(S_{0,\underline{I}_0} S_{1,\underline{I}_1} \cdots S_{i,\underline{I}_i})(S_{i+1,\underline{I}_{i+1}} \cdots S_{n-1,\underline{I}_{n-1}}). \tag{9.4.39}$$

Lemma 28 *Every assigned gluing MIMO design in an n-MIMO invengory* **A** *made by joint composition only has a strong MIMO joint composition.*

PROOF. 58 *Given two assigned MIMO unicellulars $Q_{\mathbf{A}_1}(\overrightarrow{\mathcal{K}_{\mathbf{M},1}})$ and $Q_{\mathbf{A}_2}(\overrightarrow{\mathcal{K}_{\mathbf{M},2}})$ containing $(n+1)$-prime components σ_1 and σ_2 respectively, such that $\partial_{\mathbf{M}}^-(\overrightarrow{\mathcal{K}_{\mathbf{M},2}}) = \partial_{\mathbf{M}}^+(\overrightarrow{\mathcal{K}_{\mathbf{M},1}})$, $\partial_{\mathbf{M}}^-(\sigma_2) = \partial_{\mathbf{M}}^+(\sigma_1)$ and $\overrightarrow{\mathcal{K}_{\mathbf{M},1}}, \overrightarrow{\mathcal{K}_{\mathbf{M},2}}$ disjoint at other components. Our first claim (First Claim) is that the top joint composition of the joint compositions of the assigned unicellulars equals to the joint composition of the assigned unicellulars provided by the top joint composition of σ_1 and σ_2.*

Since the i-sources and i-targets of $a_1(\sigma_1)$ (objects and relations in $\mathbf{A}_1$ assigned by σ_1) and $a_2(\sigma_2)$ (objects and relations in $\mathbf{A}_2$ assigned by σ_2) agree for $0 \le i \le n-1$, it follows from the interchange laws, by Lemma 27, between monads $T_{n,\underline{I}_n}$ and $T_{j_0,\underline{I}_{j_0}} T_{j_1,\underline{I}_{j_1}} \cdots T_{j_{n-1},\underline{I}_{j_{n-1}}}$ where $\{j_0, j_1, \cdots, j_{n-1}\}$ are distinct and selected from $\{0, 1, 2, \cdots, n-1\}$ that the top MIMO joint composition of these expressions equals to the joint composition determined by replacing $a_1(\sigma_1)$ in the original expression by the top MIMO joint composition of $a_1(\sigma_1)$ and $a_2(\sigma_2)$, as claimed.

Let $Q_{\mathbf{A}}(\overrightarrow{\mathcal{K}_{\mathbf{M}}})$ be an assigned gluing MIMO design made by non-top MIMO joint compositions, and assume that $\overrightarrow{\mathcal{K}_{\mathbf{M}}}$ contains at least one $(n+1)$-prime MIMO component. We claim (Second Claim) that the non-top MIMO composition for $Q_{\mathbf{A}}(\overrightarrow{\mathcal{K}_{\mathbf{M}}})$ is formed by the top MIMO composition of assigned MIMO unicellulars with any order. This argument is verified by induction on the number of $(n+1)$-prime MIMO components in $\overrightarrow{\mathcal{K}_{\mathbf{M}}}$. If $\overrightarrow{\mathcal{K}_{\mathbf{M}}}$ has one $(n+1)$-prime MIMO component, the result is trivial. If $\overrightarrow{\mathcal{K}_{\mathbf{M}}}$ has $(k+1)$ $(n+1)$-prime MIMO components, one choose any two of them, say σ_1 and σ_2. By considering the top MIMO joint composition of $\overrightarrow{\mathcal{K}_{\mathbf{M},1}}$ and $\overrightarrow{\mathcal{K}_{\mathbf{M}}}$, where $\overrightarrow{\mathcal{K}_{\mathbf{M},1}}$ is given by removing $\partial_{\mathbf{M}}^-(\sigma_1)$ from $\overrightarrow{\mathcal{K}_{\mathbf{M}}}$ and replacing it by $\partial_{\mathbf{M}}^+(\sigma_1)$ and $\overrightarrow{\mathcal{K}_{\mathbf{M},2}}$ is obtained similarly by removing $\partial_{\mathbf{M}}^-(\sigma_2)$ from $\overrightarrow{\mathcal{K}_{\mathbf{M}}}$ and replacing it by $\partial_{\mathbf{M}}^+(\sigma_2)$, we have the result due to the First Claim and the number of $(n+1)$-prime MIMO components in the oriented complex $\overrightarrow{\mathcal{K}_{\mathbf{M},2}}$ (become k).

At this status, we are ready to prove this lemma. If $n = 1$, the result is obvious. We assume that the statement in lemma is true for n-MIMO invengory and wish to prove $(n+1)$-MIMO invengory. Existence is true since every $(n+1)$-gluing MIMO design has an $[n, n, \cdots, n]$-invenrelation process by Lemma 26 and every assigned MIMO unicellular has an unique MIMO *joint composition. For uniqueness, If the gluing MIMO design $\overrightarrow{\mathcal{K}_{\mathbf{M}}}$ contains at most one $(n+l)$ prime MIMO component, unicity holds by induction on n and by the definition of the MIMO joint composition of an assigned MIMO unicellular. If $\overrightarrow{\mathcal{K}_{\mathbf{M}}}$ has $k+l$ $(n+l)$ prime MIMO components, suppose we have two $[n, n, \cdots, n]$-invenrelation process in $\overrightarrow{\mathcal{K}_{\mathbf{M}}}$. Either they commence with the same $(n+l)$ prime MIMO component, in which case we have proved it by induction, or they commence with different $(n+l)$ prime MIMO components. In the latter case, the result follows by induction and the Second Claim.*

Before stating our main theorem, we have several definitions about the decomposition of a gluing MIMO design.

Definition 74 *An $(n+1)$-gluing MIMO design, $\overrightarrow{\mathcal{K}_{\mathbf{M}}}$, is called MIMO-indecomposable if $\overrightarrow{\mathcal{K}_{\mathbf{M}}}$ consists of one k-prime MIMO component and its domain and codomain for some $k \leq n$.*

Definition 75 *If an $(n+1)$-gluing MIMO design, $\overrightarrow{\mathcal{K}_{\mathbf{M}}}$, is not indecomposable, then its decomposition consists of two sub $(n+1)$-gluing MIMO design $\overrightarrow{\mathcal{K}_{\mathbf{M},1}}$ and $\overrightarrow{\mathcal{K}_{\mathbf{M},2}}$ such that*

- $\partial_{\mathbf{M},k}^{-}(\overrightarrow{\mathcal{K}_{\mathbf{M},2}}) = \partial_{\mathbf{M},k}^{+}(\overrightarrow{\mathcal{K}_{\mathbf{M},1}})$ *for some $k \leq n$;*

- $\overrightarrow{\mathcal{K}_{\mathbf{M},1}}$ *and* $\overrightarrow{\mathcal{K}_{\mathbf{M},2}}$ *are disjoint except common parts at the first item;*

- $\overrightarrow{\mathcal{K}_{\mathbf{M}}} = \overrightarrow{\mathcal{K}_{\mathbf{M},1}} \bigcup \overrightarrow{\mathcal{K}_{\mathbf{M},2}}$;

- *neither* $\overrightarrow{\mathcal{K}_{\mathbf{M},1}}$ *nor* $\overrightarrow{\mathcal{K}_{\mathbf{M},2}}$ *is a sub gluing MIMO design of the other.*

Definition 76 *An $(n+1)$-gluing MIMO joint composition of an assigned $(n+1)$-gluing MIMO design $Q_{\mathbf{A}}(\overrightarrow{\mathcal{K}_{\mathbf{M}}})$ consists of evaluation in $\mathbf{A}$ for all decompositions $\overrightarrow{\mathcal{K}_{\mathbf{M}}} = \overrightarrow{\mathcal{K}_{\mathbf{M},1}} \bigcup_k \overrightarrow{\mathcal{K}_{\mathbf{M},2}}$, where $\bigcup_k$ indicates k-MIMO joint composition and $0 \leq k \leq n$.*

Now, we have prepared enough ingredients to establish the main theorem of this section about derivability for algebraic invenrelation terms from source with n_s MSAs to terminal with n_r MSAs through n-MIMO joint compositions and/or parallel compositions.

Theorem 34 *For $1 \leq l \leq n_s$, the MSA $(\mathcal{S}_{i_l}, \mathcal{R}_{i_l})$ is the i_l-th object in the MSA source invengory, denoted as $\mathbf{C}_{\mathcal{R}_l}$, with the initial object $T_{\mathcal{R}_l}$, and $t^{(i_l)}$ is used to represent an algebraic term made from $(\mathcal{S}_{i_l}, \mathcal{R}_{i_l})$. Similarly, for $1 \leq l' \leq n_r$, the MSA $(\mathcal{S}'_{k_{l'}}, \mathcal{R}'_{k_{l'}})$ are the $k_{l'}$-th object in the MSA terminal invengory, denoted as $\mathbf{C}_{\mathcal{R}'_{l'}}$, with the initial object $T_{\mathcal{R}'_{l'}}$, and $t'^{(k_{l'})}$ is used to represent an algebraic term made from $(\mathcal{S}'_{k_{l'}}, \mathcal{R}'_{k_{l'}})$. If following conditions hold:*

- There are MSA invengories $\mathbf{C}_{\mathcal{R}_{e_1},1}, \cdots, \mathbf{C}_{\mathcal{R}_{e_1},n_{e_1}}, \mathbf{C}_{\mathcal{R}_{b_1},1}, \cdots, \mathbf{C}_{\mathcal{R}_{b_1},n_{b_1}}, \mathbf{C}_{\mathcal{R}_{e_2},1}, \cdots, \mathbf{C}_{\mathcal{R}_{e_2},n_{e_2}},$ $\mathbf{C}_{\mathcal{R}_{b_2},1}, \cdots, \mathbf{C}_{\mathcal{R}_{b_2},n_{b_2}}, \cdots, \mathbf{C}_{\mathcal{R}_{e_p},1}, \cdots, \mathbf{C}_{\mathcal{R}_{e_p},n_{e_p}}, \mathbf{C}_{\mathcal{R}_{b_p},1}, \cdots, \mathbf{C}_{\mathcal{R}_{b_p},n_{b_p}},$ which satisfy following :

  1. there is an assigned gluing MIMO design between $\{\mathbf{C}_{\mathcal{R}_1}, \cdots, \mathbf{C}_{\mathcal{R}_{n_s}}\}$ to $\{\mathbf{C}_{\mathcal{R}_{e_1},1}, \cdots, \mathbf{C}_{\mathcal{R}_{e_1},n_{e_1}}\}$, named as $\mathbf{thread}_0$;

  2. for $1 \leq q \leq p-1$, there is an assigned gluing MIMO design between $\{\mathbf{C}_{\mathcal{R}_{b_q},1}, \cdots, \mathbf{C}_{\mathcal{R}_{b_q},n_{b_q}}\}$ to $\{\mathbf{C}_{\mathcal{R}_{e_{q+1}},1}, \cdots, \mathbf{C}_{\mathcal{R}_{e_{q+1}},n_{e_{q+1}}}\}$, named as $\mathbf{thread}_q$;

  3. there is an assigned gluing MIMO design between $\{\mathbf{C}_{\mathcal{R}_{b_p},1}, \cdots, \mathbf{C}_{\mathcal{R}_{b_p},n_{b_p}}\}$ to $\{\mathbf{C}_{\mathcal{R}',1}, \cdots, \mathbf{C}_{\mathcal{R}',n_r}\}$, named as $\mathbf{thread}_p$;

  4. for $1 \leq q \leq p$, there is an parallel composition between $\mathbf{thread}_{q-1}$ to $\mathbf{thread}_q$ with the operation $\otimes_{m_q}$;

  Note that only joint compositions involved in each $\mathbf{thread}$.

- there is an assigned gluing MIMO design $Q_{\mathbf{A}}(\overrightarrow{\mathcal{K}_{\mathbf{M}}})$ such that all invengories provided by previous item are 0-dimensional components of n-MIMO invengory $\mathbf{A}$;

- there are isomorphic homomorphisms $f_{i_l} : T_{\mathcal{R}_l} \longrightarrow (\mathcal{S}_{i_l}, \mathcal{R}_{i_l})$ and $f'_{k_{l'}} : T_{\mathcal{R}'_l} \longrightarrow (\mathcal{S}'_{k_{l'}}, \mathcal{R}'_{k_{l'}})$ for each i_l and $k_{l'}$;

- given any object in each terminal invengory $\mathbf{C}_{\mathcal{R}'_{l'}}$, represented as $(\mathcal{S}'_{j_{l'}}, \mathcal{R}'_{j_{l'}})$, there exists a function $\mathbf{I}_{j_1,j_2,\cdots,j_{n_r}}$ that maps terms in each $T_{\mathcal{R}_l}$ for $1 \leq l \leq n_s$ to terms in each $(\mathcal{S}'_{j_{l'}}, \mathcal{R}'_{j_{l'}})$ for $1 \leq l' \leq n_r$;

then algebraic invenrelation terms $t^{(i_l)}$ for $1 \leq l \leq n_s$ and $t'^{(k_{l'})}$ for $1 \leq l' \leq n_r$ can be derived from each other using rules mentioned in Sec. 9.1.3 and relations between objects and invengories, for instances, functions and functors.

PROOF. 59 *We first show that there exists an unique n-gluing MIMO joint composition in $Q_{\mathbf{A}}(\overrightarrow{\mathcal{K}_{\mathbf{M}}})$ with respect to each $\mathbf{thread}$ for every positive natural number n. The proof is based on induction for n. The case for $n = 1$ is true by associativity of joint composition in the n-MIMO invengory $\mathbf{A}$ made by joint compositions.*

Let us assume that the result true for n and we wish to prove it for $n+1$. If $\overrightarrow{\mathcal{K}_{\mathbf{M}}}$ has at most one $(n+1)$-prime MIMO component, then there exists an n-gluing composition in $Q_{\mathbf{A}}(\overrightarrow{\mathcal{K}})$ by the *definition of strong MIMO composition. If $\overrightarrow{\mathcal{K}_{\mathbf{M}}}$ has more than one $(n+1)$-prime MIMO components, then a strong composition is a top joint composition of MIMO unicellulars, each containing fewer prime MIMO components than $\overrightarrow{\mathcal{K}_{\mathbf{M}}}$ and there still exists an n-gluing joint composition in $Q_{\mathbf{A}}(\overrightarrow{\mathcal{K}_{\mathbf{M}}})$ by induction. Hence, we have existence by Lemma 28.*

For uniqueness of each thread, if $\overrightarrow{\mathcal{K}_{\mathbf{M}}}$ is indecomposable, then the result is obvious. If the gluing MIMO design $\overrightarrow{\mathcal{K}_{\mathbf{M}}}$ is a top joint composition of the $(n+1)$-gluing joint composition of $\overrightarrow{\mathcal{K}_{\mathbf{M},1}}$ and $\overrightarrow{\mathcal{K}_{\mathbf{M},2}}$, then by induction, one takes the unique n-gluing joint composition of $\overrightarrow{\mathcal{K}_{\mathbf{M},1}}$ followed by the unique n-gluing composition of $\overrightarrow{\mathcal{K}_{\mathbf{M},2}}$ to get the uniqueness of n-gluing joint composition in $Q_{\mathbf{A}}(\overrightarrow{\mathcal{K}_{\mathbf{M}}})$.

Since there is an n-gluing MIMO composition in $Q_{\mathbf{A}}(\overrightarrow{\mathcal{K}_{\mathbf{A}}})$, the indices $j_1, j_2, \cdots, j_{n_r}$ in $\mathbf{I}_{j_1,j_2,\cdots,j_{n_r}}(\tau_1, \tau_2, \cdots, \tau_{n_s})$ can be determined through the functor from invengories $\mathbf{C}_{\mathcal{R}_l}$ to the invengory $\mathbf{C}_{\mathcal{R}'_{l'}}$. By Theorem 30 and previous paragraphs, we have

$$\underline{t^{(i_l)}} \xoverset{f_{i_l}^{-1}}{\Longrightarrow} \underline{\tau_{1,l} = f_{i_l}^{-1}(t^{(i_l)})} \xoverset{The.\ 2}{\to} \underline{\tau_{2,l}} \xoverset{\pi_{i_{l'}}(\mathbf{I}_{j_1,\cdots,j_{n_r}}(\tau_{2,1},\cdots,\tau_{2,n_s})),\mathbf{A}}{\longrightarrow} \underline{t'^{(k_{l'})}}$$

$$\xoverset{f_{k_{l'}}'^{-1}}{\to} \underline{\zeta_{1,l'} = f_{k_{l'}}'^{-1}(t'^{(k_{l'})})} \xoverset{The.\ 2}{\to} \underline{\zeta_{2,l'}} \xoverset{f_{k_l}'}{\to} \underline{t'^{(k_{l'})}},$$

where $\pi_{i_{l'}}$ is the projection to the $i_{l'}$-th argument, $\tau_{1,l}, \tau_{2,l} \in T_{\mathcal{R}_l}$ and $\zeta_{1,l'}, \zeta_{2,l'} \in T_{\mathcal{R}'_{l'}}$.

In Fig. 9.10, we illustrate those objects and relations involved in this theorem.

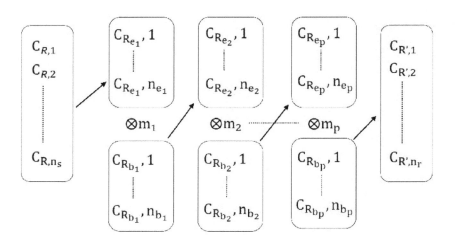

Figure 9.10: Derivability of a MIMO system.

9.5 Invenrelation Complexity

In this section, we try to propose a problem about derivation complexity in algebraic invenrelation systems. In proof complexity theory, a Frege system is a propositional proof system whose proofs are sequences of formulas derived using a finite set of sound and implicationally complete inference rules. However, the complexity of derivation in algebraic invenrelation systems cannot be obtained by adopting Frege systems directly due to following reasons: (1) the difference of MSA operations' hardness should be considered, and (2) the difference of knowledge level of each set involved in MSA operation should also be addressed.

We suggest the following issues in quantifying the complexity in algebraic invenrelation systems. They are

1. Cost assignment to each MSA operation with involved set (knowledge) created age and hardness;

2. Cost assignment to each function (relation) with involved set (knowledge) created age and hardness;

3. Cost assignment to each dimension of functor with involved invengory (knowledge) created age and hardness.

Then, the invenrelation complexity is obtained by summing up cost at each step provided by above items from Theorems 32 and 34. Such invenrelation complexity depends on knowledge involved and manipulation methods in algebraic invenrelation procedures. Such invenrelation complexity can measure difference between two invenrelation procedures. Further problems include

- Minimal complexity problem with constraints in knowledge domain and manipulation method (algebraic invenrelation systems)

- Relativity characteristic measure of invenrelation complexity between two procedures sharing the same sources and the same targets of invenrelation objects (invengories). This measure depends on knowledge domains and manipulation method involved in algebraic invenrelation systems.

- Existence of gluing design (SISO or MIMO) between given sources and targets objects (invengories) for some derivation complexity requirements.

Chapter 10

Unification of Perspectives

Although many scholars believe that intrinsic motivation fuels capability of creation, research has returned ambiguous results [52]. We suggest that the relationship between intrinsic motivation and creativity is enhanced by other-focused psychological processes. *Perspective taking*, as generated by prosocial motivation, encourages individuals to develop ideas that are useful as well as novel after adopting others perspectives. The main purpose of this chapter is to provide a systematic way to enlarge one's perspectives domain and its associated algebraic invention systems (invenrelations).

This chapter is organized as follows. In Sec. 10.1, we suggest that perspective can help individual to increase his/her creativity through *perspective taking* and propose a model for algebraic invenrelation systems parameterized by perspectives. Two important technical results required to show our extension theorem of parameterized algebraic invenrelation systems are provided in Sec. 10.2 and Sec. 10.3. Finally, we show that one can expand one's perspectives domain and its associated algebraic invenrelation systems by keeping his/her model of algebraic invenrelation systems parameterized by perspectives (extension theorem of parameterized algebraic invenrelation systems) in Sec. 10.4. An example about applying extension theorem of parameterized algebraic invenrelation systems are presented in Sec. 10.5.

10.1   Perspectives

To choose a perspective is to choose a belief system. Perspective in theory of cognition is the choice of a context from which to sense, categorize, measure or evaluate experience, cohesively forming a coherent belief, typically for comparing with another. For instance, when we look at a business perspective, we are looking at a monetary base values system; when we look at a human perspective, we are looking with a social value system and its associated beliefs.

Perspective taking is a cognitive process in which individuals adopt viewpoints from others in an attempt to understand their preferences, values, needs and beliefs. Perspective taking is crucial and basic to social interaction. Since interactions are multilateral, people evaluate other people's beliefs, goals, and intentions in order to interpret their actions. Consideration of mental states is important in both competitive and cooperative circumstances. In competitive settings such as economic actions, and in cooperative activities such as coordination actions, one attempts to evaluate another person's mental condition in order to predict his or her future actions.

Indeed, comprehensive research in both psychology and management has shown that prosocially motivated peoples are more likely to adopt the perspectives from other persons in contact, including coworkers, supervisors, suppliers, customers, and clients. Hence, perspective taking will strengthen the effect of intrinsic motivation on creativity. For example, when a motivated product development team member generates some novel possibilities, taking a customer's perspective is likely to concentrate her/his attention and energy on further developing the possibilities that are most useful for solving the customer's problems.

10.1.1 A Model for Parameterized Algebraic Invenrelation Systems

We begin with a mathematical model about algebraic invenrelation systems parameterized by perspectives. A system of algebraic invenrelation systems parameterized by perspectives is represented as $(\mathbf{C}, \{X_{[i]}^{\#}\})$, where $\mathbf{C}$ is an n-MIMO-invengory of perspectives [1] and $\{X_{[i]}^{\#}\}$ is a set of algebraic invenrelation systems and their higher dimensional maps indexed by i, for example, $X_{[0]}$ may be algebraic invenrelation systems such as invengories, multi-invengories or n-invengories, $X_{[1]}$ are maps among $X_{[0]}$, $X_{[2]}$ are maps among $X_{[1]}$, and so on. Such system of algebraic invenrelation systems parameterized by perspectives consists:

- Every 0-dimensional object $X_{[0]}$ in $\mathbf{C}$ is assigned an algebraic invenrelation system $X_{[0]}^{\#}$.

- For $1 \leq k \leq n$, every k-dimensional map (arrow) $f_{[k]} : \underline{X_{[k-1]}} \longrightarrow \underline{Y_{[k-1]}}$ in $\mathbf{C}$ is assigned a k-dimensional map (arrow) $f_{[k]}^{\#} : \underline{X_{[k-1]}^{\#}} \longrightarrow \underline{Y_{[k-1]}^{\#}}$, where $\underline{X_{[k-1]}}$ and $\underline{Y_{[k-1]}}$ are lists of $(k-1)$-dimensional objects in $\mathbf{C}$.

---

[1] The objects in $\mathbf{C}$ are perspectives and the relations (morphisms) are transformations between perspectives.

- For $1 \leq k \leq n$, every consecutive maps $X_{[k-1]} \xrightarrow{f_{[k]}} Y_{[k-1]} \xrightarrow{g_{[k]}} Z_{[k-1]}$ in $\mathbf{C}$ is assigned an isomorphism $\chi^{\#}_{f_{[k]}, g_{[k]}} : f^{\#}_{[k]}(g^{\#}_{[k]}) \xrightarrow{\cong} (g_{[k]}(f_{[k]}))^{\#}$ such that the following conditions hold:

  - $\chi^{\#}_{-,-}$ is associative ($\chi^{\overline{\#}}_{-,-}$ for extension functions).

  - $(1_{X_{[k]}})^{\#} = 1_{X^{\#}_{[k]}}$ for all objects $X_{[k]}$ in $\mathbf{C}$.

  - For any $f_{[k]} : X_{[k-1]} \longrightarrow Y_{[k-1]}$, the following isomorphisms are identity

$$f^{\#}_{[k]} = (f_{[k]}(1_{X_{[k]}}))^{\#} \xrightarrow{\chi^{\#}_{1_{X_{[k]}}, f_{[k]}}} f^{\#}_{[k]}; \tag{10.1.1}$$

and

$$f^{\#}_{[k]} = 1_{Y^{\#}_{[k]}} f^{\#}_{[k]} \xrightarrow{\chi^{\#}_{f_{[k]}, 1_{Y_{[k]}}}} f^{\#}_{[k]}. \tag{10.1.2}$$

A morphism of $(\mathbf{C}, \{X^{\#}_{[i]}\})$ to $(\mathbf{C}, \{X^{\$}_{[i]}\})$ consists of the following for $0 \leq k \leq n$:

- For every list of k-dimensional objects $X_{[k]}$ in $\mathbf{C}$, there is a functor $\mathbf{F}_{X_{[k]}} : X_{[k]}{}^{\#} \longrightarrow X_{[k]}{}^{\$}$.

- For the map $f_{[k]} : X_{[k-1]} \longrightarrow Y_{[k-1]}$ in $\mathbf{C}$, there is a natural transformation : $\mathbf{F}_{X_{[k-1]}} f^{\#}_{[k]} \longrightarrow f^{\$}_{[k]} \mathbf{F}_{Y_{[k-1]}}$, such that for any pair of consecutive maps $X_{[k-1]} \xrightarrow{f_{[k]}} Y_{[k-1]} \xrightarrow{g_{[k]}} Z_{[k-1]}$, the following diagram commutes:

$$\mathbf{F}_{X_{[k-1]}} f^{\#}_{[k]} g^{\#}_{[k]} \to f^{\$}_{[k]} \mathbf{F}_{Y_{[k-1]}} g^{\#}_{[k]} \to f^{\$}_{[k]} g^{\$}_{[k]} \mathbf{F}_{Z_{[k-1]}}$$

$$\downarrow \qquad\qquad\qquad\qquad \downarrow$$

$$\mathbf{F}_{X_{[k-1]}} (g_{[k]} f_{[k]})^{\#} \qquad \longrightarrow \qquad (g_{[k]} f_{[k]})^{\$} \mathbf{F}_{Z_{[k-1]}} \tag{10.1.3}$$

10.1.2 Conditions for Extension Theorem

This section will present input conditions for extension theorem of parameterized algebraic invenrelation systems. For $1 \leq k \leq n$, the maximum value of k, which is valid in all following input conditions, is named as the *degree of extension*.

[A] There are n-MIMO-invengories $\mathbf{C}$, $\mathbf{O}$ and $\mathbf{P}$ such that every i-dimensional object in $\mathbf{C}$ is also in $\mathbf{O}$ and $\mathbf{P}$. Moreover, we require that the following holds

- For any map $f_{[k]} : X_{[k-1]} \longrightarrow Y_{[k-1]}$ in $\mathbf{P}$ (or $\mathbf{O}$) and any map $g_{[k]} : Z_{[k-1]} \longrightarrow Y_{[k-1]}$ in $\mathbf{C}$, the fibered product of $f_{[k]}$ with $g_{[k]}$ exists and the induced map $f'_{[k]} : X'_{[k-1]} \longrightarrow Z_{[k-1]}$ is also in $\mathbf{P}$ (or $\mathbf{O}$).

- Let $X_{[k-1]} \xrightarrow{f_{[k]}} Y_{[k-1]} \xrightarrow{g_{[k]}} Z_{[k-1]}$ be morphisms in $\mathbf{C}$ such that each map in $g_{[k]}f_{[k]}$ is in $\mathbf{C}$. If $g_{[k]}$ is in $\mathbf{O}$ or in $\mathbf{P}$, then each map in $f_{[k]}$ is in $\mathbf{P}$.

[B] There is a system of algebraic invenrelation systems parameterized by perspectives on $\mathbf{P}$ for objects with dimension $k-1$, represented as $(\mathbf{P}, \{X_{[k-1]}^{\#}\})$, and there is another system of algebraic invenrelation systems parameterized by perspectives on $\mathbf{O}$, denoted as $(\mathbf{O}, \{Y_{[k-1]}^{\#}\})$. If $X_{[k-1]}$ in $\mathbf{C}$ (so $X_{[k-1]} = Y_{[k-1]}$ in $\mathbf{C}$), we set $\mathcal{D}_{X_{[k-1]}}$ as the cartesian product of $X_{[k-1]}^{\#}$ and $Y_{[k-1]}^{\#}$. Then we have an extended system of algebraic invenrelation systems parameterized by perspectives on $\mathbf{P}$, denoted as $(\mathbf{P}, \{X_{[k-1]}^{\overline{\#}}\})$, such that $(\mathbf{P}, \{X_{[k-1]}^{\overline{\#}}\}) = (\mathbf{P}, \{X_{[k-1]}^{\#}\})$ for $X_{[k-1]}$ not in $\mathbf{C}$ and $(\mathbf{P}, \{X_{[k-1]}^{\overline{\#}}\}) = (\mathbf{P}, \{\mathcal{D}_{X_{[k-1]}}\})$, otherwise. Similarly, we also have an extended system of algebraic invenrelation systems parameterized by perspectives on $\mathbf{O}$, denoted as $(\mathbf{O}, \{Y^{\overline{\$}}\})$, such that $(\mathbf{O}, \{Y_{[k-1]}^{\overline{\$}}\}) = (\mathbf{O}, \{Y_{[k-1]}^{\$}\})$ for $Y_{[k-1]}$ not in $\mathbf{C}$ and $(\mathbf{O}, \{Y_{[k-1]}^{\overline{\$}}\}) = (\mathbf{O}, \{\mathcal{D}_{X_{[k-1]}}\})$, otherwise. If the functor $f_{[k]}^{\#}$ $(f_{[k]}^{\$})$ is induced by $(\mathbf{P}, \{X_{[k-1]}^{\#}\})$ $((\mathbf{O}, \{Y_{[k-1]}^{\$}\}))$, then its extension functor is $f_{[k]}^{\overline{\#}}$ $(f_{[k]}^{\overline{\$}})$ induced by $(\mathbf{P}, \{X_{[k-1]}^{\overline{\#}}\})$ $((\mathbf{O}, \{Y_{[k-1]}^{\overline{\$}}\}))$ through composition of $f_{[k]}^{\#}$ $(f_{[k]}^{\$})$ and projection or inclusion maps with respect to $\mathcal{D}_{X_{[k-1]}}$ or through the product of $f_{[k]}^{\$} \times f_{[k]}^{\#}$.

[C] [2] For any cartesian square $\mathfrak{s}_{[k]}$ (k-dimensional objects involved) in $\mathbf{C}$ with $f_{[k]}, f'_{[k]} \in \mathbf{P}$ and $i_{[k]}, i'_{[k]} \in \mathbf{O}$,

$$
\begin{array}{ccc}
U_{[k-1]} & \xrightarrow{i'_{[k]}} & X_{[k-1]} \\
f'_{[k]} \downarrow & \mathfrak{s}_{[k]} & \downarrow f_{[k]} \\
V_{[k-1]} & \xrightarrow{i_{[k]}} & Y_{[k-1]}
\end{array}
\tag{10.1.4}
$$

there is an isomorphism $\alpha_{\mathfrak{s}_{[k]}} : i'^{\$}_{[k]} f^{\#}_{[k]} \longrightarrow f'^{\#}_{[k]} i^{\$}_{[k]}$. The isomorphism $\alpha_{\mathfrak{s}_{[k]}}$ possesses the following transitivity rules :

(1) Horizontal transitivity: Considering the horizontal extension of the cartesian square $\mathfrak{s}_{[k]}$ by another cartesian square $\mathfrak{s}_{H,[k]}$ as

$$
\begin{array}{ccccc}
U_{1,[k-1]} & \xrightarrow{j'_{[k]}} & U_{[k-1]} & \xrightarrow{i'_{[k]}} & X_{[k-1]} \\
f''_{[k]} \downarrow & \mathfrak{s}_{H,[k]} & f'_{[k]} \downarrow & \mathfrak{s}_{[k]} & \downarrow f_{[k]} \\
V_{1,[k-1]} & \xrightarrow{j_{[k]}} & V_{[k-1]} & \xrightarrow{i_{[k]}} & Y_{[k-1]}
\end{array}
\tag{10.1.5}
$$

---

[2]This item characterizes rules about synthesizing different perspectives transformations.

then we have the following commutative diagram

$$
\begin{array}{ccc}
j'^{\overline{\$}}_{[k]} i'^{\overline{\$}}_{[k]} f^{\overline{\#}}_{[k]} & \xrightarrow{\;j'^{\overline{\$}}_{[k]}\alpha_{\mathfrak{s}_{[k]}}\;} & j'^{\overline{\$}}_{[k]} f'^{\overline{\#}}_{[k]} i^{\overline{\$}}_{[k]} & \xrightarrow{\;\alpha_{\mathfrak{s}_{H,[k]}} i^{\overline{\$}}_{[k]}\;} & f''^{\overline{\#}}_{[k]} j^{\overline{\$}}_{[k]} i^{\overline{\$}}_{[k]} \\[2mm]
\chi^{\overline{\$}}_{j'_{[k]},i'_{[k]}} f^{\overline{\#}}_{[k]} \downarrow & & & & \downarrow f''^{\overline{\#}}_{[k]} \chi^{\overline{\$}}_{j_{[k]},i_{[k]}} \\[2mm]
(i'_{[k]} j'_{[k]})^{\overline{\$}} f^{\overline{\#}}_{[k]} & & \xrightarrow{\;\alpha_{\mathfrak{c}_{[k]}}\;} & & f''^{\overline{\#}}_{[k]} (i_{[k]} j_{[k]})^{\overline{\$}}
\end{array}
\tag{10.1.6}
$$

where $\mathfrak{c}_{[k]}$ is the composite cartesian squares of $\mathfrak{s}_{[k]}$ and $\mathfrak{s}_{H,[k]}$.

(2) Vertical transitivity: Considering the vertical extension of the cartesian square $\mathfrak{s}_{[k]}$ by another cartesian square $\mathfrak{s}_{V,[k]}$ as

$$
\begin{array}{ccc}
\underline{U_{1,[k-1]}} & \xrightarrow{\;i''_{[k]}\;} & \underline{X_{1,[k-1]}} \\[2mm]
g'_{[k]} \downarrow & \mathfrak{s}_{V,[k]} & \downarrow g_{[k]} \\[2mm]
\underline{U_{[k-1]}} & \xrightarrow{\;i'_{[k]}\;} & \underline{X_{[k-1]}} \\[2mm]
f'_{[k]} \downarrow & \mathfrak{s}_{[k]} & \downarrow f_{[k]} \\[2mm]
\underline{V_{[k-1]}} & \xrightarrow{\;i_{[k]}\;} & \underline{Y_{[k-1]}}
\end{array}
\tag{10.1.7}
$$

then we have the following commutative diagram

$$
\begin{array}{ccc}
i''^{\overline{\$}}_{[k]} g^{\overline{\#}}_{[k]} f^{\overline{\#}}_{[k]} & \xrightarrow{\;\alpha_{\mathfrak{s}_{V,[k]}} f^{\overline{\#}}_{[k]}\;} & g'^{\overline{\#}}_{[k]} i'^{\overline{\$}}_{[k]} f^{\overline{\#}}_{[k]} & \xrightarrow{\;g'^{\overline{\#}}_{[k]}\alpha_{\mathfrak{s}_{[k]}}\;} & g'^{\overline{\#}}_{[k]} f'^{\overline{\#}}_{[k]} i^{\overline{\$}}_{[k]} \\[2mm]
i''^{\overline{\$}}_{[k]} \chi^{\overline{\#}}_{g_{[k]},f_{[k]}} \downarrow & & & & \downarrow \chi^{\overline{\#}}_{g'_{[k]},f'_{[k]}} i^{\overline{\$}}_{[k]} \\[2mm]
i''^{\overline{\$}}_{[k]} (f_{[k]} g_{[k]})^{\overline{\#}} & & \xrightarrow{\;\alpha_{\mathfrak{c}_{[k]}}\;} & & (f'_{[k]} g'_{[k]})^{\overline{\#}} i^{\overline{\$}}_{[k]}
\end{array}
\tag{10.1.8}
$$

where $\mathfrak{c}_{[k]}$ is the composite cartesian squares of $\mathfrak{s}_{[k]}$ and $\mathfrak{s}_{V,[k]}$.

[D] [3] For any list of $(k-1)$-dimensional objects $\underline{X_{[k-1]}}$ in $\mathbf{C}$ and for any decomposition of the identity map on $\underline{X_{[k-1]}}$, $\underline{X_{[k-1]}} \xrightarrow{f_{[k]}} \underline{Y_{[k-1]}} \xrightarrow{g_{[k]}} \underline{X_{[k-1]}}$, there is an isomorphism $\eta_{f_{[k]},g_{[k]}}$: $f^{\overline{\#}}_{[k]} g^{\overline{\$}}_{[k]} \xrightarrow{\cong} 1_{\mathcal{D}_{\underline{X_{[k-1]}}}}$ [4] if $g_{[k]} \in \mathbf{O}$ and $f_{[k]} \in \mathbf{P}$. The isomorphism $\eta_{f_{[k]},g_{[k]}}$ should satisfy the following two compatible conditions:

(1) (Parallel Compatibility) Let $h_{[k]} : \underline{X'_{[k-1]}} \longrightarrow \underline{X_{[k-1]}}$ be a map in $\mathbf{C}$ and the decomposition

---

[3] This item characterizes rules about analyzing a perspectives transformation.

[4] $\mathcal{D}_{\underline{X_{[k-1]}}}$ is obtained by collected a list of $\mathcal{D}_{X_{[k-1]}}$.

map $X'_{[k-1]} \xrightarrow{f'_{[k]}} Y'_{[k-1]} \xrightarrow{g'_{[k]}} X'_{[k-1]}$. Consider the following diagram

$$X'_{[k-1]} \xrightarrow{f'_{[k]}} Y'_{[k-1]} \xrightarrow{g'_{[k]}} X'_{[k-1]}$$
$$h_{[k]} \downarrow \quad \mathfrak{s}_{1,[k]} \quad h'_{[k]} \downarrow \quad \mathfrak{s}_{2,[k]} \quad h_{[k]} \downarrow$$
$$X_{[k-1]} \xrightarrow{f_{[k]}} Y_{[k-1]} \xrightarrow{g_{[k]}} X_{[k-1]} \tag{10.1.9}$$

where $\mathfrak{s}_{1,[k]}$ and $\mathfrak{s}_{2,[k]}$ are cartesian squares.

(a) If $h_{[k]}$ is in $\mathbf{P}$, then we have following commutative diagram:

$$f'^{\overline{\#}}_{[k]} g'^{\overline{\$}}_{[k]} h^{\overline{\#}}_{[k]} \xrightarrow{f'^{\overline{\#}}_{[k]} \alpha_{\mathfrak{s}_{2,[k]}}} f'^{\overline{\#}}_{[k]} h'^{\overline{\#}}_{[k]} g^{\overline{\$}}_{[k]} \xrightarrow{\mathrm{by}\mathfrak{s}_{1,[k]}} h^{\overline{\#}}_{[k]} f^{\overline{\#}}_{[k]} g^{\overline{\$}}_{[k]}$$
$$\eta_{f'_{[k]}, g'_{[k]}} h^{\overline{\#}}_{[k]} \downarrow \qquad\qquad \downarrow h^{\overline{\#}}_{[k]} \eta_{f_{[k]}, g_{[k]}}$$
$$\mathbf{1}_{\mathcal{D}_{X'_{[k-1]}}} h^{\overline{\#}}_{[k]} \qquad = \qquad h^{\overline{\#}}_{[k]} \mathbf{1}_{\mathcal{D}_{X_{[k-1]}}} \tag{10.1.10}$$

(b) If $h_{[k]}$ is in $\mathbf{O}$, then we have following commutative diagram:

$$f'^{\overline{\#}}_{[k]} g'^{\overline{\$}}_{[k]} h^{\overline{\$}}_{[k]} \xrightarrow{\mathrm{by}\mathfrak{s}_{2,[k]}} f'^{\overline{\#}}_{[k]} h'^{\overline{\#}}_{[k]} g^{\overline{\$}}_{[k]} \xrightarrow{\alpha_{\mathfrak{s}_{1,[k]}} g^{\overline{\$}}_{[k]}} h^{\overline{\$}}_{[k]} f^{\overline{\#}}_{[k]} g^{\overline{\$}}_{[k]}$$
$$\eta_{f'_{[k]}, g'_{[k]}} h^{\overline{\$}}_{[k]} \downarrow \qquad\qquad \downarrow h^{\overline{\$}}_{[k]} \eta_{f_{[k]}, g_{[k]}}$$
$$\mathbf{1}_{\mathcal{D}_{X'_{[k-1]}}} h^{\overline{\$}}_{[k]} \qquad = \qquad h^{\overline{\$}}_{[k]} \mathbf{1}_{\mathcal{D}_{X_{[k-1]}}} \tag{10.1.11}$$

(2) (Serial Compatibility) We concatenate $X_{[k-1]} \xrightarrow{h'_{[k]}} Y_{[k-1]} \xrightarrow{g'_{[k]}} X_{[k-1]}$ and $X_{[k-1]} \xrightarrow{f_{[k]}} Z_{[k-1]} \xrightarrow{h_{[k]}} X_{[k-1]}$ serially as following diagram:

$$X_{[k-1]} \xrightarrow{h'_{[k]}} Y_{[k-1]} \xrightarrow{g'_{[k]}} X_{[k-1]}$$
$$f'_{[k]} \downarrow \quad \mathfrak{s}_{[k]} \quad f_{[k]} \downarrow$$
$$W_{[k-1]} \xrightarrow{g_{[k]}} Z_{[k-1]} \xrightarrow{h_{[k]}} X_{[k-1]} \tag{10.1.12}$$

such that $\mathfrak{s}_{[k]}$ is a cartesian square with $f_{[k]}, f'_{[k]}, h'_{[k]} \in \mathbf{P}$ and $g_{[k]}, g'_{[k]}, h_{[k]} \in \mathbf{O}$. Then there is a commutative diagram

$$h'^{\overline{\#}}_{[k]} f'^{\overline{\#}}_{[k]} g^{\overline{\$}}_{[k]} h^{\overline{\$}}_{[k]} \xrightarrow{\alpha_{\mathfrak{s}[k]}} h'^{\overline{\#}}_{[k]} g'^{\overline{\$}}_{[k]} f^{\overline{\#}}_{[k]} h^{\overline{\$}}_{[k]}$$
$$\chi^{\overline{\#}}_{h'_{[k]}, f'_{[k]}}, \chi^{\overline{\$}}_{g_{[k]}, h_{[k]}} \downarrow \qquad\qquad \downarrow \eta_{h'_{[k]}, g'_{[k]}}, \eta_{f_{[k]}, h_{[k]}}$$
$$(f'_{[k]} h'_{[k]})^{\overline{\#}} (h_{[k]} g_{[k]})^{\overline{\$}} \xrightarrow{\eta_{f'_{[k]} h'_{[k]}, h_{[k]} g_{[k]}}} \mathbf{1}_{\mathcal{D}_{X_{[k-1]}}} \tag{10.1.13}$$

10.2 Chain Rule of Isomorphism

The purpose of this section is to show the chain rule of isomorphism between sequences of k-dimensional maps among algebraic invenrelation systems. For example, if $k = 1$, the chain rule will operate at isomorphisms between sequences of composite functors.

10.2.1 Isomorphisms between Labeled Sequences

Labeled Sequences

Given a map $f_{[k]}$ which is both, in $\mathbf{O}$ and in $\mathbf{P}$, the input conditions of 10.1.2 provide us with two choices for a k-dimensional map among algebraic invenrelation systems, $f_{[k]}^{\overline{\$}}$ and $f_{[k]}^{\overline{\#}}$. Following definitions suggest a way of keeping track of the choice between $\mathbf{O}$ or $\mathbf{P}$.

Definition 77 *A k-dimensional labeled map in $\mathbf{C}$ is a pair $F_{[k]} := (f_{[k]}, \mathfrak{L})$ where $f_{[k]}$ is a map in $\mathbf{O}$ or $\mathbf{P}$ and $\mathfrak{L}$, the label, is an element of the set $\{\mathbf{O}, \mathbf{P}\}$. For a k-dimensional labeled map $F_{[k]} : \underline{X_{[k-1]}} \longrightarrow \underline{Y_{[k-1]}}$, we define a map from $\mathcal{D}_{X_{[k-1]}}$ to $\mathcal{D}_{Y_{[k-1]}}$ by $F_{[k]}^{\dagger} = f_{[k]}^{\overline{\$}}$ if $\mathfrak{L} = \mathbf{O}$, and $F_{[k]}^{\dagger} = f_{[k]}^{\overline{\#}}$ if $\mathfrak{L} = \mathbf{P}$.*

Definition 78 *A labeled sequence of k-dimensional maps is a sequence of labeled maps*

$$\underline{X_{1,[k-1]}} \overset{F_{1,[k]}}{\longrightarrow} \underline{X_{2,[k-1]}} \overset{F_{2,[k]}}{\longrightarrow} \cdots \underline{X_{m,[k-1]}} \overset{F_{m,[k]}}{\longrightarrow} \underline{X_{m+1,[k-1]}}, \tag{10.2.1}$$

which is denoted as $\varsigma_{[k]} = \{F_{1,[k]}, \cdots, F_{m,[k]}\}$. The source of $\varsigma_{[k]}$ is $\underline{X_{1,[k-1]}}$ and the target of $\varsigma_{[k]}$ is $\underline{X_{m+1,[k-1]}}$. The term $|\varsigma_{[k]}|$ is used to represent the composition of map $f_{m,[k]} \cdots f_{1,[k]}$ and $\varsigma_{[k]}^{\dagger}$ is defined as $F_{1,[k]}^{\dagger} F_{2,[k]}^{\dagger} \cdots F_{m,[k]}^{\dagger}$.

Let $\varsigma_{1,[k]} = \{F_{1,[k]}, \cdots, F_{m,[k]}\}$ and $\varsigma_{2,[k]} = \{G_{1,[k]}, \cdots, G_{l,[k]}\}$ such that the target of $\varsigma_{1,[k]}$ equals the source of $\varsigma_{2,[k]}$. Then the concatenation of $\varsigma_{1,[k]}$ and $\varsigma_{2,[k]}$ is a new labeled sequence of k-dimensional maps

$$\varsigma_{1,[k]} \diamond \varsigma_{2,[k]} = \{F_{1,[k]}, \cdots, F_{m,[k]}, G_{1,[k]}, \cdots, G_{l,[k]}\}. \tag{10.2.2}$$

Moreover, $|\varsigma_{1,[k]} \diamond \varsigma_{2,[k]}| = |\varsigma_{2,[k]}||\varsigma_{1,[k]}|$ and $(\varsigma_{1,[k]} \diamond \varsigma_{2,[k]})^{\dagger} = \varsigma_{2,[k]}^{\dagger} \varsigma_{1,[k]}^{\dagger}$.

For maps $\underline{X_{[k-1]}} \overset{F_{1,[k]}}{\longrightarrow} \underline{Y_{[k-1]}} \overset{F_{2,[k]}}{\longrightarrow} \underline{Z_{[k-1]}}$ with $f_{3,[k]} = f_{2,[k]} f_{1,[k]}$, we have an isomorphism $\chi_{F_{1,[k]}, F_{2,[k]}} : F_{1,[k]}^{\dagger} F_{2,[k]}^{\dagger} \overset{\cong}{\longrightarrow} F_{3,[k]}^{\dagger}$ such that

$$\chi_{F_{1,[k]}, F_{2,[k]}} = \begin{cases} \chi_{f_{1,[k]}, f_{2,[k]}}^{\overline{\$}} & \text{if } \mathfrak{L}_1 = \mathfrak{L}_2 = \mathbf{O}; \\ \chi_{f_{1,[k]}, f_{2,[k]}}^{\overline{\#}} & \text{if } \mathfrak{L}_1 = \mathfrak{L}_2 = \mathbf{P}. \end{cases} \tag{10.2.3}$$

For the decomposition map $X_{[k-1]} \xrightarrow{F_{1,[k]}} Y_{[k-1]} \xrightarrow{F_{2,[k]}} X_{[k-1]}$ with $\mathfrak{L}_1 = \mathbf{P}$ and $f_{2,[k]}f_{1,[k]} = 1_{X_{[k-1]}}$, we have an isomorphism $\eta_{F_{1,[k]},F_{2,[k]}} : F_{1,[k]}^\dagger F_{2,[k]}^\dagger \xrightarrow{\cong} 1_{\mathcal{D}_{X_{[k-1]}}}$ such that

$$\eta_{F_{1,[k]},F_{2,[k]}} = \begin{cases} \chi^{\overline{\#}}_{f_{1,[k]},f_{2,[k]}} & \text{if } \mathfrak{L}_2 = \mathbf{P}; \\ \eta^{\overline{\#}}_{f_{1,[k]},f_{2,[k]}} & \text{if } \mathfrak{L}_2 = \mathbf{O}. \end{cases} \tag{10.2.4}$$

Similarly, for the decomposition map $X_{[k-1]} \xrightarrow{F_{1,[k]}} Y_{[k-1]} \xrightarrow{F_{2,[k]}} X_{[k-1]}$ with $\mathfrak{L}_1 = \mathbf{O}$ and $f_{2,[k]}f_{1,[k]} = 1_{X_{[k-1]}}$, we have an isomorphism $\eta_{F_{1,[k]},F_{2,[k]}} : F_{1,[k]}^\dagger F_{2,[k]}^\dagger \xrightarrow{\cong} 1_{\mathcal{D}_{X_{[k-1]}}}$ such that

$$\eta_{F_{1,[k]},F_{2,[k]}} = \begin{cases} \chi^{\overline{\#}}_{f_{1,[k]},f_{2,[k]}} & \text{if } \mathfrak{L}_2 = \mathbf{O}; \\ \eta^{\overline{\#}}_{f_{1,[k]},f_{2,[k]}} & \text{if } \mathfrak{L}_2 = \mathbf{P}. \end{cases} \tag{10.2.5}$$

A *k-dimensional labeled square*, denoted as $\mathfrak{S}_{[k]}$, has the following diagram

$$\begin{array}{ccc} U_{[k-1]} & \xrightarrow{F'_{2,[k]}} & X_{[k-1]} \\ {\scriptstyle F'_{1,[k]}}\downarrow & \mathfrak{s}_k & \downarrow{\scriptstyle F_{1,[k]}} \\ V_{[k-1]} & \xrightarrow{F_{2,[k]}} & Y_{[k-1]} \end{array} \tag{10.2.6}$$

such that $f_{1,[k]}, f_{2,[k]}, f'_{1,[k]}, f'_{2,[k]}$ is a cartesian square $\mathfrak{s}_k$ and $\mathfrak{L}'_i = \mathfrak{L}_i$ for $1 \leq i \leq 2$. The transpose of a labeled cartesian square $\mathfrak{S}_{[k]}$, denoted as $\mathfrak{S}_{[k]}^\top$, has diagram as

$$\begin{array}{ccc} U_{[k-1]} & \xrightarrow{F'_{1,[k]}} & X_{[k-1]} \\ {\scriptstyle F'_{2,[k]}}\downarrow & \mathfrak{s}_k^\top & \downarrow{\scriptstyle F_{2,[k]}} \\ V_{[k-1]} & \xrightarrow{F_{1,[k]}} & Y_{[k-1]} \end{array} \tag{10.2.7}$$

For the cartesian square $\mathfrak{S}_{[k]}$, one defines a base change isomorphism $\alpha_{\mathfrak{S}_{[k]}} : F_{2,[k]}^{'\dagger} F_{1,[k]}^\dagger \xrightarrow{\cong} F_{1,[k]}^{'\dagger} F_{2,[k]}^\dagger$ as

$$\alpha_{\mathfrak{S}_{[k]}} = \begin{cases} (\chi^{\overline{\#}}_{f'_{1,[k]},f_{2,[k]}})^{-1} \chi^{\overline{\#}}_{f'_{2,[k]},f_{1,[k]}} & \text{if } \mathfrak{L}_1 = \mathfrak{L}_2 = \mathbf{P}; \\ (\chi^{\overline{\$}}_{f'_{1,[k]},f_{2,[k]}})^{-1} \chi^{\overline{\$}}_{f'_{2,[k]},f_{1,[k]}} & \text{if } \mathfrak{L}_1 = \mathfrak{L}_2 = \mathbf{O}; \\ \alpha_{\mathfrak{S}_{[k]}} & \text{if } \mathfrak{L}_1 = \mathbf{P}, \mathfrak{L}_2 = \mathbf{O}; \\ \alpha^{-1}_{\mathfrak{S}_{[k]}^\top} & \text{if } \mathfrak{L}_1 = \mathbf{O}, \mathfrak{L}_2 = \mathbf{P}. \end{cases} \tag{10.2.8}$$

According to input conditions [C] and [D], we have following lemma immediately about compatibility of $\chi_{-,-}$, $\eta_{-,-}$ and α_-.

Lemma 29 *(i) The base change isomorphism of the cartesian square $\mathfrak{S}_{[k]}$ is horizontally. Consider the following diagram with a horizontal extension by another cartesian square $\mathfrak{S}_{H,[k]}$:*

$$
\begin{array}{ccccc}
\underline{U_{1,[k-1]}} & \xrightarrow{F'_{3,[k]}} & \underline{U_{[k-1]}} & \xrightarrow{F'_{2,[k]}} & \underline{X_{[k-1]}} \\
F''_{1,[k]} \downarrow & \mathfrak{S}_{H,[k]} \; F'_{1,[k]} \downarrow & \mathfrak{S}_{[k]} & \downarrow F_{1,[k]} & \\
\underline{V_{1,[k-1]}} & \xrightarrow{F_{3,[k]}} & \underline{V_{[k-1]}} & \xrightarrow{F_{2,[k]}} & \underline{Y_{[k-1]}}
\end{array}
\tag{10.2.9}
$$

such that $\mathfrak{L}_2 = \mathfrak{L}_3$ and $\mathfrak{L}'_2 = \mathfrak{L}'_3$. Let $\mathfrak{C}_{[k]}$ be the composite quare of $\mathfrak{S}_{H,[k]}$ and $\mathfrak{S}_{[k]}$, then we have the following commutative diagram:

$$
\begin{array}{ccccc}
F'^{\dagger}_{3,[k]} F'^{\dagger}_{2,[k]} F^{\dagger}_{1,[k]} & \xrightarrow{F'^{\dagger}_{3,[k]} \alpha_{\mathfrak{S}_{H,[k]}}} & F'^{\dagger}_{3,[k]} F'^{\dagger}_{1,[k]} F^{\dagger}_{2,[k]} & \xrightarrow{\alpha_{\mathfrak{S}_{[k]}} F^{\dagger}_{2,[k]}} & F''^{\dagger}_{1,[k]} F^{\dagger}_{3,[k]} F^{\dagger}_{2,[k]} \\
\chi_{F'_{3,[k]}, F'_{2,[k]}} F^{\dagger}_{1,[k]} \downarrow & & & & \downarrow F''^{\dagger}_{1,[k]} \chi_{F_{3,[k]}, F_{2,[k]}} \\
F'^{\dagger}_{4,[k]} F^{\dagger}_{1,[k]} & & \xrightarrow{\alpha_{\mathfrak{C}_{[k]}}} & & F''^{\dagger}_{1,[k]} F^{\dagger}_{4,[k]}
\end{array}
\tag{10.2.10}
$$

where $F_{4,[k]} = F_{2,[k]} F_{3,[k]}$ and $F'_{4,[k]} = F'_{2,[k]} F'_{3,[k]}$.

(ii) The base change isomorphism of the cartesian square $\mathfrak{S}_{[k]}$ is vertically. Consider the following diagram with a horizontal extension by another cartesian square $\mathfrak{S}_{V,[k]}$:

$$
\begin{array}{ccc}
\underline{U_{1,[k-1]}} & \xrightarrow{F''_{2,[k]}} & \underline{X_{1,[k-1]}} \\
F'_{3,[k]} \downarrow & \mathfrak{S}_{V,[k]} & \downarrow F_{3,[k]} \\
\underline{U_{[k-1]}} & \xrightarrow{F'_{2,[k]}} & \underline{X_{[k-1]}} \\
F'_{1,[k]} \downarrow & \mathfrak{S}_{[k]} & \downarrow F_{1,[k]} \\
\underline{V_{[k-1]}} & \xrightarrow{F_{2,[k]}} & \underline{Y_{[k-1]}}
\end{array}
\tag{10.2.11}
$$

such that $\mathfrak{L}_1 = \mathfrak{L}_3$ and $\mathfrak{L}'_1 = \mathfrak{L}'_3$. Let $\mathfrak{C}_{[k]}$ be the composite quare of $\mathfrak{S}_{V,[k]}$ and $\mathfrak{S}_{[k]}$, then we have the following commutative diagram:

$$
\begin{array}{ccccc}
F''^{\dagger}_{2,[k]} F'^{\dagger}_{3,[k]} F^{\dagger}_{1,[k]} & \xrightarrow{\alpha_{\mathfrak{S}_{V,[k]}} F'^{\dagger}_{1,[k]}} & F'^{\dagger}_{3,[k]} F'^{\dagger}_{2,[k]} F^{\dagger}_{1,[k]} & \xrightarrow{F'^{\dagger}_{3,[k]} \alpha_{\mathfrak{S}_{[k]}}} & F'^{\dagger}_{3,[k]} F'^{\dagger}_{1,[k]} F^{\dagger}_{2,[k]} \\
F''^{\dagger}_{2,[k]} \chi_{F_{3,[k]}, F_{1,[k]}} \downarrow & & & & \downarrow \chi_{F'_{3,[k]}, F'_{1,[k]}} F^{\dagger}_{2,[k]} \\
F''^{\dagger}_{2,[k]} F^{\dagger}_{4,[k]} & & \xrightarrow{\alpha_{\mathfrak{C}_{[k]}}} & & F'^{\dagger}_{4,[k]} F^{\dagger}_{2,[k]}
\end{array}
\tag{10.2.12}
$$

where $F_{4,[k]} = F_{1,[k]} F_{3,[k]}$ and $F'_{4,[k]} = F'_{1,[k]} F'_{3,[k]}$.

(iii) Consider the following diagram such that the composition of each row is identity, $\mathfrak{S}_{1,[k]}$ is the labeled cartesian square on the left and $\mathfrak{S}_{2,[k]}$ is the labeled cartesian square on the right as

follows

$$
\begin{array}{ccccc}
\underline{X'_{[k-1]}} & \xrightarrow{F'_{1,[k]}} & \underline{Y'_{[k-1]}} & \xrightarrow{F'_{2,[k]}} & \underline{X'_{[k-1]}} \\
F_{3,[k]} \downarrow & \mathfrak{S}_{1,[k]} \ \ F'_{3,[k]} \downarrow & & \mathfrak{S}_{2,[k]} \ \ F_{3,[k]} \downarrow \\
\underline{X_{[k-1]}} & \xrightarrow{F_{1,[k]}} & \underline{Y_{[k-1]}} & \xrightarrow{F_{2,[k]}} & \underline{X_{[k-1]}}
\end{array}
\qquad (10.2.13)
$$

then we have following commutative diagram:

$$
\begin{array}{ccccc}
F'^{\dagger}_{1,[k]} F'^{\dagger}_{2,[k]} F^{\dagger}_{3,[k]} & \xrightarrow{F'^{\dagger}_{1,[k]} \alpha_{\mathfrak{S}_{2,[k]}}} & F'^{\dagger}_{1,[k]} F'^{\dagger}_{3,[k]} F^{\dagger}_{2,[k]} & \xrightarrow{\alpha_{\mathfrak{S}_{2,[k]}} F^{\dagger}_{2,[k]}} & F^{\dagger}_{3,[k]} F^{\dagger}_{1,[k]} F^{\dagger}_{2,[k]} \\
\eta_{F'_{1,[k]},F'_{2,[k]}} F^{\dagger}_{3,[k]} \downarrow & & & & \downarrow F^{\dagger}_{3,[k]} \eta_{F_{1,[k]},F_{2,[k]}} \\
\mathbf{1}_{\mathcal{D}_{\underline{X'_{[k-1]}}}} F^{\dagger}_{3,[k]} & = & F^{\dagger}_{3,[k]} & = & F^{\dagger}_{3,[k]} \mathbf{1}_{\mathcal{D}_{\underline{X_{[k-1]}}}}
\end{array}
\qquad (10.2.14)
$$

(iv) We concatenate $\underline{X_{[k-1]}} \xrightarrow{F_{1,[k]}} \underline{Y_{[k-1]}} \xrightarrow{F_{2,[k]}} \underline{X_{[k-1]}}$ and $\underline{X_{[k-1]}} \xrightarrow{F_{4,[k]}} \underline{Z_{[k-1]}} \xrightarrow{F_{6,[k]}} \underline{X_{[k-1]}}$ *serially as following diagram:*

$$
\begin{array}{ccccc}
\underline{X_{[k-1]}} & \xrightarrow{F_{1,[k]}} & \underline{Y_{[k-1]}} & \xrightarrow{F_{2,[k]}} & \underline{X_{[k-1]}} \\
F_{3,[k]} \downarrow & \mathfrak{S}_{[k]} \ \ F_{4,[k]} \downarrow & & & \\
& \underline{W_{[k-1]}} & \xrightarrow{F_{5,[k]}} & \underline{Z_{[k-1]}} & \xrightarrow{F_{6,[k]}} \underline{X_{[k-1]}}
\end{array}
\qquad (10.2.15)
$$

such that $\mathfrak{S}_{[k]}$ *is a cartesian. Then there is a commutative diagram*

$$
\begin{array}{ccc}
F^{\dagger}_{1,[k]} F^{\dagger}_{3,[k]} F^{\dagger}_{5,[k]} F^{\dagger}_{6,[k]} & \xrightarrow{\alpha_{\mathfrak{S}_{[k]}}} & F^{\dagger}_{1,[k]} F^{\dagger}_{2,[k]} F^{\dagger}_{4,[k]} F^{\dagger}_{6,[k]} \\
\chi_{F_{1,[k]},F_{3,[k]}}, \chi_{F_{5,[k]},F_{6,[k]}} \downarrow & & \downarrow \eta_{F_{1,[k]},F_{2,[k]}}, \eta_{F_{4,[k]},F_{6,[k]}} \\
(F_{3,[k]} F_{1,[k]})^{\dagger} (F_{6,[k]} F_{5,[k]})^{\dagger} & \xrightarrow{\eta_{F_{3,[k]} F_{1,[k]},F_{6,[k]} F_{5,[k]}}} & \mathbf{1}_{\mathcal{D}_{\underline{X_{[k-1]}}}}
\end{array}
\qquad (10.2.16)
$$

Products of Labeled Sequences

In this section, we consider the fiber product of two labeled sequences having the same final object.

Let σ_1 and σ_2 be two labeled sequences of k-dimensional maps having the same final object $T_{[k]}$. They are expressed as

$$
\sigma_1 : \ \underline{X_{1,[k-1]}} \xrightarrow{(f_{1,[k]}, \mathcal{L}_{X_1})} \underline{X_{2,[k-1]}} \xrightarrow{(f_{2,[k]}, \mathcal{L}_{X_2})} \cdots \underline{X_{n,[k-1]}} \xrightarrow{(f_{n,[k]}, \mathcal{L}_{X_n})} \underline{X_{n+1,[k-1]}} = T_{[k]},
$$

$$
\sigma_2 : \ \underline{Y_{1,[k-1]}} \xrightarrow{(g_{1,[k]}, \mathcal{L}_{Y_1})} \underline{Y_{2,[k-1]}} \xrightarrow{(g_{2,[k]}, \mathcal{L}_{Y_2})} \cdots \underline{Y_{m,[k-1]}} \xrightarrow{(g_{n,[k]}, \mathcal{L}_{Y_n})} \underline{Y_{m+1,[k-1]}} = T_{[k]}. \quad (10.2.17)
$$

The fiber-product diagram on σ_1, σ_2 is an $n \times m$ array $[\mathfrak{s}_{i,j,[k]}]$ of labeled cartesian squares, represented by $\mathfrak{S}_{[k]}$, as follows where $\mathfrak{s}_{i,j,[k]}$ is the square that is the i-th one from the top row and the j-th one from the left column,

$$
\begin{array}{ccccccc}
\underline{Z_{1,1,[k-1]}} & \xrightarrow{H_{1,1,[k]}} & \underline{Z_{1,2,[k-1]}} & \xrightarrow{H_{1,2,[k]}} & \cdots \underline{Z_{1,m,[k-1]}} & \xrightarrow{H_{1,m,[k]}} & \underline{Z_{1,m+1,[k-1]}} \\
\downarrow V_{1,1,[k]} & & \downarrow V_{1,2,[k]} & & \downarrow V_{1,m,[k]} & & \downarrow V_{1,m+1,[k]} \\
\underline{Z_{2,1,[k-1]}} & \xrightarrow{H_{2,1,[k]}} & \underline{Z_{2,2,[k-1]}} & \xrightarrow{H_{2,2,[k]}} & \cdots \underline{Z_{2,m,[k-1]}} & \xrightarrow{H_{2,m,[k]}} & \underline{Z_{2,m+1,[k-1]}} \\
\downarrow V_{2,1,[k]} & & \downarrow V_{2,2,[k]} & & \downarrow V_{2,m,[k]} & & \downarrow V_{2,m+1,[k]} \\
\vdots & & \vdots & & \vdots & & \vdots \\
\underline{Z_{n,1,[k-1]}} & \xrightarrow{H_{n,1,[k]}} & \underline{Z_{n,2,[k-1]}} & \xrightarrow{H_{n,2,[k]}} & \cdots \underline{Z_{n,m,[k-1]}} & \xrightarrow{H_{n,m,[k]}} & \underline{Z_{n,m+1,[k-1]}} \\
\downarrow V_{n,1,[k]} & & \downarrow V_{n,2,[k]} & & \downarrow V_{n,m,[k]} & & \downarrow V_{n,m+1,[k]} \\
\underline{Z_{n+1,1,[k-1]}} & \xrightarrow{H_{n+1,1,[k]}} & \underline{Z_{n+1,2,[k-1]}} & \cdots \underline{Z_{n+1,m,[k-1]}} & & \xrightarrow{H_{n+1,m,[k]}} & \underline{Z_{n+1,m+1,[k-1]}}
\end{array}
$$

where $\underline{Z_{i,m+1,[k-1]}} = \underline{X_{i,[k-1]}}$, $V_{i,m+1,[k]} = (f_{i,[k]}, \mathcal{L}_{X_i})$, $\underline{Z_{n+1,j,[k-1]}} = \underline{Y_{j,[k-1]}}$, $H_{n+1,j,[k]} = (g_{j,[k]}, \mathcal{L}_{Y_i})$, $\underline{Z_{i,j,[k-1]}} = \underline{X_{i,[k-1]}} \times_T \underline{Y_{j,[k-1]}}$ (pushout), $V_{i,j,[k]} = (f_{i,[k]}, \mathcal{L}_{X_i}) \times_T Id_{Y_{j,[k-1]}}$, and $H_{i,j,[k]} = Id_{X_{i,[k-1]}} \times_T (g_{j,[k]}, \mathcal{L}_{Y_j})$. We denote the i-th row of horizontal maps by $H_{i,[k]}$, where $H_{i,[k]}$ is the sequence consisting of $H_{i,j,[k]}$ and the j-th column of vertical maps by $V_{j,[k]}$, where $V_{j,[k]}$ is the sequence consisting of $V_{i,j,[k]}$.

The next step is to associate the above cartesian diagram $\mathfrak{S}_{[k]}$ a generalized base-change isomorphism

$$
\alpha_{\mathcal{S}_{[k]}} : H^\dagger_{1,[k]} V^\dagger_{m+1,[k]} \xrightarrow{\cong} V^\dagger_{1,[k]} H^\dagger_{n+1,[k]}. \tag{10.2.18}
$$

The sequences $H_{1,[k]} \diamond V_{m+1,[k]}$ and $V_{1,[k]} \diamond H_{n+1,[k]}$ are the two outermost directed paths from $\underline{Z_{1,1,[k-1]}}$ to $\underline{Z_{n+1,m+1,[k-1]}}$. The base-change isomorphism $\alpha_{f_{i,j,[k]}}$ associated to $f_{i,j,[k]}$ can be viewed as a "flip" from $H_{i,j,[k]} \diamond V_{i,j+1,[k]}$ to $V_{i,j,[k]} \diamond H_{i+1,j,[k]}$ (as directed paths between $\underline{Z_{i,j,[k-1]}}$ and $\underline{Z_{i+1,j+1,[k-1]}}$). The definition of $\alpha_{\mathcal{S}}$ becomes choosing a sequence of flips that transforms $H_{1,[k]} \diamond V_{m+1,[k]}$ to $V_{1,[k]} \diamond H_{n+1,[k]}$. Any such sequence of flips must start from $\mathfrak{s}_{1,m,[k]}$ and ends with $\mathfrak{s}_{n,1,[k]}$ and uses each of the $m \times n$ squares exactly once. However, the order where the intermediate flips can be chosen is not unique. Thus, we need to address the problem why the resulting definition of $\alpha_{\mathcal{S}}$ is independent of the choice of the sequence of flips. This is answered by the following Lemma.

Lemma 30 *The definition of $\alpha_{\mathcal{S}_{[k]}}$ is well-define.*

PROOF. 60 *Given two directed paths* $p_{[k]}, p'_{[k]}$ *of objects on* $\mathfrak{S}_{[k]}$, *we define* $p'_{[k]} \geq p_{[k]}$ *if both share the same starting object and the same ending object and if for any object* $\underline{Z_{i,j,[k]}}$ *in* $p_{[k]}$ *there exists an object* $\underline{Z_{i',j',[k]}}$ *in* $p'_{[k]}$ *such that* $i' \leq i$ *and* $j' \geq j$. *We say* $p'_{[k]} > p_{[k]}$ *if* $p'_{[k]} \geq p_{[k]}$ *and* $p'_{[k]} \neq p_{[k]}$. *A square* $\mathfrak{s}_{i,j,[k]}$ *flips a path* $p_{1,[k]}$ *to another one* $p_{2,[k]}$ *if the upper-right half of the boundary of* $\mathfrak{s}_{i,j,[k]}$ *is contained in* $p_{1,[k]}$ *and the other half* $V_{i,j,[k]} \diamond H_{i+1,j,[k]}$ *is in* $p_{2,[k]}$. *A path* $p_{1,[k]}$ *is said to be* adjacent *to another path* $p_{2,[k]}$ *if* $p_{1,[k]} > p_{2,[k]}$ *and for any path* $p_{[k]}$ *such that* $p_{1,[k]} \geq p_{[k]} \geq p_{2,[k]}$ *we have* $p_{[k]} = p_{1,[k]}$ *or* $p_{[k]} = p_{2,[k]}$. *A* maximal chain of paths *is a sequence* $p_{1,[k]} > p_{2,[k]} > \cdots > p_{N,[k]}$, $(N > 1)$ *such that* $p_{i,[k]}$ *is adjacent to* $p_{i+1,[k]}$ *for all* i. *Two maximal chains* $c_{[k]} : p_{1,[k]} > p_{2,[k]} > \cdots > p_{N,[k]}$ *and* $c'_{[k]} : p'_{1,[k]} > p'_{2,[k]} > \cdots > p'_{N,[k]}$ *are said* flip-neighbors with dimension k *if* $c_{[k]} = c'_{[k]}$ *or there exists an integer* i *such that* $1 < i < N$ *with* $p_{j,[k]} = p'_{j,[k]}$ *for* $i \neq j$. *We claim that any two maximal chains with dimension* k, $c_{[k]} : p_{1,[k]} > p_{2,[k]} > \cdots > p_{N,[k]}$ *and* $c'_{[k]} : p'_{1,[k]} > p'_{2,[k]} > \cdots > p'_{N,[k]}$ *satisfying* $p_{1,[k]} = p'_{1,[k]}$ *and* $p_{N,[k]} = p'_{N,[k]}$, *there exists a sequence of maximal chains with dimension* k $c_{1,[k]}, c_{2,[k]}, \cdots, c_{l,[k]}$ *such that* $c_{1,[k]} = c_{[k]}$, $c_{l,[k]} = c'_{[k]}$, *and* $c_{i,[k]}, c_{i+1,[k]}$ *are flip-neighbors for all* i. *[Claim 1]*

This claim is proved by induction on the length of the chains $c_{[k]}, c'_{[k]}$. *If* $N < 4$, *then the claim holds trivially. If* $N \geq 4$, *we assume that there exists another maximal chain* $c''_{[k]} := p''_{1,[k]} > p''_{2,[k]} > \cdots > p''_{N,[k]}$ *satisfying* $p''_{1,[k]} = p_{1,[k]}$, $p''_{N,[k]} = p_{N,[k]}$ *and there are integers* i, j *such that* $1 < i, j < N$ *and such that* $p''_{i,[k]} = p_{i,[k]}$ *and* $p''_{j,[k]} = p'_{j,[k]}$. *Then, we can find flip-neighbors between* $c_{[k]}, c''_{[k]}$ *and between* $c''_{[k]}, c'_{[k]}$. *In the case of* $c_{[k]}, c''_{[k]}$, *we can separate them as*

$$c_{\leq i, [k]} : p_{1,[k]} > p_{2,[k]} > \cdots > p_{i,[k]}, c_{\geq i, [k]} : p_{i,[k]} > p_{i+1,[k]} > \cdots > p_{N,[k]},$$

$$c''_{\leq i, [k]} : p''_{1,[k]} > p''_{2,[k]} > \cdots > p''_{i,[k]}, c''_{\geq i, [k]} : p''_{i,[k]} > p''_{i+1,[k]} > \cdots > p''_{N,[k]}. \tag{10.2.19}$$

By induction, there exists a sequence of flip neighbors with dimension k *between* $c_{\leq i, [k]}$ *and* $c''_{\leq i, [k]}$ *and between* $c_{\geq i, [k]}$ *and* $c''_{\geq i, [k]}$. *Hence, these can be catenate to give* $c_{[k]}$ *and* $c''_{[k]}$. *Similarly, In the case of* $c'_{[k]}, c''_{[k]}$, *we can separate them as*

$$c'_{\leq i, [k]} : p'_{1,[k]} > p'_{2,[k]} > \cdots > p'_{i,[k]}, c'_{\geq i, [k]} : p'_{i,[k]} > p'_{i+1,[k]} > \cdots > p'_{N,[k]},$$

$$c''_{\leq i, [k]} : p''_{1,[k]} > p''_{2,[k]} > \cdots > p''_{i,[k]}, c''_{\geq i, [k]} : p''_{i,[k]} > p''_{i+1,[k]} > \cdots > p''_{N,[k]}. \tag{10.2.20}$$

By induction, there exists a sequence of flip neighbors with dimension k *between* $c'_{\leq i, [k]}$ *and* $c''_{\leq i, [k]}$ *and between* $c'_{\geq i, [k]}$ *and* $c''_{\geq i, [k]}$. *Hence, these also can be catenate to give* $c'_{[k]}$ *and* $c''_{[k]}$.

For any path $p_{[k]}$ *from* $\underline{Z_{1,1,[k]}}$ *to* $\underline{Z_{n+1,m+1,[k]}}$, *let* $p^{\dagger}_{[k]}$ *be the functor* $\mathcal{D}_{Z_{n+1,m+1,[k]}} \longrightarrow \mathcal{D}_{Z_{1,1,[k]}}$ *generated by* $p_{[k]}$. *For any chain* $c_{[k]} : p_{1,[k]} > p_{2,[k]} > \cdots p_{n+m,[k]}$ *such that* $p_{1,[k]} = H_{1,[k]} \diamond V_{m+1,[k]}$

and $p_{m+n,[k]} = V_{1,[k]} \diamond H_{n+1,[k]}$, one has an isomorphism $\alpha_{\mathcal{S}_{[k]}}(c_{[k]})$ from $p^{\dagger}_{1,[k]}$ to $p^{\dagger}_{n+m,[k]}$ given by

$$p^{\dagger}_{1,[k]} \xrightarrow{\alpha_{\int_{(1),[k]}}} p^{\dagger}_{2,[k]} \cdots \xrightarrow{\alpha_{\int_{(n+m-1),[k]}}} p^{\dagger}_{n+m,[k]}, \qquad (10.2.21)$$

where $\int_{(i),[k]}$ is the square that flips $p_{i,[k]}$ to $p_{i+1,[k]}$. If there are two maximal chains $c_{[k]}$ and $c'_{[k]}$ that both start from $H_{1,[k]} \diamond V_{m+1,[k]}$ and end with $V_{1,[k]} \diamond H_{n+1,[k]}$, we claim that $\alpha_{\mathcal{S}_{[k]}}(c_{[k]}) = \alpha_{\mathcal{S}_{[k]}}(c'_{[k]})$. From [Claim 1], it is sufficient to prove $\alpha_{\mathcal{S}_{[k]}}(c_{[k]}) = \alpha_{\mathcal{S}_{[k]}}(c'_{[k]})$ in the case that $c_{[k]}$ and $c'_{[k]}$ are flip neighbors with $c_{[k]} \neq c'_{[k]}$. Let i be the unique integer such that $p_{i,[k]} \neq p'_{i,[k]}$. since we have the following diagram commutes

$$
\begin{array}{ccc}
p^{\dagger}_{i-1,[k]} & \xrightarrow{\alpha_{\int_{(i-1),[k]}}} & p^{\dagger}_{i,[k]} \\
\alpha_{\int_{(i),[k]}} \downarrow & & \downarrow \alpha_{\int_{(i),[k]}} \\
p'^{\dagger}_{i,[k]} & \xrightarrow{\alpha_{\int_{(i-1),[k]}}} & p^{\dagger}_{i+1,[k]}
\end{array}
$$

Hence, $\alpha_{\mathcal{S}_{[k]}}(c_{[k]}) = \alpha_{\mathcal{S}_{[k]}}(c'_{[k]})$ follows.

The following lemma is provided about the identity of isomorphism between functors induced by labeled sequenced.

Lemma 31 Let $\sigma : X_{[k-1]} \Longrightarrow Y_{[k-1]}$ be a labeled sequence. Consider the following diagram

$$
\begin{array}{ccc}
X_{[k-1]} & \xRightarrow{\sigma} & Y_{[k-1]} \\
(Id_{X_{[k-1]}}, \mathfrak{L}) \downarrow & \mathcal{S}_{[k]} & \downarrow (Id_{Y_{[k-1]}}, \mathfrak{L}) \\
X_{[k-1]} & \xRightarrow{\sigma} & Y_{[k-1]}
\end{array}
$$

where the label $\mathfrak{L}$ can be **P** or **O**. Then we have the identity isomorphism $\sigma^{\dagger} = \sigma^{\dagger}(Id_{Y_{[k-1]}}, \mathfrak{L})^{\dagger} \xrightarrow{\alpha_{\mathcal{S}}} (Id_{X_{[k-1]}}, \mathfrak{L})^{\dagger}\sigma^{\dagger} = \sigma^{\dagger}$.

PROOF. 61 *The proof is based on induction with respect to the length of σ. If the length of σ is one, we have following cartesian diagram*

$$
\begin{array}{ccc}
X_{[k-1]} & \xrightarrow{F_{[k]}} & Y_{[k-1]} \\
(Id_{X_{[k-1]}}, \mathfrak{L}) \downarrow & \mathcal{S}_{[k]} & \downarrow (Id_{Y_{[k-1]}}, \mathfrak{L}) \\
X_{[k-1]} & \xrightarrow{F_{[k]}} & Y_{[k-1]}
\end{array}
$$

such that the isomorphism $F^{\dagger}_{[k]} = F^{\dagger}_{[k]}(Id_{Y_{[k-1]}}, \mathfrak{L})^{\dagger} \xrightarrow{\alpha_{\mathcal{S}_{[k]}}} (Id_{X_{[k-1]}}, \mathfrak{L})^{\dagger}F^{\dagger} = F^{\dagger}$ is the identity. Hence, this lemma is true when the length of σ is one.

Let $\sigma = \sigma_1 \diamond \sigma_2$ and consider the following diagram obtained by horizontal composition of two cartesian squares:

$$\underline{X_{[k-1]}} \overset{\sigma_1}{\Longrightarrow} \underline{Z_{[k-1]}} \overset{\sigma_2}{\Longrightarrow} \underline{Y_{[k-1]}}$$

$$(Id_{\underline{X_{[k-1]}}}, \mathfrak{L}) \downarrow \quad \mathcal{S}_{1,[k]} \quad \downarrow J \ \mathcal{S}_{2,[k]} \quad \downarrow (Id_{\underline{Y_{[k-1]}}}, \mathfrak{L})$$

$$\underline{X_{[k-1]}} \overset{\sigma_1}{\Longrightarrow} \underline{Z_{[k-1]}} \overset{\sigma_2}{\Longrightarrow} \underline{Y_{[k-1]}} \tag{10.2.22}$$

where $J = (Id_{\underline{Z_{[k-1]}}}, \mathfrak{L})$. Since the outer border of the following diagram commutes:

$$\sigma_1^\dagger \sigma_2^\dagger \quad = \quad \sigma_1^\dagger \sigma_2^\dagger \quad = \quad \sigma_1^\dagger \sigma_2^\dagger$$

$$\| \qquad\qquad \| \qquad\qquad \|$$

$$\sigma_1^\dagger \sigma_2^\dagger (Id_{\underline{Y_{[k-1]}}}, \mathfrak{L})^\dagger \overset{\sigma_1^\dagger \alpha_{\mathcal{S}_{2,[k]}}}{\longrightarrow} \sigma_1^\dagger J^\dagger \sigma_2^\dagger \overset{\alpha_{\mathcal{S}_{1,[k]}} \sigma_2^\dagger}{\longrightarrow} (Id_{\underline{X_{[k-1]}}}, \mathfrak{L})^\dagger \sigma_1^\dagger \sigma_2^\dagger \tag{10.2.23}$$

Therefore, we have the identity isomorphism $\sigma^\dagger = \sigma^\dagger (Id_{\underline{Y_{[k-1]}}}, \mathfrak{L})^\dagger \overset{\alpha_{\mathcal{S}_{2,[k]}}}{\longrightarrow} (Id_{\underline{X_{[k-1]}}}, \mathfrak{L})^\dagger \sigma^\dagger = \sigma^\dagger$.

Automorphism by A Labeled Sequence

In this section, we will consider automorphism of the object $\underline{X_{[k-1]}}$ formed by a labeled sequence with dimension k. Consider a labeled sequence σ given by

$$\underline{X_{[k-1]}} = \underline{Y_{1,[k-1]}} \overset{(f_{1,[k]}, \mathfrak{L}_1)}{\longrightarrow} \underline{Y_{2,[k-1]}} \overset{(f_{2,[k]}, \mathfrak{L}_2)}{\longrightarrow} \cdots \overset{(f_{n,[k]}, \mathfrak{L}_n)}{\longrightarrow} \underline{Y_{n+1,[k-1]}} = \underline{X_{[k-1]}}, \tag{10.2.24}$$

the goal is to define an isomorphism $\sigma^\dagger \overset{\cong}{\longrightarrow} 1_{\mathcal{D}_{\underline{X_{[k-1]}}}}$. A *staircase* diagram based on σ is a collection of $n(n-1)/2$ cartesian squares expressed as follows

$$\underline{X_{[k-1]}}$$
$$\downarrow V_{1,1,[k]}$$
$$\underline{Z_{2,1,[k-1]}} \overset{H_{2,1,[k]}}{\longrightarrow} \underline{X_{[k-1]}}$$
$$\vdots \qquad\qquad \vdots \qquad \vdots \qquad \ddots$$
$$\underline{Z_{n-1,1,[k-1]}} \overset{H_{n-1,1,[k]}}{\longrightarrow} \underline{Z_{n-1,2,[k-1]}} \overset{H_{n-1,2,[k]}}{\longrightarrow} \cdots \qquad \underline{X_{[k-1]}}$$
$$\downarrow V_{n-1,1,[k]} \quad \downarrow V_{n-1,2,[k]} \qquad\qquad \downarrow V_{n-1,n-1,[k]}$$
$$\underline{Z_{n,1,[k-1]}} \overset{H_{n,1,[k]}}{\longrightarrow} \underline{Z_{n,2,[k-1]}} \overset{H_{n,2,[k]}}{\longrightarrow} \cdots \overset{H_{n,n-2,[k]}}{\longrightarrow} \underline{Z_{n,n-1,[k-1]}} \overset{H_{n,n-1,[k]}}{\longrightarrow} \underline{X_{[k-1]}}$$
$$\downarrow V_{n,1,[k]} \quad \downarrow V_{n,2,[k]} \qquad\qquad \downarrow V_{n,n-1,[k]} \quad \downarrow V_{n,n,[k]}$$
$$\underline{X_{[k-1]}} \longrightarrow \underline{Y_{2,[k-1]}} \longrightarrow \cdots \longrightarrow \underline{Y_{n-1,[k-1]}} \longrightarrow \underline{Y_{n,[k-1]}} \longrightarrow \underline{X_{[k-1]}}$$

satisfying the following requirements:

- $\underline{Z_{i,j,[k-1]}} = \underline{Y_{j,[k-1]}} \times_{\underline{Y_{i,[k-1]}}} \underline{X_{[k-1]}}$.

- The vertical maps are all with label **P**.

- Let $v_{i,j,[k]}$ and $h_{i,j,[k]}$ be maps of $V_{i,j,[k]}$ and $H_{i,j,[k]}$, respectively. Then, for $1 \leq i \leq n$, $h_{i+1,i,[k]}v_{i,i} = 1_{X_{[k-1]}}$ and $v_{n,i,[k]}v_{n-1,i,[k]} \cdots v_{i,i,[k]} = f_{i-1,[k]}f_{i-2,[k]} \cdots f_{1,[k]}$. Note, $v_{n,1,[k]}v_{n-1,1,[k]}$ $\cdots v_{1,1,[k]} = 1_{X_{[k-1]}}$.

However, there is no uniqueness of a staircase diagram. Morphisms and objects like $H_{i,j,[k]}$ and $Z_{i,j,[k-1]}$ should vary with staircase diagram. For any labeled sequence σ such that its map is an identity map, denoted as $\rho_\sigma(\mathfrak{S}_{[k]})$, for any choice of a staircase $\mathfrak{S}_{[k]}$ based on σ. Next lemma is provided to show that the isomorphism $\rho_\sigma(\mathfrak{S}_{[k]}) : \sigma^\dagger \longrightarrow 1_{\mathcal{D}_{X_{[k-1]}}}$ is independent on the choice of S.

Lemma 32 *The isomorphism of $\rho_\sigma(\mathfrak{S}_{[k]})$ is independent on the choice of the staircase $\mathfrak{S}_{[k]}$.*

PROOF. 62 *Suppose $\mathfrak{S}_{[k]}$ and $\mathfrak{S}'_{[k]}$ are two staircase diagrams based on σ. There are three isomorphic relations to be established first since they are building blocks for the procedure of transforming $\mathfrak{S}_{[k]}$ to $\mathfrak{S}'_{[k]}$.*

(1)(First Isomorphic Relation) We consider the following two diagrams :

$$
\begin{array}{c}
\underline{X_{2,[k-1]}} \\
\downarrow \\
\underline{X_{5,[k-1]}} \longrightarrow \underline{X_{6,[k-1]}} \\
\downarrow \quad \mathfrak{S}_{[k]} \quad \downarrow \\
\underline{X_{8,[k-1]}} \longrightarrow \underline{X_{9,[k-1]}}
\end{array}
\tag{10.2.25a}
$$

$$
\begin{array}{c}
\underline{X_{2,[k-1]}} \\
\downarrow \\
\underline{X'_{5,[k-1]}} \longrightarrow \underline{X_{6,[k-1]}} \\
\downarrow \quad \mathfrak{S}'_{[k]} \quad \downarrow \\
\underline{X_{8,[k-1]}} \longrightarrow \underline{X_{9,[k-1]}}
\end{array}
\tag{10.2.25b}
$$

such that $\underline{X_{2,[k-1]}} = \underline{X_{6,[k-1]}} = \underline{X_{[k-1]}}$, $\underline{X_{5,[k-1]}} \xrightarrow{J} \underline{X'_{5,[k-1]}}$ (existing an invertible isomorphism) and $|F_{2,5,[k]}F_{5,6,[k]}| = |F'_{2,5,[k]}F'_{5,6,[k]}| = 1_{X_{[k-1]}}$, where $F_{i,j,[k]}$ is the map from $\underline{X_{i,[k-1]}}$ to $\underline{X_{j,[k-1]}}$.

Then we have

$$
\begin{array}{ccc}
F^\dagger_{2,5,[k]}F^\dagger_{5,6,[k]}F^\dagger_{6,9,[k]} & = & F'^\dagger_{2,5,[k]}F'^\dagger_{5,6,[k]}F^\dagger_{6,9,[k]} \\[2mm]
F^\dagger_{2,5,[k]}\alpha_{\mathfrak{s}_{[k]}}\downarrow & & \downarrow F'^\dagger_{2,5,[k]}\alpha_{\mathfrak{s}'_{[k]}} \\[2mm]
F^\dagger_{2,5,[k]}F^\dagger_{5,8,[k]}F^\dagger_{8,9,[k]} \xrightarrow{1} F^\dagger_{2,5,[k]}J^\dagger F'^\dagger_{5,8,[k]}F^\dagger_{8,9,[k]} & \xrightarrow{2} & F'^\dagger_{2,5,[k]}F'^\dagger_{5,8,[k]}F^\dagger_{8,9,[k]}
\end{array}
\tag{10.2.26}
$$

where the horizontal map 1 is $\chi^{-1}_{J,F_{5,8,[k]}}$ *and the the horizontal map 2 is* $\chi_{F_{2,5,[k]},J}$*. Hence, we have isomorphic relation* $F^\dagger_{6,9,[k]} \xrightarrow{\cong} F^\dagger_{2,8,[k]}F^\dagger_{8,9,[k]}$.

(2)(Second Isomorphic Relation) We consider the following two diagrams :

$$
\begin{array}{ccc}
\underline{X_{2,[k-1]}} & \longrightarrow & \underline{X_{3,[k-1]}} \\[1mm]
\downarrow \quad \mathfrak{s}_{1,[k]} & & \downarrow \\[2mm]
\underline{X_{5,[k-1]}} & \longrightarrow & \underline{X_{6,[k-1]}} \\[1mm]
\downarrow \quad \mathfrak{s}_{2,[k]} & & \downarrow \\[2mm]
\underline{X_{8,[k-1]}} & \longrightarrow & \underline{X_{9,[k-1]}}
\end{array}
\tag{10.2.27a}
$$

$$
\begin{array}{ccc}
\underline{X'_{2,[k-1]}} & \longrightarrow & \underline{X_{3,[k-1]}} \\[1mm]
\downarrow \quad \mathfrak{s}'_{1,[k]} & & \downarrow \\[2mm]
\underline{X'_{5,[k-1]}} & \longrightarrow & \underline{X_{6,[k-1]}} \\[1mm]
\downarrow \quad \mathfrak{s}'_{2,[k]} & & \downarrow \\[2mm]
\underline{X_{8,[k-1]}} & \longrightarrow & \underline{X_{9,[k-1]}}
\end{array}
\tag{10.2.27b}
$$

such that $\underline{X_{5,[k-1]}} \xrightarrow{J} \underline{X'_{5,[k-1]}}$ *(existing an invertable isomorphism) and* $|F_{2,5,[k]}F_{5,8,[k]}| = |F'_{2,5,[k]}F'_{5,8,[k]}|$. *Then we have*

$$
\begin{array}{ccc}
F^\dagger_{2,3,[k]}F^\dagger_{3,6,[k]}F^\dagger_{6,9,[k]} & = & F'^\dagger_{2,3,[k]}F'^\dagger_{3,6,[k]}F^\dagger_{6,9,[k]} \\[2mm]
\alpha_{\mathfrak{s}_{1,[k]}}F^\dagger_{6,9,[k]}\downarrow & & \downarrow \alpha_{\mathfrak{s}'_{1,[k]}}F'^\dagger_{6,9,[k]} \\[2mm]
F^\dagger_{2,5,[k]}F^\dagger_{5,6,[k]}F^\dagger_{6,9,[k]} \xrightarrow{1} F^\dagger_{2,5,[k]}J^\dagger F'^\dagger_{5,6,[k]}F^\dagger_{6,9,[k]} & \xrightarrow{2} & F'^\dagger_{2,5,[k]}F'^\dagger_{5,6,[k]}F^\dagger_{6,9,[k]} \\[2mm]
F^\dagger_{2,5,[k]}\alpha_{\mathfrak{s}_{2,[k]}}\downarrow & & \downarrow F'^\dagger_{2,5,[k]}\alpha_{\mathfrak{s}'_{2,[k]}} \\[2mm]
F^\dagger_{2,5,[k]}F^\dagger_{5,8,[k]}F^\dagger_{8,9,[k]} & = & F'^\dagger_{2,5,[k]}F'^\dagger_{5,8,[k]}F^\dagger_{8,9,[k]}
\end{array}
\tag{10.2.28}
$$

where the horizontal map 1 is $\chi^{-1}_{J,F_{5,6,[k]}}$ *and the the horizontal map 2 is* $\chi_{F_{2,5,[k]},J}$*. Hence, we have isomorphic relation* $F^\dagger_{2,3,[k]}F^\dagger_{3,9,[k]} \xrightarrow{\cong} F^\dagger_{2,8,[k]}F^\dagger_{8,9,[k]}$.

(3)(Third Isomorphic Relation) We consider the following two diagrams :

$$
\begin{array}{ccc}
\underline{X_{1,[k-1]}} & \longrightarrow & \underline{X_{2,[k-1]}} \\
\downarrow & \mathfrak{s}_{1,[k]} & \downarrow \\
\underline{X_{4,[k-1]}} & \longrightarrow \underline{X_{5,[k-1]}} \longrightarrow & \underline{X_{6,[k-1]}} \\
\downarrow & \mathfrak{s}_{2,[k]} \quad \downarrow \quad \mathfrak{s}_{3,[k]} & \downarrow \\
\underline{X_{7,[k-1]}} & \longrightarrow \underline{X_{8,[k-1]}} \longrightarrow & \underline{X_{8,[k-1]}}
\end{array}
\qquad (10.2.29a)
$$

$$
\begin{array}{ccc}
\underline{X_{1,[k-1]}} & \longrightarrow & \underline{X_{2,[k-1]}} \\
\downarrow & \mathfrak{s}'_{1,[k]} & \downarrow \\
\underline{X_{4,[k-1]}} & \longrightarrow \underline{X'_{5,[k-1]}} \longrightarrow & \underline{X_{6,[k-1]}} \\
\downarrow & \mathfrak{s}'_{2,[k]} \quad \downarrow \quad \mathfrak{s}'_{3,[k]} & \downarrow \\
\underline{X_{7,[k-1]}} & \longrightarrow \underline{X_{8,[k-1]}} \longrightarrow & \underline{X_{8,[k-1]}}
\end{array}
\qquad (10.2.29b)
$$

such that $|F^\dagger_{2,5,[k]} F^\dagger_{5,6,[k]}| = |F'^\dagger_{2,5,[k]} F'^\dagger_{5,6,[k]}| = 1$ *and* $\underline{X_{5,[k-1]}} \xrightarrow{J} \underline{X'_{5,[k-1]}}$ *(existing an invertable isomorphism). Then we have*

$$
\begin{array}{ccccc}
F^\dagger_{1,2,[k]} F^\dagger_{6,9,[k]} & & = & & F^\dagger_{1,2,[k]} F^\dagger_{6,9,[k]} \\
\alpha_{\mathfrak{s}_{1,[k]}} F^\dagger_{6,9,[k]} \downarrow & & \ddagger & & \downarrow \alpha_{\mathfrak{s}'_{1,[k]}} F'^\dagger_{6,9,[k]} \\
F^\dagger_{1,2,[k]} F^\dagger_{2,5,[k]} F^\dagger_{5,6,[k]} F^\dagger_{6,9,[k]} & \xrightarrow{1} F^\dagger_{1,2,[k]} F^\dagger_{2,5,[k]} J^\dagger F'^\dagger_{5,6,[k]} F^\dagger_{6,9,[k]} & \xrightarrow{2} & F^\dagger_{1,2,[k]} F'^\dagger_{2,5,[k]} F'^\dagger_{5,6,[k]} F^\dagger_{6,9,[k]} \\
\alpha_{\mathfrak{s}_{1,[k]}} F^\dagger_{5,6,[k]} F^\dagger_{6,9,[k]} \downarrow & \downarrow \alpha_{\mathfrak{s}_{1,[k]}} J^\dagger F'^\dagger_{5,6,[k]} F^\dagger_{6,9,[k]} & & \downarrow \alpha_{\mathfrak{s}'_{1,[k]}} F'^\dagger_{5,6,[k]} F'^\dagger_{6,9,[k]} \\
F^\dagger_{1,4,[k]} F^\dagger_{4,5,[k]} F^\dagger_{5,6,[k]} F^\dagger_{6,9,[k]} & \xrightarrow{1} F^\dagger_{1,4,[k]} F^\dagger_{4,5,[k]} J^\dagger F'^\dagger_{5,6,[k]} F^\dagger_{6,9,[k]} & \xrightarrow{3} & F^\dagger_{1,4,[k]} F'^\dagger_{4,5,[k]} F'^\dagger_{5,6,[k]} F^\dagger_{6,9,[k]} \\
F^\dagger_{1,4,[k]} F^\dagger_{4,5,[k]} \alpha_{\mathfrak{s}_{3,[k]}} \downarrow & \downarrow F'^\dagger_{1,4,[k]} F^\dagger_{4,5,[k]} J^\dagger \alpha_{\mathfrak{s}'_{3,[k]}} & & \downarrow F'^\dagger_{1,4,[k]} F'^\dagger_{4,5,[k]} \alpha_{\mathfrak{s}'_{3,[k]}} \\
F^\dagger_{1,4,[k]} F^\dagger_{4,5,[k]} F^\dagger_{5,8,[k]} F^\dagger_{8,9,[k]} & \xrightarrow{4} F^\dagger_{1,4,[k]} F^\dagger_{4,5,[k]} J^\dagger F'^\dagger_{5,8,[k]} F^\dagger_{8,9,[k]} & \xrightarrow{3} & F^\dagger_{1,4,[k]} F'^\dagger_{4,5,[k]} F'^\dagger_{5,8,[k]} F^\dagger_{8,9,[k]} \\
F^\dagger_{1,4,[k]} \alpha_{\mathfrak{s}_{2,[k]}} F^\dagger_{8,9,[k]} \downarrow & & & \downarrow F'^\dagger_{1,4,[k]} \alpha_{\mathfrak{s}'_{2,[k]}} F'^\dagger_{8,9,[k]} \\
F^\dagger_{1,4,[k]} F^\dagger_{4,7,[k]} F^\dagger_{7,8,[k]} F^\dagger_{8,9,[k]} & & = & & F^\dagger_{1,4,[k]} F^\dagger_{4,7,[k]} F^\dagger_{7,8,[k]} F^\dagger_{8,9,[k]}
\end{array}
$$

where the following conditions are satisfied

- *the horizontal map 1 is* $\chi^{-1}_{J,F'_{5,6,[k]}}$ *;*

- *the horizontal map 2 is* $\chi_{F_{2,5,[k]},J}$ *;*

- *the horizontal map 3 is* $\chi_{F_{4,5,[k]},J}$ *;*

- *the horizontal map 4 is* $\chi^{-1}_{J,F'_{5,8,[k]}}$;

- *the diagram of part* ‡ *commutes due to*

$$
\begin{array}{ccccc}
X_{2,[k-1]} & \longrightarrow & X_{5,[k-1]} & \longrightarrow & X_{6,[k-1]} \\
\| & & \downarrow J & & \| \\
X_{2,[k-1]} & \longrightarrow & X'_{5,[k-1]} & \longrightarrow & X_{6,[k-1]}
\end{array}
\tag{10.2.30}
$$

Hence, we have isomorphic relation $F^{\dagger}_{1,2,[k]} F^{\dagger}_{2,5,[k]} F^{\dagger}_{5,6,[k]} F^{\dagger}_{6,9,[k]} \xrightarrow{\cong} F^{\dagger}_{1,4,[k]} F^{\dagger}_{4,7,[k]} F^{\dagger}_{7,8,[k]} F^{\dagger}_{8,9,[k]}$.

Suppose $\mathfrak{S}_{[k]}$ *and* $\mathfrak{S}'_{[k]}$ *are two staircase diagrams based on* σ. *We will proceed by successively modifying* $\mathfrak{S}_{[k]}$, *one vertex at a time, till it is transformed into* $\mathfrak{S}'_{[k]}$ *by applying above three isomorphic relations. If* $n = 2$, *we adopt First Isomorphic Relation to conclude that* $\rho_\sigma(\mathfrak{S}_{[k]}) = \rho_\sigma(\mathfrak{S}'_{[k]})$. *For* $n > 2$, *the Third Isomorphic Relation is applied first to replace* $Z_{n,n-1,[k-1]}$ *by* $Z'_{n,n-1,[k-1]}$. *Next, we replace* $Z_{n,n-2,[k-1]}$ *by* $Z'_{n,n-2,[k-1]}$ *through the Second Isomorphic Relation. Arguing the same fashion as above we continue westward till the bottom row of* $\mathfrak{S}_{[k]}$ *is assumed to be replaced as the bottom row of* $\mathfrak{S}'_{[k]}$ *through the Second Isomorphic Relation. Then we start with* $Z_{n-1,n-2,[k-1]}$ *by the Third Isomorphic Relation. Continuing in this procedure, the lemma is proved.*

10.3   Cancelation Rule

The main goal of this section is to define an isomorphic relation between two functors induced by two labeled sequences with $k-1$-dimensional objects, denoted as $\Upsilon^{\mathfrak{S}_{[k]}}_{\sigma_1,\sigma_2} : \sigma_1 \xrightarrow{\cong} \sigma_2$, and to show a cancelation rule associated to $\Upsilon^{\mathfrak{S}_{[k]}}_{\sigma_1,\sigma_2}$.

Consider the following diagram for the diagonal map in $\mathbf{P}$, $X_{[k-1]} \xrightarrow{(\delta,\mathbf{P})} X_{[k-1]} \times_{Y_{[k-1]}} X_{[k-1]}$,

$$
\begin{array}{ccccc}
X_{[k-1]} & \xrightarrow{(\delta,\mathbf{P})} & X_{[k-1]} \times_{Y_{[k-1]}} X_{[k-1]} & \xrightarrow{\sigma'_2} & X_{[k-1]} \\
& & \sigma'_1 \downarrow \qquad \mathfrak{S}_{[k]} & & \downarrow \sigma_1 \\
& & X_{[k-1]} & \xrightarrow{\sigma_2} & Y_{[k-1]}
\end{array}
\tag{10.3.1}
$$

where $|\sigma_1|$ is equal to $|\sigma_2|$ with $X_{[k-1]}$ as the source of σ_1, σ_2 and $Y_{[k-1]}$ as the target of σ_1, σ_2. One defines $\Upsilon^{\mathfrak{S}_{[k]}}_{\sigma_1,\sigma_2}$ to be the composition of the following sequence of isomorphisms:

$$
\sigma^{\dagger}_2 \xrightarrow{\rho^{-1}_{(\delta,\mathbf{P})\diamond\sigma'_1}} [(\delta,\mathbf{P}) \diamond \sigma'_1]^{\dagger}\sigma^{\dagger}_2 \cong [(\delta,\mathbf{P}) \diamond \sigma'_2]^{\dagger}\sigma^{\dagger}_1 \xrightarrow{\rho_{(\delta,\mathbf{P})\diamond\sigma'_2}} \sigma^{\dagger}_1.
\tag{10.3.2}
$$

For example, if σ is a sequnce such that the map $g \in \mathbf{P}$ is equal to $|\sigma|$, then we have an isomophism $\Upsilon_{G,\sigma}^{\mathfrak{S}_{[k]}} : \sigma^\dagger \xrightarrow{\cong} g^{\overline{\#}}$, where $G = (g, \mathbf{P})$. If σ is a sequnce such that the map $g \in \mathbf{O}$ is equal to $|\sigma|$, then we have an isomophism $\Upsilon_{G,\sigma}^{\mathfrak{S}_{[k]}} : \sigma^\dagger \xrightarrow{\cong} g^{\overline{\$}}$, where $G = (g, \mathbf{O})$.

10.3.1 Commutative Hexagon Lemma

The target of this section is to show the following lemma. The first ingredient in establishing the cancelation rule of $\Upsilon_{-,-}^-$.

Lemma 33 *Let $\sigma_1, \sigma_2, \sigma_3$ be labeled sequences having the same target $\underline{Y_{[k-1]}}$ such that the source of σ_i is $\underline{X_{i,[k-1]}}$ for $1 \le i \le 3$. Then we have the following cartesian cube as*

$$
\begin{array}{c}
\underline{Z_{[k-1]}} \xrightarrow{\pi_1} \bullet_1 \\
\searrow \pi_3 \quad \mathfrak{S}_{5,[k]} \quad \gamma_{13} \swarrow \\
\bullet_2 \xrightarrow{\gamma_{23}} \underline{X_{2,[k-1]}} \\
\pi_2 \downarrow \mathfrak{S}_{1,[k]} \downarrow \gamma_{32} \quad \mathfrak{S}_{3,[k]} \quad \sigma_2 \downarrow \mathfrak{S}_{6,[k]} \downarrow \gamma_{31} \\
\underline{X_{1,[k-1]}} \xrightarrow{\sigma_1} \underline{Y_{[k-1]}} \\
\nearrow \gamma_{12} \quad \mathfrak{S}_{2,[k]} \quad \sigma_3 \nwarrow \\
\bullet_3 \xrightarrow{\gamma_{21}} \underline{X_{3,[k-1]}}
\end{array}
\quad (10.3.3)
$$

where $\bullet_1 = \underline{X_{2,[k-1]}} \times_{\underline{Y_{[k-1]}}} \underline{X_{3,[k-1]}}$, $\bullet_2 = \underline{X_{1,[k-1]}} \times_{\underline{Y_{[k-1]}}} \underline{X_{2,[k-1]}}$, $\bullet_3 = \underline{X_{3,[k-1]}} \times_{\underline{Y_{[k-1]}}} \underline{X_{1,[k-1]}}$, and $\underline{Z_{[k-1]}}$ is the product of all $\underline{X_{i,[k-1]}}$ over $\underline{Y_{[k-1]}}$. Then we have the following hexagon of isomorphisms commutes:

$$
\begin{array}{c}
\pi_3^\dagger \gamma_{32}^\dagger \sigma_1^\dagger \xrightarrow{\pi_3^\dagger \alpha_{\mathfrak{S}_{3,[k]}}} \pi_3^\dagger \gamma_{23}^\dagger \sigma_2^\dagger \\
\alpha_{\mathfrak{S}_{1,[k]}} \sigma_1^\dagger \nearrow \qquad\qquad \searrow \alpha_{\mathfrak{S}_{5,[k]}} \sigma_2^\dagger \\
\pi_2^\dagger \gamma_{12}^\dagger \sigma_1^\dagger \qquad\qquad\qquad \pi_1^\dagger \gamma_{13}^\dagger \sigma_2^\dagger \\
\pi_2^\dagger \alpha_{\mathfrak{S}_{2,[k]}} \searrow \qquad\qquad \nearrow \pi_1^\dagger \alpha_{\mathfrak{S}_{6,[k]}} \\
\pi_2^\dagger \gamma_{21}^\dagger \sigma_3^\dagger \xrightarrow{\alpha_{\mathfrak{S}_{4,[k]}} \sigma_3^\dagger} \pi_1^\dagger \gamma_{31}^\dagger \sigma_3^\dagger
\end{array}
\quad (10.3.4)
$$

PROOF. 63 *The proof is based on induction. The basis of induction is the case when σ_1, σ_2 and σ_3 in Eq. (10.3.4), all are assumed to have length one. Without loss of generality, we assume that $\sigma_1 \in \mathbf{O}$ and $\sigma_2, \sigma_3 \in \mathbf{P}$. Let $\sigma_1, \sigma_2, \sigma_3$ be labeled sequences having the same target $\underline{Y_{[k-1]}}$ such* *that the source of σ_i is $\underline{X_{i,[k-1]}}$ for $1 \leq i \leq 3$. Then we have the following cartesian cube as*

$$
\begin{array}{ccc}
\underline{Z_{[k-1]}} & \xrightarrow{\pi_1} & \bullet_1 \\
\searrow \pi_3 \quad \mathfrak{S}_{5,[k]} & \gamma_{13} \swarrow & \\
\bullet_2 & \xrightarrow{\gamma_{23}} & \underline{X_{2,[k-1]}} \\
\pi_2 \downarrow \mathfrak{S}_{1,[k]} \downarrow \gamma_{32} \quad \mathfrak{S}_{3,[k]} & \sigma_2 \downarrow \mathfrak{S}_{6,[k]} \downarrow \gamma_{31} & \\
\underline{X_{1,[k-1]}} & \xrightarrow{\sigma_1} & \underline{Y_{[k-1]}} \\
\nearrow \gamma_{12} \quad \mathfrak{S}_{2,[k]} & \sigma_3 \nwarrow & \\
\bullet_3 & \xrightarrow{\gamma_{21}} & \underline{X_{3,[k-1]}}
\end{array}
\tag{10.3.5a}
$$

$$
\begin{array}{ccc}
\underline{Z_{[k-1]}} & \xrightarrow{\pi_1} & \bullet_1 \\
\downarrow \pi_4 \quad \mathfrak{S}_{7,[k]} & \sigma_4 \downarrow & \\
\underline{X_{1,[k-1]}} & \xrightarrow{\sigma_1} & \underline{Y_{[k-1]}}
\end{array}
\tag{10.3.5b}
$$

where $\bullet_1 = \underline{X_{2,[k-1]}} \times_{\underline{Y_{[k-1]}}} \underline{X_{3,[k-1]}}$, $\bullet_2 = \underline{X_{1,[k-1]}} \times_{\underline{Y_{[k-1]}}} \underline{X_{2,[k-1]}}$, $\bullet_3 = \underline{X_{3,[k-1]}} \times_{\underline{Y_{[k-1]}}} \underline{X_{1,[k-1]}}$, and $\underline{Z_{[k-1]}}$ is the product of all $\underline{X_{i,[k-1]}}$ over $\underline{Y_{[k-1]}}$. Note that the induced maps $\sigma_4 : \bullet_1 \to \underline{Y_{[k-1]}}$ and $\pi_4 : \underline{Z_{[k-1]}} \to \underline{X_{1,[k-1]}}$ have the same label as π_2 which makes $(\sigma_4, \sigma_1, \pi_4, \pi_1)$ into a cartesian square.

One has the following induced diagram of isomorphisms from Eq. (10.3.5) as

$$
\begin{array}{ccccc}
\pi_3^\dagger \gamma_{32}^\dagger \sigma_1^\dagger & \xrightarrow{\pi_3^\dagger \alpha_{\mathfrak{S}_{3,[k]}}} & & \pi_3^\dagger \gamma_{23}^\dagger \sigma_2^\dagger & \\
\alpha_{\mathfrak{S}_{1,[k]}} \nearrow \quad \searrow \chi_{\pi_3,\gamma_{32}} \sigma_1^\dagger & & \S_1 & \searrow \alpha_{\mathfrak{S}_{5,[k]}} \sigma_2^\dagger & \\
\pi_2^\dagger \gamma_{12}^\dagger \sigma_1^\dagger \xrightarrow{\chi_{\pi_2,\gamma_{12}} \sigma_1^\dagger} \pi_4^\dagger \sigma_1 \xrightarrow{\mathfrak{S}_{7,[k]}} \pi_1^\dagger \sigma_4 & \xleftarrow{\sigma_1^\dagger \chi_{\gamma_{13},\sigma_2}} & & \pi_1^\dagger \gamma_{13}^\dagger \sigma_2^\dagger \\
\pi_2^\dagger \alpha_{\mathfrak{S}_{2,[k]}} \searrow \quad \S_2 & \pi_1^\dagger \chi_{\gamma_{31},\sigma_3} \nwarrow & & \nearrow \sigma_1^\dagger \alpha_{\mathfrak{S}_{6,[k]}} \\
\pi_2^\dagger \gamma_{21}^\dagger \sigma_3^\dagger & \xrightarrow{\alpha_{\mathfrak{S}_{4,[k]}} \sigma_3^\dagger} & & \pi_1^\dagger \gamma_{31}^\dagger \sigma_3^\dagger
\end{array}
\tag{10.3.6}
$$

Then the commutativity of $\S_1$ is obtained by applying Lemma 29 (i) to the following diagram

$$
\begin{array}{ccccc}
\underline{Z_{[k-1]}} & \xrightarrow{\pi_3} & \bullet_2 & \xrightarrow{\gamma_{32}} & \underline{X_{1,[k-1]}} \\
\downarrow \pi_1 & & \downarrow \gamma_{23} & & \downarrow \sigma_2 \\
\underline{X_{4,[k-1]}} & \xrightarrow{\gamma_{13}} & \underline{X_{2,[k-1]}} & \xrightarrow{\sigma_2} & \underline{Y_{[k-1]}}
\end{array}
\tag{10.3.7}
$$

Similarly, he commutativity of §2 is obtained by applying Lemma 29 (i) to the following diagram

$$
\begin{array}{ccccc}
\underline{Z}_{[k-1]} & \xrightarrow{\pi_2} & \bullet_3 & \xrightarrow{\gamma_{12}} & \underline{X}_{1,[k-1]} \\
\downarrow \pi_1 & & \downarrow \gamma_{21} & & \downarrow \sigma_1 \\
\underline{X}_{4,[k-1]} & \xrightarrow{\gamma_{31}} & \underline{X}_{3,[k-1]} & \xrightarrow{\sigma_3} & \underline{Y}_{[k-1]}
\end{array}
\qquad (10.3.8)
$$

Hence, from the outer border of the diagram shown by Eq. (10.3.6), we therefore conclude that this lemma holds in the case when all the σ_i have length one.

In the sequel, we consider the case where one of the $\sigma_1, \sigma_2, \sigma_3$ has length greater than one so that we may decompose it as a concatenation of two sequences. Without loss of generality, one assume that σ_3 factors as $\underline{X}_{3,[k]} \xrightarrow{\sigma_4} \underline{W}_{[k]} \xrightarrow{\sigma_5} \underline{Y}_{[k]}$. A double cube obtained by decomposing the original cube into two cubes is illustrated below

$$(10.3.9)$$

where the following relations hold:

- $\bullet_1 = \underline{X}_{1,[k-1]} \times_{\underline{Y}_{[k-1]}} \underline{X}_{2,[k-1]}$, $\bullet_2 = \underline{X}_{1,[k-1]} \times_{\underline{Y}_{[k-1]}} \underline{W}_{[k-1]}$, $\bullet_3 = \underline{X}_{1,[k-1]} \times_{\underline{Y}_{[k-1]}} \underline{X}_{2,[k-1]} \times_{\underline{Y}_{[k-1]}} \underline{W}_{[k-1]}$, $\bullet_4 = \underline{X}_{2,[k-1]} \times_{\underline{Y}_{[k-1]}} \underline{W}_{[k-1]}$, $\bullet_5 = (\underline{X}_{1,[k-1]} \times_{\underline{Y}_{[k-1]}} \underline{W}_{[k-1]}) \times_{\underline{W}_{[k-1]}} \underline{X}_{3,[k-1]}$, *and* $\bullet_6 = (\underline{X}_{2,[k-1]} \times_{\underline{Y}_{[k-1]}} \underline{W}_{[k-1]}) \times_{\underline{W}_{[k-1]}} \underline{X}_{3,[k-1]}$

- $\pi_3 = \iota_4 \diamond \iota_5$.

- $\gamma_{12} = \gamma_{42} \diamond \gamma_{52}$.

- $\gamma_{13} = \gamma_{43} \diamond \gamma_{53}$.

- $\sigma_3 = \sigma_4 \diamond \sigma_5$.

- *Vertices $\underline{W_{[k-1]}}, \bullet_2, \bullet_3$ and $\bullet_4$ form the cartesian square $\mathfrak{S}_{6,[k]}$.*

- *Vertices $\underline{X_{3,[k-1]}}, \bullet_5, \underline{Z_{[k-1]}}$ and $\bullet_6$ form the cartesian square $\mathfrak{S}_{11,[k]}$.*

Then, one has the following diagram of isomorphisms induced from Eq. (10.3.9)

$$
\pi_3^\dagger \gamma_{32}^\dagger \sigma_1^\dagger = \imath_4^\dagger \imath_5^\dagger \gamma_{32}^\dagger \sigma_1^\dagger \xrightarrow{\imath_4^\dagger \imath_5^\dagger \alpha_{\mathfrak{S}_{1,[k]}}} \imath_4^\dagger \imath_5^\dagger \gamma_{23}^\dagger \sigma_2^\dagger = \pi_3^\dagger \gamma_{23}^\dagger \sigma_2^\dagger
$$

with the diagram of isomorphisms (10.3.10):

Outer and inner subdiagrams involving $\alpha_{\mathfrak{S}_{2,[k]}\circ\mathfrak{S}_{7,[k]}}\sigma_1^\dagger$, H_1, $\alpha_{\mathfrak{S}_{3,[k]}\circ\mathfrak{S}_{8,[k]}}\sigma_2^\dagger$, the vertices $\pi_2^\dagger \gamma_{42}^\dagger \gamma_{25}^\dagger \sigma_5^\dagger$ and $\pi_1^\dagger \gamma_{43}^\dagger \gamma_{35}^\dagger \sigma_5^\dagger$; $\pi_2^\dagger \gamma_{42}^\dagger \alpha_{\mathfrak{S}_{5,[k]}}$, $\alpha_{\mathfrak{S}_{7,[k]}} \gamma_{25}^\dagger \sigma_5^\dagger$, $\alpha_{\mathfrak{S}_{8,[k]}} \gamma_{35}^\dagger \sigma_5^\dagger$, $\pi_1^\dagger \gamma_{43}^\dagger \alpha_{\mathfrak{S}_{4,[k]}}$;

$$
\pi_2^\dagger \gamma_{12}^\dagger \sigma_1^\dagger = \pi_2^\dagger \gamma_{42}^\dagger \gamma_{52}^\dagger \sigma_1^\dagger \quad \imath_4^\dagger \imath_2^\dagger \gamma_{25}^\dagger \sigma_5^\dagger \xrightarrow{\imath_4^\dagger \alpha_{\mathfrak{S}_{6,[k]}} \sigma_5^\dagger} \imath_4^\dagger \imath_1^\dagger \gamma_{35}^\dagger \sigma_5^\dagger \quad \pi_1^\dagger \gamma_{43}^\dagger \gamma_{53}^\dagger \sigma_2^\dagger = \pi_1^\dagger \gamma_{13}^\dagger \sigma_2^\dagger
$$

$\alpha_{\mathfrak{S}_{7,[k]}} \gamma_{52}^\dagger \sigma_1^\dagger$, $\imath_4^\dagger \imath_2^\dagger \alpha_{\mathfrak{S}_{5,[k]}}$, $\imath_4^\dagger \imath_1^\dagger \alpha_{\mathfrak{S}_{4,[k]}}$, $\alpha_{\mathfrak{S}_{8,[k]}} \gamma_{53}^\dagger \sigma_2^\dagger$;

$$
\imath_4^\dagger \imath_2^\dagger \gamma_{52}^\dagger \sigma_1^\dagger \qquad \imath_4^\dagger \imath_1^\dagger \gamma_{53}^\dagger \sigma_2^\dagger
$$

$\pi_2^\dagger \alpha_{\mathfrak{S}_{5,[k]}\circ\mathfrak{S}_{10,[k]}}$, H_2, $\pi_1^\dagger \alpha_{\mathfrak{S}_{4,[k]}\circ\mathfrak{S}_{9,[k]}}$;

$$
\pi_2^\dagger \gamma_{21}^\dagger \sigma_3^\dagger = \pi_2^\dagger \gamma_{21}^\dagger \sigma_4^\dagger \sigma_5^\dagger \xrightarrow{\alpha_{\mathfrak{S}_{11,[k]}} \sigma_4^\dagger \sigma_5^\dagger} \pi_1^\dagger \gamma_{31}^\dagger \sigma_4^\dagger \sigma_5^\dagger = \pi_1^\dagger \gamma_{31}^\dagger \sigma_3^\dagger \tag{10.3.10}
$$

The two hexagons, H_1 and H_2, is assumed to commute by the induction hypothesis; for H_1 we use the cube constructed from γ_{25}, γ_{35} and σ_4 while for H_2 we use the cube constructed from σ_1, σ_2 and σ_5. The remaining four outer subdiagrams commute by definition of the base-change isomorphism; the equalities in these subdiagrams are obtained by comparing the double cube with the original one. The outer border of the preceding diagram comprising the six vertices, $\pi_2^\dagger \gamma_{12}^\dagger \sigma_1^\dagger$, $\pi_3^\dagger \gamma_{32}^\dagger \sigma_1^\dagger$, $\pi_3^\dagger \gamma_{23}^\dagger \sigma_2^\dagger$, $\pi_1^\dagger \gamma_{13}^\dagger \sigma_2^\dagger$, $\pi_1^\dagger \gamma_{31}^\dagger \sigma_3^\dagger$, $\pi_2^\dagger \gamma_{21}^\dagger \sigma_3^\dagger$, and the induced maps now proves commutativity of the hexagon corresponding to the original cube provided by Eq. (10.3.4). By induction, this lemma follows.

10.3.2 First Commutative Triangle Lemma

The purpose of this section is to show the following lemma. The second component in establishing the cancelation rule of $\Upsilon_{-,-}^-$.

Lemma 34 Let $\underline{X_{[k-1]}} \xrightarrow{\sigma_1} \underline{Y_{[k-1]}} \xrightarrow{\sigma_2} \underline{X_{[k-1]}}$ and $F = (|\sigma_1|, \mathbf{P})$, then the following diagram commutes with respect to any choice of $\mathfrak{S}_{[k]}$:

$$\sigma_1^\dagger \sigma_2^\dagger \xrightarrow{\Upsilon_{F,\sigma_1}^{\mathfrak{S}_{[k]}} \sigma_2^\dagger} F^\dagger \sigma_2^\dagger$$

$$\rho_{\sigma_1 \diamond \sigma_2} \searrow \qquad \swarrow \rho_{F \diamond \sigma_2}$$

$$\mathbf{1}_{\mathcal{D}_{\underline{X_{[k-1]}}}} \tag{10.3.11}$$

We have to provide the following lemma first before proving Lemma 34.

Lemma 35 Given the following cartesian diagram $\mathfrak{S}_{[k]}$

$$
\begin{array}{ccc}
\underline{X'_{[k-1]}} & \xrightarrow{\sigma_1} & \underline{Y'_{[k-1]}} \\
H \downarrow & \mathfrak{S}_{[k]} & \downarrow E \\
\underline{X_{[k-1]}} & \xrightarrow{\sigma_2} & \underline{Y_{[k-1]}}
\end{array}
\tag{10.3.12}
$$

where maps E and H both have length one. Moreover, the length of σ_1 is equal to the length of σ_2. Let $\sigma_3 : \underline{Y'_{[k-1]}} \longrightarrow \underline{Y_{[k-1]}}$ be a sequence such that $|\sigma_3| = |E|$. Then there exists a cartesian square $\mathfrak{T}_{[k]}$ as follows

$$
\begin{array}{ccc}
\underline{X'_{[k-1]}} & \xrightarrow{\sigma_1} & \underline{Y'_{[k-1]}} \\
\sigma_4 \downarrow & \mathfrak{T}_{[k]} & \downarrow \sigma_3 \\
\underline{X_{[k-1]}} & \xrightarrow{\sigma_2} & \underline{Y_{[k-1]}}
\end{array}
\tag{10.3.13}
$$

such that $|\sigma_4| = |H|$ and the length of σ_3 is equal to the length of σ_4.

PROOF. 64 *The proof is based on induction. If the length of σ_3 is one, the result holds immediately. If the length of σ_3 is greater then one, then σ_3 can be decomposed as $\underline{Y'_{[k-1]}} \xrightarrow{D} \underline{Y_{1,[k-1]}} \xrightarrow{\kappa} \underline{Y_{[k-1]}}$. At this point, we have the following two cases.*

CASE I: The length of σ_2 is less than 3.

If the length of σ_2 is one, we can choose any cartesian diagram $\mathfrak{T}_{0,[k]}$ as

$$
\begin{array}{ccc}
\widetilde{\underline{X_{[k-1]}}} & \xrightarrow{\tilde{G}} & \underline{Y'_{[k-1]}} \\
\downarrow \tilde{K} & & \downarrow D \\
\underline{X_{1,[k-1]}} & \longrightarrow & \underline{Y_{1,[k-1]}} \\
\downarrow \rho & & \downarrow \kappa \\
\underline{X_{[k-1]}} & \xrightarrow{\sigma_2} & \underline{Y_{[k-1]}}
\end{array}
$$

$$\tag{10.3.14}$$

Then there exists an inverse isomorphism pair $r : \widetilde{X_{[k-1]}} \xrightarrow{\cong} X'_{[k-1]}$ and $r^{-1} : X'_{[k-1]} \xrightarrow{\cong} \widetilde{X_{[k-1]}}$ such that $|\tilde{G}|r^{-1} = |\sigma_1|$ and $|\rho||\tilde{K}|r = |\sigma_4|$. Let $\mathfrak{T}_{1,[k]}$ be the diagram obtained by making the following replacement in $\mathfrak{T}_{0,[k]}$:

- $\widetilde{X_{[k-1]}}$ replaced by $X'_{[k-1]}$;

- $\tilde{G}$ replaced by σ_1;

- $\tilde{K}$ replaced by $\tilde{K}r^{-1}$.

Then the cartesian square $\mathfrak{T}_{[k]}$ is obtained ($\mathfrak{T}_{[k]} = \mathfrak{T}_{1,[k]}$).

If the length of σ_2 is two, then we can decompose $\mathfrak{S}_{[k]}$ as

$$
\begin{array}{ccccc}
X'_{[k]} & \xrightarrow{F'} & Z'_{[k]} & \xrightarrow{G'} & Y'_{[k]} \\
\downarrow & & \downarrow K & & \downarrow E \\
X_{[k]} & \xrightarrow{F} & Z_{[k]} & \xrightarrow{G} & Y_{[k]}
\end{array}
\tag{10.3.15}
$$

Let us find any cartesian diagram $\mathfrak{T}_{0,[k]}$ as

$$
\begin{array}{ccccc}
\widetilde{X_{[k-1]}} & \xrightarrow{\tilde{F}} & \widetilde{Z_{[k-1]}} & \xrightarrow{\tilde{G}} & Y'_{[k-1]} \\
\downarrow & & \downarrow \tilde{K} & & \downarrow D \\
X_{1,[k-1]} & \longrightarrow & Z_{1,[k-1]} & \longrightarrow & Y_{1,[k-1]} \\
\downarrow & & \downarrow \rho & & \downarrow \kappa \\
X_{[k-1]} & \xrightarrow{F} & Z_{[k-1]} & \xrightarrow{G} & Y_{[k-1]}
\end{array}
\tag{10.3.16}
$$

Then there exists an inverse isomorphism pair $r : \widetilde{Z_{[k-1]}} \xrightarrow{\cong} Z'_{[k-1]}$ and $r^{-1} : Z'_{[k-1]} \xrightarrow{\cong} \widetilde{Z_{[k-1]}}$ such that $|\tilde{G}|r^{-1} = |G'|$ and $|\rho||\tilde{K}|r = K$. Let $\mathfrak{T}_{1,[k]}$ be the diagram obtained by making the following replacement in $\mathfrak{T}_{0,[k]}$:

- $\widetilde{Z_{[k-1]}}$ replaced by $Z'_{[k-1]}$;

- $\tilde{F}$ replaced by $r|F'|$;

- $\tilde{G}$ replaced by G';

- $\tilde{K}$ replaced by K.

375

Then $\mathfrak{T}_{1,[k]}$ is also a cartesian diagram and it agrees with $\mathfrak{S}$ in the rightmost column of squares. We proceed in a similar manner replacing one by one the vertices and edges in the top row of $\mathfrak{T}_{2,[k]}$ with that of $\mathfrak{S}$. Then the cartesian square $\mathfrak{T}_{2,[k]}$ is obtained ($\mathfrak{T}_{[k]} = \mathfrak{T}_{2,[k]}$).

CASE II: The length of σ_2 is greater or equal than 3.

If the length of σ_2 is greater or equal than 3, then we can decompose $\mathfrak{S}_{[k]}$ as

$$
\begin{array}{ccccccc}
X'_{[k]} & \xrightarrow{\sigma'} & W'_{[k]} & \xrightarrow{F'} & Z'_{[k]} & \xrightarrow{G'} & Y'_{[k]} \\
\downarrow & & \downarrow & & \downarrow K & & \downarrow E \\
X_{[k]} & \xrightarrow{\sigma''} & W_{[k]} & \xrightarrow{F} & Z_{[k]} & \xrightarrow{G} & Y_{[k]}
\end{array} \qquad (10.3.17)
$$

where σ' and σ'' are two labeled sequences of maps. Let us find any cartesian diagram $\mathfrak{T}_{0,[k]}$ as

$$
\begin{array}{ccccccc}
\widetilde{X_{[k-1]}} & \longrightarrow & \widetilde{W_{[k-1]}} & \xrightarrow{\tilde{F}} & \widetilde{Z_{[k-1]}} & \xrightarrow{\tilde{G}} & Y'_{[k-1]} \\
\downarrow & & \downarrow & & \downarrow \tilde{K} & & \downarrow D \\
X_{1,[k-1]} & \longrightarrow & W_{1,[k-1]} & \longrightarrow & Z_{1,[k-1]} & \longrightarrow & Y_{1,[k-1]} \\
\downarrow & & \downarrow & & \downarrow \rho & & \downarrow \kappa \\
X_{[k-1]} & \longrightarrow & W_{[k-1]} & \xrightarrow{F} & Z_{[k-1]} & \xrightarrow{G} & Y_{[k-1]}
\end{array} \qquad (10.3.18)
$$

Then there exists an inverse isomorphism pair $r : \widetilde{Z_{[k-1]}} \xrightarrow{\cong} Z'_{[k-1]}$ and $r^{-1} : Z'_{[k-1]} \xrightarrow{\cong} \widetilde{Z_{[k-1]}}$ such that $|\tilde{G}|r^{-1} = |G'|$ and $|\rho||\tilde{K}|r = K$. Let $\mathfrak{T}_{1,[k]}$ be the diagram obtained by making the following replacement in $\mathfrak{T}_{0,[k]}$:

- $\widetilde{Z_{[k-1]}}$ replaced by $Z'_{[k-1]}$;

- $\tilde{F}$ replaced by $r|F'|$;

- $\tilde{G}$ replaced by G';

- $\tilde{K}$ replaced by K.

Then $\mathfrak{T}_{1,[k]}$ is also a cartesian diagram and it agrees with $\mathfrak{S}$ in the rightmost column of squares. We proceed in a similar manner replacing one by one the vertices and edges in the top row of $\mathfrak{T}_{i,[k]}$ with that of $\mathfrak{S}$. By induction, the cartesian square $\mathfrak{T}_{[k]}$ is obtained.

Now, we are ready to prove Lemma 34.

PROOF. 65 *Let us consider a staircase diagram based on* $\sigma_1 \diamond \sigma_2$ *as*

$$
\begin{array}{l}
\underline{X_{[k-1]}} \\
\imath_3 \downarrow \qquad\qquad \searrow T_{3,[k]} \\
\quad \underline{W_{[k-1]}} \xrightarrow{\sigma_3} \underline{X_{[k-1]}} \\
\quad \imath_1 \downarrow \quad \mathfrak{S}_{1,[k]} \;\; \imath_2 \downarrow \qquad \searrow T_{2,[k]} \\
\quad \underline{X_{[k-1]}} \xrightarrow{\sigma_1} \underline{Y_{[k-1]}} \xrightarrow{\sigma_2} \underline{X_{[k-1]}}
\end{array}
$$

$$(10.3.19)$$

where $\underline{W_{[k-1]}} = \underline{X_{[k-1]}} \times_{\underline{Y_{[k-1]}}} \underline{X_{[k-1]}}$.

By setting $H = (|\imath_3|, \mathbf{P})$, $Q = (|\sigma_3|, \mathbf{P})$ and $F = (|\sigma_1|, \mathbf{P})$, we have a staircase diagram based on $F \diamond \sigma_2$ as

$$
\begin{array}{l}
\underline{X_{[k-1]}} \\
H \downarrow \qquad \searrow T_{3,[k]} \\
\quad \underline{W_{[k-1]}} \xrightarrow{Q} \underline{X_{[k-1]}} \\
\quad \imath_1 \downarrow \quad \mathfrak{S}_{2,[k]} \;\; \imath_2 \downarrow \qquad \searrow T_{2,[k]} \\
\quad \underline{X_{[k-1]}} \xrightarrow{F} \underline{Y_{[k-1]}} \xrightarrow{\sigma_2} \underline{X_{[k-1]}}
\end{array}
$$

$$(10.3.20)$$

where $\underline{W_{[k-1]}} = \underline{X_{[k-1]}} \times_{\underline{Y_{[k-1]}}} \underline{X_{[k-1]}}$.

By setting $G = (|\imath_1|, \mathbf{P})$ and $F = (|\sigma_1|, \mathbf{P})$, we have a staircase diagram based on $\imath_3 \diamond G$ as

$$
\begin{array}{l}
\underline{X_{[k-1]}} \\
\imath_3 \downarrow \qquad\qquad \searrow T_{3,[k]} \\
\quad \underline{W_{[k-1]}} \xrightarrow{\sigma_3} \underline{X_{[k-1]}} \\
\quad G \downarrow \quad \mathfrak{S}_{3,[k]} \;\; F \downarrow \qquad \searrow T_{2,[k]} \\
\quad \underline{X_{[k-1]}} \xrightarrow{\sigma_1} \underline{Y_{[k-1]}} \xrightarrow{\sigma_2} \underline{X_{[k-1]}}
\end{array}
$$

$$(10.3.21)$$

where $\underline{W_{[k-1]}} = \underline{X_{[k-1]}} \times_{\underline{Y_{[k-1]}}} \underline{X_{[k-1]}}$.

For $i = 2, 3$, let $\imath_i^\dagger \sigma_i^\dagger \xrightarrow{\beta_i} T_{i,[k]}^\dagger$ and $T_{i,[k]}^\dagger \xrightarrow{\epsilon_i} \mathbf{1}_{\mathcal{D}_{X_{[k-1]}}}$ be natural isomorphisms. From Lemma 35, given a cartesian diagram $T_{[k]}$, one can choose the diagram as in Eq. (10.3.19) that *the resulting square in Eq. (10.3.20) (or Eq. (10.3.21)) is the same as $T_{[k]}$. Then, we have the following diagram:*

$$
\begin{array}{ccccc}
\sigma_1^\dagger \sigma_2^\dagger & & = & & \sigma_1^\dagger \sigma_2^\dagger \\[2pt]
\eta_{\imath_3 \diamond \imath_1} \downarrow & & \square_1 & & \downarrow \eta_{\imath_3 \diamond G} \\[2pt]
\imath_3^\dagger \imath_1^\dagger \sigma_1^\dagger \sigma_2^\dagger & & \xleftarrow{\;\Upsilon_{\imath_1,G}\;} & & \imath_3^\dagger G \sigma_1^\dagger \sigma_2^\dagger \\[2pt]
\beta_3 \alpha_{\mathfrak{S}_{1,[k]}} \downarrow & & \square_2 & & \downarrow \beta_3 \alpha_{\mathfrak{S}_{3,[k]}} \\[2pt]
T_{3,[k]}^\dagger \quad \xleftarrow{\;\epsilon_2 \beta_2\;} \quad T_{3,[k]}^\dagger \imath_2^\dagger \sigma_2^\dagger & & \xleftarrow{\;\Upsilon_{\imath_2,F}\;} & & T_{3,[k]}^\dagger F^\dagger \sigma_2^\dagger \\[2pt]
\eta_{T_{3,[k]}} \downarrow \quad \square_3 \quad \eta_{T_{3,[k]}} \downarrow & & \square_4 & & \downarrow \eta_{T_{3,[k]}} \\[2pt]
\mathbf{1}_{\mathcal{D}_{X_{[k-1]}}} \quad \xleftarrow{\;\epsilon_2 \beta_2\;} \quad \imath_2^\dagger \sigma_2^\dagger & & \xleftarrow{\;\Upsilon_{\imath_2,F}\;} & & F^\dagger \sigma_2^\dagger \\[2pt]
\eta_{H \diamond Q} \uparrow \quad \square_5 \quad \eta_{H \diamond Q} \uparrow & & \square_6 & & \uparrow \eta_{H \diamond \imath_1} \\[2pt]
H^\dagger Q^\dagger \quad \xleftarrow{\;\epsilon_2 \beta_2\;} \quad H^\dagger Q^\dagger \imath_2^\dagger \sigma_2^\dagger & & \xleftarrow{\;\alpha_{\mathfrak{S}_{2,[k]}}\;} & & H^\dagger \imath_1^\dagger F^\dagger \sigma_2^\dagger
\end{array}
\tag{10.3.22}
$$

By canceling $\sigma_1^\dagger \sigma_2^\dagger$ from each vertex in the square $\square_1$, the square $\square_1$ commutes from the staircase diagrams provided by Eqs. (10.3.19) and (10.3.21) and the definition of $\Upsilon_{-,-}^-$ given by Eq. (10.3.2). By canceling $\imath_3^\dagger$ on the left and $\sigma_2^\dagger$ on the right from each vertex in the square $\square_2$, the square $\square_2$ commutes from transitivity of $\alpha_{\mathfrak{S}_{1,[k]}}$ and $\alpha_{\mathfrak{S}_{3,[k]}}$. By canceling $\sigma_2^\dagger$ on the right from each vertex in the square $\square_6$, the square $\square_6$ commutes from the staircase diagrams provided by Eq. (10.3.20) and the definition of $\Upsilon_{-,-}^-$. For remaining squares, $\square_2, \square_3, \square_4, \square_5$, they commutes by functoriality from maps besides each arrow in these squares.

10.3.3 Second Commutative Triangle Lemma

The goal of this section is to prove the last lemma in establishing the cancelation rule of $\Upsilon_{-,-}^-$.

Lemma 36 *Given the diagram below:*

$$
\begin{array}{ccccc}
\underline{X_{[k-1]}} & \xrightarrow{\;\sigma_1\;} & \underline{V_{[k-1]}} & \xrightarrow{\;\sigma_2\;} & \underline{W_{[k-1]}} \\[2pt]
\sigma_3 \downarrow & & \mathfrak{S}_{[k]} & & \downarrow \sigma_4 \\[2pt]
\underline{Y_{[k-1]}} & \xrightarrow{\;\sigma_5\;} & \underline{Z_{[k-1]}} & \xrightarrow{\;\sigma_6\;} & \underline{X_{[k-1]}},
\end{array}
\tag{10.3.23}
$$

one has the following commutative diagram :

$$\sigma_1^\dagger\sigma_3^\dagger\sigma_5^\dagger\sigma_6^\dagger \xrightarrow{\ \alpha_{\mathfrak{S}_{[k]}}\ } \sigma_1^\dagger\sigma_2^\dagger\sigma_4^\dagger\sigma_6^\dagger$$

$$\rho_{\sigma_1\diamond\sigma_3\diamond\sigma_5\diamond\sigma_6}\searrow \qquad \swarrow \rho_{\sigma_1\diamond\sigma_2\diamond\sigma_4\diamond\sigma_6}$$

$$\mathbf{1}_{\mathcal{D}_{X_{[k-1]}}} \tag{10.3.24}$$

There are three Lemmas to be provided first before establishing Lemma 36.

Lemma 37 *Lengths of labeled sequences $\sigma_2, \sigma_3, \sigma_4$ and σ_5 in Lemma 36 can all be reduced as one.*

PROOF. 66 *The proof is based on induction. We first prove this by induction on the sum of the length σ_4. If $\sigma_4 = \nu_1 \diamond \nu_2$, Eq. (10.3.23) is modified as*

$$
\begin{array}{ccc}
\underline{X_{[k-1]}} & \xrightarrow{\sigma_1} \underline{V_{[k-1]}} & \xrightarrow{\sigma_2} \underline{W_{[k-1]}} \\
& \mu_1 \downarrow \quad \mathfrak{S}_{3,[k]} \quad \downarrow \nu_1 & \\
& \underline{Y_{1,[k-1]}} \xrightarrow{\sigma_2} \underline{Z_{1,[k-1]}} & \\
& \mu_2 \downarrow \quad \mathfrak{S}_{4,[k]} \quad \downarrow \nu_2 & \\
& \underline{Y_{[k-1]}} \xrightarrow{\sigma_5} \underline{Z_{[k-1]}} \xrightarrow{\sigma_6} \underline{X_{[k-1]}} &
\end{array}
\tag{10.3.25}
$$

Then, we have the following diagram of isomorphisms

$$\sigma_1^\dagger\sigma_3^\dagger\sigma_5^\dagger\sigma_6^\dagger \xrightarrow{\ \alpha_{\mathfrak{S}_{[k]}}\ } \sigma_1^\dagger\sigma_2^\dagger\sigma_4^\dagger\sigma_6^\dagger$$

$$\rho_{\sigma_1\mu_1\mu_2\sigma_5\sigma_6}\searrow \qquad \S_1 \quad \swarrow \rho_{\sigma_1\sigma_2\sigma_4\sigma_6}$$

$$\| \qquad \mathbf{1}_{\mathcal{D}_{X_{[k-1]}}} \qquad \|$$

$$\rho_{\sigma_1\mu_1\mu_2\sigma_5\sigma_6}\nearrow \quad \S_2 \ \uparrow\rho_-\ \S_3 \ \nwarrow \rho_{\sigma_1\sigma_2\nu_1\nu_2\sigma_6}$$

$$\sigma_1^\dagger\mu_1^\dagger\mu_2^\dagger\sigma_5^\dagger\sigma_6^\dagger \xrightarrow{\ \alpha_{\mathfrak{S}_{3,[k]}}\ } \sigma_1^\dagger\mu_1^\dagger\theta^\dagger\nu_2^\dagger\sigma_6^\dagger \xrightarrow{\ \alpha_{\mathfrak{S}_{4,[k]}}\ } \sigma_1^\dagger\sigma_2^\dagger\nu_1^\dagger\nu_2^\dagger\sigma_6^\dagger \tag{10.3.26}$$

where ρ_- is $\rho_{\sigma_1\mu_1\theta\nu_2\sigma_6}$. Hence, if we have that $\S_2$ and $\S_3$ commute, then so dose $\S_1$.

The next is to prove the sum of the length σ_5. If $\sigma_5 = \nu_1 \diamond \nu_2$, Eq. (10.3.23) is modified as

$$
\begin{array}{ccc}
\underline{X_{[k-1]}} \xrightarrow{\sigma_1} \underline{V_{[k-1]}} \xrightarrow{\mu_1} \underline{W_{1,[k-1]}} \xrightarrow{\mu_2} \underline{W_{[k-1]}} \\
\sigma_3 \downarrow \quad \mathfrak{S}_{1,[k]} \quad \downarrow \theta \quad \mathfrak{S}_{2,[k]} \quad \downarrow \sigma_4 \\
\underline{Y_{[k-1]}} \xrightarrow{\nu_1} \underline{Z_{1,[k-1]}} \xrightarrow{\nu_2} \underline{Z_{[k-1]}} \xrightarrow{\sigma_6} \underline{X_{[k-1]}}
\end{array}
\tag{10.3.27}
$$

379

Then, we have the following diagram of isomorphisms

$$
\begin{array}{ccc}
\sigma_1^\dagger \sigma_3^\dagger \sigma_5^\dagger \sigma_6^\dagger & \xrightarrow{\;\alpha_{\mathfrak{S}_{[k]}}\;} & \sigma_1^\dagger \sigma_2^\dagger \sigma_4^\dagger \sigma_6^\dagger \\
\rho_{\sigma_1 \sigma_3 \sigma_5 \sigma_6} \searrow \quad \S_1 \quad \swarrow \rho_{\sigma_1 \sigma_2 \sigma_4 \sigma_6} \\
\| \qquad \mathbf{1}_{\mathcal{D}_{X_{[k-1]}}} \qquad \| \\
\rho_{\sigma_1 \sigma_3 \nu_1 \nu_2 \sigma_6} \nearrow \quad \S_2 \;\uparrow \rho_- \S_3 \;\nwarrow \rho_{\sigma_1 \mu_1 \mu_2 \sigma_4 \sigma_6} \\
\sigma_1^\dagger \sigma_3^\dagger \nu_1^\dagger \nu_2^\dagger \sigma_6^\dagger \xrightarrow{\;\alpha_{\mathfrak{S}_{1,[k]}}\;} \sigma_1^\dagger \mu_1^\dagger \theta^\dagger \nu_2^\dagger \sigma_6^\dagger \xrightarrow{\;\alpha_{\mathfrak{S}_{2,[k]}}\;} \sigma_1^\dagger \mu_1^\dagger \mu_2^\dagger \sigma_4^\dagger \sigma_6^\dagger
\end{array} \tag{10.3.28}
$$

where ρ_- is $\rho_{\sigma_1 \mu_1 \theta \nu_2 \sigma_6}$. Hence, if we have that $\S_2$ and $\S_3$ commute, then so dose $\S_1$. Therefore, by induction, this lemma is valid.

The next Lemma is about the nullity about labeled maps σ_6 in Eq. (10.3.23).

Lemma 38 *The labeled sequence σ_6 in Lemma 36 can be reduced as nullity.*

PROOF. 67 *From Lemma 37, we assume that the length for labeled sequences $\sigma_2, \sigma_3, \sigma_4$ and σ_6 all have length one. Set the map f as $|\sigma_1 \diamond \sigma_3 \diamond \sigma_5|$ and $F := (f, \mathbf{P})$. Consider the following diagram*

$$
\begin{array}{ccc}
\sigma_1^\dagger \sigma_3^\dagger \sigma_5^\dagger \sigma_6^\dagger & \xrightarrow{\;\alpha_{\mathfrak{S}_{[k]}}\;} & \sigma_1^\dagger \sigma_2^\dagger \sigma_4^\dagger \sigma_6^\dagger \\
\Upsilon_{F, \sigma_1 \diamond \sigma_3 \diamond \sigma_5} \sigma_6^\dagger \searrow \quad \S_1 \quad \swarrow \Upsilon_{F, \sigma_1 \diamond \sigma_2 \diamond \sigma_4} \sigma_6^\dagger \\
\rho_{\sigma_1 \sigma_3 \sigma_5 \sigma_6} \downarrow \quad \S_2 \quad F^\dagger \sigma_6^\dagger \quad \S_3 \quad \downarrow \rho_{\sigma_1 \sigma_2 \sigma_4 \sigma_6} \\
\rho_{F \sigma_6} \swarrow \qquad \searrow \rho_{F \sigma_6} \\
\mathbf{1}_{\mathcal{D}_{X_{[k-1]}}} \qquad = \qquad \mathbf{1}_{\mathcal{D}_{X_{[k-1]}}}
\end{array} \tag{10.3.29}
$$

where the outer border is Eq. (10.3.24), the left and the right two sub-triangles, $\S_2$ and $\S_3$, on either side commute, and commutativity of the sub-triangle on $\S_1$ reduces to the following diagram:

$$
\begin{array}{ccc}
\sigma_1^\dagger \sigma_3^\dagger \sigma_5^\dagger & \xrightarrow{\;\alpha_{\mathfrak{S}_{[k]}}\;} & \sigma_1^\dagger \sigma_2^\dagger \sigma_4^\dagger \\
\Upsilon_{F, \sigma_1 \diamond \sigma_3 \diamond \sigma_5} \searrow \qquad \swarrow \Upsilon_{F, \sigma_1 \diamond \sigma_2 \diamond \sigma_4} \\
F^\dagger
\end{array} \tag{10.3.30}
$$

Consider the following two concatenate cartesian diagrams obtained by taking product of

Eq. (10.3.23) with F

$$X_{[k-1]} \xrightarrow{(\delta,\mathbf{P})} X_{[k-1]}^2 \xrightarrow{\imath_1} V'_{[k-1]} \xrightarrow{\imath_2} W'_{[k-1]} \xrightarrow{\imath_4} X_{[k-1]}$$
$$\mu_1 \downarrow \quad \mathfrak{S}_{1,[k]} \;\; \mu_2 \downarrow \quad \mathfrak{S}_{2,[k]} \;\; \mu_3 \downarrow \quad \mathfrak{S}_{3,[k]} \;\; F \downarrow$$
$$X_{[k-1]} \xrightarrow{\sigma_1} V_{[k-1]} \xrightarrow{\sigma_2} W_{[k-1]} \xrightarrow{\sigma_4} Z_{[k-1]} \qquad (10.3.31\mathrm{a})$$

$$X_{[k-1]} \xleftarrow{\imath_5} Y'_{[k-1]} \xleftarrow{\imath_3} V'_{[k-1]} \xleftarrow{\imath_1} X_{[k-1]}^2 \xleftarrow{(\delta,\mathbf{P})} X_{[k-1]}$$
$$F \downarrow \;\; \mathfrak{S}_{6,[k]} \;\; \mu_5 \downarrow \;\; \mathfrak{S}_{5,[k]} \;\; \mu_2 \downarrow \;\; \mathfrak{S}_{4,[k]} \;\; \mu_1 \downarrow$$
$$Z_{[k-1]} \xleftarrow{\sigma_5} Y_{[k-1]} \xleftarrow{\sigma_2} V_{[k-1]} \xleftarrow{\sigma_1} X_{[k-1]} \qquad (10.3.31\mathrm{b})$$

Then we have the following diagram of isomorphisms

$$
\begin{array}{ccc}
\sigma_1^\dagger \sigma_3^\dagger \sigma_5^\dagger & \xrightarrow{\;\alpha_{\mathfrak{S}_{[k]}}\;} & \sigma_1^\dagger \sigma_2^\dagger \sigma_4^\dagger \\[2pt]
\searrow \; \Upsilon_{F,\sigma_1\sigma_3\sigma_5}^{\mathfrak{S}_{4,[k]}\mathfrak{S}_{5,[k]}\mathfrak{S}_{6,[k]}} \quad \square_1 \quad \Upsilon_{F,\sigma_1\sigma_2\sigma_4}^{\mathfrak{S}_{1,[k]}\mathfrak{S}_{2,[k]}\mathfrak{S}_{3,[k]}} \; \swarrow & & \\[2pt]
F^\dagger & = & F^\dagger \\[2pt]
\rho_{\Delta\mu_1} \uparrow \;\; \square_3 \;\; \uparrow \rho_{\Delta\imath_1\imath_3\imath_5} & \square_2 & \rho_{\Delta\imath_1\imath_2\imath_4} \uparrow \;\; \square_4 \;\; \uparrow \rho_{\Delta\mu_1} \\[2pt]
\Delta\imath_1^\dagger \imath_3^\dagger \imath_5^\dagger F^\dagger & \xrightarrow{\;\alpha_{\mathfrak{S}_{7,[k]}}\;} & \Delta\imath_1^\dagger \imath_2^\dagger \imath_4^\dagger F^\dagger \\[2pt]
\nearrow \alpha_{\mathfrak{S}_{4,[k]}\mathfrak{S}_{5,[k]}\mathfrak{S}_{6,[k]}} \quad \square_5 \quad \alpha_{\mathfrak{S}_{1,[k]}\mathfrak{S}_{2,[k]}\mathfrak{S}_{3,[k]}} \nwarrow & & \\[2pt]
\Delta^\dagger \mu_1^\dagger \sigma_1^\dagger \sigma_3^\dagger \sigma_5^\dagger & \xrightarrow{\;\alpha_{\mathfrak{S}_{[k]}}\;} & \Delta^\dagger \mu_1^\dagger \sigma_1^\dagger \sigma_2^\dagger \sigma_4^\dagger
\end{array} \qquad (10.3.32)
$$

where $\Delta = (\delta,\mathbf{P})$ and $\mathfrak{S}_{7,[k]}$ is the cartesian square made by

$$
\begin{array}{ccc}
V'_{[k-1]} & \xrightarrow{\imath_3} & Y'_{[k-1]} \\
\imath_2 \downarrow & \mathfrak{S}_{7,[k]} & \imath_5 \downarrow \\
W'_{[k-1]} & \xrightarrow{\imath_4} & X_{[k-1]}
\end{array} \qquad (10.3.33)
$$

The outer border of Eq. (10.3.32) commutes from functorial reasons. From the definition of $\Upsilon_{F,\sigma_1\sigma_3\sigma_5}^{\mathfrak{S}_{4,[k]}\mathfrak{S}_{5,[k]}\mathfrak{S}_{6,[k]}}$ and $\Upsilon_{F,\sigma_1\sigma_2\sigma_4}^{\mathfrak{S}_{1,[k]}\mathfrak{S}_{2,[k]}\mathfrak{S}_{3,[k]}}$, diagrams $\square_3$ and $\square_4$ commute. By canceling the item $\Delta^\dagger$ in each vertex of the square $\square_5$, we can expand the square $\square_5$ as

$$
\begin{array}{ccccccc}
\mu_1^\dagger \sigma_1^\dagger \sigma_3^\dagger \sigma_5^\dagger & \xrightarrow{\alpha_{\mathfrak{S}_{1,[k]}}} & \imath_1^\dagger \mu_2^\dagger \sigma_3^\dagger \sigma_5^\dagger & \xrightarrow{\alpha_{\mathfrak{S}_{5,[k]}}} & \imath_1^\dagger \imath_3^\dagger \mu_5^\dagger \sigma_5^\dagger & \xrightarrow{\alpha_{\mathfrak{S}_{4,[k]}}} & \imath_1^\dagger \imath_3^\dagger \imath_5^\dagger F^\dagger \\[2pt]
\alpha_{\mathfrak{S}_{[k]}} \downarrow & & \alpha_{\mathfrak{S}_{[k]}} \downarrow & & & & \alpha_{\mathfrak{S}_{7,[k]}} \downarrow \\[2pt]
\mu_1^\dagger \sigma_1^\dagger \sigma_3^\dagger \sigma_5^\dagger & \xrightarrow{\alpha_{\mathfrak{S}_{1,[k]}}} & \imath_1^\dagger \mu_2^\dagger \sigma_3^\dagger \sigma_5^\dagger & \xrightarrow{\alpha_{\mathfrak{S}_{2,[k]}}} & \imath_1^\dagger \imath_3^\dagger \mu_5^\dagger \sigma_5^\dagger & \xrightarrow{\alpha_{\mathfrak{S}_{3,[k]}}} & \imath_1^\dagger \imath_3^\dagger \imath_5^\dagger F^\dagger
\end{array} \qquad (10.3.34)
$$

Since the left square commutes for functorial reasons and the right square commutes by Lemma 33, the square $\Box_5$ commutes.

Consider the following two diagrams

$$
\begin{array}{ccc}
\underline{X}_{[k-1]} & \xrightarrow{\Delta \diamond \imath_1} \underline{V}'_{[k-1]} \xrightarrow{\imath_2} \underline{W}'_{[k-1]} \\
& \imath_3 \downarrow \qquad\qquad \downarrow \imath_4 \\
& \underline{Y}'_{[k-1]} \xrightarrow{\imath_5} \underline{Z}'_{[k-1]} = \underline{X}_{[k-1]}
\end{array}
\tag{10.3.35a}
$$

$$
\begin{array}{ccc}
\Delta^\dagger \imath_1^\dagger \imath_3^\dagger \imath_5^\dagger & \xrightarrow{\alpha_{\mathfrak{S}_{[k]}}} & \Delta^\dagger \imath_1^\dagger \imath_2^\dagger \imath_4^\dagger \\
\rho_{\Delta \imath_1 \imath_3 \imath_5} \searrow & & \swarrow \rho_{\Delta \imath_1 \imath_2 \imath_4} \\
& \mathbf{1}_{\mathcal{D}_{\underline{X}_{[k-1]}}} &
\end{array}
\tag{10.3.35b}
$$

The diagram in Eq. (10.3.35a) is an instance of the cartesian diagram in Eq. (10.3.23) with nullity of σ_6. The diagram in Eq. (10.3.35b) corresponds to Eq. (10.3.24). By canceling $F^\dagger$ in all vertices of diagram $\S_2$, the results becomes the diagram shown in Eq. (10.3.35b). Hence, proving that $\S_1$ commutes, reduces to proving that the diagram in Eq. (10.3.35b) commutes.

Since the square $\Box_1$ commutes if and only if $\Box_2$ commutes, the commutativity of the diagrams in Eq. (10.3.35) implies the commutativity of the diagram in Eq. (10.3.24). Therefore, Lemma 38 is proved.

The last Lemma used to establish Lemma 36 is about the labeled map σ_1 in Eq. (10.3.23).

Lemma 39 *The sequence σ_1 can be assumed as a single map.*

PROOF. 68 *Let the labeled map F be $(|\sigma_1|, \mathbf{P})$, consider the following diagram*

$$
\begin{array}{ccc}
\sigma_1^\dagger \sigma_3^\dagger \sigma_5^\dagger & \xrightarrow{\alpha_{\mathfrak{S}_{[k]}}} & \sigma_1^\dagger \sigma_2^\dagger \sigma_4^\dagger \\
& \searrow \rho_{\sigma_1 \sigma_3 \sigma_5} \quad \rho_{\sigma_1 \sigma_2 \sigma_4} \swarrow & \\
\Upsilon^{\mathfrak{S}_{[k]}}_{F,\sigma_1} \downarrow & \mathbf{1}_{\mathcal{D}_{\underline{X}_{[k-1]}}} & \downarrow \Upsilon^{\mathfrak{S}_{[k]}}_{F,\sigma_1} \\
& \nearrow \rho_{F \sigma_3 \sigma_5} \quad \rho_{F \sigma_2 \sigma_4} \nwarrow & \\
F^\dagger \sigma_3^\dagger \sigma_5^\dagger & \xrightarrow{\alpha_{\mathfrak{S}_{[k]}}} & F^\dagger \sigma_2^\dagger \sigma_4^\dagger
\end{array}
\tag{10.3.36}
$$

The outer border commutes for functorial reasons. The two triangles on the left and right sides commute by Lemma 34. Therefore for the top triangle to commute, it suffices that the bottom triangle commutes.

Similarly, if the labeled map G becomes $(|\sigma_1|, \mathbf{O})$, consider the following diagram

$$\sigma_1^\dagger \sigma_3^\dagger \sigma_5^\dagger \quad \xrightarrow{\alpha_{\mathfrak{S}_{[k]}}} \quad \sigma_1^\dagger \sigma_2^\dagger \sigma_4^\dagger$$

$$\searrow \rho_{\sigma_1\sigma_3\sigma_5} \quad \rho_{\sigma_1\sigma_2\sigma_4} \swarrow$$

$$\Upsilon_{G,\sigma_1}^{\mathfrak{T}_{[k]}} \downarrow \qquad \mathbf{1}_{\mathcal{D}_{X_{[k-1]}}} \qquad \downarrow \Upsilon_{G,\sigma_1}^{\mathfrak{T}_{[k]}}$$

$$\nearrow \rho_{F\sigma_3\sigma_5} \quad \rho_{F\sigma_2\sigma_4} \nwarrow$$

$$G^\dagger \sigma_3^\dagger \sigma_5^\dagger \quad \xrightarrow{\alpha_{\mathfrak{S}_{[k]}}} \quad G^\dagger \sigma_2^\dagger \sigma_4^\dagger \qquad\qquad (10.3.37)$$

The two triangles on the left and right sides commute by Lemma 34. For the top triangle to commute, it suffices that the bottom triangle commutes. Finally, from both cases of $(|\sigma_1|, \mathbf{P})$ and $(|\sigma_1|, \mathbf{O})$, these are precisely the reduction of σ_1 as a single map.

The proof of Lemma 36 is ready to present now.

PROOF. 69 *From Lemmas 37, 38 and 39, the diagram provided by Eq. (10.3.23) can be reduced as*

$$X_{[k-1]} \xrightarrow{\sigma_1} V_{[k-1]} \xrightarrow{\sigma_2} W_{[k-1]}$$

$$\sigma_3 \downarrow \quad \mathfrak{S}_{[k]} \quad \downarrow \sigma_4$$

$$Y_{[k-1]} \xrightarrow{\sigma_5} X_{[k-1]} \qquad\qquad (10.3.38)$$

where each labeled map has length one and σ_1 is assumed with label $\mathbf{O}$ without loss of generality. Moreover, the diagram provided by Eq. (10.3.24) can be reduced as

$$\sigma_1^\dagger \sigma_3^\dagger \sigma_5^\dagger \quad \xrightarrow{\alpha_{\mathfrak{S}_{[k]}}} \quad \sigma_1^\dagger \sigma_2^\dagger \sigma_4^\dagger$$

$$\searrow \rho_{\sigma_1\sigma_3\sigma_5} \quad \rho_{\sigma_1\sigma_2\sigma_4} \swarrow$$

$$\mathbf{1}_{\mathcal{D}_{X_{[k-1]}}} \qquad\qquad (10.3.39)$$

Set $\imath_4$ as $(\sigma_1 \diamond \sigma_2, \mathbf{O})$ and $\imath_5$ as $(\sigma_1 \diamond \sigma_3, \mathbf{O})$, then we consider the fiber product of labeled maps
$X_{[k-1]} \xrightarrow{\imath_4} W_{[k-1]} \xrightarrow{\sigma_4} X_{[k-1]}$ *and* $X_{[k-1]} \xrightarrow{\imath_5} Y_{[k-1]} \xrightarrow{\sigma_5} X_{[k-1]}$

$$X_{[k-1]} \xrightarrow{\imath_5} Y_{[k-1]} \xrightarrow{\sigma_5} X_{[k-1]}$$

$$\imath_4 \downarrow \quad \mathfrak{S}_{1,[k]} \quad \imath_3 \downarrow \quad \mathfrak{S}_{2,[k]} \quad \imath_4 \downarrow$$

$$W_{[k-1]} \xrightarrow{\imath_2} V_{[k-1]} \xrightarrow{\sigma_2} W_{[k-1]}$$

$$\sigma_4 \downarrow \quad \mathfrak{S}_{3,[k]} \quad \sigma_3 \downarrow \quad \mathfrak{S}_{[k]} \quad \sigma_4 \downarrow$$

$$X_{[k-1]} \xrightarrow{\imath_5} Y_{[k-1]} \xrightarrow{\sigma_5} X_{[k-1]} \qquad\qquad (10.3.40)$$

where ι_2 and ι_3 are induced maps from above fiber product.

By defining another two natural isomorphisms $\pi_1 : \sigma_1^\dagger \longrightarrow \iota_4^\dagger \sigma_2^\dagger$ and $\pi_2 : \iota_4^\dagger \sigma_2^\dagger \longrightarrow \iota_5^\dagger \iota_3^\dagger$, one obtains the following diagram

$$
\begin{array}{ccccc}
\sigma_1^\dagger \sigma_3^\dagger \sigma_5^\dagger & \xrightarrow{\;\alpha_{\mathfrak{S}_{[k]}}\;} & & & \sigma_1^\dagger \sigma_2^\dagger \sigma_4^\dagger \\[4pt]
\pi_1 \downarrow & & & & \downarrow \pi_1 \\[4pt]
\iota_4^\dagger \iota_2^\dagger \sigma_3^\dagger \sigma_5^\dagger & \xrightarrow{\;\alpha_{\mathfrak{S}_{[k]}}\;} & & & \iota_4^\dagger \iota_2^\dagger \sigma_2^\dagger \sigma_4^\dagger \\[4pt]
\searrow \alpha_{\mathfrak{S}_{3,[k]}} & & \S1 & \rho_{\iota_4\iota_2} \swarrow & \\[4pt]
& \iota_4^\dagger \sigma_4^\dagger \iota_5^\dagger \sigma_5^\dagger & \xrightarrow{\;\rho_{\iota_5\sigma_5}\;} & \iota_4^\dagger \sigma_4^\dagger & \\[4pt]
& & & \rho_{\iota_4\sigma_4} \swarrow & \\[6pt]
\pi_2 \downarrow \;\; \S2 \;\; \downarrow \rho_{\iota_4\sigma_4} & & \mathbf{1}_{\mathcal{D}_{X_{[k-1]}}} & \rho_{\iota_5\sigma_5} \uparrow \;\; \S3 \;\; \downarrow \pi_2 \\[4pt]
& \nearrow \rho_{\iota_5\sigma_5} & & \\[4pt]
\iota_5^\dagger \sigma_5^\dagger & \xleftarrow{\;\rho_{\iota_4\sigma_4}\;} & & \iota_5^\dagger \sigma_5^\dagger \iota_4^\dagger \sigma_4^\dagger \\[4pt]
\nearrow \rho_{\iota_3\sigma_3} & & \S4 & \alpha_{\mathfrak{S}_{2,[k]}} \nwarrow \\[4pt]
\iota_5^\dagger \iota_3^\dagger \sigma_3^\dagger \sigma_5^\dagger & \xrightarrow{\;\mathfrak{S}_{[k]}\;} & & \iota_5^\dagger \iota_3^\dagger \sigma_2^\dagger \sigma_4^\dagger
\end{array}
$$

$$(10.3.41)$$

The unmarked subdiagrams commute for functorial reasons. By canceling $\iota_4^\dagger$, commutativity of the diagram $\S1$ is based on the following diagram

$$
\begin{array}{ccccc}
\underline{W_{[k]}} & \xrightarrow{\;\iota_2\;} & \underline{V_{[k]}} & \xrightarrow{\;\sigma_2\;} & \underline{W_{[k]}} \\[4pt]
\sigma_4 \downarrow & \mathfrak{S}_{3,[k]} \;\; \sigma_3 \downarrow & \mathfrak{S}_{[k]} \;\; \sigma_4 \downarrow & & \\[4pt]
\underline{X_{[k]}} & \xrightarrow{\;\iota_5\;} & \underline{Y_{[k]}} & \xrightarrow{\;\sigma_5\;} & \underline{X_{[k]}}
\end{array}
\qquad (10.3.42)
$$

By canceling $\sigma_5^\dagger$, commutativity of the diagram $\S2$ is based on the following diagram

$$
\begin{array}{ccc}
\underline{X_{[k]}} & \xrightarrow{\;\iota_5\;} & \underline{Y_{[k]}} \\[4pt]
\iota_4 \downarrow & \mathfrak{S}_{1,[k]} \;\; \iota_3 \downarrow & \\[4pt]
\underline{W_{[k]}} & \xrightarrow{\;\iota_2\;} & \underline{V_{[k]}} \\[4pt]
\sigma_4 \downarrow & \mathfrak{S}_{3,[k]} \;\; \sigma_3 \downarrow & \\[4pt]
\underline{X_{[k]}} & \xrightarrow{\;\iota_5\;} & \underline{Y_{[k]}}
\end{array}
\qquad (10.3.43)
$$

By canceling $\sigma_4^\dagger$, commutativity of the diagram $\S_3$ is based on the following diagram

$$
\begin{array}{ccccc}
\underline{X_{[k]}} & \xrightarrow{\imath_5} & \underline{Y_{[k]}} & \xrightarrow{\sigma_5} & \underline{X_{[k]}} \\
\imath_4 \downarrow & \mathfrak{S}_{1,[k]} & \imath_3 \downarrow & \mathfrak{S}_{2,[k]} & \imath_4 \downarrow \\
\underline{W_{[k]}} & \xrightarrow{\imath_2} & \underline{V_{[k]}} & \xrightarrow{\sigma_2} & \underline{W_{[k]}}
\end{array}
\tag{10.3.44}
$$

By canceling $\imath_5^\dagger$, commutativity of the diagram $\S_4$ is based on the following diagram

$$
\begin{array}{ccc}
\underline{Y_{[k]}} & \xrightarrow{\sigma_5} & \underline{X_{[k]}} \\
\imath_3 \downarrow & \mathfrak{S}_{12[k]} & \imath_4 \downarrow \\
\underline{V_{[k]}} & \xrightarrow{\sigma_2} & \underline{W_{[k]}} \\
\sigma_3 \downarrow & \mathfrak{S}_{[k]} & \sigma_4 \downarrow \\
\underline{Y_{[k]}} & \xrightarrow{\sigma_5} & \underline{X_{[k]}}
\end{array}
\tag{10.3.45}
$$

Hence, the diagram in Eq. (10.3.41) commutes.

Consider the following staircase diagram induced by the labeled map $\sigma_1 \diamond \sigma_2 \diamond \sigma_4$ as

$$
\begin{array}{l}
\underline{X_{[k-1]}} \\
\kappa_1 \downarrow \\
\quad \bullet_2 \xrightarrow{\kappa_2} \underline{X_{[k-1]}} \\
\kappa_3 \downarrow \qquad \imath_5 \downarrow \\
\quad \bullet_1 \xrightarrow{\kappa_4} \underline{Y_{[k-1]}} \xrightarrow{\sigma_5} \underline{X_{[k-1]}} \\
\kappa_5 \downarrow \qquad \imath_3 \downarrow \; \mathfrak{S}_{2,[k]} \; \imath_4 \downarrow \\
\underline{X_{[k-1]}} \xrightarrow{\sigma_1} \underline{V_{[k-1]}} \xrightarrow{\sigma_2} \underline{W_{[k-1]}} \xrightarrow{\sigma_4} \underline{X_{[k-1]}}
\end{array}
\tag{10.3.46}
$$

where κ_i are constructed by cartesian condition. Then, we have the following diagram of isomorphisms

$$
\begin{array}{ccccccc}
\sigma_1^\dagger \sigma_2^\dagger \sigma_4^\dagger & \xrightarrow{\pi_1 \pi_2} & \imath_5^\dagger \imath_3^\dagger \sigma_2^\dagger \sigma_4^\dagger & \xrightarrow{\alpha_{\mathfrak{S}_{2,[k]}}} & \imath_5^\dagger \sigma_5^\dagger \imath_4^\dagger \sigma_4^\dagger & \xrightarrow{\rho_{\imath_5 \sigma_5} \rho_{\imath_4 \sigma_4}} & \mathbf{1}_{\mathcal{D}_{\underline{X_{[k-1]}}}} \\
\rho_{\kappa_1 \kappa_3 \kappa_5} \uparrow & & \rho_{\kappa_1 \kappa_2} \uparrow & & \rho_{\kappa_1 \kappa_2} \uparrow & & \| \\
\kappa_1^\dagger \kappa_3^\dagger \kappa_5^\dagger \sigma_1^\dagger \sigma_2^\dagger \sigma_4^\dagger & \xrightarrow{\alpha_{\mathfrak{S}_{4,[k]}}} & \kappa_1^\dagger \kappa_2^\dagger \imath_5^\dagger \imath_3^\dagger \sigma_2^\dagger \sigma_4^\dagger & \xrightarrow{\alpha_{\mathfrak{S}_{2,[k]}}} & \kappa_1^\dagger \kappa_2^\dagger \imath_5^\dagger \sigma_5^\dagger \imath_4^\dagger \sigma_4^\dagger & \xrightarrow{\rho_{\kappa_1 \kappa_2} \rho_{\imath_5 \sigma_5} \rho_{\imath_4 \sigma_4}} & \mathbf{1}_{\mathcal{D}_{\underline{X_{[k-1]}}}}
\end{array}
\tag{10.3.47}
$$

where $\mathfrak{S}_{4,[k]}$ is the cartesian square made by objects $\bullet_2, \underline{X_{[k-1]}}, \underline{V_{[k-1]}}, \underline{X_{[k-1]}}$. Since each rectangle in Eq. (10.3.47) commutes due to functorail reason, the diagram provided by Eq. (10.3.47) commutes. Hence, the top row of Eq. (10.3.47) gives the right arrow of Eq. (10.3.39).

Now, we will prove the right arrow of Eq. (10.3.39). Consider the following staircase diagram induced by the labeled map $\sigma_1 \diamond \sigma_3 \diamond \sigma_5$ as

$$
\begin{array}{l}
\underline{X_{[k-1]}} \\[2pt]
\kappa_1' \downarrow \\[4pt]
\quad \bullet_2' \xrightarrow{\;\kappa_2'\;} \underline{X_{[k-1]}} \\[2pt]
\kappa_3' \downarrow \qquad \imath_4 \downarrow \\[4pt]
\quad \bullet_1' \xrightarrow{\;\kappa_4'\;} \underline{W_{[k-1]}} \xrightarrow{\;\sigma_4\;} \underline{X_{[k-1]}} \\[2pt]
\kappa_5' \downarrow \qquad \imath_2 \downarrow \;\; \mathfrak{S}_{3,[k]} \;\; \imath_5 \downarrow \\[4pt]
\underline{X_{[k-1]}} \xrightarrow{\;\sigma_1\;} \underline{V_{[k-1]}} \xrightarrow{\;\sigma_3\;} \underline{Y_{[k-1]}} \xrightarrow{\;\sigma_5\;} \underline{X_{[k-1]}}
\end{array}
$$

$$(10.3.48)$$

where κ_i' are constructed by cartesian condition based on $\sigma_1 \diamond \sigma_3 \diamond \sigma_5$. Then, we have the following diagram of isomorphisms

$$
\begin{array}{ccccccc}
\sigma_1^\dagger \sigma_3^\dagger \sigma_5^\dagger & \xrightarrow{\;\pi_1\;} & \imath_4^\dagger \imath_2^\dagger \sigma_3^\dagger \sigma_5^\dagger & \xrightarrow{\;\alpha_{\mathfrak{S}_{3,[k]}}\;} & \imath_4^\dagger \sigma_4^\dagger \imath_5^\dagger \sigma_5^\dagger & \xrightarrow{\;\rho_{\imath_4 \sigma_4} \rho_{\imath_5 \sigma_5}\;} & \mathbf{1}_{\mathcal{D}_{X_{[k-1]}}} \\[6pt]
\rho_{\kappa_1' \kappa_3' \kappa_5'} \uparrow & & \rho_{\kappa_1' \kappa_2'} \uparrow & & \rho_{\kappa_1' \kappa_2'} \uparrow & & \| \\[6pt]
\kappa_1'^\dagger \kappa_3'^\dagger \kappa_5'^\dagger \sigma_1^\dagger \sigma_3^\dagger \sigma_5^\dagger & \xrightarrow{\;\alpha_{\mathfrak{S}_{4,[k]}'}\;} & \kappa_1'^\dagger \kappa_2'^\dagger \imath_4^\dagger \imath_2^\dagger \sigma_3^\dagger \sigma_5^\dagger & \xrightarrow{\;\alpha_{\mathfrak{S}_{3,[k]}}\;} & \kappa_1'^\dagger \kappa_2'^\dagger \imath_4^\dagger \sigma_4^\dagger \imath_5^\dagger \sigma_5^\dagger & \xrightarrow{\;\rho_{\kappa_1' \kappa_2'} \rho_{\imath_4 \sigma_4} \rho_{\imath_5 \sigma_5}\;} & \mathbf{1}_{\mathcal{D}_{X_{[k-1]}}}
\end{array}
$$

$$(10.3.49)$$

where $\mathfrak{S}_{4,[k]}'$ is the cartesian square made by objects $\bullet_2', \underline{X_{[k-1]}}, \underline{V_{[k-1]}}, \underline{X_{[k-1]}}$. Since each rectangle in Eq. (10.3.49) commutes due to functorail reason, the diagram provided by Eq. (10.3.49) commutes. Hence, the top row of Eq. (10.3.49) gives the left arrow of Eq. (10.3.39). Therefore, we have shown that the diagram in Eq. (10.3.39) commutes. This completes the proof of Lemma 36.

10.3.4 Proof of Cancelation Rule and its Implications

Theorem 35 *(Cancelation Rule) Given three labeled sequences $\sigma_1, \sigma_2, \sigma_3$ such that $|\sigma_1| = |\sigma_2| = |\sigma_3|$, the isomorphism $\Upsilon_{-,-}^-$ satisfies the cancelation rule below:*

$$
\Upsilon_{\sigma_3,\sigma_2}^{\mathfrak{V}_{[k]}} \Upsilon_{\sigma_2,\sigma_1}^{\mathfrak{S}_{[k]}} = \Upsilon_{\sigma_3,\sigma_1}^{\mathfrak{U}_{[k]}}
$$

$$(10.3.50)$$

with respect to each choice of product diagrams $\mathfrak{S}_{[k]}, \mathfrak{U}_{[k]}, \mathfrak{V}_{[k]}$ at dimension k.

PROOF. 70 *Let $\sigma_1, \sigma_2, \sigma_3$ be labeled sequences having the same target $\underline{Y_{[k-1]}}$ such that all the source of σ_i is $\underline{X_{[k-1]}}$ for $1 \leq i \leq 3$. Then, according to Lemma 33, we have the following* cartesian cube as

$$
\begin{array}{ccc}
\underline{Z_{[k-1]}} & \xrightarrow{\pi_1} & \bullet_1 \\
\searrow \pi_3 \quad \mathfrak{S}_{5,[k]} & \gamma_{13} \swarrow & \\
\bullet_2 \xrightarrow{\gamma_{23}} & \underline{X_{[k-1]}} & \\
\pi_2 \downarrow \mathfrak{S}_{1,[k]} \downarrow \gamma_{32} \quad \mathfrak{S}_{3,[k]} & \sigma_2 \downarrow \mathfrak{S}_{6,[k]} \downarrow \gamma_{31} \\
\underline{X_{[k-1]}} \xrightarrow{\sigma_1} & \underline{Y_{[k-1]}} & \\
\nearrow \gamma_{12} \quad \mathfrak{S}_{2,[k]} & \sigma_3 \nwarrow & \\
\bullet_3 \xrightarrow{\gamma_{21}} & \underline{X_{[k-1]}} &
\end{array}
\tag{10.3.51}
$$

moreover, we have four more diagonal maps from $\underline{X_{[k-1]}}$ to $\underline{Z_{[k-1]}}, \bullet_1, \bullet_2, \bullet_3$ as

- $\underline{X_{[k-1]}} \xrightarrow{\sigma_0} \underline{Z_{[k-1]}}$;

- $\underline{X_{[k-1]}} \xrightarrow{\sigma_1} \bullet_1$;

- $\underline{X_{[k-1]}} \xrightarrow{\sigma_2} \bullet_2$;

- $\underline{X_{[k-1]}} \xrightarrow{\sigma_3} \bullet_3$.

Then we have the following diagram of isomorphisms.

$$
\begin{array}{ccc}
\sigma_0^\dagger \pi_2^\dagger \gamma_{12}^\dagger \sigma_1^\dagger & \xrightarrow{\alpha_{\mathfrak{S}_{2,[k]}}} & \sigma_0^\dagger \pi_2^\dagger \gamma_{21}^\dagger \sigma_3^\dagger \\
\searrow \rho_{\delta_0 \diamond \pi_2 \diamond \gamma_{12}} \sigma_1^\dagger & \rho_{\delta_0 \diamond \pi_2 \diamond \gamma_{21}} \sigma_3^\dagger \swarrow & \\
\alpha_{\mathfrak{S}_{1,[k]}} \uparrow \quad \sigma_1^\dagger & \xrightarrow{\Upsilon^{\mathfrak{S}_{2,[k]}}_{\sigma_3,\sigma_1}} \quad \sigma_3^\dagger & \downarrow \alpha_{\mathfrak{S}_{4,[k]}} \\
\nearrow \rho_{\delta_0 \diamond \pi_3 \diamond \gamma_{32}} \sigma_1^\dagger & \rho_{\delta_0 \diamond \pi_1 \diamond \gamma_{31}} \sigma_3^\dagger \nwarrow & \\
\sigma_0^\dagger \pi_3^\dagger \gamma_{32}^\dagger \sigma_1^\dagger \quad \downarrow \Upsilon^{\mathfrak{S}_{3,[k]}}_{\sigma_2,\sigma_1} & \Upsilon^{\mathfrak{S}_{6,[k]}}_{\sigma_3,\sigma_2} \uparrow \quad \sigma_0^\dagger \pi_1^\dagger \gamma_{31}^\dagger \sigma_3^\dagger \\
\alpha_{\mathfrak{S}_{3,[k]}} \downarrow \quad \sigma_2^\dagger & = \quad \sigma_2^\dagger & \uparrow \alpha_{\mathfrak{S}_{6,[k]}} \\
\nearrow \rho_{\delta_0 \diamond \pi_3 \diamond \gamma_{23}} \sigma_2^\dagger & \rho_{\delta_0 \diamond \pi_1 \diamond \gamma_{13}} \sigma_2^\dagger \nwarrow & \\
\sigma_0^\dagger \pi_3^\dagger \gamma_{23}^\dagger \sigma_2^\dagger & \xrightarrow{\alpha_{\mathfrak{S}_{5,[k]}}} & \sigma_0^\dagger \pi_1^\dagger \gamma_{13}^\dagger \sigma_2^\dagger
\end{array}
\tag{10.3.52}
$$

We claim that the inner rectangle, which is made by $\sigma_1^\dagger, \sigma_2^\dagger, \sigma_3^\dagger$, in Eq. (10.3.52) commutes.

By canceling $\delta_0^\dagger$ at each vertex of the outer border, the outer border, which is a hexagon, commutes by using the Lemma 33. The following diagrams

- 1. composed by $\sigma_0^\dagger \pi_2^\dagger \gamma_{12}^\dagger \sigma_1^\dagger$, $\sigma_1^\dagger$ and $\sigma_0^\dagger \pi_3^\dagger \gamma_{32}^\dagger \sigma_1^\dagger$,

- *2. composed by $\sigma_0^\dagger \pi_2^\dagger \gamma_{21}^\dagger \sigma_3^\dagger$, $\sigma_3^\dagger$ and $\sigma_0^\dagger \pi_1^\dagger \gamma_{31}^\dagger \sigma_3^\dagger$,*

- *3. composed by $\sigma_0^\dagger \pi_3^\dagger \gamma_{23}^\dagger \sigma_2^\dagger$, $\sigma_2^\dagger$ and $\sigma_0^\dagger \pi_1^\dagger \gamma_{13}^\dagger \sigma_2^\dagger$,*

commute due to Lemma 36. For those three 4-vertices diagrams

- *1. composed by $\sigma_0^\dagger \pi_2^\dagger \gamma_{12}^\dagger \sigma_1^\dagger$, $\sigma_1^\dagger$, $\sigma_3^\dagger$, and $\sigma_0^\dagger \pi_2^\dagger \gamma_{21}^\dagger \sigma_3^\dagger$,*

- *2. composed by $\sigma_0^\dagger \pi_3^\dagger \gamma_{23}^\dagger \sigma_2^\dagger$, $\sigma_2^\dagger$, $\sigma_1^\dagger$, and $\sigma_0^\dagger \pi_3^\dagger \gamma_{32}^\dagger \sigma_1^\dagger$,*

- *3. composed by $\sigma_0^\dagger \pi_1^\dagger \gamma_{13}^\dagger \sigma_2^\dagger$, $\sigma_2^\dagger$, $\sigma_3^\dagger$, and $\sigma_0^\dagger \pi_1^\dagger \gamma_{31}^\dagger \sigma_3^\dagger$,*

commute due to Lemma 34. Let us illustrate the 4-vertices diagram composed by $\sigma_0^\dagger \pi_2^\dagger \gamma_{12}^\dagger \sigma_1^\dagger$, $\sigma_1^\dagger$, $\sigma_3^\dagger$, and $\sigma_0^\dagger \pi_2^\dagger \gamma_{21}^\dagger \sigma_3^\dagger$ only since the other three cases can be obtained similarly.

Consider the following diagram

$$
\begin{array}{ccc}
\sigma_0^\dagger \pi_2^\dagger \gamma_{12}^\dagger \sigma_1^\dagger & \xrightarrow{\alpha_{\mathfrak{S}_{2,[k]}}} & \sigma_0^\dagger \pi_2^\dagger \gamma_{21}^\dagger \sigma_3^\dagger \\
{}_{\rho_{\delta_0 \diamond \pi_2 \diamond \gamma_{12}} \sigma_1^\dagger} \downarrow \searrow {}^{\Upsilon^{\mathfrak{S}'_{1,[k]}}_{\delta_3, \delta_0 \diamond \pi_2}} & & {}^{\Upsilon^{\mathfrak{S}'_{1,[k]}}_{\delta_3, \delta_0 \diamond \pi_2}} \swarrow \downarrow {}_{\rho_{\delta_0 \diamond \pi_2 \diamond \gamma_{21}} \sigma_3^\dagger} \\
\sigma_1^\dagger \xleftarrow{\rho_{\delta_3 \diamond \gamma_{12}} \sigma_1^\dagger} \delta_3^\dagger \gamma_{12}^\dagger \sigma_1^\dagger & \xrightarrow{\alpha_{\mathfrak{S}_{2,[k]}}} & \delta_3^\dagger \gamma_{21}^\dagger \sigma_3^\dagger \xrightarrow{\rho_{\delta_3 \diamond \gamma_{21}} \sigma_3^\dagger} \sigma_3^\dagger
\end{array}
\tag{10.3.53}
$$

Since the right triangle diagram, by canceling the common term $\sigma_3^\dagger$, is

$$
\begin{array}{c}
\sigma_0^\dagger \pi_2^\dagger \gamma_{21}^\dagger \\
{}^{\Upsilon^{\mathfrak{S}'_{1,[k]}}_{\delta_3, \delta_0 \diamond \pi_2}} \swarrow \downarrow {}_{\rho_{\delta_0 \diamond \pi_2 \diamond \gamma_{21}}} \\
\delta_3^\dagger \gamma_{21}^\dagger \xrightarrow{\rho_{\delta_3 \diamond \gamma_{21}}} \mathbf{1}_{\mathcal{D}_{X_{[k-1]}}}
\end{array}
\tag{10.3.54}
$$

which commutes due to Lemma 34. Same argument can be applied to the left triangle diagram. Then, the 4-vertices diagram composed by $\sigma_0^\dagger \pi_2^\dagger \gamma_{12}^\dagger \sigma_1^\dagger$, $\sigma_1^\dagger$, $\sigma_3^\dagger$, and $\sigma_0^\dagger \pi_2^\dagger \gamma_{21}^\dagger \sigma_3^\dagger$ commutes.

Therefore, the inner rectangle in Eq. (10.3.52) commutes which implies that $\Upsilon^{\mathfrak{V}_{[k]}}_{\sigma_3, \sigma_2} \Upsilon^{\mathfrak{S}_{[k]}}_{\sigma_2, \sigma_1} = \Upsilon^{\mathfrak{U}_{[k]}}_{\sigma_3, \sigma_1}$.

Proposition 1 *The isomorphism $\Upsilon^{\mathfrak{S}_{[k]}}_{\sigma_1, \sigma_2}$ is independent of the choice of $\mathfrak{S}_{[k]}$. Moreover, the isomorphism $\Upsilon^{\mathfrak{S}_{[k]}}_{-,-}$ is reflexive, transitive and symmetric.*

PROOF. **71** *From Theorem 35, we have*

$$
\Upsilon^{\mathfrak{S}_{[k]}}_{\sigma, \sigma} \Upsilon^{\mathfrak{S}_{[k]}}_{\sigma, \sigma} = \Upsilon^{\mathfrak{S}_{[k]}}_{\sigma, \sigma},
\tag{10.3.55}
$$

and $\Upsilon^{\mathfrak{S}_{[k]}}_{\sigma, \sigma}$ is an identity.

If $\mathfrak{S}_{[k]}$ and $\mathfrak{S}'_{[k]}$ are two diagrams such that $\Upsilon^-_{\sigma_1,\sigma_2}$ is defined. We have

$$\Upsilon^{\mathfrak{S}_{[k]}}_{\sigma_1,\sigma_2}\Upsilon^{\mathfrak{T}_{[k]}}_{\sigma_2,\sigma_2} = \Upsilon^{\mathfrak{S}'_{[k]}}_{\sigma_1,\sigma_2}, \tag{10.3.56}$$

and since $\Upsilon^{\mathfrak{T}_{[k]}}_{\sigma,\sigma}$ is an identity, hence, $\Upsilon^{\mathfrak{S}_{[k]}}_{\sigma_1,\sigma_2} = \Upsilon^{\mathfrak{S}'_{[k]}}_{\sigma_1,\sigma_2}$.

From Theorem 35 again, we have

- $\Upsilon^{\mathfrak{S}_{[k]}}_{\sigma,\sigma}$ *is an identity;*

- $\Upsilon^{\mathfrak{S}_{[k]}}_{\sigma_1,\sigma_3}$ *if* $\Upsilon^{\mathfrak{S}_{[k]}}_{\sigma_1,\sigma_2}$ *and* $\Upsilon^{\mathfrak{S}'_{[k]}}_{\sigma_2,\sigma_3}$ *hold;*

- $\Upsilon^{\mathfrak{S}_{[k]}}_{\sigma_1,\sigma_2} = \Upsilon^{\mathfrak{S}^{-1}_{[k]}}_{\sigma_2,\sigma_1}$.

Therefore, the isomorphism $\Upsilon^{\mathfrak{S}_{[k]}}_{-,-}$ is reflexive, transitive and symmetric.

10.4   Extension of Algebraic Invenrelation Systems through Perspectives

The main goal of this section is to prove extension theorem of parameterized algebraic invenrelation systems.

10.4.1   Expression $\chi_{-,-}$, ρ_- and $\alpha_{\mathfrak{S}_{[k]}}$ by $\Upsilon_{-,-}$

In Proposition 1, we have showed that $\Upsilon^{\mathfrak{S}_{[k]}}_{-,-}$ is independent of choosing $\mathfrak{S}_{[k]}$. In the later on of this section, we will adopt the notation $\Upsilon_{-,-}$, instead of the notation $\Upsilon^{\mathfrak{S}_{[k]}}_{-,-}$. The purpose of this section is to express $\chi_{-,-}$, ρ_- and $\alpha_{\mathfrak{S}_{[k]}}$ by $\Upsilon_{-,-}$.

Following Lemma is required to prove expressions of $\chi_{-,-}$ and ρ_- by $\Upsilon_{-,-}$.

Lemma 40 *Let σ_1 be the sequence $X_{[k-1]} \xrightarrow{F_1} Y_{[k-1]} \xrightarrow{F_2} Z_{[k-1]} \xrightarrow{F_3} X_{[k-1]}$ and σ_2 be the sequence $X_{[k-1]} \xrightarrow{F_1} Y_{[k-1]} \xrightarrow{F_4} X_{[k-1]}$ such that F_2, F_3, F_4 have same label (**O** or **P**) with $|F_3||F_2| = |F_4|$. Then the following diagram commutes*

$$
\begin{array}{ccc}
F_1^\dagger F_2^\dagger F_3^\dagger & \xrightarrow{\chi_{F_2,F_3}} & F_1^\dagger F_4^\dagger \\
{}_{\rho_{\sigma_1}}\searrow & & \swarrow{}_{\rho_{\sigma_2}} \\
& \mathbf{1}_{\mathcal{D}_{X_{[k-1]}}} &
\end{array}
\tag{10.4.1}
$$

PROOF. 72 *Consider the following staircase diagram induced by the labeled map* $F_1 \diamond F_2 \diamond F_3$
as

$$
\begin{array}{ccccc}
\underline{X}_{[k-1]} & & & & \\
\kappa_1 \downarrow & & & & \\
\underline{X}''_{[k-1]} & \xrightarrow{\kappa_2} & \underline{X}_{[k-1]} & & \\
\kappa_3 \downarrow & & \kappa_4 \downarrow & & \\
\underline{X}'_{[k-1]} & \mathfrak{S}_{[k]} \; \underline{Y}'_{[k-1]} & \xrightarrow{\kappa_6} & \underline{X}_{[k-1]} & \\
\kappa_7 \downarrow & \kappa_8 \downarrow & & \kappa_9 \downarrow & \\
\underline{X}_{[k-1]} & \xrightarrow{F_1} & \underline{Y}_{[k-1]} & \xrightarrow{F_2} & \underline{Z}_{[k-1]} & \xrightarrow{F_3} & \underline{X}_{[k-1]}
\end{array}
$$

$$(10.4.2)$$

where κ_i *are constructed by cartesian condition. Then, we have the following diagram of isomorphisms*

$$
\begin{array}{ccccc}
\kappa_3^\dagger \kappa_7^\dagger F_1^\dagger F_2^\dagger F_3^\dagger & \xrightarrow{\alpha_{\mathfrak{S}_{[k]}}} & \kappa_2^\dagger \kappa_4^\dagger \kappa_8^\dagger F_2^\dagger F_3^\dagger & \longrightarrow & \kappa_2^\dagger \kappa_4^\dagger \kappa_6^\dagger \kappa_9^\dagger F_3^\dagger \\
\| & & \downarrow & & \downarrow \\
\kappa_3^\dagger \kappa_7^\dagger F_1^\dagger (F_3 F_2)^\dagger & \xrightarrow{\alpha_{\mathfrak{S}_{[k]}}} & \kappa_2^\dagger (\kappa_8 \kappa_4)^\dagger (F_3 F_2)^\dagger & \longrightarrow & \kappa_2^\dagger
\end{array}
$$

$$(10.4.3)$$

where the right square is based on Eqs. (10.1.12) and (10.1.13). Hence, by canceling the term $\kappa_2^\dagger$ *in each vertex of the right square in Eq. (10.4.3), one has*

$$
\begin{array}{ccc}
F_1^\dagger F_2^\dagger F_3^\dagger & \longrightarrow & \kappa_4^\dagger \kappa_6^\dagger \kappa_9^\dagger F_3^\dagger \\
\downarrow & & \downarrow \\
F_1^\dagger F_4^\dagger & \longrightarrow & \mathbf{1}_{\mathcal{D}\underline{X}_{[k-1]}}
\end{array}
$$

$$(10.4.4)$$

which proves Lemma 40.

The following theorem is about expressing $\chi_{-,-}$ by $\Upsilon_{-,-}$.

Theorem 36 *Let* $\underline{X}_{[k-1]} \xrightarrow{F_1} \underline{Y}_{[k-1]} \xrightarrow{F_2} \underline{Z}_{[k-1]}$ *be maps having same label* λ. *If* F_3 *is* $(|F_2||F_1|, \lambda)$, *then we have* $\chi_{F_1, F_2} = \Upsilon_{F_3, F_1 \diamond F_2}$.

390

PROOF. 73 *Consider the following diagram*

$$X_{\underline{[k-1]}} \xrightarrow{\Delta} X_{\underline{[k-1]}} \times_{Z_{\underline{[k-1]}}} X_{\underline{[k-1]}} \xrightarrow{\grave{F}_1} Y_{\underline{[k-1]}} \times_{Z_{\underline{[k-1]}}} X_{\underline{[k-1]}} \xrightarrow{\grave{F}_2} X_{\underline{[k-1]}}$$

$$\grave{F}_3 \downarrow \qquad\qquad \mathfrak{S}_{[k]} \qquad\qquad F_3 \downarrow$$

$$X_{\underline{[k-1]}} \xrightarrow{F_1} Y_{\underline{[k-1]}} \xrightarrow{F_2} Z_{\underline{[k-1]}} \qquad (10.4.5)$$

then we have following diagram of isomorphisms

$$F_1^\dagger F_2^\dagger \;=\; \Delta^\dagger \grave{F}_3^\dagger F_1^\dagger F_2^\dagger \xrightarrow{\alpha_{\mathfrak{S}_{[k]}}} \Delta^\dagger \grave{F}_1^\dagger \grave{F}_2^\dagger F_3^\dagger \;=\; F_3^\dagger$$

$$\chi_{F_1,F_2}\downarrow \qquad \chi_{F_1,F_2}\downarrow \qquad\qquad \downarrow \chi_{F_1,F_2} \qquad \|$$

$$F_3^\dagger \;=\; \Delta^\dagger \grave{F}_3^\dagger F_3^\dagger \;=\; \Delta^\dagger \grave{F}_3^\dagger F_3^\dagger \;=\; F_3^\dagger \qquad (10.4.6)$$

The square on the left commutes for functorial reasons, the one in the middle commutes by base-change, and the one on the right commutes by 40. Thus the diagram commutes. Since the bottom row is the identity and the upper row is $\Upsilon_{F_3, F_1 \diamond F_2}$, the theorem follows by looking at the outer border of the diagram.

The next theorem is to represent ρ_- by $\Upsilon_{-,-}$.

Theorem 37 *Let σ be a sequence such that $|\sigma|$ is an identity map $Id_{X_{\underline{[k-1]}}}$. Set $I := (Id_{X_{\underline{[k-1]}}}, \lambda)$. Then $\rho_\sigma = \Upsilon_{I,\sigma}$.*

PROOF. 74 *Consider the following diagram*

$$X_{\underline{[k-1]}} \xrightarrow{\Delta} X_{\underline{[k-1]}} \xrightarrow{\sigma'} X_{\underline{[k-1]}}$$

$$I'\| \qquad \mathfrak{S} \qquad \| I$$

$$X_{\underline{[k-1]}} \xrightarrow{\sigma} X_{\underline{[k-1]}} \qquad (10.4.7)$$

where $\sigma' = \sigma$ and $I' = I$. Then, one has the following commutative diagram

$$I'^\dagger \sigma^\dagger \xrightarrow{\alpha_{\mathfrak{S}}} \sigma'^\dagger I'^\dagger \xrightarrow{\rho_{\sigma'}} I^\dagger$$

$$\| \qquad\qquad \| \qquad\qquad \|$$

$$\sigma^\dagger \;=\; \sigma'^\dagger \xrightarrow{\rho_{\sigma'}} 1_{\mathcal{D}_{X_{\underline{[k-1]}}}}$$

$$(10.4.8)$$

Hence, $\rho_\sigma = \Upsilon_{I,\sigma}$ is valid from outer border of Eq. (10.4.8).

The next theorem is to represent α_- by $\Upsilon_{-,-}$. However, we have to provide some lemmas before establishing such theorem.

Lemma 41 *Let σ_1, σ_2 be two sequences such that $|\sigma_1| = |\sigma_2| = \mathbf{1}_{\mathcal{D}_{X_{[k-1]}}}$. Then the following diagram commutes*

$$
\begin{array}{ccc}
\sigma_1^\dagger \sigma_2^\dagger & \xrightarrow{\rho_{\sigma_2}} & \sigma_1^\dagger \\
\rho_{\sigma_1} \downarrow \searrow {\scriptstyle \rho_{\sigma_1 \diamond \sigma_2}} \downarrow \rho_{\sigma_1} & & \\
\sigma_2^\dagger & \xrightarrow{\rho_{\sigma_2}} & \mathbf{1}_{\mathcal{D}_{X_{[k-1]}}}
\end{array}
\tag{10.4.9}
$$

PROOF. 75 *This diagram commutes due to ρ_- definition.*

Lemma 42 *Given the following cartesian diagram with $|\sigma_1| = |\sigma_3| = \mathbf{1}_{\mathcal{D}_{X_{[k-1]}}}$*

$$
\begin{array}{ccc}
\underline{Z_{[k-1]}} & \xrightarrow{\sigma_3} & \underline{Z_{[k-1]}} \\
\sigma_2 \downarrow & \mathfrak{S}_{[k]} & \downarrow \sigma_2 \\
\underline{X_{[k-1]}} & \xrightarrow{\sigma_1} & \underline{X_{[k-1]}}
\end{array}
\tag{10.4.10}
$$

Then the following diagram commutes

$$
\begin{array}{ccc}
\sigma_2^\dagger \sigma_1^\dagger & \xrightarrow{\mathfrak{S}_{[k]}} & \sigma_3^\dagger \sigma_2^\dagger \\
\rho_{\sigma_1} \searrow & & \swarrow \rho_{\sigma_3} \\
& \sigma_2^\dagger &
\end{array}
\tag{10.4.11}
$$

PROOF. 76 *The proof of this Lemma is based on induction with respect to lengths of $\sigma_1(\sigma_3)$ (horizontal) and σ_2 (vertical).*

(basic step) For case that lengths of σ_1, σ_2 and σ_3 are one is obvious from definitions of ρ_- and $\alpha_{\mathfrak{S}_{[k]}}$.

We begin by performing induction at horizontal direction. Suppose that σ_1 is decomposed as

$\sigma_4 \diamond G$ *and* σ_3 *is decomposed as* $\sigma_7 \diamond G'$. *Consider the following diagram*

$$
\begin{array}{ccccccc}
\underline{Z_{[k-1]}} & \xrightarrow{\sigma_7} & & Y'_{[k-1]} & \xrightarrow{G'} & \underline{Z_{[k-1]}} \\[2pt]
H' \nwarrow & \mathfrak{S}_{1,[k]} & \nearrow F' & & & \\[2pt]
& \underline{Z_{[k-1]}} & \xrightarrow{\sigma_6} & \underline{Z_{[k-1]}} & & \\[2pt]
\sigma_2 \downarrow & \sigma_2 \downarrow & & \sigma_2 \downarrow \quad \downarrow \sigma'_2 & \mathfrak{S}_{3,[k]} & \downarrow \sigma_2 \\[2pt]
& \underline{X_{[k-1]}} & \xrightarrow{\sigma_5} & \underline{X_{[k-1]}} & & \\[2pt]
H \swarrow & \mathfrak{S}_{2,[k]} & & \searrow F & & \\[2pt]
\underline{X_{[k-1]}} & \xrightarrow{\sigma_4} & & Y_{[k-1]} & \xrightarrow{G} & \underline{X_{[k-1]}}
\end{array}
\qquad (10.4.12)
$$

where $H = H' = I$. *Then, we have following diagram of isomorphisms*

$$
\begin{array}{ccccccc}
\sigma_2^\dagger \sigma_4^\dagger G^\dagger & \xrightarrow{H=I} & \sigma_2^\dagger H^\dagger \sigma_4^\dagger G^\dagger & \xrightarrow{\alpha_{\mathfrak{S}_{2,[k]}}} & \sigma_2^\dagger \sigma_5^\dagger F^\dagger G^\dagger & \xrightarrow{\rho_{\sigma_5 FG}} & \sigma_2^\dagger \\[4pt]
\alpha_{\mathfrak{S}_{4,[k]}} \downarrow & & \alpha_{\mathfrak{S}_{4,[k]}} \downarrow & & \alpha_{\mathfrak{S}_{5,[k]}} \downarrow & & \\[4pt]
\sigma_7^\dagger \sigma_2'^\dagger G^\dagger & \xrightarrow{H'=I} & H'^\dagger \sigma_7^\dagger \sigma_2'^\dagger G^\dagger & \xrightarrow{\alpha_{\mathfrak{S}_{1,[k]}}} & \sigma_6^\dagger F'^\dagger \sigma_2'^\dagger G^\dagger & & \| \\[4pt]
\alpha_{\mathfrak{S}_{3,[k]}} \downarrow & & \alpha_{\mathfrak{S}_{3,[k]}} \downarrow & & \alpha_{\mathfrak{S}_{3,[k]}} \downarrow & & \\[4pt]
\sigma_7^\dagger G'^\dagger \sigma_2^\dagger & \xrightarrow{H'=I} & H'^\dagger \sigma_7^\dagger G'^\dagger \sigma_2^\dagger & \xrightarrow{\alpha_{\mathfrak{S}_{1,[k]}}} & \sigma_6^\dagger F'^\dagger G'^\dagger \sigma_2^\dagger & \xrightarrow{\rho_{\sigma_6 F'G'}} & \sigma_2^\dagger
\end{array}
\qquad (10.4.13)
$$

where $\mathfrak{S}_{4,[k]}$ *is a cartesian square*

$$
\begin{array}{ccc}
\underline{Z_{[k-1]}} & \xrightarrow{\sigma_7} & Y'_{[k-1]} \\[2pt]
\sigma_2 \downarrow & \mathfrak{S}_{4,[k]} & \downarrow \sigma_2 \\[2pt]
\underline{X_{[k-1]}} & \xrightarrow{\sigma_4} & Y_{[k-1]}
\end{array}
$$

$$(10.4.14)$$

and $\mathfrak{S}_{5,[k]}$ *is a cartesian square*

$$
\begin{array}{ccccc}
\underline{Z_{[k-1]}} & \xrightarrow{\sigma_6} & \underline{Z_{[k-1]}} & \xrightarrow{F'} & Y'_{[k-1]} \\[2pt]
\sigma_2 \downarrow & & \mathfrak{S}_{5,[k]} & & \downarrow \sigma'_2 \\[2pt]
\underline{X_{[k-1]}} & \xrightarrow{\sigma_5} & \underline{X_{[k-1]}} & \xrightarrow{F'} & Y_{[k-1]}
\end{array}
$$

$$(10.4.15)$$

By considering the four vertices at outer border of Eq. (10.4.13), *the Lemma is valid in horizontal direction* (σ_1 *and* σ_3) *since* $\sigma_2^\dagger \sigma_4^\dagger G^\dagger = \sigma_2^\dagger \sigma_1^\dagger$ *and* $\sigma_7^\dagger G'^\dagger \sigma_2^\dagger = \sigma_3^\dagger \sigma_2^\dagger$.

For vertical direction (σ_2), we assume that σ_2 is decomposed as $\sigma_8 \diamond \sigma_9$. Consider the following cartesian diagram

$$
\begin{array}{ccc}
\underline{Z_{[k-1]}} & \xrightarrow{\sigma_3} & \underline{Z_{[k-1]}} \\
\sigma_8 \downarrow & \mathfrak{S}_{6,[k]} \quad \downarrow \sigma_8 & \\
\underline{Z_{1,[k-1]}} & \xrightarrow{\sigma_{10}} & \underline{Z_{1,[k-1]}} \\
\sigma_9 \downarrow & \mathfrak{S}_{7,[k]} \quad \downarrow \sigma_9 & \\
\underline{X_{[k-1]}} & \xrightarrow{\sigma_1} & \underline{X_{[k-1]}}
\end{array}
\qquad (10.4.16)
$$

Correspondingly, we have following diagram of isomorphisms

$$
\begin{array}{ccc}
\sigma_8^\dagger \sigma_9^\dagger \sigma_1^\dagger & \xrightarrow{\alpha_{\mathfrak{S}_{7,[k]}}} \sigma_8^\dagger \sigma_9^\dagger \sigma_1^\dagger & \xrightarrow{\alpha_{\mathfrak{S}_{6,[k]}}} \sigma_3^\dagger \sigma_8^\dagger \sigma_9^\dagger \\
\rho_{\sigma_1} \searrow & \rho_{\sigma_{10}} \downarrow & \swarrow \rho_{\sigma_3} \\
& \sigma_8^\dagger \sigma_9^\dagger &
\end{array}
\qquad (10.4.17)
$$

By the induction hypothesis, the two sub-triangles commute and hence from the outer border we get the Lemma in vertical direction, too.

Lemma 43 *Let $F : \underline{X_{[k-1]}} \longrightarrow \underline{Y_{[k-1]}}$ and $\sigma : \underline{Y_{[k-1]}} \longrightarrow \underline{Y_{[k-1]}}$ with $|\sigma| = Id_{Y_{[k-1]}}$. Then the following two isomorphisms are equal*

$$
F^\dagger \sigma^\dagger \xrightarrow{F^\dagger \rho_\sigma} F^\dagger, \quad F^\dagger \sigma^\dagger \xrightarrow{\Upsilon_{F, F \diamond \sigma}} F^\dagger.
\qquad (10.4.18)
$$

PROOF. 77 *Consider the following diagram*

$$
\begin{array}{ccc}
\underline{X_{[k-1]}} & \xrightarrow{\sigma'} & \underline{X_{[k-1]}} \\
F \downarrow & \mathfrak{S}_{[k]} \quad \downarrow F & \\
\underline{Y_{[k-1]}} & \xrightarrow{\sigma} & \underline{Y_{[k-1]}}
\end{array}
\qquad (10.4.19)
$$

Then, one has

$$
\begin{array}{ccc}
F^\dagger \sigma^\dagger & \xrightarrow{\alpha_{\mathfrak{S}_{[k]}}} & \sigma'^\dagger F^\dagger \\
\rho_\sigma \searrow & \swarrow \rho_{\sigma'} & \\
& F^\dagger &
\end{array}
\qquad (10.4.20)
$$

The commutativity of Eq. (10.4.20) proves the claim in this Lemma.

Theorem 38 *Consider a cartesian diagram*

$$
\begin{array}{ccc}
\underline{X_{[k-1]}} & \xrightarrow{\sigma_4} & \underline{Z_{1,[k-1]}} \\
\sigma_3 \downarrow & \mathfrak{S} & \downarrow \sigma_1 \\
\underline{Z_{2,[k-1]}} & \xrightarrow{\sigma_2} & \underline{Y_{[k-1]}}
\end{array}
\qquad (10.4.21)
$$

Then $\alpha_{\mathfrak{S}} = \Upsilon_{\sigma_4 \diamond \sigma_1, \sigma_3 \diamond \sigma_2}$.

PROOF. 78 *The proof of this Theorem is based on induction with respect to lengths of $\sigma_2(\sigma_4)$ (horizontal) and $\sigma_1(\sigma_3)$ (vertical). We will show horizontal part only since the vertical part can be obtained similarly by exchanging roles between $\sigma_2(\sigma_4)$ and $\sigma_1(\sigma_3)$.*

(basic step) For case that lengths of $\sigma_1, \sigma_2, \sigma_3$ and σ_4 are one is obvious from definitions of $\Upsilon_{-,-}$ and $\alpha_{\mathfrak{S}_{[k]}}$.

We begin by performing induction at horizontal direction. Suppose that σ_2 is decomposed as $\sigma_5 \diamond G$ and σ_4 is decomposed as $\sigma_6 \diamond G'$. Consider the following diagram

$$
\begin{array}{ccccccc}
\underline{X_{[k-1]}} & & \xrightarrow{\sigma_6} & & \underline{Y'_{1,[k-1]}} & \xrightarrow{G'} & \underline{Y_{1,[k-1]}} \\
& H' \nwarrow & & \mathfrak{S}_{1,[k]} & & \nearrow F' & \\
& \underline{X_{[k-1]}} & \xrightarrow{\sigma_4} & \underline{Y_{1,[k-1]}} & & & \\
\sigma_3 \downarrow & \sigma_3 \downarrow & \mathfrak{S}_{3,[k]} & \sigma_1 \downarrow & \downarrow \sigma'_1 \; \mathfrak{S}_{4,[k]} & \downarrow \sigma_1 & \\
& \underline{Y_{2,[k-1]}} & \xrightarrow{\sigma_2} & \underline{Z_{[k-1]}} & & & \\
& H \swarrow & \mathfrak{S}_{2,[k]} & & \searrow F & & \\
\underline{Y_{2,[k-1]}} & & \xrightarrow{\sigma_5} & & \underline{Y'_{2,[k-1]}} & \xrightarrow{G} & \underline{Z_{[k-1]}}
\end{array}
\qquad (10.4.22)
$$

where $H = H' = I$. Then, we have following commutative diagram of isomorphisms

$$
\begin{array}{ccccccc}
\sigma_3^\dagger \sigma_5^\dagger G^\dagger & \xrightarrow{H=I} & \sigma_3'^\dagger H^\dagger \sigma_5^\dagger G^\dagger & \xrightarrow{\alpha_{\mathfrak{S}_{2,[k]}}} & \sigma_3'^\dagger \sigma_2^\dagger F^\dagger G^\dagger & \xrightarrow{\rho_{FG}} & \sigma_3^\dagger \sigma_2^\dagger \\
\alpha_{\mathfrak{S}_{5,[k]}} \downarrow & & \alpha_{\mathfrak{S}_{6,[k]}} \downarrow & & \alpha_{\mathfrak{S}_{3,[k]}} \downarrow & & \\
\sigma_6^\dagger \sigma_1'^\dagger G^\dagger & \xrightarrow{H'=I} & H'^\dagger \sigma_6^\dagger \sigma_1'^\dagger G^\dagger & \xrightarrow[\alpha_{\mathfrak{S}_{1,[k]}}]{\alpha_{\mathfrak{S}_{8,[k]}}} & \sigma_4^\dagger \sigma_1^\dagger F^\dagger G^\dagger & & \downarrow \alpha_{\mathfrak{S}_{3,[k]}} \\
\alpha_{\mathfrak{S}_{4,[k]}} \downarrow & & \alpha_{\mathfrak{S}_{4,[k]}} \downarrow & & \alpha_{\mathfrak{S}_{7,[k]}} \downarrow & & \\
\sigma_6^\dagger G'^\dagger \sigma_1^\dagger & \xleftarrow{H'=I} & H'^\dagger \sigma_6^\dagger G'^\dagger \sigma_1^\dagger & \xleftarrow{\alpha_{\mathfrak{S}_{1,[k]}^{-1}}} & \sigma_4^\dagger F'^\dagger G'^\dagger \sigma_1^\dagger & \xleftarrow{\rho_{F'G'}^{-1}} & \sigma_4^\dagger \sigma_1^\dagger
\end{array}
\qquad (10.4.23)
$$

where $\mathfrak{S}_{5,[k]}$ *is a cartesian square*

$$
\begin{array}{ccc}
\underline{X_{[k-1]}} & \xrightarrow{\sigma_6} & \underline{Y'_{1,[k-1]}} \\
\sigma_3 \downarrow & \mathfrak{S}_{5,[k]} & \downarrow \sigma'_1 \\
\underline{Y_{2,[k-1]}} & \xrightarrow{\sigma_5} & \underline{Y'_{2,[k-1]}}
\end{array}
$$

$$(10.4.24)$$

and $\mathfrak{S}_{6,[k]}$ *is a cartesian square*

$$
\begin{array}{ccccc}
\underline{X_{[k-1]}} & \xrightarrow{H'} & \underline{X_{[k-1]}} & \xrightarrow{\sigma_6} & \underline{Y'_{1,[k-1]}} \\
\sigma'_3 \downarrow & & \mathfrak{S}_{6,[k]} & & \downarrow \sigma'_1 \\
\underline{Y_{[k-1]}} & \xrightarrow{H} & \underline{Y_{2,[k-1]}} & \xrightarrow{\sigma_5} & \underline{Y'_{2,[k-1]}}
\end{array}
$$

$$(10.4.25)$$

and $\mathfrak{S}_{7,[k]}$ *is a cartesian square*

$$
\begin{array}{ccccc}
\underline{Y_{1,[k-1]}} & \xrightarrow{F'} & \underline{Y'_{1,[k-1]}} & \xrightarrow{G'} & \underline{Y_{1,[k-1]}} \\
\sigma_1 \downarrow & & \mathfrak{S}_{7,[k]} & & \downarrow \sigma_1 \\
\underline{Z_{[k-1]}} & \xrightarrow{F} & \underline{Y'_{2,[k-1]}} & \xrightarrow{G} & \underline{Z_{[k-1]}}
\end{array}
$$

$$(10.4.26)$$

and $\mathfrak{S}_{8,[k]}$ *is a cartesian square*

$$
\begin{array}{ccc}
\underline{Y_{1,[k-1]}} & \xrightarrow{F'} & \underline{Y'_{1,[k-1]}} \\
\sigma_1 \downarrow & \mathfrak{S}_{8,[k]} & \downarrow \sigma'_1 \\
\underline{Z_{[k-1]}} & \xrightarrow{F} & \underline{Y'_{2.[k-1]}}
\end{array}
$$

$$(10.4.27)$$

By considering the four vertices at outer border of Eq. (10.4.23), the Lemma is valid in horizontal direction (σ_2 and σ_4) from the commutativity of the diagram provided by Eq. (10.4.23).

10.4.2 Linearity of $\Upsilon_{-,-}$

The goal of this section is to demonstrate that $\Upsilon_{-,-}$ satisfies linearity. It can be stated formally by the following Theorem.

Theorem 39 *Let* $\sigma_1 : \underline{X_{[k-1]}} \longrightarrow \underline{Y_{[k-1]}}$ *and* $\sigma_2 : \underline{X_{[k-1]}} \longrightarrow \underline{Y_{[k-1]}}$ *be two labeled maps such that* $|\sigma_1| = |\sigma_2|$. *For any two labeled maps* $\varrho : \underline{W_{[k-1]}} \longrightarrow \underline{X_{[k-1]}}$ *and* $\tau : \underline{Y_{[k-1]}} \longrightarrow \underline{Z_{[k-1]}}$, *the following two isomorphisms are equal*

$$\varrho^\dagger \sigma_2^\dagger \tau^\dagger \xrightarrow{\Upsilon_{\varrho \diamond \sigma_1 \diamond \tau, \varrho \diamond \sigma_2 \diamond \tau}} \varrho^\dagger \sigma_1^\dagger \tau^\dagger, \quad \varrho^\dagger \sigma_2^\dagger \tau^\dagger \xrightarrow{\varrho \Upsilon_{\sigma_1, \sigma_2} \tau} \varrho^\dagger \sigma_1^\dagger \tau^\dagger. \tag{10.4.28}$$

PROOF. 79 *The proof is divided into two parts. The first part is to show the equality of the following two isomorphisms*

$$\varrho^\dagger \sigma_2^\dagger \xrightarrow{\Upsilon_{\varrho \diamond \sigma_1, \varrho \diamond \sigma_2}} \varrho^\dagger \sigma_1^\dagger, \quad \varrho^\dagger \sigma_2^\dagger \xrightarrow{\varrho \Upsilon_{\sigma_1, \sigma_2}} \varrho^\dagger \sigma_1^\dagger. \tag{10.4.29}$$

Consider the following diagram made by fiber product of maps $\underline{W_{[k-1]}} \xrightarrow{\varrho} \underline{X_{[k-1]}} \xrightarrow{\sigma_2} \underline{Y_{[k-1]}}$ *and* $\underline{W_{[k-1]}} \xrightarrow{\varrho} \underline{X_{[k-1]}} \xrightarrow{\sigma_1} \underline{Y_{[k-1]}}$

$$
\begin{array}{ccccccc}
\underline{W_{[k-1]}} & \xrightarrow{a} & \bullet_1 & \xrightarrow{b} & \bullet_2 & \xrightarrow{c} & \underline{W_{[k-1]}} \\
d \downarrow & \mathfrak{S}_{1,[k]} & \downarrow e & \mathfrak{S}_{2,[k]} & & \downarrow \varrho & \\
& & \bullet_3 & \xrightarrow{f} & \bullet_4 & \xrightarrow{g} & \underline{X_{[k-1]}} \\
h \downarrow & \mathfrak{S}_{3,[k]} & \downarrow i & \mathfrak{S}_{4,[k]} & & \downarrow \sigma_1 & \\
\underline{W_{[k-1]}} & \xrightarrow{\varrho} & \underline{X_{[k-1]}} & \xrightarrow{\sigma_2} & \underline{Y_{[k-1]}} & &
\end{array}
$$

$$\tag{10.4.30}$$

We also construct a cartesian cube based on $\mathfrak{S}_{1,[k]}$ *as*

$$
\begin{array}{ccccc}
\bullet_1 & & \xrightarrow{b} & & \bullet_2 \\
& \nwarrow j & \mathfrak{S}_{5,[k]} & k \nearrow & \\
& \underline{W_{[k-1]}} \xrightarrow{p} \bullet_5 & \xrightarrow{o} & \underline{W_{[k-1]}} & \\
d \downarrow & \mathfrak{S}_{6,[k]} \quad n \downarrow & \mathfrak{S}_{7,[k]} & \varrho \downarrow \mathfrak{S}_{8,[k]} \downarrow e & \\
& \underline{W_{[k-1]}} & \xrightarrow{\varrho} & \underline{X_{[k-1]}} & \\
& \swarrow l & \mathfrak{S}_{9,[k]} & m \searrow & \\
\bullet_3 & & \xrightarrow{f} & & \bullet_4
\end{array}
$$

$$\tag{10.4.31}$$

Then we can have the following diagram of isomorphisms

$$
\varrho^\dagger \sigma_2^\dagger \qquad\qquad\qquad\qquad\qquad\qquad\qquad\qquad\qquad\qquad \varrho^\dagger \sigma_1^\dagger
$$

$$
\rho_{adh}^{-1} \downarrow \qquad\qquad\qquad\qquad\qquad\qquad\qquad\qquad\qquad\qquad\qquad \uparrow \rho_{abc}
$$

$$
a^\dagger d^\dagger h^\dagger \varrho^\dagger \sigma_2^\dagger \xrightarrow{\alpha_{\mathfrak{S}_{3,[k]}}} a^\dagger d^\dagger f^\dagger i^\dagger \sigma_2^\dagger \xrightarrow{\alpha_{\mathfrak{S}_{1,[k]}}} a^\dagger b^\dagger e^\dagger i^\dagger \sigma_2^\dagger \xrightarrow{\alpha_{\mathfrak{S}_{4,[k]}}} a^\dagger b^\dagger e^\dagger g^\dagger \sigma_1^\dagger \xrightarrow{\alpha_{\mathfrak{S}_{2,[k]}}} a^\dagger b^\dagger c^\dagger \varrho^\dagger \sigma_1^\dagger
$$

$$
\chi_{a,pj} \downarrow \qquad\quad \chi_{a,pj} \downarrow \qquad\quad \chi_{a,pj} \downarrow \qquad\quad \chi_{a,pj} \downarrow \qquad\quad \chi_{a,pj} \downarrow
$$

$$
p^\dagger j^\dagger d^\dagger h^\dagger \varrho^\dagger \sigma_2^\dagger \xrightarrow{\alpha_{\mathfrak{S}_{3,[k]}}} p^\dagger j^\dagger d^\dagger f^\dagger i^\dagger \sigma_2^\dagger \xrightarrow{\alpha_{\mathfrak{S}_{1,[k]}}} p^\dagger j^\dagger b^\dagger e^\dagger i^\dagger \sigma_2^\dagger \xrightarrow{\alpha_{\mathfrak{S}_{4,[k]}}} p^\dagger j^\dagger b^\dagger e^\dagger g^\dagger \sigma_1^\dagger \xrightarrow{\alpha_{\mathfrak{S}_{2,[k]}}} p^\dagger j^\dagger b^\dagger c^\dagger \varrho^\dagger \sigma_1^\dagger
$$

$$
\alpha_{\mathfrak{S}_{6,[k]}} \downarrow \qquad \alpha_{\mathfrak{S}_{6,[k]}} \downarrow \qquad \alpha_{\mathfrak{S}_{5,[k]}} \downarrow \qquad \alpha_{\mathfrak{S}_{5,[k]}} \downarrow \qquad \alpha_{\mathfrak{S}_{5,[k]}} \downarrow
$$

$$
p^\dagger n^\dagger l^\dagger h^\dagger \varrho^\dagger \sigma_2^\dagger \xrightarrow{\alpha_{\mathfrak{S}_{3,[k]}}} p^\dagger n^\dagger l^\dagger f^\dagger i^\dagger \sigma_2^\dagger \quad \S_1 \quad p^\dagger o^\dagger k^\dagger e^\dagger i^\dagger \sigma_2^\dagger \xrightarrow{\alpha_{\mathfrak{S}_{4,[k]}}} p^\dagger o^\dagger k^\dagger e^\dagger g^\dagger \sigma_1^\dagger \xrightarrow{\alpha_{\mathfrak{S}_{1,[k]}}} p^\dagger o^\dagger k^\dagger c^\dagger \varrho^\dagger \sigma_1^\dagger
$$

$$
\rho_{lh} \downarrow \qquad \S_2 \qquad \alpha_{\mathfrak{S}_{9,[k]}} \downarrow \qquad\quad \alpha_{\mathfrak{S}_{8,[k]}} \downarrow \qquad\quad \alpha_{\mathfrak{S}_{5,[k]}} \downarrow \qquad \S_3 \quad \rho_{kc} \downarrow
$$

$$
p^\dagger n^\dagger \varrho^\dagger \sigma_2^\dagger \xrightarrow{\rho_{mi}^{-1}} p^\dagger n^\dagger \varrho^\dagger m^\dagger i^\dagger \sigma_2^\dagger \longrightarrow p^\dagger o^\dagger \varrho^\dagger m^\dagger i^\dagger \sigma_2^\dagger \xrightarrow{\alpha_{\mathfrak{S}_{4,[k]}}} p^\dagger o^\dagger \varrho^\dagger m^\dagger g^\dagger \sigma_1^\dagger \xrightarrow{\rho_{mq}} p^\dagger o^\dagger \varrho^\dagger \sigma_1^\dagger
$$

$$
\rho_{pn} \searrow \qquad\quad \rho_{pn} \searrow \qquad\quad \rho_{po} \swarrow \qquad\quad \rho_{po} \downarrow \qquad\quad \rho_{po} \downarrow
$$

$$
\varrho^\dagger \sigma_2^\dagger \xrightarrow{\rho_{mi}^{-1}} \varrho^\dagger m^\dagger i^\dagger \sigma_2^\dagger \xrightarrow{\alpha_{\mathfrak{S}_{4,[k]}}} \varrho^\dagger m^\dagger g^\dagger \sigma_1^\dagger \xrightarrow{\rho_{mq}} \varrho^\dagger \sigma_1^\dagger \quad (10.4.32)
$$

Note that that the topmost row of maps in the diagram provided by Eq. (10.4.32) defines $\Upsilon_{\varrho \diamond \sigma_1, \varrho \diamond \sigma_2}$ while the bottommost row defines $\varrho^\dagger \Upsilon_{\sigma_1, \sigma_2}$. The commutativity of the square $\S_1$ is based on Lemma 33 and the commutativity of squares $\S_2$ and $\S_3$ is based on Lemma 42. Hence, the first part is proved from commutativity of Eq. (10.4.32).

The second part is to show the equality of the following two isomorphisms

$$
\sigma_2^\dagger \tau^\dagger \xrightarrow{\Upsilon_{\sigma_1 \diamond \tau, \sigma_2 \diamond \tau}} \sigma_1^\dagger \tau^\dagger, \quad \sigma_2^\dagger \tau^\dagger \xrightarrow{\Upsilon_{\sigma_1, \sigma_2} \tau} \sigma_1^\dagger \tau^\dagger. \tag{10.4.33}
$$

Consider the following diagram made by fiber product of maps $\underline{X}_{[k-1]} \xrightarrow{\sigma_1} \underline{Y}_{[k-1]} \xrightarrow{\tau} \underline{Z}_{[k-1]}$ and $\underline{X}_{[k-1]} \xrightarrow{\sigma_2} \underline{Y}_{[k-1]} \xrightarrow{\tau} \underline{Z}_{[k-1]}$

$$
\begin{array}{ccccccc}
\underline{Z}_{[k-1]} & \xleftarrow{\hat{a}} & \hat{\bullet}_1 & \xleftarrow{\hat{b}} & \hat{\bullet}_2 & \xleftarrow{\hat{c}} & \underline{Z}_{[k-1]} \\
\hat{d} \uparrow & \hat{\mathfrak{S}}_{1,[k]} & \uparrow \hat{e} & \hat{\mathfrak{S}}_{2,[k]} & & \uparrow \tau & \\
& & \hat{\bullet}_3 & \xleftarrow{\hat{f}} & \hat{\bullet}_4 & \xleftarrow{\hat{g}} & \underline{Y}_{[k-1]} \\
\hat{h} \uparrow & \hat{\mathfrak{S}}_{3,[k]} & \uparrow \hat{i} & \hat{\mathfrak{S}}_{4,[k]} & & \uparrow \sigma_2 & \\
\underline{Z}_{[k-1]} & \xleftarrow{\tau} & \underline{Y}_{[k-1]} & \xleftarrow{\sigma_1} & \underline{X}_{[k-1]} & &
\end{array}
$$

$$
\tag{10.4.34}
$$

We also construct a cartesian cube based on $\hat{\hat{\mathfrak{S}}}_{1,[k]}$ as

$$
\begin{array}{ccccccc}
\bullet_1 & & \xleftarrow{\;\hat{b}\;} & & \bullet_2 & & \\
& \searrow \hat{j} & & \hat{\hat{\mathfrak{S}}}_{5,[k]} & & \hat{k} \swarrow & \\
& \underline{Z_{[k-1]}} \xleftarrow{\;\hat{p}\;} \bullet_5 & & \xleftarrow{\;\hat{o}\;} & & \underline{Z_{[k-1]}} & \\
\hat{d} \uparrow & \hat{\hat{\mathfrak{S}}}_{6,[k]} \quad \hat{n} \uparrow & & \hat{\hat{\mathfrak{S}}}_{7,[k]} & & \tau \uparrow \hat{\hat{\mathfrak{S}}}_{8,[k]} \quad \uparrow \hat{e} & \\
& \underline{Z_{[k-1]}} & \xleftarrow{\;\tau\;} & & \underline{Y_{[k-1]}} & & \\
& \nearrow \hat{l} & & \hat{\mathfrak{S}}_{9,[k]} & & \hat{m} \nwarrow & \\
\bullet_3 & & \xleftarrow{\;\hat{f}\;} & & \bullet_4 & &
\end{array}
\tag{10.4.35}
$$

Then we can have the following diagram of isomorphisms

$$
\begin{array}{ccccccccc}
\sigma_2^\dagger \tau^\dagger & & & & & & & & \sigma_1^\dagger \tau^\dagger \\
\rho_{cba}^{-1} \downarrow & & & & & & & & \uparrow \rho_{hda} \\
\sigma_2^\dagger \tau^\dagger \hat{c}^\dagger \hat{b}^\dagger \hat{a}^\dagger & \xrightarrow{\alpha_{\hat{\mathfrak{S}}_{2,[k]}}} & \sigma_2^\dagger \hat{g}^\dagger \hat{e}^\dagger \hat{b}^\dagger \hat{a}^\dagger & \xrightarrow{\alpha_{\hat{\mathfrak{S}}_{1,[k]}}} & \sigma_2^\dagger \hat{g}^\dagger \hat{f}^\dagger \hat{d}^\dagger \hat{a}^\dagger & \xrightarrow{\alpha_{\hat{\mathfrak{S}}_{4,[k]}}} & \sigma_1^\dagger \hat{i}^\dagger \hat{f}^\dagger \hat{d}^\dagger \hat{a}^\dagger & \xrightarrow{\alpha_{\hat{\mathfrak{S}}_{3,[k]}}} & \sigma_1^\dagger \tau^\dagger \hat{h}^\dagger \hat{d}^\dagger \hat{a}^\dagger \\
\chi_{\hat{a},\hat{j}\hat{p}} \downarrow & & \chi_{\hat{a},\hat{j}\hat{p}} \downarrow & & \chi_{\hat{a},\hat{j}\hat{p}} \downarrow & & \chi_{\hat{a},\hat{j}\hat{p}} \downarrow & & \chi_{\hat{a},\hat{j}\hat{p}} \downarrow \\
\sigma_2^\dagger \tau^\dagger \hat{c}^\dagger \hat{b}^\dagger \hat{j}\hat{p} & \xrightarrow{\alpha_{\hat{\mathfrak{S}}_{2,[k]}}} & \sigma_2^\dagger \hat{g}^\dagger \hat{e}^\dagger \hat{b}^\dagger \hat{j}\hat{p} & \xrightarrow{\alpha_{\hat{\mathfrak{S}}_{1,[k]}}} & \sigma_2^\dagger \hat{g}^\dagger \hat{f}^\dagger \hat{d}^\dagger \hat{j}\hat{p} & \xrightarrow{\alpha_{\hat{\mathfrak{S}}_{4,[k]}}} & \sigma_1^\dagger \hat{i}^\dagger \hat{f}^\dagger \hat{d}^\dagger \hat{j}\hat{p} & \xrightarrow{\alpha_{\hat{\mathfrak{S}}_{3,[k]}}} & \sigma_1^\dagger \tau^\dagger \hat{h}^\dagger \hat{d}^\dagger \hat{j}\hat{p} \\
\alpha_{\hat{\mathfrak{S}}_{5,[k]}} \downarrow & & \alpha_{\hat{\mathfrak{S}}_{5,[k]}} \downarrow & & \alpha_{\hat{\mathfrak{S}}_{6,[k]}} \downarrow & & \alpha_{\hat{\mathfrak{S}}_{6,[k]}} \downarrow & & \alpha_{\hat{\mathfrak{S}}_{6,[k]}} \downarrow \\
\sigma_2^\dagger \tau^\dagger \hat{c}^\dagger \hat{k}^\dagger \hat{o}\hat{p} & \xrightarrow{\alpha_{\hat{\mathfrak{S}}_{2,[k]}}} & \sigma_2^\dagger \hat{g}^\dagger \hat{e}^\dagger \hat{k}^\dagger \hat{o}\hat{p} & \S_1 & \sigma_2^\dagger \hat{g}^\dagger \hat{f}^\dagger \hat{l}^\dagger \hat{n}\hat{p} & \xrightarrow{\alpha_{\hat{\mathfrak{S}}_{4,[k]}}} & \sigma_1^\dagger \hat{i}^\dagger \hat{f}^\dagger \hat{l}^\dagger \hat{n}\hat{p} & \xrightarrow{\alpha_{\hat{\mathfrak{S}}_{3,[k]}}} & \sigma_1^\dagger \tau^\dagger \hat{h}^\dagger \hat{l}^\dagger \hat{n}\hat{p} \\
\rho_{\hat{c}\hat{k}} \downarrow & \S_2 & \alpha_{\hat{\mathfrak{S}}_{8,[k]}} \downarrow & & \alpha_{\hat{\mathfrak{S}}_{8,[k]}} \downarrow & & \alpha_{\hat{\mathfrak{S}}_{8,[k]}} \downarrow & \S_3 & \rho_{\hat{h}\hat{l}} \downarrow \\
\sigma_2^\dagger \tau^\dagger \hat{o}\hat{p} & \xrightarrow{\rho_{\hat{g}\hat{m}}^{-1}} & \sigma_2^\dagger \hat{g}^\dagger \hat{m}^\dagger \tau^\dagger \hat{o}^\dagger \hat{p}^\dagger & \longrightarrow & \sigma_2^\dagger \hat{g}^\dagger \hat{m}^\dagger \tau^\dagger \hat{n}^\dagger \hat{p}^\dagger & \xrightarrow{\alpha_{\hat{\mathfrak{S}}_{4,[k]}}} & \sigma_1^\dagger \hat{i}^\dagger \hat{m}^\dagger \tau^\dagger \hat{n}^\dagger \hat{p}^\dagger & \xrightarrow{\rho_{\hat{i}\hat{m}}} & \sigma_1^\dagger \tau^\dagger \hat{n}^\dagger \hat{p}^\dagger \\
\rho_{\hat{o}\hat{p}} \searrow & & \rho_{\hat{o}\hat{p}} \searrow & & \rho_{\hat{n}\hat{p}} \swarrow & & \rho_{\hat{n}\hat{p}} \downarrow & & \rho_{\hat{n}\hat{p}} \downarrow \\
& \sigma_2^\dagger \tau^\dagger & \xrightarrow{\rho_{\hat{g}\hat{m}}^{-1}} & \sigma_2^\dagger \hat{g}^\dagger \hat{m}^\dagger \tau^\dagger & \xrightarrow{\alpha_{\mathfrak{S}_{4,[k]}}} & \sigma_1^\dagger \hat{i}^\dagger \hat{m}^\dagger \tau^\dagger & \xrightarrow{\rho_{\hat{i}\hat{m}}} & \sigma_1^\dagger \tau^\dagger &
\end{array}
\tag{10.4.36}
$$

Note that that the topmost row of maps in the diagram provided by Eq. (10.4.36) defines $\Upsilon_{\sigma_1 \diamond \tau, \sigma_2 \diamond \tau}$ while the bottommost row defines $\Upsilon_{\sigma_1, \sigma_2} \tau$. The commutativity of the square $\S_1$ is based on Lemma 33 and the commutativity of squares $\S_2$ and $\S_3$ is based on Lemma 42. Hence, the second part is proved from commutativity of Eq. (10.4.36).

Therefore, from the first and second part, this Theorem is established.

10.4.3 Extension Theorem of Algebraic Invenrelation Systems

The main goal of this Chapter is to show the extension theorem of parameterized algebraic invenrelation systems. We begin with some definitions.

Definition 79 *Let* $Q = \overline{\{\mathbf{P}, \mathbf{O}\}}$ *be the smallest n-MIMO-invengory containing* $\mathbf{P}$ *and* $\mathbf{O}$. *According to conditions for extension theorem ([A], [B], [C] and [D]) provided in Sec. 10.1.2, a cover with dimension* $k-1$ *($1 \leq k \leq n$), denoted as* $\zeta_{[k-1]}$, *of algebraic invenrelation systems parameterized by perspectives is a triple* $((Q, \{Z^{\times}_{[k-1]}\}), F^{\times}_{\#}, F^{\times}_{\$})$ *consisting of*

(1) an algebraic invenrelation system $(Q, \{Z^{\times}_{[k-1]}\})$;

(2) a morphism between algebraic invenrelation systems $F^{\times}_{\#} : (Q, \{Z^{\times}_{[k-1]}\})|_{\mathbf{P}} \longrightarrow (\mathbf{P}, \{X^{\overline{\#}}_{[k-1]}\})$ [5];

(3) a morphism between algebraic invenrelation systems $F^{\times}_{\$} : (Q, \{Z^{\times}_{[k-1]}\})|_{\mathbf{O}} \longrightarrow (\mathbf{O}, \{Y^{\overline{\$}}_{[k-1]}\})$ [6];

subject to the following conditions

- *(a) For any objects* $\underline{X_{[k-1]}} \in \mathbf{C}$, *one has functor* $S_{\underline{X_{[k-1]}}} : X^{\times}_{[k-1]} \longrightarrow \mathcal{D}_{\underline{X_{[k-1]}}}$, *where* $\mathcal{D}_{\underline{X_{[k-1]}}}$ *is made by the list of* $\mathcal{D}_{X_{[k-1]}}$ *for each* $X_{[k-1]} \in \underline{X_{[k-1]}}$.

- *(b) For every cartesian square* $\mathfrak{S}_{[k]}$ *in* $\mathbf{C}$ *as follows such that* $f \in \mathbf{P}$ *and* $i \in \mathbf{O}$,

$$
\begin{array}{ccc}
\underline{U_{[k-1]}} & \xrightarrow{i'} & \underline{X_{[k-1]}} \\
f' \downarrow & \mathfrak{S} & \downarrow f \\
\underline{V_{[k-1]}} & \xrightarrow{i} & \underline{Y_{[k-1]}}
\end{array}
\tag{10.4.37}
$$

we have the following commutative diagram

$$
\begin{array}{ccc}
S_{\underline{X_{[k-1]}}} i'^{\times} f^{\times} & \xrightarrow{\text{by } (-)^{\times} \text{ functorial}} & S_{\underline{X_{[k-1]}}} f'^{\times} i^{\times} \\
\text{by (3)} \downarrow & & \downarrow \text{by (2)} \\
i'^{\overline{\$}} S_{\underline{X_{[k-1]}}} f^{\times} & & f'^{\overline{\#}} S_{\underline{V_{[k-1]}}} i^{\times} \\
\text{by (2)} \downarrow & & \downarrow \text{by (3)} \\
i'^{\overline{\$}} f^{\overline{\#}} S_{\underline{Y_{[k-1]}}} & \xrightarrow{\alpha_{\mathfrak{S}}} & f'^{\overline{\#}} i^{\overline{\$}} S_{\underline{Y_{[k-1]}}}
\end{array}
\tag{10.4.38}
$$

- *(c) For every sequence* $\underline{X_{[k-1]}} \xrightarrow{i} \underline{Y_{[k-1]}} \xrightarrow{h} \underline{X_{[k-1]}}$ *such that* $hi = 1_{\underline{X_{[k-1]}}}$ *with* $i \in \mathbf{P}$ *and*

---

[5] Note that the projection of $(\mathbf{P}, \{X^{\overline{\#}}_{[k-1]}\})$ to $\mathbf{P}$ part in $\mathbf{C}$ becomes $(\mathbf{P}, \{X^{\#}_{[k-1]}\})$

[6] Note that the projection of $(\mathbf{O}, \{Y^{\overline{\$}}_{[k-1]}\})$ to $\mathbf{O}$ part in $\mathbf{C}$ becomes $(\mathbf{O}, \{Y^{\$}_{[k-1]}\})$

$h \in \mathbf{O}$, *the following diagram commutes.*

$$
\begin{array}{ccc}
\underline{S_{X_{[k-1]}}} i^{\times} h^{\times} & \xrightarrow{\ by\ (-)^{\times}\ functorial\ } & \underline{S_{X_{[k-1]}} \mathbf{1}_{X_{[k-1]}^{\times}}} \\[4pt]
by\ (2) \downarrow & & \| \\[4pt]
\overline{i^{\#}} \underline{S_{Y_{[k-1]}}} h^{\times} & & \underline{S_{X_{[k-1]}}} \\[4pt]
by\ (3) \downarrow & & \| \\[4pt]
\overline{i^{\#}} h^{\overline{\$}} \underline{S_{X_{[k-1]}}} & \xrightarrow{\ \eta_{i,h}\ } & \mathbf{1}_{\mathcal{D}_{X_{[k-1]}}} \underline{S_{X_{[k-1]}}}
\end{array}
\qquad (10.4.39)
$$

The following definition is provided to describe the morphism between two covers with dimension $k-1$.

Definition 80 *Let* $\zeta_{1,[k-1]} = ((Q, \{Z_{[k-1]}^{\times}\}), F_{\#}^{\times}, F_{\$}^{\times})$ *and* $\zeta_{2,[k-1]} = ((Q, \{Z_{[k-1]}^{\square}\}), F_{\#}^{\square}, F_{\$}^{\square})$ *be two covers. Then a morphism* $\zeta_{2,[k-1]} \longrightarrow \zeta_{1,[k-1]}$ *of covers is a morphism of* $(Q, \{Z_{[k-1]}^{\times}\}) \xrightarrow{\xi} (Q, \{Z_{[k-1]}^{\square}\})$ *such that the following two diagrams commute*

$$
\begin{array}{ccc}
(Q, \{Z_{[k-1]}^{\times}\})|_{\mathbf{P}} & \xrightarrow{\ \xi|_{\mathbf{P}}\ } & (Q, \{Z_{[k-1]}^{\square}\})|_{\mathbf{P}} \\[4pt]
F_{\#}^{\times} \searrow & & \swarrow F_{\#}^{\square} \\[4pt]
& (\mathbf{P}, \{X_{[k-1]}^{\overline{\#}}\}) &
\end{array}
\qquad (10.4.40)
$$

and

$$
\begin{array}{ccc}
(Q, \{Z_{[k-1]}^{\times}\})|_{\mathbf{O}} & \xrightarrow{\ \xi|_{\mathbf{O}}\ } & (Q, \{Z_{[k-1]}^{\square}\})|_{\mathbf{O}} \\[4pt]
F_{\$}^{\times} \searrow & & \swarrow F_{\$}^{\square} \\[4pt]
& (\mathbf{O}, \{X_{[k-1]}^{\overline{\$}}\}) &
\end{array}
\qquad (10.4.41)
$$

A cover $\zeta_{1,[k-1]} = ((Q, \{Z_{[k-1]}^{\times}\}), F_{\#}^{\times}, F_{\$}^{\times})$ *is called* an ideal cover *if* $F_{\#}^{\times}$ *and* $F_{\$}^{\times}$ *are isomorphisms.*

Let $\zeta_{[k-1]} = ((Q, \{Z_{[k-1]}^{\square}\}), F_{\#}^{\square}, F_{\$}^{\square})$ be a cover. For any labeled sequence σ with $k-1$-dimensional objects as

$$
\underline{X_{1,[k-1]}} \xrightarrow{F_1} \underline{X_{2,[k-1]}} \xrightarrow{F_2} \cdots \underline{X_{n,[k-1]}} \xrightarrow{F_n} \underline{X_{n+1,[k-1]}}
\qquad (10.4.42)
$$

we set $\sigma^{\square} = F_1^{\square} \cdots F_n^{\square}$.

Some Lemmas should be provide first in later proving of main extension Theorem.

Lemma 44 *Let* $\zeta_{[k-1]} = ((Q, \{Z^{\square}_{[k-1]}\}), F^{\square}_{\#}, F^{\square}_{\$})$ *be a cover. For any labeled sequence* σ *such that* $|\sigma|$ *is an identity map with respect to the object* $X_{[k-1]}$, *the following diagram commutes:*

$$S_{X_{[k-1]}} \sigma^{\square} \longrightarrow \sigma^{\dagger} S_{X_{[k-1]}}$$

$$\searrow \qquad \swarrow$$

$$S_{X_{[k-1]}} \tag{10.4.43}$$

PROOF. 80 *The map from* $S_{X_{[k-1]}} \sigma^{\square}$ *to* $S_{X_{[k-1]}}$ *is based on the functor* $(-)^{\square}$ *with respect to the following cartesian diagram*

$$
\begin{array}{ccc}
X^{\square}_{[k-1]} & \xrightarrow{S_{X_{[k-1]}}} & \mathcal{D}_{X_{[k-1]}} \\
\sigma^{\square} \downarrow & & \downarrow Id \\
X^{\square}_{[k-1]} & \xrightarrow{S_{X_{[k-1]}}} & \mathcal{D}_{X_{[k-1]}}
\end{array}
$$

$$\tag{10.4.44}$$

The map from $\sigma^{\dagger} S_{X_{[k-1]}}$ *to* $S_{X_{[k-1]}}$ *is based on the definition of* ρ_{σ} *since* $|\sigma|$ *is an identity map.*

To every labeled map F_i *as in Eq. (10.4.42), we associate a map* $S_{X_{[k-1]}} F^{\square}_i \to F^{\dagger}_i S_{Y_{[k-1]}}$, *which, for* $\lambda = \mathbf{P}$, *is the map* $S_{X_{[k-1]}} f^{\square}_i \to f^{\overline{\#}}_i S_{Y_{[k-1]}}$ *obtained from* $F^{\square}_{\#}$ *and for* $\lambda = \mathbf{O}$, *is the map* $S_{X_{[k-1]}} f^{\square}_i \to f^{\overline{\$}}_i S_{Y_{[k-1]}}$ *obtained from* $F^{\square}_{\$}$. *By successively using* $S_{X_{i,[k-1]}} F^{\square}_i \to F^{\dagger}_i S_{X_{i+1,[k-1]}}$, *we can have the map from* $S_{X_{[k-1]}} \sigma^{\square}$ *to* $\sigma^{\dagger} S_{X_{[k-1]}}$. *Hence, the diagram in Eq. (10.4.43) commutes.*

Lemma 45 *Let* $\zeta_{[k-1]} = ((Q, \{Z^{\square}_{[k-1]}\}), F^{\square}_{\#}, F^{\square}_{\$})$ *be a cover. For any cartesian square* $\mathfrak{S}$

$$
\begin{array}{ccc}
W_{[k-1]} & \xrightarrow{\sigma_1} & X_{[k-1]} \\
\sigma_2 \downarrow & \mathfrak{S} & \downarrow \sigma_3 \\
Z_{[k-1]} & \xrightarrow{\sigma_4} & Y_{[k-1]}
\end{array}
$$

$$\tag{10.4.45}$$

we have the following diagram commutes

$$
\begin{array}{ccc}
S_{W_{[k-1]}} \sigma^{\square}_1 \sigma^{\square}_3 & \xrightarrow{\text{by } (-)^{\square} \text{ functorial}} & S_{W_{[k-1]}} \sigma^{\square}_2 \sigma^{\square}_4 \\
1 \downarrow & & \downarrow 2 \\
\sigma^{\dagger}_1 S_{X_{[k-1]}} \sigma^{\square}_3 & & \sigma^{\dagger}_2 S_{Z_{[k-1]}} \sigma^{\square}_4 \\
3 \downarrow & & \downarrow 4 \\
\sigma^{\dagger}_1 \sigma^{\dagger}_3 S_{Y_{[k-1]}} & \xrightarrow{\alpha_{\mathfrak{S}}} & \sigma^{\dagger}_2 \sigma^{\dagger}_4 S_{Y_{[k-1]}}
\end{array}
$$

$$\tag{10.4.46}$$

PROOF. 81 *We will prove the arrow 1 since the other three arrows can be proved similarly. If all vertical arrows are established, then diagram in Eq. (10.4.46) commutes.*

If the labeled sequence σ_1 is

$$\sigma_1 : \underline{W_{[k-1]}} = \underline{W_{0,[k-1]}} \xrightarrow{F_1} \underline{W_{1,[k-1]}} \xrightarrow{F_2} \underline{W_{2,[k-1]}} \cdots \xrightarrow{F_n} \underline{W_{n,[k-1]}} = \underline{X_{[k-1]}} \tag{10.4.47}$$

To every labeled map F_i as in Eq. (10.4.47), we associate a map $S_{W_{i-1,[k-1]}} F_i^{\square} \to F_i^{\dagger} S_{W_{i,[k-1]}}$, which, for $\lambda = \mathbf{P}$, is the map $S_{W_{i-1,[k-1]}} f_i^{\square} \to f_i^{\overline{\#}} S_{W_{i,[k-1]}}$ obtained from $F_{\overline{\#}}^{\square}$ and for $\lambda = \mathbf{O}$, is the map $S_{W_{i-1,[k-1]}} f_i^{\square} \to f_i^{\overline{\$}} S_{W_{i,[k-1]}}$ obtained from $F_{\overline{\$}}^{\square}$. By successively using $S_{W_{i-1,[k-1]}} F_i^{\square} \to F_i^{\dagger} S_{W_{i,[k-1]}}$, we can have the map from $S_{W_{[k-1]}} \sigma_1^{\square} \sigma_3^{\square}$ to $S_{W_{[k-1]}} \sigma_2^{\square} \sigma_4^{\square}$ (arrow 1).

Lemma 46 *Let $\zeta_{[k-1]} = ((Q, \{Z_{[k-1]}^{\square}\}), F_{\#}^{\square}, F_{\$}^{\square})$ be a cover. For any two labeled sequences σ_1 and σ_2 such that $|\sigma_1| = |\sigma_2|$ with source as $\underline{X_{[k-1]}}$ and target as $\underline{Y_{[k-1]}}$. Then following diagram commutes.*

$$
\begin{array}{ccc}
S_{\underline{X_{[k-1]}}} \sigma_1^{\square} & \xrightarrow{\text{by } (-)^{\square} \text{ functorial}} & S_{\underline{X_{[k-1]}}} \sigma_2^{\square} \\
\downarrow & & \downarrow \\
\sigma_1^{\dagger} S_{\underline{Y_{[k-1]}}} & \xrightarrow{\Upsilon_{\sigma_2,\sigma_1}} & \sigma_2^{\dagger} S_{\underline{Y_{[k-1]}}}
\end{array} \tag{10.4.48}
$$

PROOF. 82 *By using the following diagram*

$$
\begin{array}{ccccc}
\underline{X_{[k-1]}} & \xrightarrow{\Delta} & \underline{X_{[k-1]}} \times_{\underline{Y_{[k-1]}}} \underline{X_{[k-1]}} & \xrightarrow{\sigma_2'} & \underline{X_{[k-1]}} \\
 & \sigma_1' \downarrow & \mathfrak{S}_{[k]} & \sigma_1 \downarrow & \\
 & \underline{X_{[k-1]}} & \xrightarrow{\sigma_2} & \underline{Y_{[k-1]}} &
\end{array} \tag{10.4.49}
$$

the commutativity of the diagram in Eq. (10.4.48) is equivalent to check the commutativity of the following diagram

$$
\begin{array}{ccccccc}
\sigma_1^{\square} & \xrightarrow{\rho_{\Delta\sigma_2'}^{-1}} & \Delta^{\square}\sigma_2'^{\square}\sigma_1^{\square} & \xrightarrow{\alpha_{\mathfrak{S}_{[k]}}} & \Delta^{\square}\sigma_1'^{\square}\sigma_2^{\square} & \xrightarrow{\rho_{\Delta\sigma_1'}} & \sigma_2^{\square} \\
F_{\underline{\ }}^{\square} \downarrow & & F_{\underline{\ }}^{\square} \downarrow & & F_{\underline{\ }}^{\square} \downarrow & F_{\underline{\ }}^{\square} \downarrow & \\
\sigma_1^{\dagger} & \xrightarrow{\rho_{\Delta\sigma_2'}^{-1}} & \Delta^{\dagger}\sigma_2'^{\dagger}\sigma_1^{\dagger} & \xrightarrow{\alpha_{\mathfrak{S}_{[k]}}} & \Delta^{\dagger}\sigma_1'^{\dagger}\sigma_2^{\dagger} & \xrightarrow{\rho_{\Delta\sigma_1'}} & \sigma_2^{\dagger}
\end{array} \tag{10.4.50}
$$

where $F_{\underline{\ }}^{\square}$ is a sequence of $F_{\#}^{\square}$ or $F_{\$}^{\square}$ based on labels in each map within σ_1 or σ_2.

Now, we are ready to present our extension theorem.

Theorem 40 *According to conditions for extension theorem ([A], [B], [C] and [D]) provided in Sec. 10.1.2, there exists an extension of* **P** *(or* **O***) by an ideal cover. Moreover, any two ideal covers are isomorphic via a unique isomorphism.*

PROOF. 83 *The existence of such cover is based on the construction.*

For any object in $\underline{X_{[k-1]}}$, we set $X_{[k-1]}^{\square}$ as $\mathcal{D}_{X_{[k-1]}}$. For every map f in Q, we select a labeled sequence σ_f such that $|\sigma_f| = f$ and $f^{\square} = \sigma_f^{\dagger}$. For any pair of maps $\underline{X_{[k-1]}} \xrightarrow{f} \underline{Y_{[k-1]}} \xrightarrow{g} \underline{Z_{[k-1]}}$ in Q, we can set $\chi_{f,g}^{\square} = \Upsilon_{\sigma_{gf}, \sigma_f \diamond \sigma_g}$ by Theorem 36.

We claim that the constructed $((Q, \{W_{[k-1]}^{\square}\})$ is a parameterized algebraic invenrelation system defined in Sec. 10.1.1. We will show the associativity of $\chi_{-,-}^{\square}$ since other requirements for a parameterized algebraic invenrelation system are obvious valid. Let $\underline{X_{[k-1]}} \xrightarrow{f} \underline{Y_{[k-1]}} \xrightarrow{g} \underline{Z_{[k-1]}} \xrightarrow{h} \underline{V_{[k-1]}}$ be a map in Q, we wish to show that

$$\chi_{gf,h}^{\square} \chi_{f,g}^{\square}(h^{\square}) = \chi_{f,hg}^{\square} f^{\square} \chi_{g,h}^{\square}. \tag{10.4.51}$$

Then, this is equivalent to verify

$$\Upsilon_{\sigma_{hgf}, \sigma_{gf} \diamond \sigma_h} \Upsilon_{\sigma_{gf}, \sigma_f \diamond \sigma_g}(\sigma_h^{\dagger}) = \Upsilon_{\sigma_{hgf}, \sigma_f \diamond \sigma_{hg}} \sigma_f^{\dagger}(\Upsilon_{\sigma_{hg}, \sigma_g \diamond \sigma_h}). \tag{10.4.52}$$

For the L.H.S. of Eq. (10.4.52), we have $\Upsilon_{\sigma_{gf}, \sigma_f \diamond \sigma_g}(\sigma_h^{\dagger}) = \Upsilon_{\sigma_{gf} \diamond \sigma_h, \sigma_f \diamond \sigma_g \diamond \sigma_h}$ from linearity of $\Upsilon_{-,-}$ by Theorem 39. Hence, the L.H.S. of Eq. (10.4.52) becomes

$$\Upsilon_{\sigma_{hgf}, \sigma_{gf} \diamond \sigma_h} \Upsilon_{\sigma_{gf}, \sigma_f \diamond \sigma_g}(\sigma_h^{\dagger}) = \Upsilon_{\sigma_{hgf}, \sigma_{gf} \diamond \sigma_h} \Upsilon_{\sigma_{gf} \diamond \sigma_h, \sigma_f \diamond \sigma_g \diamond \sigma_h} = \Upsilon_{\sigma_{hgf}, \sigma_f \diamond \sigma_g \diamond \sigma_h} \tag{10.4.53}$$

by Theorem 35.

For the R.H.S. of Eq. (10.4.52), we have $\sigma_f^{\dagger}(\Upsilon_{\sigma_{hg}, \sigma_g \diamond \sigma_h}) = \Upsilon_{\sigma_f \diamond \sigma_{hg}, \sigma_f \diamond \sigma_g \diamond \sigma_h}$ from linearity of $\Upsilon_{-,-}$ by Theorem 39 again. Hence, the R.H.S. of Eq. (10.4.52) becomes

$$\Upsilon_{\sigma_{hgf}, \sigma_f \diamond \sigma_{hg}} \sigma_f^{\dagger}(\Upsilon_{\sigma_{hg}, \sigma_g \diamond \sigma_h}) = \Upsilon_{\sigma_{hgf}, \sigma_f \diamond \sigma_{hg}} \Upsilon_{\sigma_f \diamond \sigma_{hg}, \sigma_f \diamond \sigma_g \diamond \sigma_h} = \Upsilon_{\sigma_{hgf}, \sigma_f \diamond \sigma_g \diamond \sigma_h} \tag{10.4.54}$$

by Theorem 35. Since both sides of Eq. (10.4.52) are equal to $\Upsilon_{\sigma_{hgf}, \sigma_f \diamond \sigma_g \diamond \sigma_h}$, the associativity of $\chi_{-,-}^{\square}$ is established.

Define $F_{\#}^{\square}$ as $\Upsilon_{F, \sigma_f} : f^{\square} \longrightarrow f^{\overline{\#}}$ for any map $f : X_{[k-1]} \longrightarrow Y_{[k-1]}$ in **P***. Then, for any pair of morphisms $\underline{X_{[k-1]}} \xrightarrow{f} \underline{Y_{[k-1]}} \xrightarrow{g} \underline{Z_{[k-1]}}$ with $F = (f, \mathbf{P})$, $G = (g, \mathbf{P})$ and $H = (gf, \mathbf{P})$, the following diagram*

$$
\begin{array}{ccccc}
f^{\square} g^{\square} & \xrightarrow{\Upsilon_{F \diamond \sigma_g, \sigma_f \diamond \sigma_g}} & f^{\overline{\#}} g^{\square} & \xrightarrow{\Upsilon_{F \diamond F, F \diamond \sigma_g}} & f^{\overline{\#}} g^{\overline{\#}} \\
\Upsilon_{\sigma_{gf}, \sigma_f \diamond \sigma_g} \downarrow & & & & \downarrow \Upsilon_{H, F \diamond G} \\
(gf)^{\square} & \xrightarrow[\Upsilon_{H, \sigma_{gf}}]{} & & & (gf)^{\overline{\#}}
\end{array}
\tag{10.4.55}
$$

commutes by Theorems 35, 36 and 39. This shows that $F_{\#}^{\square}$ is a morphism between algebraic invenrelation systems.

Define $F_{\$}^{\square}$ as $\Upsilon_{F,\sigma_f} : f^{\square} \longrightarrow f^{\overline{\$}}$ for any map $f : \underline{X_{[k-1]}} \longrightarrow \underline{Y_{[k-1]}}$ in $\mathbf{O}$. Then, for any pair of morphisms $\underline{X_{[k-1]}} \xrightarrow{f} \underline{Y_{[k-1]}} \xrightarrow{g} \underline{Z_{[k-1]}}$ with $F = (f, \mathbf{O})$, $G = (g, \mathbf{O})$ and $H = (gf, \mathbf{O})$, the following diagram

$$f^{\square}g^{\square} \xrightarrow{\Upsilon_{F\diamond\sigma_g,\sigma_f\diamond\sigma_g}} f^{\overline{\$}}g^{\square} \xrightarrow{\Upsilon_{F\diamond F,F\diamond\sigma_g}} f^{\overline{\$}}g^{\overline{\$}}$$

$$\Upsilon_{\sigma_{gf},\sigma_f\diamond\sigma_g} \downarrow \qquad\qquad\qquad\qquad \downarrow \Upsilon_{H,F\diamond G}$$

$$(gf)^{\square} \xrightarrow{\Upsilon_{H,\sigma_{gf}}} \qquad (gf)^{\overline{\$}} \tag{10.4.56}$$

commutes by Theorems 35, 36 and 39. This shows that $F_{\$}^{\square}$ is also a morphism between algebraic invenrelation systems.

The remaining tasks to complete the construction of $((Q, \{W_{[k-1]}^{\square}\})$ as a cover are to checking (b) and (c) in Definition 79. By using Theorems 36 and 38 to transform all maps encountered within (b) and (c) into $\Upsilon_{-,-}$ form, then, repeatedly applying the cancelation rule (Theorem 35) gives the desired commutativity.

Let $\zeta_{1,[k-1]} = ((Q, \{W_{[k-1]}^{\times}\}), F_{\#}^{\times}, F_{\$}^{\times})$ and $\zeta_{2,[k-1]} = ((Q, \{W_{[k-1]}^{\square}\}), F_{\#}^{\square}, F_{\$}^{\square})$ be two covers. We will show that there exists a map between $\zeta_{1,[k-1]} = ((Q, \{W_{[k-1]}^{\times}\}), F_{\#}^{\times}, F_{\$}^{\times})$ and $\zeta_{2,[k-1]} = ((Q, \{W_{[k-1]}^{\square}\}), F_{\#}^{\square}, F_{\$}^{\square})$ on Q. Let $\underline{X_{[k-1]}} \xrightarrow{f} \underline{Y_{[k-1]}} \xrightarrow{g} \underline{Z_{[k-1]}}$ be maps in Q, the existence of such map is based on the following diagram

$$f^{\times}g^{\times} \longrightarrow \sigma_f^{\times}\sigma_g^{\times} \longrightarrow \sigma_f^{\dagger}\sigma_g^{\dagger} \longrightarrow \sigma_f^{\square}\sigma_g^{\square} \longrightarrow f^{\times}g^{\times}$$

$$\downarrow \qquad\quad \downarrow \qquad\quad \downarrow \qquad\quad \downarrow \qquad\quad \downarrow$$

$$(gf)^{\times} \longrightarrow \sigma_{gf}^{\times} \longrightarrow \sigma_{gf}^{\dagger} \longrightarrow \sigma_{gf}^{\square} \longrightarrow (gf)^{\square} \tag{10.4.57}$$

which commutes by Lemma 46 (in two middle squares). Let $\mathbf{t}_i : \zeta_{1,[k-1]} \longrightarrow \zeta_{2,[k-1]}$ for $i = 1, 2$. Now recall that for any map f in $\mathbf{O}$ or $\mathbf{P}$, the choice for a map $f^{\times} \longrightarrow f^{\square}$ is uniquely determined by the commutativity of the corresponding diagram in Definition 80. Therefore, on $\mathbf{O}$ and on $\mathbf{P}$, the restrictions of $\mathbf{t}_i$ coincide. Since any map in Q is a composite of maps in $\mathbf{O}$ or $\mathbf{P}$, the map $\zeta_{1,[k-1]} \longrightarrow \zeta_{2,[k-1]}$ implies uniqueness in general.

10.5   Example

In this section, we will provide an example about applying Theorem 40 to enlarge one's creation space.

Let $\mathbf{P}$ be the invengory composed by elements (objects) with different color, i.e., each object has its own color (distinct each other) and its geometric shape (may same at some of them). Let $\mathbf{O}$ be the invengory composed by elements with different geometric shape, i.e., each object has its own geometric shape (distinct each other) and its color (may same at some of them). And let $\mathbf{C}$ be the invengory composed by elements with different color and different geometric shape. Every element (object) X in $\mathbf{P}$ (or $\mathbf{O}$) is assigned a two-dimensional pattern design made by X (an invengory) $X^{\overline{\#}}$ (or $X^{\overline{\$}}$). We now verify that above specification satisfies those conditions for extension theorem provided by Sec. 10.1.2.

[A] There are 1-SISO-invengories $\mathbf{C}$, $\mathbf{O}$ and $\mathbf{P}$ such that every 0-dimensional object in $\mathbf{C}$ is also in $\mathbf{O}$ and $\mathbf{P}$. Moreover, the following items hold

- For any map $f : X \longrightarrow Y$ in $\mathbf{P}$ (or $\mathbf{O}$) and any map $g : Z \longrightarrow Y$ in $\mathbf{C}$, the fibered product of f with g exists and the induced map $f' : X' \longrightarrow Z$ is also in $\mathbf{P}$ (or $\mathbf{O}$).

- Let $X \xrightarrow{f} Y \xrightarrow{g} Z$ be morphisms in $\mathbf{C}$ such that each map in gf is in $\mathbf{C}$. If g is in $\mathbf{O}$ or in $\mathbf{P}$, then each map in f is in $\mathbf{P}$.

[B] There is a system of algebraic invenrelation systems parameterized by perspectives on $\mathbf{P}$ for objects with dimension 0, represented as $(\mathbf{P}, \{X^{\overline{\#}}\})$, and there is another system of algebraic invenrelation systems parameterized by perspectives on $\mathbf{O}$, denoted as $(\mathbf{O}, \{Y^{\overline{\#}}\})$. Since $X^{\overline{\#}} = Y^{\overline{\#}}$ for any object $X = Y \in \mathbf{C}$, we use $\mathcal{D}_X$ for $X^{\overline{\#}}$ or $Y^{\overline{\#}}$.

[C] For any cartesian square $\mathfrak{s}_{[0]}$ (0-dimensional objects involved) in $\mathbf{C}$ with $f, f' \in \mathbf{P}$ and $i, i' \in \mathbf{O}$,

$$
\begin{array}{ccc}
U & \xrightarrow{i'} & X \\
f' \downarrow & \mathfrak{s}_{[0]} & \downarrow f \\
V & \xrightarrow{i} & Y
\end{array}
\tag{10.5.1}
$$

there is an isomorphism $\alpha_{\mathfrak{s}_{[0]}} : i'^{\overline{\$}} f^{\overline{\#}} \longrightarrow f'^{\overline{\#}} i^{\overline{\$}}$. The isomorphism $\alpha_{\mathfrak{s}_{[0]}}$ possesses the following transitivity rules :

(1) Horizontal transitivity: Considering the horizontal extension of the cartesian square $\mathfrak{s}_{[0]}$

by another cartesian square $\mathfrak{s}_{H,[0]}$ as

$$U_1 \xrightarrow{\ j'\ } U \xrightarrow{\ i'\ } X$$
$$f'' \downarrow \ \mathfrak{s}_{H,[0]} \quad f' \downarrow \ \mathfrak{s}_{[0]} \quad \downarrow f$$
$$V_1 \xrightarrow{\ j\ } V \xrightarrow{\ i\ } Y \tag{10.5.2}$$

then we have the following commutative diagram

$$
\begin{array}{ccccc}
j'^{\bar{\$}} i'^{\bar{\$}} f^{\overline{\#}} & \xrightarrow{\ j'^{\bar{\$}}\alpha_{\mathfrak{s}_{[0]}}\ } & j'^{\bar{\$}} f'^{\overline{\#}} i^{\bar{\$}} & \xrightarrow{\ \alpha_{\mathfrak{s}_{H,[0]}} i^{\bar{\$}}\ } & f''^{\overline{\#}} j^{\bar{\$}} i^{\bar{\$}} \\
\chi^{\bar{\$}}_{j',i'} f^{\overline{\#}} \downarrow & & & & \downarrow f''^{\overline{\#}} \chi^{\bar{\$}}_{j,i} \\
(i'j')^{\bar{\$}} f^{\overline{\#}} & & \xrightarrow{\ \alpha_{\mathfrak{c}_{[0]}}\ } & & f''^{\overline{\#}} (ij)^{\bar{\$}}
\end{array}
\tag{10.5.3}
$$

where $\mathfrak{c}_{[0]}$ is the composite cartesian squares of $\mathfrak{s}_{[0]}$ and $\mathfrak{s}_{H,[0]}$.

(2) Vertical transitivity: Considering the vertical extension of the cartesian square $\mathfrak{s}_{[0]}$ by another cartesian square $\mathfrak{s}_{V,[0]}$ as

$$U_1 \xrightarrow{\ i''\ } X_1$$
$$g' \downarrow \ \mathfrak{s}_{V,[0]} \quad \downarrow g$$
$$U \xrightarrow{\ i'_{[0]}\ } X$$
$$f' \downarrow \ \mathfrak{s}_{[0]} \quad \downarrow f$$
$$V \xrightarrow{\ i\ } Y \tag{10.5.4}$$

then we have the following commutative diagram

$$
\begin{array}{ccccc}
i''^{\bar{\$}} g^{\overline{\#}} f^{\overline{\#}} & \xrightarrow{\ \alpha_{\mathfrak{s}_{V,[0]}} f^{\overline{\#}}\ } & g'^{\overline{\#}} i'^{\bar{\$}} f^{\overline{\#}} & \xrightarrow{\ g'^{\overline{\#}}\alpha_{\mathfrak{s}_{[0]}}\ } & g'^{\overline{\#}} f'^{\overline{\#}} i^{\bar{\$}} \\
i''^{\bar{\$}} \chi^{\overline{\#}}_{g,f} \downarrow & & & & \downarrow \chi^{\overline{\#}}_{g',f'} i^{\bar{\$}} \\
i''^{\bar{\$}} (fg)^{\overline{\#}} & & \xrightarrow{\ \alpha_{\mathfrak{c}_{[0]}}\ } & & (f'g')^{\overline{\#}} i^{\bar{\$}}
\end{array}
\tag{10.5.5}
$$

where $\mathfrak{c}_{[0]}$ is the composite cartesian squares of $\mathfrak{s}_{[0]}$ and $\mathfrak{s}_{V,[0]}$.

[D] For any decomposition of the identity map on X, $X \xrightarrow{\ f\ } Y \xrightarrow{\ g\ } X$, there is an isomorphism $\eta_{f,g} : f^{\overline{\#}} g^{\bar{\$}} \xrightarrow{\ \cong\ } \mathbf{1}_{\mathcal{D}_X}$ if $g \in \mathbf{O}$ and $f \in \mathbf{P}$. The isomorphism $\eta_{f,g}$ should satisfy the following two compatible conditions:

(1) (Parallel Compatibility) Let $h : X' \longrightarrow X$ be a map in $\mathbf{C}$ and the decomposition map

$X' \xrightarrow{f'} Y' \xrightarrow{g'} X'$. Consider the following diagram

$$X' \xrightarrow{f'} Y' \xrightarrow{g'} X'$$

$$h \downarrow \mathfrak{s}_{1,[0]} h' \downarrow \mathfrak{s}_{2,[0]} h \downarrow$$

$$X \xrightarrow{f} Y \xrightarrow{g} X \qquad (10.5.6)$$

where $\mathfrak{s}_{1,[0]}$ and $\mathfrak{s}_{2,[0]}$ are cartesian squares.

(a) If h is in $\mathbf{P}$, then we have following commutative diagram:

$$f'^{\overline{\#}} g'^{\overline{\$}} h^{\overline{\#}} \xrightarrow{f'^{\overline{\#}}\alpha_{\mathfrak{s}_{2,[0]}}} f'^{\overline{\#}} h^{\overline{\#}} g^{\overline{\$}} \xrightarrow{\mathrm{by}\mathfrak{s}_{1,[0]}} h^{\overline{\#}} f^{\overline{\#}} g^{\overline{\$}}$$

$$\eta_{f',g'} h^{\overline{\#}} \downarrow \qquad\qquad \downarrow h^{\overline{\#}} \eta_{f,g}$$

$$\mathbf{1}_{\mathcal{D}_{X'}} h^{\overline{\#}} \qquad = \qquad h^{\overline{\#}} \mathbf{1}_{\mathcal{D}_X} \qquad (10.5.7)$$

(b) If h is in $\mathbf{O}$, then we have following commutative diagram:

$$f'^{\overline{\#}} g'^{\overline{\$}} h^{\overline{\$}} \xrightarrow{\mathrm{by}\mathfrak{s}_{2,[0]}} f'^{\overline{\#}} h'^{\overline{\#}} g^{\overline{\$}} \xrightarrow{\alpha_{\mathfrak{s}_{1,[0]}} g^{\overline{\$}}} h^{\overline{\$}} f^{\overline{\#}} g^{\overline{\$}}$$

$$\eta_{f',g'} h^{\overline{\$}} \downarrow \qquad\qquad \downarrow h^{\overline{\$}} \eta_{f,g}$$

$$\mathbf{1}_{\mathcal{D}_{X'}} h^{\overline{\$}} \qquad = \qquad h^{\overline{\$}} \mathbf{1}_{\mathcal{D}_X} \qquad (10.5.8)$$

(2) (Serial Compatibility) We concatenate $X \xrightarrow{h'} Y \xrightarrow{g'} X$ and $X \xrightarrow{f} Z \xrightarrow{h} X$ serially as following diagram:

$$X \xrightarrow{h'} Y \xrightarrow{g'} X$$

$$f' \downarrow \mathfrak{s}_{[0]} f \downarrow$$

$$W \xrightarrow{g} Z \xrightarrow{h} X \qquad (10.5.9)$$

such that $\mathfrak{s}_{[0]}$ is a cartesian square with $f, f', h' \in \mathbf{P}$ and $g, g', h \in \mathbf{O}$. Then there is a commutative diagram

$$h'^{\overline{\#}} f'^{\overline{\#}} g^{\overline{\$}} h^{\overline{\$}} \xrightarrow{\alpha_{\mathfrak{s}_{[0]}}} h'^{\overline{\#}} g'^{\overline{\$}} f^{\overline{\#}} h^{\overline{\$}}$$

$$\chi_{h',f'}^{\overline{\#}}, \chi_{g,h}^{\overline{\$}} \downarrow \qquad\qquad \downarrow \eta_{h',g'}, \eta_{f,h}$$

$$(f'h')^{\overline{\#}}(hg)^{\overline{\$}} \xrightarrow{\eta_{f'h',hg}} \mathbf{1}_{\mathcal{D}_X} \qquad (10.5.10)$$

Therefore, by Theorem 40, there exists an extension of $\mathbf{P}$ (or $\mathbf{O}$) by an ideal cover such that one can have an algebraic invenrelation system parameterized by both color and geometric shape jointly.

Figure 10.1: Invention Perspective Taking

Chapter 11

Invenrelation Networks

In movie "The Butterfly Effect", we recognize that the tiny variation of initial conditions at one place can induce significant different outcomes at another place. With globalization, the economy, information and the people at different local area are getting closer than before. With this trend, a more radically superior mode of invenrelation than before is generated due to globalization. Such invenrelation mode is *coordinating invenrelation networks*. Thanks to the maturity of communication network technology, organizations [1] at different local area are allowed to invent together. Coordinating invenrelation begins when organizations come together to invent common objects or solve common problems that are beyond the scope, scale or capabilities of individual organizations.

This chapter is organized as follows. Concepts and three basic ingredients about coordinating invenrelation networks are introduced in Sec. 11.1. In 11.2, notions about random relations and random functors, which are used to model uncertain effect from information communication, are presented. The tensor product of many-sorted algebra (MSA) multi-invengories which plays as a building block for higher dimensional tensor product is the main topic in Sec. 11.3. Then, the tensor product of n-MIMO invengories is presented in Sec. 11.4. Finally, an example about a network of invenrelations is given in Sec. 11.5.

---

[1] An organization is an entity which distributes tasks for a collective goal, for example, a social group, a government or a cluster of computing machines.

11.1 Coordinating Invenrelation Networks

Coordinating Invenrelation Networks (CINs) is a network of entities (organizations) which work collaboratively to achieve a common goal by utilizing their knowledge domains and invenrelation methods individually. CIN implies that a dominant organization coordinates other involved organizations to invent jointly and share final innovation results. Hence, CIN is an unification of distributive and integrated invenrelation. From enterprise perspective, invenrelation may be required in procedures of research and development, production and test, and sale. Contrary from traditional enterprises, which focus internal invenrelation inside a company, CIN requests enterprises to adopt more open and collaborative mode of invenrelation instead of internal invenrelation procedure. CINs management requires enterprises to familiarize with communication network, coordination of cross-cultural and cross-organizational invenrelation results exchange.

11.1.1 Advantages of Adopting CINs

The advantages to organizations that embrace the concept of CINs are significant. A recent and typical case is that Boeing adopted CIN's mode to product Boeing 787 aircraft. From invention aviation techniques, shape determination, transformation and even financing, almost all these parts in producing Boeing 787 aircraft are realized through CINs' mode. Boeing 787 manufacturing and R & D are related to suppliers and research institutions in the United States, Japan, France, Britain, Italy, Sweden, Canada, South Korea, Australia and other countries, and Boeing's global network of innovation shortens Boeing 787 time to market and save considerable R & D costs. We provide some potential advantages about CINs as sequel.

CINs make organizations more adaptive in facing environmental changes. In the biological world, a species must evolve to adapt to the current environment where it lives, or the species will be eliminated by environment. This is a natural rule of the biological world. However, such rule also applies to the business world. As the world changes, the enterprise needs to change along with it. It must adjust its speed, processes, and pace of invention and be able to keep tract future trends in markets. Since invention and development are much quicker than before which reduces products life. For example, Apple's iPod debuted and made a storm in consumer electronics. Very shortly after the first iPod, an even better one came with more functions with lighter design. Then came devices that can play MP3 files. How about the shelf life for that original iPod? Much shorter than the shelf life of a CD player when it debuted on the market.

With a truly global corporation through consolidated investment, planning, decision-making, trade and supply networks, no matter where you are, the product you buy is the same. Let us inspect at Apple again. In Hong Kong, Moscow, Bombay, Paris, or Los Angeles, the latest, lightest, highest-memory iPod MP3 player is the same product: that is a truly wonderful result after global corporation. Therefore, organizations that support CINs are better in dealing with market and technology changes.

CINs make organizations more creative and collaborative. Researchers and scientists do not work complete independently as they inevnt and develop new products. In general, they collaborate and work with a team, leveraging each other's knowledge domain and invention methods to continually improve the idea and design. CINs supports this collaborative team approach, allowing teams of organizations to innovate together on projects and share results. CINs further shortens time to solution by allowing innovators to easily seek input and assistance from experts within the CIN. Users can ask their questions and receive and review responses from anywhere within the CIN. Subject matter organizations are automatically identified by CINs using algebraic processing capabilities on invention content. Each organization profile in CINs can be augmented manually by the organizations themselves or by CIN system administrators. Multiple organizations can comment on the same question and all responses may be collected by CIN system administrators for future innovation and problem solving.

Members in CINs could learn new knowledge domains and invention methods rapidly. The rapid growth of communication network technology, regarded it as the fastest growth of any technology in human history, plays a crucial rule in realizing CINs. The number of regional and national electrical resources, for example, multimedia presentation, related to online knowledge learning has expanded exponentially in recent years. Some important features about applying communication network technology in CINs are (a) multi-sensory interaction, (b) time and location independence, and (c) many-to-many communication. These feature are explained following.

The first feature of CIN based learning is that it allows multimedia documents to be published and distributed through communication links among computers around the world. Multi-sensory interaction over communication networks can provide access to up-to-date, authentic information, which can then be incorporated into R&D office collaborative activities. For example, researchers can work collaboratively to plan and implement tasks (e.g., designing and carrying out advertising activities) using current information (e.g., transport schedules, prices, consuming habit, social information, weather, news) related to their own personal invention methods gathered from a variety of sites all over the world. The most potent collaborative activities involve not just finding and using information via multimedia networks, but rather making use of technologies to construct new knowledge together interactively.

The second feature-time and location independence cooperation-allows users to present and receive ideas at any time of the day from any computing devices through internet connection. Time and place independent communication increase the chance of online collaboration in several ways. First, it allows researchers to initiate communication with each other or with other researchers located in other areas. Second, it allows for more in-depth analysis and critical response, because emails or documents at blogs can be answered more cautiously than synchronous information. Third, CIN realizes the cross-cultural possibilities of long distance cooperation.

The third feature is that CIN allows many-to-many communication among inventors. CIN has three major advantages in performing cooperative innovation: (a) it reduces emotional estrangement, such as frowning and hesitating, which can intimidate people, especially those with less power and authority; (b) it reduces social and cultural distance among inventors related to religion, accent, gender, and status; and (c) it allows individuals to contribute at their own knowledge domains and invention methods. Hence, CIN results in cooperation that is more equal in participation than face-to-face discussion, with those inventors who are traditionally excluded out of discussions benefiting most from the increased participation.

CINs reduce resources, e.g., costs and time, to market. Another way CINs can reduce resources required for products to market is by leveraging the complementary resource endowments of a cooperative partner. There are three significant reasons to support this notion. (1) The ability of cooperative partners to generate new ideas from complementary resources increases with the degree of compatibility in their organizational systems and processes. (2) The ability of organizations involved in CINs increases with the organization's prior experience and potential to occupy an information-rich position in its economic networks. (3) As the proportion of resources in the possible partners in CINs increases, so dose the potential for earning new ideas or products by combining the complementary resources. In conclusion, both knowledge domains and invention methods complementarity are critical for realizing the potential benefits of combining complementary resources.

CINs uncover hidden business opportunities. A new market, which is about business to deal invention ideas exchange among organizations within CINs, is generated. Possible ways to appear in such market include: (1) Use the home page for ideas exchange and products advertisement; (2)

Make inventors available to customers and investors on-line; (3) Give every inventors a web pages; and (4) Replace ideas communication through multimedia over data networks. We conclude that creating Web-enabled invention model called for a new set of invention development principles, which they summarized and shared within the burgeoning CIN community: (1) Start simple but grow very fast; (2) Wherever one go, there one is; (3) Take risks and make mistakes easily, but fix them quickly; (4) Just enough is good enough; and (5) One is not impeded by any other way of thinking.

CINs help to build a more secure environment among collaborative organizations. The higher transparency and the high-trust cooperating environment of CINs have significant advantages, as transparent information flow exposes security risks early on. This is apparent in the examples of several CINs, such as the Institute of Electrical and Electronics Engineers (IEEE) standard developments and Linux developers. They operate in complete transparency: every member posting to a mailing list in IEEE and Linux working groups knows that everyone else can read their postings. Pretenders, swindlers, and anyone trying to use the groups and their lists for any reason other than to benefit the community are immediately exposed, admonished, and ejected-if unwilling to rectify organization rules.

Although we have provided some advantages induced by CINs, there are still many other quantitative and qualitative benefits organizations can realize through CINs.

Ingredients of CINs

In this section, we discuss three components of CINs. They are invenrelation capability, communication and coordination.

Invention Capability

An invenrelation is an unique or novel device, method, composition, process manipulated from known facts or objects. An invenrelation may also be referred as an improvement, or a different approach, of achieving an existing result or function. An invenrelation that is not derived from an existing model or idea easily, or that achieves a completely exceptional function or result, will be called as a breakthrough invenrelation. Invenrelation often enlarges the boundaries of human knowledge, facts or methods. An invenrelation that is novel and not obvious to others skilled in the same field may be able to obtain the legal protection of a patent.

Invenrelation capability is the ability to create new devices and methods from known facts or objects. An open and curious intelligence allows an invenrelator to aware beyond what is known. Observing a new possibility, connection, or relationship can inspire an invenrelation. Sometimes invenrelators disregard the boundaries between separate knowledge fields by combining concepts or elements from different realms that would not normally be put together. Playing games can lead to invenrelation. As a famous and great inventor-Thomas Edison-said, "I never did a day's work in my life, it was all fun". Perspective is a vital element of invenrelation capability. It may begin with questions, doubt or a intuition. It may begin by recognizing that something unusual or accidental may be useful or that it could open a new avenue for exploration. For example, on 8 Nov, 1895, Wilhelm Conrad Rontgen discovered an image project from his cathode ray generator, projected far beyond the possible range of the cathode rays (now known as an electron beam). Further investigation showed that the rays were generated at the point of contact of the cathode ray beam on the interior of the vacuum tube and they penetrated many kinds of matter. Some days after his discovery, Rontgen took an X-ray photograph of his wife's hand which clearly revealed her wedding ring and bones. The photograph astonished the general public and aroused great scientific interest in the new type of radiation. Rontgen named the new form of radiation X-radiation (X standing for "Unknown"). Hence, invenrelation capability is the basic requirement for members in CINs.

Communication

Communication is the process of conveying information. We present a diagram to illustrate the proposed communication model in Fig. 11.1. Our model is an extension model from Shannon and Weavers (1949) linear model (no feedback), David Berlo (1960) Sender-Message-Channel-Receiver Model (no room for noise), and Barnlund (2008) transaction model (no information interpretation based on communicators' knowledge and experiences). Each component in our model is explained as follows.

Communicators: It combines functions of information sender and receiver. A more realistic communication is an interactive information exchange process.

Information Manipulation: It transforms information generated by communicator into proper form suitable to be transferred and understandable via coding, modulation or translation.

Information Interpretation: After transferred information sensed by the communicator, the communicator will explain its meaning according to the instant environment (social and cultural) context, possessed knowledge and experiences. Information may be sensed through seeing, hearing, touching, smelling, tasting or whatever action which can extract meanings from transferred information. The interpretation may require the communicator to think, analyze and infer true meanings from sensed information. A successful communication is that interpretation results made by one communicator match the meaning for information to be manipulated by the other communicator.

Transfer: It is about the way in which the manipulated information is conveyed or the way in which the manipulated information is passed on or deliver it. The purpose of transfer is to make information exchangeable between communicators without barriers, e.g., physical barriers like time or space, or physiological barriers like ill health, poor eye sight or hearing difficulties.

In the proposed communication model, noise is interference with the interpretating of messages transferred. There are many examples of noise:

Physical Noise: Noise that physically destroys information in communication, for example, the noise from a construction site next to a church making it difficult to hear the paster.

Physiological and Psychological Noise: Physiological defects that prevent effective communication, such as actual deafness or blindness preventing information sensed from outer environment. Certain psychological problems can also make communication difficult. A mental disorder person, e.g., delirium, will have troubles in interacting and communicating with other persons.

Semantic Noise: Different interpretations of the meanings of some words due to different communicators' knowledge backgrounds. For example, the word "group" can be interpreted as a crowd of persons by soldiers, or as an algebraic structure consisting of a set together with an operation by mathematicians.

Structural Noise: Poorly structured information pieces in communication can prevent the receiver from accurate interpretation. For example, disorganized directions statements can make the receiver even lost more. Another kind of structural noise is made by syntactical misuse. Errors in grammar can disrupt communication, such as incorrect changes in verb tense during a sentence.

Social and Cultural Noise: Many misunderstanding circumstances are induced by social and cultural difference. In the West, it is regarded as polite to open gifts as soon as they are given to express appreciation. In China, the situation is totally reverse. Normally, Chinese feel that if one opens the gift as soon as it is given, one might embarrass the person who gives the gift and one might be thought greedy. Chinese tend to open the gifts after the visitors have left. However, when we receive gifts from a West friend, in order to avoid misunderstanding, we may follow their custom by opening the gifts in front of him or her and express our appreciation immediately. We present the Fig 11.1 to illustrate the proposed communication model.

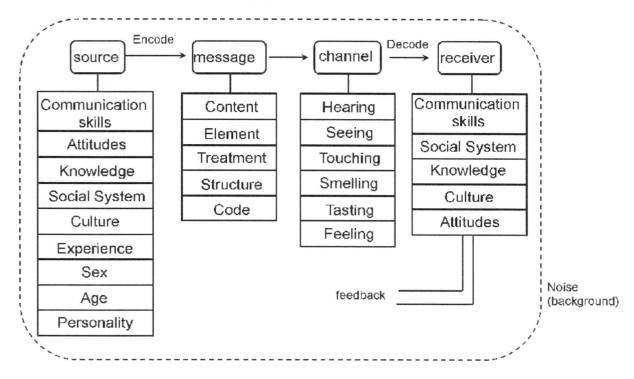

Figure 11.1: Communication model.

Coordination

Coordination is a recursive process where two or more entities work together to realize shared goals. Following three reasons are provided to support that coordination is a necessary essence in CINs.

(1) The dramatic improvements in the costs and functions of information technologies are changing-by orders of magnitude-the ways on how people communicate and coordinate. Compared to last century, larger numbers of people have acquired direct access to computers. These computers are now beginning to be connected to each other through internet or other wireless networks. We now have, for the first time, an opportunity for vastly larger numbers of organizations to use resourceful computing and communications capabilities to help coordinate their common invenrelation goals. For example, new web-based software has been developed to (a) support authors from different countries working together on the same document, (b) help people transfer and manipulate multimedia information more effectively, and (c) enable people who use various computer operating systems to work on a same project. Therefore, there is a pervasive feeling in current global business that the pace of change is accelerating and that we need to coordinate more flexible and adaptive organizations.

(2) There appears to be a growing recognition of the commonality of invenrelation problems in a variety of different disciplines that deal with the coordination of separate academic fields. For example, management theorists and economists have found concepts about information processing useful in analyzing human behavior, and computer scientists have used social and other political concepts in designing and analyzing parallel and distributed computer systems. These cross-disciplinary connections offer the possibility of more approaches adopted to solve the same problem due to various perspectives involved. Such interdisciplinary approach enables us to explore parallels between: (a) coordinating groups of invenrelators, (b) coordinating groups of invenrelation machines, and (c) coordinating "hybrid" groups that include both invenrelators and invenrelation machines.

(3) In order to share a larger market and reduce risk, related business entities (enterprises) often form an alliance. A business alliance is a cooperation between businesses, usually motivated by cost reduction and improved service for the customer. Because alliances are getting more prevalent in many industries, and because they inherently challenge the concept that organizations are discretely bounded entities, researchers have tried to understand the antecedent

conditions that lead to study the network of business alliance. Alliances are often bounded by a single agreement with equitable risk and benefits share for all parties involved and are typically coordinated by an integrated unit. We can classify alliances as following types: (1) Marketing alliance, (2) Service alliance, (3) Geographic alliance, (4) Intellectural properties alliance. All types of alliances require proper coordination rules to make members in alliances to achieve their common goals. Finally, relationships among these three components (invenrelation capability, communication and coordination) can be illustrated by Fig. 11.2.

11.2   Random Invengory

Noise is anything that disturbs information being transmitted from a sender to a receiver. It results from both internal and external factors. Communication savants classify noise as four types: physical, psychological, physiological and semantic. In communication systems made by electrical devices, noise is a random fluctuation in an electrical signal, a characteristic of all electronic devices. Noise generated by electronic devices can be produced by several different effects. The most important one is thermal noise, which is unavoidable since electric devices are always operated above absolute zero (absolute temperature scales). Because noise phenomena in communication limit the range in which truly invenrelation ideas generated by one entity can be reproduced by other entities in CINs, this motives us to introduce a statistical viewpoint about functions and invengories-*random functions* and *random invengories*.

11.2.1   Random Functions and Relations

A random function f from the domain X to the codomain Y is a random choice from a set of functions (non-random), denoted as V, from the domain X to the codomain Y. The probability to choose a random function is determined by the probability density (or mass) function for elements in V. Similarly, a random relation F from the domain X to the codomain Y is a random choice from a set of relations (non-random), denoted as V, from the domain X to the codomain Y. The probability to choose a random relation is determined by the probability density (or mass) function for elements in V. By classifying mappings for those one-to-many elements in domain as before, a random relation F can be expressed as $F = \bowtie_{i=1}^{I_F} f_i$, where I_F is an integer for mapping layers and f_i are random functions. We say that two random functions f and g are equal if random variables $f(x)$ and $g(x)$ are equal in distribution for each element x in the domain.

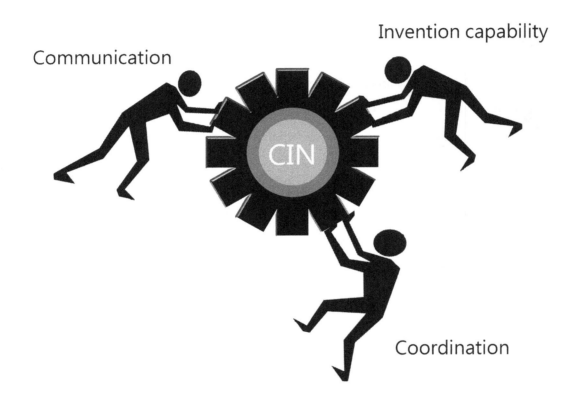

Figure 11.2: Three components of CIN.

11.2.2 Random Invengory Definition

From the previous discussions, we have to collect a set of objects with specific random relations among them to form a random invengory for analogy invenrelation under noise communication environment. A random invengory is defined below to characterize these features (objects and their random relations in a random invengory) mathematically.

Definition 81 *A random invengory* **C** *consists of:*

1. *A collection of objects;*

2. *A collection of random relations;*

3. *Operations assigning to each random relation F an object $domF$, its domain, and an object $ranF$, its range (codomain) (we write $F : A \rightarrow B$ to show that $domF = A$ and $ranF = B$; the collection of all random relations with domain A and range B is written as $\mathbf{C}(A, B)$);*

4. *The random relations F, G and H can be expressed by random functions as $F =\bowtie_{i=1}^{I_F} f_i$, $G =\bowtie_{j=1}^{I_G} g_j$ and $H =\bowtie_{k=1}^{I_H} h_k$, where each f_i, g_j and h_k is a random function. A composition operator assigning to each pair of random functions f_i and g_j, with $ranf_i = domg_j$ for some indices $i \in I_F$ and $j \in I_G$, respectively. A composite random function $g_j \circ f_i : domf_i \rightarrow rang_j$, satisfying the following associative law:*

   For any random relations $F : A \rightarrow B, G : B \rightarrow C$, and $H : C \rightarrow D$ where $A, B, C,$ and D are not necessarily distinct, we always have

$$h_k \circ (g_j \circ f_i) = (h_k \circ g_j) \circ f_i, \tag{11.2.1}$$

   where indices i, j and k satisfy $ran\ f_i = dom\ g_j$ and $ran\ g_j = dom\ h_k$.

5. *For each object A, an identity relation $id_A : A \rightarrow A$ satisfying the following identity law with respect to any random relation $F : A \rightarrow B$ and each index i:*

$$id_B \circ f_i = f_i,\ and\ f_i \circ id_A = f_i, \tag{11.2.2}$$

   where $F =\bowtie_{i=1}^{I_F} f_i$.

Example 45 *The invengory* $\mathbf{Set}_n$ *has sets with n distinct elements as objects and total random functions between sets as random relations. Let V_n be the set of n^n functions from $\{1, 2, \cdots, n\}$*

421

to $\{1, 2, \cdots, n\}$ and let $f_1, f_2, \cdots$ be a sequence of random functions chosen independently and uniformly from V_n.

By checking the validity for the following laws:

1. An object in $\mathbf{Set}_n$ is a set.

2. A random relation $f : A \longrightarrow B$ in $\mathbf{Set}_n$ is a total random function from the set A to the set B.

3. For each total random function f with domain A and codmain B, we have dom $f = A$, ran $f = B$ and $f \in \mathbf{Set}_n(A, B)$.

4. The composition of a total random function $f : A \longrightarrow B$ with another total random function $g : B \longrightarrow C$ is the total random function from A to C mapping each element $a \in A$ to $g(f(a)) \in C$. Such composition of total random functions is associative since $h \circ (g \circ f) = (h \circ g) \circ f$, where $f : C \longrightarrow D$.

5. For any random function $f : A \longrightarrow B$, the identity functions on A and B satisfy the equations $id_B \circ f = f$ and $f \circ id_A = f$.

we can conclude that $\mathbf{Set}_n$ is a random invengory.

Let $h_1 = f_1$, and for $t > 1$ let $h_t = f_t \circ h_{t-1}$ be the composition of the first t random functions. Define T to be the smallest t for which h_t is a constant function. An interesting problem about such invengory is the distribution of the random variable T.

11.2.3 Random Functor

A *random functor* is a structure-preserving of analogical random relations between two random invengories. Given two random invengories $\mathbf{C}$ and $\mathbf{D}$, a random functor $\mathbf{F}$ from $\mathbf{C}$ to $\mathbf{D}$ is a random choice from a set of functors (non-random), denoted as $\mathbf{V}$, from the random invengory $\mathbf{C}$ to the random invengory $\mathbf{D}$. The probability to choose a random functor is determined by the probability density (or mass) function for elements in $\mathbf{V}$. Hence, we define a random functor as:

Definition 82 *Let $\mathbf{C}$ and $\mathbf{D}$ be two random invengories. A random functor satisfies that*

$$\mathbf{F}(id_A) = id_{\mathbf{F}(A)},$$
$$\mathbf{F}(g_j \circ_{\mathbf{C}} f_i) = \mathbf{F}(g_j) \circ_{\mathbf{D}} \mathbf{F}(f_i) \tag{11.2.3}$$

for all **C**-*objects* A, *all composable* **C**-*random relations* $F = \bowtie_{i=1}^{I_F} f_i$ *and* $G = \bowtie_{j=1}^{I_G} g_j$, *and all random functions* f_i *and* g_j *with* ran f_i = dom g_j. *Formulas in Eq. (11.2.3) are equal in probability distribution sense.*

Having defined random mappings from one random invengory to another-random functors-we proceed to define structure-preserving mappings for random functors, named *random natural transformations.*

Definition 83 *Let* **C** *and* **D** *be random invengories and let* **F** *and* **G** *be two random functors from* **C** *to* **D**. *A random natural transformation* $\mathbf{\Psi}$ *from the random functor* **F** *to the random functor* **G** *is a relation that assigns to every* **C**-*object* A *a* **D**-*random relation* $\mathbf{\Psi}_A$ ($\mathbf{\Psi}_A = \bowtie_{i=1}^{I_A} \psi_{A,i}$ *if such relation can be expressed by several but finite random functions.) such that for any* **C**-*random relation* $F : A \to B(F = \bowtie_{k=1}^{I_F} f_k)$ *the following diagram commutes in* **D** *with respect to all indices* i, j *and* k *when* cod $\psi_{A,i}$ = dom $\mathbf{G}(f_k)$ *and* cod $\mathbf{F}(f_k)$ = dom $\psi_{B,j}$:

$$\psi_{A,i} \circ_{\mathbf{D}} \mathbf{G}(f_k) = \mathbf{F}(f_k) \circ_{\mathbf{D}} \psi_{B,j}$$

Moreover, if $\mathbf{\Psi}_A$ *is an isomorphic relation in* **D** *for every object* A, *then* $\mathbf{\Psi}$ *is called a* natural isomorphism.

11.3   Building Block: Tensor Product of Random Multi-invengories

In this section, we will consider the tensor product of two random symmetric multi-invengories, the building block in tensor product of two n-MIMO invengories with objects as symmetric multi-invengories. This is the key step for operations in CINs since coordinators have to combine inven-relations from different sources. We begin by definition of *random symmetric multi-invengory.*

Definition 84 *A random symmetric multi-invengory consists of the following:*

1. *a class* $\mathbf{C}_0$, *whose elements are called the objects of* **C**.

2. *for each* $n \in \mathbb{N}$ *and* $a_1, \cdots, a_n, a, \in \mathbf{C}_0$, *a set* $\mathbf{C}(a_1, \cdots, a_n; a)$, *whose elements* F *are called random relations expressed as*

$$a_1, \cdots, a_n \xrightarrow{F} a$$

3. *for each* $n, i_1, \cdots, i_n \in \mathbb{N}$ *and* $a, a_j, a_{j,k} \in \mathbf{C}_0$, *a function*

$$\mathbf{C}(a_1, \cdots, a_n; a) \times \mathbf{C}(a_{1,1}, \cdots, a_{1,i_1}; a_1) \times \cdots \times \mathbf{C}(a_{n,1}, \cdots, a_{n,i_n}; a_n)$$

$$\longrightarrow \mathbf{C}(a_{1,1}, \cdots, a_{1,i_1}, \cdots, a_{n,1}, \cdots, a_{n,i_n}; a), \qquad (11.3.1)$$

called composition and written as

$$(F, F_1, \cdots, F_n) \longrightarrow F \circ (F_1, \cdots, F_n) \tag{11.3.2}$$

4. *For each permutation action $\sigma \in \Sigma_n$ (a permutation group with n distinct elements), we have a map associated to σ as*

$$\mathbf{C}(a_1, a_2, \cdots, a_n; a) \xrightarrow{\sigma^*} \mathbf{C}(a_{\sigma(1)}, a_{\sigma(2)}, \cdots, a_{\sigma(n)}; a) \tag{11.3.3}$$

5. *Associativity. For random relations $F, F_i, F_{i,j} \in \mathbf{C}(a_1, \cdots, a_n; a)$ expressed by random functions as $F = \bowtie_{l=1}^{I_F} f_{;l}$, $F_i = \bowtie_{l_i=1}^{I_{F_i}} f_{i;l_i}$, and $F_{i,j} = \bowtie_{l_{i,j}=1}^{I_{F_{i,j}}} f_{i,j;l_{i,j}}$, respectively, they have to satisfy*

$$f_{;l} \circ (f_{1;l_1} \circ (f_{1,1;l_{1,1}}, \cdots, f_{1,i_1;l_{1,i_1}}), \cdots, f_{n;l_n} \circ (f_{n,1;l_{n,1}}, \cdots, f_{n,i_n;l_{n,i_n}})$$

$$= (f_{;l} \circ (f_{1;l_1}, \cdots, f_{n;l_n})) \circ (f_{1,1;l_{1,1}}, \cdots, f_{1,i_1;l_{1,i_1}}, \cdots, f_{n,1;l_{n,1}}, \cdots, f_{n,i_n;l_{n,i_n}}) \tag{11.3.4}$$

with respect to all indices l, l_i and $l_{i,j}$.

6. *For each object a, an identity relation $id_a : a \to a$ satisfying the following identity law with respect to each index i:*

$$f_i \circ (id_{a_1}, \cdots, id_{a_n}) = f_i = id_a \circ f_i, \tag{11.3.5}$$

where $F : a_1, a_2, \cdots, a_n \to a$ and $F = \bowtie_{i=1}^{I_F} f_i$.

7. *Given $\sigma \in \Sigma_n$, we have following diagram to commute:*

$$\mathbf{C}(a_1, ., a_n; a) \times \mathbf{C}(a_{1,1}, ., a_{1,i_1}; a_1) \times . \times \mathbf{C}(a_{n,1}, ., a_{n,i_n}; a_n) \longrightarrow \mathbf{C}(a_{1,1}, \cdots, a_{n,i_n}; a)$$

$$\sigma \downarrow \qquad\qquad\qquad\qquad\qquad\qquad\qquad \downarrow \sigma$$

$$\mathbf{C}(a_{\sigma(1)}, ., a_{\sigma(n)}; a) \times \mathbf{C}(a_{\sigma(1),1}, ., a_{\sigma(1),i_{\sigma(1)}}; a_{\sigma(1)}) \times \cdots \times$$

$$\mathbf{C}(a_{\sigma(n),1}, ., a_{\sigma(n),i_{\sigma(n)}}; a_{\sigma(n)}) \longrightarrow \mathbf{C}(a_{\sigma(1),1}, ., a_{\sigma(n),i_{\sigma(n)}}; a) \tag{11.3.6}$$

8. *For each object a, an identity relation $id_a : a \to a$ satisfying the following identity law with respect to each index i:*

$$f_i \circ (id_{a_1}, \cdots, id_{a_n}) = f_i = id_a \circ f_i, \tag{11.3.7}$$

where $F : a_1, a_2, \cdots, a_n \to a$ and $F = \bowtie_{i=1}^{I_F} f_i$.

9. Given $\sigma \in \Sigma_n$, we have following diagram to commute:

$$\mathbf{C}(a_1,..,a_n;a) \times \mathbf{C}(a_{1,1},..,a_{1,i_1};a_1) \times . \times \mathbf{C}(a_{n,1},..,a_{n,i_n};a_n) \longrightarrow \mathbf{C}(a_{1,1},\cdots,a_{n,i_n};a)$$

$$\sigma \downarrow \qquad\qquad\qquad\qquad\qquad \downarrow \sigma$$

$$\mathbf{C}(a_{\sigma(1)},..,a_{\sigma(n)};a) \times \mathbf{C}(a_{\sigma(1),1},..,a_{\sigma(1),i_{\sigma(1)}};a_{\sigma(1)}) \times \cdots \times$$

$$\mathbf{C}(a_{\sigma(n),1},..,a_{\sigma(n),i_{\sigma(n)}};a_{\sigma(n)}) \longrightarrow \mathbf{C}(a_{\sigma(1),1},..,a_{\sigma(n),i_{\sigma(n)}};a) \qquad (11.3.8)$$

10. Given $\sigma_t \in \Sigma_{i_t}$ for $1 \leq t \leq n$, we have following diagram to commute:

$$\mathbf{C}(a_1,..,a_n;a) \times \mathbf{C}(a_{1,1},..,a_{1,i_1};a_1) \times . \times \mathbf{C}(a_{n,1},..,a_{n,i_n};a_n) \longrightarrow \mathbf{C}(a_{1,1},\cdots,a_{n,i_n};a)$$

$$\sigma_1,\sigma_2,\cdots,\sigma_n \downarrow \qquad\qquad\qquad\qquad \downarrow \sigma_1 \oplus \cdots \oplus \sigma_n$$

$$\mathbf{C}(a_1,..,a_n;a) \times \mathbf{C}(a_{1,\sigma_1(1)},..,a_{1,\sigma_1(i_1)};a_1) \times \cdots \times$$

$$\mathbf{C}(a_{n,\sigma_n(1)},..,a_{n,\sigma_n(i_n)};a_n) \longrightarrow \mathbf{C}(a_{1,\sigma_1(1)},..,a_{n,\sigma_n(i_n)};a) \qquad (11.3.9)$$

A *functor* is a structure-preserving of analogical relations between two invengories. By coping similar ideas from functor between two random symmetric multi-invengories, we define a *random multi-functor* for mapping between two multi-invengories as:

Definition 85 *Let $\mathbf{C}$ and $\mathbf{D}$ be two random symmetric multi-invengories. A* random multifunctor $\mathbf{F} : \mathbf{C} \to \mathbf{D}$ *is a random choice from a set of multifunctors (non-random), denoted as $\mathbf{V}$, from the random invengory $\mathbf{C}$ to the random invengory $\mathbf{D}$. The probability to choose a random functor is determined by the probability density (or mass) function for elements in $\mathbf{V}$. The random functor $\mathbf{F}$ satisfies following equalities in distribution as*

$$\mathbf{F}(id_a) = id_{\mathbf{F}(a)},$$

$$\mathbf{F}(g_j \circ_C (f_{1;k_1},\cdots,f_{n;k_n})) = \mathbf{F}(g_j) \circ_{\mathbf{D}} (\mathbf{F}(f_{1,k_1}),\cdots,\mathbf{F}(f_{n,k_n})) \qquad (11.3.10)$$

for all $\mathbf{C}$-objects $a_1,\cdots,a_n,a$, all composable $\mathbf{C}$-relations $G = \bowtie_{j=1}^{I_G} g_j$ and $F_i = \bowtie_{k_i=1}^{I_{F_i}} f_{i;k_i}$ for $1 \leq i \leq n$, and all random functions indices j and k_i.

Hence, we can form an invengory of random symmetric multi-invengories, denoted as $\mathbf{S} - \mathbf{Mult}$, according to Definitions 84 and 85.

Given two random symmetric multi-invengories $\mathbf{M}$ and $\mathbf{N}$, the notion about *bilinear map* can be adopted to form a new random symmetric multi-invengory $\mathbf{P}$ that mirrors algebraic invenrelation procedures in $\mathbf{M}$ and $\mathbf{N}$ separately. The precise definition follows.

Definition 86 *Let* $\mathbf{M}$, $\mathbf{N}$ *and* $\mathbf{P}$ *be random symmetric multi-invengories. A bilinear map* $\mathbf{F}$: $(\mathbf{M}, \mathbf{N}) \longrightarrow \mathbf{P}$ *consists of :*

1. *A function* $f : \mathbf{M}_0 \times \mathbf{N}_0 \longrightarrow \mathbf{P}_0$, *where* $\mathbf{M}_0, \mathbf{N}_0$ *and* $\mathbf{P}_0$ *are objects in invengories* $\mathbf{M}$, $\mathbf{N}$ *and* $\mathbf{P}$, *respectively.*

2. *For each random relation* $F : (a_1, \cdots, a_m) \longrightarrow a$ *of* $\mathbf{M}$ *and object* b *of* $\mathbf{N}$, *an random relation* $\mathbf{F}(F, b) : (f(a_1, b), \cdots, f(a_m, b)) \longrightarrow f(a, b)$ *of* $\mathbf{P}$.

3. *For each random relation* $G : (b_1, \cdots, b_n) \longrightarrow b$ *of* $\mathbf{N}$ *and object* a *of* $\mathbf{M}$, *an random relation* $\mathbf{F}(a, G) : (f(a, b_1), \cdots, f(a, b_n)) \longrightarrow f(a, b)$ *of* $\mathbf{P}$.

such that

1. *For each object* b *of* $\mathbf{N}$, $\mathbf{F}(, b)$ *is a random multifunctor from* $\mathbf{M}$ *to* $\mathbf{P}$.

2. *For each object* a *of* $\mathbf{M}$, $\mathbf{F}(a,)$ *is a random multifunctor from* $\mathbf{N}$ *to* $\mathbf{P}$.

3. *Given random relations* $F : (a_1, \cdots, a_m) \longrightarrow a$ *and* $G : (b_1, \cdots, b_n) \longrightarrow b$, *we have following commutative diagram:*

$$\langle \langle f(a_i, b_j) \rangle_{i=1}^m \rangle_{j=1}^n \xrightarrow{\mathbf{F}(F, b_j)} \langle f(a, b_j) \rangle_{j=1}^n$$

$$\equiv \downarrow$$

$$\langle \langle f(a_i, b_j) \rangle_{j=1}^n \rangle_{i=1}^m \qquad \downarrow \mathbf{F}(a, G)$$

$$\mathbf{F}(a_i, G) \downarrow$$

$$\langle f(a_i, b) \rangle_{i=1}^m \xrightarrow{\mathbf{F}(F, b)} f(a, b) \tag{11.3.11}$$

where $\langle \rangle$ *denotes a sequence and* $\equiv$ *denotes for index exchange.*

The naturality for bilinear maps from $\mathbf{M}, \mathbf{N}$ to $\mathbf{P}$ is provided by the following definition.

Definition 87 *Given bilinear maps* $\mathbf{F}_1, \mathbf{F}_2, \cdots, \mathbf{F}_k$ *and* $\mathbf{G}$, *a k-natural transformation in each variable, denoted as* $\zeta : (\mathbf{F}_1, \mathbf{F}_2, \cdots, \mathbf{F}_k) \longrightarrow \mathbf{G}$, *will assign a k-tuples random relation,* $\zeta_{a,b}$: $(\mathbf{F}_1(a, b), \cdots, \mathbf{F}_k(a, b)) \longrightarrow \mathbf{G}(a, b)$, *in* $\mathbf{P}$ *for each pair of objects* $(a, b) \in \mathbf{M}_0 \times \mathbf{N}_0$. *For each random relation* $F : (a_1, \cdots, a_m) \longrightarrow a$ *of* $\mathbf{M}$ *and each random relation* $G : (b_1, \cdots, b_n) \longrightarrow b$ *of*

N, *we have the following commutative diagrams:*

$$
\langle\langle \mathbf{F}_j(a_i,b)\rangle_{i=1}^m\rangle_{j=1}^k \xrightarrow{\langle \mathbf{F}_j(F,b)\rangle_{j=1}^k} \langle \mathbf{F}_j(a,b)\rangle_{j=1}^k
$$

$$
\equiv\downarrow
$$

$$
\langle\langle \mathbf{F}_j(a_i,b)\rangle_{j=1}^k\rangle_{i=1}^m \qquad\qquad \downarrow \zeta(a,b)
$$

$$
\langle\zeta(a_i,b)\rangle_{i=1}^m \downarrow
$$

$$
\langle \mathbf{G}(a_i,b)\rangle_{i=1}^m \xrightarrow{\mathbf{G}(F,b)} \mathbf{G}(a,b) \tag{11.3.12}
$$

$$
\langle\langle \mathbf{F}_j(a,b_i)\rangle_{i=1}^n\rangle_{j=1}^k \xrightarrow{\langle \mathbf{F}_j(a,G)\rangle_{j=1}^k} \langle \mathbf{F}_j(a,b)\rangle_{j=1}^k
$$

$$
\equiv\downarrow
$$

$$
\langle\langle \mathbf{F}_j(a,b_i)\rangle_{j=1}^k\rangle_{i=1}^n \qquad\qquad \downarrow \zeta(a,b)
$$

$$
\langle\zeta(a,b_i)\rangle_{i=1}^n \downarrow
$$

$$
\langle \mathbf{G}(a,b_i)\rangle_{i=1}^n \xrightarrow{\mathbf{G}(a,G)} \mathbf{G}(a,b) \tag{11.3.13}
$$

The remaining part of this section is to show that there exists a tensor product random multi-invengory for any given two random symmetric multi-invengoreis **M** and **N**. Some definitions and Lemmas have to be addressed first before establishing tensor theorem.

Definition 88 *Let* $\mathbb{M}$ *be the free monoid monad in* **Set***. A random* $\mathbb{M}$*-graph* X *consists of two sets,* X_0 *(the objects) and* X_1 *(the random relations with multiple input objects), with two functions, the source function* $s : X_1 \longrightarrow \mathbb{M}X_0$ *and the target* $t : X_1 \longrightarrow X_0$*. A map of* $\mathbb{M}$*-graphs* $f : X \longrightarrow Y$ *consists of function for objects* $f_0 : X_0 \longrightarrow Y_0$ *and function for arrows* $f_1 : X_1 \longrightarrow Y_1$ *such that the following diagram commutes*

$$
\mathbb{M}X_0 \xleftarrow{s} X_1 \xrightarrow{t} X_0
$$

$$
\mathbb{M}f_0 v \downarrow \qquad f_1 \downarrow \qquad f_0 \downarrow
$$

$$
\mathbb{M}Y_0 \xleftarrow{s} Y_1 \xrightarrow{t} Y_0 \tag{11.3.14}
$$

Based on this definition, we have an invengory of $\mathbb{M}$-graphs, denoted as $\mathbb{M} - \mathbf{Graph}$. Following lemma is about the relationship between $\mathbb{M} - \mathbf{Graph}$ and $\mathbf{S} - \mathbf{Mult}$.

Lemma 47 *Multi-invengories* $\mathbb{M} - \mathbf{Graph}$ *and* $\mathbf{S} - \mathbf{Mult}$ *are adjoint pair.*

PROOF. 84 *There is a forgetful functor* $\mathbf{U} : \mathbf{S} - \mathbf{Mult} \longrightarrow \mathbb{M} - \mathbf{Graph}$ *by omitting identities, permutations and compositions.*

Let X be a random $\mathbb{M}$-graph, the free random multi-invenegory $\mathcal{F}X$ on X has the same objects: $(\mathcal{F}X)_0 = X_0$. Its random relations are obtained by gluing those random relations of X recursively by rules:

- *if $a \in X_0$ then $id_a \in (FX)(a; a)$;*

- *if $F \in X(a_1, \cdots, a_n; a)$ and $F_1 \in (\mathcal{F}X)(a_{1,1}, \cdots, a_{1,i_1}; a_1)$..., $F_n \in (\mathcal{F}X)(a_{n,1}, \cdots, a_{n,i_n}; a_n)$ then $F(F_1, \cdots, F_n) \in (FX)(a_{1,1}, \cdots, a_{n,i_n}; a)$.*

Hence, we obtain a left adjoint of U by the free multi-invengory functor.

The following theorem is provided to construct the tensor of two $\mathbf{S} - \mathbf{Mult}$.

Theorem 41 *For any two random symmetric multi-invengoreis $\mathbf{M}$ and $\mathbf{N}$, there is a tensor product random symmetric multi-invengories $\mathbf{M} \otimes \mathbf{N}$ with a bilinear map $(\mathbf{M}, \mathbf{N}) \longrightarrow \mathbf{M} \otimes \mathbf{N}$.*

PROOF. 85 *We first construct the coproducts with respect to $\mathbf{M}$ and $\mathbf{N}$ as*

$$\coprod_{a \in \mathbf{M}_0} (a, \mathbf{N}), \tag{11.3.15}$$

and

$$\coprod_{b \in \mathbf{N}_0} (\mathbf{M}, b). \tag{11.3.16}$$

Each of these coproducts has $\mathbf{M}_0 \times \mathbf{N}_0$ as its objects. Let $Free(\mathbf{M}_0 \times \mathbf{N}_0)$ be the free random multi-invengory on the set of objects $\mathbf{M}_0 \times \mathbf{N}_0$, we consider the following pushout

$$
\begin{array}{ccc}
Free(\mathbf{M}_0 \times \mathbf{N}_0) & \xrightarrow{R_1} & \coprod_{b \in \mathbf{N}_0} (\mathbf{M}, b) \\
R_2 \downarrow & & \downarrow \\
\coprod_{a \in \mathbf{M}_0} (a, \mathbf{N}) & \longrightarrow & \mathbf{M} \bullet \mathbf{N},
\end{array}
\tag{11.3.17}
$$

where R_1, R_2 are restricting maps and $\mathbf{M} \bullet \mathbf{N}$ is the pushout.

Given one random relation from each random multi-invengory, say $\alpha : (a_1, \cdots, a_m) \longrightarrow a$ in $\mathbf{M}$ and $\beta : (b_1, \cdots, b_n) \longrightarrow b$ in $\mathbf{N}$. One defines $\mathbb{M} - \mathbf{Graphs}$ $X(\alpha, \beta)$ and $Y(\alpha, \beta)$ as :

- *Both having objects as $\{(a_1, \cdots, a_m) \times (b_1, \cdots, b_n)\} \bigcup \{(a, b)\}$*

- In $X(\alpha, \beta)$, there are two random relations, both with source $\langle\langle(a_i, b_j)\rangle_{i=1}^m\rangle_{j=1}^n$ and target (a, b).

- In $Y(\alpha, \beta)$, there is only one random relations with source $\langle\langle(a_i, b_j)\rangle_{i=1}^m\rangle_{j=1}^n$ and target (a, b).

Be setting following maps:

- *A collapsing map from $X(\alpha, \beta)$ (two relations) to $Y(\alpha, \beta)$ (one relation);*

- *There is a map from $X(\alpha, \beta)$ to $U(\mathbf{M} \bullet \mathbf{N})$ (forgetful functor) by sending each random relation to one way at digram in Definition 86;*

we have the following pushout diagram to generate $\mathbf{M} \times \mathbf{N}$

$$
\begin{array}{ccc}
\coprod_{\alpha,\beta} \mathfrak{L}X(\alpha, \beta) & \longrightarrow & \mathbf{M} \bullet \mathbf{N} \\
\downarrow & & \downarrow \\
\coprod_{\alpha,\beta} \mathfrak{L}Y(\alpha, \beta) & \longrightarrow & \mathbf{M} \otimes \mathbf{N},
\end{array} \tag{11.3.18}
$$

where $\mathfrak{L}$ is the left adjoint operator to $\mathbb{M} - \mathbf{Graphs}$ $X(\alpha, \beta)$ and $Y(\alpha, \beta)$ according to Lemma 47. Therefore, we have a bilinear map $(\mathbf{M}, \mathbf{N}) \longrightarrow \mathbf{M} \otimes \mathbf{N}$.

11.4 Tensor Product of n-MIMO Random Invengories

The goal of this section is the systematic construction of the higher dimensional tensor product of n-MIMO invengories [2], which represent algebraic invenrelation systems for entities in CINs. The key idea is to associate tensor and plurioperad through enrich structure. The enrich construction is adopted from [53].

11.4.1 Monad Structure on MIMO Invengory

We begin by introducing random MIMO invengory then discuss monad structure with respect to it induced by free construction of random MIMO.

Let S be a set of random multi-invengoires and $\mathcal{A}$ be a symmetric monoidal invengory whose monoid of objects is the free monoid on S. A random MIMO in a symmetric monoidal invengory $\mathcal{A}$ is a symmetric monoidal random invengory $\mathbf{P}$, enriched over $\mathcal{A}$, which has the nonnegative

---

[2]The tensor product of random multi-invegories provided in Theorem 41 is used to build 0-dimensional objects of the tensor product of n-MIMO invengories.

integers $n \in \mathbb{N}$ as objects and whose tensor product is given by the addition law $m \otimes n = m + n$ on objects $(m, n) \in \mathbb{N}^2$. The structure of a MIMO is fully determined by the structure of the double sequence $\mathbf{P}(m, n) \in \mathcal{A}$ for $(m, n) \in \mathbb{N}^2$. The composition structures of homomorphisms consist of:

- horizontal products: $\mathbf{P}(m, n) \otimes \mathbf{P}(k, l) \xrightarrow{\circ_h} \mathbf{P}(m + k, n + l)$ for $m, n, k, l \in \mathbb{N}$;

- vertical products: $\mathbf{P}(k, m) \otimes \mathbf{P}(n, k) \xrightarrow{\circ_v} \mathbf{P}(n, m)$ for $k, m, n \in \mathbb{N}$;

- units: $1 \xrightarrow{Id} \mathbf{P}(1, 1)$

Naturally, a morphism of random MIMOs consists of a symmetric monoidal functor $\phi : \mathbf{P} \to \mathbf{Q}$, which is fully determined by a collection of morphisms preserving structures. The invengory of random MIMOs is denoted by $\mathbf{R} - \mathbf{MIMO}$.

Let $\mathbb{B}$ be the invengory formed by pairs $(m, n) \in \mathbb{N}^2$ as objects with morphisms sets :

$$\{(m, n) \longrightarrow (p, q)\} = \begin{cases} \Sigma_m^{op} \times \Sigma_n, \text{if } m = p \text{ and } n = q \\ \emptyset, \text{otherwise} \end{cases}$$

where Σ_m represents a right action of the symmetric group with n elements and Σ_n represents a left action of the symmetric group with m elements. The invengory of random MIMOs is endowed with an obvious forgetful functor $U : \mathbf{R} - \mathbf{MIMO} \to \mathcal{A}^{\mathbb{B}}$. This forgetful functor induces a left adjoint functor $F : \mathcal{A}^{\mathbb{B}} \to \mathbf{R} - \mathbf{MIMO}$, which maps a biobject $M \in \mathcal{A}^{\mathbb{B}}$ to a corresponding free object $F(M) \in \mathbf{R} - \mathbf{MIMO}$.

The identity morphism of a random MIMO $id : \mathbf{P} \to \mathbf{P}$ determines the augmentation of the adjunction between biobjects and random MIMOs. This construction applied to the free MIMO $\mathbf{P} = F(M)$ gives a universal composition product $\mu : F(F(M)) \to F(M)$ that makes $F : \mathcal{A}^{\mathbb{B}} \to \mathcal{A}^{\mathbb{B}}$. With the other morphism $\eta : M \to F(M)$, we have a monad structure for $\mathcal{A}^{\mathbb{B}}$. Because we have following commutative diagrams:

$$
\begin{array}{ccc}
F^3 & \xrightarrow{F\mu} & F^2 \\
{\scriptstyle \mu F} \downarrow & & \downarrow {\scriptstyle \mu} \\
F^2 & \xrightarrow{\mu} & F
\end{array}
\tag{11.4.1}
$$

and

$$F \xrightarrow{\eta F} F^2$$

$$F\eta \downarrow \qquad \downarrow \eta$$

$$F^2 \xrightarrow{\mu} F \qquad\qquad (11.4.2)$$

where $F^2 = F \circ F$ and $F^3 = F \circ F \circ F$.

11.4.2 Distributive Tensors

We understand that monads on an invengory $\mathbf{C}$ are monoids in the strict monoidal invengory end-ofunctors of $\mathbf{C}$ whose tensor product is given by composition. Given the analogy between monads and tensors over a random MIMO $\mathcal{A}^{\mathbb{B}}$, one natural question to ask is under what conditions are tensors monoids in a certain monoidal random MIMO. The answer, that we will illustrate in this section, is to consider *distributive tensor* structure over $\mathcal{A}^{\mathbb{B}}$. We begin by defining tensor structure over $\mathcal{A}^{\mathbb{B}}$.

Definition 89 *By setting* $\mathcal{M}\mathcal{A}^{\mathbb{B}}$ *as* $\coprod_{n \geq 0} (\mathcal{A}^{\mathbb{B}})^n$, *we have a functor* $E : \mathcal{M}\mathcal{A}^{\mathbb{B}} \to \mathcal{A}^{\mathbb{B}}$. *A tensor on a random MIMO* $\mathcal{A}^{\mathbb{B}}$ *is a* $\mathcal{M}$-*algebra structure* (E, u, σ) *on* $\mathcal{A}^{\mathbb{B}}$, *i.e.*,

$$\mathcal{A}^{\mathbb{B}} \xrightarrow{\eta_{\mathcal{A}^{\mathbb{B}}}} \mathcal{M}\mathcal{A}^{\mathbb{B}}$$

$$1_{\mathcal{A}^{\mathbb{B}}} \searrow \quad u \quad \swarrow E$$

$$\mathcal{A}^{\mathbb{B}} \qquad\qquad (11.4.3)$$

and

$$\mathcal{M}^2 \mathcal{A}^{\mathbb{B}} \xrightarrow{\mu_{\mathcal{A}^{\mathbb{B}}}} \mathcal{M}\mathcal{A}^{\mathbb{B}}$$

$$\mathcal{M}E \downarrow \quad \sigma \quad \downarrow E$$

$$\mathcal{M}\mathcal{A}^{\mathbb{B}} \xrightarrow{E} \mathcal{A}^{\mathbb{B}} \qquad\qquad (11.4.4)$$

A random MIMO invengory $\mathcal{A}^{\mathbb{B}}$ *equipped with a tensor structure is called a* monoidal random MIMO.

The next definition is about the enrichment over $\mathcal{A}^{\mathbb{B}}$.

Definition 90 *An invengory enriched in* $(\mathcal{A}^{\mathbb{B}}, E)$, *denoted as* X, *consists of*

- a set of objects X_0;

- for all pairs of sequences $(\underline{x}_0, \underline{x}_1)$ of elements of X_0, an object $X(\underline{x}_0, \underline{x}_1)$ of $\mathcal{A}^{\mathbb{B}}$. These objects are called the relations of X.

- for all $n \in \mathbb{N}$ and $(n+1)$-tuples $(\underline{x}_0, \underline{x}_1, \cdots, \underline{x}_n)$ of elements of X_0, one has maps $\kappa_n :$ $E_{1 \leq i \leq n} X(\underline{x}_{i-1}, \underline{x}_i) \longrightarrow X(\underline{x}_0, \underline{x}_n)$, named as compositions of X, satisfying unit and associative laws as

$$X(\underline{x}_0, \underline{x}_1) \xrightarrow{u} E_1 X(\underline{x}_0, \underline{x}_1)$$

$$Id \searrow \qquad \downarrow \kappa_1$$

$$X(\underline{x}_0, \underline{x}_1) \qquad\qquad (11.4.5)$$

and

$$E_{1 \leq i \leq n} E_{1 \leq j \leq m_i} X(\underline{x}_{(ij)-1}, \underline{x}_{ij}) \xrightarrow{\sigma} E_{1 \leq i \leq n, 1 \leq j \leq m_i} X(\underline{x}_{(ij)-1}, \underline{x}_{ij})$$

$$E_{1 \leq i \leq n} \kappa_{m_i} \downarrow \qquad\qquad\qquad \downarrow \kappa_{m_1 + \cdots + m_n}$$

$$E_{1 \leq i \leq n} X(\underline{x}_{(i1)-1}, \underline{x}_{im_i}) \xrightarrow{\kappa_n} X(\underline{x}_0, \underline{x}_{nm_n}) \qquad (11.4.6)$$

The map between two enriched invengories in $(\mathcal{A}^{\mathbb{B}}, E)$ is given by the following definition.

Definition 91 *Let X and Y be two enriched invengories in $(\mathcal{A}^{\mathbb{B}}, E)$, the functor $\mathbf{F} : X \longrightarrow Y$ consists of a function $f_0 : X_0 \longrightarrow Y_0$, and for all pairs $(\underline{x}_0, \underline{x}_1)$ from X_0, maps $f_{\underline{x}_0, \underline{x}_1} :$ $X(\underline{x}_0, \underline{x}_1) \longrightarrow Y(f_0(\underline{x}_0), f_0(\underline{x}_1))$ satisfying :*

$$E_{1 \leq i \leq n} X(\underline{x}_{i-1}, \underline{x}_i) \xRightarrow{E_{1 \leq i \leq n} f_0} E_{1 \leq i \leq n} Y(f_0(\underline{x}_{i-1}), f_0(\underline{x}_i))$$

$$\kappa_{X,n} \downarrow \qquad\qquad\qquad \downarrow \kappa_{Y,n}$$

$$X(\underline{x}_0, \underline{x}_n) \xrightarrow{f_0} Y(f_0(\underline{x}_0), f_0(\underline{x}_n)) \qquad (11.4.7)$$

From definitions 89, 90 and 91, we have following lemma

Lemma 48 *Set $\mathfrak{E}$ as a functor $\mathcal{M}\mathcal{A}^{\mathbb{B}} \to \mathcal{A}^{\mathbb{B}}$ when $\mathcal{M}\mathcal{A}^{\mathbb{B}}$ is $\coprod_{0 \leq n \leq 1} (\mathcal{A}^{\mathbb{B}})^n$. We have following facts:*

1. *$(\mathfrak{E}, u, \sigma)$ is a monad on $\mathcal{A}^{\mathbb{B}}$.*

2. *$\sigma : \mathfrak{E} E_{1 \leq i \leq n} X(\underline{x}_{i-1}, \underline{x}_i) \longrightarrow E_{1 \leq i \leq n} X(\underline{x}_{i-1}, \underline{x}_i)$ is an $\mathfrak{E}$-algebra structure on $_{1 \leq i \leq n} X(\underline{x}_{i-1}, \underline{x}_i)$.*

3. *Each relation of an enriched invengory X is an $\mathfrak{E}$-algebra with composition map as κ_1 :*

$$\mathfrak{E}X(\underline{x}_0, \underline{x}_1) \longrightarrow X(\underline{x}_0, \underline{x}_1).$$

The following lemma is used to build the correspondence between free algebra on $\mathcal{A}^{\mathbb{B}}$ presented at Eq. (11.4.1) and monoidal structure on $\mathcal{A}^{\mathbb{B}}$.

Lemma 49 *Let F induce a monad structure for $\mathcal{A}^{\mathbb{B}}$. By treating F-Algebra as a monoidal invengory through cartesian produce, we have*

$$F^{\#} - \mathbf{Cat} \cong (F - Algebra) - \mathbf{Cat} \tag{11.4.8}$$

where $F^{\#} - \mathbf{Cat}$ is the invengory for monoidal structure on $\mathcal{A}^{\mathbb{B}}$.

PROOF. 86 *Let X_0 be a set and, for a pair of sequences $\underline{x}_0, \underline{x}_1 \in X_0$, let $X(\underline{x}_0, \underline{x}_1) \in \mathcal{A}^{\mathbb{B}}$. For each $n \in \mathbb{N}$ and $\underline{x}_0, \cdots, \underline{x}_n \in X_0$, following maps:*

$$\lambda_n : \prod_{1 \le i \le n} FX(\underline{x}_{i-1}, \underline{x}_i) \longrightarrow X(\underline{x}_0, \underline{x}_n) \tag{11.4.9}$$

are the maps for a $F^{\#} - \mathbf{Cat}$.

By Lemma 48, the maps $\lambda_{\underline{x}_0, \underline{x}_1} : FX(\underline{x}_0, \underline{x}_1) \longrightarrow X(\underline{x}_0, \underline{x}_1)$ are algebra structures for relations, and for $\underline{x}_{ij} \in X_0$ with $1 \le i \le k$ and $1 \le j \le n_i$, we have following commutative diagram:

$$
F \prod_{1 \le i \le k} X(\underline{x}_{i-1}, \underline{x}_i) \xrightarrow{\prod_{1 \le i \le k} \eta} F \prod_{1 \le i \le k} FX(\underline{x}_{i-1}, \underline{x}_i) \xrightarrow{\lambda_n} FX(\underline{x}_0, \underline{x}_n)
$$

$$
F \leftrightarrow \prod \downarrow
$$

$$
\prod_{1 \le i \le k} FX(\underline{x}_{i-1}, \underline{x}_i) \qquad\qquad\qquad \downarrow \lambda_{\underline{x}_0, \underline{x}_n}
$$

$$
\prod_{1 \le i \le k} \lambda_{\underline{x}_{i-1}, \underline{x}_i} \downarrow
$$

$$
\prod_{1 \le i \le k} X(\underline{x}_{i-1}, \underline{x}_i) \xrightarrow{\prod_{1 \le i \le k} \eta} \prod_{1 \le i \le k} FX(\underline{x}_{i-1}, \underline{x}_i) \xrightarrow{\lambda_n} X(\underline{x}_0, \underline{x}_n) \tag{11.4.10}
$$

By setting map λ'_n as following composition

$$\lambda'_n : \prod_{1 \le i \le k} X(\underline{x}_{i-1}, \underline{x}_i) \xrightarrow{\prod_{1 \le i \le k} \eta} \prod_{1 \le i \le k} FX(\underline{x}_{i-1}, \underline{x}_i) \xrightarrow{\lambda_n} X(\underline{x}_0, \underline{x}_n) , \tag{11.4.11}$$

then the commutativity of Eq. (11.4.10) implies that the map λ'_n satisfies associativity. The unit axiom for λ'_n is established since

$$\lambda'_n Id_{\prod_{1 \leq i \leq k} X(\underline{x}_{i-1}, \underline{x}_i)} = Id_{X(\underline{x}_0, \underline{x}_n)} \lambda'_n = \lambda'_n. \tag{11.4.12}$$

Conversely, we wish to construct λ_n from λ'_n as

$$\lambda'_n : \prod_{1 \leq i \leq k} FX(\underline{x}_{i-1}, \underline{x}_i) \xrightarrow{\prod_{1 \leq i \leq k} \lambda_{\underline{x}_{i-1}, \underline{x}_i}} \prod_{1 \leq i \leq k} X(\underline{x}_{i-1}, \underline{x}_i) \xrightarrow{\lambda'_n} X(\underline{x}_0, \underline{x}_n). \tag{11.4.13}$$

Hence, one has following commutative diagram about such construction

$$
\begin{array}{ccccc}
\prod\limits_{1 \leq i \leq k} F \prod\limits_{1 \leq j \leq n_i} FX(\underline{x}_{(ij)-1}, \underline{x}_{ij}) & \xrightarrow{T \leftrightarrow \prod} & \prod\limits_{1 \leq i \leq k, 1 \leq j \leq n_i} F^2 X(\underline{x}_{(ij)-1}, \underline{x}_{ij}) & \xrightarrow{\prod\limits_{ij} \mu} & \prod\limits_{1 \leq i \leq k, 1 \leq j \leq n_i} FX(\underline{x}_{(ij)-1}, \underline{x}_{ij}) \\[2mm]
\prod\limits_{i} F \prod\limits_{j} \lambda_{\underline{x}_{(ij)-1}, \underline{x}_{ij}} \downarrow & & \downarrow \prod\limits_{ij} F\lambda_{\underline{x}_{(ij)-1}, \underline{x}_{ij}} & & \downarrow \prod\limits_{ij} \lambda_{\underline{x}_{(ij)-1}, \underline{x}_{ij}} \\[2mm]
\prod\limits_{1 \leq i \leq k} F \prod\limits_{1 \leq j \leq n_i} X(\underline{x}_{(ij)-1}, \underline{x}_{ij}) & \xrightarrow{\lambda_n} & \prod\limits_{1 \leq i \leq k, 1 \leq j \leq n_i} FX(\underline{x}_{(ij)-1}, \underline{x}_{ij}) & \xrightarrow{\prod\limits_{ij} \lambda_{\underline{x}_{(ij)-1}, \underline{x}_{ij}}} & \prod\limits_{1 \leq i \leq k, 1 \leq j \leq n_i} X(\underline{x}_{(ij)-1}, \underline{x}_{ij}) \\[2mm]
\prod\limits_{i} F\lambda'_{n_i} \downarrow & & \downarrow \prod\limits_{i} F\lambda'_{n_i} & & \downarrow \lambda'_n \\[2mm]
\prod\limits_{1 \leq i \leq k} FX(\underline{x}_{i-1}, \underline{x}_i) & \xrightarrow{\prod\limits_{i} \lambda_{\underline{x}_{i-1}, \underline{x}_i}} & \prod\limits_{1 \leq i \leq k} X(\underline{x}_{i-1}, \underline{x}_i) & \xrightarrow{\lambda'_n} & X(\underline{x}_0, \underline{x}_n)
\end{array} \tag{11.4.}
$$

which shows the associativity for map λ_n from the outer components in Eq. (11.4.14). The unit axiom for λ_n holds because

$$\lambda_n Id_{\prod_{1 \leq i \leq k} FX(\underline{x}_{i-1}, \underline{x}_i)} = Id_{X(\underline{x}_0, \underline{x}_n)} \lambda_n = \lambda_n. \tag{11.4.15}$$

The correspondence between between λ_n and λ'_n. is clearly a bijection, and builds isomorphism on objects over Set.

In the reaming part, we will try to build the correspondence between functors in $F^\# - \mathbf{Cat}$ and functors in $(F - Algebra) - \mathbf{Cat}$.

Let $f_0 : X_0 \longrightarrow Y_0$ be a function,

$$\lambda_n : \prod_{1 \leq i \leq k} FX(\underline{x}_{i-1}, \underline{x}_i) \longrightarrow X(\underline{x}_{i-1}, \underline{x}_i) \tag{11.4.16}$$

$$\gamma_n : \prod_{1 \leq i \leq k} FY(\underline{y}_{i-1}, \underline{y}_i) \longrightarrow Y(\underline{y}_{i-1}, \underline{y}_i) \tag{11.4.17}$$

434

be maps for $F^{\#} - \mathbf{Cat}$ invengories X, Y, and λ'_n and γ'_n be associated maps constructed from λ_n and γ_n with

$$f_{\underline{x}_0, \underline{x}_1} : X(\underline{x}_0, \underline{x}_1) \longrightarrow Y(f_0(\underline{x}_0), f_0(\underline{x}_1)) \tag{11.4.18}$$

for $\underline{x}_0, \underline{x}_1 \in X_0$.

The diagram below

$$
\begin{array}{ccc}
\prod_{1 \le i \le k} X(\underline{x}_{i-1}, \underline{x}_i) & \xrightarrow{\prod_i \mathbf{F}} & \prod_{1 \le i \le k} Y(\underline{y}_{i-1}, \underline{y}_i) \\
\prod_i \eta \downarrow & & \downarrow \prod_i \eta \\
\prod_{1 \le i \le k} FX(\underline{x}_{i-1}, \underline{x}_i) & \xrightarrow{\prod_i F\mathbf{F}} & \prod_{1 \le i \le k} FY(\underline{y}_{i-1}, \underline{y}_i) \\
\lambda_n \downarrow & & \downarrow \gamma_n \\
X(\underline{x}_0, \underline{x}_n) & \xrightarrow{f_{\underline{x}_0, \underline{x}_n}} & Y(\underline{y}_0, \underline{y}_n)
\end{array}
\tag{11.4.19}
$$

illustrates how maps in $F^{\#} - \mathbf{Cat}$ for functor $\mathbf{F}$ imply maps in $(F - Algebra) - \mathbf{Cat}$. Similarly, the next diagram

$$
\begin{array}{ccc}
\prod_{1 \le i \le k} FX(\underline{x}_{i-1}, \underline{x}_i) & \xrightarrow{\prod_i F\mathbf{F}} & \prod_{1 \le i \le k} FY(\underline{y}_{i-1}, \underline{y}_i) \\
\prod_i \lambda_{\underline{x}_{i-1}, \underline{x}_i} \downarrow & & \downarrow \prod_i \gamma_{\underline{x}_{i-1}, \underline{x}_i} \\
\prod_{1 \le i \le k} X(\underline{x}_{i-1}, \underline{x}_i) & \xrightarrow{\prod_i \mathbf{F}} & \prod_{1 \le i \le k} Y(\underline{y}_{i-1}, \underline{y}_i) \\
\lambda'_n \downarrow & & \downarrow \gamma'_n \\
X(\underline{x}_0, \underline{x}_n) & \xrightarrow{f_{\underline{x}_0, \underline{x}_n}} & Y(\underline{y}_0, \underline{y}_n)
\end{array}
\tag{11.4.20}
$$

explains how maps in $(F - Algebra) - \mathbf{Cat}$ for functor $\mathbf{F}$ imply maps in $F^{\#} - \mathbf{Cat}$. Therefore, we have the correspondence between $F^{\#} - \mathbf{Cat}$ and $(F - Algebra) - \mathbf{Cat}$ from dual relation between λ_n and λ'_n.

The following definition is given for *distributive tensor*.

Definition 92 *A functor $E : \mathcal{MA}^{\mathbb{B}} \longrightarrow \mathcal{A}^{\mathbb{B}}$ is a distributive when, for all $n \in \mathbb{N}$, $E_{1 \le i \le n}$ preserves coproducts in each variable. The term $\mathbf{Dist}(\mathcal{A}^{\mathbb{B}})$ denotes for the invengory whose objects are such functors, and whose morphisms are natural transformations between them. A tensor (E, u, σ) is said to be distributive if E is distributive.*

When E is distributive and $p, q_i \in \mathbb{N}$, we have isomorphism

$$E_{1\leq i \leq p} \coprod_{j \in q_i} X_{ij} \cong \coprod_{j_1 \in q_1} \cdots \coprod_{j_p \in q_p} E_{1 \leq i \leq p} X_{ij_i} \qquad (11.4.21)$$

for double indexed objects in $\mathcal{A}^{\mathbb{B}}$. It is more convenient for us to introduce terminologies about coproduct cocones for distributive structure. For each $1 \leq i \leq p$, we collect a family of maps

$$c_{ij} : X_{ij} \longrightarrow X_{i\bullet}, \qquad (11.4.22)$$

where $\bullet \in [1, 2, \cdots, q_i]$, and c_{ij} forms a coproduct cocone in $\mathcal{A}^{\mathbb{B}}$. Given i and $j \in q_i$, one has map

$$E_{1\leq i \leq p} c_{ij} : E_{1\leq i \leq p} X_{ij} \longrightarrow E_{1\leq i \leq p} X_{i\bullet}, \qquad (11.4.23)$$

and distributivity of E makes all such maps form a coproduct cocone. By the fact that "a coproduct of coproduct is a coproduct" and coproduct cocone

$$c_i : X_{i\bullet} \longrightarrow X_{\bullet\bullet}, \qquad (11.4.24)$$

one has following new coproduct cocone obtained by composing c_{ij} and c_i as

$$X_{ij} \xrightarrow{c_{ij}} X_{i\bullet} \xrightarrow{c_{i\bullet}} X_{\bullet\bullet}. \qquad (11.4.25)$$

Given $E, F \in \mathbf{Dist}(\mathcal{A}^{\mathbb{B}})$, the tensor product $E \circ F$ in $\mathbf{Dist}(\mathcal{A}^{\mathbb{B}})$ is defined as:

$$(E \circ F)_{ij} = \coprod_{1 \leq i \leq p} E_i \coprod_{1 \leq j \leq q_i} F_j, \qquad (11.4.26)$$

then, we have map

$$E_i \circ F_j \xrightarrow{c_{ij}} (E \circ F)_{ij}. \qquad (11.4.27)$$

In case that $E = Id$, we have an invertible map, denoted as κ:

$$(Id \circ F)_j \xrightarrow{\kappa} F_j. \qquad (11.4.28)$$

In case that $F = Id$, we have an invertible map, denoted as ρ:

$$(E \circ Id)_i \xrightarrow{\rho} E_i. \qquad (11.4.29)$$

From definitions c_{ij}, κ and ρ, we have following commutative diagram [3]

$$
\begin{array}{ccc}
E_i F_j G_k \xrightarrow{c_{ij}} (E \circ F)_{ij} G_k \xrightarrow{c_{(ij)k}} ((E \circ F) \circ G)_{(ij)k} & & \\
c_{jk} \downarrow & & \downarrow \alpha_{E,F,G} \\
E_i \circ (F \circ G)_{jk} \xrightarrow{\quad c_{i(jk)} \quad} (E \circ (F \circ G))_{i(jk)} & &
\end{array}
\qquad (11.4.30)
$$

Given data $(\circ, \alpha, Id, \kappa, \rho)$, we have following lemma about $\mathbf{Dist}(\mathcal{A}^{\mathbb{B}})$.

---

[3]The ranges of indices i, j, k are omitted for simplified notations purpose.

Lemma 50 *The data $(\circ, \alpha, Id, \kappa, \rho)$ possesses a monoidal structure for $\mathbf{Dist}(\mathcal{A}^{\mathbb{B}})$.*

PROOF. 87 *If we set $F = Id$ and $G = F$ in Eq. (11.4.30), the following diagram is obtained:*

$$(E \circ Id)_i F_k \xrightarrow{c_{ik}} ((E \circ Id) \circ F)_{ik}$$

$$\rho^{-1} F_k \nearrow \quad = \quad \rho^{-1} F_k \nearrow$$

$$E_i F_k \xrightarrow{c_{ik}} (E \circ F)_{ik} \qquad \alpha_{E, Id, F} \downarrow$$

$$E_i \lambda^{-1} \searrow \quad = \quad E_i \lambda^{-1} \searrow$$

$$E(Id \circ F)_k \xrightarrow{c_{ik}} (E \circ (Id \circ F))_{ik} \tag{11.4.31}$$

The right triangle in Eq. (11.4.31) indicates the unit coherence for $\mathbf{Dist}(\mathcal{A}^{\mathbb{B}})$.

The next goal is to prove coherence condition for E, F, G and H in $\mathbf{Dist}(\mathcal{A}^{\mathbb{B}})$. We assume indices $i, j, k, l, p, q_i, r_{ij}, s_{ijk} \in \mathbb{N}$ for functors $E_{1 \le i \le p}, F_{1 \le j \le q_i}, G_{1 \le k \le r_{ij}}$ and $H_{1 \le l \le s_{ijk}}$, however, these functors are expressed as E_i, F_j, G_k and H_l for notation simplicity.

Consider the following diagram [4]*:*

$$E_i F_j G_k H_l \xrightarrow{\quad Id \quad} E_i F_j G_k H_l$$

$$Id \downarrow \searrow c_{ij} \qquad\qquad c_{ij} \swarrow \downarrow Id$$

$$(EF)_{ij} G_k H_l \xrightarrow{\quad Id \quad} (EF)_{ij} G_k H_l$$

$$Id \downarrow \searrow c_{(ij)k} \qquad c_{(ij)k} \alpha_{EFG} \swarrow \downarrow c_{(ij)k} \alpha_{EFG}$$

$$((EF)G)_{(ij)k} H_l \xrightarrow{Id} (E(FG))_{i(jk)} H_l$$

$$\alpha_{(EF)GH} \downarrow \qquad \downarrow \alpha_{E(FG)H}$$

$$E_i F_j G_k H_l \xrightarrow{c_{ij}} (EF)_{ij} G_k H_l \xrightarrow{c_{kl}} (EF)_{ij} GH_{kl} \; E_i((FG)H)_{(jk)l} \xleftarrow{c_{(jk)l}} E_i(FG)_{jk} H_l \xleftarrow{c_{jk}} E_i F_j G_k H_l$$

$$\alpha_{EF(GH)} \searrow \qquad \swarrow \alpha_{FGH}$$

$$\alpha_{EFG} \searrow \qquad E_i(F(GH))_{j(kl)} \qquad \swarrow Id$$

$$\uparrow$$

$$Id \searrow \qquad E_i(FG)_{jk} H_l \qquad \swarrow Id$$

$$\uparrow$$

$$E_i F_j G_k H_l \tag{11.4.32}$$

From the commutative of the outer-most pentagon, we can have the commutative of the inner-most pentagon from Eq. (11.4.32), which is the requirement of coherence condition for functors

---

[4]$\circ$ is removed for simplicity.

E, F, G and H in $\mathbf{Dist}(\mathcal{A}^{\mathbb{B}})$.

11.4.3 Correspondence between Tensors and Plurioperads

The purpose of this section is to build the correspondence between tensors and plurioperads. Define the functor $\Gamma : \mathbf{Dist}(\mathcal{A}^{\mathbb{B}}) \longrightarrow \mathbf{End}(\mathcal{A}^{\mathbb{B}})$ [5] as

$$\Gamma(E)X = \coprod_{1 \leq n} E_{1 \leq i \leq n} X \tag{11.4.33}$$

with respect to each $X \in \mathcal{A}^{\mathbb{B}}$. Then, we have a coproduct cocone for $p \in \mathbb{N}$ as

$$d_i : E_{1 \leq i \leq p} X \longrightarrow \Gamma(E)X. \tag{11.4.34}$$

If E is an identity functor $\mathbf{I}$, we have an isomorphism $\varrho : \mathbf{I}_{\mathcal{A}^{\mathbb{B}}} \longrightarrow \Gamma(\mathbf{I})$. For X in $\mathcal{A}^{\mathbb{B}}$ and $1 \leq i \leq p, 1 \leq j \leq q_i$, we have a composition:

$$E_{1 \leq i \leq p} F_{1 \leq j \leq q_i} X \xrightarrow{d_j} E_{1 \leq i \leq p} \Gamma(F)X \xrightarrow{d_i} \Gamma(E)\Gamma(F)X, \tag{11.4.35}$$

where $\Gamma(E)\Gamma(F)X$ is a coproduct structure. Moreover, we also have a composition:

$$E_{1 \leq i \leq p} F_{1 \leq j \leq q_i} X \xrightarrow{c_{ij}} (E \circ F)_{ij} X \xrightarrow{d_{(ij)}} \Gamma(E \circ F)X, \tag{11.4.36}$$

where $\Gamma(E \circ F)$ is a coproduct structure. We then have following commutative diagram for map $\acute{\varrho}_{E,F} : \Gamma(E)\Gamma(F)X \longrightarrow \Gamma(E \circ F)X$:

$$
\begin{array}{ccc}
E_i\Gamma(F)X \xrightarrow{d_i} \Gamma(E)\Gamma(F)X \xrightarrow{\acute{\varrho}_{E,F}} \Gamma(E \circ F)X \\
d_j \uparrow \qquad\qquad\qquad\qquad \uparrow d_{(ij)} \\
E_i F_j X \qquad \xrightarrow{c_{ij}} \qquad (E \circ F)_{(ij)}X
\end{array}
\tag{11.4.37}
$$

Lemma 51 *The maps $\varrho, \acute{\varrho}_{-,-}$ make Γ into a monoidal functor, i.e., Γ sends distributive tensors to monads.*

PROOF. 88 *Let $(TR, \circ, Id_{TR})$ be monoidal invengory (tensors) and $(MD, ;Id_{MD})$ be monoidal invengory (monads). For functor Γ from $(TR, \circ, Id_{TR})$ to $(MD, ;Id_{MD})$, it induces a natural transformation $\acute{\varrho}_{E,F} : \Gamma(E)\dot{\Gamma}(F) \longrightarrow \Gamma(E \circ F)$ and a morphism $\varrho : Id_{MD} \longrightarrow \Gamma(Id_{TR})$.*

---

[5] The invengory for endomorphic maps from $\mathcal{A}^{\mathbb{B}}$.

438

We begin by verifying the left unit monoidal coherence axiom about Γ. Considering the following commutative diagram:

$$
\begin{array}{ccc}
Id_{MD} \cdot \Gamma(F) & \xrightarrow{\varrho} & \Gamma(Id_{MD}) \cdot \Gamma(F) \\
\kappa_{MD} \downarrow & & \downarrow \acute{\varrho}_{Id_{MD},F} \\
\Gamma(F) & \xleftarrow{\Gamma(\kappa_{TR})} & \Gamma(Id_{TR} \circ F)
\end{array}
\qquad (11.4.38)
$$

the left unit monoidal coherence axiom is satisfiedfrom by Eq. (11.4.38).

About the right unit monoidal coherence axiom about Γ, we consider the following commutative diagram:

$$
\begin{array}{ccc}
\Gamma(E) \cdot Id_{MD} & \xrightarrow{\varrho} & \Gamma(E) \cdot \Gamma(Id_{TR}) \\
\rho_{MD} \downarrow & & \downarrow \acute{\varrho}_{E,Id_{TR}} \\
\Gamma(E) & \xleftarrow{\Gamma(\rho_{TR})} & \Gamma(E \circ Id_{TR})
\end{array}
\qquad (11.4.39)
$$

the right unit monoidal coherence axiom is satisfied by Eq. (11.4.39).

For tensors E, F and G, we have following commutative diagram

$$
\begin{array}{ccccccc}
E_i \circ F_j \circ G_k & & \xrightarrow{Id} & & & & E_i \circ F_j \circ G_k \\
& \searrow d_i d_j d_k & & & & d_i d_j d_k \swarrow & \\
& \Gamma(E) \cdot \Gamma(F) \cdot \Gamma(G) & \xrightarrow{Id} & & \Gamma(E) \cdot \Gamma(F) \cdot \Gamma(G) & & \\
Id \uparrow & \searrow c_{E,F} & & & c_{F,G} \swarrow & & \uparrow Id \\
d_i d_j \uparrow & (\Gamma(E) \cdot \Gamma(F)) \cdot \Gamma(G) & \xrightarrow{\alpha^{MD}_{EFG}} \Gamma(E) \cdot (\Gamma(F) \cdot \Gamma(G)) & & \uparrow d_j d_k & \\
& \downarrow \acute{\varrho}_{E,F} & & \acute{\varrho}_{F,G} \downarrow & & \\
E_i F_j G_k \xrightarrow{d_k} E_i F_j \Gamma(G) & \xrightarrow{d_{(ij)} c_{ij}} \Gamma(EF)\Gamma(G) & & \Gamma(E)\Gamma(FG) \xleftarrow{d_{(jk)} c_{jk}} \Gamma(E) F_j G_k \xleftarrow{d_i} E_i F_j G_k \\
& \downarrow \acute{\varrho}_{E\circ F,G} & & \acute{\varrho}_{E,F\circ G} \downarrow & & \\
c_{ij} \downarrow & \Gamma((E \circ F) \circ G) & \xrightarrow{\Gamma(\alpha^{TR}_{EFG})} \Gamma(E \circ (F \circ G)) & & \downarrow c_{jk} \\
Id \uparrow & \nearrow \acute{\varrho}_{E\circ F,G} d_{(ij)} & & \acute{\varrho}_{E,F\circ G} d_{(jk)} \nwarrow & & \uparrow Id \\
& (E \circ F)_{(ij)} \Gamma(G) & & \Gamma(E)(F \circ G)_{(jk)} & \\
& \nearrow c_{ij} d_k & & c_{jk} d_i \nwarrow & \\
E_i \circ F_j \circ G_k & & \xrightarrow{Id} & & & & E_i \circ F_j \circ G_k
\end{array}
$$

$$(11.4.40)$$

then the inner hexagon in Eq. (11.4.40) *will demonstrate the associativity coherence for monoidal functor Γ from Lemma 50.*

Given a cartesian monad F (free monad on $\mathcal{A}^{\mathbb{B}}$) on a finitely complete invengory, one has an induced F-plurioperad. The remaining part of this section wishs to show an analogous notion of F-tensor. Under certain conditions the given monad F distributes with the monoid monad $\mathbb{M}$ on $\mathcal{A}^{\mathbb{B}}$ and the composite monad $\mathbb{M}F$ is again cartesian, in which case one has an equivalence of invengories between F-tensors and $\mathbb{M}F$-plurioperads. We require that F is a *local right adjoint* (lra) monad, and that $\mathcal{A}^{\mathbb{B}}$ is *lextensive*. A functor for MIMO caetgories $T : \mathbf{A} \to \mathbf{B}$ is local right adjoint when for all $\underline{A} \in \mathbf{A}$, the induced functors

$$T_{\underline{A}} : \mathbf{A}/\underline{A} \to \mathbf{B}/T\underline{A}, \tag{11.4.41}$$

are right adjoint. We also assume that $\mathcal{A}^{\mathbb{B}}$ is lextensive in this chapter. A MIMO-invengory $\mathcal{A}^{\mathbb{B}}$ is lextensive when it has finite limits, coproducts and for each family of sequence objects $(\underline{X}_i : i \in I)$ of $\mathcal{A}^{\mathbb{B}}$, following functor is an equivalence functor:

$$\prod_{i \in I} \mathcal{A}^{\mathbb{B}}/\underline{X}_i \longrightarrow \mathcal{A}^{\mathbb{B}}/(\coprod_{i \in I} \underline{X}_i). \tag{11.4.42}$$

Following lemmas are provided about lra and lextensive.

Lemma 52 *Let $T_i : \mathbf{A}_i \to \mathbf{B}_i$ be a family of lra functors. Then*

$$\prod_{i \in I} \mathbf{A}_i \xrightarrow{\prod_i T_i} \prod_{i \in I} \mathbf{B}_i \tag{11.4.43}$$

is lra.

PROOF. 89 *Given $\underline{X}_i \in \mathbf{A}_i$, we have $(\prod_i T_i)_{(\underline{X}_i)} = \prod_i((T_i)_{\underline{X}_i})$, which as a product of right adjoints is a right adjoint.*

Lemma 53 *Let $\mathbf{A}$ and $\mathbf{B}$ be lextensive and I be a set for indices. We have following facts:*

1. *The functor $\Upsilon : \mathbf{A}^I \longrightarrow \mathbf{A}$, which takes an I-indexes family of sequence of objects of $\mathbf{A}$ to its coproduct, is lra.*

2. *If functors $F_i : \mathbf{A} \longrightarrow \mathbf{B}$ for $i \in I$ are lra, then $\coprod_i F_i : \mathbf{A} \longrightarrow \mathbf{B}$ is lra.*

3. *If $F_i : \mathbf{A} \longrightarrow \mathbf{B}$ for $i \in I$ are functors and $\phi_i : F_i \longrightarrow G_i$ are cartesian transformations, then $\coprod_i \phi_i : \coprod_i F_i \longrightarrow \coprod_i G_i$ is cartesian.*

440

PROOF. 90 *1) Given a family $(\underline{X}_i, i \in I)$ of sequence of objects of* **A**, *the functor* Υ *is the functor*

$$\prod_{i \in I} \mathbf{A}/\underline{X}_i \longrightarrow \mathbf{A}/(\coprod_{i \in I} \underline{X}_i), \tag{11.4.44}$$

which is an equivalence (lra).

2) Consider the following composition

$$\mathbf{A} \xrightarrow{diagonal\ map} \mathbf{A}^I \xrightarrow{\prod_{i \in I} F_i} \mathbf{B}^I \xrightarrow{\Upsilon} \mathbf{B} \tag{11.4.45}$$

of a right adjoint (since **A** *has coproducts) followed by a lra (by Lemma 52 followed by another lra by 1), and so* $\coprod_i F_i$ *is a lra.*

3) Since the naturality for $\coprod_i \phi_i$ *is the coproduct of the cartesian naturality squares*

$$
\begin{array}{ccc}
F_i\underline{X} & \xrightarrow{\phi_i} & G_i\underline{X} \\
F_if \downarrow & & \downarrow G_if \\
F_i\underline{Y} & \xrightarrow{\phi_i} & G_i\underline{Y}
\end{array}
\tag{11.4.46}
$$

where $f : \underline{X} \longrightarrow \underline{Y}$ *is a relation in* **A**, *then* $\coprod_i \phi_i$ *is a cartesian functor.*

Let **LraDist** and **LraEnd** be subinvengories of **Dist** and **End**, respectively. We have following lemma about the existence for the functor from **LraDist**$/F^{\#}$ to **LraEnd**$/\Gamma(F^{\#})$.

Lemma 54 *Let* $\mathcal{A}^{\mathbb{B}}$ *be lextensive. One has a functor*

$$\Gamma_F : \mathbf{LraDist}/F^{\#} \longrightarrow \mathbf{LraEnd}/\Gamma(F^{\#}). \tag{11.4.47}$$

PROOF. 91 *We first claim that the monoidal structure of* **Dist** *restricts to* **LraDist**, *and there is a monoidal functor from* **LraDist**$(\mathcal{A}^{\mathbb{B}})$ *to* **LraEnd**$(\mathcal{A}^{\mathbb{B}})$.

Since $1_{\mathcal{A}^{\mathbb{B}}}$ *is lra, the unit of* **Dist**$(\mathcal{A}^{\mathbb{B}})$ *is lra. For lra functors* $E, F \in \mathbf{Dist}(\mathcal{A}^{\mathbb{B}})$, *we have to show that* $E \circ F$ *is lra. By Lemmas 51 and 53 and expression*

$$(E \circ F)_{(n)} = \coprod_{n_1 + \cdots n_k = n} E_{(k)}(F_{(n_1)}, \cdots, F_{(n_k)}), \tag{11.4.48}$$

it is enough to show $E_{(k)}(F_{(n_1)}, \cdots, F_{(n_k)})$ *is lra. Because* $E_{(k)}(F_{(n_1)}, \cdots, F_{(n_k)})$ *can be obtained by compositions as*

$$\prod_i (\mathcal{A}^{\mathbb{B}})^{n_i} \xrightarrow{\prod_i F_{n_i}} (\mathcal{A}^{\mathbb{B}})^k \xrightarrow{E_k} \mathcal{A}^{\mathbb{B}} \tag{11.4.49}$$

441

this is lra by Lemma 52.

Given $\varphi : E \longrightarrow E'$ and $\phi : F \longrightarrow F'$, the next is to show that $\varphi \circ \phi$ is cartesian. From Lemma 53, it is enough to show that

$$E_k(F_{n_1}, \cdots, F_{n_k}) \xrightarrow{\varphi_k(\phi_{n_1}, \cdots, \phi_{n_k})} \qquad (11.4.50)$$

is cartesian. By observing the following compositions:

$$
\begin{array}{ccc}
\prod_i F_{n_i} & \prod_i E_k & \\
\longrightarrow & \longrightarrow & \\
\prod_i (\mathcal{A}^{\mathbb{B}})^{n_i} \Downarrow \prod_i \phi_{n_i} \; (\mathcal{A}^{\mathbb{B}})^k \Downarrow \varphi_k & \mathcal{A}^{\mathbb{B}}, & \qquad (11.4.51) \\
\longrightarrow & \longrightarrow & \\
\prod_i F'_{n_i} & \prod_i E'_k &
\end{array}
$$

*we have $\varphi \circ \phi$ is cartesian by horizontal composite of cartesian transformations between pullback preserving functors. Thus the monoidal structure of **Dist** restricts to **LraDist**.*

*Before finishing the claim, we have to show that there is a monoidal functor from $\mathbf{LraDist}(\mathcal{A}^{\mathbb{B}})$ to $\mathbf{LraEnd}(\mathcal{A}^{\mathbb{B}})$. Since the monoidal structure of **Dist** restricts to **LraDist**, the remaining part is to show that the monoidal functor $\Gamma : \mathbf{Dist} \longrightarrow \mathbf{End}$ preserves lra objects and cartesian transformations. Let $E \in \mathbf{Dist}$ be lra, the lra property of $\Gamma(E)$ is obtained from the composition*

$$\mathcal{A}^{\mathbb{B}} \xrightarrow{diagonal \; map} (\mathcal{A}^{\mathbb{B}})^n \xrightarrow{E_{1 \leq i \leq n}} \mathcal{A}^{\mathbb{B}} \qquad (11.4.52)$$

where $n \in \mathbb{N}$. Let $\phi : F \longrightarrow F'$ in $\mathbf{Dist}(\mathcal{A}^{\mathbb{B}})$ be cartesian and $\Gamma(\phi)$ is a cartesian map again from Lemma 53.

For the existence of Γ_F, we first make the following observation. If $\mathcal{N}$ is a monoidal invengory with a monoid (M, ι, m) therein, where $\iota : Id \longrightarrow M$ and $m : M \otimes M \longrightarrow M$. The tensor product of relations $\alpha : A \longrightarrow M$ and $\beta : B \longrightarrow M$ is the composition

$$A \otimes B \xrightarrow{\alpha \otimes \beta} M \otimes M \xrightarrow{m} M \qquad (11.4.53)$$

and the forgetful functor $\mathcal{N}/M \longrightarrow \mathcal{N}$ is monoidal. To give $\alpha : A \longrightarrow M$ into a monoid structure in $\mathcal{N}/M$, we require the isomorphism between $Mon(\mathcal{N}/M) \equiv Mon(\mathcal{N})/M$. Hence, given a monoidal functor $H : \mathcal{N} \longrightarrow \mathcal{N}'$ such that HM is a monoid, one has a commutative *diagram*

$$\mathcal{M}/M \overset{H_M}{\longrightarrow} \mathcal{M}'/HM$$

$$\downarrow \qquad\qquad \downarrow$$

$$\mathcal{M} \overset{H}{\longrightarrow} \mathcal{M}'$$

$$(11.4.54)$$

for monoidal functors.

Applying this observation to $\Gamma : \mathbf{LraDist}(\mathcal{A}^{\mathbb{B}}) \longrightarrow \mathbf{LraEnd}(\mathcal{A}^{\mathbb{B}})$, one has

$$\Gamma_E : \mathbf{LraDist}(\mathcal{A}^{\mathbb{B}})/E \longrightarrow \mathbf{LraEnd}(\mathcal{A}^{\mathbb{B}})/\Gamma(E) \qquad (11.4.55)$$

for each lra distributive tensor E*. An object of* $\mathbf{LraDist}(\mathcal{A}^{\mathbb{B}})/E$ *amounts to a functor* $A :$ $\mathcal{M}\mathcal{A}^{\mathbb{B}} \longrightarrow \mathcal{A}^{\mathbb{B}}$ *together with a cartesian transformation* $: A \longrightarrow E$*. The distributivity of* A *is a consequence of the cartesian of , the distributivity of* E *and* $\mathcal{A}^{\mathbb{B}}s$ *coproducts. The lra of* A *is also a consequence, because the domain of any cartesian transformation into a lra functor is again lra. A morphism in* $\mathbf{LraDist}(\mathcal{A}^{\mathbb{B}})/E$ *from to* $: B \longrightarrow E$ *is a natural transformation* $\phi : A \longrightarrow B$ *such that* $\beta\phi = \alpha$*,* ϕ *is automatically cartesian by pullback property. Thus a monoid in* $\mathbf{LraDist}(\mathcal{A}^{\mathbb{B}})/E$ *is simply a cartesian multitensor morphism into* E*. Similarly a monoid in* $\mathbf{LraEnd}(\mathcal{A}^{\mathbb{B}})/E$ *is also a cartesian monad morphism into* $\Gamma(E)$*, Therefore, by considering the special case for* $E = F^{\#}$*, one has a desired functor*

$$\Gamma_F : \mathbf{LraDist}/F^{\#} \longrightarrow \mathbf{LraEnd}/\Gamma(F^{\#}). \qquad (11.4.56)$$

For convenience, we will denote $\mathbf{LraDist}/F^{\#}$ as $F - \mathbf{Tensor}$ and $\mathbf{LraEnd}/\Gamma(F^{\#})$ as $\mathbb{M}F - \mathbf{Plurioperad}$. From Lemma 54, we have following theorem about Γ_F.

Theorem 42 *Let* $\mathcal{A}^{\mathbb{B}}$ *be lextensive and* F *a coproduct preserving lra monad on* $\mathcal{A}^{\mathbb{B}}$*. We have the equivalence for functor* Γ_F *as*

$$\Gamma_F : F - \mathbf{Tensor} \longrightarrow \mathbb{M}F - \mathbf{Plurioperad}. \qquad (11.4.57)$$

PROOF. 92 *For equivalence of* Γ_F*, we have to show that* Γ_F *is surjective on objects and fully faithful. Let* $\alpha : A \longrightarrow \Gamma(F)$ *be a cartesian transformation. For each finite sequence of sequence* of objects $(\underline{X}_i : 1 \leq i \leq n)$ of $\mathcal{A}^{\mathbb{B}}$, we construct pullbacks as

$$
\begin{array}{ccc}
\tilde{A}_i(\underline{X}_i) & \longrightarrow & A(\underline{1}) \\
\tilde{\alpha} \downarrow & & \downarrow \alpha(1) \\
F_i(\underline{X}_i) & \overset{E_i \varsigma_{\underline{X}_i}}{\longrightarrow} F_i(\underline{1}) \overset{d_i}{\longrightarrow} & \Gamma F(\underline{1})
\end{array}
\qquad (11.4.58)
$$

where $\varsigma_{\underline{X}_i}$ is a constant map for domain with objects $\underline{X}_i$. Then, we have a cartesian transformation $\tilde{\alpha} : \tilde{A} \longrightarrow F$. The stability of $\mathcal{A}^{\mathbb{B}}s$ coproducts applied to the pullbacks

$$
\begin{array}{ccc}
\tilde{A}_i(\underline{1}) & \overset{\tilde{\alpha}}{\longrightarrow} & F_i(\underline{1}) \\
\downarrow & & \downarrow d_i \\
A(\underline{1}) & \overset{\alpha(1)}{\longrightarrow} & \Gamma F(\underline{1})
\end{array}
\qquad (11.4.59)
$$

implies that $\Gamma_F(\tilde{\alpha}) \equiv \alpha$ (surjectivity).

Let $\alpha : A \longrightarrow F$, $\beta : B \longrightarrow F$ and $\phi : \Gamma A \longrightarrow \Gamma B$ with $\Gamma(\beta)\phi = \Gamma(\alpha)$, we have to show the uniqueness for $\phi' : A \longrightarrow B$. For the uniqueness of $\phi'(\underline{1})$, it is established from the following diagram:

$$
\begin{array}{ccc}
A_i(\underline{1}) & \overset{\phi_i'(\underline{1})}{\longrightarrow} & B_i(\underline{1}) \\
\alpha(\underline{1}) \searrow & & \swarrow \beta(\underline{1}) \\
& F_i(\underline{1}) & \\
d_i \downarrow \quad \downarrow d_i & & \downarrow d_i \\
& \Gamma F(\underline{1}) & \\
\nearrow \Gamma\alpha(\underline{1}) & \Gamma\beta(\underline{1}) \nwarrow & \\
\Gamma A(\underline{1}) & \overset{\Gamma\phi'(\underline{1})}{\longrightarrow} & \Gamma B(\underline{1})
\end{array}
\qquad (11.4.60)
$$

444

For the uniqueness of $\phi'(\underline{X}_i)$, it is obtained from the following diagram:

$$
\begin{array}{ccc}
A_i(\underline{X}_i) & \overset{\phi_i'(\underline{X}_i)}{\longrightarrow} & B_i(\underline{X}_i) \\
\alpha(\underline{X}_i) \searrow & & \swarrow \beta(\underline{X}_i) \\
& F_i(\underline{X}_i) & \\
A_i(\varsigma_{\underline{X}_i}) \downarrow & \downarrow F_i(\varsigma_{\underline{X}_i}) \quad \downarrow B_i(\varsigma_{\underline{X}_i}) & \\
& F(\underline{1}) & \\
\alpha(\underline{1}) \nearrow & & \nwarrow \beta(\underline{1}) \\
A(\underline{1}) & \overset{\phi'(\underline{1})}{\longrightarrow} & B(\underline{1})
\end{array}
$$

$$(11.4.61)$$

11.4.4 Induction to Higher Dimension

The goal of this section is to introduce the inductive nature of the plurioperadic approach to higher dimension invengorical tensor product. We begin by presheaf invengories.

Let $\hat{\mathbf{B}}$ be a presheaf invengory induced by the MIMO invengory $\mathbf{B}$, $\hat{\mathbf{C}}$ be a presheaf invengory induced by the MIMO invengory $\mathbf{C}$ and a lra functor $T : \hat{\mathbf{B}} \longrightarrow \hat{\mathbf{C}}$. For $\mathbb{H} \in \hat{\mathbf{C}}$, we have an induced functor $E_T : \hat{\mathbf{C}}/\mathbb{H} \longrightarrow \hat{\mathbf{B}}$. Given a presheaf (functor), $H = E_T(\mathbb{H})$, in $\hat{\mathbf{B}}$ and a morphism $f : \underline{D} \longrightarrow \underline{C}$ in the MIMO invengory $\mathbf{C}$, we will denote by $H(f)$ the element of a presheaf invengory induced by the functor H over $\mathbf{C}$ and by $\tilde{f}$ as the map $H(f) \longrightarrow H$.

If we have a lra functor $T : \hat{\mathbf{B}} \longrightarrow \hat{\mathbf{C}}$ and a presheaf X in $\hat{\mathbf{B}}$, then, we can define a functor TX as

- For objects: $TX(\underline{C}) = (H, h)$, where h is a natural transformation $h : H \longrightarrow X$;

- For morphisms: $TX(f)(H, h) = (H(f), h\tilde{f})$ with identities $(H, h) = TX(Id)$.

Given a map $e : A \longrightarrow TX$, we can factorize it through its colimit Z as

$$A \overset{g_a}{\longrightarrow} TZ \overset{Th'}{\longrightarrow} TX,$$

$$(11.4.62)$$

where g_a are components of the universal cocone and $h' : Z \longrightarrow X$. A lra $T : \hat{\mathbf{B}} \longrightarrow \hat{\mathbf{C}}$ is tight when for all G, H in $E_T(\mathbb{H})$ and $\iota : G \equiv H$ in $\hat{\mathbf{B}}$, we have $G = H$ and $\iota = Id$. We then have following lemmas.

Lemma 55 *Let $T : \hat{\mathbf{B}} \longrightarrow \hat{\mathbf{C}}$ be a tight lra. Then for all $T' : \hat{\mathbf{B}} \longrightarrow \hat{\mathbf{C}}$ there exists at most one cartesian transformation $T' \longrightarrow T$.*

PROOF. 93 *We assume that α, β are two cartesian transformations $T' \longrightarrow T$ with $a \in T'X(\underline{C})$. For a given $\mathbb{H}$, one has a factorization as*

$$\underline{C} \xrightarrow{a} T'X \xrightarrow{\alpha_X} TX$$

$$g_\alpha \searrow \qquad \nearrow Tf_\alpha$$

$$Th_\alpha \tag{11.4.63}$$

by using the cartesian naturality square for α corresponding to f_α. We then have $g'_\alpha : \underline{C} \longrightarrow T'h_\alpha$ with $\alpha g'_\alpha = g_\alpha$ and $a = T'(f_\alpha) g'_\alpha$ (factorization of a).

Similarly, by replacing α as β, we have another factorization about a as $a = T'(f_\beta) g'_\beta$. Then, there is an isomorphism $\iota : h_\alpha = h_\beta$ such that $T(\iota) g'_\alpha = g'_\beta$ and $f_\alpha \iota = f_\beta$. By tightness of T, ι is an identity which implies $\alpha = \beta$.

Following lemma is about monad $F^\#$.

Lemma 56 *Let (F, η, μ) be a lra monad on $\hat{\mathbf{C}}$ such that F is right. Then for all $E : athcalM\hat{\mathbf{C}} \longrightarrow \hat{\mathbf{C}}$ there exists at most one cartesian transformation $\epsilon : E \longrightarrow F^\#$.*

PROOF. 94 *By Lemma 55, it is enough to show that $F_n^\# : \hat{\mathbf{C}}^n \longrightarrow \hat{\mathbf{C}}$ is tight for all $n \in \mathbb{N}$. Considering the map $E_{F_n^\#} : ((h_1, \cdots, h_n), \underline{C}) \longrightarrow (h_1, \cdots, h_n)$, if we have another $(h'_1, \cdots, h'_n) \in \hat{\mathbf{C}}^n$ with an isomorphism $\iota : (h_1, \cdots, h_n) \equiv (h'_1, \cdots, h'_n)$, then we have identities $\iota_i : h'_i = h_i$ for $1 \le i \le n$. This shows that $F_n^\#$ is tight.*

The invengory $\mathbb{G}$ has objects as finite sequences of natural numbers and maps for $\underline{n} < \underline{m}$ as

$$\underline{n} \underset{\tau}{\overset{\sigma}{\underset{\longrightarrow}{\rightrightarrows}}} \underline{m}, \tag{11.4.64}$$

which satisfy $\sigma\tau = \tau\tau$ and $\tau\sigma = \sigma\sigma$. Then an object of the presheaf invengory induced by $\mathbb{G}$, denoted as $\hat{\mathbb{G}}$ (named as MIMO Globular Set), is a diagram

$$\underline{X_0} \underset{\longleftarrow}{\overset{s_0}{\longleftarrow}} \underline{X_1} \underset{t_1}{\overset{s_1}{\underset{\longleftarrow}{\leftleftarrows}}} \underline{X_2} \cdots \tag{11.4.65}$$

446

of sets and functions with $s_i s_j = s_i t_j$ and $t_i t_j = t_i s_j$, where i, j are indices in $0 \bigcup \mathbb{N}$. The elements of $\underline{X}_n$ are called n-cells. For an $(n+1)$-cell $\underline{x}$, the n-cells $s\underline{x}$ and $t\underline{x}$ are called the source and target of $\underline{x}$ respectively. Given a pair $(\underline{a}, \underline{b})$ of n-cells of $\underline{X}$, we can define the globular set $X(\underline{a}, \underline{b})$. A k-cell of $X(\underline{a}, \underline{b})$ is an $(n+k)$-cell $\underline{x}$ of $\underline{X}$ with $s_k \underline{x} = \underline{a}$ and $t_k \underline{x} = \underline{b}$. In particular the globular sets $X(\underline{a}, \underline{b})$ where $\underline{a}$ and $\underline{b}$ are 0-cells are called the homomorphisms of X. A morphism $f : \underline{X} \longrightarrow \underline{Y}$ of globular sets induces maps $\underline{X}(\underline{a}, \underline{b}) \longrightarrow \underline{Y}(f_0(\underline{a}), f_0(\underline{b}))$, where f_0 is a function $\underline{X}_0 \longrightarrow \underline{Y}_0$. A finite sequence $(\underline{X}_0, \underline{X}_1, \cdots, \underline{X}_n)$ of globular sets can be treated as globular set by setting 0-cells as collection of $\{\underline{X}_i\}$ for $0 \le i \le n$ and its homomorphisms are provided by $(\underline{X}_0, \underline{X}_1, \cdots, \underline{X}_n)(i-1, i) \longrightarrow \underline{X}_i$ for $0 \le i \le n$. This constructs a functor $\hat{\mathbb{G}}^n \longrightarrow \hat{\mathbb{G}}$.

The role of $\mathbb{H}$ is replaced by the globular set $\mathbf{TR}$ of trees. The set $\mathbf{TR}_0$ contains one element denoted as 0 and its associated globular set contains one 0-cell. By induction an element of $\mathbf{TR}_{n+1}$ is a finite sequence $(\xi_1, \cdots, \xi_k)$ of elements of $\mathbf{TR}_n$ and its associated globular set is the sequence of globular sets $(\xi_1, \cdots, \xi_k)$ regarded as a globular set. The object map of E_T is defined as $E_T : \hat{\mathbb{G}}/\mathbf{TR} \longrightarrow \hat{\mathbb{G}}$.

The source and target maps $s, t : \mathbf{TR}_{n+1} \longrightarrow \mathbf{TR}_n$ are identical and are set as ∂. For each dimension n, we wish to define maps $\sigma : \partial\xi \longrightarrow \xi$ and $\tau : \partial\xi \longrightarrow \xi$ satisfying $\tau\sigma = \sigma\sigma$ and $\sigma\tau = \tau\tau$. We can define ∂, σ, τ by induction of dimension. For $n = 0$, we define σ as $0 \longrightarrow \xi$, which is the map that selects the object $0 \in \xi$. We define τ as $0 \longrightarrow \xi$, which is the map that selects the minimum vertex of ξ. The initial step ∂ is uniquely determined since $\mathbf{TR}_0$ is singleton with σ, τ just defined. For the inductive step, we set $\xi = (\xi_1, \cdots, \xi_k) \in \mathbf{TR}_{n+2}$, then $\partial\xi = (\partial\xi_1, \cdots, \partial\xi_k)$ and the maps σ, τ are the identities on 0-cells. The non-empty homomorphism maps are given by $\sigma, \tau : \partial\xi_i \longrightarrow \xi_i$ for $1 \le i \le k$. Under such definitions, it is obvious to see that $\tau\sigma = \sigma\sigma$ and $\sigma\tau = \tau\tau$ for higher dimension of n.

Given a lra functor $T : \hat{\mathbb{G}} \longrightarrow \hat{\mathbb{G}}$, we will demonstrate that T is tight. If $n = 0$, the result follows due to $\mathbf{TR}_0 = \{0\}$ and the only automorphism of $0 \in \hat{\mathbb{G}}$ is the identity. For the inductive step, we assume that $\xi, \xi' \in \mathbf{TR}_{n+1}$ with $\iota : \xi \equiv \xi'$. Since the only non-empty homomorphism for ξ and ξ' are between consecutive elements of their vertex sets, any $f : \xi \longrightarrow \xi'$ in $\hat{\mathbb{G}}$ is order preserving in dimension 0. Because the 0-cell map of ι is an order preserving bijection, such map must be the identity. The homomorphic maps of ι must also be identities by induction. Since the globular sets associated to $\xi \in \mathbf{TR}_n$ are also connected, we have the following result.

Lemma 57 *Let $T : \hat{\mathbb{G}} \longrightarrow \hat{\mathbb{G}}$ defined as below is lra, tight and coproduct preserving:*

- *an n-cell of TX is a pair (ξ, f), where $\xi \in \mathbf{TR}_n$;*

- *for $n \geq 1$, $s(\xi, f) = (\partial \xi, f\sigma)$ and $t(\xi, f) = (\partial \xi, f\tau)$;*

- *for $g : X \longrightarrow Y$, $T(g)(\xi, f) = (\xi, gf)$.*

11.4.5 n-MIMO Tensor Theorem

In this section, we wish to prove n-MIMO tensor theorem by representing n-MIMO tensor as plurioperads. We begin by following definition.

Definition 93 *An endofunctor U of $\hat{\mathbb{G}}$ is normalized, when for all $X \in \hat{\mathbb{G}}$, $\{UX\}_0 \equiv X_0$. A monad (U, η, μ) is normalized when U is normalized as endofunctor, a cartesian transformation $\alpha : U \longrightarrow T$ is a normalized collection when U is normalized. A T-plurioperad $\alpha : U \longrightarrow T$ is normalized when U is normalized as a monad or endofunctor. We use the term $T - \mathbf{COL}_0$ to represent the sub-invengory of $\mathbf{LraEnd}(\hat{\mathbb{G}})/T$ consisting of the normalised collections, and adopt the term $T - \mathbf{OP}_0$ to represent the sub-invengory of $T - \mathbf{OP}$ consisting of the normalized plurioperads.*

Before later derivation, we have to introduce some notations. A finite sequence $(\underline{X}_1, \cdots, \underline{X}_k)$ of globular sets may be regarded as a globular set: the set of sequences of 0-cells is

$$[k]_0 = \{0, \cdots, k\}, \tag{11.4.66}$$

where k are positive integers; $(\underline{X}_1, \cdots, \underline{X}_k)(i-1, i) = \underline{X}_i$ and all the other homomorphisms are empty. We regard sequences $(\underline{x}_0, \cdots, \underline{x}_k)$ of 0-cells of a globular set X as maps $\Xi : [k]_0 \longrightarrow \underline{X}$ in $\hat{\mathbb{G}}$. Given the map Ξ, we will define

$$\Xi^* \underline{X} = \{\underline{X}(\underline{x}_{i-1}, \underline{x}_i)\}, \tag{11.4.67}$$

where $1 \leq i \leq k$, and a map $\check{\Xi} : \Xi^* \underline{X} \longrightarrow \underline{X}$. Note that the maps $\check{\Xi}$ and Ξ agree on 0-cells. We have following lemma about $T\underline{X}$, where T is a monad.

Lemma 58 *Let $\underline{X}$ be a MIMO globular set and $\underline{a}, \underline{b} \in \underline{X}_0$. For all $m \in \mathbb{N}$ and $\Xi : [m]_0 \longrightarrow \underline{X}$, if $\Xi(0) = \underline{a}$ and $\Xi(m) = \underline{b}$, the maps*

$$\{T\Xi^* \underline{X}\}(0, m) \longrightarrow \{T\underline{X}\}(\underline{a}, \underline{b}), \tag{11.4.68}$$

form a coproduct cocone.

PROOF. 95 *Since the map $f : \xi \longrightarrow \underline{X}$ can be factorized uniquely as*

$$\xi \xrightarrow{f'} \Xi^*\underline{X} \xrightarrow{\breve{\Xi}} \underline{X}, \tag{11.4.69}$$

we have $(\xi, f') \in T\Xi^*\underline{X}$, which is sent to (ξ, f) by $T\breve{\Xi}$. Note that f' is the identity on 0-cells, which is to say that (ξ, f) is an n-cell of $\{T\Xi^*\underline{X}\}(0, m)$. Hence, an n-cell θ of $\{T\underline{X}\}(\underline{a}, \underline{b})$ is determined uniquely by (1) $m \in \mathbb{N}$, $\Xi : [m]_0 \longrightarrow \underline{X}$ such that $\Xi(0) = \underline{a}$ and $\Xi(m) = \underline{b}$, and an n-cell θ' of $\{T\Xi^*\underline{X}\}(0, m)$ with $\{T\breve{\Xi}\}(0, m)\theta' = \theta$. If any of the $\underline{X}(\underline{x}_{i-1}, \underline{x}_i)$ is empty, one has that $\{T\xi^*\underline{X}\}(0, m)$ is empty since T preserves the initial object. Thus one can specify an n-cell θ of $\{T\underline{X}\}(\underline{a}, \underline{b})$ uniquely by giving (m, θ', Ξ) as above with the additional condition that homomorphisms $\underline{X}(\underline{x}_{i-1}, \underline{x}_i)$ are non-empty for all $1 \le i \le k$.

Following lemma is provided about pullbacks and homomorphisms in $\hat{\mathbb{G}}$.

Lemma 59 *Given following the commutative square I*

$$
\begin{array}{ccc}
\underline{W} & \xrightarrow{h} & \underline{X} \\
f \downarrow & I & \downarrow g \\
\underline{Y} & \xrightarrow{k} & \underline{Z}
\end{array}
\tag{11.4.70}
$$

in $\hat{\mathbb{G}}$, one has, for each $\underline{a}, \underline{b} \in \underline{W}_0$, the commutative square II indicated as below

$$
\begin{array}{ccc}
\underline{W}(\underline{a}, \underline{b}) & \xrightarrow{h_{\underline{a},\underline{b}}} & \underline{X}(h\underline{a}, h\underline{b}) \\
f_{\underline{a},\underline{b}} \downarrow & II & \downarrow g_{h\underline{a},h\underline{b}} \\
\underline{Y}(\underline{a}, \underline{b}) & \xrightarrow{k_{\underline{a},\underline{b}}} & \underline{Z}(h\underline{a}, h\underline{b})
\end{array}
\tag{11.4.71}
$$

The square I is a pullback if and only if the square II is a pullback for each $\underline{a}, \underline{b} \in \underline{W}_0$.

PROOF. 96 *If the square II is a pullback with $\underline{y} \in \underline{Y}(\underline{a}, \underline{b})_n$ (n-dimensional component), $\underline{x} \in \underline{X}(h\underline{a}, h\underline{b})_n$ and $k\underline{y} = g\underline{x}$, then there is a unique $\underline{w} \in \underline{W}_{n+1}$ such that $f\underline{w} = \underline{y}$ and $h\underline{w} = \underline{x}$. Because $f_{0,0} = Id$ and its components commute with sources and targets, one has $\underline{w} \in \underline{W}_n$, which says that the square II is a pullback for each $\underline{a}, \underline{b} \in \underline{W}_0$.*

On the other hand, if the square II is a pullback for each $\underline{a}, \underline{b} \in \underline{W}_0$, we have the square I is a pullback when the dimension is 0 since $f_{\underline{0},\underline{0}} = g_{\underline{0},\underline{0}} = Id$. For higher dimension n, let $\underline{y} \in \underline{Y}_{n+1}$ and $\underline{x} \in \underline{X}_{n+1}$ such that $k\underline{y} = g\underline{x}$. Set $\underline{a} = s\underline{y}$ and $\underline{b} = t\underline{y}$ so that $\underline{y} \in \underline{Y}(\underline{a}, \underline{b})_n$. Since the components of maps in $\hat{\mathbb{G}}$ commutes with sources and targets, there is a unique $\underline{w} \in \underline{W}(\underline{a}, \underline{b})_n$

449

such that $f\underline{w} = \underline{y}$ and $h\underline{w} = \underline{x}$. Any $\underline{w}' \in \underline{W}_{n+1}$ such that $f\underline{w}' = \underline{y}$ and $h\underline{w}' = \underline{x}$ is in $\underline{W}(\underline{a}, \underline{b})_n$ because the components of f commute with sources and targets, which implies that $w' = w$.

Lemma 60 *Fix a choice of initial object and pullbacks in $\hat{\mathbb{G}}$, such that the pullback of an identity arrow is an identity. Let $\alpha : A \longrightarrow T$ be a normalised collection. Fro all $m \in \mathbb{N}$ and $\Xi : [m]_0 \longrightarrow \underline{X}$ with $\Xi(0) = \underline{a}$ and $\Xi(m) = \underline{b}$, the maps*

$$\{A\Xi^*\underline{X}\}(0, m) \longrightarrow \{A\underline{X}\}(\underline{a}, \underline{b}), \tag{11.4.72}$$

form a coproduct cocone.

PROOF. 97 *By Lemma 58, Lemma 59 and the following diagram:*

$$
\begin{array}{ccc}
\{A\Xi^*\underline{X}\}(0, m) & \overset{\{A\tilde{\Xi}\}_{0,m}}{\longrightarrow} & \{A\underline{X}\}(\underline{a}, \underline{b}) \\
\{\alpha_{\Xi^*\underline{X}}\}_{0,m} \downarrow & & \downarrow \{\alpha_{\underline{X}}\}_{\underline{a},\underline{b}} \\
\{T\Xi^*\underline{X}\}(0, m) & \overset{\{T\tilde{\Xi}\}_{0,m}}{\longrightarrow} & \{T\underline{X}\}(\underline{a}, \underline{b})
\end{array}
\tag{11.4.73}
$$

this lemma is established.

Lemma 61 *The assignment $A \longrightarrow \grave{A}$ is the object map of a monoidal functor as*

$$\grave{()} : F - \mathbf{COL}_0 \longrightarrow \mathbf{Dist}(\hat{\mathbb{G}}). \tag{11.4.74}$$

We have an isomorphism A-Algebra $\equiv \grave{A}$-Invengory commuting with the forgetful functors into **Set**.

PROOF. 98 *The above definition is functorial in each $\underline{X}_i$, so one has $\grave{A} : \mathcal{M}\hat{\mathbb{G}} \longrightarrow \hat{\mathbb{G}}$. A morphism of normalised collections $\omega : A \longrightarrow B$ is a cartesian transformation between A and B, and such ω induces a natural transformation $\grave{\omega} : \grave{A} \longrightarrow \grave{B}$ by the formula $\grave{\omega}_{\underline{X}_i} = \{\omega_{\underline{X}}\}_{(0,k)}$. The cartesianess of ω and Lemma 59 imply that $\grave{\omega}$ is cartesian. For a given normalized collection $\alpha : A \longrightarrow F$, one has a cartesian transformation $\grave{\alpha} : \grave{A} \longrightarrow F^{\#}$. Since $F^{\#}$ is distributive, the functor $\grave{A}$ is also distributive due to the cartesianess of $\grave{\alpha}$ and the stability of coproducts in $\hat{\mathbb{G}}$. Therefore, the assignment $\omega \longrightarrow \grave{\omega}$ is a well-defined functor.*

Let A and B be normalized collections. For $k, m \in \mathbb{N}$, $\Xi : [k]_0 \longrightarrow B\underline{X}$, $\Xi(0) = 0$ and $\Xi(k) = m$, the maps

$$\{A\Xi^*B\underline{X}\}(0, k) \longrightarrow \{AB\underline{X}\}(0, m) \tag{11.4.75}$$

form a coproduct cocone. By the definition of the tensor product in $\mathbf{Dist}(\hat{\mathbb{G}})$, this induces an isomorphism $\grave{AB} \equiv \grave{A} \circ \grave{B}$. We claim that these isomorphisms satisfy the coherence conditions of a monoidal functor. Recall that the tensor product in $\mathbf{Dist}(\hat{\mathbb{G}})$ is defined using coproducts. A different choices of coproducts give rise to different monoidal structures on $\mathbf{Dist}(\hat{\mathbb{G}})$, however, these choices have unique coherence isomorphisms that make $\mathbf{Dist}(\hat{\mathbb{G}})$ monoidal. Because of this reason, one can easily check that if a given monoidal coherence diagram commutes for a particular choice of defining coproducts of the monoidal structure of $\mathbf{Dist}(\hat{\mathbb{G}})$, then this diagram commutes for any such choice. Thus, it is enough to see that such diagram commutes for some choice of coproducts for coherence condition. For simplicity, one can simply choose the coproducts so that all the coherence isomorphisms involved in the diagram are identities. This finishes the proof that $\grave{()}$ is monoidal.

Let A be a normalised plurioperad and Z be a set. To give a MIMO globular set $\underline{X}$ with $\underline{X}_0 = \underline{Z}$ (a finite sequence composed by elements from Z) and $x : A\underline{X} \longrightarrow \underline{X}$, which gives maps $x_{\underline{y},\underline{z}} : \{A\underline{X}\}(\underline{y}, \underline{z}) \longrightarrow \underline{X}(\underline{y}, \underline{z})$ for all $\underline{y}, \underline{z} \in \underline{Z}$. For each $k \in \mathbb{N}$ and $f : [k]_0 \longrightarrow \underline{X}$ such that $f(0) = \underline{y}$ and $f(k) = \underline{z}$, we have a map

$$x_f : \grave{A}_i \underline{X}(f_{i-1}, f_i) \longrightarrow \underline{X}\}(\underline{y}, \underline{z}). \tag{11.4.76}$$

For $\underline{y}, \underline{z} \in \underline{Z}$, one has a unique $f : [1]_0 \longrightarrow \underline{X}$ provided by $f(0) = \underline{y}$ and $f(1) = \underline{z}$. The naturality square for η at f implies that $\{\eta_{\underline{X}}\}_{\underline{y},\underline{z}} = \{A\grave{f}\}_{0,1}\{\eta_{(\underline{X}(\underline{y},\underline{z}))}\}_{0,1}$ and the definition of $\grave{()}$ says that $\{\eta_{(\underline{X}(\underline{y},\underline{z}))}\}_{0,1} = \grave{\eta}_{\underline{X}(\underline{y},\underline{z})}$. Hence, a map $x : A\underline{X} \longrightarrow \underline{X}$ satisfies the unit law of an A-algebra is equivalent that x is the identity on 0-cells and that x_f satisfies the unit axioms of an A-invengory.

For associativity of x, we have to verify the commutativity of the following diagram

$$
\begin{array}{ccc}
\{A^2\underline{X}\}(\underline{y}, \underline{z}) & \xrightarrow{\{\mu_{\underline{X}}\}_{\underline{y},\underline{z}}} & \{A\underline{X}\}(\underline{y}, \underline{z}) \\
{\scriptstyle \{Ax\}_{\underline{y},\underline{z}}}\downarrow & & \downarrow{\scriptstyle x_{\underline{y},\underline{z}}} \\
\{A\underline{X}\}(\underline{y}, \underline{z}) & \xrightarrow{x_{\underline{y},\underline{z}}} & \underline{X}(\underline{y}, \underline{z})
\end{array}
\tag{11.4.77}
$$

Given $f : [m]_0 \longrightarrow \underline{X}$ with $f(0) = \underline{y}$ and $f(m) = \underline{x}$, and $g : [k]_0 \longrightarrow Af^*\underline{X}$ with $g(0) = 0$ and $g(k) = m$, if precomposing the map

$$\{A^2 g^* f^* \underline{X}\}(0, k) \xrightarrow{\{A\grave{g}\}_{0,k}} \{A^2 f^* \underline{X}\}(0, m) \xrightarrow{\{A\grave{f}\}_{0,m}} \{A^2 \underline{X}\}(\underline{y}, \underline{z}) \tag{11.4.78}$$

and using Lemma 60, one has the following commutative digram as

$$\grave{A}_i\grave{A}_j\underline{X}(f_{(i,j)-1}, f_{(i,j)}) \xrightarrow{\acute{\mu}} \grave{A}_{ij}\underline{X}(f_{(i,j)-1}, f_{(i,j)})$$

$$\grave{A}x_{\{A\grave{y}\}f} \downarrow \qquad\qquad\qquad \downarrow x_f$$

$$\grave{A}_i\underline{X}(g_{i-1}, g_i) \quad \xrightarrow{\acute{\mu}} \quad \underline{X}(\underline{y}, \underline{z}) \tag{11.4.79}$$

where $1 \leq i \leq k$ and $1 \leq j \leq m_i$. The associative law for x, namely Eq. (11.4.77), implies the A-invengory associative laws as shown by Eq. (11.4.79). Conversely, since the composites Eq. (11.4.78) over all choices of f and g form a coproduct cocone by Lemma 60, Eq. (11.4.79) also implies Eq. (11.4.77). This completes the description of the object part of isomorphism: A-Algebra $\equiv \grave{A}$-Invengory.

Let $(\underline{X}, x)$ and $(\underline{X}', x')$ be A-Algebra and $F_0 : \underline{X}_0 \longrightarrow \underline{Y}_0$ be a function, we have maps $F : \underline{X} \longrightarrow \underline{Y}$ as $F_{\underline{x},\underline{y}} : \underline{X}(\underline{x}, \underline{y}) \longrightarrow \underline{X}'(F_0(\underline{x}), F_0(\underline{y}))$ for all $\underline{x}, \underline{y} \in \underline{X}_0$. By Lemma 60, to verify that F is an algebra map is equivalent to say that F_0 and $F_{\underline{x},\underline{y}}$ form an A-functor. The isomorphism A-Algebra $\equiv \grave{A}$-invengory introduced above commutes with the forgetful functors into **Set** by definition.

The invengory $\mathbb{G}_{\leq n}$ is defined to be the full sub-invengory of $\mathbb{G}$ consisting of those dimensions $0 \leq k \leq n$. The objects of $\hat{\mathbb{G}}_{\leq n}$ are called n-MIMO globular sets. Since the monad F on $\hat{\mathbb{G}}$ restricts to n-MIMO globular sets, one has a monad $F_{\leq n}$ on $\hat{\mathbb{G}}_{\leq n}$. By restricting F to $F_{\leq n}$, the description of F from Sec. 11.4.3 implies that the monads $F_{\leq n}$ are lra, coproduct preserving and tight. Now, we are ready to present the main theorem in this Chapter: the tensor product theorem for n-MIMO invengories.

Theorem 43 We have the equivalence for

$$F_{\leq n+1} - \mathbf{Plurioperad}_0 \equiv F_{\leq n} - \mathbf{Tensor} \equiv \mathbb{M}F_{\leq n} - \mathbf{Plurioperad}. \tag{11.4.80}$$

PROOF. 99 By Lemmas 56 and 57, the functor $F^\#$ is right. Then, there is a monoidal functor

$$\grave{()} : F - \mathbf{COL}_0 \longrightarrow \mathbf{LraDist}(\hat{\mathbb{G}})/F^\# \tag{11.4.81}$$

from Lemma 61. We claim that the functor $\grave{()}$ induces an equivalence: $F-\mathbf{COL}_0 \equiv \mathbf{LraDist}(\hat{\mathbb{G}})/F^\#$. There are two tasks to verify about this equivalence. We first verify that $\grave{()}$ is surjective.

For a cartesian $\epsilon : E \longrightarrow F^\#$, we define $\alpha : A \longrightarrow F$ such that $\grave{\alpha} \equiv \epsilon$. For $\underline{x}, \underline{y} \in \underline{X}_0$, we define $\{A\underline{X}\}(\underline{x}, \underline{y})$ as a coproduct of maps

$$c_f : E_i\underline{X}(f(i-1), f(i)) \longrightarrow \{A\underline{X}\}(\underline{x}, \underline{y}), \tag{11.4.82}$$

for each $f : [k]_0 \longrightarrow \underline{X}$ such that $f(0) = \underline{x}$ and $f(k) = \underline{y}$. For all f, the components of α are identities on 0-cells with the homomorphic maps determined by the commutativity of

$$
\begin{array}{ccc}
E_i \underline{X}(f(i-1), f(i)) & \xrightarrow{c_f} & \{A\underline{X}\}(\underline{x}, \underline{y}) \\
\epsilon \downarrow & & \downarrow \{\alpha_{\underline{X}}\}_{\underline{x},\underline{y}} \\
\{Ff^*\underline{X}\}(0,k) & \xrightarrow{\{T\dot{f}\}_{0,k}} & \{T\underline{X}\}(\underline{x}, \underline{y})
\end{array}
$$

$$(11.4.83)$$

The cartesianess of α is based on Lemma 59 and lextensive of $\hat{\mathbb{G}}$. If $\underline{X} = (\underline{X}_1, \cdots, \underline{X}_k)$ with f is the identity on 0-cells, one has $\grave{\alpha} \equiv \epsilon$, which is required for surjectivity.

The next goal is to verify faithfulness. Let $\alpha : A \longrightarrow F$ and $\beta : B \longrightarrow F$ be normalized collections with a cartesian transformation $\psi : A \longrightarrow B$. From Lemma 55 and tightness of F, we have following identities for $\underline{X} \in \hat{\mathbb{G}}$ and $f : [k]_0 \longrightarrow \underline{X}$ such that

$$
\{\psi_{f^*\underline{X}}\}(0,k) = \grave{\psi}_{\underline{X}(f(i-1), f(i))}. \tag{11.4.84}
$$

For $\underline{x}, \underline{y} \in \underline{X}_0$ and by Lemma 60 (coproduct cocone), the map $\{\psi_{\underline{X}}\}_{\underline{x},\underline{y}}$ with respect to all f is determined as

$$
\begin{array}{ccc}
\{Af^*\underline{X}\}(0,k) & \xrightarrow{\{A\dot{f}\}_{0,k}} & \{A\underline{X}\}(\underline{x}, \underline{y}) \\
\{\psi_{f^*\underline{X}}\}(0,k) \downarrow & & \downarrow \{\psi_{\underline{X}}\}_{\underline{x},\underline{y}} \\
\{Bf^*\underline{X}\}(0,k) & \xrightarrow{\{B\dot{f}\}_{0,k}} & \{B\underline{X}\}(\underline{x}, \underline{y})
\end{array}
$$

$$(11.4.85)$$

Note also that this square is a pullback by the extensivity of $\hat{\mathbb{G}}$. To finish the proof of faithfulness, we have to verify that $\psi_{\underline{X}}$ are cartesian natural in $\underline{X}$.

Let $F : \underline{X} \longrightarrow \underline{Y}$ and $f : [k]_0 \longrightarrow \underline{X}$ with $F\dot{f} = \grave{F}f$, one has the following pullback diagram

$$
\begin{array}{ccccc}
\{Af^*\underline{X}\}(0,k) & \xrightarrow{\{A\dot{f}\}_{0,k}} & \{A\underline{X}\}(\underline{x}, \underline{y}) & \xrightarrow{\{AF\}_{\underline{x},\underline{y}}} & \{A\underline{Y}\}(F_0(\underline{x}), F_0(\underline{y})) \\
\{\psi_{f^*\underline{X}}\}(0,k) \downarrow & & \downarrow \{\psi_{\underline{X}}\}_{\underline{x},\underline{y}} & & \downarrow \{\psi_{\underline{Y}}\}_{F_0(\underline{x}), F_0(\underline{y})} \\
\{Bf^*\underline{X}\}(0,k) & \xrightarrow{\{B\dot{f}\}_{0,k}} & \{B\underline{X}\}(\underline{x}, \underline{y}) & \xrightarrow{\{BF\}_{\underline{x},\underline{y}}} & \{B\underline{Y}\}(F_0(\underline{x}), F_0(\underline{y}))
\end{array}
$$

$$(11.4.86)$$

By Lemma 59 and Eq. (11.4.86), the following squares are pullback with respect to all $\underline{x}, \underline{y} \in \underline{X}_0$:

$$
\begin{array}{ccc}
\{A\underline{X}\}(\underline{x}, \underline{y}) & \xrightarrow{\{AF\}_{\underline{x},\underline{y}}} & \{A\underline{Y}\}(F_0(\underline{x}), F_0(\underline{y})) \\
\downarrow \{\psi_{\underline{X}}\}_{\underline{x},\underline{y}} & & \downarrow \{\psi_{\underline{Y}}\}_{F_0(\underline{x}), F_0(\underline{y})} \\
\{B\underline{X}\}(\underline{x}, \underline{y}) & \xrightarrow{\{BF\}_{\underline{x},\underline{y}}} & \{B\underline{Y}\}(F_0(\underline{x}), F_0(\underline{y}))
\end{array}
$$

$$(11.4.87)$$

which shows that maps $\psi_{\underline{X}}$ are cartesian natural in $\underline{X}$. Hence, the claim about the equivalence of the functor $\grave{()}$ is established.

For $n \in \mathbb{N}$, the invengory of normalized $(n+1)$-collections, denoted by $F_{\leq n+1} - \mathbf{COL}_0$, whose objects are cartesian transformations $\alpha : A \longrightarrow F_{\leq n+1}$, one has a functor

$$\grave{()}_{\leq n} : F_{\leq n+1} - \mathbf{COL}_0 \longrightarrow \mathbf{Dist}(\hat{\mathbb{G}}_{\leq n}), \tag{11.4.88}$$

whose object map is given by

$$\grave{A}_{\leq n, i} \underline{X}_i = \{A\underline{X}\}(0, k), \tag{11.4.89}$$

where A is a normalized $n + 1$-collection, $\underline{X}_i \in \hat{\mathbb{G}}_{\leq n}$ for $1 \leq i \leq k$ and $\underline{X} = (\underline{X}_1, \cdots, \underline{X}_k) \in \hat{\mathbb{G}}_{\leq n+1}$. By restriction to finite dimensional cases, the functor $\grave{()}_{\leq n}$ is an equivalence of invengories $F_{\leq n+1} - \mathbf{Col}_0 \equiv \mathbf{LraDist}(\hat{\mathbb{G}}_{\leq n})/F_{\leq n}^{\#}$. Therefore, we have

$$F_{\leq n+1} - \mathbf{Plurioperad}_0 \equiv F_{\leq n} - \mathbf{Tensor} \equiv \mathbb{M}F_{\leq n} - \mathbf{Plurioperad}. \tag{11.4.90}$$

11.5 Example: A Network of Invenrelators with 2-MIMO Invengory

In this section, we will provide an example of tensor product of 2-MIMO-invengories. The example is based on work [54]. We begin with some definitions.

Definition 94 *Gray-MIMO* is the monoidal invengory of 2-MIMO-invengories and 2-functors with tensor product the pseudo-version of Gray's tensor product of 2-invengories.

Definition 95 A *Gray-MIMO*-invengory is an invengory enriched in the monoidal invengory *Gray-MIMO*.

Then, a **Gray-MIMO**-invengory $\mathbb{C}$ can be described as consisting of collections C_0 of objects, C_1 of MIMO arrows, C_2 of 2 dimensional MIMO arrows and C_3 of 3 dimensional MIMO arrows, together with

- functions $s_n, t_n : C_i \to C_n$ for all $0 \leq n < i \leq 3$, also denoted d_n^- and d_n^+ and called *n-source* and *n-target*,

- functions $\circ_n : C_{n+1} {}_{s_n} \times_{t_n} C_{n+1} \to C_{n+1}$ for all $0 \leq n < 3$, called *vertical composition*,

454

- functions $\circ_n : C_i \; {}_{s_n}\times_{t_n} \; C_{n+1} \to C_i$ and $\circ_n : C_{n+1} \; {}_{s_n}\times_{t_n} \; C_i \to C_i$ for all $0 \le n \le 1, n+1 < i \le 3$, called *whiskering*,

- a function $\circ_0 : C_2 \; {}_{s_0}\times_{t_0} \; C_2 \to C_3$, called *horizontal composition*, and

- functions $id_{\_} : C_i \to C_{i+1}$ for all $0 \le i \le 2$, called *identity*,

such that:

1. $\mathbb{C}$ is a 3-skeletal reflexive globular set.

2. for every $\underline{C}, \underline{C}' \in C_0$, the collection of elements of $\mathbb{C}$ with 0-source $\underline{C}$ and 0-target $\underline{C}'$ forms a 2-category $\mathbb{C}(\underline{C}, \underline{C}')$, with n-composition in $\mathbb{C}(\underline{C}, \underline{C}')$ given by $\circ_{n+1}$ and identities given by id_i.

3. for every $g : \underline{C}' \to \underline{C}''$ in C_1 and every $\underline{C}$ and $\underline{C}''' \in C_0$, $- \circ_0 g$ is a 2-functor $\mathbb{C}(\underline{C}'', \underline{C}''') \to \mathbb{C}(\underline{C}', \underline{C}''')$ and $g \circ_0 -$ is a 2-functor $\mathbb{C}(\underline{C}, \underline{C}') \to \mathbb{C}(\underline{C}, \underline{C}'')$.

4. for every $\underline{C}' \in C_0$ and every $\underline{C}$ and $\underline{C}'' \in C_0$, $- \circ_0 id_{\underline{C}'}$ is equal to the identity functor $\mathbb{C}(\underline{C}', \underline{C}'') \to \mathbb{C}(\underline{C}', \underline{C}'')$, and $id_{\underline{C}'} \circ_0 -$ is equal to the identity functor $\mathbb{C}(\underline{C}, \underline{C}') \to \mathbb{C}(\underline{C}, \underline{C}')$.

5. for every $\gamma : \underline{C} \overset{f}{\underset{f'}{\Rightarrow}} \underline{C}'$ in C_2 and $\delta : \underline{C}' \overset{g}{\underset{g'}{\Rightarrow}} \underline{C}''$ in C_2,

$$s_1(\delta \circ_0 \gamma) = (g' \circ_0 \gamma) \circ_1 (\delta \circ_0 f)$$

$$t_1(\delta \circ_0 \gamma) = (\delta' \circ_0 f') \circ_1 (g \circ_0 \delta)$$

and $\delta \circ_0 \gamma$ is an iso-3-arrow.

6. for every $\varphi : \underline{C} \overset{f}{\underset{f'}{\Rrightarrow}} \underline{C}'$ in C_3 and $\delta : \underline{C}' \overset{g}{\underset{g'}{\Rightarrow}} \underline{C}''$ in C_2,

$$((\delta \circ_0 f') \circ_1 (g \circ_0 \varphi)) \circ_2 (\delta \circ_0 \gamma) = (\delta \circ_0 \gamma') \circ_2 ((g' \circ_0 \varphi) \circ_1 (\delta \circ_0 f)),$$

and for every $\gamma : \underline{C} \overset{f}{\underset{f'}{\Rightarrow}} \underline{C}'$ in C_2 and $\psi : \underline{C}' \overset{g}{\underset{g'}{\Rrightarrow}} \underline{C}''$ in C_3,

$$(\delta' \circ_0 \gamma) \circ_2 ((g' \circ_0 \gamma) \circ_1 (\psi \circ_0 f)) = ((\psi \circ_0 f') \circ_1 (g \circ_0 \gamma)) \circ_2 (\delta \circ_0 \gamma),$$

.

7. for every $\underline{C} \xrightarrow{\ f''\ } \underline{C}'$ with f (top, γ) and f'' (bottom, γ') and $\delta : \underline{C}' \xrightarrow[g']{g} \underline{C}''$ (with ψ) in $\mathbb{C}$,

$$\delta \circ_0 (\gamma' \circ_1 \gamma) = ((\delta \circ_0 \gamma') \circ_1 (g \circ_0 \gamma)) \circ_2 ((g' \circ_0 \gamma') \circ_1 (\delta \circ_0 \gamma)),$$

and for every $\gamma : \underline{C} \xrightarrow[f']{f} \underline{C}'$ (with ψ) and $\underline{C}' \xrightarrow{\ g''\ } \underline{C}''$ with g (top, δ) and g'' (bottom, δ') in $\mathbb{C}$,

$$(\delta' \circ_1 \delta) \circ_0 \gamma = ((\delta' \circ_0 f') \circ_1 (\delta \circ_0 \gamma)) \circ_2 ((\delta' \circ_0 \gamma) \circ_1 (\delta \circ_0 f)),$$

.

8. for every $f : \underline{C} \to \underline{C}'$ in C_1 and $\delta : \underline{C}' \xrightarrow[g']{g} \underline{C}''$ (with ψ) in C_2,

$$\delta \circ_0 id_f = id_{\delta \circ_0 f},$$

and for every $\gamma : \underline{C} \xrightarrow[f']{f} \underline{C}'$ (with ψ) in C_2 and $g : \underline{C}' \to \underline{C}''$ in C_1,

$$id_g \circ_0 \gamma = id_{g \circ_0 \gamma},$$

.

9. for every $c \in \mathbb{C}(\underline{C}, \underline{C}')_p$, $c' \in \mathbb{C}(\underline{C}', \underline{C}'')_q$ and $c'' \in \mathbb{C}(\underline{C}'', \underline{C}''')_r$ with $p + q + r \leq 2$,

$$(c'' \circ_0 c') \circ_0 c = c'' \circ_0 (c' \circ_0 c).$$

.

Let $\mathbb{C}$ and $\mathbb{D}$ be **Gray-MIMO**-categories. Define a **Gray-MIMO**-category $\mathbb{C} \otimes \mathbb{D}$ by the following presentation. We begin by introducing generators for tensor product.

11.5.1 Generators

Generators are expressions $\underline{c} \otimes \underline{d}$, with $\underline{c} \in \underline{C}_p$ and $\underline{d} \in \underline{D}_q$, of dimension $p + q$, for $p + q \leq 3$. Face of these are :

- for $p \leq 3$ and $q = 0$, if $\varphi : \underline{C} \; \gamma' \; {}_3 \; \gamma \; \underline{C}'$ in $\mathbb{C}$ and $\underline{D} \in \mathbb{D}$, then $\varphi \otimes \underline{D}$ is given by the

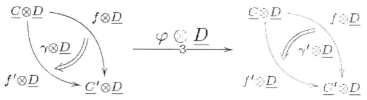

diagram

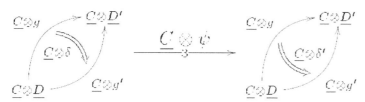

- for $p = 0$ and $q < 3$, if $\underline{C} \in \mathbb{C}$ and $\psi : \underline{D} \; \delta' \; {}_3 \; \delta \; \underline{D}'$ in $\mathbb{D}$, then

$\underline{C} \otimes \psi$ is given by the diagram

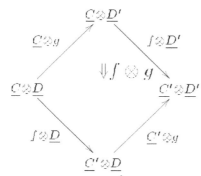

- for $p, q = 1$, if $f : \underline{C} \to \underline{C}'$ in $\mathbb{C}$ and $g : \underline{D} \to \underline{D}'$ in $\mathbb{D}$, then $f \otimes g$ is given by the diagram

- for $p = 2$, $q = 1$, if $\gamma : \underline{C} \Downarrow \underline{C}'$ in $\mathbb{C}$ and $\mathbf{g} : \underline{D} \longrightarrow \underline{D}'$ in $\mathbb{D}$, then $\gamma \otimes \mathbf{g}$ is given by

the diagram

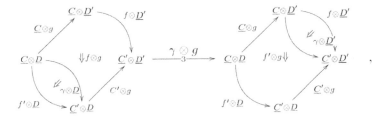

- for $p = 1$, $q = 2$, if $f : \underline{C} \longrightarrow \underline{C}'$ in $\mathbb{C}$ and $\delta: \underline{D} \overset{g}{\underset{g'}{\Downarrow}} \underline{D}'$ in $\mathbb{D}$, then $f \otimes \delta$ is given by

the diagram

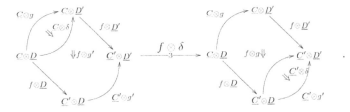

11.5.2 Naturality relations

The naturality relations are:

- for $p = 3$, $q = 1$, if $\varphi : \underline{C} \overset{f}{\underset{f'}{\Rrightarrow}} \underline{C}'$ in $\mathbb{C}$ and g : $\underline{D} \longrightarrow \underline{D}'$ in $\mathbb{D}$, then the diagram

commutes,

- for $p = 1$ and $q = 3$, if $f : \underline{C} \to \underline{C}'$ in $\mathbb{C}$ and $\psi :$ 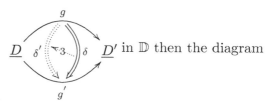 $\underline{D}'$ in $\mathbb{D}$ then the diagram

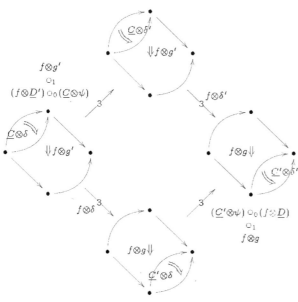

- for $p = 2$ and $q = 2$, if $\gamma : \underline{C} \xrightarrow[f']{f} \underline{C}'$ in $\mathbb{C}$ and $\delta : \underline{D} \xrightarrow[g']{g} \underline{D}'$ in $\mathbb{D}$, then the diagram

- for $p = 2$ and $q = 2$, if $\gamma : \underline{C} \xrightarrow[f']{f} \underline{C}'$ in $\mathbb{C}$ and $\delta : \underline{D} \xrightarrow[g']{g} \underline{D}'$ in $\mathbb{D}$, then the diagram

- for $p = 2$ and $q = 2$, if $\gamma : \underline{C} \xrightarrow[f']{f} \underline{C}'$ in $\mathbb{C}$ and $\delta : \underline{D} \xrightarrow[g']{g} \underline{D}'$ in $\mathbb{D}$, then the diagram

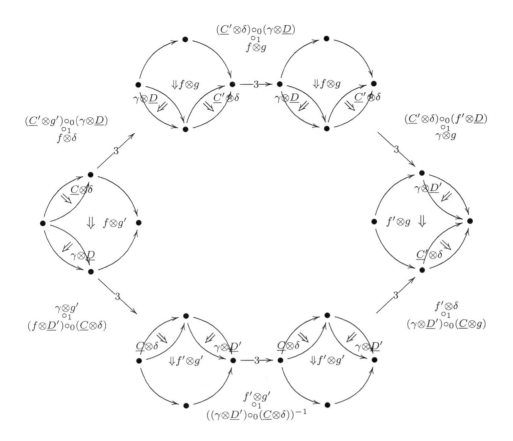

commutes.

11.5.3 Functorial relations

The functorial relations are:

- for $p \leq 3$ and $q = 0$, if $c' \circ_n c$ is defined in $\mathbb{C}$ and $\underline{D} \in \mathbb{D}$, then

$$(c' \circ_n c) \otimes \underline{D} = (c' \otimes \underline{D}) \circ_n (c \otimes \underline{D}),$$

- for $p = 0$ and $q \leq 3$, if $\underline{C} \in \mathbb{C}$ and $d' \circ_n d$ is defined in $\mathbb{D}$, then

$$\underline{C} \otimes (d' \circ_n d) = (\underline{C} \otimes d') \circ_n (\underline{C} \otimes d),$$

- for $p, q = 1$, if $\underline{C} \xrightarrow{f} \underline{C}' \xrightarrow{f'} \underline{C}''$ in $\mathbb{C}$ and $g : \underline{D} \to \underline{D}'$ in $\mathbb{D}$, then

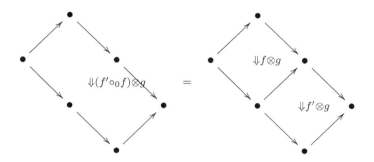

and if $f : \underline{C} \to \underline{C}'$ in $\mathbb{C}$ and $\underline{D} \xrightarrow{g} \underline{D}' \xrightarrow{g'} \underline{D}''$ in $\mathbb{D}$, then

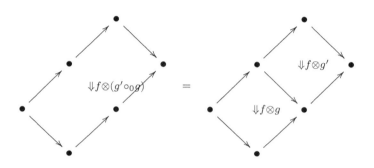

- for $p = 2, q = 1$, composition in left factor, if $\underline{C} \overset{f}{\underset{f''}{\rightrightarrows}} \underline{C}'$ in $\mathbb{C}$ and $g : \underline{D} \to \underline{D}'$

in $\mathbb{D}$, then the diagram

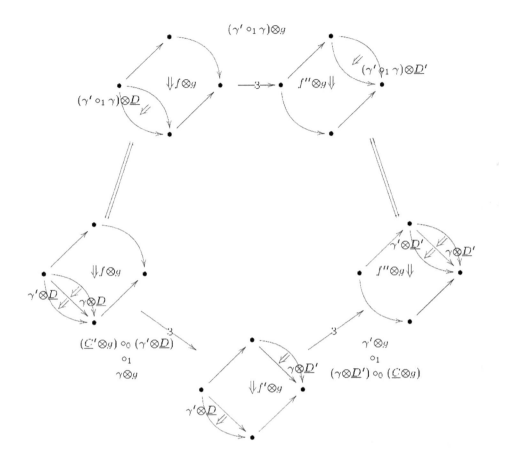

commutes, if $\underline{C} \underset{f'}{\overset{f}{\Downarrow \gamma}} \underline{C'} \overset{f''}{\longrightarrow} \underline{C''}$ in $\mathbb{C}$ and $g : \underline{D} \to \underline{D'}$ in $\mathbb{D}$, then the diagram

462

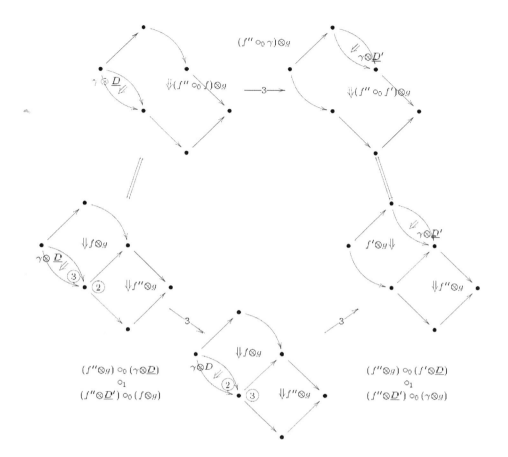

commutes, if $\underline{C} \xrightarrow{f} \underline{C'} \underset{f''}{\overset{f'}{\Downarrow \gamma'}} \underline{C'}$ in $\mathbb{C}$ and $g : \underline{D} \to \underline{D'}$ in $\mathbb{D}$, then the diagram

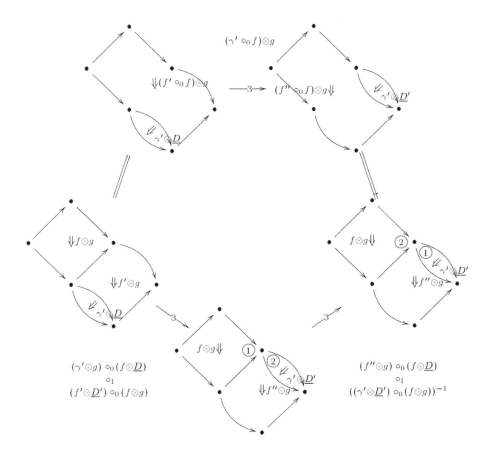

$$(\gamma' \circ_0 f) \otimes g$$

$$(\gamma' \otimes g) \circ_0 (f \otimes \underline{D})$$
$$\circ_1$$
$$(f' \otimes \underline{D}') \circ_0 (f \otimes g)$$

$$(f'' \otimes g) \circ_0 (f \otimes \underline{D})$$
$$\circ_1$$
$$((\gamma' \otimes \underline{D}') \circ_0 (f \otimes g))^{-1}$$

commutes,

- for $p = 2, q = 1$, composition in right factor, if $\gamma : \underline{C} \overset{f}{\underset{f'}{\Downarrow}} \underline{C}'$ in $\mathbb{C}$ and $\underline{D} \overset{g}{\longrightarrow} \underline{D}' \overset{g''}{\longrightarrow} \underline{D}''$

  in $\mathbb{D}$, then the diagram

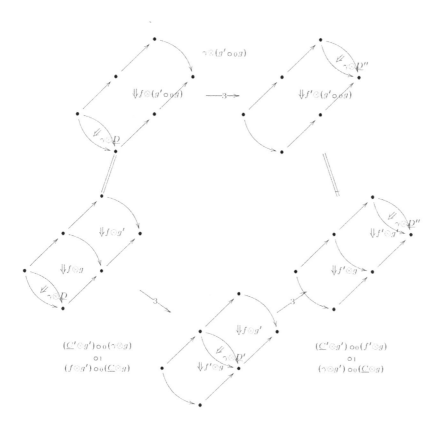

- for $p = 1$, $q = 2$, composition in left factor, analogous to $p = 2$, $q = 1$.

11.5.4 Identity relations

The identity relations are:

- for $p + q \leq 2$, if $id_{\underline{c}}$ is defined in $\mathbb{C}$ and $\underline{d} \in \mathbb{D}$, then

$$id_{\underline{c}} \otimes \underline{d} = id_{\underline{c} \otimes \underline{d}},$$

and if $\underline{c} \in \mathbb{C}$ and $id_{\underline{d}}$ is defined in $\mathbb{D}$, then

$$\underline{c} \otimes id_{\underline{d}} = id_{\underline{c} \otimes \underline{d}},$$

11.5.5 Interchange relations

The interchange relation is:

- for $p, q = 1$, if $\underline{C} \xrightarrow{f} \underline{C}' \xrightarrow{f'} \underline{C}''$ in $\mathbb{C}$ and $\underline{D} \xrightarrow{g} \underline{D}' \xrightarrow{g'} \underline{D}''$ in $\mathbb{D}$ then the diagram

465

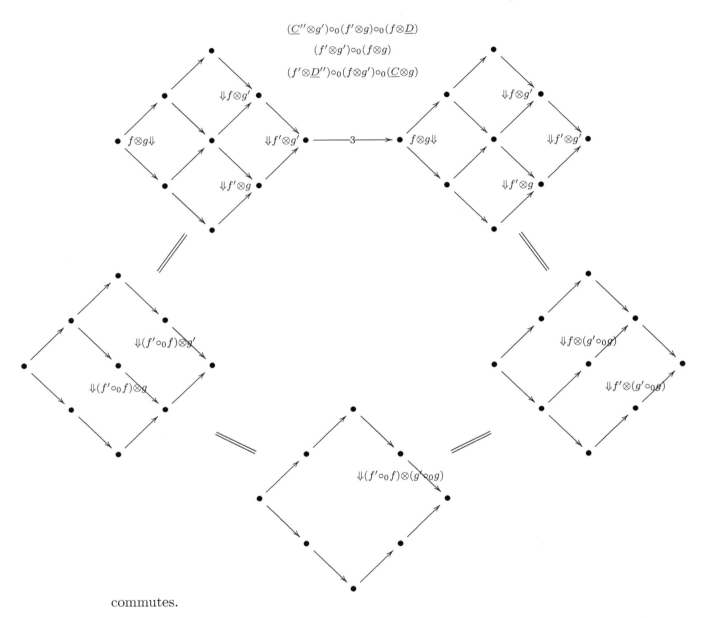

$(\underline{C}''\otimes g')\circ_0(f'\otimes g)\circ_0(f\otimes\underline{D})$

$(f'\otimes g')\circ_0(f\otimes g)$

$(f'\otimes\underline{D}'')\circ_0(f\otimes g')\circ_0(\underline{C}\otimes g)$

$\Downarrow f\otimes g'$

$f\otimes g\Downarrow$ $\Downarrow f'\otimes g'$ —3→ $f\otimes g\Downarrow$ $\Downarrow f'\otimes g'$ $\Downarrow f\otimes g'$

$\Downarrow f'\otimes g$ $\Downarrow f'\otimes g$

$\Downarrow(f'\circ_0 f)\otimes g'$ $\Downarrow f\otimes(g'\circ_0 g)$

$\Downarrow(f'\circ_0 f)\otimes g$ $\Downarrow f'\otimes(g'\circ_0 g)$

$\Downarrow(f'\circ_0 f)\otimes(g'\circ_0 g)$

commutes.

Until now, we can conclude that $\otimes$ (tensor product) is a functor from **Gray-MIMO-Invengories** $\times$ **Gray-MIMO-Invengories** to **Gray-MIMO-Invengories**.

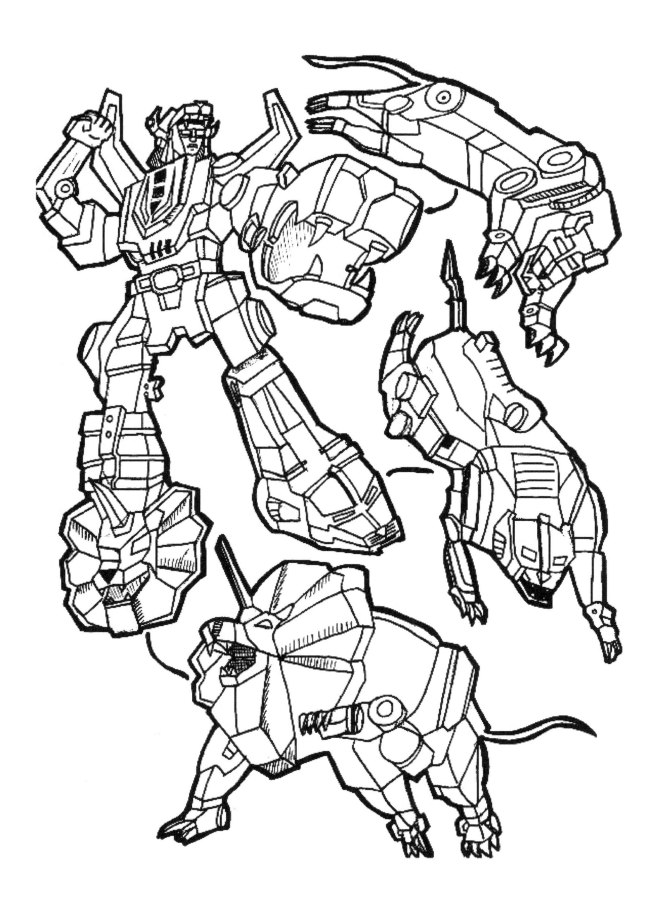

Figure 11.3: CIN

Chapter 12

Final Remarks

In this chapter, we will discuss several issues about the future of Invenrelation.

12.1 Education

This section describes the importance of education and two key capabilities, abstraction and mathematics, in applying Invenrelation.

12.1.1 Importance of Education

Although education is not in the list of the three basic human needs, education is equally important. For the progress of a country, education is necessary and important. A country's literate population is an important index to measure its competition capability. The number of institutes offering vocational courses and schools offering online education is increasing by the maturity of information technologies. Vocational courses are bases for further specialized education. Online degree programs help the adults and workers in general to pursue education even while working. Distance education has helped those who are unable to attend classes due to geographical limitation. In today's competitive and knowledge-explosion world, it won't be wise to neglect the importance of education. And most countries have realized this. This has led to many government-aided educational programs and government grants to schools and educational institutions.

Education is the process by which society transmits its accumulated knowledge, skills, customs and values from one group of persons to another group of persons. A right to education has been created and recognized by several judicial systems, for example, the United Nations'

International Covenant on Economic, Social and Cultural Rights of 1966 guarantees the right of being educated by government under its Article 13. It should be no doubt about the importance of education. Why is education so important?

Civilization of a society is achieved by education. Education is crucial because it teaches us the proper behavior and manners in a society thus making us civilized. It is the backbone of society. Education is the basis of civilization and culture. Education cultivates us into mature individuals, then individuals are capable of planning for their own future and taking the right decisions in life by developing of individuals' values and virtues. Education forms a support system for individuals to excel in life by teaching individuals with an insight into their lives and teaching individuals to learn from experience. The future of a nation is safe in the hands of educated individuals. Education is important for the economic growth of a nation by fostering principles of equality and socialism.

Education helps us to recognize our world by providing knowledge. It helps us build opinions and have perspective on things in life. People argue over the subject of whether education is the only thing that provides knowledge. Some may say that knowledge can be obtained easier from information technological products, e.g., computers and internet. However, information cannot be converted into knowledge without the catalyst called education. Education helps us capable of interpreting things rightly. Education is not just about introducing knowledge in textbooks. It is about the lessons of life.

Education is important because it equips us with skills that are required to realize our dreams. Education opens doors to bright career future chances. Every employer of today requires his/her prospective employees to be well-educated. Hence, education becomes an eligibility criterion for employment in any sector of professional careers. We are evaluated in the market on the basis of our educational backgrounds and how well we can apply those skills learned from education.

12.1.2 Capabilities Required to Apply Invenrelation: Abstraction and Mathematics

In Chap. II, we mentioned that the basic step to apply Invenrelation is to recognize the constitutive elements with their properties and relations for things to be invented (or problems to be solved) through abstraction method. Hence, the first important capability for one to apply Invenrelation is abstraction. How do we develop the ability about abstraction?

Mathematics is often considered the mother of science. It can be applied to a wide range of academic fields. What is the main characteristic of mathematics that makes mathematics applicable in various fields? In fact, one of the most simple answer is: abstract. Actually, it is quite "abstract" to explain the meaning of the word: abstraction. For example: the expression, $1 + 1 = 2$, is an abstract concept. One may add an unit, for instance, apple, dog or person, after numbers to represent concrete objects being added. Because the expression $1 + 1 = 2$ represents an abstract concept, it can serve as the results of adding two identical objects, like $1person + 1person = 2persons$ or $1ball + 1ball = 2balls$.

The reason why that abstraction is difficult to understand is that people's learning process itself is not begin from abstraction, but from comprehending specific examples. In childhood, we do not learn the concept *animal* first, instead, we learn meanings for dogs, cats, or tigers (some kinds of animals) at beginning. Thence, by abstracting their behaviors and characteristics, these specific objects are grouped into animals. It is much easier to learn concrete things since they tend to match general life experience. However, there are too many concrete things around us. Hence, we can not remember too many specific things, or even apply them. If we can process induction to obtain those same characteristics and principles behind interesting specific things, this process is an abstract process. Regardless of experience or knowledge, the higher level of abstraction we can extract, the more extensive range can be applied by such abstraction. However, it will be more difficult to learn. Mathematics is often regarded as a profound subject due to its high level of abstraction.

It will be very beneficial in applying the abstraction process in learning knowledge. For example, we learn algorithms, data structures in information science but these subjects are abstract disciplines. Therefore, one can implement relevant content by various computer languages or apply these abstract disciplines in various occasions. Because primitive human instinct is to learn things from concrete examples at the beginning instead of learning things from abstraction principles, what we have to be educated before applying Invenrelation properly is to extract the abstract elements from the learning process and experience.

Usually, experts admonish new learners to understand well the meta-spirit of a certain knowledge. The purpose of such advisement is to tell learners to extract those abstract components from learning objectives. In the age of knowledge explosion, learners are often anxious about increasing new knowledge. Hence, the burden of future learners in learning process is getting heavier. At this circumstance, the ability to perform abstract thinking becomes more important. If we can capture the abstract parts of knowledge and applied them to learn new related fields of study, we can learn new things efficiently. Otherwise, we will waste a lot of energy and time in learning those repeated elements and be drowned by a flood of knowledge.

How to cultivate abstraction capability from the specific learning examples should be an important topic of the learner. A rule of thumb is: "In the process of learning, one always thinks about what the abstract elements and what are the specific elements in current learning targets. Abstract part must be thoroughly absorbed and the specific part should be treated as experience. Finally, the accumulated experience will also be transformed into abstraction."

The other important skill required to apply Invenrelation is mathematics capability. There are three components in mathematics capability: Memory Capability, Deriving Capability and Patten Recognition Capability. Let us explain these components serially.

Memory Capability: It is not easy to memorize facts in Mathematics. One cannot just memorize a lot of theorems and formulas in Mathematics, the more difficult part is to memorize those complex concepts represented by abstract symbols. Since experiences are abstracted as concepts represented by mathematical symbols, the connotation of a symbol is rich which makes general persons hard to solve problems by understanding its original concept. One must be accompanied by a certain degree of understanding in memorizing those mathematical facts. If one just blindly memorizes them, those facts will be forgotten soon. Not to mention about applying them to solve problems. In learning a new language, experts believe that three different aspects: forms, pronunciations and meanings, must be memorized before communicating thoughts fluently with others. Similarly, mathematical expressions also have forms (symbols), pronunciations (reading methods), and meanings (the meta-concepts represented by symbols). Moreover, one must memorize the conditions and methods to utilize those mathematical expressions. If one does not delve in how to memorize in mathematics, he or she will have difficulty in applying mathematics to solve problems in practice.

Deriving Capability (Calculation Capability): It is the most basic ability in a problem-solving process. Perhaps it is not the key part in obtaining answers, but bad computing capability always leads to errors in a problem-solving process. For further deriving capability, it requires one to be able to transform the original problems into mathematical symbols. This deriving capability is not just the ability to manipulate basic four operations in calculation, but the ability to analyze and integrate. If one has better such ability, one will be able to verify his/her conjectures more efficiently.

Patten Recognition Capability: Pattern recognition capabilities is not only the intuition of mathematics, but also the sensitivity of mathematical problems. Such ability enables one to distinguish problem types by applying the structure and the template of concepts, then one can point out those subtle differences and adopt the best way to solve the problem accordingly. But, how can one develop such intuition and sensitivity of mathematics? In addition to memorize a lot of mathematical facts, one has to apply his/her deriving capability to classify these facts into a structure of concepts. When a new problem is posed later on, one can compare the new problem with his/her structure of mathematical concepts and decide what is the best approach to solve the new problem. Relationship among mathematics, abstraction and invenrelation is presented by Fig. 12.1.

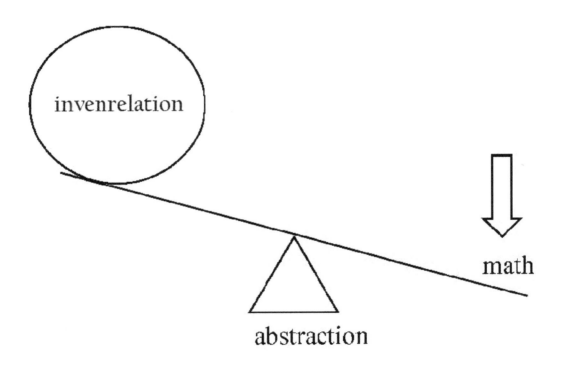

Figure 12.1: Three basic ingredients for invenrelation.

Note: Since Invenrelation is based on mathematics frameworks, it would be an important issue to build structures for Invenrelation processes. When such structures are established, they will serve as the building blocks of meaningful learning, retention of instructional materials about Invenrelation and invention process models created by great inventor (a person or even a machine). Identifying the learners Invenrelation structures will help instructors to organize materials, identify knowledge and creation gaps, and relate new materials to existing slots or anchors within the learners Invenrelation structures. The purpose of such structure is to track the development of Invenrelation structures over time. Accordingly, one may design various indicators derived from graph theory to provide a precise description and analysis of Invenrelation structures. Then several patterns can help us to better understand the construction and development of Invenrelation structures over time. In the future, an automated system to diagnosis the changing of Invenrelation structures will be further developed and implemented as a standard analysis tool for web applications.

12.2 Research

In this section, we will propose several research topics about Invenrelation. These topics can be classified into following categories:

- Random phenomenons are natural in our world. Many-sorted algebras and invengories are two bases in building Invenrelation, however, they are built on deterministic sense in previous chapters (except random invengory notions in communicating Invenrelation information among inventors). In Sec. 12.2.1, we explore possible future research topics about considering random effects within many-sorted algebras and invengories.

- By the early 21st century, nearly every child in places with mature information technology (IT) construction, knew how to use a personal computer. Businesses' information technology departments have gone from using storage tapes created by a single machine to interconnected networks of employee workstations that store information in a server array, often somewhere far away from the main business office. Undoubtedly, we are at the Age of information which defines an industry that uses computers, networking, software programming, and other equipment and processes to store, process, retrieve, transmit, and protect information. In Sec. 12.2.2, we will discuss issues about implementing Invenrelation over computer networks and managing information generated by Invenrelation over them.

- Since Inverelation is built on mathematics heavily, we will image several issues about the interaction between mathematics and Invenrelation in Sec. 12.2.3.

- If we wish to invent new knowledge, it is crucial to abstract existing knowledge as structured components before processing by Invenrelation. In Sec. 12.2.4, we consider questions about representing existing knowledge with new form for Invenrelation.

12.2.1 Random

Einstein wrote: "I, at any rate, am convinced that He [God] does not throw dice." in a 1926 letter to Max Born to reject the proposal that mechanics was to be understood as a probability without any causal explanation. During the debate over 30 years between Bohr and Einstein about quantum mechanics , a central issue is: Weather God dose or dose not throw dice? This is equivalent to ask the essence about scientific principles, i.e., dose scientific principles follow causality or randomness? The debate between Bohr and Einstein can not be concluded with win or loss simply. By retrospecting history of philosophy and science, the debate over the relation between causality and randomness indicates that more insightful and fluent contents are generated in our human history. I think each scientist possessing with historical responsibility should expect two great persons from any fields (art or science) to debate and cooperate over a more deeper problem.

Aristotle (384 BC − 322 BC) was a Greek philosopher and polymath, a student of Plato and teacher of Alexander the Great. Aristotle suggested that the reason for anything coming about can be classified to four different types of causal factors: material cause, final cause, formal cause and efficient cause. The later development of concepts about causality is based on Aristotle's efficient cause. In the history of science, Laplace's demon was the first published articulation of causal or scientific determinism by Pierre-Simon Laplace in 1814. In article *A Philosophical Essay on Probabilities*, Pierre Simon Laplace wrote (English Translation): "We may regard the present state of the universe as the effect of its past and the cause of its future. An intellect which at a certain moment would know all forces that set nature in motion, and all positions of all items of which nature is composed, if this intellect were also vast enough to submit these data to analysis, it would embrace in a single formula the movements of the greatest bodies of the universe and those of the tiniest atom; for such an intellect nothing would be uncertain and the future just like the past would be present before its eyes." Causality provides a perspective and a framework that one can follow to develop ones thoughts. In this framework, one can image an omniscient person who can predict future and infer past by knowing everything at current state and its evolution rules.

Newton's laws of motion make people with great imagination generate illusion that one can approach omniscience by applying these laws. However, omniscience is only an illusion after all. Human mind is not possible to get a point that can overlook and understand everything. Hence, randomness can be treated as a temporary expedient for human to recognize our universe. If we take causality perspective as the top of a skyscraper, randomness perspective is treated as the middle level of a skyscraper analoglly. The height of level depends on how complete we understand our interesting things.

The notion of randomness originated from gambling. The mathematical theory of randomess has its roots in attempts to analyze games of chance by Gerolamo Cardano in the sixteenth century, and by Blaise Pascal and Pierre de Fermat in the seventeenth century. Christiaan Huygens published a book about probability in 1657. An application of probability in science with deeper level is at the subject of Statistical mechanics. Statistical mechanics is a branch of physics that applies probability and statistics, which contains mathematical tools for dealing with large populations, to the study of the thermodynamic behavior of systems consisted by a large number of particles. Statistical mechanics provides a framework for associating the microscopic properties of individual particles to the macroscopic bulk properties of materials that can be observed in daily life. Hence, thermodynamics can be explained as a result of classical and quantum mechanics at the microscopic level.

The concepts of randomness and causality are not conflict! An illustrative example is the notion about temperature. It is impossible to measure the temperature of a single particle. Temperature is a measure of a macroscopic phenomenon. In 18th century, thermodynamic behaviors can only be treated by basic concepts like forces, time and space with Newton's laws of motion. However, several natural phenomenons can not be explained by Newton's laws of motion satisfactorily. The framework built by Newton based on causality becomes dangerous. Randomness helps us to explain the notion of temperature at this point. By statistical hypothesis for large amount of particles, the concept about temperature can be obtained again according to Newton's laws.

What is the relation between randomness and causality at aforementioned example? First, the concept about randomness becomes the supplementation for causality inevitably. At this moment, the perspective from randomness shows its own power and independence in exploring science. Second, the concept of randomness compromises with framework built by causality. Although statistical hypothesis are applied to characterize behavior of large amount of particles, each particle follows Newton's law (causality) in microscopic view. We must admit that causality and randomness, two different perspective, works jointly at some circumstance.

We suggest several interesting topics below about Invenrelation with randomness effects.

(1) In Chap II, we present the algebraic model for Invenrelation. In such model, two key components f_ω (operations) and $S_{ij,\omega}$ (sets) are involved. If f_ω or/and $S_{ij,\omega}$ are endowed with random structure, we can ask the mean, the variance and the distribution (convergence) of results made by Invenrelation.

(2) When distribution is obtained, one can apply detection theory to measure the way we make decisions under conditions of uncertainty, such as how we would perceive distances in unclear conditions. Detection theory assumes that the decision maker is not a passive receiver of information, but an active decision-maker who makes judgements under conditions of uncertainty. In unclear circumstances, we are forced to decide how far away from the current result to the goal, based solely available information which is impaired by the uncertain circumstance. On the other hand, we also can quantify the degree of bizarre thoughts by adjusting criterion with respect to distribution of Inverelation results.

(3) Estimation-Inverelation theory is an intersection field between Invenrelation and statistics that deals with estimating the outcomes of invenrelation model parameters based on measured/empirical data that have random components. The parameters describe an underlying Invenrelational setting in such a way that their values affect the distribution of the measured Invenrelation results. An estimator attempts to approximate the unknown parameters using the measurements. For example, it is desired to estimate the proportion of a group of Invenrelation results which satisfy some particular characteristcs. That proportion is the unobservable parameter; the estimation is based on a small random sample of Invenrelation results.

(4) In Chap. IX, we mentioned about the algorithm and complexity issues about the derivation in Invenrelation. A *randomized invenrelation algorithm* is an algorithm which employs a degree of randomness as part of its procedure. In general, the algorithm adopts uniformly random bits as an auxiliary input to guide its behavior, in the wish of achieving good performance over all possible choices of random bits with higher chance. The performance of algorithms will be a random variable determined by the algorithm procedures and random bits; thus either the

running time, running storage or the output are random variables.

(5) When we need to perform logical operation in Invenrelation, e.g., quasi-varieties of MSA introduced in Chap. VIII, we may adopt probabilistic logical operations that have truth value that ranges in degree between 0 and 1. At this point, many results in Fuzzy can be applied to Invenrelation and this enable us to process incomplete data and provide approximate solutions in Invenrelation.

12.2.2 Computer Implementation and Invenrelation Networks

Since Invenrelation is a system of methods to derive new things which involve mathematics heavily, we wish to discuss computer implementation and network issues for Invenrelation in this computer Age.

Computer Language Systems for Invenrelation

A computer language is an artificial language designed to communicate instructions to a machine, particularly a computer. Computer languages can be used to create programs that control the behavior of machines and to express algorithms precisely. Isn't Invenrelation supposed to be a subject in which mathematical structures are analyzed on such a high level of generality that computations are neither desirable nor possible? One of the main purposes of designing computer language for Invenrelation is the unrelenting way in which it proceeds from algorithm to algorithm until all of Invenrelation theory is presented in precise computational form. This of course cannot be the whole story because there are several results in Invenrelation theory that are non-constructive and that cannot therefore be captured by any algorithm. However, for many purposes, the constructive aspects are central to the language design for Invenrelation.

There are some reasons to support such issue. First, one of the most important features of Invenrelation theory is that it is a computational approach for creating new things. The conceptual clarity obtained from an Invenrelational understanding of some particular circumstance in mathematics enables one to see how a computation of relevant entities can be carried out for special cases. When the special case of inventions is itself very complex, as frequently is the case, then it is a great advantage to know exactly what one is trying to do and in principle how to carry out the computation. The idea of mechanizing such computations is very inspiring. The present computer language systems do not enable one to do this. Invenrelation language as well as many particular examples must be present in the computer before computation of Invenrelational entities can be implemented.

Secondly, the fact that Inverelation theory is essentially algebraic means that it can be learned by understanding these basic constructions. One may argue that Invenrelation theory is just a collection of hierarchical abstraction procedures. However, it is particularly important for computer programmers that there should be a programming language dedicated for Invenrelation. Because mathematicians have accumulated geometric and algebraic intuitions, many things can be eliminated in current Invenrelation theory to them. But computer programmers generally lack these intuitions, so these elisions can induce a great obstacle for them. Computer language does not permit such elisions and thus presents the basic material in a form that makes computer programmers to gain an advantage for creation similar to the mathematicians' advantage from their knowledge of geometry and algebra.

Operating Systems and Hardware Architecture Design for Invenrelation

In order to realize Invenrelation in machines, hierarchical functional programming has to be adopted since it is built based on meta-relational (meta-functional) constructions. However, hierarchical functional (relational) programming languages are typically less efficient in their use of central processing unit (CPU) and memory than imperative languages such as Pascal and C. Accordingly, new hardware design should be dedicated for machines running Invenrelation. The art of hardware architecture has three main subcategories:

- Instruction set architecture, or ISA. The ISA is the code that an Invenrelation processor reads and acts upon. It is the machine language (or assembly language), including the instruction set, memory address arrangement, word size, processor registers, data formats.

- Microarchitecture. Such organization describes the data paths, data processing elements and data storage elements, and describes how they should realize the ISA coordinately.

- System architecture. This includes all of remaining hardware components within a computing system. These include:

  1. Data communication protocols, such as computer buses and switches;

  2. Memory controllers and hierarchies;

  3. Input/Output, or I/O, refers to the interaction between an Invenrelation processing system, and the outside world, possibly a human, or another information processing

system.

4. Resources controller which assigns hardware resources properly to achieve performance goal and balance.

5. Miscellaneous issues such as parallel processing or virtualization for machines running Invenrelation.

Since new hardware architecture and software language have to be proposed for Invenrelation, a new operating system (OS) for machines running Invenrelation that manages computer hardware resources and provides common services for computer programs should also be designed. The operating system is a crucial component of the system software in a computer system. Application programs require an operating system to function.

Networks of Machines Implementing Invenrelation

The networking that we use today are developed in the 1960s and 1970s. At that time, the problem that people wished to solve was what we call a resource-sharing problem today. There were not many computers, and they were big and expensive. Move forward 50 years, every PC that you buy today has four cores. Computers are just these ordinary items, and people really do not care about resource sharing. If computers can form a coordinating invention network as we described in Chap. XI, what we care about is creating and moving content around. In the sequel, we will present a very preliminary sketch of a research agenda for networks of machines implementing invenrelation.

Empirical studies of machines coordination. This category can include a variety of empirical methodologies, such as:

- laboratory experiments with group innovation;

- econometric studies of firms and markets running CINs;

- culture-graphic field observations of organizational Invenrelational processes.

These studies can be used to stimulate the development of new theory, e.g., a classification of organizational Invenrelational processes and the reduction of coordinating invenrelation cost.

Invenrelation is better to be implemented by hierarchical functional language as discussed in Sec. 12.2.2. If one can express computations with primitives in functional programming, then parallelization often becomes easier and makes programs more robust. Design and experimentation with new methods for coordinating distributed and parallel processing computer systems running hierarchical functional language also provides a category of research topics. This category includes experimentation with different methods for solving the coordination problems that arise in distributed and parallel computer systems such as synchronization, and task assignment.

Design of new technologies for supporting entities (human, machines, human and machines) coordination. This area includes designing new computer and communications systems to support a wide variety of kinds of coordination Invenrelation tasks at different levels of generality: interacting, design, project management, meetings, decision-making, etc. In some cases, a good idea for such system design will stimulate new theory.

Invenrelation network planning and design. Invenrelation network planning process involves three main steps:

- The first stage involves determining where to place the machines and how to connect them.

- The second stage determines the operation and capabilities of the machines used, subject to performance criteria such as the Quality of Service (QoS).

- The last stage involves determining how to meet capacity requirements, and ensure reliability within the Invenrelation network.

If we treat machines as vertices and machines connections as adding edges between machines with random, a random graph is generated by some random process. The theory of random graphs, which lies at the intersection between graph theory and probability theory, can be applied to figure out characteristics of random Invenrelation networks.

Data Management and Mining for Invenrelation Results

Because Invenrelation results [1] can be generated by machines automatically, it is an important topic to consider Invenrelational data management and mining. From Invenrelation theory, invention results have to be represented by richly structured datasets, where the prime components are structured in some way. Structures among the prime components may demonstrate certain patterns, which can be helpful for many data management and mining tasks and are usually hard

---

[1]Actually, many other data about Invenrelation can be mined, for example, input components, Invenrelational procedures or hierarchical analog relations. Here, we take Invenrelation results as a sample case for data mining.

to capture with traditional statistical models. We discuss several issues about structure mining tasks.

The most direct transforming of a classic data mining task to structured domains is structure-based classification. In structure-based classification, we are interested in predicting the category of an Invenrelation result, based not just on its attributes, but on the structures it participates in, and on attributes of objects structured by some relational paths. For instance, we may apply structure-based classification to predict the invention category based on characteristics of the invenrelational procedure and its input components.

The goal in cluster analysis for Invenrelation is to find distinct characteristics in each subclass. This is made by segmenting the data into groups, where members in a group are similar to each other and are very dissimilar from members in different groups. Different from classification, clustering is unsupervised and can be applied to discover hidden patterns within Invenrelation results. This makes it an ideal technique for applications such as invention exploration, related patents and many others. There has been extensive research work on clustering in pattern recognition, machine and statistics learning. In the case of clustering structured data, even the definition of an element in a cluster is an open research problem. We can cluster individual objects, collections of structured objects, or some other sub-structure of the original. How do we compare the similarity of two of these elements or sub-structures, with potentially different structures? As this may necessitate tests for structural isomorphism, problems will become more intractable.

There may be a wide range of applications related to predicting the existence of structures. One of the simplest application is to predict the type of structure between two entities. For example, we may face the problem of predicting whether two inventions (patents) which share some common characteristics are belonged to a product family or designed by the same Invenrelation procedure. The structure type may be modeled in several ways. In some cases, the structure type may simply be an attribute of the structure. In this case, we may know the existence of a structure between two entities, and we are interested in predicting its type. For example, perhaps we know there is some connection between two patents, and we must predict whether it is a familial relation, a co-family relation or evolution relation. In other instances, there may be different kinds of structures. These may be different potential relationships between entities; in the second example, there are two possible relationships: a co-inventor relationship and an employer-employee relationship. We may wish to make inferences about the existence of one kind of structure through observing another type of structure.

Another challenge work in Invenrelation data mining is coherently handling two different types of dependence structures: the logical relationships between objects and the statistical relationship between attributes of objects. Typically, we often restrict the probabilistic dependence to be among objects that are logically related. In statistical learning models for multi-relational data, we must not only search over probabilistic dependencies, but also figuring out the different possible logical relationships between objects. This search over logical relationships has been a focus of research in inductive logic programming, and the methods and machinery developed in this area should be used to solve this problem.

12.2.3 New Methods and Mathematical Representation

The purpose of Invenrelation is try to model invention (creation) thought processes as mathematical operations. Mathematics arises from many different kinds of problems. At the beginning, problems about mathematics were found in commerce, architecture, land measurement and astronomy. Nowadays, all sciences try to formulate problems about quantities and structures by mathematics. Furthermore, many new mathematical problems are induced within studying other fields. For example, today's string theory, a still-expanding scientific area which attempts to unify the four fundamental forces of nature, continues to inspire new mathematics. In the following, we provide several discussions about new mathematics directions which may be inspired by Invenrelation.

In Chap. IX, we consider the problem for derivation complexity of Invenrelation procedures. An interesting problem is how dose one quantify the difference between two Invenrelation results based on some criteria, for example, the hardness of mathematical operations or the knowledge level involved in Invenrelation. This measure may help us to grade the invention competition or patents importance. Another measure is to calibrate the psychological distance between the observer and an Invenrelation result based on one's personal knowledge level and thoughts patterns. Such distance will affect interpretation level between the observer and an Invenrelation result. Possible dimensions to consider about such measure are: (a) spatial : how much distance in physical space is the target from the observer; (b) temporal : how much time separates between the observers present time and the target event; (c) hypotheticality : how likely is the target invention to happen, or how close it is to reality, as construed by the inventor; and (d) environmental : how distinct is the target from the observer's self environmental backgrounds.

Many mathematical objects, such as sets of, points, numbers and functions, possess internal structure as a consequence of operations or relations that are defined on the set. Mathematics then studies properties of those sets that can be expressed in terms of that structure, for example, geometry studies properties of the set of points in a space that can be expressed in terms of arithmetic operations. In the development of Invenrelation, we adopted various mathematical objects to model invention processes. Is it possible for us to give the geometric space for a collection of interesting objects? Then one can parametrize and classify those objects by introducing coordinates on the resulting space. We may name such space as "Invenrelation map". For example, one might think of an Invenrelation map as a map or a picture of a set of invention processes. A map of the China is, roughly speaking, an Invenrelation map for the set of 22 provinces. If you had a table of the 22 provinces and their sizes and shapes, and another table detailing which provinces bordered on which other provinces, one might still have only a fuzzy idea of what China looks like and how it is put together. But with a map, you would perceive invention types clearly.

Understanding and characterizing change is a common theme in the natural sciences, and calculus was, developed by Newton and Leibniz, a powerful tool to investigate it. In Chap. V, the general definition of derivative is provided. However, many properties about such derivatives have not explored in details. Many problems about thought processes lead naturally to relationships between a quantity and its rate of change, and these are suitable to be studied by differential equations. Many phenomena in invention processes can also be described by dynamical systems [2]; chaos theory with general derivative definition makes precise the ways in which many of these systems exhibit unpredictable yet still deterministic behavior.

In Chap XI, we discussed about coordinating invention networks. Mathematical tools should be developed to build and analyze formal representations of coordination processes. These problems can include at least two kinds of formal modelling. (a) Mathematical modelling: Much of the work in economical issues about applying Invenrelation in business falls in this category. (b) Computer simulations: It may also be useful, in some cases, to use knowledge representation techniques (will be discussed at next section) as a verification platforms without actually running experiments.

---

[2]The change of Inverelation results can vary with respect to interesting quantities, e.g., time, place, persons or minds.

12.2.4 New Knowledge Representation

We redefine the meaning of knowledge here for more general sense. Knowledge is anything that can be interpreted with relations by humans.

In order to develop more new knowledge based on Invenrelation, the first important task is to find prime components in each knowledge field. However, there are still have many problems in this issue:

- Is it possible for us to regulate prime components in all knowledge domain, e.g., physics, biology or even painting? These prime components should satisfy following requirements based on desired abstraction level: (a) they are independent each other; (b) they are able to derive all knowledge facts; and (c) there is no contradiction among them. We have to note that prime components may change with time. For instance, humans change prime components for materials many times in history.

- A machine-support information system that can record, search and modification for facts relations with prime components in each knowledge domain and for relations between each knowledge domain.

- Can we verify the validity of new generated knowledge and explore its relation with others existing knowledge fields. Ideal situation is to perform verification on computers.

12.3 Industry

Industrial Revolution was a period over the 18th and 19th centuries where changes in manufacturing, mining, agriculture, transportation, and technology had a deep effect on the social, economic and cultural conditions of the times. It began in the United Kingdom, then generally spread throughout Western Europe, North America, Asia, and eventually the rest of the world. At those times, inventions and scientific discoveries played an important role in modernization of the world, when an era of global industrial liberalization played a significant role in the scientific advancement of the world. It all began with the advancement of the liberal invention of humans after the Renaissance, which eventually led to the industrial revolution. We select following areas in industry to discuss possible future stories affected by Invenrelation. They are intellectual property, business, art and articles for daily use.

12.3.1 Intellectual Property

The combined use of computers and communications and the future evolution in the field of machine-generated works by Invenrelation will bring new scenes of creating intellectual property. The question is, how far we can go in considering Invenrelator [3] intelligence and autonomy, how can we legally deal with a new form of Invenrelational behavior capable of autonomous action? This section addresses and analyzes the issues concerning the ownership of works generated by Invenrelation within patents and copyright, and concludes that the current regime is insufficient to deal with the future use of more and more Invenrelation systems in the producing of such works.

From moral consideration, it may not proper to grant intellectual property to Invenrelator (machines). Can an Invenrelator hold such rights despite not being mankind? The body corporate seems provide an insightful example. A company which does not even exist in physical form is nonetheless regarded as an entity capable of possessing property, earning money and being subject to and entitled to enjoy certain rights and share obligation. More particularly, company is able to acquire and hold intellectual property rights. So there is no reason why similar rights could not be granted to an Invenrelator to allow it to hold the intellectual property rights in what it has generated.

In considering the possibility of providing separate legal personality to Invenrelators, we may inspect the reasoning behind the grant of personality to a body corporate. Generally, the grant to a corporation of separate personality rooted in three main considerations - the first is the requirement for certain organizations to exist in some duration, the second is the need for such organizations to be able of holding and dealing with property and being accountable for losses, and last is the benefits rewardable to society. Hence, if we plan to grant authorship to such Invenrelator personalities, then we must consider responsibility. In the same approach as a company can be sued, an Invenrelator could be sued but how would it meet any financial obligations imposed? Possible solutions are the establishment of some forms for deposit accounts and insurance schemes.

As intellectual property rights play a more important part in commerce and become more valuable, we shall find more interesting and fancy attacks on the ownership of such rights in infringement cases. Many people may say that we will never be able to understand intelligence

---

[3]Machines use Invenerlation to create new contents.

and therefore never be able to produce a true artificial intelligence system. Let us retrospect that twenty years ago the same was said about life. Life was a gift from God something that could never be comprehended or created. Nnowadays, we have broken the genetic code and are able to produce new life through cloning. Remember the following aphorism:

"We must prepare now for a future that will surely come."

12.3.2 Business

In this section, we discuss two business issues affected by Invenrelation. The first is brain-sport industry and the second is the explosion of business concepts.

Humans may become weak in their brain functions due to more and more creation works replaced by Invenrelators. In order to keep brain functions normally, it is beneficial to have brain-sports industry. Industry is a collection of similar organizations which involve products and services, customers and value activities. Brain-sports industry is a *market which provides customers activities, places, staffs, concepts and products associated to enhance invention and creation functions of human brains.* Following diagram, Fig. 12.2, is provided to classify the relationship among each sub-industry of brain-sports.

The history of thought and ideas teaches us that invention fosters more invention. Invention feeds on itself, so we can expect that there will be more and more periodical literatures in investigating business concepts. Thus, it is becoming more arduous to be acquainted with all areas of business and to keep up with even that sample of journals covered in the reference volumes on business literature. How do we face such an explosion of business concepts and literature discussing them?

Of course, some core ideas and methodologies will have become and will continue to be fundamental for financial economist and financial manager. These include:

- Increased intelligence of relatively low-cost computing devices in dealing e-commerce, e.g., how to regulate legal status for computing devices which can perform commercial behaviors.

- Global markets require an understanding of the international dimensions of asset value and return.

- Behavioral theory, e.g., how individuals make decisions and react to risk.

- Notions of microeconomics, e.g., demand-supply elasticity equilibrium; behavior and reactions of rivals.

- Notions of macroeconomics, e.g., the field of studying wide phenomena such as changes in unemployment, national income, rate of growth, gross domestic product, inflation and price levels.

- Creation event analysis techniques, e.g., to analyze the markets' initial assessment of the commercial value impacts of change made by new created products or services.

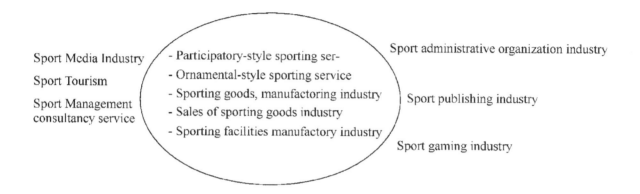

Figure 12.2: Possible future industries for brain-sports.

12.3.3 Art

One definition about art is the expression of human spirit. There are many reasons for the important role that creativity and art plays within spirit. First, art excites the expression of our truest meanings, which is the kernel process of spiritual growth. It makes us examine what is within and without — the very nature within us and around us as well as the concordance of this cosmos. Then, this transformative inner introspecting and creativity naturally induces more beauty in our outer world. Second, artistic creativity is one of the best healing therapies to heal human minds in the world. Some even say art is beyond healing in that it saves our spirit by connecting us to our deepest spirit, to each other in profound new ways as well as to the reality itself. Finally, the beauty of art reflects reality in its boundlessly artistic and creative characteristics. The beauty of art is spirituality in the form of creativity. Developing and continually exercising ones creativity will enable one to experience the inspiration of all creativity.

People tend to think that any manufactured conflicts are dramatic, however, true dramatic conflicts are conflicts in the sense of people life and between emotions and inner thoughts. Superficial understanding of the dramatic art itself is only a partial representation of superficial understanding of art for general people. Currently, many people working for art totally disregard the essence of art. Instead, they pay more and more attention to artificial skills rather than the essence art. Some people even think good art can be generated by money. However, facts disprove such perspective. If money can produce excellent art, modern people should produce great and unprecedented art since we are in the most affluent era of human history. Most people should agree that most great classical works of art are not made by modern people.

When we try to apply Invenrelation in creating new art objects, the theme of such art objects can not be understood as skills or techniques only. It should be understood as thoughts (philosophy) to be transferred to audience. Here, the notion of "philosophy" is not an abstract concept, but is the depth of understanding things and emotions expression by artists. The level of an art object is determined crucially by this. Nowadays, there are very few authors as the 19th century Russian novelists in writing works to sympathize unfortunates with humanitarianism and to contemplate the tragedy with the enthusiasm of religious saints. When I read their books (19th century Russian novelists), I just feel like reading philosophical works since they continued to ask questions, and did not necessarily provide answers for these questions. Similarly, life always prepares problems for us, but not necessarily gives us satisfactory answers. After reading such kinds of books, those problems posted in books must also remain in our minds by repeating interrogations with no hope of resolving. Just such feelings make us filled with imagination for possible answers. Of course, the Russian classical literature may be an extreme example. Undeniably, great works to survive for centuries must possess philosophy. Ancient Chinese has recognized this for a long time, for instance, the traditional Chinese painting pays much more attention in philosophy spirit than in forms. Artists must first to comprehend principles of everything, i.e., that is, an understanding of the meaning of all things (philosophy). Then, artists are able to represent the invisible principles to tangible things with life and meaning. Now, the reason why many of our literary and artistic works are flat and insipid is that many creators for those works are lack of understanding principles behind everything, thoughts and philosophy.

12.3.4 Articles for Daily Use

Time: morning, December 1, 2200 . Location: my villa in Utopian at Earth-0. "Ding......", a burst of ringing followed by a beautiful melody. I open my eyes to see the clock and the time is 6:00 AM exactly. The curtains open automatically and the ray of sunshine shines into my room which makes me feel very comfortable. Wait a moment, why the sky is not dark at 6:00 AM in December? Well, in 2200, humans have launched an artificial sun into the sky and it begins to work from 5:00 AM every day in winter. This artificial sun can control heat distribution over earth area in winter and reduces the chance of winter storms. The artificial sun stops working in summer.

"My lord, it is time to wake up!" This is my housekeeping robot and it will help me to wash up and arrange my bed. My housekeeping robot help me to wear clothes which can adjust temperature, colors and styles with respect to my surrounding environments automatically. Furthermore, my clothes can enhance my physical strength during my body movements. There are many intelligent robots at my home for different purposes. For example, I also have a sporting robot who can be my partner in playing basketball and tennis. After washing up my face, I begin to train my body by jogging and raising weights. Although I am 90 years old, my health status is at age of 30. Scientists have developed nano-robots which can drill into all parts of my body to probe and treat various diseases, for example, those tiny robots even can drill into cerebrovascular and clear the obstruction which enables a paralyzed patient can stand up again. Because all blood vessels are smooth, people will feel very spiritual. Moreover, scientists also make various artificial organs which can be used to replace broken organs.

I sit beside dinning table and turn on radio to listen news. At this moment, my housekeeping robot has prepared breakfast already. I drink fresh milk and eat freshly baked bread, fried meat and eggs. You may say that these things are common and one enjoys these every morning. If I tell you, the milk is shipped by spaceship just from the Earth-1. You will not be surprised in 2200 since milk drunk by the people on Earth-0 is shipped from Earth-1, a planet outside the solar system. This is a great achievement of our planet exploration team. Our detection teams travelled in space by spaceships, and found many original planets proper to raise animals and plants. Earth-1 is one of them. Earth-1 is covered by the sea and large areas of virgin forest with fresh air. Humans shipped calves from Earth-0 to Earth-1 and made them blooming. Since cows eat grass without any pollution and drink clear water, the production of milk is very nutritious and very safe.

After breakfast, I take my flying car and go to my lab. In 2200, there are no cars for personal transportation. In order to protect environment, we have invented flying cars. There are several distinct features provided by flying cars. First, flying cars can be driven automatically and it can avoid obstacles by itself without humans commands. Second, the flying car utilizes solar energy and the excess solar energy will be stored in a battery for later usage when there is no sun. Third, the flying car has suckers on the feet which can climb and stop on walls to save a parking place. The flying car flies into my lab, which is at level 900 in the Building of Computer Protection. I drive my flying car into my lab directly from windows of my lab. I just park my flying car and my assistant runs to me worriedly. He bring me with a sample program scripts and yell to me: "Our detective team has discovered a new kind of computer virus". I begin to test this computer virus and try to figure out the solution to combat this virus. During recess time, I will call my sporting-robot to play basketball with me. My sporting-robot can also play other kinds of sports with me. Time passes quickly and I begin to collect my items at 6:00 pm. When I arrive home, my housekeeping-robot has cooked dinner already for me. Although I can use ultrasound to remove the dirt of my body, I still wish to have a hot shower. After showering, I check my office documents for a while and fall in sleep quickly within a lullaby.

A few days later, my vacation will begin. I plan to go Earth-1 and there are a lot of animals and plants with fresh air at Earth-1. By gene technologies, many extinct animals can live at Earth-II again. Since the natural environment at Earth-1 is so nice, plenty of people even hope to immigrate into this vivid planet.

12.4 Ethical Issues

Let us consider a situation in the future. Invention or creation may be regarded as the most difficult (or advanced) function of our brains. If machines which apply Invenrelation to invent or create new things are widely deployed in our world, we will suffer an Age of *invention explosion*. Below, we will point out several ethical issues about such Age.

Privacy and Security: Privacy and security are problems associated to invenrelation systems and applications. Privacy is an issue that concerns the invenrelation society in connection with maintaining personal (or organizational) information on individual residents in invenrelation systems. It deals with the rights of the individual regarding the collection of information in an invenrelation system about one's processing, disseminating, saving, and using of this information in making decisions. These aspects are long standing legal and social problems that have become associated with the computer (machines) field because invenrelation systems are much more efficient than current information systems (without utilizing AI in generating new information extensively) they have replaced, and because they allow more closer relations among intelligent machines on a much greater scale than current information systems. Therefore, damages to individuals privacy from current information systems are potentially enlarged in current invenrelation systems.

Security of invenrelation systems has to achieve the following goals: (1) to prevent intentional denial of service, (2) to prevent unauthorized access, (3) to protect the system from malicious attack and (4) to recover from system failures. The access control requirements are specially crucial in time-shared and parallel-programmed invenrelation systems where multiple users are served simultaneously-invention jobs processed concurrently must be prevented from interfering with each other and users must be prevented from gaining unauthorized access to each others' programs or data. When classified information is stored or processed in an invenrelation system, a problem is induced: how can an invenrelation system allow concurrent processing of information in different security classification categories, and simultaneous use of the system by users who have different security requirements while no classified information is leaked to unauthorized users.

Property:

It is a complex issue to deal with intellectual property rights. Several questions are induced: Who owns results generated by invenrelation? What are the just and fair prices for its exchange?

Who owns the channels of networks among inventors, especially the bandwidth of wireless medium and cables, through which information is transmitted?

There are substantial economic and ethical concerns surrounding these rights; concerns revolving around the special attributes of invenrelation itself and the means by which it is transmitted. Any individual item of invenrelation can be extremely costly to produce at the first time. However, once it is produced, that information has the illusive quality of being easy to reproduce and to broadcast. Furthermore, this replication can take place without destroying the original. This makes invenrelation hard to protected at today e-environment since, unlike substantial property, it becomes communicable and hard to keep it to one's self. It is even difficult to design an appropriate reimbursement scheme because many invenrelation results are obtained by combing or analogizing from other invented results.

To fully understand our moral predicament regarding invenrelation systems, it is better to retrospect England about 250 years ago, industry revolution in England. By comparing it with future times when invention is an easy and automatic task, we may anticipate some of the problems of the invenrelation society. As the industrial age launched in England, a significant change took place in the relationship between people and their work. The steam engine replaced man power by reducing much personal physical energy required to perform a job. The factory system, as Adam Smith described in his essay about textile mills, effectively replaced the laborer's contribution of his energy and of his skills. This was done by means of new machines and new organization forms.

In the future, the same moral spirit may face us again. Practitioners of invenrealtion systems proceed by extracting invention ideas from experts, inventors and the knowledgeable, and then implanting them into computer software where it becomes capital in the economic sense. This process of transferring invention ideas from an individual, and subsequently implanting it into machines transfers control of the property to those who own the hardware and software. Is this exchange of property authorized? Consider some of the most successful commercial artificial intelligence systems of the day. Who owns, for example, the medical knowledge contained in MYCIN, How is the contributor of his knowledge to be compensated? More complicated cases are hybrid intellectual property right problems where invenrelation results are generated from natural persons and machines. These are among the issues we must resolve as more invenrelation systems are created.

Concern over intellectual property rights relates to the content generated by invenrelation.

There are some equally urgent property rights issues surrounding the information processing (Computation Power), transmitting (Bandwidth) and saving (Storage Space). These properties are belonged to commons in current and future Cloud environment. In an age in which people benefit by the communication of information, there is a tendency for us to treat computation power, bandwidth and storage space as commons in the same way as did the herdsmen in Garrett Hardin's essay, *The Tragedy of the Commons*. Each shepherd receives direct benefits from adding an animal to a pastureland shared in common. As long as there is plenty of grazing capacity the losses due to the animal's consumption are reduced among them and each shepherd feels only indirectly and proportionally much less. So each shepherd was motivated to increase the size of his own animals group. However, the commons were destroyed and every shepherd lost finally.

In the future, devices surrounding us may be clogged with an explosion of data, voice, video, and digital contents generated by invenrelation systems. Organizations and individuals will expand their use of processing, communicating and saving information generated by invenrelation because it is beneficial for them to do so. But if the social checks on the expanded usage of computation power, bandwidth and storage are inadequate, and a certain degree of temperance isn't followed, we may find that shortage, congestion and noise will destroy the flow of invenrelation information through the devices. It will be a crucial issue to allocate these limited resources if invenrelation Age comes true.

Peaceful Usage:

The invention of nuclear technology is an important event in 20th century. If one dose not apply such technology in peaceful purposes, for example, to design a weapon, it may induce a tragedy in human history. Only two nuclear weapons have been used in the course of war until now, both by the United States near the end of World War II. On August 6, 1945, an uranium gun-type device named as "Little Boy" was detonated over the Japanese city of Hiroshima. Three days later, on August 9, a plutonium implosion-type device named as "Fat Man" was exploded over Nagasaki, Japan. These two bombings resulted in the deaths of approximately 200,000 Japanese people - mostly civilians -from acute injuries sustained from the explosions

However, if one applies nuclear technology in peaceful purposes, it can be adopted in seven principal areas: mining and processing of nuclear raw materials; the production of enriched uranium; the fabrication of nuclear fuel elements; the design, construction and operation of nuclear reactors; bio-medical applications; environmental applications and fuel reprocessing. The origins of a commitment to develop nuclear energy for peaceful purposes can be traced to President Eisen-

493

howers speech, *Atoms for Peace*, in 1953 and the subsequent establishment of the International Atomic Energy Agency (IAEA) in 1956.

In the future, there will be more and more new technologies invented. They can be applied for peaceful purposes or non-peaceful purposes which depend on our human attitude. Therefore, one has to be careful in applying invenrelation to generate new things. New things should be generated by keeping ***public order, morality and health***, especially for new thoughts or policies about religions and political affairs. For example, the Protestant Reformation (a big change in religion thoughts) was the 16th-century schism within Western world pioneered by Martin Luther, John Calvin and other early Protestants. It was begun by the 1517 posting of Luther's Ninety-five theses. Unfortunately, the Reformation led to a series of religious wars that culminated in the Thirty Years' War (1618 − 1648), which ruined much of Germany, killing about 40 % of its population.

Bibliography

[1] N. Bohr, "Atomic physics and human knowledge," *Dover Publications Inc.*, 2011.

[2] S. E. Keene, "A programmer's guide to object-oriented programming in Common LISP," *Addison-Wesley*, 1988.

[3] A. Snyder, "Encapsulation and inheritance in object-oriented programming languages," *ACM SIGPLAN Notices*, vol. 21, no. 11, pp. 38-45, Nov. 1986.

[4] J. Hendler, "Enhancement for multiple-inheritance," *Proc. ACM SIGPLAN workshop on Object-oriented programming*, New York, USA, pp. 98-106, 1986.

[5] G. Booch, "Object-oriented analysis and design with applications," *Addison-Wesley*, 1994.

[6] G. W. F. Hegel, "G. W. F. Hegel's Theory of Right, Duties and Religion: Translation, with a Supplementary Essay on Hege," *BiblioLife*, 2009.

[7] J. Hyppolite and J. O'Neill, "Studies on Marx and Hegel," *Heinemann Educational Publishers*, 1969.

[8] S. Toulmin, "Criticism in the history of science: Newton on absolute space, time, and motion," *The Philosophical Review*, vol. 68, no. 1, pp. 1-29, Jan. 1959.

[9] T. Burge, "Belief de re," *The Journal of Philosophy*, vol. 74, no. 6, pp. 338-362, Jun. 1977.

[10] J. Ivar, G. Booch, and J. Rumbaugh, "The Unified Software Development Process," *Addison-Wesley*, 1988.

[11] R. Hekmat, "Ad-hoc Networks: Fundamental Properties and Network Topologies," *Springer*, 2006.

[12] J, McQuillan, "Adaptive routing algorithms for distributed computer networks," *Bolt Beranek and Newman Inc.*, 1974.

[13] Kamoun, Farouk and Leonard Kleinrock, "Stochastic Performance Evaluation of fierarchical Routing for Large Network," *Computer Networks*, vol. 3, pp. 337-353, 1979.

[14] G. S. Lauer, "Hierarchical routing design for SURAN," *Proceedings of IEEE ICC*, pp. 93-102, Jun., 1986.

[15] C. V. Ramamoorthy and W. T. Tsai, "An adaptive hierarchical routing algorithm," *Proceedings of IEEE COMPSAC*, pp. 93-104, 1983.

[16] E. Sakhaee and A. Jamalipour, "Stable clustering and communications in pseudolinear highly mobile ad hoc networks," *IEEE Transactions on Vehicular Technology*, vol. 57, no. 6, pp. 3769-3777, November 2008.

[17] D. Stoyan, W. Kendall, and J. Mecke, "Stochastic Geometry and its Applications", *John Wiley*, 1995.

[18] J. L. Rougier, D. Kofman, and A. Gravey, "Optimization of hierarchical routing protocols", *Performance Evaluation*, vol. 41, no. 3, pp. 227-245, 2000.

[19] D. Burton, "Elementary number theory", *McGraw-Hill*, 2010.

[20] D. S. Dummit and R. M. Foote, "Abstract Algebra", *Wiley*, 2004.

[21] C. L. Liu, "Elements of Discrete Mathemtics", *McGraw-Hill*, 1998.

[22] S. Y. Chang, "Generating Function Analysis of Wireless Networks and ARQ Systems", *Ph. Dissertation, University of Michigan*, 2006.

[23] G. Bianchi, "Performance analysis of the IEEE 802.11 distributed coordination function", *IEEE J. Select. Areas Commun.*, vol. 18, no. 3, pp. 535-547, Mar. 2000.

[24] G. F. Franklin, J. D. Powell, and A. Emami-Naeini, "Feedback Control of Dynamic Systems", *Addision Wesely*, 1994.

[25] S. Y. Chang, H. C. Wu, F. Neubrander, and J. C. Principe, "Theories, analysis and bounds of the fi

nite-support approximation for the inverses of mixing-phase FIR systems", *IEEE Transactions on Circuits and Systems I: Regular Papers*, vol. 56, no. 10, pp. 2181-2194, Oct. 2009.

[26] S. K. Mitra, "Digital Signal Processing", 4th ed. *McGraw Hill*, 2005.

[27] S. J. Champagne, "M. S. Thesis: The Asymptotic Z-transform", Department of Mathematics, Louisiana State University, 2005.

[28] C. T. Chen, "Linear System Theory and Design", 3rd ed, 1998.

[29] T. M. Connolly and C. E. Begg, "DataBase Systems: A Practical Approach to Design, Implementation and Management", 4th ed, *Addision Wesely*, 2004.

[30] M. Fowler, "UML Distilled: A Brief Guide to the Standard Object Modeling Language", *Addision Wesely*, 2003.

[31] M. Chein and M. L. Mugnier, " Graph-based Knowledge Representation", *Springer-Verlag*, 2009.

[32] J. Munkres, "Topology", *Prentice-Hall*, 2000.

[33] M. G. Moehrle, "What is triz? from conceptual basics to a framework for research," *CREATIVITY AND INNOVATION MANAGEMENT*, vol. 14, no. 1, pp. 3-13, Mar. 2005.

[34] L. Z. et al, "Rsvp: A new resource reservation protocol," *IEEE Network Magazine*, vol. 7, no. 5, pp. 116-127, Sept. 1993.

[35] M. Burgeruthor, B. HacklE, and W. Ring, "Incorporating topological derivatives into level set methods," *Journal of Computational Physics*, vol. 194, no. 10, pp. 344-362, Feb. 2004.

[36] I. J. GOOD, "The interaction algorithm and practical fourier analysis," *IEEE Communications Letters*, vol. 20, no. 2, pp. 361-372, 1958.

[37] L. R. Rabiner and B. H. Juang, "An introduction to hidden Markov models," *IEEE ASSP Magazine*, pp. 4-16, Jan. 1986.

[38] P. W. Foulk, "Directed-graph models and their application to software development," *Software and Microsystems*, vol. 1, no. 7, pp. 192-199, 1982.

[39] S. Vosniadou and A. Ortony, "Similarity and Analogical Reasoning," *Cambridge University Press*, 1989.

[40] J. H. Huang, "Aalogy within civil law," *Master's thesis*, National Taiwan University, Taipei, Taiwan, 1987.

[41] O. Holmes, "The Path of the Law," *Applewood Books*, 2006.

[42] T. Leinster, "Higher Operads, Higher Categories," *Cambridge University Press*, 2004.

[43] H. S. Seung and D. D. Lee, "The manifold ways of perception," *Science*, vol. 290, no. 22, pp. 2268-2269, Dec. 2000.

[44] B. J. Gardner, "How to make many-sorted algebras one-sorted," *Com- mentationes Mathematicae Universitatis Carolinae*, vol. 30, no. 4, pp. 627-635, 1989.

[45] J. Plonka, "Diagonal algebras," *Fund. Mathematics*, vol. 58, pp. 309-322, 1966.

[46] S. Albeverio, J. E. Fenstad, R. Hoegh-Krohn, and T. Lindstrm, "Nonstandard methods in stochastic analysis and mathematical physics," *Academic Press*, 1986.

[47] V. A. Molchanov, "On nonstandard axiomatization of elementarily nonaxiomatizable classes of discrete algebraic systems," Siberian Mathematical Journal, vol. 40, no. 2, pp. 363-373, 1999.

[48] A. Hatcher, "Algebraic Topology," *Cambridge University Press*, 2001.

[49] R. Steiner, "The algebra of directed complexes," *Applied Categorical Structures*, vol. 1, no. 3, pp. 247-284, 1993.

[50] O. Klima, P. Tesson, and D. Therien, "Dichotomies in the complexity of solving systems of equations over

nite semigroups," *Theory of Computing systems*, vol. 40, no. 3, pp. 263-297, 2007.

[51] D. Yau, "Higher dimensional algebras via colored PROPs,", arXiv preprint, 2008.

[52] T. Dewetta and A. S. Denisib, "What motivates organizational citizenship behaviours? exploring the role of regulatory focus theory," *European Journal of Work and Organizational Psychology*, vol. 16, no. 3, pp. 241-260, Feb. 2007.

[53] M. Batanin and M. Weber, "Algebras of higher operads as enriched categories," *Appl. Category Struct.*, vol. 19, pp. 93-135, 2011.

[54] S. E. Crans, "A tensor product for gray-categories," *Theory and Application of Categories*, vol. 5, no. 2, pp. 12-69, 1999.

INVENRELATION

作　者/張適宇（Shih Yu Chang）

出版者/美商 EHGBooks 微出版公司

發行者/漢世紀數位文化（股）公司

臺灣學人出版網：http://www.TaiwanFellowship.org

地　　址/106 臺北市大安區敦化南路 2 段 1 號 4 樓

電　　話/02-2707-9001 轉 616-617

印　　刷/漢世紀古騰堡®數位出版 POD 雲端科技

出版日期/2013 年 9 月（亞馬遜 Kindle 電子書同步出版）

總經銷/Amazon.com

臺灣銷售網/三民網路書店：http://www.sanmin.com.tw

　　　　　三民書局復北店

　　　　　地址/104 臺北市復興北路 386 號

　　　　　電話/02-2500-6600

　　　　　三民書局重南店

　　　　　地址/100 臺北市重慶南路一段 61 號

　　　　　電話/02-2361-7511

　　　　　全省金石網路書店：http://www.kingstone.com.tw

定　　價/新臺幣 750 元（美金 25 元 / 人民幣 150 元）

www.ingramcontent.com/pod-product-compliance
Lightning Source LLC
Chambersburg PA
CBHW081454050326
40690CB00015B/2793